IRISH AMERICAN
CHRONICLE

FOREWORD
Maureen O'Hara

PREFACE
Peter Quinn

CONSULTANT
Thomas Fleming

ESSAYIST
Terry Golway

CONTRIBUTING WRITERS
Dan Brekke
Tom Deignan
Vincent Feeney
Richard Jensen
Christy Nadalin
Ray O'Hanlon
Tina Pisco
Bradley Shreve

LEGACY

Publisher & CEO
Louis Weber

Editor-in-Chief
David J. Hogan

Editor
David Aretha

Art Director
James Slate

Creative Director
Marissa Conner

Acquisitions Editor
Robert A. Rodriguez

**Director of Acquisitions
& Visual Resources**
Doug Brooks

Manager of Acquisitions
Jamie Santoro

Administrative Coordinator
Kathline Jones

Special Projects Editor
Valerie A. Iglar-Mobley

Production Director
Steven Grundt

Assistant Production Director
Margaret McConnell

Digital Publishing Programmer
Michael A. Anderson

Visual Resources Specialist
Dustin Drase

Art Buyer
Rebecca Gizicki

Legacy Logo Designer
James Schlottman

Contract Manager
Renee G. Haring

Editorial Assistant
Mariel Demler

Prepress Manufacturing Director
Dave Darian

Prepress Assistants
Eddy Mirko
Patrick Mulcrone

Imaging Development Manager
Paul Fromberg

Imaging Technician
Sherese Hopkins

Imaging Assistant
Juliana Schneider

**Executive Vice President, Business
Development**
Rocky Wu

Manufacturing Manager
Jared Svoboda

Legal Adviser
Dorothy Weber

Legacy Publishing is a division of Publications International, Ltd.

ISBN-13: 978-1-4127-1536-2
ISBN-10: 1-4127-1536-9

Manufactured in China.

8 7 6 5 4 3 2 1

Front cover photo: An immigrant family gazes at the New York skyline after disembarking at Ellis Island in August 1925.
Back cover photo: Members of the heavily Irish Knights of Labor pose with the tools of their trades.

Library of Congress Cataloging-in-Publication Data

Fleming, Thomas J.
   Irish American chronicle / primary consultant, Thomas Fleming ; essayist and consultant, Terry J. Golway ; contributing writers,
Dan Brekke ... [et al.].
      p. cm.
   Includes index.
   ISBN-13: 978-1-4127-1536-2
   ISBN-10: 1-4127-1536-9
   1. Irish Americans--History. 2. Irish Americans--History--Sources. I. Golway, Terry, 1955- II. Brekke, Dan. III. Title.
   E184.I6F595 2009
   973'.049162--dc22
                                        2008033986

Contributors

Foreword Author

Born Maureen FitzSimons outside of Dublin, actress **Maureen O'Hara** became one of Hollywood's best-loved stars with such films as *How Green Was My Valley* (1941) and *Miracle on 34th Street* (1947). O'Hara held her own alongside actor John Wayne in five films, most notably 1952's *The Quiet Man*. In 1946 she battled (and won) the right for recognition by the U.S. government as "Irish" (rather than British). Her memoir, *'Tis Herself*, was published in 2004.

Preface Author

Peter Quinn was raised and educated in the Bronx. A speechwriter for two New York governors, he also served as corporate editorial director for Time Warner, retiring in 2006. He is the author of two novels, *Banished Children of Eve*—a 1995 American Book Award winner—and *Hour of the Cat*. His most recent book is *Looking for Jimmy: A Search for Irish America*. He cowrote the script for the television documentary *McSorley's New York*, which won a 1987 New York-area Emmy Award for best historical programming.

Consultant

Author of 23 novels and nearly as many nonfiction books, **Thomas Fleming** is one of America's most distinguished writers. He has served as president of the Society of American Historians and of the American Center of PEN, a writer's organization. All four of his grandparents were born in Ireland. He grew up in Jersey City, where his father, "Teddy" Fleming, was a prominent politician. His first five novels chronicled the heartbreak and conflicts of the Irish in New Jersey's brutal "us against them" politics. A later novel, *Hours of Gladness*, dealt with the hopes and disillusions of the Irish in post-Vietnam America. His 2005 memoir, *Mysteries of My Father*, won wide praise.

Essayist

Terry Golway is the director of the Kean Center for American History at Kean University and has taught Irish history at New York University. He is author of *The Irish in America*, a companion book to the PBS series *Long Journey Home*; *Irish Rebel*, a biography of John Devoy; and *For the Cause of Liberty*, a history of Irish nationalism. He has appeared on Irish television in several documentaries, and writes for *The New York Times*, *The Irish Echo*, and *America*.

Contributing Writers

A native of Chicago, **Dan Brekke** is the descendant of O'Malleys, Morans, and Hogans from County Mayo. He is a longtime journalist and lifelong student of history. A former editor at the *San Francisco Examiner* and *Wired*, his features have appeared in *Wired*, *The New York Times Magazine*, *Business 2.0*, and numerous other publications.

Tom Deignan is the author of *Irish Americans: Coming to America*. For almost a decade, he has written the weekly "Sidewalks" column for *The Irish Voice* newspaper. He also writes columns about books, movies, and history for *Irish America* magazine. His writing has appeared in *The New York Times*, *The* (Newark) *Star-Ledger*, *The New York Observer*, and *The New York Sun*. He has taught history, cinema, and English at St. John's University and CUNY.

Vincent Feeney, Ph.D., has been an adjunct professor of Irish history at the University of Vermont since 1977. He has published scholarly articles in *Eire-Ireland*, *Vermont History*, *The Encyclopedia of the Irish in America*, and *The Vermont Encyclopedia*. Dr. Feeney received his Ph.D. from the University of Washington. Currently he is at work on a history of the Irish in Vermont.

Richard Jensen, Ph.D., graduated from the University of Notre Dame in 1962 and took his Ph.D. in American Studies at Yale University in 1966. He has taught American political and social history, and historical methods, at schools across the U.S. and has lectured widely around the world. He has written 11 books and 53 articles, and he has given numerous papers to scholarly conferences.

Christy Nadalin is a freelance writer, editorial researcher, and documentary television producer whose work has appeared in publications and productions by the National Geographic Society, the Discovery Channel, A&E Television Networks, and Time-Life Books. She contributed to *Civil Rights Chronicle*, *The Sixties Chronicle*, *The Fifties Chronicle*, *American West Chronicle*, and *World War II Chronicle*.

Ray O'Hanlon is editor of *The Irish Echo*, published weekly in New York since 1928. A journalist for 30 years, Dublin-born O'Hanlon worked for *The Irish Press* until he immigrated to the United States in 1987. A graduate of University College Dublin with a degree in politics and economics, O'Hanlon is the author of *The New Irish Americans*. He has been a frequent media guest on Irish issues and matters of interest to Irish America.

Tina Pisco had a successful career as a journalist and television news producer in the Brussels press corps before moving to West Cork and turning her hand to writing full-time. She is the author of the best-selling novels *Only a Paper Moon* and *To Catch a Magpie* as well as the book *For the Love of the Irish*. She writes regularly for newspapers, books, and magazines as well working as a screenwriter and script doctor.

Bradley Shreve, Ph.D., is a scholar of race and ethnicity. He has lived and worked in Belfast, Northern Ireland, Bogotá, Colombia, and, most recently, on the Navajo Reservation, where he teaches history at Diné College. He served as contributing writer to *The Sixties Chronicle*, *The Fifties Chronicle*, and *American West Chronicle*.

Factual Verification and Research

Brian Hannon is a Ph.D. candidate in European History at Edinburgh University. A journalist, he holds a B.A. in English, an M.A. in modern European history, and an MSc in Second World War history.

Marci McGrath, M.A., holds a master's degree in history from the University of New Orleans. She has taught history at the secondary school level.

Christy Nadalin (professional information above)

Chris Smith is a New Orleans-based writer and researcher.

National Archives photo research by **Jane Martin.**

Genealogical information for the Introduction provided by **Colleen Hebebrand.**

Index by **Ina Gravitz.**

Contents

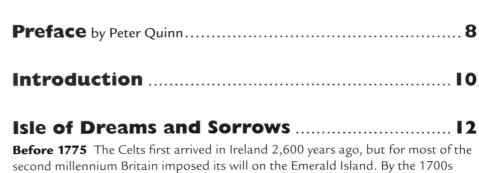

Isle of Dreams and Sorrows 12

Before 1775 The Celts first arrived in Ireland 2,600 years ago, but for most of the second millennium Britain imposed its will on the Emerald Island. By the 1700s many weary Irish were looking for a better life elsewhere—specifically, in America.

1775–1799 When the British waged war against the rebelling colonists, they faced large numbers of Scots-Irish. In fact, at one point during the war, about a third of the Continental Army was Irish-born or of Irish ancestry.

1800–1829 Unable to find work in Ireland, hordes of laborers journeyed to the United States, where they dug canals, built roads, and helped the young nation grow and prosper.

1830–1844 The new immigrants who poured into America's eastern cities were not just Irish, they were Irish Catholics. Anglo-Saxon Protestants resented their presence, resulting in discrimination and, at times, violence.

1845–1860 Irish peasants depended on the potato for sustenance, and when the crop repeatedly failed in the mid- to late 1840s, a million of them died. Another million set sail for America, where they fought for survival in urban enclaves.

1861–1870 During the Civil War, some 150,000 Irish Americans wore Union blue, including the men of the "Irish Brigade." Yet across the battlefields, they faced thousands of Confederate soldiers who were also of Irish descent.

Irish *and* American

Iremember so clearly the beautiful sunny day my father brought me to the high point on Tara in County Meath. As we stood there in silence, looking out over rolling green fields, hills, trees, and blue skies, he took my hand. With his other hand, he waved wide and said, "Maureen, look at this. This is your land. All that you can see, as far as you can see belongs to you." Being the great patriot that he was (he was christened Charles Stewart Parnell FitzSimons), I knew exactly how he meant it, and it made me so proud to belong to this pastoral beauty; proud to be Irish.

I come from a culture steeped in music, dance, and song. I come from men and women who conquered 800 years of oppression, genocide, famine, bondage, and conscription. In spite of all these things, we sent out into the world priests, archbishops, cardinals, presidents, senators, governors, judges, policemen, firemen, lawyers, doctors, writers, directors, producers, musicians, singers, and—yes—actors. We sent the rich and the poor, the beggars and the thieves. Above all, we sent out our Irishness.

It has always amazed me throughout my career and my life in the United States how much the Irish are loved. How so many wish to be Irish and look for the smallest connection to their bloodlines—and find it! I

Maureen O'Hara

think this is so unique and such an honour for Ireland and for the Irish everywhere.

I come from a people who toiled their way across the United States of America, helping to form and build a nation. Our labour and our desire to be free men and women went into the very foundations of that great country. Our blood, sweat, and tears became part of our DNA, and a people evolved that was resilient to adversity. We left oppression from foreigners, church, state, and education behind us. We were a new breed born from men and women of courage.

Little did those early Irish immigrants know that our numbers would one day amount to millions across their new land. Little did they know that our love and loyalty to our traditions and culture would weave into the very fibers of the newfound country. That we would melt into the immigration pot, enriching the blend, without losing where we came from. We would become known as Irish Americans.

I went to Hollywood as a teenage girl. I had Irish values engrained in me by a family that lived well and honestly. We worshipped as a family at church and in the home. Through our parents, we were taught by example what it meant to be Christian. It was the mainstay of our lives. You studied hard, you obeyed the rules, and you gave an honest day's labour for your pay. My parents showed and taught us charity of mind, heart, and spirit. My mother was much loved for her caring and generosity of heart. My parents were never prejudiced toward any man or woman. We were privileged children in so many ways. Our family was very close, and we shared everything together. In many ways, we were very protected in that family womb. Our parents were successful in all their endeavours. My mother ran her own business, which in itself showed great strength and determination for the times. She was also an accomplished actress and opera singer. My father enjoyed a lovely tenor voice, and many nights were spent around the fire, listening and joining in to old Irish songs carried down the generations. This kind of upbringing prepared me for the trials and tribulations of Hollywood.

There were many Irish men and women in every walk of the film industry. The sad part was that most of us were under contract, and that meant that when you were given a part, you took it. Being raised the way I was, I gave an honest day's work. I was never idle. Keeping a roof over my daughter's head and food on the table was my priority. I took, as I call them, some "stinkeroo" roles. I was working so much that I never really had the time to make close friends in the Irish community, but it was great to know that we were there for one another in time of need. It was the same in Ireland. You always knew that you had a community behind you if the hard times showed up.

I must say that the making of *The Quiet Man* was not only a joy for those of us involved; it seemed to express what Irish men and women everywhere felt about the old soil. It stirred people to come back and see their roots. It was the catalyst that brought the Irish back home—and still does to this day. That movie changed my life. As Mary Kate, I became a symbol of the strength and the fire, the fairness, the discipline, and the softness that lives in every Irish woman. I was seen as Ireland's own.

No one will ever break the bond between Mother Ireland and her children in America. I have been proud to be from both these wonderful nations.

Thanks to the opportunities I was given in America, my life took many different turns. Back in Ireland, I had achieved status in the Abbey Theatre, Dublin. I was cast in an original play in the Abbey and would have been recognised as the creator of the role. This was a great position to attain, and it was very hard for me to decide to leave and not take the role. I left to sign a seven-year contract with Mayflower Productions (a British film company) and eventually go to America. I'll never be able to say what would have happened had I stayed in Ireland, but in the end I'm happy with whom I became as an actress and in my business life. It was far beyond my expectations of where my life could go. In America, I was given opportunities to thrive in business ventures that women were traditionally closed out of. I became the first woman president of a commercial airline.

The United States is where I made my life. It is the second nation to touch my heart and soul and make me proud to belong. It is another land that is mine. I'm sure many of you have not heard the story of my U.S. citizenship. Times were turbulent: World War II, fanatical investigations, everything was topsy-turvy. I had a new baby daughter, born an American citizen. As a noncitizen, I felt vulnerable. I had to think of our future. I made my decision to become a U.S. citizen. I knew I would be raising my daughter in the United States and felt that I wanted and needed to be a greater part of this country, for her and for me. In that pursuit, I created complications for myself but was very proud of the outcome.

To make a long story short, I had completed all the paperwork and passed the naturalization exam when an officer of the court told me that the next step was to forswear allegiance to my former country. She told me to raise my right hand and declare that I forswore

Maureen O'Hara's certificate of naturalization

my allegiance to Great Britain. I was shocked! Great Britain? I politely explained to her that I was born in Ireland. I could therefore not forswear allegiance that I did not have. She then showed me the stack of papers I had filled out: Everywhere that I had written "Irish" as my nationality had been crossed out and replaced with "British." I refused outright and was sent into the courtroom to see the judge. I explained my position to him, and we argued the finer points of Irish history for a long time, each refusing to give way to the other. Finally the judge asked for consultation with Washington. To my surprise, Washington's response was that I was considered British!

I had no choice but to refuse my American citizenship. I carefully explained to the judge that I could not let them take our pride in being Irish away from my child and future grandchildren. The judge gave in. He ordered that they put whatever I wanted on my papers just as long as I got out of his courtroom! "British" was erased from the certificate of naturalization, and "Irish"

was typed over it. This was the first time in American history that the government recognised an Irish citizen as being Irish.

The story made it to the papers, and the news reached Ireland in a few days. Eamon de Valera, head of the Irish government, reacted by issuing this statement: "We are today an independent republic. We acknowledge no sovereignty except that of our own people. A fact that our attitude during the recent war should have amply demonstrated. Miss O'Hara was right when she asserted she owed no allegiance to Britain and therefore had none which she could renounce."

I am Irish American. If you ask me what that means, I would tell you that Ireland and America are two great countries and that I have embraced the very best of both. I have integrated those cultures into one being, into who I am. I am proud of and would defend both countries to the death. My soul finds home amongst both peoples and in both countries.

This chronicle will foster a greater understanding of the blending of two nations. It will make you so proud to be Irish and American. American and Irish. Happy reading.

Maureen O'Hara

Born in County Dublin, Ireland, actress and singer Maureen O'Hara starred in more than 50 films, including such timeless classics as Miracle on 34th Street *and* The Quiet Man. *She is a dual citizen of Ireland and the United States, with homes in both countries.*

Proud and Triumphant

A funny thing happened to Irish America on the way to the future: a collection of immigrant outsiders became quintessential insiders. There was no shortage of those who thought such an outcome impossible. The 19th century cartoonist Thomas Nast, for example, depicted the Irish as brutish, semi-simian disrupters of America's cities. British historian Edward Freeman observed sardonically that the United States could perhaps become a world power "if only every Irishman would kill a Negro, and be hanged for it."

The tale of how the Irish became players in every aspect of American life while insisting on their connection to their ancient homeland begins on an island so far out on the fringe of Europe that the Romans called it Hibernia (from *hiberna:* winter quarters). Left to their own devices/vices, the Hibernians, a collection of querulous Celts, occupied themselves with local disputes that poets and bards, with a characteristic penchant for eloquence and exaggeration, turned into epics.

The old order was jolted by the return of a former slave who'd been kidnapped from Roman Britain. Patricius/Patrick brought Christianity to the Irish, who enthusiastically embraced the new religion while clinging tenaciously to the old, with its fairies and miraculous wells. Eventually, thanks to a cadre of scholarly monks, the Irish famously saved civilization, only to lose their franchise to marauding Vikings, meddlesome Normans, and empire-building Englishmen.

Peter Quinn

The contest for control of the island reached a conclusion of sorts when the natives (known as "mere" or pure Irish) and the descendants of the Norman settlers (known as "old English") joined in prolonged and unsuccessful resistance to Tudor conquistadors, Cromwellian zealots, and a Dutch prince with an English wife and a large following of Scot Presbyterians. The Protestant minority celebrated and cemented its triumph, while the Catholic majority suffered confiscation, humiliation, and disenfranchisement, a condition it lamented and yearned to overthrow.

The reason this history is important is that you can't understand America or Ireland or Irish America without it. Right from the start, Irish America reflected Ireland's divided heritage. First off the boats were the Scots-Irish, a hard-fighting, hard-working collection of flinty individualists—Protestants with attitude—who flocked to the frontier.

The Scots-Irish influence on America is profound. A short list of those with Scots-Irish blood in their veins includes Ulysses Grant, Teddy Roosevelt, Elvis Presley, and the James brothers (the big-time bandits Jesse and Frank as well as the highbrow intellectuals Henry and William). Their contradictions are perhaps best epitomized by the seventh president of the United States, Andrew Jackson, vanquisher of the British, champion of the common man, enemy of privilege and plutocracy, as well as slave-owner and remorseless foe of Native Americans.

The Catholic Irish, though fewer in number at the outset, were far more problematic. For much of the English-speaking world, popery and papists were bugbear and nightmare, agents of Satan and instruments of the French and Spanish empires. Immediately suspect, they were quick to suffer the consequences. Ann Glover, for instance, one of the thousands of Catholics deported during the Cromwellian settlement, ended up in Boston, where she worked as a housekeeper and made no secret of her origins. Described by Cotton Mather as an "an old Irishwoman...obstinate in idolatry," she didn't aid her cause by speaking only Irish at her trial. She was hanged as a witch in 1688.

The mass entry of the Catholic Irish into America didn't get underway until the 1840s, when a ruinous crop failure was turned by an imperial government into a brutal instrument of social engineering. The Great Hunger left a million dead and sent a million or more abroad in what was often as much rout as mass migration. The governor of Massachusetts famously compared their arrival to the barbarian hordes that invaded the Roman Empire. Others not only lamented the growing numbers of Irish, but organized a powerful third party movement—the "Know-Nothings"—to deny them full status as Americans.

The saga of these immigrants' struggle for acceptance takes up a large part of this book. Without trying to prescribe a single approach to its telling, let me suggest an underlying theme: America wouldn't be America without the Irish. Simply by being themselves, by refusing to abandon their culture and faith, by insisting on their rights as workers, by building their own educational, charitable, and political organizations, the Irish helped make the country safe for diversity.

The Irish didn't act out an idealized love of humanity. Their elbows were often sharp and their instincts tribal. But their toughness made it impossible for would-be homogenizers to coerce them out of being themselves. And toughness was at the heart of the matter. Anyone who grew up Irish or around them can tell you that. Try studying the history of the fight game, or reading the pulp fiction of the '30s or '40s, or watching noir films without encountering a procession of Irish names and types—cops, robbers, molls, *et al.*—the hardest of the hardboiled.

America today, in all its promise, pain, and glorious complexity, is what the Irish have helped make it. They've shaped its music, politics, literature, and slang. Thanks to them, the ancient Celtic feast of Samhain is now the American holiday of Halloween (and how the ghost of Ann Glover must enjoy the spectacle of the Puritans' descendants dressed as witches and goblins!). Whether it was the Scots-Irish who pushed across the Alleghenies in search of new frontiers or the Irish-Catholic politicians who put in place the foundations of the New Deal, the Irish have been the working realists of the American Dream.

Like all human stories, the chronicle of Irish America has its share of sins and shortcomings. But at its center is a message of hope. Thanks to the energy, vitality, and obstinacy of the Irish, the American Dream got bigger, not smaller. Paths were blazed. Doors were open that would have otherwise stayed shut—doors through which millions of other immigrants, people of different races, religions, and nationalities, continue to pass in pursuit of the Dream.

Peter Quinn

Peter Quinn is an Irish American writer and novelist. His first novel, Banished Children of Eve, *won a 1995 American Book Award. His most recent book is* Looking for Jimmy: A Search for Irish America *(2007).*

Inventing America

In Cleveland, Ohio, on December 5, 1905, a 38-year-old Irish immigrant named Patrick Hogan completed his day as a warehouseman and began his walk home. Darkness was falling as he made his way through the industrial area known as The Flats. He detoured to a small tavern for a drink, and then resumed his journey. As he approached an alley near the Central Viaduct, two gunmen accosted him. The 5'5" Hogan, whom the *Cleveland Leader* later described as "a particularly athletic man possessed of much courage," ripped a cloth mask from one of the men. A moment later, Hogan lay dead. If robbery had been the attackers' motive, they panicked without completing their job, because $7.25—nearly all of Hogan's weekly pay—remained in his pocket.

Patrick Hogan had come to America around 1885. His wife, Mary, and four young children survived him.

Fifty-five years after Hogan's murder, another Irish American, John F. Kennedy, was elected president of the United States, putting an end to speculation about Protestant America's supposed distrust of Catholics, specifically Irish Catholics.

Facile observers will claim that JFK's assassination "ended America's innocence"—as though prior to 1963 we had been a society of wide-eyed cherubs. But no nation created out of armed revolution, and preserved and enlarged in blood and fire—including the sacrifices of immigrants—can be innocent.

The Irish learned this first-hand in the 19th and early 20th centuries, when Ireland's failed potato crop and subsequent economic and political turmoil motivated their immigration to a nation that, though wealthy, was unwilling to allow them little beyond poverty and humiliation.

Strong cultural and familial ties to Ireland, and the nurture of the American Catholic Church, helped the Irish newcomers survive those early years in America. Their capacity for toil was virtually limitless. Gradually, they discovered how American cities "worked." They learned the importance of solidarity and contacts, and the crucial principle of a favor for a favor. Equally important, Irish American leaders reached out to the poor, the sick, and the friendless. Street by street, parish by parish, many of America's important Northeastern and Midwestern cities were transformed.

Today, Americans of all backgrounds enjoy Irish pubs, dance, and other accessible elements of Irish culture. They like to get into the Irish spirit.

On an early spring day in 1984, a male descendant of the ill-fated Patrick Hogan jogged around the Rose Bowl. It probably was gray and cool in Ireland on that morning, but in Southern California the weather was bright and mild. It was St. Patrick's Day, and as the runner came around a large outbuilding, a woman who was jogging the other way approached him. "Hey, runner," she called out in a Spanish accent as she passed, "you're not wearing green!"

The man smiled and called back over his shoulder. "Don't need to!" he said. "My blood is green!"

Later that year, the jogger and his wife had a baby boy, who would be called Patrick.

Everybody is Irish on St. Patrick's Day. For those who have been born Irish, the grip of heritage and tradition is uniquely strong, and wonderful.

Isle of Dreams and Sorrows

Essay by Thomas Fleming

Many years ago, my wife and I were driving through Ireland. We made a wrong turn and were soon wandering through County Mayo totally lost. Night fell. We decided to return to a recent crossroads and drive in another direction. As I backed up, the motor went dead and refused to start. I turned off the headlights to save the battery and got out of the car. There was not a light visible anywhere. Nor were there any stars. Never had I experienced such darkness. Around us sighed a sea wind that seemed like a living, breathing creature. It was as if *Ireland,* the invisible green fields and barren hills and winding rivers, the ruined castles and ancient tombs and haunted battlefields, was embracing me.

I became acutely conscious of the Irish blood in my veins. In this total blackness, time ceased. The modern world, symbolized by the inert automobile, vanished. I was back a thousand, no, two thousand years, in the ancient Ireland of myths and sagas, a land where Celtic warriors came howling out of the night swinging swords, where imperious, willful women whispered silken words of promise and passion. I understood why generations of Irish believed they were surrounded by a supernatural world of angels and demons, saints and devils. I understood how Ireland became a woman capable of capturing a soul—both a sorrowful mother and a joyous daughter that

> **"In Ireland the inevitable never happens and the unexpected constantly occurs."**
>
> —SIR JOHN PENTLAND MAHAFFY

The Celtic cross stands as the symbol of Celtic Christianity. In the 5th century, the Celts—the pagan inhabitants of Ireland—welcomed St. Patrick and his teachings about Jesus Christ. Ireland has been a Christian country ever since.

BEFORE 1775

c. 8000 BCE: Ireland's first inhabitants arrive from Scotland by traversing a land bridge between the two islands.

c. 2000 BCE: The Beaker People, known for producing bell-shaped drinking vessels, arrive in Ireland from Western Europe.

c. 600 BCE: The Celts, a polytheistic culture that once ranged from the Balkans to the Iberian Peninsula and east through Turkey, first arrive in Ireland. They will begin to migrate en masse in another 400 years.

c. 200 BCE: The Celtic migration continues with the arrival of the La Tene, a Celtic warrior culture. By this time, the country is divided into about 150 tuaths—self-governing mini-kingdoms.

c. 150 BCE: As the Roman Empire expands west, Gaels from Spain flee to Ireland. The Gaelic culture will dominate the island for more than a millennium.

43: Roman emperor Claudius invades England. Rome will spend a century trying to subjugate the British Isles, but it will ultimately fail to take Scotland and it will abandon plans to attack Ireland.

431: Pope Celestine I sends Palladius to Ireland to serve as its first bishop. Palladius finds the Irish less than welcoming, and soon he will go back to England.

432: Saint Patrick arrives in Ireland from Britain and establishes his mission, introducing monotheistic Christianity to the island's people.

March 17, 461: Saint Patrick dies. Though he will never be canonized by the pope, Patrick will be venerated as a saint of the church shortly after his death.

c. 500: Saint Brendan—who according to legend was the first Irishman in America, some 900 years before Columbus—is born in County Kerry.

people loved and sometimes died to rescue from evil enemies.

I stumbled back to the car and turned the ignition key again. The motor started! A click and the headlights cast their brilliant electric eyes into the night. Soon we were relaxing in a modern hotel room. But the experience of Ireland's darkness was too profound to ignore. That night I began a journey into my Irish ancestors' astonishing, anguished past. I would even say that the experience marked the moment when I became convinced that in order to understand the Irish American experience, it is essential to know Ireland's history.

The Green Island

For Ireland, geography has been fate. Tens of thousands of years ago, she was linked to the landmass we now call Europe. Geological shocks created a channel that separated her and the lands to her east from the rest of the continent. Further shocks tore Ireland asunder from these lands, and through this gash in the Earth's crust surged saltwater wide enough and deep enough to create a sea. Ireland became Europe's westernmost island, facing the empty Atlantic Ocean on one side and Britain across the Irish Sea on the other side. If you look at a map, you will notice that Britain, the larger island, seems to tilt forward, as if it were eager to seize Ireland in a brutal embrace. There are a thousand years of suffering in that tilt.

The first people came to Ireland about 9,000 years ago. We know lit-

This entrance to a burial chamber at Newgrange dates to 3200 BCE, but people lived in Ireland at least 4,000 years before that. During the high Neolithic Age (after 4000 BCE), agriculture was undertaken and culture prospered.

tle about them beyond traces of their bones and flint tools discovered by archaeologists. They were small and apparently very primitive, with no knowledge of agriculture. They were succeeded by more sophisticated people who planted and harvested and tamed some wild animals, such as dogs and horses. They left behind them impressive graves, where they deposited the ashes of their dead. The huge tombs in the valley of the river Boyne—in Dowth, Knowth, and Newgrange—were built, scholars estimate, 5,000 years ago.

Newgrange is the most impressive of these tombs. Its burial chambers are at the end of a long tunnel in an immense hill comprised of some 200,000 tons of stone. It was built around the time the Egyptians were constructing their pyramids, and it must have taken a similar amount of backbreaking labor. The builders left no trace of a written language. But they dragged enormous curbstones to the bases of their tombs, many carved with geometric spirals that may have had religious or philosophical meanings. These silent guardians are rimmed with white quartz pebbles from the Wicklow Hills. Archaeologists think that similar pebbles once covered the entire 35 foot high mound with a brilliant shimmering mantle. On a summer day, the effect must have been stun-

The distinctive interwoven knots of Celtic art date back to the Iron Age. This Ardagh chalice, from the 8th or 9th century, was discovered in 1868 by a boy digging for potatoes.

ning. Was it a kind of declaration of faith in the soul's immortality?

The tombs themselves—there are 300 of them scattered throughout the northern half of Ireland—bear some resemblance to shrines. An opening in the ceiling at Newgrange is positioned so that on the shortest day of the year, the rising sun fills the corridor and the inner chamber with annunciatory light. These ancient people may have worshipped a sun god and offered thanks and supplications to him at this time, when preparations for planting the crops of the coming year began.

Eventually these people, probably joined by others from Europe, progressed from stone implements to metals. Ireland began mining copper in County Cork, and gold was discovered in the Wicklow Hills. Soon, ancient mariners plied the seas around Europe trading in woven cloth and bronze and gold

artifacts. Thanks to that mysterious "river in the ocean" now known as the Gulf Stream, Ireland had a climate distinctly warmer and more benign than Europe's or Britain's. The ancient mariners began calling her the Green Island. While Minoan artists were painting spectacular frescos in Knossos, Irish artisans created gorgeous gold necklaces and strikingly beautiful decorations on pottery. They traded these treasures for bronze daggers and axes from Portugal, amber from the shores of the Baltic Sea, and glassy faience beads from distant Egypt. The merchant ships carried news of the Green Island to distant lands, and soon men and women began coming to Ireland not just to trade but to live and prosper—and rule.

The Rise of the Celts

Starting in 900 BCE, tall, blond, ferociously adventurous Celtic warriors began surging from their homeland on the steppes of Russia. Soon their war-bands were sweeping south and west on magnificent horses. They rode so recklessly that in some parts of Europe, stories were told of strange half-man, half-beast creatures called centaurs. The Celtic armies were equipped with iron swords and spears and armor—a huge advance over bronze. Iron had been discovered in the Caucasus

BEFORE 1775

June 9, 597: St. Columcille, an Irish-born missionary who is also known as Saint Columba, dies at age 75 after a life spent converting the Scots to Christianity. He will be credited with spreading monastic Christianity into the void left by the fallen pagan Roman Empire.

664: The Synod of Whitby, a council convened to decide the date of Easter, follows the decree of the Roman Church over that of the Irish Church.

795: The Vikings invade Ireland for the first time, raiding coastal monasteries. War parties will work their way inland, build settlements, and within a half-century establish alliances with the Irish.

1002: Brian Boru, credited with building alliances between Ireland's many chieftains and kings, becomes high king of Ireland.

1066: The Normans conquer England, decisively defeating the Saxons at the Battle of Hastings.

1142: Ireland's first Cistercian monastery is established at Mellifont, introducing a new, austere form of monasticism to the cultural landscape.

1155: King Henry II of England is granted dominion over Ireland on the authority of Pope Adrian IV.

August 23, 1170: The Welsh Earl of Pembroke, known as Strongbow, leads his Norman army to the south coast of Ireland near what is now Waterford. He captures the Viking settlement there before moving on to Dublin.

1171: Strongbow becomes the first British-born person to rule any part of Ireland when he becomes king of Leinster.

1172: The Second Synod of Cashel decrees that the Irish Church should follow the model of the Church of England, which is under the jurisdiction of the Church of Rome.

around 1100 BCE, and by 900 BCE the Celts were using it in numerous ways. By the end of the 4th century BCE, they were Europe's dominant power, in control of the entire continent from Spain and the British Isles to Romania. Inevitably, these swaggering, half-naked warriors reached Ireland.

The Celtic empire was a haphazard affair. The Celts had no written language and little interest in founding cities or organizing provinces. They were essentially a huge tribe of often-contentious war-chiefs. Slowly, over the next 200 years, a more methodical and determined people began to conquer them: the Romans. Again and again, their carefully trained legions marched into battle against the Celts, almost invariably winning the fights.

Not only did the Romans have a vision of empire, they knew how to realize it. They built roads, cre-

In this Celtic artwork, a god holds the arms of two men. Each tribe had their gods, which were associated with nature. Though more than 300 deities are recorded, fewer than 20 were common to all tribes.

ated cities, and offered citizenship to those who submitted to their laws. They raised great temples to their gods and amphitheaters for plays and communal festivals; they founded schools to teach the arts and sciences. By the end of the 2nd century AD, Spain, France, and Britain had become Roman provinces. But Ireland remained beyond their grasp—a fact of enormous consequence for the Irish soul.

For more than 600 years, the Celts ruled Ireland. Their language, their religion, their gods, the tales of their wars and heroes—their entire way of life—was unchallenged. It was a warrior culture. The Celtic temperament was explosive; they were always ready for battle. But they also loved beauty. An exquisite gold torque was around each warrior's neck when he went into a fight—often it was the only thing he wore. As the war frenzy gripped them, it was not uncommon for members of an entire Celtic army to fling off their armor and clothes and rush naked at the enemy, screaming curses and threats. Warriors were also prone to fight each other. Duels, often to the death, frequently occurred.

The Celts believed in the immortality of the soul, and in reincarnation. Death, while sorrowful, was largely unfeared. A slain man's soul would return, hopefully in another warrior's body. Celtic priests, known as druids, studied as long as 20 years to acquire their arcane arts of divination, prophecy, and magic. They had no written language, beyond a crude alphabet (called Ogam) used for brief inscriptions. Everything they learned from older druids was committed to memory. Druids were feared because they had the power to deal with the Otherworld, where the gods and evil spirits lived. An angry druid could utter a curse over a wisp of hay and fling it in the face of an enemy. Within hours, according to legend, the victim's body would be covered with boils and he might become a hopeless lunatic.

Celtic society was organized around kings. Each king ruled a *tuath*—in Celtic, "a people"—a cluster of families usually translated as a tribe. There were about 150 *tuaths* in Ireland, each one a minor kingdom capable of turning out as many as 3,000 soldiers. A king could form an alliance with other kings, or submit to the rule of a more powerful king—or win the submission of all the kings in his part of Ireland if he had the power and prestige to insist on it. Eventually, four or five confederacies emerged, ruling different sections of Ireland. Sometimes this local supremacy was due to the gifted leadership of various kings, but often it was the influence of geography.

Ancient Irish society had a cultured upper class that included aristocrats, warriors, bards, and the priestly druids (*pictured*). Celtic druids were healers, scholars, and arbitrators. They were polytheistic, and they venerated nature.

Connaught and Ulster, for instance, had barrier rivers and mountains on their borders, which made them easier to defend and rule.

A king was a leader in war and a judge in peace. Originally, he claimed descent from one of the god-heroes of Celtic mythology. As time passed, ambitious or talented warriors could claim a kingship by exploits in battle. War was the king's chief business. Throughout Ireland to this day exist the ruins of thousands of *raths* (forts), which were built to resist attacks from enemies. Often these circular earthworks, each surrounded by an outer ditch, were large enough to contain houses and pens for animals. In the stony west of Ireland, their walls

were often made of rocks. Kings and upper-class Celts (the *flaithi*) lived in *duns* (more formidable forts), often at the head of easily defended narrow valleys or on top of steep hills.

In peace, the king's will was not the only law. Within a *tuath*, everyone was protected by the Brehon Laws. This elaborate set of rules eventually covered every possible action or infraction, from being stung by a neighbor's bees to homicide. Most wrongs, even murder, were punished by a fine called an *eric;* the payment was in the only currency in use: cows. A fine was levied not only against the guilty man but five generations of his family. If they failed to pay, the plaintiff often resorted to a weapon that has reappeared throughout Irish history: the hunger strike. The injured man sat before the offender's door and refused to eat or drink. Almost always the offender, fearful of the wrath of the gods, capitulated.

Every king had in his *tuath* men from the *oes dana*—the class of learning. Besides druids, these men included judges, doctors, skilled craftsmen in metal working, harpists, and poets. The poets—*filids*—ranked second only to the druids in their importance to the king and his family. The highest ranking poet, an *ollamh,* was almost equal to the king and sometimes intimidated royalty

BEFORE 1775

October 6, 1175: King Henry II and Irish high king Rory O'Connor agree to the Treaty of Windsor. The pact makes O'Connor king of Connaught but subservient and obligated to pay tribute to Henry II.

1314: Scottish king Robert the Bruce gives one-half of the Stone of Scone to Cormac McCarthy, lord of Blarney, in gratitude for his help at the Battle of Bannockburn. The stone will be set into Blarney castle in 1446 and, according to legend, kissing it will imbue a person with great eloquence.

May 26, 1315: Edward the Bruce, younger brother of Scottish king Robert the Bruce, lands on Ireland's shores with a 6,000-man fleet and declares himself king of Ireland.

October, 1318: The Anglo-Norman army of John de Birmingham routs the Scots-Irish army of Edward the Bruce at the Battle of Faughart. Bruce is drawn and quartered, and his head is sent to English king Edward II.

1348–51: Like much of the rest of Europe, Ireland is brought to its knees by the "Black Death." The Plague claims the lives of one out of three people in Ireland.

1366: In an effort to reverse the trend of Anglo-Norman assimilation in Irish culture, the English leadership in Ireland passes a series of laws known as the Statutes of Kilkenny. They forbid, among other things, marriage between English and Irish.

December 1, 1494: Sir Edward Poyning, Ireland's viceroy under King Henry VII, comes before the Irish Parliament at Drogheda and asserts that the legislative body will hereafter be subject to the authority of the British Parliament.

1536: In Dublin, a parliament passes a version of the English Act of Supremacy, making England's King Henry VIII head of the Irish Church.

with the threat of his satire, which could supposedly disfigure the victim. Most of the time, the poet devoted himself to praising the king and his ancestors. At feasts, he entertained listeners by reciting the poems that celebrated the semi-mythical events in the early history of Celtic Ireland. Only a poet could travel beyond the boundaries of his *tuath* and still claim the protection of the Brehon Laws.

Not far behind Celtic faith in the sorcery of words was their near worship of music. The harpist had a seat of honor at each king's banquet table, just below the poet. The harmonies that the Celts loved best were divided into laughing music (*Geantraighe*), crying music (*Goltraighe*), and sleeping music (*Suantraighe*). The harpists played six-string instruments similar to the lyres that were plucked by the worshippers of Orpheus, the Greek god of music and revels. Anyone who injured a harpist's plucking finger was obliged to pay a heavy fine.

The poems of the Greek heroic age, the *Iliad* and the *Odyssey*, are justly honored around the world. The Celtic heroic poems are equally powerful and dramatic—and they provide us with a vivid portrait of the Celtic way of life. The central

IRELANDS HISTORICAL EMBLEMS.

Such Irish emblems as the harp, the shamrock, the roundtower, and the ancient goddess Eire made an important contribution to national unity and pride in the long struggle for independence.

figure in many of the poems is the semi-divine warrior Cuchulain, son of the war god Lugh. Once Cuchulain went into his "warp-spasm," he was invincible in battle. The poems describe how his body contorted into fearful shapes: *On his head his temple sinews stretched to the nape of his neck, each … measureless knob as big as the head of a month-old child.… The hair of his head twisted like the tangle of a red thornbush … then tall and thick, steady and strong, high as the mast of a noble ship, rose up from the dead center of his skull a straight spout of black blood darkly and magically smoking.* Hyperbole is one of the hallmarks of Celtic poetry.

Into the ranks of the enemy Cuchulain would charge, mowing down warriors by the hundreds with his whirling sword and plunging spear. Like the Greek heroes, he sometimes met a great warrior from

Irish DNA

Ireland is more than a little remote. The Romans, who called the island Hibernia—the land of eternal winter—did not bother to conquer it. Others, however, were not so choosy. Vikings, Normans, and Saxons all sailed to Ireland with mostly conquest and plunder in mind.

In the 1990s, an Irish government advertising campaign promoted the country's many qualities. The ad suggested that contemporary visitors would have a grand time, especially since the visitors, unlike the Vikings and the rest, would be folks "we" actually invited.

But who were the "we"? Were the Irish of the late 20th century drawing some line between themselves and these uninvited outsiders? Had these invaders not become "Irish" through centuries of cohabitation?

The question of who is absolutely Irish is often judged at a mere glance: red hair, freckles—the "map of Ireland" on someone's face. Probing more deeply, it can be decided by family name. But none of these can match a determination based on deoxyribonucleic acid (DNA).

Ireland has been inhabited for roughly 10,000 years. The Celts were not the first arrivals, but they are the people who more than any other have established a scientific standard for "Irishness."

Oxford University geneticist Bryan Sykes, author of *Saxons, Vikings and Celts: The Genetic Roots of Britain and Ireland,* argues that the Celts—who first arrived from the Iberian Peninsula around 6,000 years ago—remain the core of the Irish population. As many as 98 percent of citizens in counties Mayo and Roscommon have Celtic roots, though that percentage is much lower in Leinster counties, where about a quarter of DNA can be attributed to Anglo-Norman invaders.

Sykes, armed with approximately 10,000 DNA research samples, contends that Ireland has remained "stubbornly Celtic." If so, then even all those uninvited arrivals mentioned in that tourist ad failed to significantly dilute "Irish" DNA—or make the island anything less than Celtic Central.

the other side in single battle, while the armies watched. Unlike Achilles, for whom vengeance was a primary motive, Cuchulain was sometimes torn by anguish when he killed a man he respected or in some cases loved.

In *The Tain Bo Cuailnge,* considered the best of the Celtic epics, Cuchulain is forced to fight his foster brother, Ferdia, when an army from Connaught, led by the warrior queen, Maeve, invades Ulster. For days the heroes clash, inflicting fearful wounds, until Ferdia slumps to the ground dead. A weeping Cuchulain clutches him to his chest and sobs, *Ill-met, Ferdia, like this/ You crimson and pale in my sight/...Bravery is battle madness!*

Women also figure strongly in the Celtic sagas. Queen Maeve is a semi-divine, outspoken wife who gets into an argument with her husband, King Ailill, about which of them has the most wealth. When she discovers that he has a great white-horned bull superior to any in her herds, she decides to obtain a huge brown bull in Ulster. When the owners reject her offer, Maeve leads an army to seize it. Her warriors are defeated by Cuchulain, and the triumphant warrior and his followers come upon the queen, defenseless, in the field. She begs him to spare her. "I am not wont to slay women," Cuchulain says, and Maeve lives to fight another day.

Cuchulain—a mortal man, though the son of the god Lugh—exemplifies Irish mythological figures. These were not so much gods as heroes possessing superhuman powers. Cuchulain defended Ulster against Queen Maeve.

BEFORE 1775

1542: The Irish Parliament passes the Crown of Ireland Act, naming England's King Henry VIII king of Ireland.

January 28, 1547: Edward VI becomes king of England and Ireland, ushering in an era of Protestant reforms. These include the implementation of the *Book of Common Prayer* as the "handbook" for Anglican liturgy.

July 1553: Mary I becomes queen of England and Ireland. A staunch Roman Catholic, she will bring Britain back to the Church of Rome.

1556: Queen Mary I establishes plantations of English settlers in the Irish interior at Laois and Offaly. She names them Queen's County and King's County in honor of herself and her husband, King Philip II of Spain.

November 17, 1558: On the death of her half-sister, Mary I, Elizabeth I takes the English and Irish throne. Elizabeth is a committed Protestant, and her reign will see the Church of England turn away from Rome once again.

1558: Queen Elizabeth enacts The Oath of Supremacy, the first of many anti-Catholic "penal laws." It will be the first step toward condemning the Catholics of Ireland to a life of poverty and near-starvation as tenant farmers and servants to Protestant landowners.

1584: Richard Butler, among the first Irishmen to reach North America, explores North Carolina's Outer Banks as a member of Sir Walter Raleigh's first expedition to the East Coast.

1586: Edward Nugent, an Irish colonist on Virginia's Roanoke Island, murders the king of the local native Indian tribe. This murder, among other acts of hostility between natives and the European newcomers, may be a reason for the mysterious disappearance of the Roanoke Island settlement.

Women were the equals of men in pre-Christian Ireland. They owned property and held power. Queen Maeve, depicted here as a huntress in this early woodcut, is one of many strong female figures in Irish mythology.

Finn Mac Cumail is another famous semi-mythical Celtic warrior whose story is told in a cycle of poems. Rather than marching at the head of an army like Cuchulain, Finn lived by his wits in the forests with a band of devoted followers, the Fianna. To join these heroes, a young man had to pass seemingly impossible tests. He had to stand up to his waist in a hole while warriors threw spears at him. He had only his shield and a stick of wood to deflect them. If he suffered the slightest wound, he failed the test. He also had to run noiselessly through the forest without so much as a single twig cracking under his feet. If a thorn pierced his foot, he had to extract it while running at top speed. These supermen defended Ireland's coasts against invaders, and had the first pick of the young girls in their *tuath* when they were ready for marriage.

The Fianna loved the land with a passion that more than equaled Cuchulain's devotion to honor and glory. Their favorite poet, Caeilte, described an island where the Fianna hunted and relaxed: *Skittish deer are on her pinnacles and blackberries on her waving heather…in all her glades a faultless grass….her wild swine, they were fat; cheerful her fields, her nuts hung on her forest-hazel boughs…under her rivers' brinks trout lie, the sea gulls wheeling around her grand cliff….* For the Fianna, Ireland was a living creature.

The upper-class Celts lived well. Their dining tables groaned beneath whole roasted pigs, slabs of beef, and great haunches of deer. Wine and mead (a kind of beer made from fermented honey) flowed copiously from silver flagons. The women wore bright silks, red or purple cloaks, and gleaming gold and silver jewelry. One poet described an aristocratic beauty's coiffure: *two tresses of golden hair upon her head, and a plaiting of four strands in each tress, and a ball of gold upon the end of each plait.* Men wore equally bright colors; often their cloaks were dyed a half dozen hues to attract the attention of local beauties. Sexual desire was frequently and openly an accepted part of their lives. When Queen

The Fenian Cycle tells of Finn Mac Cumhail and his band, known as the Fianna. These professional soldiers were learned in poetry as well as in the art of warfare.

Maeve was trying to persuade Ferdia to fight Cuchulain, she offered him her daughter's hand in marriage and added: "My own friendly thighs on top of that if need be."

Enter Saint Patrick

In what the Celts called the Outerworld, in Britain and Europe and lands around the Mediterranean Sea, vast changes were taking place. Toward the end of the 3rd century the Roman Empire began to collapse. Power-hungry generals organized armies and marched on Rome to make themselves emperors. With the frontiers unguarded, across the Rhine River surged thousands of ragged, hungry German warriors: Vandals, Goths, Sueves. The Romans called all of them barbarians. In the growing chaos, a new religion, Christianity, based on the teachings of a Jewish prophet, Jesus of Nazareth, began to appeal to many people. In the 4th century, Christianity became the official religion of the Roman Empire. But the triumph of the new faith did not stop the barbarian warriors from continuing to dismantle the empire.

Gradually, the empire split into western and eastern sections, with two emperors; one ruled from Constantinople, the other from Rome. The eastern empire would flourish for another thousand years. But the western empire, already overrun by barbarians, continued to disintegrate. In 410, a barbarian army stormed through Italy and sacked Rome. Here and there, pockets of Roman civilization survived and the Christian Church acquired some of the empire's dwindling power and prestige. A pope continued to speak from ravaged Rome and urged the conversion of the barbarians. Most of them embraced Christianity in a vague, unlettered way as a gesture of respect for the glory that once had been Rome.

There is little evidence of this turmoil touching Celtic Ireland at first. Britain, now mostly Christian, had only random contacts with the Green Island. Occasionally, Celtic warriors were hired to help the Roman British in their struggle with invading tribes of Angles, Saxons, and Jutes. Celtic kings soon perceived that the pickings were easy in this near anarchy. They began sailing across the Irish Sea on raids that brought back loot and captives, whom they sold as slaves. One of those unfortunates was a 16-year-old boy named Patricius. He was the son of an affluent Roman official who was probably a nominal Christian.

Bought by a farmer in County Antrim, Patricius was assigned the task of tending sheep and cattle in the countryside. It was not a pleasant job. For weeks, he was alone on Antrim's craggy steep-sided Slemish Mountain. His owner/master sent him little food; often he was forced to eat roots and grass. What pride he may have acquired from his father's status soon vanished. He faced a future of desolating ignominy. A slave was on the lowest rung of Ireland's Celtic society.

Patricius began to think about the Christian religion into which he had been baptized. He had never taken it seriously; priests were boring nuisances, always asking his father for money. He was not even sure he believed in God. But his misery drove him to reach out to the only being in the universe who

BEFORE 1775

August 8, 1588: King Phillip II of Spain sends the Spanish Armada to attack England. After engaging a larger British fleet, the Armada will attempt to escape back to Spain but will suffer significant casualties on the north and west coasts of Ireland.

1594: Displeased with English dominion over Ireland, Gaelic chieftains Hugh O'Neill and Hugh O'Donnell lead their subjects in a series of skirmishes against the army of Elizabeth I. Collectively, these battles will come to be known as the Nine Years War.

1600s: The Irish begin to immigrate to coastal settlements on the eastern shores of North America. These immigrants include indentured servants and economic or political refugees.

December 24, 1601: Gaelic chieftains suffer defeat at the hands of the English at the Battle of Kinsale. The battle proves to be the turning point of the Nine Years War; Gaelic rule in Ireland will become increasingly marginalized.

September 1607: The chieftains of Ulster's most prominent clans, including the O'Neills and O'Donnells, set sail for Spain from the Irish port of Rathmullan. This event, which will become known as the Flight of the Earls, marks the end of centuries of Gaelic rule in Ulster.

1638: Dubliner George Downing arrives in Boston. An early Irish American success story, Downing will rise to prominence as a Harvard graduate and nephew of the first governor of the Massachusetts Bay Colony, John Winthrop.

October 1641: In Ireland, violence breaks out between Irish Catholic gentry and English Protestant plantation settlers, primarily in Ulster. The unrest, which will continue for 12 years, will be known as the Irish Confederate Wars.

St. Patrick, patron saint of Ireland, brought Christianity to Irish pagans in the 5th century. His feast day on March 17 is celebrated all over the world.

might care about him; he began praying to Jesus.

Gradually, Patricius later recalled, faith came alive in his soul. His prayers were being heard, he was sure of it. But six long, unhappy years passed before a voice whispered: *Your hungers are rewarded. You are going home.* That night, Patricius fled toward the coast, trudging in the darkness and hiding by day. In a seaport, he found a ship that took him to Europe, probably as a deckhand. Eventually, he returned to his parents' home in Britain, where he was welcomed with joy and relief. But Patricius could not stop thinking about Ireland. By now deeply religious, he began having dreams in which the voices of men he had met in Ireland called out to him,

beseeching his help. Finally, Jesus spoke in his heart, asking him why he would not serve the one "who gave his life for you."

Upon returning to Europe, Patricius studied at a monastery in France and was ordained not only a priest but a bishop, to give him more authority. He made no secret of his intention to return to Ireland to bring Christ's message to the pagan Celts. In 432, he arrived with 24 followers. Their work was difficult and even dangerous at first. They were successful with the slaves and lower-class people, but the kings and their druids and chief warriors regarded Patricius with fear and suspicion. A chief druid warned King Laoghaire, the ruler of northern Ireland: *This man shall destroy our gods and overturn our altars.... He will seduce the people and bring them after him.... He will free the slaves... he will magnify kindreds of low degree... and he shall subdue unto himself the kings that resist him....*

In some versions of his story, Patricius narrowly escaped assassination several times. But his charisma and fervor were irresistible. He faced down King Laoghaire and his druids and lesser kings and their followers, often converting druids on the spot. Roving Ireland, he made a point of appearing at shrines such as the great mound at Newgrange and declaring the supremacy and power of the Christian faith. Soon Patrick, as the Celts called him, was a kind of king in his own right, traveling with a retinue of believers that included sons of kings and household servants. Rich converts showered gifts on him, but he invariably gave his new wealth to the poor.

Patrick's personal life was austere. He slept on stone and immersed himself in icy water while he said his daily prayers. His clothing was a rough hair shirt and a robe of unbleached wool. He began founding churches in all parts of Ireland. By the time he returned to King Laoghaire's palace in the north, the missionary bishop was so powerful that the king asked him to join a group of druids and historians to revise and write down the laws and customs of the land from a Christian point of view. Finally, Patrick founded a main church at Armagh, from which he hoped to oversee his spiritual domain.

In little more than 30 years, Patrick transformed Ireland from a pagan to a Christian country. Not everyone surrendered his or her worship of the old gods, but everywhere, north and south, east and west, churches rose in the vicinity of the Celtic shrines. Pagan feast days became Christian holy days. The kings and their favorite *flaithi* continued to rule, and the wealthy farmers continued to own their herds of cows and sheep. But they grudgingly agreed that slavery was an abomination that had to be extinguished in Ireland. To Celts who already believed in the immortality of the soul and a future life in a mysterious Underworld, it was not too difficult to accept a Christian paradise in which Jesus waited to embrace his followers and a netherworld where evil men and women were punished. Especially important, Christianity brought the Latin alphabet, giving the Irish a written language.

Christian Ireland Versus Barbarian Europe

In these same decades, in Europe and Britain, Roman civilization all but expired. *Bybliothecis sepulcrorum in perpetuum clausis,* sighed one Roman writer. "The libraries, like

St. Bridgid, or "Mary of the Gael," lived in the 5th century and is second only to St. Patrick in the affections of the Irish. She founded Ireland's first convent.

tombs, were closed forever." The last Western emperor, Romulus Augustulus, was deposed by the Gothic barbarian chief, Odoacer, in 476. St. Patrick, by now a very old man, died around this time. The centuries known as the Dark Ages began. But in Ireland, Christianity flourished and grew at an astonishing pace. Thousands of men and women responded to St. Patrick's summons to seek holiness through self-denial. They retreated to austere hermitages and to monasteries, where they devoted their lives to prayer and scholarship.

They were joined by refugees from monasteries in Europe, who brought with them much of the learning of the Romans and Greeks. Over the next three centuries, these monks and nuns created richly illustrated books, which rescued from oblivion great philosophers such as Aristotle and Plato, poets such as Homer and Virgil, and historians such as Herodotus and Tacitus. They also wrote down—and often brilliantly revised—the epic sagas of the Celts, giving Ireland a sense of history and local pride that the rest of Europe was rapidly losing. Most beautiful of all were the monks' illustrated copies of the Bible. Visitors to modern Dublin can see one of the greatest of these works of art, the 9th century *Book of Kells,* named

BEFORE 1775

1642: The English Civil War begins. Actually a series of three wars over nine years, it will lead to the end—however briefly—of the English monarchy and ultimately see the empire ruled as a protectorate under Oliver Cromwell.

August 15, 1649: Lord Protector Oliver Cromwell lands in Dublin with his formidable New Model Army. He will spend the next several years brutally persecuting Catholics and massacring Irish civilians, notably in Drogheda and Wexford.

1650s: More than 100,000 Irish children are sold into slavery in the West Indies during Cromwell's decade of terror.

September 3, 1651: The Parliamentarians and Cromwell's New Model Army defeat the Royalists of Charles II at the Battle of Worcester, marking the end of the English Civil War.

1652: England's Parliament passes the Act of Settlement, which is meant to penalize Irish Catholics for their participation in the Irish rebellion of 1641. They will be barred from positions of power, stripped of their lands, and exiled to Connaught.

September 3, 1658: Oliver Cromwell dies at Whitehall at age 59 and is buried in an elaborate service at Westminster Abbey. In the decade after his arrival in Ireland, the island's population plummeted from 1.5 million to about 500,000.

January 30, 1661: Oliver Cromwell's body is exhumed, hanged, drawn and quartered, and decapitated in a bizarre "posthumous execution" ritual. His body is dumped into a common pit. His head will spend the next 300 years touring greater London before a final burial in February 1960.

for the monastery where it was created, in County Meath.

In these centuries, the Irish can be said without too much exaggeration to have preserved Western civilization and rescued Christianity from ignorance. This epochal accomplishment included a reverse flow of missionaries, such as Saints Columba and Columbanus, who brought the Irish Christian message and its love of learning to Scots, English, and Europeans. Their followers traveled as far as Switzerland and Italy, where they founded monasteries and churches.

Another traveler, whose life is a perplexing mix of myth and possible fact, was a County Kerry priest named Brendan. He too was a founder of monasteries in distant lands. But he is especially remembered for a voyage he described in the book *Navigato Sancti Brendani*. It tells how he and his companions sailed across the vast Atlantic Ocean in a small skin-covered *curragh* and discovered the "Land of Promise and of Saints"—America. The book notes islands that resemble Iceland and Newfoundland, where they stopped along the way. The voyagers called them "God's stepping stones." Despite these assertions, most historians regard St. Brendan's story as unproven.

Secular learning and literature also flourished in Ireland during these times. Poets sang of love and

The *Book of Kells,* containing the four gospels, was created around 800 A.D. Considered the most beautifully illuminated manuscript in the world, it is on display at Trinity College in Dublin.

sorrow with a marvelous poignancy. One of the most beautiful poems is the lament of Liadain, an attractive maiden who rejects her suitor Cuirithir, causing him to become a monk:

> *No pleasure*
> *that deed I did, tormenting him*
> *tormenting what I treasure*

Another vivid poem is the sigh of an old woman for her lost youth:

> *When my arms are seen,*
> *all bony and thin!*
> *the craft they used to practice*
> *was pleasant:*
> *they used to be about glorious kings*

The Rise and Fall of Brian Boru

The brutal, mostly illiterate European world that emerged from the wreckage of the Roman Empire continued history's age-old struggle for wealth and power. Ireland ruefully discovered that her devotion to religion, learning, and poetry on the outer edge of the continent did not guarantee her immunity from its violence. In 795, fierce, helmeted warriors began appearing off the Irish coast. They beached their swift, high-prowed ships and stormed ashore to loot and pillage and kidnap. The Vikings, Ireland's first invaders in a thousand years, had arrived. Monasteries, with their gold and silver altar pieces, book covers, and rich priestly vestments, were a favorite target. These raiding expeditions soon grew bigger and more ambitious. Within 50 years, the Norsemen were establishing settlements and marching inland to wreak wider havoc.

Christianity had unified Ireland culturally. But her political organization remained the ever-shifting confederacies of the Celtic era. There was no central government to raise armies or fleets to protect the Green Island from attack and abuse by a determined, well-armed enemy. Soon the Vikings had established an enclave around Dublin Bay. Their goal was no longer plunder; they wanted land. The population of Scandinavia had grown at a rapid pace, and surplus men and women were seeking a new life beyond its borders.

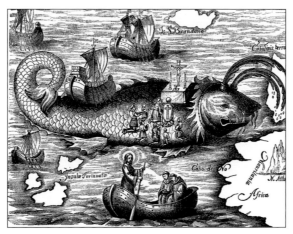

According to legend, St. Brendan made a voyage to the Isle of Delight, where he met a sea monster. Some scholars have speculated that Brendan discovered America during his journey.

For another century, the Irish and the "White Gentiles," as the Vikings were called because of their blond hair, made war on each other. The Irish fiercely resisted the invaders' attempts to occupy large areas of land. They confined them to trading settlements at Dublin, Wexford, Cork, and Limerick, which became Ireland's first cities. Many Vikings

Brian Boru, a self-declared high king of Ireland, slaughtered the Vikings of Dublin. He died in 1014 at the Battle of Clontarf, where the Vikings were defeated and fled.

grew discouraged and sailed away to Iceland and Greenland, but others replaced them. Most fearsome were the "Black Gentiles," dark-haired warriors who came from Denmark and soon ruled all of Munster. They imposed a "nose tax," an ounce of silver for every nose. It was either pay or have their noses slit. Ireland was not the only country that these warriors invaded. Much of England became known as the Danelaw, and a large chunk of western France became Normandy, land of the Northmen.

Vikings, both blond and dark-haired, found the Irish more and more difficult to defeat in battle. Irishmen had acquired weapons and learned tactics that enabled them to fend off the invaders. They even captured a Viking king, whom they ceremoniously drowned in a convenient lake. The Irish also learned how to combine their forces. Eventually, a leader emerged from the hard fighting against the Danes in Munster: Brian Boru. The latter term was a title bestowed on him by his chief poet, Mac Liag. It meant "tribute of cows." For about 30 years, Brian ruled the southern half of Ireland from his fortress-palace, Kincora (near the modern town of Killaloe) while another warrior king,

Malachy, ruled Ulster and the rest of the north. In 1002, Brian pressured Malachy into resigning and declared himself, with the help of poet Mac Liag, *Imperator Scottorum,* emperor of all Ireland.

Even the Vikings, who were writing sagas glorifying their conquests, called Brian the noblest of all kings. He was noted for his kindness to wrongdoers, often forgiving a man twice for the same offense. He saw himself as a feudal ruler like France's Charlemagne, claiming the fealty of all the other petty and not so petty Irish kings as a matter of law, not sentiment. Under his shrewd, benevolent rule, Ireland became a unified country for the first time. He even forced all the Viking towns and settlements to pay him tribute. But the Celtic habit of loyalty to local kings made Brian's reign all too temporary.

Leinster's warriors revolted, and the Vikings in Dublin sent them men and money. The Norsemen were persuaded to enter the fray by Queen Gormflaith, one of those headstrong Irish women who were descendants in spirit if not in fact of mythical Queen Maeve. Gormlaith had been married three times, the last time to Brian, who divorced her for adultery. She was notoriously unfaithful to all of her husbands. Gormlaith's hatred of Brian was intense. She convinced King Sitric

King Magnus in the Marsh at Downpatrick

King Magnus of Norway is killed by Irish at a battle near Downpatrick in 1103. After first landing in Ireland in 795, Vikings continued raids on the island for 40 years before establishing the settlements of Dublin, Cork, and Waterford.

of Dublin, her son by an earlier marriage, to share her animosity, even though he was married to Brian's sister. It was said of Gormlaith that she was "the fairest of all women" but that she "did all things ill over which she had any power."

When Brian marched into Leinster with a warrior host from Munster and Connacht to restore his rule, the two armies met at Clontarf outside Dublin. The battle lasted from dawn to dusk, and thousands died. Brian's warriors won, but in the chaotic aftermath a Viking warrior found the king without his bodyguards; they were chasing the routed enemy. The Viking killed Brian, mak-

ing Good Friday, April 23, 1014, one of the saddest days in Irish history.

Brian's chief poet, Mac Liag, wrote a lament for his loss:

> Oh where, Kincora, is Brian the great
> And where is the beauty
>   that once was thine
> Oh where are the princes
>   and nobles that sate
> At the feast in thy halls and
>   drink the red wine,
> Where, O Kincora.

Brian's son had been killed in the early stages of the fighting at Clontarf, and no other heir was strong enough to inherit his power. For 150 years, Ireland relapsed into instability, with various local kings intriguing and occasionally fighting to become the high king without success. Murtagh O'Brien, a great grandson of Brian Boru, ruled from 1086 to 1119, displaying much of his ancestor's shrewdness and personal charm. But he and other high king claimants reigned "with opposition." Much of this hostility emanated from Leinster, where powerful families still brooded over their defeat at Clontarf. The Irish had a profound sense of their identity as a people, but not as a nation.

The Norman Semi-Conquest

So we come to the fateful year 1166, when Rory O'Connor became high king of Ireland. He was from Connacht, the western province, and was opposed by Dermot Mac Murrough, king of Leinster. King Rory backed a rival for the kingship of Leinster, and Mac Murrough was expelled. Mac Murrough immediately did what hundreds of other ousted kings had done during the previous centuries—he looked elsewhere for alliances.

By this time, Ireland was no longer isolated from Britain and the rest of Europe. The Viking trading ports, especially Dublin, maintained merchant fleets that sailed regularly to British and European ports and to Scandinavia. They also had war fleets that they rented out to Irish kings. Over the centuries, the Norse had become Christian and mostly Irish in their blood and outlook. So Mac Murrough did not think it was either treacherous or dangerous to board one of their ships and seek allies in Britain.

In the Britain to which Mac Murrough sailed, the Roman past was only a dim memory, and the Angles and the Saxons had been conquered by another warrior tribe: the Normans. In 1066 the Normans had defeated Harold, the last Saxon king, whose reign had been as unstable as the high kings of Ireland since Brian Boru's death. Like the Romans, the Normans had a strong sense of identity and they knew how

In the 12th century, England's King Henry II (of Norman descent) firmly established his "lordship" over Ireland. In subsequent decades, Normans seized more and more Irish land for themselves.

to rule. They parceled out England, Scotland, and Wales to their barons, and within a generation had created a somewhat unified nation.

Soon Mac Murrough had an audience with Henry II, great grandson of William the Conqueror, the man who had led the Normans to victory in 1066. The deposed Irish chieftain had no idea that Henry had been thinking about invading Ireland for the previous decade. Henry had even persuaded Pope Adrian IV (the first and only English pope) to "give" him the Green Island, in return for his promise to reform the Irish church. Irish priests and monks still followed practices and policies that were too Celtic to please the Roman authorities.

Among other things, they tolerated married priests and trial marriages.

Henry II's interest in religious matters was minimal, however. Church reform was merely an excuse to seize as much of Ireland as possible and take over the booming port of Dublin, whose near monopoly of the fur trade was depriving many English ports of profits. But Henry shrewdly waited for an opportunity to mask his intentions. Mac Murrough's plea (for Henry to help him regain the kingship of Leinster) was the answer to his greedy prayers.

Henry sent the Irish chieftain to Wales to confer with some of his barons there. The Celtic Welsh were still unruly subjects, reluctant to pay tribute to the Norman conquerors. The barons of Wales were always broke and looking for new worlds to plunder. Soon Mac Murrough found an ally: Richard de Clare, locally known as Strongbow. In traditional Irish style, Mac Murrough promised him the hand of his daughter, Aoife, if the baron would come to his aid in Leinster.

In 1170, Strongbow landed near Waterford with 3,000 men. Sword-swinging, mail-clad Norman knights on armored horses hacked down terrified Irish foot soldiers by the dozens. Hundreds more fell when superbly trained archers poured swarms of deadly arrows

BEFORE 1775

April 23, 1661: The English monarchy returns to power, as King Charles II is crowned in London. Charles's government will reverse the policies of the Cromwell years, and some Irish Catholics will get their land back.

1665: Ireland's Parliament passes the Act of Explanation, ordering the return of one-third of all lands taken from Catholics who did not join the 1641 rebellion but lost their lands to Cromwell nonetheless.

c. 1680: The Shamrock takes its place as one of Ireland's most enduring symbols when Irish citizens begin to wear the three-leafed clover on their clothes in honor of St. Patrick's Day.

July 1, 1681: Oliver Plunkett, archbishop of Armagh, is hanged, then drawn and quartered, following a treason conviction in London. He remains England's last Catholic martyr.

April 23, 1685: James II is crowned king of England. His accession puts Catholics back in the seat of power in England as well as Ireland.

November 1688: As King James II struggles for his political life, his viceroy in Ireland attempts to secure the garrison at Derry, the only one apparently disloyal to the Catholic James. However, 13 apprentice boys lock the gates to the fortified city, and when James's soldiers arrive at the gates, they will lay siege to Derry for more than 100 days.

1688: William of Orange and a consortium of Parliamentarians capture the crown from James II following the Glorious Revolution. Taking the throne as William III, the new king will oversee an end to absolute monarchy. He also will reign during the final defeat of Catholicism as England's state religion.

into their ranks. The Normans were an army; the Irish were a courageous disorganized horde, relying on leather armor, antiquated iron swords, and slings that flung stones. Adding to the terror, the Normans gave no quarter to those who tried to surrender. Even when Irish towns, all lacking walls, gave up without a fight, their inhabitants were frequently butchered.

Mac Murrough died in 1171 and Strongbow, who had married his daughter, proclaimed himself king of Leinster. Watching from England, Henry II became alarmed. He did not trust Strongbow, who now controlled the crucial port of Dublin and was acting as if he were an independent ruler. It was time to reveal Henry's royal role in this adventure. Late in 1171, he arrived in Ireland at the head of a large army, piously announcing that Pope Adrian had authorized him to take over the country "to proclaim the truths of the Christian religion to a rude and ignorant people."

Strongbow and his fellow barons grudgingly submitted to Henry II's supremacy. Henry confirmed Strongbow's claim to Leinster. Henry gave the province of Meath to a more loyal baron, Hugh de Lacy. Henry also confirmed the sovereignty of numerous Irish kings who submitted to him. But the Norman king retained in his personal control (for his personal profit) the Norse ports, including Dublin.

Henry II returned to England, satisfied that he had established his "lordship" over Ireland. It was a vague term, but during the next century, it justified a gradual Norman takeover of Ireland. They bolstered their rule with huge castles and forts and vast cathedrals. They practiced their own brand of Christianity, which justified and even encouraged aggressive warfare. Their chief interest was making money. On their seized lands, they began practicing a new kind of agriculture, aimed at producing large crops to sell abroad. Year by year, they forced the remaining Irish kings to give up more and more of their ancestral domains. It was rule by force, and the Irish never accepted the legitimacy of the invaders' lordship. Their poets consistently called the parts of Ireland ruled by the Normans "the swordland."

The Normans attempted to establish English law in the areas they ruled. They created counties and nominated sheriffs. But in practice the policy proved unworkable. Within too many Norman-ruled districts there were semi-independent enclaves of Irish. Meanwhile, lesser Normans were intermarrying with the Irish and abandoning their

The Normans (*pictured*) invaded Ireland in 1171. They returned the exiled king of Leinster, who was backed by Henry II (who would become the first king of England to set foot in Ireland). This led to 800 years of English rule.

native French for Gaelic. The baffled kings of England, who had their hands full trying to control rebellious Scots and Welsh and their own unruly barons, largely ignored Ireland for the next 200 years. Through dynastic intermarriages with Irish kings, the Fitzgeralds, the de Lacys, the Marshalls, and other Norman barons gradually turned into Celtic monarchs, ready and willing to fight wars for territory and power.

Then came an earthshaking shock from Scotland: Edward Bruce, brother of King Robert, who had won Scotland's temporary independence from the English, invaded Ireland in 1315 with a 6,000-man army. One of the O'Neills, with a long tradition of kingship in Ulster, transferred his claim to that province to the Scottish Celtic liberator. A huge war exploded, with many Irish and even a few Norman barons rallying to "the Bruce." But in much of Ireland, local kings preferred to seize the chance to regain lands from the Normans. After three years of carnage, compounded by crop failures and a famine, Edward Bruce's army was a depleted remnant and his Irish support grew thin. In 1318 he was killed in battle at Faughart in County Louth, but his ghost would haunt Ireland for a long time.

Bruce's invasion left Anglo-Norman authority in Ireland in shambles. Any hope of unifying the country along English lines vanished. A group of Irish kings sent a petition to the pope pleading with him to revoke the English kings' lordship of Ireland. It was ignored, but it was a sign of growing defiance. Then came another catastrophe: the Black Death. This horrendous plague, which killed millions in Asia and Europe, devastated towns and ports in Ireland, which were heavily Norman in population. Distracted by Scottish and French wars, the English kings could do little to help their weakened subjects in Ireland. Many became embittered—and far less loyal. The Irish took advantage of this situation to reclaim land and power throughout Ireland.

From Anglo-Normans to Englishmen

In 1361 King Edward III of England sent his son and heir, Lionel, to Ireland with an army that was much too small. Lionel was soon sending home frantic calls for help. He summoned a parliament in Kilkenny that revealed the Anglo-Normans' growing desperation. The parliament's famous (or better, infamous) statutes ordered the Anglo-Normans to stop hiring Irish poets and musicians and otherwise "comporting themselves according to the customs, fashion, and language of the Irish enemies." It was an attempt to erect a permanent barrier between the two peoples in Ireland. Among the Irish, the Statutes of Kilkenny were largely scorned and ignored. But the pope, still angry at the largely unreformed Irish church, supported them and sternly segregated the English and Irish churches—an omen of religious trouble to come.

For the next 150 years, Ireland grew steadily more Irish and less Anglo-Norman, even in Dublin, where the kings of England retained theoretical control. Everywhere, Anglo-Norman landowners paid "danegelds" (protection money) to local Irish chiefs. More and more Normans abandoned the French language for Irish, while their com-

BEFORE 1775

July 1, 1690: James II fails to recapture his crown from William III, suffering defeat at the Battle of the Boyne.

July 12, 1691: Some 7,000 die as the Catholic Jacobites and Protestant Williamites clash at Aughrim. It remains the bloodiest battle in Irish history.

October 3, 1691: The Treaty of Limerick is signed, ending both the Siege of Limerick and the wider war between the Jacobites and Williamites that had been waged since James II first attempted to recapture his throne in 1689.

1695: A Penal Act forbidding the education of Catholic children, whether in Ireland or abroad, is passed in Britain. In response, so-called "hedge schools"—secret schools that meet privately in barns, cottages, and even behind hedges—emerge.

1697: The Protestant Parliament attempts to eradicate Catholicism in Ireland by passing the Bishop's Banishment Act, legislation that orders exile for Catholic clergy. It is largely ignored and unenforced.

1698: In an effort to curb the influx of Irish indentured servants, South Carolina enacts a personal tax on each new immigrant.

1703: The Irish Parliament passes the Act to Prevent the Further Growth of Popery. By mandating that Catholic estates be divided equally among heirs unless a sole heir converts to Protestantism, Parliament ensures the eventual breakup of large Catholic land holdings.

1704: With the passage of the Registration Act, Ireland's Parliament requires Catholic clergy to register with local authorities, pay a substantial bond, and agree not to preach outside their jurisdiction.

patriots in England began speaking English. In the trading ports and towns of Ireland, the Irish began referring to the Anglo-Normans as "Englishmen."

The English kings deplored the erosion of their power in Ireland. But they were distracted for the better part of a century by the see-saw Wars of the Roses between the families of Lancaster and York for control of their own country. English authority in Ireland dwindled to the area around Dublin, known as "The Pale." The rest of Ireland was ruled by locally powerful lords, such as Burke of Mayo, Fitzgerald of Kildare, and O'Neill of Tyrone. Gradually the Fitzgeralds, thanks to their proximity to Dublin, emerged as the most powerful family in Ireland, and the English kings made them their legates. But the Earls of Kildare, as the Fitzgeralds were known, began taking sides in English politics and often were in rebellion against the king of the moment in London.

In 1485 a cold-eyed earl named Henry Tudor became King Henry VII by defeating and killing his unpopular predecessor, Richard III. In Europe, nation states were taking shape in France and Spain. During Henry VII's reign, a new world was discovered on the other side of the Atlantic Ocean. Henry decided it

was time to make England an organized, centralized nation, with Scots and Welsh ruling with an iron fist from London. Ireland, that turbulent, perpetually rebellious island, also had to be brought under control. England's lordship had to be made more than just a word.

Henry VII grew even more determined to subdue the Irish when those who attempted to overthrow his reign recruited soldiers in Ireland and won the support of several Norman-Irish lords. His wrath led him to send one of his most trusted deputies, Sir Edward Poyning, to Ireland with an army. Sir Edward summoned a parliament and issued an edict that came to be known as "Poyning's Law." It stated that no Irish parliament could meet without the permission of the king of England.

Henry's son, King Henry VIII, was wholly in accord with this domineering policy. But Poyning and his law, like previous attempts to impose English control, were ignored everywhere in Ireland except Dublin. Here is a report on the state of the Green Island that the ambitious Henry VIII read a few years after he took the throne in 1509: *more than sixty counties called regions...inhabited by the king's Irish enemies...where reigneth more than sixty chief captains whereof some call themselves kings…some princes, some dukes, some archdukes that liveth only by the sword and obeyeth unto no other temporal person.…Also there be thirty great captains of the English folk that follow the same Irish order…and every of them maketh war and peace for himself without any licence of the King.…*

Henry VIII's solution to this independence was a proclamation that henceforth, the king of England owned all the land in Ireland and would grant portions of it only to those lords and chiefs who accepted his rule. This clever stroke legitimized the king's power in Ireland for centuries to come. The transformation acquired even more threatening overtones when Henry became embroiled in a quarrel with the pope. His Spanish queen, Catherine of Aragon, had failed to give him a male heir. He wanted a divorce to marry an English woman, Anne Boleyn. When the pope yielded to Spanish pressure and refused to grant his request, Henry declared that henceforth England would have a separate church with himself as its stand-in pope.

Elsewhere in Europe, men such as Martin Luther were issuing similar declarations of defiance to Rome's religious authority. The western world was dividing into Catholics and Protestants, and England began its slide into the Protestant orbit.

In 1536 Henry VIII became head of the Church in Ireland. Catholics resisted the split with Rome and the break-up of the monasteries. The Reformation coincided with the colonization of the island.

Henry VIII seized the immense wealth of the monasteries in England, Scotland, and Ireland and used the stolen riches to fund a fleet and army that soon made Britain a major power.

Under Henry VIII's daughter, Queen Elizabeth I, the English determination to subjugate Ireland grew tinged with hatred between the two peoples. "The Irish live like beasts," wrote one Englishman involved in the struggle. "They are more uncivil, more uncleanly, more barbarous in their customs and demeanors than in any part of the world that is known." If Anglo-Normans, whose people had been living in Ireland for centuries, sided with the Irish,

they were called "degenerate English." Queen Elizabeth thoroughly approved the use of brutal force to bring this "rude and barbarous nation to civility." By the latter word, she meant obedience to English law.

At times, English tactics transcended any and all civilized limits. During a campaign in Ulster, Sir Humphrey Gilbert, one of Elizabeth's deputies, killed several dozen Irish. He ordered the heads of all the corpses brought to his camp to form a lane that led to his tent. An English eyewitness gleefully recounted how it "did bring great terror to the people" when they came to plead with Gilbert for mercy and "saw the heads of their dead fathers, brothers, children, kinsfolk and friends on the ground before their faces."

Some sensitive Englishmen were appalled by the carnage. Poet Edmund Spenser described the suffering he saw in Munster as "such wretchedness as that any stony heart would have rued the same." Starving refugees crept "out of every corner of the woods and glens…upon their hands for their legs would not bear them. They looked like anatomies of death, they spake like ghosts crying out of their graves…" But most of the invaders only hardened their hearts. "A barbarous country must first be broken by war before it will be capable of good government," wrote another Elizabethan deputy, Sir John Davies.

It is hardly surprising that such treatment made ludicrous any hope of turning the Irish into Protestants. Henry VIII had proclaimed himself head of the Irish as well as the English Church. The two churches, though united in an overall Catholic faith, had never really blended. When Henry's Irish Church became Protestant, the Catholic Irish reached out for allies in their struggle for survival and found them in Spain and France. With England in the ranks of the Protestant enemy, the popes—in an ironic about-face—exhorted the Irish to remain loyal to the old faith. For the first time, religion became a binding force in the Irish soul.

Celtic Ireland's Last Stand

In the closing years of Elizabeth's reign, the English seemed triumphant everywhere in Ireland. But in Ulster, Hugh O'Neill, the earl of Tyrone, was a troubled man. Elizabeth had given him his title, and he had fought in her armies against rebellious Old English in Munster. He had been a royal favorite since he was a boy, living for years in the Dublin Pale under her protection. But he never forgot that he had descended from the Ui Nialls, high kings of

In 1541 Henry VIII upgraded Ireland to a full kingdom to bring it under the Crown's control. However, brutal repression of Catholics (*pictured*) failed to convert the Irish to Protestantism.

ancient Ireland. Another Ulster chieftain, "Red Hugh" O'Donnell, the earl of Tyrconnell, married his daughter and persuaded O'Neill that together they could rescue Ireland—or at least Ulster—from English rule. They rebelled, and in 1598 they smashed an English army at a place called the Yellow Ford, north of Armagh. The entire English government in Ireland reeled from the shock.

The rebels sent envoys to Spain to seek guns and money. In 1601 a Spanish fleet and army seized the port of Kinsale, in County Cork. It was the first of a series of blunders. Kinsale was at the wrong (southern) end of Ireland. The British besieged the invaders, and O'Neill and O'Donnell had no choice but to march their army from Ulster to rescue them. It was a long, exhausting journey, which involved evading and occasionally fighting an English

army sent to intercept them. Their soldiers were footsore and weary when they reached Kinsale. But they besieged the startled British and demanded their surrender.

By this time, the Spanish were running out of food and ammunition. They had only 3,500 men—half what the Irish had urged them to send. The panicky Spanish commander demanded that the Irish attack without a moment's delay. O'Donnell and O'Neill felt they had no choice and decided that an assault on Christmas Eve might be their best hope of success. Alas, their battalions got lost in the darkness. O'Neill's men appeared before the English battle line without the O'Donnells. The English cavalry promptly attacked and routed them. O'Donnell and his men arrived as the O'Neills were fleeing and shouted themselves hoarse trying to rally them. But the virus of defeat was loose in the Irish ranks. O'Donnell's men also were routed, and the survivors reeled back to Ulster, a beaten mob. The Spanish condemned the Irish as cowards and surrendered.

Red Hugh O'Donnell fled to Spain to plead in vain for another army. He died there, a heartsick man. Hugh O'Neill retreated to Ulster, where he rallied enough men to keep fighting until 1603, when he negotiated a pardon from Queen Elizabeth and was permitted to retain his lands. The English in Ireland were outraged, and they soon concocted evidence that O'Neill was plotting another rebellion with Rory O'Donnell, Red Hugh's brother and heir to the earldom of Tyrconnell. In 1607 the two earls, in fear of imminent arrest and execution, boarded a French ship in the little seaside town of Rathmullen and fled to Europe, never to return.

Triumph of the Protestants

The flight of the earls marked the end of Celtic Ireland as a political force. The British seized their lands—the four counties of Donegal, Tyrone, Derry, and Armagh—and began a systematic program to transform Ulster from the most rebellious province in Ireland to a bastion of English and Protestant loyalty. They imported thousands of Scots-Presbyterians to Ireland, evicting Catholic Irish from land they had farmed for centuries. The project was called "The Ulster Plantation"—a name that signified permanence. In County Derry, 90 percent of the land was given to the newcomers, leaving 10 percent to the Irish who had previously owned all of it. The planners in London made

Irish lords joined forces with Spain in the hope of ridding Ireland of Queen Elizabeth's rule. After losing the Battle of Kinsale (1601), they fled in 1607 in the famous "Flight of the Earls." Pictured is Hugh O'Neill, earl of Tyrone.

sure that this 10 percent was hilly, rocky land on which it was difficult to grow much. Today, we would call this ethnic cleansing.

The bitterness between the Scots and English newcomers and the Irish was pervasive. The usurpers lived on farms and in towns that had been fortified. Lurking in the bogs and forests like the Fianna of old were as many as 5,000 swordsmen of the vanquished earls. However, the number of Protestants continued to grow, as Scottish settlers swarmed into eastern Ulster. The enraged Irish watched and waited for an opportunity to strike. In Britain, tension between Protestants and Catholics mounted, and

King Charles I sided with the Catholics. From Spain came Owen Roe O'Neill, nephew of the now dead Hugh O'Neill, earl of Tyrone. Owen was a soldier who had proven himself in the Spanish army. The Irish decided that the moment for liberation—and revenge—had come.

In October 1641, the Irish of Ulster erupted, and Catholics elsewhere in Ireland followed their example. In Ulster, acts of terrible brutality took place. In Portadown, more than 100 Protestant women and children were driven onto a bridge, stripped of most of their clothes, and flung into the river. Thousands of Protestant refugees crowded the roads, hoping to reach fortified towns that were holding out. Hundreds were killed by roving bands of Irish; many more died from hunger and disease. The leaders of the rebellion deplored these acts of revenge, but it took them weeks to get their embittered followers under control. In England, rumor soon swelled the toll of dead to numbers that exceeded 150,000—the entire Protestant population of Ireland. Historians now estimate that about 12,000 men and women lost their lives.

For the next decade, Ireland writhed in the grip of a chaotic civil war. It was complicated by the civil war that exploded in England between King Charles I and Parlia-

BEFORE 1775

1706: In Philadelphia, Francis Makemie—minister, native of County Donegal, and the father of American Presbyterianism—founds the first Presbytery in the American colonies.

1713: Satirist and *Gulliver's Travels* author Jonathan Swift is named dean of Dublin's St. Patrick's Cathedral.

1720: The General Court of the Massachusetts Bay Colony decrees that all Irish immigrants must leave the colony within seven months.

1727: The Irish Parliament passes the Disenfranchising Act, denying suffrage to Irish Catholics.

1729: Jonathan Swift pens his satirical masterpiece, *A Modest Proposal: For Preventing the Children of Poor People in Ireland from Being a Burden to their Parents or Country, and for Making Them Beneficial to the Public.*

March 17, 1737: The Charitable Irish Society, the first Irish fraternal organization in the Americas, is founded in Boston.

1740–41: Persistent cold and inclement weather, and the resulting depleted harvests, lead to a famine that claims more than one in ten Irish citizens. It will be referred to as the "forgotten famine" because unlike the potato blight a century later, it does not lead to mass emigration.

April 13, 1742: Handel first performs his timeless *Messiah* in Dublin.

1745: England bans the long-standing practice of allowing foreign armies to recruit Irish Catholic troops, commonly called "Wild Geese," after realizing that these troops were being used against the British crown.

1759: Arthur Guinness signs a 9,000-year lease on a brewery at St. James's Gate in Dublin, ensuring that Irish Americans will enjoy quality stout on St. Patrick's Day through the year 10759.

ment. The Irish proclaimed their loyalty to Charles, whose Catholic grandmother, Queen Mary, had been beheaded by Queen Elizabeth. But Charles tried to have it both ways, deploring the Irish rebellion and accepting their pledges of loyalty. Meanwhile, his armies were being defeated in England by a Protestant military genius, Oliver Cromwell. By 1649 Cromwell had triumphed, beheaded Charles I, and turned to Ireland. Sounding a cry that would be echoed by Irish Protestants for the next 300 years, he vowed to avenge the "saints" who had been "martyred" by the Catholics in 1641.

The horrid MASSACRE of the Protestants, at the Bridge over the River Ban, in IRELAND in the Year 1641.

In 1641 the Irish Catholic gentry tried to seize power, but soon this "rising" descended into a cycle of violence between Irish Catholics and Protestant settlers. In this English engraving, Catholics throw Protestant women and children off a bridge.

Cromwell invaded Ireland with an army of 8,000 veteran infantry and 4,000 cavalry, plus heavy siege guns that could smash the walls of any fortified town. He began by battering his way into Drogheda and massacring most of the inhabitants. Thereafter, most towns surrendered, but that did not save the Irish of Wexford, who were massacred after they negotiated a peaceful capitulation. Cromwell went back to England to rule as lord protector, but he left behind his army and grim orders to extirpate Irish landowners east of the Shannon River. All of them were driven to Connaught, and their lands were parceled out to his army officers and English investors.

When the Irish Confederate Wars ended in 1650, Ireland was a wreck. An estimated 600,000 people had died from battle wounds and malnutrition—almost a third of the population. After Cromwell, land ownership by Irish Catholics sank from 59 percent to 22 percent. Cromwell banned the public practice of Catholicism. Mass was an "abomination." The oppression only deepened the Irish determination to persevere in St. Patrick's faith.

Oliver Cromwell died in 1658, leaving his son Richard as his heir. He was an inept ruler and Parliament dismissed him. Another civil war loomed until Cromwellian gen-

Oliver Cromwell (*left*), "Lord Protector of the Commonwealth," is infamous for his brutal conquest of Ireland, with killings, mass evictions, and deportations of many Irish. He is still hated in Ireland.

erals agreed to invite Charles II, son of the murdered king, to accept the throne. The Irish hoped he might restore their religious rights—and their lands. But the king's position was too precarious to risk turning the Protestant majority in England against him. Not until 1685 did Irish Catholic hopes revive, when Charles II died and his brother, James II, inherited the throne. James had long made no secret of his conversion to Catholicism, and he began a campaign to restore Catholic influence in Ireland and England.

James appointed a Catholic, Richard Talbot, commander of the army in Ireland. Talbot began giv-

ing commissions to Catholic officers. When the Protestant viceroy objected, James removed him and gave his job to Talbot, now the earl of Tyrconnell—a name that resounded with those who remembered Red Hugh O'Donnell. Talbot announced plans to summon an Irish parliament that would restore to Catholic owners most of the land seized by Cromwell. Tensions between Protestants and Catholics escalated in both Ireland and England.

In 1688 England exploded into revolution. Parliament denounced James II and invited the king's Protestant daughter, Mary, and her husband, William of Orange (ruler of the Netherlands), to accept the throne. The English army turned against the king, and he fled to France. William and Mary were wel-

comed with acclamations when they arrived in London.

In England, the so-called "Glorious Revolution" was bloodless. But in Ireland, it was a different and far more tragic story. The French, already at war with England, saw an opportunity to damage their enemy through Ireland. They gave James II money and an army of French and English and Scottish Catholics. The king landed in Ireland in 1689. Irish Catholics flocked to his standard, but heavily Protestant Ulster supported the Glorious Revolution. William of Orange responded with a Protestant army under his personal leadership, including troops sent by his fellow Protestant, the king of Denmark.

James II proved to be a timid, uninspiring leader. At the 1690 Bat-

The Protestant victory of William of Orange over the Catholics in 1690 is still commemorated today by Orangemen during the marching season in the North.

BEFORE 1775

1760: The Protestant Ascendancy, the comparatively small community of Protestants who held power over the majority Irish Catholics since Queen Elizabeth's reign, officially consolidates its power base with the establishment of the Protestant-only Patriot Party.

November 1761: County Limerick is the site of the first significant acts of what will come to be known as "whiteboyism." These self-styled "White Boys" wear white while vandalizing Protestant agrarian infrastructure as a protest against the Protestant Ascendancy's treatment of Catholic subsistence farmers.

1765: Hugo Oconór, a Spanish army colonel, becomes the first Irish-born soldier to be stationed in the American West.

March 17, 1766: New York City's first confirmed St. Patrick's Day parade steps off at dawn.

March 5, 1770: The Boston Massacre claims five lives including that of Patrick Carr, a 30-year-old Irish immigrant and leather craftsman.

1771: Benjamin Franklin tours Ireland and, stunned by the destitute state of the Irish peasantry, returns to America determined to rid the colonies of British oppression.

March 17, 1771: One of the earliest Irish American aid organizations, the Society of the Friendly Sons of St. Patrick for the Relief of Emigrants from Ireland, is founded in Philadelphia.

December 1774: Militiamen under the leadership of Irish American general John Sullivan capture Fort William and Mary in the port of Portsmouth, New Hampshire. They confiscate the fort's gunpowder supplies and small arms.

tle of the Boyne, his army was outmaneuvered and forced to retreat, although casualties were light. Nevertheless, James II abandoned his soldiers and fled to France. Leadership of the largely Irish Catholic army passed to Patrick Sarsfield, who had Celtic and Old English ancestors. In a battle at Aughrim in 1691, the English scored a decisive victory and the Irish retreated to Limerick. The Protestants, now commanded by a Dutch general named Ginkel, besieged the city. The situation soon became hopeless. Sarsfield negotiated a treaty that permitted him and 11,000 of his men to sail to France, where they entered the service of the French army. Henceforth, the Irish would mourn them as the "Wild Geese" who had been forced to abandon their native land.

The other articles of the Treaty of Limerick were seemingly generous. Irish Catholic troops who surrendered elsewhere in Ireland would be permitted to keep their lands if they took an oath of allegiance to King William and Queen Mary. Catholics were told they would be permitted to practice their religion, but the details were left ominously vague. Noblemen and gentlemen could carry arms. Since most of the noblemen and many gentlemen had left with Sarsfield, this too sounded better on paper than in fact.

Ireland's Dark Night of the Soul

During the next decade, the generosity of the Treaty of Limerick evaporated under the icy pressure of Protestant enmity. With the Catholics disarmed, the Irish Parliament began passing "penal laws" that severely restricted their rights. Catholics were banned from parliament, professions, and the army. They could not buy land or lease it except for ruinously short terms, and they could not marry Protestants. They could not educate their children abroad, and Catholic schools were prohibited at home. They could not carry weapons and were forbidden to own a horse worth more than five pounds. They were also deprived of the vote. This was essential to the evolving Protestant tyranny, as Catholics still constituted two-thirds of the population of Ireland.

The banshee's wail announces a death nearby. Dressed in white, she often washes her hands or combs her long, gray hair. Moreover, she can shapeshift into a black cat or raven.

The Wild Geese

Centuries ago, thousands of exiled Irish soldiers left Ireland and fought for nations around the world. They were called the "Wild Geese." To Irish satirist Jonathan Swift, these warriors proved that the Irish were brave and noble rather than an inferior race, as many in England believed. Wrote Swift, "It ought to make the English ashamed."

During the 18th century, the term Wild Geese referred to Irish brigades in European armies. They were particularly prominent in France. Eventually, however, Irish brigades and soldiers in America, Spain, Russia, Poland, Germany, Austria, and Peru were seen as part of a broader Wild Geese tradition.

Patrick Sarsfield was the most famous of the Wild Geese. Following the Siege of Limerick in 1691, Sarsfield negotiated a treaty with England's William of Orange. The agreement allowed Irish Catholic forces to peacefully relocate to France and granted Catholics equal rights in Ireland. Sarsfield and his troops settled in France. Catholics, however, remained second-class citizens in Ireland.

For decades afterward, the Wild Geese cried the Gaelic phrase *Cuimnidh ar Luimneach agus ar Feall na Sasanach,*

Patrick Sarsfield

which means "Remember Limerick and the Saxon Faith" (that is, remember English betrayal). France's Irish Brigade gained a measure of revenge in 1745 with a famous victory over the British at Fontenoy.

Elsewhere in the world, Ambrose O'Higgins and his son, Bernardo, served in South America. Limerick native Peter de Lacy became a general in the Russian army, and more than a dozen Irish immigrants became generals in the Austrian army.

Irish officers also took part in the American Revolution. They belonged to French regiments that helped General George Washington defeat the British at Yorktown. Just as notable are the Irish soldiers under Count de Dillon who played an important role in the unsuccessful French American attack on Savannah in 1779.

Irish regiments were also an important part of the Spanish army. Led by Lieutenant Colonel Arturo O'Neil, they played a major role in the assault that captured Florida from the British in 1780–81. Among the officers were Captains Juan Hogan, Eduardo Nugent, and Pedro O'Reilly.

So began the dark night of the Irish soul. Soon, Catholics' ownership of Ireland's land dropped to about seven percent. More and more Catholics were driven into degrading poverty, toiling as tenants for English landlords, many of whom were absentees who never left London. The Gaelic language was slowly eliminated from Irish life; with it went remnants of the old Celtic culture. Poets no longer lived with the wealthy families, passing on the traditions and tales of the heroic past. An eyewitness to this gathering agony was Kerry poet Egan O'Rahilly, who lived from 1670 to 1726. Here is O'Rahilly addressing an English landlord:

> *That my old bitter heart is pierced*
> *in this black gloom*
> *That foreign devils have made*
> *my land a tomb*
> *That the sun that was Munster's*
> *glory has gone down*

> *Has made me a beggar before you,*
> *Valentine Brown*
> *That royal Cashel is bare*
> *of house and guest*
> *That Brian's turreted home*
> *is the Otter's nest*
> *That the kings of the land*
> *have neither land nor crown*
> *Has made me a beggar before you,*
> *Valentine Brown.*

Ironically, in Protestant Ulster, a similar despair began seeping through the lives of average men and women. They slowly discovered that they too were regarded by the English as colonial pawns in the vast empire under construction in London. Ulster industries and products, such as woolen goods and linen, were taxed and manipulated to give British manufacturers an advantage in world markets. More and more of the Protestant Irish sank into poverty and began to feel and think like Irishmen, with a grudge against their imperial masters in Britain.

Adding to Ireland's woes were crop failures in the 1720s and a famine in the 1740s. In 1729 one man wrote of thousands "crowded along the roads, scarce able to walk and infinite numbers starved in every ditch." Many people gave up on Ireland. In the words of one observer, they were ready to "ship themselves" to other parts of the world "to get food." Once wealthy Catholics, reduced to indigence by Cromwellian confiscations, made similar decisions.

Both the distressed Protestants and the desperate Catholics began looking beyond Ireland's shores. More and more of them became aware of a land 3,000 miles away on the other side of the ocean—the 13 colonies that England had created along the Atlantic seaboard. The Irish had played a role in their growth and development for more

Irish peat-gatherers toil on the land. In 1600 Protestants owned 10 percent of Ireland's land, but by 1778 they owned more than 90 percent, resulting in widespread poverty for Irish Catholics.

than a century. Richard Butler of County Tipperary was a prominent member of Sir Walter Raleigh's 1584 expedition to Virginia and North Carolina. The following year, Butler helped establish the short-lived "lost colony" on Roanoke Island.

As the various colonies developed, a steady stream of Irish arrived each year. Many came as indentured servants, and some of these men prospered. George Downing arrived in Boston in 1638 at the age of 14. He graduated from Harvard and later married the daughter of Governor John Winthrop. Thomas Burke's once-affluent Catholic clan chose to emigrate rather than endure humiliating poverty in Ireland. The Burkes moved to North Carolina and became one of the most prominent families in the colony.

Historians have concluded that about 20 percent of these early Irish comers were Catholics. The

settlers often encountered hostility. Boston's Puritans hanged Ann "Goody" Glover as a witch in 1688. Irish Protestants, almost all Presbyterians, were equally unwelcome in many colonies. In tolerant Quaker-run Pennsylvania, they were encouraged, and they came by the thousands. New York, already populated by numerous Dutch, was also ready to welcome the Irish.

Reverend Francis Makemie of County Donegal founded the first American presbytery in Philadelphia in 1706. By 1737 James Murray of New York was writing home, urging "my fether and mether and my three sisters to come here." He would pay their passage. "There is servants comes here out of Ereland wha [who] are now justices of the peace." That

Those seeking a new start in America could sign an indenture agreement, in which they repaid the cost of the trip by laboring for a set period after reaching their destination.

An article lists appearances of witch-craft in America. Ann Glover was the last person to be hanged for witchcraft in Boston (1688). Puritan Cotton Mather was instrumental in her sen-tencing, describing her as a "scandal-ous old Irishwoman."

same year, on St. Patrick's Day, the Irish in Boston founded the first of their many fraternal organizations, the Charitable Irish Society.

By 1750 the colonists began to call themselves Americans, though they still professed a perfunctory loyalty to the king of England. Most of them were happy with their lives. They had the highest per capita income in the Western world, and they were the lowest taxed. On their western border, land was abundant and seemed open to anyone willing to claim, clear, and farm it. In their ports, merchants—not a few of them Irish—grew rich trading with the West Indies and Europe.

News of this amazing country traveled through Ireland, induc-ing thousands of Irish to borrow or beg for the money to get there. They often settled in groups on the frontier. Catholics, confronted by prejudice in this new world, often dropped the traditional "O" or "Mac" from the names and tried to blend in with the overwhelmingly Protestant population. Irish Prot-estants were more numerous, and they retained their identity. But in both groups, anger at England con-tinued to churn in their souls.

By the 1770s, the Irish in America had swelled to more than 300,000, and alarmed British aristocrats talked of forbidding them to emi-grate without permission. Around this time, an already famous Ameri-can paid a visit to Ireland. Benjamin Franklin had won worldwide acclaim for his discovery of electricity. A book he had written for aspiring entrepre-neurs, *The Way to Wealth*, was a huge seller in England and France. For the previous decade and a half, he had been living in England, trying to play the peacemaker in the quarrels that repeatedly erupted over Britain's determination to tax the Americans without their consent.

Franklin was beginning to won-der if British greed was a force that could be countered only with angry defiance. His visit to Ireland gave

a strong impetus to his thinking in this direction. He was horrified by the "extreme poverty" he saw everywhere. Most people, he stated, "live in wretched hovels of mud and straw, are clothed in rags, and sub-sist chiefly on potatoes. Our New England farmers of the poorest sort, in regard to the enjoyment of all the comforts of life, are princes when compared to them." Would this be America's fate, Franklin wondered, if it did not resist London's insatia-ble arrogance?

The stage was set for a new branch of the Irish nation to play a major role in one of history's epochal turning points, the Ameri-can Revolution.

In 1771 Ben Franklin toured Ireland. He was appalled at the poverty he saw and feared that America would suffer a simi-lar fate under continuing British rule.

Yankee Doodle with a Brogue

1775–1799

As protests and boycotts gave way to gunfire and bloodshed at Lexington and Concord in 1775, a young boy in the backwoods of South Carolina was doing his best to help his widowed mother cope with the chores of farm life on the American frontier. For young Andrew Jackson and his family, Lexington and Concord might as well have been in County Antrim, where Andrew's parents and two of his brothers had been born. The revolution that would so change their lives was imminent, but in the Irish community of Waxhaw, South Carolina, history hardly seemed around the corner.

The Jacksons were Irish, but they were more than just that. They were Scots-Irish, meaning they could trace their roots back to Scotland—a land conquered by the English and ensnared in religious, political, and tribal conflicts during the 17th and 18th centuries. Many Scots left their native land, crossed the narrow channel between the west coast of Scotland and County Antrim in Ireland, and started new lives. For families like the Jacksons, however, Ireland was not the end of the journey, but a stepping-stone. More than 250,000 Scots-Irish moved on to the New World in the 18th century.

Most were Presbyterians, which meant they were not members of the established Church of Ireland. Like Catholics, they were subjected to dis-

Andrew Jackson's family migrated from County Antrim to the Carolina backcountry. While fighting in the Revolution, young Andrew was captured—and took a saber blow (*pictured*) for refusing to polish British boots. He got revenge in 1815 when he defeated the British in the Battle of New Orleans. The Irish American hero was elected president in 1828.

crimination in Ireland, and while Catholics certainly were treated far worse, Presbyterians were barred from public office along with Catholics in 1704. Thus, many of them moved to the Americas. In the backwoods and hollows of Pennsylvania, the Carolinas, Virginia, and other regions, they could practice their religion and preserve their culture, music, and folkways. Bluegrass and the distinctive way of life that Americans associate with Appalachia began with the arrival of the Scots-Irish.

When the British sailed into New York Harbor in the summer of 1776 to begin a full-scale war against the rebellious colonies, Irish Americans joined local Patriot militias and the regular Continental Army in conspicuous numbers. While there surely was an Irish Catholic presence in the Revolution—Charles Carroll of Maryland signed the Declaration of Independence, Wexford native John Barry was considered the "father" of the U.S. Navy, and John Sullivan of New Hampshire served as a major general in the Continental Army—Scots-Irish dominated the rank and file of George Washington's army.

"Call this war by whatever name you may, only call it not an American rebellion;…" wrote one Hessian soldier of his experience in fighting in America. "…it is nothing more or less than a Scotch Irish Presbyterian rebellion." Like so many other Scots-Irish, the Jackson boys of South Carolina eagerly signed up to fight the British. One was killed in action, while their mother died while caring for American prisoners of war.

Midway through the war, about a third of the Continental Army was Irish-born or of Irish ancestry. But not every Irish soldier was a Patriot. When Britain's Lord Cornwallis marched through the South near the war's end, he sent Irish American troops—most of them deserters from the Patriot cause—into the South Carolina backwoods because he believed they "would be received with a better temper by the settlers…who were universally Irish…."

The success of the American Revolution and the creation of a republic inspired political radicals in Ireland. They organized a group called the Society of United Irishmen. These rebels had read Thomas Jefferson and Thomas Paine, and they celebrated not only the success of the American rebellion but of the French Revolution as well. A young leader named Theobold Wolfe Tone landed in Philadelphia in 1795 to meet with Irish Americans about launching a republican rebellion in Ireland. They put him in touch with French diplomats in the city.

Immigrants who had fled oppression in Ireland flocked to the Patriot cause. They dominated the frontier, where the British enlisted Indians to attack them. Irishmen, crying "Don't Tread on Me," were conspicuous at Bunker Hill in 1775 and fought in multi-ethnic regiments in all the campaigns. Sixteen became generals.

Three years later, the Irish rose against the British with the assistance of a small French force. But the Rebellion of 1798 did not meet with the same success as the American Revolution. It was crushed in less than five months, with some 30,000 people dead. (By comparison, the American Revolution of 1775 to the early 1780s cost the lives of about 25,000 Americans.) Tone was among the casualties. He was taken prisoner but managed to commit suicide before being sent to the gallows.

Some agitators were rounded up even before the 1798 Rebellion broke out. They were imprisoned for a short time and then released. Staunchly republican, they boarded ships bound for the new United States. There they joined other Irish Americans in the founding of the American Society of United Irishmen, which advertised its goal as "the emancipation of Ireland from the tyranny of the British government." It was the first political exile movement in the young nation's history. Most of these activists were middle-class professionals and a mix of Catholics and Church of Ireland Anglicans. They were not the Scots-Irish Presbyterians of the frontier, and they would not follow the trails being blazed beyond the Appalachians. They settled into urban life in New York and Philadelphia.

Rebels are arrested during the failed Rebellion of 1798. The uprising split Irishmen. Protestants loyal to the king warned that home rule meant "Rome Rule"—that is, control by Catholics subservient to the pope in Rome. For decades thereafter, the British used the slogan whenever they felt threatened by Irish independence.

These politically active Irish were not shy about expressing their views. Journalists Mathew Carey and William Duane, and Vermont Congressman Matthew Lyon, became vociferous critics of President John Adams, whom they believed to be pro-British. They also attacked the Federalist Party, which they saw as aristocratic and soft on monarchy. A Federalist congressman complained of the "hordes of wild Irishmen" who were attempting to "disturb our tranquility." In response, in part, to the power of the Irish exile community, Congress passed a law that put immigrants at risk of instant deportation if they were deemed a threat to the nation.

In 1800 the Irish exiles and their Irish American allies organized what could be called the first ethnic voting bloc in U.S. history. They supported Thomas Jefferson, whom they regarded as a true republican, in his quest to oust Adams. The election ended in an Electoral College tie between Jefferson and Aaron Burr, with Adams finishing third. The election was thrown to the House of Representatives, where Irish votes helped Jefferson prevail. It would not be the last time Irish Americans made an impact on U.S. politics.

June 12, 1775: In the first naval engagement of the American Revolution, the five sons of Irish-born rebel Maurice O'Brien capture the British sloop *Margaretta*, in Machias Harbor, Maine.

June 17, 1775: Colonel John Stark, a son of Irish immigrants, rallies his troops at the Battle of Bunker Hill with the words "Live free or die." Though the British claim victory on this day and capture the Charlestown Peninsula, Stark's words will be immortalized as the New Hampshire state motto.

December 7, 1775: Irish-born John Barry is appointed to the rank of captain in the Continental Navy. He will serve honorably throughout the Revolution and help establish the autonomous Department of the Navy.

July 4, 1776: John Dunlap, a Philadelphia printer and northern Ireland native, prints copies of the Declaration of Independence at the request of John Hancock.

August 2, 1776: Charles Carroll, a Maryland delegate to the Continental Congress, signs the Declaration of Independence. He is the only Catholic Irish American signatory.

December 25, 1776: Under the direction of Henry Knox, a Boston-born son of Irish immigrants, George Washington crosses the Delaware to attack an enemy force at Trenton.

1776–1781: Irish Americans fight to gain America's independence from Britain in impressive numbers. As many as a third of the Continental Army's soldiers and more than 1,500 of its officers are of Irish descent.

October 7, 1777: Timothy Murphy, expert marksman and son of Irish immigrants, inspires the Patriots at the Second Battle of Saratoga by killing two British commanding officers and sending their troops into disarray.

Irish fight for American independence From the Battle of Bunker Hill in 1775 (*pictured*) to the conclusion of the war, Irishmen played a significant role in the fight for American independence. Although it was an exaggeration, Loyalist Joseph Galloway in 1779 estimated that one half of the American army was Irish. In the stout defense of Boston's Bunker Hill—the first major battle of the war—Irishmen comprised a large proportion of the American forces. One of those present at the scene, British General Sir Henry Clinton, later commented that the Irish were the chief Patriot defenders of the hill.

Stark shines on battlefields Of Ulster Presbyterian stock, John Stark commanded a regiment of his fellow New Hampshire men at Bunker Hill, fighting from behind a hastily constructed hay and rail fence. He later distinguished himself with General Washington at the battles of Trenton and Princeton. In 1777 he joined his New Hampshire militiamen with Vermont's Green Mountain Boys to defeat the British at the Battle of Bennington. He is reputed to have told his men before the battle, "There are the Redcoats and they are ours—or this night Molly Stark sleeps a widow."

Distinguished American general

Dublin-born Richard Montgomery (*bent backward*) first saw the New World in the uniform of a British soldier. He eventually became a British officer. However, he resigned his commission in 1772 and settled in New York. Montgomery opposed British colonial policy, and when hostilities broke out he was commissioned as a brigadier general in the Continental Army. In 1775 he led an American force in capturing Montreal but was killed later in the year during the siege of Quebec. A romantic figure, he was mourned by his wife for the rest of her life.

Nixon is first to read Declaration

At noon on July 8, 1776, at the Pennsylvania State House in Philadelphia, John Nixon had the honor of giving the first public reading of the Declaration of Independence. That this grandson of immigrants from County Wexford, Ireland, was given such a historic task befitted his commitment to American independence. He had opposed British policy in the colonies as early as the Stamp Act crisis in 1765, and in the days before the outbreak of hostilities, he was an active participant in the committees of correspondence.

Signers of the Declaration of Independence Of the 56 signers of the Declaration of Independence, eight had Irish backgrounds. Three—Matthew Thornton of New Hampshire and George Taylor and James Smith of Pennsylvania—were born in Ireland. Whether Irish-born or of Irish descent, most of the eight came from Scots-Irish Presbyterian backgrounds. The only Irish Catholic signer was Charles Carroll of Carrollton, Maryland, reputed to be the wealthiest member of the Second Continental Congress. He also was the longest surviving signer, living until 1832.

1777–1778: Philadelphia resident and Donegal native Gustavus Conyngham raids British ships from one end of the Atlantic to the other, eventually capturing some 60 ships for his adopted homeland.

1778: The first of several Catholic relief acts is passed. The new law allows Catholics in Ireland and England to own land and bequeath land to a sole Catholic heir.

March 17, 1778: While encamped at Valley Forge, a brawl breaks out among General Washington's troops when some of the German soldiers make an effigy of a "Paddy." The incensed Irish accuse the New Englanders of the insult. Washington quells the disturbance by mandating that the entire camp celebrate the Irish holiday with extra rum rations.

1779: The "Irish Volunteers," an armed Protestant army, is marshaled. The purpose of the army is to buffer Ireland's security at a time when Britain's army is stretched thin with multiple overseas conflicts. Its presence helps the Irish gain several concessions for independence from England.

1780: Hercules Mulligan, a New York City tailor born to Irish immigrant parents, foils a British plot to kidnap General Washington. An accomplished spy, Mulligan will spend the war posing as a Loyalist while passing valuable information to the Patriots.

1782: Ireland's Parliament is granted legislative independence from England with the repeal of Poyning's Law.

1783: Irish-born patriot Stephen Moylan is promoted to brigadier general, capping a distinguished career.

1785: St. Peter's Church, the first Catholic Church in New York, is incorporated.

"When our friendless standard was first unfurled, who were the strangers who first mustered around our staff? And when it reeled in the fight, who more brilliantly sustained it than Erin's generous sons?"

—GEORGE WASHINGTON

For whom Fort Knox is named The son of Scots-Irish immigrants, Henry Knox rose to the rank of major general during the Revolutionary War. His knowledge of heavy weapons prompted General Washington to appoint him commander of the rebel artillery in the siege of British-held Boston. Possessing few artillery pieces at the time, Knox organized a Herculean effort to haul cannons captured at Ticonderoga to Boston, some 300 miles away. After the war, he was appointed the new country's first secretary of war. The famed Fort Knox in Kentucky is named after him.

Conyngham captures 60 British ships Stranded in the Netherlands at the start of the American Revolution, Donegal-born Gustavus Conyngham received a commission in the Continental Navy from envoys of his adopted country serving in France. Over the next two years, Captain Conyngham captured some 60 British ships in the waters around Britain, Spain, and the West Indies. Unable to prove his naval commission when captured by the British in 1780, he was threatened with execution as a pirate. Only a daring escape to the Continent saved him.

Irish on the Frontier

On March 15, 1767, in the rugged South Carolina settlement of Waxhaw, Irish immigrant and recently widowed Elizabeth Jackson gave birth to a third son. Little Andrew Jackson would grow up to become the seventh president of the United States.

The Jacksons were just one of countless Irish Protestant families who settled the American frontier throughout the 18th century. Most of these so-called Scots-Irish were Presbyterians of Scottish descent. They had been encouraged by the British to settle in the Ulster region of northern Ireland. However, poor growing seasons, high land prices, and religious conflict sent many to America.

A County Donegal farmer who built a new life in western Pennsylvania spoke for many when he said: "Thank God I came to this country where we are free from landlords, rent, and the fear of eviction." So many Irish immigrants used the Great Wagon Road, which runs from Pennsylvania to Georgia, that it came to be called the "Irish Road."

The fearless frontier spirit of these Irish immigrants could be found in the likes of Davy Crockett, the "king of the wild frontier," whose father was born on a ship en route from Ireland to the United States. Life on the frontier, of course, was never easy. The seasons were harsh, the land was untamed, and Native Americans viewed Irish settlers as invaders.

Thus, the Scots-Irish became renowned for their toughness, a trait that came in handy when the Revolutionary War broke out. One British official reported that "emigrants from Ireland are our most serious opponents."

These settlers changed the new world, bringing Celtic music, a fierce code of honor, and passion for Jeffersonian politics into American culture. By opening the South and West, they made the dream of "Manifest Destiny" a reality. Even today, census figures show that outside of Irish bastions in Massachusetts and New York, parts of Mississippi and Tennessee are among the most Irish in the nation.

Murphy slays British general Timothy Murphy (*center*), the son of Irish immigrants, grew up in frontier Pennsylvania. Recognized for his skills as a marksman—he could hit a target at 250 yards—he was invited to join the elite Morgan Rifle Corps during the Revolution. He achieved fame at the Battle of Bemis Heights at Saratoga on October 7, 1777, when a shot he fired from long distance struck and killed British general Simon Fraser. Murphy then shot and killed another senior British officer, Sir Frances Clarke. The losses threw the Redcoat army into such disarray that it was forced to surrender.

August 29, 1786: Daniel Shays, a farmer of Irish descent and veteran of the American Revolution, leads an uprising of farmers (Shays's Rebellion). They are angered by a system of taxation that leads to debt, debtor's prison, and land forfeiture.

May 25, 1787: Delegates to the Constitutional Convention meet in Philadelphia to draft the United States Constitution. Influenced in part by Shays's Rebellion, the Founding Fathers recognize the inherent weaknesses in the Articles of Confederation. The new Constitution will feature a much stronger centralized government than had originally been intended.

September 17, 1787: The United States Constitution is adopted. Several Irish American signatories, including four Irish-born immigrants and two sons of Irish immigrants, are among the 39 original delegates to sign the new U.S. Constitution. The government of the Continental Congress is dismissed, as is the service of County Derry native Charles Thomson, who served as the Congress's secretary through its 15-year tenure.

1788: Irish American craftsmen organize the Society of St. Tammany in New York City. From its inauspicious beginnings as a social club, it will soon become synonymous with Democratic Party politics in the city.

November 6, 1789: Pope Pius VI appoints John Carroll, scion of a prominent Maryland family of Irish Catholic merchants, bishop of Baltimore. Carroll becomes the first Catholic bishop in the United States.

September 1791: Theobald Wolfe Tone, an Irish Protestant barrister and politician, pens an essay entitled "Argument on Behalf of the Catholics of Ireland." He argues that the English authorities have used religious strife to keep the Irish subjugated.

> **"[We planned to] march directly to Boston, plunder it, and then . . . to destroy the nest of devils, who by their influence, make the Court enact what they please, burn it and lay the town of Boston in ashes."**
>
> —DANIEL SHAYS, LEADER OF SHAYS'S REBELLION

Shays's Rebellion In the days following the Revolutionary War, the American economy was in shambles. Because the laws favored creditors, farmers in western Massachusetts were particularly hard hit, with many of them losing their farms. In their frustration, hundreds of farmers rose in rebellion (*below*). The rebels shut down law courts and even attempted to capture the arsenal at Springfield. The most outspoken leader of the rebellion was Daniel Shays (*left*), a Revolutionary War veteran and the son of an Irishman who had come to America as an indentured servant. Shays's Rebellion was quickly suppressed, and the rebels were eventually pardoned.

The Irish Who Took Over New York

The foundation for America's first Irish political dynasty was laid in 1731, when Charles Clinton and his family settled (fittingly) in Ulster County, New York. The Clintons produced generals, mayors, governors, and a vice president while becoming one of the most influential families in New York. Before that, however, the Clintons were one of many Irish families who had to endure a tragic journey across the Atlantic Ocean.

Charles Clinton was born in County Longford in 1690. He was wealthy when he decided to sail to America in 1729, but that did not make his immigrant journey a comfortable one. His ship was rife with hunger and disease, and two of his children perished. Moreover, the ship's captain attempted to extort money from the surviving passengers.

Once settled in New York, Charles's son, George, held public office and became an advocate of independence from Britain. During the Revolutionary War, George served as a general and later became the first governor of

DeWitt Clinton

New York. He served six successive terms, thus earning the nickname the "Father of New York." As with many Irish Protestants, the Clinton family passionately supported Thomas Jefferson and his Democratic-Republican Party. The Jeffersonians welcomed immigrants—as opposed to the conservative Federalists, who championed the infamous Alien and Sedition Acts of 1798.

When Jefferson was reelected president in 1804, George Clinton was his vice president. He served in the same position under James Madison after unsuccessfully bidding for the presidency himself. George's nephew, DeWitt, was born in 1769 and worked for his uncle in the governor's office. DeWitt served in the U.S. Senate in 1802–03 and later became the second Irish mayor of New York City (after James Duane). By 1817 DeWitt Clinton became New York's governor—and famously promoted the construction of the Erie Canal. When it opened in 1825, it was the most vivid example of the many ways the Clinton family had changed the course of American history.

Father of the American Navy

John Barry, a native of County Wexford, immigrated to America in 1760. Attracted to Philadelphia because of its tolerance toward Catholics and its access to the Atlantic, Barry became a successful sea captain. When the Revolution broke out, he entered the new Continental Navy and commanded the first American naval vessel to capture a British warship. For his many exploits during the conflict, he became one of the most celebrated American naval officers of the War of Independence. He has been called the "Father of the American Navy" because he served as the Navy's first flag officer.

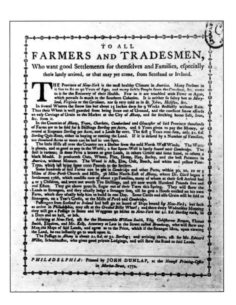

Ads in Ireland extol America's virtues

So much land and work was available in late 18th and early 19th century America that advertisements espousing the virtues of the New World were regularly published in Ireland. "New-York [has] the most healthy climate in America," reads this 1772 pamphlet, which offers "thousands of farms" for sale. Little was said about harsh frontier conditions or the grueling labor required to dig canals and build railroads. Still, the ads attracted many Irish, whose agricultural lives had been disrupted by skyrocketing rents and other factors.

October 14, 1791: Wolfe Tone is invited to speak before a group of prominent Belfast Protestants. The Society of United Irishmen is born at this first meeting. The centerpiece of their platform is the need for parliamentary reform and religious equality.

1792: In Britain and Ireland, further Catholic relief acts permit the establishment of Catholic schools without approval of Protestant bishops, intermarriage between Catholics and Protestants, and the admission of Catholics to the practice of law.

1793: The Catholic Relief Act of 1793 reestablishes Catholic suffrage, allows for admission of Catholics to Trinity College, and permits them to serve as officers in the armed forces. • In the U.S., Alexander Hamilton organizes the Federalist Party. Characterized by strong centralized government and a bent toward elitism, the party will drive most immigrants—Irish and otherwise—into the arms of the emerging Democratic-Republican Party.

1795: William Drennan, a founding member of the Society of United Irishmen, becomes the first to refer to Ireland as the "Emerald Isle" when he coins the phrase in his poem "When Erin First Rose."

September 21, 1795: A band of young Protestant men, called the Peep O'Day Boys for their habit of attacking Catholic dissenters at daybreak, kill some 30 Catholic Defenders in the brief Battle of the Diamond in County Armagh. In the wake of the battle, the Peep O'Day Boys will rechristen themselves the Orange Order.

July 12, 1796: The first Orange Order parade is held in County Armagh in honor of the 1690 defeat of Catholic king James II by William of Orange at the Battle of the Boyne.

Washington's secretary of war Trained as a physician, Ulster-born James McHenry served as a surgeon when he joined the Continental Army, but at Valley Forge he became secretary to General Washington. After the war, he retired to devote himself to politics. A staunch Federalist, he represented Maryland in Congress and participated in the convention that created the Constitution. He served as secretary of war under the first two U.S. presidents. Fort McHenry, the bombardment of which inspired the writing of "The Star-Spangled Banner," was named for him.

Georgetown emerges Today a trendy neighborhood in Washington, D.C., Georgetown in the late 18th century was a growing Irish community. Attracted by colonial Maryland's tolerant attitude toward Catholics, its proximity to the port of Baltimore, and plentiful jobs on the docks of Georgetown's riverfront, Irish men and women gravitated to the area. In 1791 the Jesuits—an order of the Roman Catholic Church—opened Georgetown College, pictured here in later years.

The Carrolls of Maryland

Before the Kennedys of Boston, the Carrolls of Maryland reigned as a multigenerational Irish Catholic clan that wielded great power and influence in the 18th century. However, none of this was easy, for this was a time of great persecution of Catholics in both Ireland and America.

The Carrolls had been a prominent family in Ireland. But by the 1680s, conflict with Protestants drove family patriarch Charles Carroll to Maryland, which had a long tradition of religious tolerance. Even when Catholics in America were disenfranchised following England's so-called Glorious Revolution of 1688, Maryland remained a relatively good place for Irish Catholics. Charles "The Settler" Carroll amassed a fortune, as did his sons—Charles and Daniel.

By the mid-18th century, as independence from Britain came to dominate public debate, the Carrolls helped bring Maryland into the revolutionary ranks. Along with many other Irish Catholics, they believed freedom from Britain and its old-world religious conflicts would encourage greater religious tolerance in the U.S.

Charles of Carrolton

Charles the Settler's grandson, who was known as Charles of Carrolton (born in 1737), played a central role in the movement for U.S. independence. He wrote anti-British essays under the name "First Citizen," and he accompanied Benjamin Franklin on a diplomatic mission to Canada in 1776. When America's Declaration of Independence was published, Carroll was the only Catholic who signed the famous document, putting his life and fortune at risk.

Following independence, Carroll served in the U.S. Senate and helped establish the Baltimore & Ohio Railroad. Meanwhile, Charles's cousin, John, was arguably the most influential Catholic clergyman of his day. In 1789 John Carroll was named leader of America's first diocese, in Baltimore. He also had a strong say in New York and Philadelphia, where Catholic immigration was growing.

John Carroll, who served as archbishop until his death in 1815, gave future American Catholic leaders a blueprint when it came to establishing a community for Catholic immigrants. This proved essential, as the trickle of Irish immigrants became a flood due to the famine of the 1840s.

The Whiskey Rebellion Among the Scots-Irish settlers of western Pennsylvania's backcountry, whiskey was an important commodity, oftentimes serving as money when currency was scarce. When President Washington's new federal government sought to raise revenue by declaring a tax on whiskey, unrest in the backcountry grew, breaking out in violence in 1794. In the Whiskey Rebellion, outraged farmers tarred and feathered some tax collectors (*pictured*) and burned their homes. Only after the arrival of 13,000 militiamen and the arrest of the insurgent leaders was peace restored.

Wielders of Wicked Pens

December 1796: Having secured French assistance, Wolfe Tone and the United Irishmen attempt rebellion, arriving in Bantry Bay, Ireland, with most of a 15,000-man fleet. Their plans are scrapped when foul weather forces their return to France.

May 24, 1798: The United Irishmen's rebellion begins, as violence erupts between the United Irishmen and government loyalists in Leinster and County Kildare.

June 21, 1798: After some initial success, the United Irishmen are decisively defeated by more than 10,000 British troops at the Battle of Vinegar Hill. The British retake County Wexford and force a turning point in the rebellion. The United Irishmen will go down in defeat in July. The failure of their rebellion will lead to a fresh wave of immigration to America.

June–July 1798: The U.S. Congress passes a series of four laws collectively known as the Alien and Sedition Acts. Though designed to protect the U.S. from noncitizens during times of war, they contain several unconstitutional provisions that are widely interpreted as an effort by the Federalist power base to purge the nation of new immigrants, who comprise a large anti-Federalist voting bloc.

October 1798: Irish American congressman Matthew Lyon is indicted under the Sedition Act for speaking out against President John Adams in a letter to the editor of a Vermont paper. Lyon will be reelected to Congress while serving a prison term.

1799: Jeffersonian Democrat publisher William Duane, a Philadelphian of Irish descent, is charged with sedition for his vehement anti-Federalist writings. He will be saved from conviction by the election of Jefferson to the presidency the following year.

Just a decade after the Revolution, the young United States endured serious growing pains. Events in Europe as well as in the U.S. placed Irish immigrants at the center of a fierce political debate. A passionate group of Irish writers, printers, and polemicists wielded their wicked pens to fight for their place in the new nation.

In 1798 Wolfe Tone and the United Irishmen led their tragic, failed uprising in Ireland, several years after the revolution in France had descended into a reign of terror. President John Adams and the Federalist Party were disturbed by these violent events in Europe. Fearing that revolutionary discontent would spread to the U.S., they passed the Alien and Sedition Acts of 1798. While the legislation was proposed as an effort to combat disloyalty, it soon became clear that the acts targeted Irish and French Catholics and any others who supported the Federalists' rival, Thomas Jefferson and his Democratic-Republican Party.

Wicklow native Matthew Lyon, a printer and militiaman who would serve with the legendary Green Mountain Boys, was among the fiercest critics of Adams and the Federalists. He had settled in Vermont, served in the state House of Representatives, and published various newspapers before being elected to the United States Congress, taking office in 1797. His passion and temper earned him the nickname "The Wild Irishman." After criticizing Adams, Lyon became the first person arrested and jailed under the Alien and Sedition Acts. While in prison, he successfully campaigned for reelection, earning him the distinction of being the first U.S. congressman elected while incarcerated.

Tipperary native William Duane, who emigrated as a teenager and went on to become a prominent Philadelphia attorney and Pennsylvania general assemblyman, was another prominent critic of the Federal-

William Duane

ists. In 1795 Duane became editor of the *Philadelphia Aurora*. Through his written words, he battled the *Porcupine's Gazette, The Gazette of the United States,* and other pro-Federalist newspapers.

Duane, Lyon, and others in the fledgling Irish American press helped swing the tide of public opinion against the Federalists. In 1800 Thomas Jefferson ran against Adams in a race that famously ended up as an electoral tie, forcing Congress to select the winner.

Jefferson would later say that his victory could not have been possible without William Duane and the *Aurora*. But Jefferson also should have mentioned fellow Irish supporter Lyon. As a member of Congress (having been released from prison), Lyon cast the deciding vote in favor of Jefferson, breaking the electoral tie.

The dimwitted O'Regan The novel *Modern Chivalry* (1792) introduced the American reading public to Teague O'Regan, the prototypical stage Irishman. Manservant to sophisticated captain John Farrago, the clownish O'Regan is dimwitted yet also cunning, deceitful, and mischievous. Through all their misadventures, O'Regan speaks in dialect—author Hugh Henry Brackenridge's

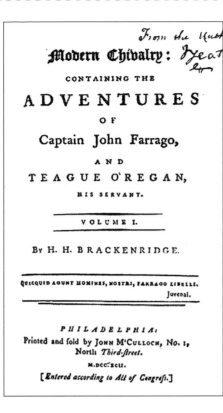

approximation of the broken English of the "bog-trotting" Irish. For the next hundred years, numerous O'Regan types would appear in novels and theaters across America.

Burk's patriotic play While a student at Trinity College in Dublin in 1796, John Daly Burk was forced to flee Ireland because of his involvement with the radical United Irishmen. During his 55-day voyage to America, he wrote a five-act play, *Bunker-Hill: Or the Death of General Warren*, which was performed in Boston in 1797. Because of its patriotic theme, it became a staple of Independence Day celebrations well into

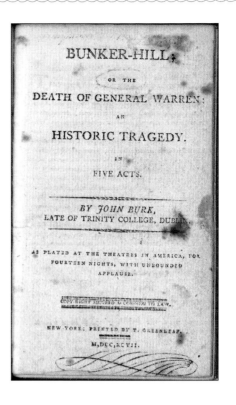

the 19th century. An outspoken critic of the Federalists, Burk barely escaped deportation by going into hiding until the election of Thomas Jefferson. He died in a duel in 1808.

Chief justice of the Supreme Court Considered one of the greatest legal minds of the age, John Rutledge (of Scots-Irish descent) was elected governor of South Carolina during the American Revolution. In 1780 his home was lost after he was forced to flee Charleston when the British occupied the city. After the war, he signed the Constitution and served as a justice of the U.S. Supreme Court. In 1795 President Washington appointed him chief justice during a recess of the U.S. Senate. But after he spent only a few months in office, the Federalist-dominated Senate rejected him for his opposition to the Jay Treaty. That treaty improved U.S. relations with Britain while empowering the Federalists.

Irish resent increased taxes In order to finance its war with France, Britain increased its taxation of Ireland. Rising taxes prompted this angry cartoon, which portrays England's "John Bull" sucking the life out of Ireland. The rising taxes became increasingly disproportionate to Ireland's resources. By 1796 even the poorest were being levied. By 1797 high food prices had contributed to soaring poverty; in Dublin, 37,000 people were deemed destitute. The cost of stationing English troops in Ireland also fell on the shoulders of hard-pressed Irish taxpayers.

The infantry came forward firing,
The ground was strew'd with men expiring;
The rest, defenceless, unprotected,
Fled ev'ry way, as fear directed.
Patt ran as fast as heels could carry,
Nor did his friends behind him tarry;
They fled together in a group,
'Till overtaken by a troop
Of horse—a pistol bullet
Found passage thro' poor Paddy's gullet.

—THE UNITED IRISHMEN, A TALE; FOUNDED ON FACTS, 1798

Irish rebel against English rule The 1798 Rebellion was an attempt to separate Ireland from English rule and the ruling Anglican class. The rebellion saw significant fighting in 11 of Ireland's 32 counties. County Wexford witnessed particularly fierce clashes between rebels and government forces. Atrocities were committed by both sides. The attackers in this illustration were members of the separatist United Irishmen movement. The picture underlines the fact that many of the rebels were armed only with spear-like pikes, which would prove ineffective against the muskets of English regulars and loyalist militia.

Priests among the rebellion's leaders The 1798 Rebellion was inspired by the American and French revolutions, but it was not just a crusade for the rights of man. It was also a violent response by Catholics in particular, whose religious rights were subordinate to the privileged position of the established Anglican Church. Some insurgent forces were led by priests, most notably Father John Murphy. His actions, though initially successful, ended in his capture and execution. In this illustration, a Father Cinch is shot by an English officer at the Battle of Vinegar Hill in County Wexford.

Rebel and martyr The British take Theobald Wolfe Tone captive in the fall of 1798. Tone and his United Irishmen Society cofounders initially attempted to secure constitutional changes to discriminatory laws aimed at Catholics, Presbyterians, and dissenters. Ireland at the end of the 18th century was a sectarian state, but one awash in revolutionary ideas from America and France. Encouraged by promised French aid, the United Irishmen ultimately fought for an Irish Republic entirely separate from Britain. However, the 1798 Rebellion had been crushed by the time Tone returned with French troops. Captured and imprisoned, he committed suicide while incarcerated in Dublin.

Lyon's revenge County Wicklow-born Matthew Lyon was a Jeffersonian congressman famous for his verbal and physical battles with Federalist Roger Griswold on the floor of the House of Representatives. Lyon (*depicted in dark brown coat*) supported the French Revolution and the United Irishmen. Griswold (*in red vest*) and his party, fearful of French and Irish "radicals," pushed through the 1798 Alien and Sedition Acts, the latter making it a crime to "defame" the government. Because he denounced President John Adams (a Federalist), Lyon was jailed for four months for sedition. However, he was reelected to Congress (while in jail!). Then, when the 1800 presidential election ended in an electoral tie and had to be decided in Congress, Lyon cast the deciding vote—for Jefferson, of course.

LYON BOOTED OUT OF THE HOUSE

Resolved, That Matthew Lyon, a member of this House, having been convicted of being a notorious and seditious person, and of a depraved mind, and wicked and diabolical disposition; and of wickedly, deceitfully, and maliciously, contriving to defame the Government of the United States; and of having, with intent and design to defame the Government of the United States, and John Adams, the President of the United States, and to bring the said Government and President into contempt and disrepute, and with intent and design to excite against the said Government and President the hatred of the good people of the United States, and to stir up sedition in the United States—wickedly, knowingly, and maliciously, written and published certain scandalous and seditions writings or libels, be therefor expelled this House."

—*ANNALS OF CONGRESS*, FEBRUARY 1799

"Refuse King" With the Federalists supporting England in war against France, Rufus King—America's ambassador to England from 1796 to 1803—blocked the transfer to the U.S. of United Irishmen imprisoned in England after the 1798 Rebellion. In so doing, King, who had fought for America's freedom, incurred the wrath of the movement's American supporters and earned the nickname "Refuse King." In 1816 King lost the election for New York governor to Democratic-Republican incumbent Daniel Tompkins. Tompkins was heavily supported by New York's Irish, who still harbored bitter memories of King's opposition to the prisoner transfer.

Irish Flock to America

1800–1829

The great construction projects of the 1820–60 era involved canals and railroads. Irish Catholics did most of the work. They were organized into work gangs, and the boss contracted their services for so many days at a dollar a day. Rival Irish gangs sometimes fought over who would do the work.

When a group of Irish Americans stormed the headquarters of New York's Tammany Hall in 1817, demanding that the group's politically potent leaders support an Irish immigrant named Thomas Addis Emmet for Congress, a new factor was introduced to American society: ethnic politics. The Irish, outsiders from the city's WASP majority, were demanding a place at the table of power.

The demand was backed by numbers, as the Irish presence in the city and throughout the country was increasing. Actually, it was about to explode. While Ireland's economy faltered, the young American republic embarked on a series of what were called "internal improvements"—roads, canals, and other public-works projects. In search of work, Irish immigrated to the United States in large numbers.

Several hundred thousand Americans were of Irish descent in 1820, when the nation's population was a little more than 9.6 million. Some of those Irish were Scots-Irish Protestants. The rest were Catholics or Anglo-Irish Anglicans, including Emmet and some of his fellow exiles from the United Irish movement in Ireland.

> *They say there's bread and work for all,*
> *And the sun shines always there.*
> —LYRICS OF A POPULAR IRISH EMIGRANT SONG ABOUT THE UNITED STATES

Most of the Catholics who had left Ireland in the 18th century did so as indentured servants, agreeing to work for free for several years in exchange for passage to America. Some of these indentured Irish worked for the Patowmack Company in Virginia, which had been formed after the Revolution to build a canal that would link the Potomac River with the western frontier. The company's most famous shareholder was an affluent planter named George Washington.

Irish immigration to the United States began to increase in the early 1800s as the Irish economy, ironically enough, felt the effects of peace. With the end of the Napoleonic Wars in 1815, agricultural prices collapsed because there were no more armies to feed. The drop in prices coincided with an increase in rents, making the hard life of an Irish tenant farmer harder still. So many Irish left that His Majesty's authorities tried to steer them to British-ruled Canada by making it cheaper to sail to Quebec than to Philadelphia, Boston, or New York. Poorer Irish, most of them Catholics, booked the cheaper passages to Canada and then continued on to the United States.

According to one estimate, as many as 100,000 Irish people emigrated from Ireland to the United States from 1783 to 1815. But that surge was nothing compared to the deluge that followed. From 1815 to the early 1840s, as many as a million Irish immigrated to the United States.

New organizations were founded to support the recent arrivals. Hibernian Societies (referring to the Roman name for Ireland, Hibernia, which means a dark, cold place) were established in Charleston in 1801, Baltimore in 1803, and New Orleans in 1824. Boston, Philadelphia, and New York had Irish organizations, including the Friendly Sons of St. Patrick and the Charitable Irish Society, well before the turn of the 19th century.

Many of the new immigrants came to the United States in search of work, as opposed to those earlier immigrants who moved with their families to start a new life and to create a new identity. The character of Irish immigration changed. Young, unmarried men left home to go to work on the Erie Canal, the canals of New Orleans, or the roads being cut through the Appalachians. This round of immigration was more Catholic than that of the 1700s. During the first quarter of the 19th century, new Catholic dioceses were created in St. Louis, New Orleans, and Cincinnati, among other places.

The Orange Order was a militant organization formed by Protestants in Ireland in 1795 to oppose the rights of Catholics. Though strong in northern Ireland (and Canada), the Orange Order was much weaker in America, where members sometimes fought pitched battles with Catholics.

Not all Catholic immigrants were Irish—many were German—but more Irish Catholics began to immigrate in the early 1800s than ever before.

The increasing presence of Catholics in a nation with solidly Protestant roots disturbed and threatened many Anglo-Saxon Americans. They were suspicious of the papacy, with its monarchial trappings, and regarded Catholics as unlikely Americans because of their presumed allegiance to the Vatican. Irish Protestants were among the first to react to the increased presence of Irish Catholics. In 1820, for example, Irish American Protestants founded an American branch of the Orange Order. The organization, still popular in Northern Ireland today, was named in honor of William of Orange, the man who had restored Protestant rule to Britain and Ireland in the late 17th century.

In 1824 a group of Scots-Irish Protestants carrying orange banners marched through the Greenwich Village section of Manhattan. The spectacle caught the attention of a group of Irish Catholics offended by the display of orange and its sectarian implications. A brawl broke out, and many rioters were arrested. The Catholic suspects were defended by two politically connected Irish Protestant attorneys, William Sampson and Thomas Addis Emmet, both of whom supported Catholic rights in Ireland as well as in America.

Emmet had not received Tammany's backing in his congressional bid, and so he was not elected. But he and his colleagues continued to voice support for republican ideals and for religious toleration in public life. They hoped, too, that Ireland one day would win the freedom America enjoyed—perhaps with America's help.

In the fall of 1828, the son of Irish immigrants received the nomination of Thomas Jefferson's party for president of the United States. Andrew Jackson, orphaned as a teenager and a hero of the War of 1812, became the first common man elected to the presidency when he defeated incumbent John Quincy Adams, son of a president and a man of privilege.

Did Jackson campaign as an Irishman made good, an immigrant's son who overcame tragedy and poverty to make a name for himself in war and peace? Certainly not. Those kinds of appeals would not appear for some time. Instead, Andrew Jackson was elected president without regard to his ethnicity, his religion, or his national origin. He was, simply, an American.

However, as the 19th century progressed, not all the Irish in America would win such ready acceptance.

Thomas Addis Emmet was an Irish patriot imprisoned for his support of the 1798 Irish Rebellion. After prison, he went to America and became a lawyer in New York City. Emmet was renowned for his oratory. In one famous Supreme Court case, he squared off against Daniel Webster.

1800-29

1800: With the general U.S. presidential election in an electoral deadlock, Congressman Matthew Lyon casts the deciding vote for Thomas Jefferson over Federalist incumbent John Adams. The Irish-born Lyon is a staunch anti-Federalist. • Irish-born physician Dr. John Crawford introduces the practice of vaccination in Baltimore, leading to the establishment of the city's Vaccine Institute in 1802. • Construction of the White House, designed by Irish American James Hoban, is completed.

July 18, 1800: John Rutledge, a son of Irish immigrants and the first Irish American chief justice of the U.S. Supreme Court, dies at age 60.

1800–1810: John Gilkey, an Irish immigrant who arrived in America in 1797, cultivates a potato from the cross-pollination of red, white, and blue Irish potato seed on his farm in western Pennsylvania. Known as the Neshannock, Mercer, or Gilkey potato, it is prized for its productivity as well as its excellent flavor and texture.

1801: The Hibernian Provident Society is founded in New York City. It is the first of many Hibernian societies that will be established in the East. Its mandate is to provide aid to Irish immigrants and their descendants.

January 1, 1801: As a result of the Act of Union, which was passed by Parliament the previous year, Ireland and Great Britain join to form the United Kingdom.

1802: Catherine O'Hare, an Irish immigrant from Ulster, becomes the first known European woman to deliver her child in the American West.

Hoban designs the White House Kilkenny-born James Hoban was already a successful architect when he left Ireland for America in 1785. He had been one of the designers of the Royal Exchange building (now Dublin's city hall), but in Ireland his prospects were limited. In the United States, he first achieved recognition for his work on South Carolina's capitol building in Columbia. However, his crowning achievement was the design of the president's residence—the White House—in the new nation's capital. Construction on the White House began in 1792, but it was not completed until 1800. The cost of construction was listed as $232,372.

Emmet's parting words Though portrayed here in uniform, Robert Emmet better played the role of impassioned orator for Irish freedom. Emmet was in France seeking aid for the United Irishmen when the 1798 Rebellion erupted. After returning to Ireland, he planned a new rising. It was a failure. He was captured, tried, hanged, drawn, and quartered in Dublin in September 1803. Nevertheless, the final line in his speech from the dock immortalized him: "When my country takes her place among the nations of the earth, then, and not till then, let my epitaph be written."

Green Ink

Facing suspicion and frequent hostility, the early Irish in America founded their own newspapers in order to fight back. The earliest papers, however, followed the habit of the times, with front pages carrying news of ship arrivals and commercial notices. Only later in the 19th century would the front pages be used as polemical weapons.

The first Irish American paper was *The Shamrock or Hibernian Chronicle*. It hit New York's streets from 1810 to 1817. A weekly published by United Irishman Thomas O'Connor, *The Shamrock* reported on births, marriages, deaths, and ships from Ireland, including their passenger manifests. *The Shamrock* gave way to *The Emerald* and *The Truth Teller*, which was strongly Catholic in tone. In Boston, *The Pilot* became popular reading for that city's rapidly growing Irish population.

The massive influx of post-famine immigrants provided Irish papers with boosted circulations and greater reason to vent against English tyranny. Indeed, the post-famine years were a golden age for Irish newspapers in America.

The Irish-American, first published in 1849, suggested an evolving sense of national identity. Other newspapers

Masthead of *The Irish World*

included *Irish Citizen*, John Devoy's *Gaelic American*, *The Chicago Citizen*, and Patrick Ford's *The Irish World*. These newspapers competed for readers by attacking each other as well as dastardly England. The Irish American press could draw on a dependable news cycle from Ireland, including its national struggle and even outright war.

In 1928, just a few years after the birth of the Irish Free State, Charles "Smash the Border" Connolly, a man whose sobriquet said it all, founded *The Irish Echo* in New York as a successor to an earlier venture, *The Sinn Feiner*. The *Echo* would become dominant in a still feisty market but would not see out the 20th century alone. Competitors such as the *Irish Voice* and, in Arizona, *The Desert Shamrock* ensured that the American Irish story would not be reported in isolation.

Fulton's steamboat Robert Fulton, whose father hailed from Kilkenny, showed an interest in boat design as a youth in Pennsylvania. While studying in England in the late 1780s, he became intrigued with the possibilities presented by the steam engine. At one point, he invented a "plunging boat" (like a submarine), but no one was interested. His fame rests on the development of the first practical steamboat, the *Clermont* (*pictured*), which in 1807 traveled from New York City to Albany in 32 hours. Fulton's steamboat revolutionized world travel.

1800-29

"...that great contractor, Mordecai Cochran...with his immortal Irish brigade, a thousand strong, with their carts, wheelbarrows, picks, shovels and blasting tools, grading the commons, and climbing the mountainside...and leaving behind them a roadway good enough for an emperor to travel over."

—A PENNSYLVANIA FARMER AFTER WITNESSING PART OF THE CONSTRUCTION OF THE NATIONAL ROAD

Building the National Road

From the birth of the United States, Americans had dreamed of building a road to connect the eastern seaboard to the lands west of the Allegheny Mountains. In 1806 Congress authorized the building of a road from Cumberland, Maryland, to the Mississippi River. Because the beginning of construction in 1811 coincided with an uptick in emigration from the Emerald Isle, the road crews were comprised of hundreds of Irishmen. Some of them were "working to pay off the dead horse"—that is, laboring their way out of indentured servitude. Work on the National Road included clearing land with axes, hoes, and shovels and crushing stone for roadbeds. For such backbreaking work, each laborer received from 12 cents to a dollar a day.

Basilica of the Assumption

Situated on a hill overlooking Baltimore Harbor, the Basilica of the Assumption was the first Catholic cathedral built in the United States. Construction took place from 1806 to 1821. Working with prominent architect Benjamin Henry Latrobe, who had volunteered his services, Bishop John Carroll purposely avoided the Gothic style, which was reminiscent of the Dark Ages of Medieval Europe. Instead, he had Latrobe design a structure similar to the U.S. Capitol in Washington, D.C. Considered a masterpiece of American architecture, the cathedral is today a national historic landmark.

Sullivans govern two states The sons of Irish parents who came to America as indentured servants, John and James Sullivan rose to become governors of, respectively, New Hampshire and Massachusetts. Younger brother James (*pictured*), who was educated as a lawyer, was active in radical politics in Massachusetts during the

Revolution and was elected governor in 1807. John first rose to prominence as a general in the Continental Army, and although his military record was mixed, he was a hero in his native New Hampshire.

Perry a hero in War of 1812 The vanquisher of a British squadron on Lake Erie during the War of 1812, Commodore Oliver Perry is best remembered for his words announcing the victory: "We have met the enemy and they are ours." His hard-fought success forced the British to abandon Detroit and fall back

to Niagara. Perry's connection to Ireland is interesting. His mother, from County Down, met his father, an American naval officer, while he was a prisoner of war being held in Cork during the American Revolution. After the war, he brought her to his home state of Rhode Island.

Hibernian societies help immigrants Very little about early 19th century Irish emigration was coordinated. But once the Irish reached America, they organized themselves with a zeal made necessary by unfamiliar and potentially hostile new surroundings. Fraternal orders and Hibernian societies, such as this Charleston Hibernian Society, were more than just help groups. They became, over time, active political clubs determined to secure influence and power for huge numbers of arriving Irish—immigrants who still harbored resentment arising from the denial of political rights in Ireland.

Macdonough prevails on Lake Champlain On September 11, 1814, a makeshift fleet of U.S. gunboats defeated a superior British naval force at the Battle of Plattsburgh Bay on Lake Champlain. The victor that day was Commodore Thomas Macdonough (*center*), whose grandfather had emigrated from Ireland in the early 18th century. Earlier, Macdonough had made a name for himself in skirmishes with the Barbary pirates. When war with Britain broke out in 1812, he was given command of U.S. ships on Lake Champlain. His rout of the British forces at Plattsburgh ensured that Lake Champlain remained safely in American hands.

September 1814: In one of the final engagements of the War of 1812, Thomas Macdonough, an Irish American commodore with the U.S. Navy, commands the *Saratoga* to victory in the Battle of Lake Champlain. The pivotal triumph prevents British troops from capturing New York and Vermont.

1817: Another wave of emigrants flees Ireland, as consecutive years of poor crop yields lead to yet another famine. A severe typhus outbreak adds to the misery. • The Shamrock Society of New York publishes a 22-page how-to immigration pamphlet entitled *Hints to Irishmen; who intend, with their families to make a permanent residence in America.*

April 24, 1817: A riot breaks out at the headquarters of the Tammany Society—the center of power for New York's Democratic Party—when the society's old guard refuses to nominate an Irish immigrant to a leadership post.

1820s: The rate of Irish immigration to America increases, and for the next four decades as many as one in three immigrants will be Irish. Additionally, there is an increase in the number of educated and skilled Irish making the crossing.

1824: Andrew Jackson, who was born just a couple of years after his parents emigrated from Ireland, becomes the first Irish American to run for president. He receives the nomination from his faction of the fragmented Democratic-Republican Party. • John McLoughlin, born in Canada to parents of Irish descent, arrives in Oregon as the newly appointed chief factor of the Hudson's Bay Company's Columbia district. He will effectively rule over the region for two decades, earning the sobriquet "Father of Oregon."

Lyric poet of Ireland In the early 19th century, Ireland's Thomas Moore emerged as one of the most popular poets and musical composers of the period. "Moore's Melodies," published from 1807 to 1834, were hit tunes of their day, and Moore was duly proclaimed national lyric poet of Ireland. His final days, however, were dominated less by melody than by mental illness and melancholy. Moore outlived all five of his children. Two died as infants, one died as a teenager, and two others passed away as young adults.

Irish pour into cities With little money to buy land on the frontier, Irish Catholic immigrants in the late 1820s transformed American cities. Men flocked to the docks of New York (*pictured*) or the factories of such cities as Lowell, Massachusetts, while women worked as seamstresses or domestic servants. Clearly defined Irish neighborhoods sprang up, as did a network of religious, social, fraternal, and political organizations designed to make the transition to city life easier. This created a foundation for the Famine Irish who went to big cities in even greater numbers during the 1840s.

The Power of Tammany Hall

It seems as if New York's Tammany Hall has always been synonymous with Irish political power. But the Irish had little to do with the creation of the Society of St. Tammany, as the organization was known when it was founded in the late 1780s.

Tammany societies were created in New York, Philadelphia, and other cities as fraternal and patriotic clubs. The name derived from Native American Lenape chief Tamanend. Tammany members even incorporated Native American jargon and rituals, calling members sachems (braves) while meeting in places called wigwams.

Tammany was seen as a workingman's alternative to aristocratic clubs. Not surprisingly, Tammany members were more comfortable with the Jeffersonian political party than the comparatively upper-class Federalists, who had supported the infamous Alien and Sedition Acts in the 1790s.

Perhaps the most prominent citizen affiliated with Tammany's early days was Aaron Burr, who organized Tammany support to help become Jefferson's vice president in 1800. Later, future president Martin Van Buren served as a grand sachem for Tammany Hall.

By the 1820s, Tammany was a loyal ally of the Democratic Party. Since Irish immigrants and other members of the lower classes were generally rejected by other political organizations, farsighted sachems recruited them to increase Tammany's power.

Tammany members fought to abolish laws that allowed only affluent landowners to vote. They also opposed jail sentences for debtors and, in 1828, supported Andrew Jackson for president. Jackson was seen as a hero of the common man. The fact that he was the son of Irish immigrants only made Tammany's appeal to the Irish—who could now vote—that much more apparent.

When Tammany headquarters moved into a grand building on 14th Street in Manhattan, the building came to be called Tammany Hall. So, too, did the organization.

The 1830s brought an increase in Irish Catholic immigration, with as many as 200,000 Irish entering New York City. Many immigrants went straight from their ship to a

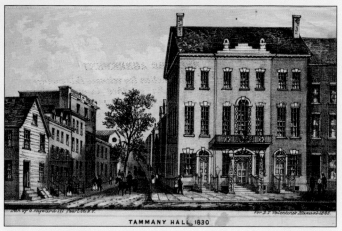

Tammany Hall, E. 14th Street, New York City

Tammany court with notes reading "Please naturalize the bearer."

As predominately Irish wards formed, Tammany spawned a broader social network. Saloons became important meeting places, and volunteer firehouses established close ties to the organization. They served as places where ambitious urban males could prove themselves and perhaps even become political candidates. Meanwhile, police officers were appointed by Tammany officials. It would not be long before Irishmen dominated the NYPD.

Of course, there was a downside to the Irish-Tammany alliance. The Irish often suffered because of widespread fraud and corruption. ("Vote early and often" became a slogan affiliated with Tammany politics.) Meanwhile, the Democratic Party was the dominant party in the slave-holding South, creating tensions between Irish immigrants and black Americans.

For all of these problems, however, Tammany's appeal to a poor Irish immigrant was clear. The machine offered jobs, shelter, coal, and even food. These were deeply anti-Irish times, with nativism rampant in many parts of New York City. (In 1844 a member of the anti-immigrant American party was elected mayor.) Tammany offered Irish immigrants protection as well as a chance to survive and perhaps even advance in a strange, often hostile land.

Irish help Spain colonize Texas Colonists gather at a settlement in Texas in 1823. In 1767, when the Spanish needed a governor for their vast colony in the American Southwest, they called on Hugo Oconór—who had been born Hugh O'Connor in Dublin. O'Connor was one of many Irishmen who changed their name, served Spain, and created the foundation for modern Texas. Father Miguel Muldoon was a prominent cleric who served under Viceroy Don Juan O'Donoju. By the early 1800s, Irish immigrants had settled such Texas towns as Refugio and San Patricio de Hibernia.

The Ditch That Made New York Rich

From 1817 to 1825, some 50,000 immigrants from Ireland found work building America's great canal system. They toiled day and night, through rain, snow, and extreme heat. To cope with the brutal tasks at hand, workers drank whiskey and beer and often sang songs. Irish labor proved indispensable in the greatest construction endeavor the United States had ever embarked upon.

The construction of an artificial waterway that connected Lake Erie with the Hudson River was nothing short of an engineering marvel. Many in New York State had believed the task impossible and staunchly rejected the proposal to build the Erie Canal. However, Governor DeWitt Clinton supported the project, believing the canal would open new markets in the Great Lakes region and bring New York unprecedented revenue. Clinton was right. The canal drastically cut transportation costs and led to the rapid growth of the region's economy. From 1830 to 1840, Michigan's population skyrocketed from 31,639 to 212,267. Moreover, the canal made both Buffalo and New York City principal financial centers.

The success of the Erie Canal would not have been possible without Irish labor. Contractors recognized that recent immigrants from Ireland could serve as a massive

Erie Canal

workforce at little cost to investors. Most worked for $8 to $12 per month. Furthermore, the Irish had a reputation as strong, diligent workers who could dig a stretch of canal faster than anyone—provided that the compensation was just.

According to one story, laborers working the Tonawanda-Buffalo leg of the canal set up kegs of beer at given intervals to spur themselves forward. Once they reached a given keg, they would down its contents and quickly move on to the next, prompting one observer to note that it was the "fastest diggin' and drinkin' the canawl has ever seen."

Irish construct the Erie Canal On November 4, 1825, New York governor DeWitt Clinton officially opened the Erie Canal by pouring water from Lake Erie into the Atlantic Ocean. A great American achievement, the canal was built on the backs of Irish laborers. An estimated 3,000 Irishmen worked on the canal in 1818 alone. According to a cliché at the time, the only things needed to build a canal were a pick, a shovel, and an Irishman. The work was dangerous. Cave-ins, explosions, and collapsing scaffolding accounted for many deaths, but by far the biggest culprit was "canal fever"—malaria. So many Irish died that it was commonly believed that for every mile of completed canal, one Irishman was buried.

Sampson defends the Irish William Sampson provided legal defense for the members of the United Irishmen—a role that landed him in hot water during the 1798 Irish Rebellion. Sampson was imprisoned and then forced to leave the Emerald Isle. Subsequently, he was shipwrecked in Wales before being imprisoned in and finally expelled from Portugal. He then moved to France and Germany before settling in the United States. In America, he continued to defend the Irish. He won a seminal case that established the confessional privilege, and he defended Irish Catholics in New York following their street battle with Scots-Irish Orangemen in 1824.

Lynch brings business to New York
Dominick Lynch, an acquaintance once said, "was the only Irishman I ever heard of that brought money to America." From a prominent Galway family, Lynch had made a fortune trading in Europe before shifting his focus to America. After purchasing a plot of land in upstate New York, he made it a bustling commercial center, with gristmills, sawmills, and cotton and woolen mills. Though he desired to name the site Lynchville, the residents—most of whom worked for Lynch—voted to name it Rome in 1819.

A Pittsburgh pioneer Arriving in America before the Revolution, James O'Hara became a prosperous merchant in Philadelphia. Once war broke out, he served as quartermaster of the Continental Army. Then, following independence, he relocated to the frontier town of Pittsburgh. There he opened a retail store, ran a sawmill and gristmill, built ships, brewed beer, made window and bottle glass, and acquired extensive real estate holdings. He justly has been called "the father" of Pittsburgh commerce and industry.

1825: William Macneven, a veteran of the 1798 United Irishmen rebellion, becomes head of the newly created Emigrant Assistance Society in New York City. • Construction is completed on the Erie Canal. The majority of the construction workers will be Irish immigrants. The working conditions are so dangerous that it is commonly claimed that along every mile of the canal, an Irishman is buried.

1827: The B&O Railroad, one of the nation's first, is chartered. Financing for the railroad is spearheaded by Alexander Brown, an industrialist and banker who emigrated from County Antrim in 1800.

1828: The Democratic Party is officially created as an offshoot of the Democratic-Republican Party during the candidacy of its first nominee, Irish American Andrew Jackson. • Daniel O'Connell is elected to the British Parliament, becoming the first Catholic to win the office in more than 150 years. However, he will refuse to take his seat because the swearing-in oath refers to Catholicism as a superstition.

November 4, 1828: Andrew Jackson becomes the first Irish American to be elected president of the United States.

1829: Charlestown, Massachusetts, erupts in three days of violence as anti-Catholic rioters attack the homes of Irish Catholic immigrants. • In the Mexican territory of Texas, Irish families establish a town they name Villa de San Patricio de Hibernia. It is part of Mexico's effort to hold the territory by offering free land to New York Irish Catholics who agree to practice their faith and speak Spanish.

April 1829: In part due to its desire to avoid further conflict in the wake of the O'Connell controversy, Irish Parliament passes the Catholic Emancipation Act, which repeals the last of the Penal Acts.

The Five Points slum In the 19th century, the Five Points neighborhood in lower Manhattan—where five streets intersected—was considered New York City's worst slum. In the 1820s, Irish immigrants and recently emancipated (in New York State) African Americans packed into tenements on this swampy land. In its crowded, disease-ridden streets, crime was rampant. Its Irish complexion peaked in the years following the Great Famine. In later decades, Jews, Italians, and other European immigrants settled in Five Points.

Catholic Relief Act For more than a century, Britain's "penal laws" had denied Irish Catholics many rights, including holding government office, voting, buying land, practicing law, attending school, and possessing weapons. The Catholic Church was outlawed and the Irish language was banned. Some, but not all, of the penal laws were repealed over the years, and by 1828 large numbers of Irish demanded more freedom. Fearing an Irish rebellion under orator Daniel O'Connell (*right*), British Parliament passed the Catholic Relief Act of 1829, which lifted many of the remaining restrictions on Irish Catholics.

Irish American Presidents

In the presidential race of 1828, Democrat Andrew Jackson challenged incumbent John Quincy Adams. To many eastern elites, Jackson symbolized the unruly, uneducated, and unsophisticated element in American society that endangered the nation's very sociopolitical structure. Many Americans disliked Jackson because of his background. Unlike any president before him, Jackson had grown up in poverty, in the backcountry of South Carolina, and he was the son of Scots-Irish immigrants.

In the end, Jackson decisively won the election, even though he failed to carry the Northeast. His election not only ushered in a new, more democratic era of politics, but it also opened the door for other candidates of Scots-Irish stock. In 1844 James K. Polk, who traced his ancestry to County Donegal, was elected to the presidency. Thirteen years later, James Buchanan, whose father had immigrated from Ireland, took up residence in the White House. In addition, presidents Chester Arthur, William McKinley, Woodrow Wilson, and Richard Nixon all claimed a strong Scots-Irish background.

While these seven presidents had roots in Ireland, as Scots-Irish their lines ultimately began in Scotland. The election of 1960, however, brought to office the first Irish Catholic president, John Fitzgerald Kennedy. He was fully and proudly Irish. In 1848 his great-grandfather had emigrated from County Wexford to the United States, settling in Boston and making his living as a cooper. John Kennedy's maternal line also was firmly rooted in the Republic of Ireland. Still today, many in County Wexford and elsewhere in Ireland consider Kennedy a true son of Erin and proudly display his portrait in public houses, shops, and cafés.

Fortieth president Ronald Reagan's paternal great-grandfather, Michael, immigrated to America from County Tipperary in 1858. But unlike Kennedy, Reagan had strong Scottish and English roots and was Protestant, not Catholic. Several other presidents also have some Irish or Scots-Irish ancestry, including Ulysses S. Grant, Grover Cleveland, Lyndon Johnson, Jimmy Carter, George H. W. Bush, Bill Clinton, and George W. Bush.

First Irish president
The election of "Old Hickory," Andrew Jackson, in 1828 as the first Irish president of the United States ushered in a new era of American politics. The son of humble Scots-Irish immigrants, Jackson became a popular military hero with his victory over the British at the Battle of New Orleans in 1815. His ascension to the presidency symbolized the victory of the common man over the privileged elite in America. The celebration at his inauguration in March 1829 was a boisterous affair in which rough western frontiersmen mingled with Washington society.

> "Civil war raging [in Philadelphia].... [T]he state of things in that city is growing worse and worse every day. I shan't be caught voting for a 'Native' ticket again in a hurry."
>
> —DIARY ENTRY OF WEALTHY NEW YORKER GEORGE TEMPLETON STRONG ABOUT
> RIOTING BETWEEN IRISH CATHOLICS AND NATIVISTS, JULY 8, 1844

During the 19th century, rioting occasionally broke out between Protestants and Catholics in American cities. Over the decades, close to 100 people were killed, but the violence died out after the 1870s. The Philadelphia riots of 1844 were triggered by the use of the Protestant Bible in public schools. As many as 18 people, mostly Protestants, were killed.

No Love for Irish Catholics

1830–1844

As thousands of native-born Philadelphians descended on that city's Irish enclave of Kensington on Monday, May 6, 1844, rain began to fall. The wet weather spoiled plans to hold a rally against the burgeoning population of Irish Catholics in the neighborhood. Would-be demonstrators were forced to take shelter in a market that catered to the very people they despised. Not surprisingly, perhaps, events quickly spun out of control. The two sides began to brawl, and an Irishman was shot in the face. The Kensington Irish rallied to one of their own, assailing the demonstrators with whatever they could lay their hands on. Other Irish, positioned in buildings near the market, opened fire on the demonstrators.

It was the beginning of three days of deadly conflict in Philadelphia between native-born citizens and Irish Catholic immigrants. Homes and Catholic churches were put to the torch, and several people were killed. A few weeks later, to celebrate the anniversary of American independence, thousands of Philadelphians marched through the city to show their support for the families of demonstrators killed in May. More violence broke out. The militia was called in, hundreds of Irish fled their homes, and the City of Brotherly Love became a combat zone pitting anti-immigrant mobs against the Irish. As many as 18 people were killed in several days of fighting. Dozens were injured.

The arrival of hundreds of thousands of Irish in the 1820s through the early 1840s profoundly disturbed not only the residents of Philadelphia but those of Boston, New York, and other urban areas where the new immigrants settled. As William Shannon noted in his classic book *The American Irish*, New Yorkers, Philadelphians, Bostonians, and other Americans might have admired such Irish figures as Charles Carroll, the well-to-do signer of the Declaration of Independence, but they found the new wave of Irish immigrants repulsive. Not only were the new arrivals overwhelmingly Catholic and, therefore, alien to the nation's Protestant culture, but they were poor and uneducated. They also were predominately rural people who chose to start their new lives in America not on the land but in its fast-growing cities, where there was work to be had.

Anti-Irish violence broke out sporadically. Much of it was fueled by anti-Catholicism, while some of it was the result of economic competition between native-born workers and Irish laborers. Street-level hostility toward Catholic immigrants in general and Irish Catholics in particular inspired a broader movement known as nativism, which encouraged politicians to adopt anti-immigrant positions. One such nativist, James Harper, was elected mayor of New York City in 1844. In 1849, the movement would give birth to a formal organization known as the Order of the Star Spangled Banner. It was better known as the "Know-Nothing" party because of its members' insistence that they knew nothing of nativist activities.

One of the most contentious issues between Irish Catholic immigrants and the native-born was education. Such clerics as Bishop John Hughes of New York, an Irish immigrant, objected to Protestant values in public schools. Led by the largely Irish Catholic hierarchy, the Catholic Church established its own, separate school system and often demanded public support for the parochial schools.

If nothing else, the Irish Catholic immigrants were accustomed to the kind of hostility they faced in America's cities. They had fled a country in which they had few rights, and where a Protestant minority kept a firm grip on power thanks to legislation known as the Penal Laws. Beginning in 1695, the British Parliament had passed a series of laws that banned Catholic education, prohibited Catholics from voting or holding some elective offices, and restricted Catholic property rights. Irish Catholic farmers rented small

In his attempt to urge Parliament to accept Catholic members, Daniel O'Connell formed the Catholic Association in Ireland and held "monster" rallies. O'Connell became the first Catholic elected to Parliament in more than a century. The British were merely placating O'Connell, as evidenced by this artwork, entitled *Keeping the Child Quiet.*

plots of land, becoming increasingly dependent on the potato as their main source of food while other crops paid the rent.

Just as the Irish in America began to defend themselves in the face of nativist violence, the Irish in Ireland began to move against oppressive forces at home. In 1823 Catholic lawyer Daniel O'Connell formed an organization called the Catholic Association, which challenged Britain's restrictions against Catholic membership in Parliament. For a penny a month, even the poorest Irishman could join, and within two years, O'Connell organized Ireland's farmers and laborers into a potent political organization. O'Connell was elected to Parliament in 1828, and the British grudgingly allowed him to take his seat in 1829.

The success of emancipation led O'Connell to begin agitation against the Act of Union, which had brought Ireland into the United Kingdom in 1801 (as opposed to being a province with limited self-government). Once again, O'Connell used the tactics of mass popular organization. He and his followers established a central Repeal Association in 1840 and a network of local affiliates throughout the countryside. His reach and influence extended beyond the parishes, villages, and cities of early Victorian Ireland. The Irish in America embraced the notion of repeal, although in O'Connell's view repeal would not necessarily mean a complete break with Britain but rather a return to self-government within the British Empire.

Branches of the Repeal Association were established in the United States, and such American politicians as future president James Buchanan and former president John Tyler supported repeal. American money flowed into O'Connell's organization, setting a precedent for future Irish political organizations that would look to the U.S. for popular support and money.

Not all of O'Connell's views, however, found favor among Irish Americans. He was a stalwart abolitionist who urged his American supporters to oppose slavery. Some Irish Americans resented criticism of their adopted country from abroad, while others saw O'Connell taking sides in American partisan politics.

By the mid-1840s, the repeal movement in Ireland began to lose energy as its leader aged and as younger Irish agitators became impatient. In the United States, Irish Catholics continued to find themselves on the defensive as nativism continued to spread.

In 1845 the potatoes in Ireland turned black with disease. From that point on, Ireland and the United States would never be the same.

James Harper cofounded Harper and Brothers, publisher of books and magazines that featured anti-Catholic polemics. An outspoken nativist, Harper was elected by the short-lived American Republican Party as mayor of New York in 1844. Later, he supported the Know-Nothings and then the Republican Party.

December 1830: The Bowie knife's legendary status is established when its namesake, Irish American Alamo hero Jim Bowie, uses it to kill three would-be assassins.

1831: An anti-Irish mob sets fire to New York City's St. Mary's Church.

March 16, 1831: Many of the most successful members of New York's Irish expatriate community attend the first annual Erina Ball.

1832: Irish nationalist leader Daniel O'Connell launches the Repeal Movement in an effort to nullify the 1801 Act of Union, which had united Britain and Ireland in the formation of the United Kingdom.

May 1832: The Western Baptist Educational Association is established in Boston. Strong anti-Catholic sentiment in the early decades of the 19th century leads to the development of this and similar groups, including the Baptist Home Mission and the General Association of Congregational Churches. Though ostensibly promoting their own religions, many are de facto hate groups.

1833: William Sampson, a United Irishmen member who was exiled after the rebellion and settled in New York, publishes his magnum opus, *History of Ireland*.

1834: Telegraph inventor Samuel Morse, who despises Irish Catholics, pens an essay suggesting a Catholic conspiracy for national domination. It eventually will become a manifesto of sorts for the short-lived Know-Nothing party.

August 11–12, 1834: Anti-Irish rioting in Charlestown, Massachusetts, culminates in the torching of an Ursuline convent by a mob of angry Protestants.

Irish a part of America's first railroad The Baltimore and Ohio (B & O) Railroad, which opened in 1830 as America's first railroad, revolutionized transportation. For the Irish, the B & O was a steady source of labor. The work was hard, but it helped create stable Irish Catholic communities for railroad laborers. Robert Garrett, who immigrated to the United States from County Down, eventually became president of the B & O. His son would hold the same position. Charles Carroll, a descendent of the prominent Carroll clan, was a key B & O investor.

Brown strikes it rich Belfast native Alexander Brown was one of America's first millionaires. He worked as a linen merchant in Ireland before immigrating to Baltimore. Brown and his sons, who imported and exported a wide variety of goods, had offices in New York, Philadelphia, and England. Brown was also a key supporter of the Baltimore and Ohio Railroad, America's first major rail line. Following his death in 1834, the Brown family focused solely on banking. Alex. Brown & Sons proclaimed itself America's foremost international banking enterprise of the 19th century.

The Rise of Paddy

In the 1871 book *New Physiognomy*, author Samuel R. Wells described what an Irishman supposedly looked like: "The untrained, blunt, coarse bog-trotter walks heavily upon his heels in parlour, church, or kitchen, his gait being more like that of a horse on a bridge than like that of the cultured gentleman."

Beginning in the 1840s, just as immigration from Ireland was reaching peak levels, stereotypes that portrayed the Irish as pugnacious, ragged, alcoholic, and prone to criminal behavior proliferated across the United States. This negative image first emerged in Great Britain, where such pseudoscientific books as Robert Knox's *The Races of Man* argued that those of Celtic stock were physically and mentally inferior to Anglo-Saxons. Across the Atlantic, Americans largely embraced these ideas, as such nativist organizations as the Order of the Star Spangled Banner called for greater restrictions on immigration.

By the 1850s, popular American periodicals and weekly comics further perpetuated anti-Irish sentiment and stereotypes, portraying Irish men and women as wild, beast-like savages. Caricaturists Thomas Nast, Joseph Keppler, and Bernhard Gillam likened the "paddy" to an ape while accusing the Irish of political corruption and contributing to a decline in American values and morality.

Morse suspicious of Catholic immigrants Best known as the inventor of the telegraph, Samuel Morse was also one of the most prominent nativists of the 1830s. He argued that Catholic immigrants were undermining democracy in the United States. "You are marked as their prey," Morse warned native-born Americans. He later published his anti-immigrant essays under the titles *Foreign Conspiracy Against the Liberties of the United States* and *Imminent Dangers to the Free Institutions of the United States Through Foreign Immigration*.

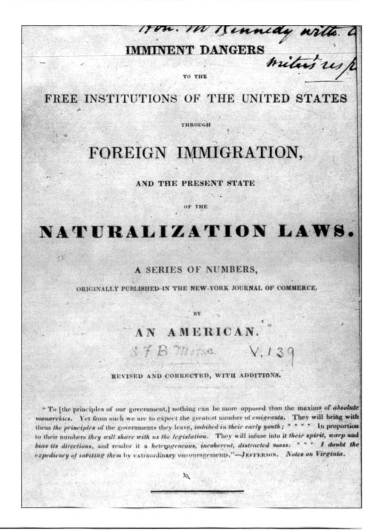

1835: Samuel Morse continues to disseminate his views on the purported Catholic takeover of the republic with the release of two essays, *Foreign Conspiracy* and *Imminent Dangers*.

1836: A Canadian woman named Maria Monk publishes *The Awful Disclosures of Maria Monk,* a sensationalized account of her alleged experience as a Catholic nun who was sexually exploited by priests. (Scholarly research has since refuted Monk's claims.) The book will succeed in exacerbating anti-Catholic discrimination. • Roger B. Taney, a Catholic of Scots-Irish ancestry and the architect of the notorious Dred Scott decision that will deny citizenship to African Americans, is sworn in as chief justice of the Supreme Court.

March 6, 1836: The siege at the Alamo ends in a pitched battle from which the Mexicans emerge victorious over the Texans. Among the 185 men who give their lives for Texas's independence are two fabled Irish Americans: Jim Bowie and Davy Crockett.

April 1836: Texas wins its independence from Mexico thanks to the military leadership of Sam Houston, a Texan of Scots-Irish ancestry. Houston will be named the first president of the new Republic of Texas.

May 4, 1836: The first division of the Ancient Order of Hibernians is officially founded at New York City's St. James Church. It is an outgrowth of a meeting held two months earlier between anti-nativist activists from Pennsylvania and New York.

1838: On the orders of Andrew Jackson, the United States' first Irish American president, thousands of Cherokee Indians are forced to leave the Southeast along the "Trail of Tears" and accept relocation to Indian reservations in the West.

NOTICE.

PATRICK M'DERMOTT, a Native of the County Kildare, and who was married in Kingston, near Dublin, is hereby informed, that his wife and four children have arrived in Boston. They understand that he left Roxbury, in this State, about twelve months since, to obtain work as a stone mason; they are extremely anxious to hear from him. He is hereby requested to write or come for his poor family, to this city, as soon as possible.

☞ Editors, with whom we exchange, will perform an act of charity by giving the above notice a few insertions.
Oct. 1.

Breakup of immigrant families A Massachusetts newspaper printed this notice to help reunite members of an Irish immigrant family. Prior to the Great Famine, other famines occurred in Ireland between 1708 and 1842. In many cases, one member of the family would leave first, then pay the passage for other family members once he or she found employment. However, poor education and communication often resulted in permanent separation—not only from the homeland, but also from loved ones who followed.

MCCORMICK.

REAPING MACHINE.

McCormick's reaper The son of an Irish American inventor, Cyrus McCormick was born in Virginia in 1809. At age 25, he earned a patent for his mechanical reaper—an invention begun by his father, Robert, but ultimately perfected by Cyrus—that would change agricultural production in America. By combining functions previously performed by separate machines, the reaper saved time and allowed farmers to dramatically increase their production. McCormack's invention won him several awards, including a prestigious gold medal at London's Crystal Palace Exhibition. His business, the McCormick Harvesting Machine Company, eventually became the foundation of the International Harvester Company.

Race Relations

Beginning in colonial times, relations between African Americans and the Irish were fraught with tension. Occupying the lowest rungs of society, free blacks and the Irish often competed for the same jobs. In the southern states, contractors frequently assigned the most dangerous jobs to Irishmen, on the assumption that a black slave was too valuable an investment to lose in case of an accident.

One historian has argued that the Irish in the early 19th century adopted the racist attitudes of white Americans to further their own efforts at assimilation. Through the 1820s and 1830s, race riots erupted in Cincinnati, Philadelphia, and Pittsburgh in which the Irish participated, although they were not specifically Irish riots.

At the same time, some Irish were empathetic toward the plight of black Americans. Irish-born John England—the first Catholic bishop of Charleston, South Carolina—established an order of nuns with the explicit mission of

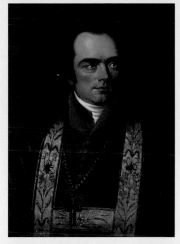

John England

educating both the African American girls and the poor white girls of the city. In the early 1830s, he opened a school for black girls. In response, he was threatened by racists and had to travel with a bodyguard. Other Irish American churchmen took similar measures to ameliorate the condition of black Americans.

Slavery presented a particular problem for working-class Irish. In general, they opposed emancipation on the grounds that free blacks would compete with them for jobs—and because the abolitionists had shown no inclination to support the workingman. Daniel O'Connell, the "Great Liberator," exhorted Irish Americans to support the cause of abolition, but his efforts fell on deaf ears. Instead, when the United States passed a draft law during the Civil War, the New York Irish rioted in opposition. Mobs burned black businesses and homes and lynched a number of African Americans. In all, some 100 people died, most of them Irish.

Protestant mob burns down convent The purpose of Boston's Ursuline Convent, which was dedicated in 1825, was to educate the Irish immigrants who were flocking to the area. By 1834, however, rumors swirled that girls were being held captive at the convent. This confirmed the anti-Catholic suspicions of local Protestants, who also believed that Irish newcomers would take their jobs. In August, a mob burned the convent. Only remnants stood (*pictured*). Just one man was convicted of the crime, and he eventually was pardoned. The Ursuline Convent was never rebuilt, but its bricks were used to build Boston's Cathedral of the Holy Cross.

Crockett defends the Alamo John Wayne was cast to play Davy Crockett in the big-screen depiction of the 1836 battle at the Alamo, and for most Americans that is confirmation enough that Crockett was a larger-than-life figure in his own time and beyond. Crockett, a frontiersman, soldier, and member of Congress, was of Irish-French stock. His name is often mentioned in conjunction with Scots-Irish heroes of his time, such as Jim Bowie. Crockett and Bowie perished at the Alamo while defending Texan independence from Santa Anna's Mexican army.

Irish hero of Texas "Scotch-Irishmen of America: I come to speak to you of that epoch-making man, General Sam Houston." So said Reverend D. C. Kelley at an 1890 meeting of the Scotch Irish Society of America. Born in Rockbridge County, Virginia, Houston epitomized the fighting spirit so closely associated with the Scots-Irish. He led the Texas Army in its battle for independence from Mexico (1835–36), and he later served as senator and governor of Texas. That state's largest city bears his name. Houston also is the only person ever to govern two states. In the late 1820s, he served as governor of Tennessee.

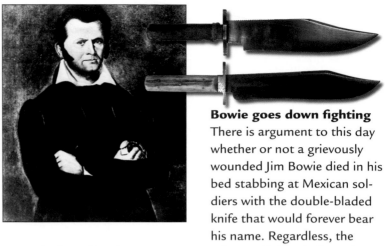

Bowie goes down fighting There is argument to this day whether or not a grievously wounded Jim Bowie died in his bed stabbing at Mexican soldiers with the double-bladed knife that would forever bear his name. Regardless, the Kentucky-born frontiersman cut an undisputedly heroic figure in the Scots-Irish pantheon, along with the likes of Davy Crockett and William Travis, both of whom fell at the Alamo on March 6, 1836. Bowie's knife owes its fame to a duel in Mississippi, but the man's name is most strongly linked with his adopted Texas.

Vicious propaganda Nativist and anti-Catholic publications were widely available in the 1830s. Newspapers such as *The Downfall of Babylon* applauded the "triumph of truth over popery." Pamphlets and books disseminated conspiracy theories about priests and made dire predictions about how the Irish would destroy America. In the illustration from this 1836 issue, a nun throws a murdered infant into a pit.

"Death" of Tammany Hall Cartoons were central to political debate in the 1830s. In 1837 New York's Democrats, including Tammany Hall as well as a faction of the Democratic Party called the Loco Focos, suffered heavy losses in the municipal elections. The Whigs, depicted on the left, were victorious. At right, a wounded Indian and an Irishwoman represent Tammany and the Democrats. Laments the woman: "Arrah be me soul Ould Tammany, your faithful Loco Foco will die wid you!"

"It went through twenty printings, sold 300,000 copies, and down to the Civil War served as the 'Uncle Tom's Cabin' of the Know-Nothing movement."

—HISTORIAN WILLIAM V. SHANNON ON *THE AWFUL DISCLOSURES OF MARIA MONK*

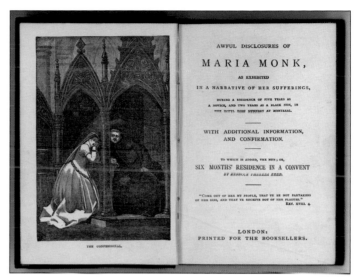

Awful disclosures Anti-Catholic literature was widely distributed in the 19th century. *The Awful Disclosures of Maria Monk*, first published in 1836, was a complete fabrication—yet hundreds of thousands of people bought the book thinking that its story was true. The narrator, Maria Monk, describes depraved conditions inside the Hotel Dieu convent in Montreal, in which priests impregnate nuns whose unwanted babies are buried in a mass grave. *The Awful Disclosures* was last reprinted in the 1990s.

"Father of Oregon" Though born in Quebec, Canada, John McLoughlin traced his roots back to Ireland's County Donegal. Eventually, he became known as the "Father of Oregon." A fur trader, McLoughlin ran the western territory for the Hudson Bay Company. Once established in Oregon, he assisted the waves of settlers who sought to begin new lives in the western territories. He even was elected mayor of Oregon City. Mount McLoughlin, a dormant volcano in southern Oregon, is named after him.

1830-44

April 10, 1838: Father Theobald Mathew convenes the first meeting of the Cork Total Abstinence Society. Members pledge to forgo alcohol entirely. Mathew will sign some seven million converts on both sides of the Atlantic before his death.

July 31, 1838: The "Poor Law" is enacted in Ireland. Intended to foster self-reliance by denying assistance to Ireland's poor, the law results in mass starvation and homelessness.

1839: Irish-born wagon maker Joseph Murphy responds to a tax levied on wagons traversing New Mexico by building an extra-large wagon. He hopes to soften the tax impact by increasing his freight load. Soon, these "J. Murphy wagons," as they will come to be known, will be ubiquitous on the trails to the western frontier.

1840: In the past decade, the percentage of unskilled to skilled Irish immigrants coming to America rose to 60 percent from a low of 28 percent in 1826, reversing an earlier trend of unskilled immigrant influx.
• Irish immigration to New Orleans, Louisiana, has doubled in the past decade, raising the number of Irish living in the city to 100,000.

1840s: As Irish immigrants continue to reach America's shores in ever greater numbers, Catholic colleges and universities are established, including Fordham in 1841, Notre Dame in 1842, and both Villanova and Holy Cross in 1843.

1841: Coadjutor Bishop John Hughes spearheads the founding of the Irish Emigrant Society in New York City. Under the leadership of Gregory Dillon, its first president, the society will have its hands full trying to aid the crush of Irish immigrants arriving in the city each year.

Indentured servants This document frees Irishman Francis O'Neill, who had spent seven years of indentured servitude in a penal colony in Australia. Though nobody knows how many impoverished British and Irish "paid" for passage to America by agreeing to a term of forced servitude, it is likely that thousands took the "opportunity." A typical term was

seven years, but servants often found themselves impoverished and forced into continued service well past the expiration of their terms.

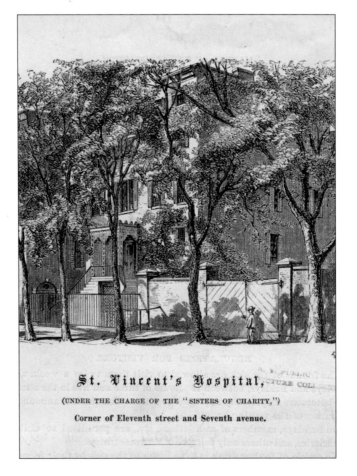

St. Vincent's Hospital,
(UNDER THE CHARGE OF THE "SISTERS OF CHARITY,")
Corner of Eleventh street and Seventh avenue.

Sisters of Charity
Along with the great wave of Irish Catholic immigrants in the 19th century came vast social needs. The Sisters of Charity was among the religious groups that ran hospitals (including St. Vincent's in New York City) and other facilities designed to aid Irish immigrants in the United States. The first Sisters of Charity hospital opened in St. Louis in 1828. In the decades that followed, the Sisters and many other Catholic-affiliated groups operated hospitals in Manhattan and big cities across the U.S.

Irish Helping Irish

Robert Hogan was disturbed by what he saw. The 1830s were drawing to a close, and more and more Irish immigrants to the United States were poor and Catholic. Hogan, the president of the Friendly Sons of St. Patrick, could see that native-born American Protestants were becoming more intolerant toward these destitute immigrants. Thus, the pillars of New York's Irish community held a meeting. Representatives from Tammany Hall joined Hogan, Bishop "Dagger" John Hughes, and others to formulate a plan to assist the Irish.

Scene at the Irish Emigrant Office in Ann street.

The result was the Irish Emigrant Society, founded in 1841. Members greeted new immigrants and warned them of schemers who preyed upon the newly arrived Irish. The society's members also helped immigrants find jobs and homes, and they even translated for those rural immigrants who spoke only Irish.

In the mid- to late 1840s, when the Famine ravaged Ireland, the Irish Emigrant Society assisted thousands of immigrants every month. The society also began to lobby for political change. It supported the 1847 creation of a New York government commission to aid immigrants and operate the nation's first immigration processing center. It was called Castle Garden, the forerunner to Ellis Island.

Since many immigrants were often cheated by banks, the Emigrant Society also facilitated Irish financial trans-actions. In 1850 society members decided to enter the banking business, forming the Emigrant Industrial Savings Bank. On September 30, 1850, Queens County-born Bridget White became the bank's first customer. Nearly 100 accounts were opened by the end of the month and 300 by the end of the year. Four of every five Emigrant Savings Bank customers had been born in Ireland.

From this humble beginning, the Emigrant Savings Bank became one of America's largest, and today has more than $10 billion in assets. One of the bank's logos—an image of Irish people disembarking a ship—helped patrons remember the company's immigrant roots.

GROCERY CART AND HARNESS FOR SA—In good order, and one chestnut horse, 8 years old excellent saddle horse; can be ridden by a lady. Also, ~~young man wanted~~ from 16 to 18 years of age, able to w~~rite~~ No Irish need apply. CLUFF & TUNIS, No. 270 W~~ash~~ington st., corner of Myrtle-av., Brooklyn.

No Irish need apply Anti-Irish notices, such as "No Irish need apply," were likely not as widespread in the United States as some believe, though they certainly did exist. They probably were more prevalent in London, which is where a folk song about such anti-Irish notices originated. "I'm a decent boy just landed from the town of Ballyfad," the song begins. When he sees a job offer, he adds: "the dirty spalpeen ended with 'No Irish need apply!'" Even if few such signs existed in the U.S., the Irish faced job discrimination—especially for well-paying jobs—through much of the 19th century.

1841: Daniel O'Connell writes "An Address of the People of Ireland to their Countrymen and Countrywomen in America." He urges Irish Americans to support the efforts of abolitionists to end the practice of slavery in the United States. Some 70,000 Irish sign the document.

1842: Writer Charles Dickens travels to the Unites States and visits, among other places, New York's destitute Irish neighborhood, Five Points. He will write about his experience in "American Notes."

December 20, 1842: Upon the death of Bishop DuBois, Irish-born John Hughes is appointed bishop of the diocese of New York. Hughes will spend his career fighting for the rights of Irish immigrants, particularly Catholics.

Autumn 1843: The potato blight is discovered in Philadelphia. Originating in Mexico's Central Highlands, where it had been dormant for perhaps centuries, it will make its way to North America (to little effect) before crossing to Ireland.

May 6, 1844: Rioting breaks out in the Philadelphia suburb of Kensington, as anti-Irish nativists attack and destroy Irish homes and Catholic churches.

Summer 1844: The Philadelphia Bible riot erupts after Protestants and Catholics haggle over the use of the Bible in public schools. When the dust clears after three days of violence, 13 people are dead.

July 1844: Discovering that the Hibernia Greens, an Irish militia, is inside Philadelphia's St. Philip Neri Church, a Protestant mob attacks the church with cannon fire. The rioters will fail to honor a promise to let the militia leave peacefully, and the ensuing gunfight will leave 18 rioters dead in the street.

Advice for emigrants
Robert McDougall's *The Emigrant's Guide to North America* (1841), written in Irish, was aimed at Scots-Gaelic immigrants to Canada. The book was one of many attempts to help those Irish who were fleeing poverty, disease, and famine in the 19th century. Many were native Irish speakers who did not speak English, and thus they were easy prey for unscrupulous profiteers. The guide gave practical advice on finding work and lodgings and dealing with contracts.

CEANN-IÙIL AN FHIR-IMRICH
DO DH'AMERICA MU-THUATH;

OR,

THE EMIGRANT'S GUIDE
TO NORTH AMERICA.

By ROBERT M'DOUGALL, Esq.

Ni fear a dh'fhalbhas 'na thràth
Biadh 'us bàrr 'sam bi toirt ;
Am feadh bhios tàchrain gun stàth,
A' dol bàs leis a ghort :
Bithidh piseach agus loinn
Air a chloinn 's air a mhnaoidh ;
Am feadh bhios truaghain gun sgoinn,
Fo na Goill air an claoidh.

GLASGOW:
J. & P. CAMPBELL, 24, GLASSFORD STREET.
OBAN: J. MILLER.—INVERNESS: J. BAIN & CO.
DINGWALL: A. KEITH.

MDCCCXLI.

Higher education for Irish Catholics In June 1841, six students comprised the student body of St. John's College in New York. This was the modest beginning of Fordham University (its chapel is pictured) and of Catholic higher education for Irish immigrants. Such Catholic colleges and universities as Villanova in Philadelphia, Holy Cross in Boston, and Notre Dame in Indiana would ensure that once the Irish found their way in America, their children would receive a world-class education while maintaining Catholic values.

Women of Courage

In the history of American immigration, Irish women were unique. Unlike other immigrant groups, more Irish women than men immigrated to America in the great diaspora of the 19th century. Many came with husbands and children, but large numbers came alone. This was due to conditions in Ireland. With few options for work and frequently lacking marriage dowries, Irish girls left their homeland. Sometimes in groups, but often singly, they bravely set out for the New World.

In an America in which few women worked outside the home, jobs for women were limited. Skilled Irish girls found work as seamstresses and milliners. Many of the unskilled took positions in the textile mills of New England. There they worked long hours, usually from seven in the morning until seven at night, with a half-day on Saturday. Too many images of 16- and 17-year-old Irish girls in bare feet standing next to looms attest to the hardships of their lives.

Female laborers in a New York City twine factory

The vast majority of Irish immigrant girls, however, went into domestic service. They were the maids, cooks, laundresses, and nannies of America's wealthier classes. By the time of the Civil War, "Bridgets" were in almost every well-heeled home in the country. They had little competition for work. Yankee women considered domestic service demeaning, and black Americans were generally excluded from live-in positions. The Irish monopoly in domestic work was so complete that one wealthy matron in Rutland, Vermont, when looking for help in the 1870s, lamented that she could get nothing but Irish.

For single Irish girls, domestic service had certain benefits. Besides steady pay, it provided them the security of a home—no small matter when living alone in a strange land. And if the pay was low, so were the living expenses. Money was put aside for dowries, for contributions to the Church, or to send home to family in Ireland. One esti-mate calculated that from 1848 to 1864, Irish immigrants sent $65 million to Ireland to help sustain family members and to help others to emigrate—much of it coming from the savings of servant girls.

It was common in Ireland at the time for an anxious family member to ask the postman whether there was an "American" in his mailbag—an "American" being a letter from the States, presumably containing sorely needed money. One other benefit of domestic service, as historian Hasia Diner has pointed out, was that Irish girls coming from impoverished rural backgrounds learned the etiquette and proprieties of middle-class American life, and in time passed these traits to their families.

Nuns comprised another group of immigrant Irish women who played a courageous role in America, particularly the Sisters of the Presentation and the Sisters of Mercy. These orders and others attracted thousands of Irish women who selflessly devoted their lives to the care of the sick and to the education of the young. That the Irish eventually became one of America's great success stories was in large measure due to the efforts of these women.

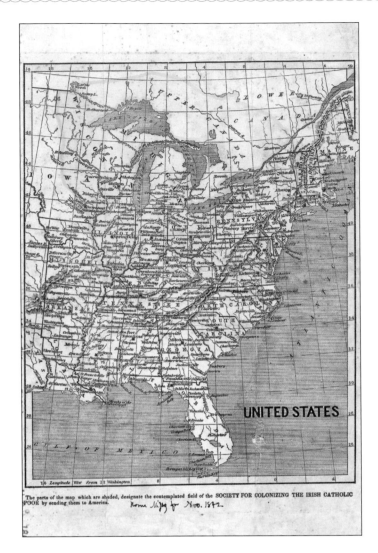

The parts of the map which are shaded, designate the contemplated field of the SOCIETY FOR COLONIZING THE IRISH CATHOLIC POOR by sending them to America.

UNITED STATES

A plan to colonize Irish poor An obscure organization called the "Society for Colonizing the Irish Catholic Poor" put together this plan in 1842. The organizers' goal was to send Ireland's impoverished potato farmers to North America's undeveloped western territory, where the land was fertile but the conditions primitive—although improving. Due to the opening of the Erie Canal, Michigan's population soared from 9,000 in 1820 to 200,000 in 1840. This relocation plan never materialized, but it might have been a good idea. Ireland's Great Famine began in 1845.

Heeney amasses a fortune Irish-born Cornelius Heeney immigrated to New York in 1784 and worked with the Astor family in the fur trading business. John Jacob Astor and Heeney eventually parted ways, but not before Heeney amassed a fortune. Heeney then became one of New York's great philanthropists for Catholic charities. He was also one of the first Catholics to hold public office, serving in New York's state assembly from 1818 to 1822. When he retired in 1837, he used his assets to help create the Brooklyn Benevolent Society, which was dedicated to serving the poor.

Repeal Associations Fed up with Ireland's ties to Great Britain, Daniel O'Connell formed the Irish Repeal Association in 1840. The association sought to nullify the 1801 Act of Union, which had united Britain and Ireland in the formation of the United Kingdom. The group was supported in Ireland as well as America, as illustrated in this poster. The figures represent Ireland (*left*) and America. Surrounded by shamrocks, one holds a shield decorated with stars and stripes while the other leans against an Irish harp. Repeal Associations eventually faded when they lost the support of forces allied with the Young Ireland movement.

Dickens comments on New York's Irish In 1842 Charles Dickens visited America and wrote his "American Notes," which were reprinted in *Brother Jonathan*, a New York news publication. Dickens described the poor conditions of Irish neighborhoods, such as the infamous Five Points in New York City's Hell's Kitchen. He also noted the Irish contribution to the formation of America, declaring: "who else would dig, and delve, and drudge, and do domestic work, and make canals and roads, and execute great lines of Internal Improvement!"

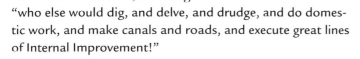

BROTHER JONATHAN.

New-York:

SATURDAY. OCTOBER 1, 1842.

OUR WEEKLY GOSSIP.

We present the reader this week with a greater variety of literary miscellany than in our last; the articles being shorter, and each of its kind excellent. The news department will also be found unusually full, as the past week has not been so barren a one for the newspapers as the one preceding. The pictorial embellishments of the sheet are numerous; and all relative to subjects of interest.

Among the advertisements in this paper will be found the announcement that Mr. Dickens's American Notes, will get the "General Circulation" for which they are intended through the publishing machinery of the Brother Jonathan—a means which will carry them farther than any of the old fashioned bookselling machinery possibly could. The next issue of the Extra Jonathan will contain Bulwer's last novel; the "Last of the Barons," and our arrangements are perfected in relation to it, to give it wings at the earliest possible hour after its reception.

Our next week's pictorial department will include as many engravings as we this week present—and possibly more. Such marked approval upon the part of the public, has attended our adoption of this feature, that we are bound by interest, as well as gratitude, to "keep the ball

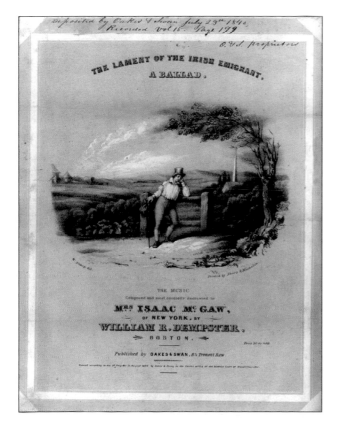

IRISH EMIGRANT'S LAMENT

Yours was the good, brave heart, Mary,
That still kept hoping on,
When the trust in God had left my soul,
And my arm's young strength was gone;
There was comfort ever on your lip,
And the kind look on your brow
I bless you, Mary, for that same,
Though you cannot hear me now.

I thank you for the patient smile
When your heart was fit to break,
When the hunger pain was gnawin' there,
And you hid it for my sake;
I bless you for the pleasant word,
When your heart was sad and sore
Oh! I'm thankful you are gone, Mary,
Where grief can't reach you more!

—EXCERPT FROM "LAMENT OF THE IRISH EMIGRANT"
(1843), BY HELEN SELINA SHERIDAN

An Irishman's lament An Irishman stands by the stile where he first met his beloved wife, now dead from starvation, as he contemplates his departure to America. The song "Lament of the Irish Emigrant" (1843) was written by Helen Selina Sheridan and published in the U.S. The words describe the pain and loneliness of a man who has lost his wife and child and must leave his beloved homeland: *In the land I'm goin' to/They say there's bread and work for all/And the sun shines always there—/But I'll not forget old Ireland,/Were it fifty times as fair!*

They Hated the Irish

When large numbers of Irish Catholics began arriving in the United States in the 1820s and 1830s, they were frequently met with hostility and even violence. This was the result of a number of factors. One was the centuries-old English prejudice against the Irish that had been transplanted to the New World. Englishmen and their American cousins considered the Irish barbaric—a crude, uncouth people incapable of assimilation into civilized society.

Religion was a major issue. The Irish were the first Roman Catholics to enter the United States in large numbers. This did not sit well in an America that was overwhelmingly Protestant—an America that had been originally settled by people militantly opposed to the Church of Rome. Moreover, the Irish Catholics of the 1820s and 1830s entered the United States at the time of the Second Great Awakening, when evangelical fervor with its anti-Catholic bias was at fever pitch. Such organizations as the American Bible Society (1816) and the American Tract Society (1825) preached that Catholicism and democracy were incompatible. It was widely believed that the pope had purposely sent the Irish to America to undermine Protestantism.

Economics also were a factor. In general, the new Irish Catholic immigrants settled in the newly industrialized cities close to the eastern seaboard, where they competed with native-born Americans for work. Competition for jobs only deepened American dislike for the Irish. Such animosity erupted in Boston in 1834, when an angry mob burned down a convent.

In 1849 nativist sentiment coalesced around a secret organization, the Order of the Star Spangled Banner, popularly known as the "Know-Nothings" due to its members' reluctance to admit any knowledge of its existence. Capitalizing on anti-Irish sentiment, the Know-Nothings had a strong political following in the early 1850s. However, the emergence of slavery as the dominant issue of the day and the formation of the Republican Party led to their demise.

"Monster" rallies On the eve of the Great Famine, growing numbers of Irish were demanding self-government for Ireland through the repeal of the Act of Union. Led by brilliant orator Daniel O'Connell, the Repeal Movement featured "monster" rallies, including one on the Hill of Tara that attracted 750,000 people. The movement peaked in Dublin in October 1843. As O'Connell and a half-million supporters prepared to gather for another monster rally, Prime Minister Robert Peel banned the demonstration. To avoid a potential massacre, O'Connell called off the rally. The 68-year-old O'Connell was then arrested. His health suffered while in prison and his Repeal Movement faded. He died just four years later.

The Kensington riots In May 1844, tensions between native Protestants and Irish Catholics led to arson and bloodshed. Debates about religious education in Kensington, a section of Philadelphia, spilled into the streets. Believing that Irish Catholics were attempting to overturn Protestant traditions, nativist mobs attacked Irish homes, a Sisters of Mercy convent, and St. Augustine's Catholic Church (*pictured*). The Irish responded by disrupting nativist meetings. The Kensington riots, which left numerous combatants dead, were part of a wave of anti-Irish Catholic violence that spread across the United States.

Nativist music Following the anti-Catholic riots in the Kensington section of Philadelphia in May 1844, nativists rallied around songs that espoused the "evils" of immigration. This particular tune was composed by James W. Porter, with lyrics written by "a Native." It was dedicated to the anti-immigrant American Republican Party, which had been formed in 1843. The torn flag was also a popular nativist symbol. Anti-Irish activists claimed that American flags had been desecrated by Irish rioters.

Carey rails for Irish freedom Born to a middle-class Dublin family, Mathew Carey began publishing incendiary pamphlets at age 17 and had to leave Ireland to avoid arrest before he was 20. He met Ben Franklin in Paris before settling in Franklin's native Philadelphia in the 1780s. Up through the 1830s, Carey continued writing and publishing, often

defending the cause of Irish freedom. He also commented widely on U.S. business, and he is considered America's first political economist. When he died in 1839, he was deemed one of America's most distinguished Catholic laymen.

The Great Hunger
1845–1860

"[T]he Almighty indeed sent the potato blight, but the English created the Famine."

—AUTHOR JOHN MITCHEL, *THE LAST CONQUEST OF IRELAND* (1861)

In the early 1840s, as Daniel O'Connell was marshalling the Irish masses on behalf of his repeal campaign, about three million of the island's eight million people depended on a single crop—the potato—for their very existence. The potato was well suited to the damp Irish climate and offered a fine source of nutrition. But Ireland's dependence on the potato was not a matter of choice or taste. It was the product of a system in which land was owned by the few and worked by the many.

Landless tenant farmers, laboring in fields that had become the spoils of war in Britain's conquest of Ireland, raised cash crops to pay rent to a landlord or agent. That person, in turn, rented the land from a larger landlord, usually of English or Anglo-Irish descent. The humble potato, which required not a plow but a simple spade to harvest, became the Irish tenant farmer's main food supply.

Though the potatoes were small, the Irish consumed them in astonishing quantities. One scholar of the period, Kevin Whelan, estimated that the island's three million so-called "potato people" ate between 50 and 80 potatoes, per person, each day. The British, Whelan noted, saw Ireland's dependence on the potato as evidence of a character flaw. "There was a prevalent ideological antipathy to the potato as a 'lazy' root grown in 'lazy' beds by

From 1845 to '49, the famine raged in Ireland as the potato blight ruined the primary food supply. A million people, too weak to resist, died from typhus, fever, and starvation. Another million migrated to America, Canada, and England. This painting by John Barker captures the hopelessness of the famine victims.

'lazy' people," he wrote. "The potato itself was an inferior food in a civilizational sense, which pinned the Irish poor to the bottom of the cultural ladder, accentuating the negatives associated with their race ('Celtic') and their religion ('Popery')."

Midsummer often was a tense time along the Irish countryside, for it was then that the old harvest began to run out just before the new harvest was ready. Starvation was no stranger to Ireland, so farmers monitored their crops with care. Their lives depended on the new harvest.

As the potato crop of 1845 neared maturity, a mysterious disease began to spread from field to field, county to county. The potatoes were rotting away, almost overnight, in their beds. *The Freeman's Journal,* an Irish newspaper, reported the case of a farmer who "had been digging potatoes—the finest he had ever seen—from a particular field…up to Monday last; and on digging in the same ridge on Tuesday he found the tubers blasted, and unfit for the use of man or beast."

The potato blight spoiled part of the crop in 1845 and the entire crop in 1846. There was hardly a crop at all in 1847 because an inadequate amount of potatoes had been planted (for fear that the blight would persist). The famine was mostly over by 1849.

A fungus, later called *Phytophthora infestans,* had invaded the soil of Ireland, targeting the sole source of food for three million people. About a third of the potato crop for 1845 was lost. One of the worst catastrophes in 19th century European history had begun.

The potato had failed several times in the quarter-century leading up to the blight of 1845. Thus, the British government and private charities were accustomed to devising relief programs for starving Irish farm families. This time, however, the disease was so aggressive, and the number of people affected was so great, that it quickly became clear that extraordinary measures might be necessary. The British government under Conservative prime minister Robert Peel ordered the purchase of American corn to be held in reserve and then sold in Ireland to avert mass starvation. But even that measure wasn't enough, leading Peel to propose the unthinkable: a repeal of laws that imposed heavy taxes on grain imported into the United Kingdom.

Called the Corn Laws, these measures protected British landlords against competition from foreign food imports. The wealth of the aristocratic, landholding class in Britain was based, to a large extent, on the protection that the Corn Laws offered. Peel's party, dominated by great landowners, regarded the Corn Laws as untouchable. The Corn Law repeal passed in 1846, despite a lack of support from the prime minister's own party, and he resigned soon afterward.

By then, the situation in Ireland was becoming a massive human tragedy. About three-quarters of the potato harvest in 1846 fell victim to the blight. Just before the blight reappeared, a British administrator in charge of relief operations, Charles Trevelyan, began to close up operations, believing the worst was past. Trevelyan wished to make sure that the poor Irish did not become "habitually dependent on government." He wrote: "The great evil with which we have to contend is not the physical evil of the famine, but the moral evil of the selfish, perverse and turbulent character of the people."

The people for whom Trevelyan had such contempt were dying by the thousands. Writer John Mitchel recalled a visit to County Galway, where suffering was great. "I could see, in front of the cottages, little children leaning against a fence...their limbs fleshless, their bodies half-naked, their faces bloated yet wrinkled, and of a pale greenish hue—children who would never, it was too plain, grow up to be men and women."

In County Cork, a young man named Jeremiah O'Donovan Rossa witnessed the slow, terrible death by starvation of his father. Years later, he still remembered how the air in his home near Skibbereen was filled with "a sickly odor of decay, as if the hand of Death had stricken the potato field." Rossa would go on to become one of Britain's fiercest enemies when he immigrated to New York in 1871.

The government changed directions when the new harvest failed in 1846. By the end of the year, a half-million Irish people were employed in public-works projects. Such assistance, while welcome, was not enough to prevent hunger, then starvation, then disease, then death. In Skibbereen and other areas, observers and travelers were shocked to see hollow-eyed men, women, and children in blackened fields, or the corpses of entire families being consumed by rats. Doctors who attempted to treat illnesses associated with starvation—typhus, dysentery, and what was called "famine fever"—noticed a peculiar smell on their patients. Gone was the "sooty and peat-smoke odor of former times," noted one physician. In its place was a "cadaverous suffocating odor" that doctors recognized as "always the forerunner of death."

Mother Ireland crucified, illustrated by Frenchman Leon Adolphe Willette in 1885, was designed to ridicule the British government. At the time of the famine, France provided little real help and accepted few refugees.

As the specter of death visited the fields and lanes of rural Ireland, other food and livestock continued to be exported from the island. If famine suggests the absence of food, then Ireland did not suffer from a famine at all, for only the potato crop failed. Even today, some Irish people in Ireland and elsewhere refer to the catastrophe not as a famine but as the Great Hunger—or *An Gorta Mor* in Irish Gaelic.

Debate over British policy in Ireland during the famine, particularly concerning the export of food from the starving island, remains contentious.

The British government and private charities set up soup kitchens that fed three million people. The "cry for help" was answered by American donations of money and food. Thousands of Irish who were seriously ill sailed for Canada and the U.S., but the so-called "coffin ships" arrived with many dead bodies.

Some scholars believe that British policy makers were simply incapable of interfering with trade—they could not conceive of a role government could play in the normal exchange of goods. But critics, then and since, have charged that authorities refused to break the rules of Victorian economics not because of ideological commitment but simply because the victims were Irish. A fiery poet named Jane Francesca Elgee wrote this angry stanza, which was printed in the nationalist newspaper *The Nation*:

> *Fainting forms, hunger-stricken, what see you in the offing?*
> *Stately ships to bear our food away, amid the stranger's scoffing.*

The potato failed again in 1847, creating such death and suffering that the Irish still remember the year as Black '47. That year, three million Irish people lived off food handed out in British-financed soup kitchens. The cost of relief was growing, so Parliament passed legislation requiring that those costs be passed to Irish landlords, many of whom could not afford such an expense. Families were evicted, often by force, and left to fend for themselves. Trevelyan, preparing to retire, said that Ireland "must be left to the operation of natural causes."

The following year, a 26-year-old man from County Wexford left his home and joined the hordes of Irish people fleeing their doomed homeland to start new lives across the Atlantic Ocean. The young man's name was Patrick Kennedy. He journeyed first, as many Irish did, to Liverpool, where he boarded a ship bound for Boston. During the monthlong trip, he met a young woman name Bridget Murphy. They married after arriving in America, but their new life was far from easy. Though they had fled the horror of starvation, they had not outrun poverty. Patrick Kennedy died in 1858, an exhausted, sick man of 35 years.

He left Bridget to raise their four children, one of whom, Patrick Joseph, would grow up to become a successful tavern owner in Boston. His son, Joseph P. Kennedy, would graduate from Harvard College, make a fortune, and serve in Franklin Roosevelt's administration. And his sons and daughters would create the most famous American family of the 20th century.

Patrick Kennedy and Bridget Murphy made it to America. Hundreds of thousands did not. The Irish population of eight million in 1840 was reduced to a little more than six million by 1850. About a million people died of starvation or disease. Another million, perhaps more, left. Many went to America (nearly 900,000 landed in New York during the famine years of 1847 to 1851), but some went to Britain and others journeyed to Canada.

Those who immigrated to the United States surely were the most wretched newcomers to arrive in America without the chains of slavery. They were poor, hungry, and unprepared for life in the cities of North America. And Americans were appalled. Boston tried to staunch the flow of Irish by imposing a tax on immigrants, but still they came—as many as 30,000 in 1847 (the city's population at the time was about 120,000). By 1860 New York was home to 200,000 Irish immigrants, one-quarter of the city's total population.

The anti-immigrant movement, already active in the port cities of the Northeast, grew in power and influence. In 1854 the "Know-Nothing" party became one of the nation's most successful third parties, capturing control of the Massachusetts legislature and the governor's office. In Philadelphia, which had witnessed anti-Catholic and anti-immigrant violence before the famine exiles arrived at its port, the new immigrants were "of the lower order of mankind," as one historian complained.

The anti-Irish, anti-immigrant forces contended that the poor Irish could never be assimilated into the American mainstream. Some of this was religious bias, as Protestant Americans believed that Catholics were loyal to the pope, not the president. Many Protestants also bemoaned that the Irish were abysmally poor and uneducated.

However, as America stumbled toward a civil war, the Irish found a way to convince their critics that they, too, could fight and die for the Stars and Stripes.

By the time the famine ended, hundreds of thousands of Irish had resettled in America. One-third went to large cities, especially New York, Philadelphia, Boston, and New Orleans. The others went to smaller cities that needed manual labor. Relatively few became farmers.

1845: In the past decade, the production of Irish whiskey has been cut in half, due in large part to the efforts of Father Theobald Mathew and his Cork Total Abstinence Society. • Frederick Douglass, American abolitionist and former slave, travels to Ireland and delivers a series of lectures throughout the country. He meets with Daniel O'Connell, who will draw parallels between American abolitionism and his own efforts to repeal the 1801 Act of Union.

March 4, 1845: James K. Polk, a Democrat of Scots-Irish descent, takes office as the 11th president of the United States.

June 8, 1845: Andrew Jackson, the nation's seventh president and the first of Irish ancestry, dies at age 78.

August 20, 1845: The emergence of the potato blight in Ireland is first noted at the National Botanic Gardens in Glasnevin.

October 4, 1845: *The New York Tribune* is the first American newspaper to publish news of the potato blight in Ireland.

November 1845: In an effort to relieve the suffering in Ireland, British prime minister Robert Peel buys American corn for redistribution to Irish peasants.

1846: Sam Houston, an Irish American hero of the War of 1812 and the Mexican-American War, is elected to serve Texas in the U.S. Senate, shortly after Texas becomes a state. He will remain in the Senate until 1859 before becoming governor of Texas. • With the onset of the Mexican-American War, a group of Catholic European immigrants, predominately Irish, deserts the U.S. Army to fight for Mexico. Regarded as heroes by Mexicans and traitors by Americans, the San Patricio Battalion will grow to some 200 strong.

O'Sullivan preaches "Manifest Destiny" By the 1830s, many Americans had come to believe that the United States was destined to expand westward and occupy the North American continent from sea to sea. That other peoples—Native Americans, Mexicans, and the British—might have legitimate claims on western lands was irrelevant. This expansionist belief was given the name "Manifest Destiny" by John L. O'Sullivan, an American journalist whose forebears came from Ireland. Writing in 1845, O'Sullivan stated that it was the United States' "Manifest destiny to overspread the continent allotted by Providence for the free development of our yearly multiplying millions." "Manifest Destiny" is personified in this painting by John Gast.

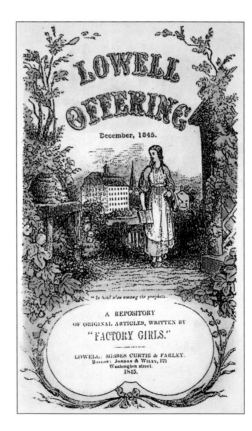

Lowell's "factory girls" The *Lowell Offering*, first published in 1840, was written by the "factory girls" of the mills in Lowell, Massachusetts. The mills were set up on a utopian model in an effort to avoid the terrible conditions of factory workers in England. Factory women (ages 15 to 35) were originally American and English, but after cotton production revived in the 1840s, Lowell's mill owners decided to employ Irish immigrants. Thousands of Irish women profited from the mills' enlightened health and education policies.

Fighting Fires

The son of dirt-poor Irish immigrants, Matthew T. Brennan joined a volunteer fire department in New York City in the early 1840s. Soon he was elected company foreman. After winning election to a plum city position, Brennan became the first known Irish Catholic to run for a statewide political office. His career illustrates the prominent role that firehouses played in the lives of Irish Americans in the mid-1800s.

The Irish were not prominent when America's first fire companies were organized in Boston and Philadelphia during the early 18th century. Even a century later, when a massive fire struck Lower Manhattan in December 1835, only about one in 10 New York firefighters were Irish.

But as the famine Irish settled in America's cities, they came to dominate urban fire companies. Firehouses were local places of refuge where immigrant Irishmen could prove themselves. Meanwhile, these colorful, brawny men fascinated the public.

The American Fireman (Currier & Ives)

Future Tammany Hall boss William Tweed was 16 years old when he became a volunteer firefighter in the late 1830s, kicking off a long career of working side by side with the Irish. By 1855 more than 25 percent of New York's firefighters were Irish-born. Twice that number claimed Irish ancestry.

As fire companies became more Irish, however, elite reformers began to target them. In the 1840s and 1850s, firefighters in Pittsburgh, Nashville, and Philadelphia were cited for violence, lewd behavior, and other transgressions.

After the Civil War, firefighting became paid work. The job remained dangerous but also offered a stable salary and a path out of poverty. These benefits were not lost on the children of immigrants, transforming firefighting into a father-son career for the Irish.

In 1889 Irish immigrant Hugh Bonner was appointed chief of New York's fire department. The Irish were on their way to ruling the firehouse—from top to bottom.

Firefighters duke it out The building is burning and the firefighters are fighting each other, not the blaze. The chaotic scene portrayed in this illustration was not uncommon in pre-Civil War cities, where volunteer fire companies—comprised heavily of Irish immigrants—competed to extinguish fires. The competition sometimes reached the point of fisticuffs—or worse. Nevertheless, young Irishmen believed that membership in a fire company was a path to greater social acceptance and respectability. For some, it would be a stepladder to a political career.

Spring 1846: Irish workers risk their lives blasting a rail bed through a rocky section of Vermont's Green Mountains near the town of Bolton. When they learn that their contractor, a man named Barker, has run out of money to pay them, workers go after him. Barker fears for his life until authorities and a priest arrive to prevent bloodshed.

April 1846: The Donner Party, consisting of families of Irish, German, and English descent, leave the Midwest bound for California. Foul weather and a tactical mistake will leave them stranded and starving for several months in the High Sierra, where they will resort to cannibalism.

June 1846: After its initial appearance in 1845, the potato blight returns to Ireland. It spreads like wildfire, claiming 90 percent of the year's crop.

June 30, 1846: Lord John Russell succeeds Sir Robert Peel as prime minister of Britain. His hands-off approach to famine relief will be in marked contrast to that of his predecessor, proving disastrous for the starving Irish.

July 1846: Daniel O'Connell's Repeal Movement splits with Young Ireland. O'Connell's followers are upset that the Young Irelanders refuse to repudiate violence as a means to an end.

Fall 1846: Averse to free food distribution, the Russell government enacts a public works policy in Ireland. Starving people are forced to labor up to 70 hours a week at wages that do not keep pace with the rising costs of food.

December 29, 1846: A consortium of Irish gentry and members of the upper class establish the General Central Relief Committee in Dublin. Over the next year, they will donate more than 60,000 pounds sterling to famine relief.

Irish peasants thrive thanks to potatoes Irish peasant women dig for potatoes. No one could have predicted the terrible scourge that befell Ireland in the mid-19th century. The population was at its highest despite several famines earlier in the century. With Britain's war with France over, peace reigned. Because the price of grain was rising, farmers broke up most grassland for tillage. Peasant families thrived after adopting a diet of potatoes, which could be produced in abundance on small plots of land. The potato is a very healthful balanced food, especially when supplemented by milk.

There was an Old Man with an Owl,
Who continued to bother and howl;
He sat on a rail, and imbibed bitter ale,
Which refreshed that Old Man and his Owl.

Irish limericks The five-line verses made popular by Edward Lear in the mid-19th century owe the origin of their name to the city of Limerick in the southwest of Ireland. A limerick is a humorous, mischievous, satirical, or obscene poem that follows a strict form and that absolutely requires rhyme. The opening line generally refers to a person or place. Pictured is a page from Lear's *Book of Nonsense* (1846), featuring one of his limericks.

> **"On July 27th I passed from Cork to Dublin, and the doomed plant bloomed in all the luxuriance of an abundant harvest. Returning on August 3rd, I beheld with sorrow mere wastes of putrefying vegetation."**
>
> —FATHER MATTHEW, 1846

Blight destroys Ireland's crops Late July 1845 was wet in Ireland, and there were no apparent signs that the potato crop would be poor. By August, however, news of potatoes rotting in the ground started to filter out of southeast England. By September, the potato blight had reached Waterford and Wexford, and it quickly spread to the rest of Ireland. Though potato blight (the effects of which are pictured) had been recorded in the United States, this was the first time it had appeared in Europe. Scientists failed to recognize the blight as a fungus and not a disease of the plant itself, and therefore none of the remedies suggested were successful.

THE POTATO DISEASE.—Accounts received from different parts of Ireland show that the disease in the potato crop is extending far and wide, and causing great alarm amongst the peasantry. Letters from resident landlords feelingly describe the misery and consternation of the poor people around them, and earnestly urge the imperative necessity of speedy intervention on the part of the Government to ascertain the actual extent of the calamity, and provide wholesome food as a substitute for the deficient supply of potatoes. Mr. John Chester, of Kilscorne House, in Magshole, in the county of Louth, in a letter to the *Dublin Evening Post*, states that he has a field of twenty acres of potatoes, which, up to the 3rd instant, had been perfectly dry and sound, when they were attacked by the blight, and three-fourths of them are so diseased and rotten that pigs decline to eat them. This, he says, is the case all through the county of Louth. The *Belfast News Letter* has a still more lamentable account. It says, "We have abstained from occupying our space with the accounts of the prevalence of this calamity in various places, for this reason, that it may be here stated, once for all, that there is hardly a district in Ireland in which the potato crops at present are uninfected—perhaps we might say, *hardly a field*."

News of the blight By October 1845, news of the mysterious Irish potato blight had filtered back to England, as evidenced by this small story in the *Illustrated London News*, dated October 18, 1845. Some thought the new locomotive trains caused it. Others blamed "mortiferous vapors." Some Catholics saw it as divine punishment for the "sins of the people," while others saw it as God's judgment against abusive landlords. The cause was actually an airborne fungus (*Phytophthora infestans*) transported in the holds of ships traveling from North America to England. Winds carried the fungus to the Irish countryside. Under ideal moist conditions, a single infected potato plant could infect thousands more in just a few days.

Irish scrounge for alternative food Without potatoes, Irish peasants quickly became desperate for food. Those lucky enough to live by the sea collected limpets, seaweed, and mussels to feed their families. Families sacrificed livestock and even domestic animals, such as dogs, for food. Others had to resort to eating berries and grass, creating a range of diseases through malnutrition on an unprecedented scale. In the second and third year of the Great Hunger, even fishing was unavailable, as many boats had been used for firewood in the harsh winters of 1845 and 1846. By 1847 (Black '47), there was nothing to eat and nothing left to burn.

"RINT" *v.* POTATOES.—THE IRISH JEREMY DIDDLER.

" You haven't got such a thing as Twelve-pence about you ?—A Farthing a week—a Penny a month—a Shilling a year ? "

O'Connell sullied in *Punch* This cartoon depicts Daniel O'Connell as a cruel landlord who continued to collect rent from his starving tenants to fund his political ambitions. The cartoon, printed in the British periodical *Punch* in November 1845 (at the beginning of the Great Famine), was an effort to sully O'Connell's reputation by making him out to be no better than the British he so passionately opposed. Propaganda against O'Connell and others fighting for Irish freedom was common in 19th century English newspapers.

Repeal of the Corn Laws The protectionist Corn Laws, enacted in Britain in 1815, imposed heavy tariffs on all imported grain—which benefited British landowners. The Corn Laws, however, proved to be a roadblock to Prime Minister Robert Peel, who strove to import grain for Ireland during the Great Famine. Grain that would have been cheap in a free market was prohibitively expensive because of the Corn Law tariffs. Peel proposed to repeal the Corn Laws for the sake of the starving Irish. However, English gentry and politicians reacted with outrage at the prospect of losing their protective tariffs. The political furor over Peel's decision soon overshadowed any concern for the threat of famine in Ireland.

Peel oversees famine relief Robert Peel, the British prime minister, took prompt relief measures to alleviate the consequences of the failed potato crop of 1845. To prevent a rise in food prices, he imported £100,000 worth of Indian corn from the United States. He also set up a relief committee to help those in distress. Relief works (mainly road building) were established to provide employment so that people could buy the cheap imported cornmeal. However, he did not want to stop exports of food from Ireland because such sales were lucrative for the British. Instead, he proposed repealing the Corn Laws, a move that led to his ouster in 1846.

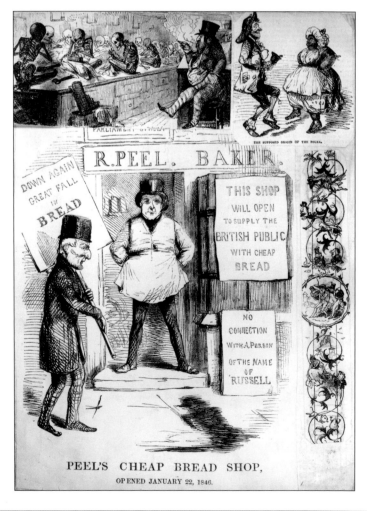

PEEL'S CHEAP BREAD SHOP,
OPENED JANUARY 22, 1846.

Russell's policy: let it be In 1846 Robert Peel was replaced by Lord John Russell, a believer in the principle of "laissez-faire" (let it be). Regarding the Irish famine, he advocated a hands-off policy, believing that problems should be solved on their own through natural means. The aim was to prevent the Irish from becoming "habitually dependent," and to make "Irish property support Irish poverty." Russell felt that Peel's policy of providing cheap Indian cornmeal to the Irish had been a mistake because it undercut market prices and discouraged private enterprises from importing food. Under Russell in 1846, the British government would do nothing to help the starving masses.

McClatchy builds newspaper empire
James McClatchy was just one of many Irish immigrants who took to newspaper work in the mid-19th century, but his legacy is certainly one of the most enduring. McClatchy worked as a journalist for the *New York Tribune* after arriving in the Big Apple in 1840. He moved to California during the Gold Rush, found none of the precious metal, and returned to journalism. He edited *The Daily Bee,* a Sacramento-based paper that would become the foundation for a respected newspaper company that bore the McClatchy name. To this day, The McClatchy Company operates more than 30 newspapers nationwide.

America expands thanks to Polk

Andrew Jackson lived to see fellow Scots-Irishman James Knox Polk take the oath of office as president in March 1845. Polk was an aggressive leader in the Jackson mold. He secured America's Northwest in a treaty with Britain after first threatening war, and he led the country to victory in the Mexican-American War. That conflict concluded with a vastly expanded contiguous United States that closely matches today's map of the continental states. Presidential historians highly rate the one-term Polk for his record of successfully finishing what he set out to accomplish.

1847: Ireland suffers through the worst year of the potato famine; hundreds of thousands of people lose their lives. • As desperate Irish citizens attempt to escape their devastated homeland, they travel aboard overcrowded, disease-ridden ships. So many will die in the attempt that these emigrant vessels will come to be known as "coffin ships." This year alone, one in five emigrants will die en route to America. • Just 16 years after their own displacement on the Trail of Tears, Choctaw Indians organize a gift of $170 for the famine-stricken Irish. • County Wexford-born surveyor Jasper O'Farrell surveys Yerba Buena, California, which will be renamed San Francisco. He is credited with designing Market Street, the city's prominent thoroughfare. • The substantial Irish immigrant population in Buffalo, New York, gets a community leader when Pope Pius IX appoints Irish American John Timon as the first bishop of Buffalo.

January 1847: Pope Pius IX donates 1,000 Roman crowns to Irish famine relief.

January 1, 1847: British benefactor Lionel de Rothschild founds the British Association for the Relief of Distress in Ireland and the Highlands of Scotland, with Ireland receiving the lion's share of the association's funds.

January–February 1847: The Shin Hollow War, a series of skirmishes between immigrant laborers—including the Irish "Corkonians" and "Far Downers"—delays construction of the Erie Railroad.

Early 1847: The British government abandons its public works programs and sets up soup kitchens throughout Ireland. By midsummer, huge numbers of Irish will be sustained on government-provided soup.

BRIG-GEN. JAMES SHIELDS.

War hero and three-state senator By 1843 Irish immigrant James Shields had fought in the Black Hawk War, studied law, won election to the Illinois state legislature, and served on the state supreme court. Commissioned as an officer at the outbreak of the Mexican-American War, he rose to the rank of brigadier general for his heroics at the Battle of Cerro Gordo. He later saw action at Churubusco and Chapultepec. Shields went on to become the only person ever to be elected U.S. senator from three different states: Illinois, Minnesota, and Missouri.

Kearny a hero in war against Mexico A descendant of Irish immigrants, Stephen Kearny helped conquer both New Mexico and California. When the Mexican-American War broke out in 1846, Kearny was made commander of the Army of the West. With a force of 1,700 men, he marched into New Mexico and, after a few brief encounters, occupied Santa Fe. (Here, he proclaims U.S. possession of New Mexico in 1846.) Then, with a cavalry force of 300 men, he moved on to California. Kearny's and Robert Stockton's forces took San Diego. After Los Angeles fell to Kearny in January 1847, Mexico surrendered California to the United States.

The San Patricios

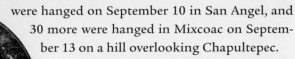

The year 1847 was the worst of Ireland's Great Famine. It also marked the largest execution of army deserters in U.S. history. These turncoats were mostly Irish or Irish American soldiers in the Mexican army's San Patricio Battalion, led by Captain John Riley from Galway. After the outbreak of the 1846–48 Mexican-American War, Riley had gathered hundreds of San Patricios around a flag depicting St. Patrick, a harp, and a shamrock.

Desertion from the U.S. Army to the Mexican army was spurred by virulent anti-Catholicism in the U.S. officer corps. There was also a more earthly reason: The Mexican government offered 320 acres to any man who switched sides.

The San Patricios fought bravely, including at the Battle of Churubusco, where 85 were captured by the Americans. U.S. general Winfield Scott ordered them court-martialed for treason and desertion. Fifty were convicted. Twenty

San Patricio medallion

were hanged on September 10 in San Angel, and 30 more were hanged in Mixcoac on September 13 on a hill overlooking Chapultepec.

America quickly forgot these anonymous men, but Mexico did not. In 1959 the Mexican government unveiled a memorial to the San Patricios in the Plaza de San Jacinto in San Angel.

The San Patricios made headlines in 1999 when a movie depicting their exploits, *One Man's Hero,* vanished from screens days after its release. Despite the presence of actors Tom Berenger and Patrick Bergin, the appearance of Prince Albert of Monaco in his first screen role, and favorable reviews in the *Los Angeles Times* and elsewhere, the movie was a dead reel walking. Some claimed that the film was pulled because the distribution company saw it as "anti-American." The movie's director said that the film did not "bomb," as MGM claimed, but was instead torpedoed.

Execution of the San Patricios The end for the San Patricios was a cruel one. After the mass hangings on September 10, 1847, the remaining 30 condemned men were put through a particularly torturous ordeal. On September 13, they were put on carts below scaffolds, with nooses placed around their necks, and forced to watch as American forces stormed the Mexican citadel of Chapultepec. When the American flag signifying an American victory went up over the citadel at the end of the battle, the carts were ordered away and the San Patricios met their deaths.

1845-60

March 1847: The USS *Jamestown* sets sail from Boston to County Cork, Ireland. Its hold is packed with supplies earmarked for famine relief. • One in three Irish peasants are currently employed in pointless, make-work public works projects at the pleasure of a British government that thinks it is more important to instill a work ethic than save people from starvation.

April 1847: The brig *Exmouth* is shipwrecked in a storm en route from Londonderry, Ireland, to Quebec. Of some 240 emigrants and crew members, only three will survive.

May 15, 1847: Daniel O'Connell, Ireland's "Liberator" and champion of Catholic emancipation, dies at age 71 in Genoa, Italy.

June 8, 1847: British Parliament enacts the Poor Law Extension Act, which shifts the fiscal responsibility for famine relief to Irish landowners. Further, the law's Gregory Clause holds that landowners with more than a quarter-acre of land are denied aid. Many landowners choose to evict their tenant farmers rather than support them.

Mid-1847: Ships teeming with typhus, dysentery, and cholera-sickened patients arrive at the quarantine station at Grosse Ile, Quebec, from famine-torn Ireland. By the time the autumn ice puts an end to the epidemic, some 3,000 will be dead.

July 1847: The USS *Macedonian,* the second of the American ships sent by the U.S. Congress to deliver supplies to the famine victims in Ireland, arrives in County Cork.

September 1847: Revisiting its concerns about handouts and the high cost of famine relief, the British government declares an end to the potato famine and closes the soup kitchens.

Ireland exports tons of food The British government was fervent about the principles of free market trade. The people of Ireland were starving, yet the country continued to export grain, butter, and cattle. In fact, Ireland was a net exporter of food throughout the five years of the Great Famine. Some sectors actually increased their exports. Free market relief plans depended on private merchants selling food to peasants. These peasants were earning wages through public works, which were financed mainly by the Irish themselves through local taxes. However, tax revenues were insufficient. Wages were too low. Paydays were irregular, and those who did get work could not afford to both pay their rent and buy food.

THE DYING WALK TO THEIR GRAVES

This miserable shed had served as a grave where the dying could bury themselves. It was seven feet in length and six in width, and was already walled around on the outside with an embankment of graves, half way to the eaves. The aperture of this horrible den of death would scarcely admit of the entrance of a common-sized person. And into this noisome sepulchre living men, women, and children went down to die—to pillow upon the rotten straw—the grave clothes vacated by preceding victims around them. Here they lay as closely to each other as if crowded, side by side, on the bottom of one grave. Six persons had been found in this fetid sepulchre at one time, and with only one able to crawl to the door to ask for water. Removing a board from the entrance of this black hole of pestilence, we found it crammed with wan victims of famine, ready and anxious to perish. A quiet, listless despair broods over the population, and death reaps a full harvest.

—ELIHU BURRITT, DESCRIBING A HUT IN THE FAMINE-RAVAGED VILLAGE OF SKIBBEREEN, FEBRUARY 20, 1847

Burritt Reports on Skibbereen

Through the writings of New England pacifist Elihu Burritt, the sufferings in the West Cork market town of Skibbereen came to represent the devastation of the Irish famine to the American public.

Burritt's background was unusual. Born into a working-class family in New Britain, Connecticut, and apprenticed as a blacksmith at an early age, he soon exhibited exceptional intellectual abilities, particularly in the study of languages. He spent every spare moment reading, and by age 30 he reportedly could speak seven languages fluently and could read more than 40 others. In Worcester, Massachusetts, he worked as a blacksmith while editing a weekly journal, *The Christian Citizen,* which advocated temperance, pacifism, and an end to slavery. Admirers called him the "Learned Blacksmith."

In the winter of 1846–47, the worst year of the Famine, Burritt visited Ireland to learn of conditions. In letters and pamphlets, he reported to America on the situation he found in Skibbereen. In one letter, he wrote of seeing "pale, emaciated children" who looked "as if they had been just thawed out of the ice in which they had been embedded until their blood had been turned to water."

Funeral of a famine victim in Skibbereen

In another letter, Burritt wrote: "We saw in every tenement we entered enough to sicken the stoutest heart... half-naked women and children would come out of their cabins, apparently in the last stages of famine fever, to beg 'a ha'penny, for the honour of God!' As they stood upon the wet ground, one could almost see it smoke beneath their bare feet, burning with the fever."

Possibly the most telling description of starvation he rendered was of a 12-year-old boy "whose body had swollen to three times its normal size and actually burst the garment he wore." Scenes like those, detailed by Burritt and others, touched American hearts and led to an outpouring of relief efforts.

Peasants succumb to famine, fever An Irish peasant family contemplates its fate. Nicholas Cummins, a Cork magistrate, visited hovels in Skibbereen. He wrote: "In the first, six famished and ghastly skeletons, to all appearances dead, were huddled in a corner on some filthy straw. . . . I approached with horror, and found by a low moaning they were alive—they were in fever, four children, a woman and what had once been a man. . . . In a few minutes I was surrounded by at least 200 such phantoms, such frightful spectres as no words can describe, [all suffering] either from famine or from fever."

September 13, 1847: On the heels of their defeat at Churubusco, 30 of the surviving captured members of the San Patricio Battalion are brought to a spot with a view of the Battle of Chapultepec. They are fitted with nooses around their necks. Per the directive of U.S. general Winfield Scott, they are executed at the moment the American flag is raised over the battlefield.

Fall 1847: The blight claims 30 percent of Ireland's potato crop for the year. While seemingly an improvement over the previous year, the reality is that the government's forced public works policy left few farmers to plant potatoes, so the crop was inadequate to begin with.

November 2, 1847: Denis Mahon, a major landowner in County Roscommon, is murdered as he returns home after a meeting. While the real reasons behind his death have never come to light, he had recently evicted some 3,000 tenants from his property, offering them an unpleasant choice of homelessness or passage to North America on board a coffin ship.

January 24, 1848: Gold is discovered at Sutter's Mill on California's American River. Irish Americans and Irish immigrants will be among the hundreds of thousands who will head west in hopes of striking it rich.

April 24, 1848: The barque *Jeanie Johnston*, carrying emigrants fleeing the famine, makes its first crossing from County Kerry to Quebec. Over the next decade, it will cross the Atlantic 16 times, carrying some 2,500 migrants to a new life in North America. Unlike most migrant ships of the age, it never loses a passenger to accident or disease.

July 29, 1848: The Young Ireland Rebellion culminates ignobly with a hostage standoff at a widow's cottage in County Tipperary.

Soup kitchens After the public works experiment failed, the British fed the starving Irish for free at soup kitchens. The Soup Kitchen Act of 1847 called for the food to be provided through taxes collected by local relief committees. Demand quickly exceeded supply. In Killarney, only one soup kitchen was available for 10,000 people. Many people refused to eat the soup after one serving, complaining of severe bowel problems. At some soup kitchens, the shame of standing in line with a begging bowl was compounded by demands that the peasants convert to Protestantism before being served.

The Quakers offer support The Quakers were the only Protestant religious group to unconditionally aid the starving masses during the Great Famine in Ireland. The Quakers established charitable works—such as soup kitchens, clothing stores, and schools—all over the country and in city centers. Some Irish Quaker volunteers contracted typhus and dysentery from those they were trying to help. Later in the 19th century, Quakers successfully campaigned for measures to improve health through better hygiene, improved housing, and proper sewerage for Dublin.

> "I attended myself a poor woman, whose infant, dead two days, lay at the foot of the bed, and four others nearly dead in the same bed; and, horrible to relate, a famished cat got up on the corpse of the poor infant and was about to gnaw it, but for my interference. I could tell you such tales of woe without end."
>
> —JOHN O'SULLIVAN, ARCHDEACON IN KENMARE, IRELAND, 1847

Mass evictions Ireland was going bankrupt. Many landlords were heavily in debt. Rents had not been collected and taxes were due. In 1847 the Irish Poor Law Extension Act shifted the cost of famine relief to Ireland's property owners. The new Poor Law required landlords to raise an estimated £10 million in tax revenue—an impossible task. To save their ruined estates, the landlords evicted the paupers. An estimated half-million people were evicted from their homes and set on the road.

The fate of the evicted Landlords used two methods to evict tenants. The first involved suing the male head of a family for being in arrears. The man would be sentenced to prison, and his family would be made homeless. The second method was to send families overseas in poorly built, overcrowded vessels that became known as "coffin ships." In this picture, an evicted family's starving neighbors dig for whatever they can find as the family is led away.

Food riots Starving residents of Galway attack a government potato store. Throughout the famine, the Irish watched with increasing anger as boatloads of homegrown food crammed the docks for export. Food riots erupted in such ports as Youghal, where peasants tried to confiscate a boatload of oats. At Dungarvan, British troops were hit with stones. The troops responded by firing into the crowd, killing two peasants and wounding several others. British soldiers escorted riverboats transporting food while starving peasants watched on shore. As the famine worsened, the British sent in more troops.

Fall 1848: The potato blight has destroyed half of Ireland's potato crop this season.

December 2, 1848: The crew aboard the steamer *Londonderry* forces 174 Irish emigrants below deck for the passage from Sligo to Liverpool. After two days at sea, the steamer comes into port at Londonderry carrying 72 dead passengers. An inquest will determine that they died of suffocation, and the ship's captain and crew will be found criminally liable.

1849: In the past three years, the number of liquor licenses in Boston has increased by nearly 50 percent.
• The Irish Emigrant Society of New York publishes *Address to the People of Ireland,* a broadside directed to would-be immigrants warning them against harboring unrealistic expectations about life in America. • An anti-immigration secret society calling itself the Order of the Star Spangled Banner emerges in New York City. The group will adopt its official name, the American Party, in 1850, but will be best known by the moniker given it by *New York Tribune* editor Horace Greeley: the "Know-Nothing" party.

July 1849: Queen Victoria makes her first official state visit to Ireland. Reasons behind the visit are cited variously as either an attempt to prove that the famine is over and thus that British aid is no longer needed, or to report on the state of the Irish so as to offer more aid.

October 1849: Some 100 emigrants die when their brig, *St. John,* founders in foul weather on the rocks off Cohasset, Massachusetts. Horrified spectators watch helplessly.

1850s: Free blacks begin to take on the role of strikebreakers in Irish-dominated labor markets, such as New York City's longshoremen, leading to hostility between the two ethnic groups.

Destitute Irish pour into Liverpool Passage to Liverpool (*pictured*) was cheap, and three out of four Irish sailing for America departed from that English city. Before the famine, Liverpool had a population of 250,000, but during the famine huge numbers of destitute Irish flooded into the city. Conditions were abysmal, and typhus and dysentery epidemics broke out. Liverpool was on the brink of ruin as authorities tried to feed those who had arrived penniless on its docks. Authorities eventually decided to deport Irish back to Ireland, returning some 15,000 to their homeland.

DISEASE AND DEATH ON THE HIGH SEAS

Before the emigrant has been a week at sea he is an altered man. How can it be otherwise? Hundreds of people, men, women, and children of all ages, from the drivelling idiot of ninety to the babe just born, huddled together without light, without air, wallowing in filth and breathing a fetid atmosphere, sick in body, dispirited in heart, the fever patients lying between the sound, in sleeping places so narrow as almost to deny them the power of indulging, by a change of position, the natural restlessness of the disease; by their ravings disturbing those around, and predisposing them, through the effects of the imagination, to imbibe the contagion; living without food or medicine, except as administered by the hand of casual charity, dying without the voice of spiritual consolation, and buried in the deep without the rites of the Church.

—IRISH LANDLORD STEPHEN E. DEVERE, WHO TRAVELED ON A SHIP TO AMERICA TO SEE THE ONBOARD CONDITIONS FIRSTHAND, 1847

Ships of Hope—and Death

One of the worst aspects of the Great Famine was the tragic story of the "coffin" ships. Thousands of Irish men, women, and children, having scraped together just enough money to escape starvation at home, sought salvation by booking passage on ships bound for America. For too many, the passage was not to salvation but to a watery grave.

In 1847, the worst year of the famine, an estimated 150,000 Irish embarked for the United States, and of that number about ten percent died either at sea or shortly after disembarkation. The British did nothing to set standards of cleanliness or limit the numbers each ship should carry. At the same time, of the 100,000 who took the less expensive route to Canada, about 30 percent perished.

What caused this tragedy? One factor was the condition of the emigrants themselves. Malnourished after months of starvation, many of them suffered from dysentery and typhus and brought these diseases aboard ship. Others in this weakened condition were susceptible to disease.

Then there were the ships. Too many of them were old sailing ships meant for the transfer of lumber from North America to Britain. For the return trip, unscrupulous owners converted them into passenger ships. Conditions were primitive. Captains crammed immigrants into holds too low to stand in. Beds were often hastily tiered planks, and privies were little more than slop buckets. Frequently, not enough food and water had been stocked for a trip that could take anywhere from a few weeks to a few months.

In these conditions, the presence of typhus—"ship fever"—quickly afflicted passengers and crew alike. The plight of the *Virginius* in 1847 was representative of many of the coffin ships. It left Liverpool with 476 Irish passengers. During the voyage, 158 people died, including the master, mate, steward, and nine sailors.

Irish blamed for the famine This cartoon depicts Ireland as Cinderella snubbed by her haughty sisters, Britannia and Caledonia. Despite an international outcry for the British to help the starving in Ireland, many religious-minded social reformers in England viewed the blight as a heaven-sent "blessing" that would finally provide an opportunity to transform Ireland's cycle of poverty. Many thought that the famine was entirely Ireland's fault. It was brought on, they claimed, by the mismanagement of its landlords, the stupidity of its peasants (who had insisted on a diet of potatoes), and by the laziness of all the Irish.

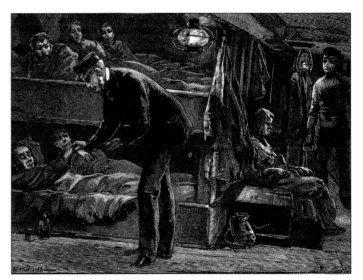

Horrors on the high seas The British ships that crossed the Atlantic were often crammed to twice their capacity. Many passengers were infected with typhus before they boarded, and disease spread quickly in the cramped, unventilated quarters below deck. Passengers were expected to bring their own food for the journey, but many Irish boarded with nothing to eat. Lack of clean drinking water compounded the horror of the trip across the ocean. Thousands died during the voyages and were dumped overboard.

1845-60

1850s: Under the watchful eyes of Dublin archbishop Paul Cullen and his New York counterpart, John Hughes, a so-called "devotional revolution" begins among the Irish on both sides of the Atlantic. The lax Catholicism that existed at the beginning of the famine years eventually will be replaced by a Catholicism firmly entrenched in Irish identity.
• This decade will see the emergence of Irish street gangs in the tough New York ghetto of Five Points, with such names as the Dead Rabbits, the Kerryonians, and the notoriously violent Plug Uglies. • The "American Wake" becomes commonplace in Ireland during this decade of heavy emigration. Held for a young emigrant the night before he or she leaves for America, it is a sorrowful event, as family and friends do not expect to ever see their loved one again.

1850: Stephen Foster, an Irish American composer and the "Father of American Music," pens "De Camptown Races," one of his most popular songs. Foster also is successful with "Oh! Susanna" and "Old Folks at Home." • Irish-born journalist Thomas D'Arcy McGee founds the newspaper *American Celt* in Boston.
• Irish comprise one-quarter of the population of the cities of New York, Philadelphia, Boston, and Baltimore.
• The rash of Irish peasant evictions, exacerbated by British policies such as the Poor Law Extension Act, peaks this year, as nearly 20,000 tenant farmers are forced from their homes.
• Members of the Irish Emigrant Society establish the Emigrant Industrial Savings Bank of New York. Through its customers, the bank will become a major departure point for monies sent overseas to Irish families in need.

1851: Ireland's census, accounting for emigration, suggests that at least a million people have died during the famine.

Success of the *Jeanie Johnston*
In contrast to the typical "coffin ships" that carried Irish famine refugees to the new world, the *Jeanie Johnston* was a remarkable success story. Despite making 16 voyages to North America during the famine years—carrying some 2,500 passengers on a transatlantic voyage of nearly 50 days—no one ever died on the ship. The vessel's good fortune is universally credited to its humane captain, James Attridge, who never overloaded the ship and ensured that a doctor was always on board. Pictured is a replica of the *Jeanie Johnston,* which was completed in Quebec in 2002 in recognition of the 150th anniversary of the Famine.

Quarantine islands This painting by Ray Butler depicts a quarantine station on Partridge Island, a medical inspection stop for those hoping to land at Saint John, New Brunswick. Quarantine islands were established in the United States and Canada in an attempt to stem the flow of disease that was carried across the Atlantic by the ships that transported Irish immigrants. At these medical stations, conditions were hellish and epidemics were rife. Immigrants were not allowed to leave until they had been given a clean bill of health. Many died before being allowed to enter the United States and Canada.

Disease on Staten Island The Marine Hospital Quarantine on Staten Island was established in 1799 to isolate anyone entering New York Harbor who showed signs of contagious disease. By the mid-19th century, Irish immigrants were arriving in unprecedented numbers, stretching the Quarantine's resources beyond capacity. Many ships arrived with cases of smallpox, yellow fever, cholera, and typhus. All on board were quarantined, even if only one case was detected, and they could be held for weeks or even months. In 1858, after yet another outbreak of yellow fever, the local population had enough and burned the entire complex down.

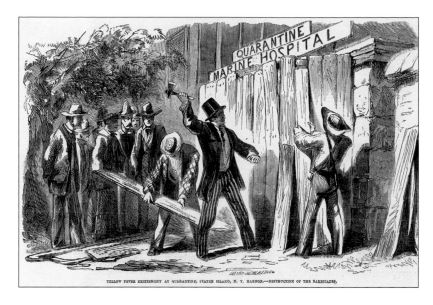

YELLOW FEVER EXCITEMENT AT QUARANTINE, STATEN ISLAND, N. Y. HARBOR.—DESTRUCTION OF THE BARRICADES.

Immigrants overwhelm Grosse Isle As the famine worsened, American authorities—fearful of great hordes of immigrants arriving at American ports—diverted ships to Canada. In Quebec, quarantine facilities were set up on Grosse Isle, a small island on the Saint Lawrence River. Grosse Isle, with only 150 beds, was soon overrun. In June 1847, 40 vessels containing 14,000 Irish immigrants waited in a line that extended two miles down the river—as alluded to in this John Falter painting entitled *The Famished*. Henry Ford's father was detained at Grosse Isle after being denied entry into the United States. He escaped and walked across the border to Detroit.

A rude welcome in New York Throughout the famine years, 75 percent (650,000) of all Irish immigrants to the United States landed in New York. In 1847 the city had a population of 372,000. That year, 52,000 Irish arrived. Vulnerable in this strange new world, they were often taken advantage of as soon as they arrived in New York. Runners, speaking Gaelic, met the newly arrived immigrants with promises of good jobs and lodgings. The reality was often filthy boarding houses in Lower Manhattan and poor-paying, backbreaking work. New York experienced a high rate of infant mortality and a dramatic rise in crime.

1851: The famine and its attendant evictions, along with British policy toward Ireland, have resulted in a 50 percent decrease in the number of Irish tenant farmers, from 600,000 in 1845 to 300,000 this year.

September 17, 1851: Thomas Fitzpatrick, Irish-born champion of Indian rights, concludes the Treaty of Fort Laramie between the U.S. and several Sioux Nations under Ogala chief Red Cloud.

October 12, 1851: Irish immigrants form the Second Regiment of Irish Volunteers in New York City. Initially a citizen militia, it will become the 69th New York State Militia and remain predominately Irish throughout much of its history.

December 1852: Violence breaks out between police and some 1,000 squatters when New York police try to evict people from the Old Brewery in the New York slum of Five Points. Dozens are injured, but the police collar some 20 wanted murderers who have been hiding in the decrepit old building.

1853: Humanitarian Charles Loring Brace founds the Children's Aid Society in New York City. Loring strives to improve the lives of poor, homeless, orphaned, and immigrant children by placing them with upstanding families in rural communities via the Society's "Orphan Train" program. Though many are helped by Brace's efforts, the fact that most of the poor are Catholic and most of the host families are Protestant leads to accusations of social engineering.

October 12, 1853: Irish-born prizefighter John "Old Smoke" Morrissey captures the American championship from Yankee Sullivan. Morrison will retire from fighting in 1859 and make a seamless transition to a successful career in New York politics.

Timon reaches out to Protestants Bishop John Timon was born in the same year as his colleague, Archbishop John Hughes, New York's "Dagger John." From his bishopric in Buffalo, Timon espoused an outgoing and integrated American Catholicism, one that would reach out and nurture contact with various Protestant denominations. A former frontier missionary, Timon also promulgated the idea of eastern Catholics migrating to the West to fill the vast empty spaces. In doing so, Timon was at odds with Hughes, who advocated a more insular, more concentrated, more controlled, and less ecumenical church.

The unconventional Father Hogan William Hogan was cut from a different cloth than most of his fellow Catholic priests. The Irish-born Hogan was already in Holy Orders when he immigrated to Philadelphia around 1810. Hogan was a popular pastor who enjoyed a less than monastic social life. When he faced sanctions from his bishop, Hogan's parishioners rallied around him. The power struggle ended with Hogan's excommunication from the church. The unfettered Hogan used his rhetorical talents to significant effect in the 1840s as an anti-Catholic polemicist.

"We are unwilling to pay taxes for the purpose of destroying our religion in the minds of our children."

—NEW YORK ARCHBISHOP JOHN HUGHES, ON PROTESTANT-INFLUENCED PUBLIC SCHOOLS

The Church Takes Care of Its Own

By the early 1840s, it was clear to New York archbishop "Dagger" John Hughes and other Irish Catholic leaders that something had to be done about America's public schools. Though technically nonreligious, education in New York and other cities was heavily Protestant and anti-Catholic. One required text in New York, *The Irish Heart*, dismissed much of Catholicism as a mix of superstition and sin. Meanwhile, the Protestant version of the Bible was dominant in classrooms.

Hughes, whose provocative nickname came from the knife-like crucifix he wore, argued that these were essentially Protestant schools. Thus, Hughes demanded that government funds be used to establish Catholic schools. (This idea had actually worked a few years earlier in Lowell, Massachusetts.)

New York archbishop John Hughes

In the end, explicit religious references were removed from public schools, but it mattered little to Hughes. He and other Irish American leaders had become convinced that "the scattered debris of the Irish nation" (Hughes's words) should be educated by the Catholic Church.

In fact, over the next several decades, the Irish constructed a separate Catholic world in America. From primary schools and orphanages to colleges and hospitals, the Church played a cradle-to-the-grave role in the lives of a vast majority of Irish Americans.

Some saw this as self-imposed segregation. Intimate ties to parish life did limit interaction with the rest of the world and, some say, instilled a narrow set of values in the American Irish. Many have argued that the church stifled Irish American assimilation, creativity, and advancement into the upper classes. Others, however, note that the Irish may never have survived—or ultimately flourished—in the U.S. without the help of the Church.

Interestingly, the Irish were not a particularly religious people before the famine—in Ireland or the U.S. The trauma of the famine created vast physical and spiritual needs on both sides of the Atlantic. At times, the Church physically protected the thousands of immigrants who were arriving weekly in the U.S. during the 1840s and 1850s.

The original St. Patrick's church in New York was built with a surrounding brick wall to ward off anti-immigrant mobs. Dagger John once proclaimed that if city officials did not do a better job protecting Catholic churches, the Irish would fight back and turn the city into "another Moscow" (referring to how the Russians burned down their capital when retreating from Napoleon). Of course, the Irish lived in places where "poverty, wretchedness, and vice [were] rife," as Charles Dickens wrote of New York's infamous Five Points.

Church leaders provided services—as well as stern moral leadership—in an effort to guide the Irish away from destructive temptation. And for all of Dickens's purple prose about the ghettoes, many immigrants forged stable new lives under the Church's watchful eye.

In one Five Points parish, more than 1,000 Irish immigrants married from 1853 to 1860. Half were from the western Irish counties of Sligo, Cork, and Kerry. As they would well into the 19th and 20th centuries, Irish Catholics were sticking together—for better or worse.

The Young Ireland Rebellion With the famine at its height in 1848, the appetite for Irish national sovereignty was as sharp as ever. However, the physical means to fight for it had been brought to a new low. It was not surprising, then, that the Young Ireland Rebellion faltered in a single gunfight outside the widow McCormack's house in Ballingarry, County Tipperary. Young Ireland leader William Smith O'Brien was arrested, but his organization nevertheless delivered a lasting legacy: the first unfurling of Ireland's tricolor flag.

Irish ties to Jim Crow character The name "Jim Crow," which today is associated with post–Civil War segregation laws, first emerged in a song and dance number in the 1820s. Irish American minstrel performer Thomas Dartmouth "Daddy" Rice heard an old black man in Louisville sing a song that ended with the lines "Wheel about and turn about, en do j's so. Eb'ry time I wheel about I jump Jim Crow." Rice made the character a part of his traveling performances. Among whites during the 1840s, the name "Jim Crow" became synonymous with a black person.

Irish Dems flex their muscles This 1848 campaign satire portrays Democratic presidential candidate Lewis Cass as an Irish Bowery Boy. Wearing the typical garb of the street-tough Bowery Boys—stovepipe hat, boots, and plaid pants—Cass is depicted as having vanquished three obstacles to his election: the issue of abolition, Free Soil candidate Martin Van Buren, and Whig vice-presidential candidate Millard Fillmore. He is accepting the surrender of his Whig opponent, Zachary Taylor. The message here is that the Democratic Party, with its Irish muscle, will defeat the Whigs. As it turned out, Taylor won the election.

Lodes o' Luck

Like those of other ethnicities, Irish Americans headed west in the 1800s hoping to find precious metals in hills, mountains, and streams. Typically, their toil resulted in disappointment rather than riches. But the luck of the Irish did shine on a select few.

During the California Gold Rush in the 1840s and '50s, the most successful Irish Americans earned their fortunes as entrepreneurs. Sam Brannan trumpeted the Gold Rush, then sold supplies at inflated prices. A minter, David C. Broderick, made his fortune by selling $10 gold coins that contained only $8 worth of gold.

In Nevada in 1859, two Irish Americans may have been the first to strike gold in the region. Peter O'Reilly and Pat McLaughlin discovered the metal in Six Mile Canyon near Virginia City. The find became known as the Comstock Lode, but these Irish finders would not be keepers. Another miner, Henry Comstock, claimed the strike was on his land. The Irishmen didn't ask questions, but they should have. Both died poor. Marcus Daly was another lucky Irishman. Born in County Cavan in 1841, Daly survived the Great Famine, immigrated to New York, and wound up in Virginia City. There, he fell in with another Irishman, William Murphy, and mine owner George Hearst, father of William Randolph Hearst. In 1876 Daly found himself in Butte, Montana. There, aided by Hearst, he purchased the Anaconda silver claim from Irish prospector Michael Hickey.

The Anaconda had riches beyond silver, specifically a huge copper vein. Demand for copper was surging due to the telegraph and electricity. Daly's success attracted many fellow Irish to Butte, including tin miners from Cork. Within a few years, Daly was rich. When he died in 1900, Butte and America bade farewell to its "Copper King." Daly, the Anaconda, and Butte's Irish connection would be fondly recalled in 2006 during a visit to the city by Ireland's president, Mary McAleese.

Scheming Brannan strikes it rich By the time gold was discovered in California in 1848, Irish American Samuel Brannan had started San Francisco's first newspaper and owned a store near the first gold strike. Brannan cunningly took advantage of the imminent Gold Rush. He collected bogus tithes from his fellow Mormons and used the money to buy all the prospecting gear in the region, which he sold to gold hunters at outrageous prices. He also ran through the streets of San Francisco, shouting, "Gold! Gold! Gold from the American River." Half of San Francisco's population fled to the gold fields, and Brannan became California's first millionaire. Bad luck eventually caught up with him, as he lost his fortune and died broke.

Gold Rush lures famine refugees Irish names crop up like so many nuggets in the story of the California Gold Rush. This had less to do with luck than a degree of historical timing. Gold fever struck on America's western seaboard at a time when untold numbers of Irish were fleeing the Great Hunger. The lure of gold was an extension of America's pull. The mass migration of the famine years did not stop on the East Coast, in part due to the promise of easy riches in California and other western states and territories.

1854: Immigrant John McSorley opens a pub he calls The Old House at Home on Manhattan's lower east side. It will endure into the 21st century as McSorley's Old Ale House. • The nativist American Party enjoys its greatest electoral success this year, gaining power in several northeastern cities and sending 62 representatives to the U.S. Congress. Party members call for immigration limits and a 21-year waiting period for citizenship. • William Hogan, an excommunicated Irish American priest, publishes *Popery as It Was and as It Is*, a negative exposé of Catholicism. • Kit Carson, an American frontiersman, trapper, and guide of Scots-Irish ancestry, is named Indian agent at Taos, New Mexico. For the next several years, he will negotiate treaties between the southwestern tribes and the U.S. government.

1855: Some 25 percent of New York City police officers are Irish-born. • James Shields, a County Tyrone-born American general and statesman, purchases a large tract of land in Minnesota for the establishment of an Irish community. Shieldsville will be settled by some 200 East Coast Irish families, who purchase land from Shields at less than $2 an acre.

June 5, 1855: The American Party, also known as the "Know-Nothing" party, opens its first national political convention.

August 1, 1855: Castle Garden opens on Manhattan Island. It will be New York City's receiving and processing center for millions of immigrants, many of them Irish, over the next 35 years.

1856: "Know-Nothing" presidential candidate Millard Fillmore suffers defeat in all but one state, Maryland.

Revolutionary writer

Born in Londonderry in 1815, John Mitchel rose to prominence by writing about the Irish famine. In 1846 he became associated with the nationalist movement Young Ireland, and his revolutionary writing led to his arrest. Mitchel was sent to Tasmania, but he escaped to the United States. While in the U.S., his radical work attracted the condemnation of even the predominately Irish U.S. bishops. Still, his book *Jail Journal* is considered a classic. Mitchel returned to Ireland and was elected to the House of Commons in 1875, but he died before he could serve.

The Mollies of Ireland

Though the name of the Molly Maguires is most often associated with Pennsylvania's mining country in the 1860s and '70s, the story of this secret society is rooted in Ireland. There, the Molly Maguires were, according to popular belief, drawn from the name of a widow who had led retaliatory raids against oppressive English landlords and their agents. Most typically, the "Mollies" were groups of tenant farmers who battled against the iniquity of the London-imposed land distribution system. They would sometimes disguise themselves in women's clothes during dead-of-night raids.

Provocative Irish dancer Lola Montez, born Eliza Rosanna Gilbert in County Sligo, Ireland, was one of the most scandalous women of the age. Noted more for her romantic liaisons than any dancing talent, she nonetheless kept male audiences captivated with her highly suggestive "spider dance." Among her lovers

were King Ludwig I of Bavaria and renowned Hungarian pianist and composer Franz Liszt. Following the Revolutions of 1848 in Europe, she fled to London and then left for the United States, where she lived for a number of years in gold-rich California. After suffering a stroke and pneumonia, Montez died in 1861 in New York City at age 39.

Father Mathew's "Pledge" In the 1830s and 1840s, Father Theobald Mathew led a massive temperance movement in Ireland. His organization, the Abstinence Society, required individuals to take "The Pledge," by which they promised to refrain from all alcoholic beverages. In 1849 Mathew took his message to America, where more than 600,000 people—mainly Irish—are said to have taken The Pledge. Recognizing Mathew's work, President Zachary Taylor invited him to dine at the White House. Moreover, both houses of Congress accorded him a congenial welcome.

MR. BRIGGS'S PLEASURES OF HOUSEKEEPING.

TWEED INTRODUCING BIG SIX'S BOYS.

Building America The Irish construction worker has been a worldwide phenomenon, but never more than in the United States during the 1800s. Laying brick upon brick in so many U.S. cities were Irish laborers, who were plentiful and worked for low wages. Though frequently lampooned, these Irish workers were of critical importance to the literal building of America. Such work often served as a stepping-stone, as many of these laborers went on to start their own construction companies.

The "Big Six" Through much of the 19th century, volunteer fire departments were as much social and political organizations as they were instruments of public safety. In their engine houses, men met to play cards, share gossip, and plot politics. Companies were rigidly stratified. Some were comprised only of professional men while others consisted entirely of laborers. Manhattan's Americus Engine Company No. 6, known as "Big Six," was comprised primarily of Irishmen, strong supporters of the Democratic Party. In 1850 they elected William Tweed (*holding hat*) foreman and launched his political career.

Irish, Germans share common bond The Irish and German immigrants who crowded America's eastern cities in the 19th century might have spoken different languages, but they often shared a vital characteristic: Catholicism. Consequently, both groups were similarly depicted by Anglo-Protestant nativists afraid of being swamped by "papist" newcomers. Inevitably, the Irish and Germans found common cause. An interesting case is that of Irishwoman Annie Moore, the first recorded immigrant at Ellis Island. Moore married a German immigrant, Joseph Schayer, and bore 11 children.

A trailblazing hero You could well say that they don't make them like Kit Carson anymore. From his humble Scots-Irish beginnings in Kentucky, Christopher Houston Carson grew up to become one of the frontier's most celebrated scouts—both foe and friend of Indian tribes. At his death in 1868 in Colorado Territory, Carson was fluent in three European languages and several Native American tongues. In key respects, Carson—and other Scots-Irish trailblazers of the mid-19th century— were the prototype populist heroes of an emerging American mass culture.

Irish settle in Texas This house was built by Irish settlers in Port O'Connor, Texas (on the Gulf of Mexico), around 1850. The connection of the Irish with Texas is a long one. As early as 1806, a number of Irish families resided at Villa de Santisima Trinidad on the Trinity River in northeastern Texas. Two Irish communities resulted from conscious efforts at colonization. After receiving a grant of Texas land in 1828, Irish-born James Power returned to Ireland and recruited families to his settlement at Refugio near Corpus Christi. In a similar venture at about the same time, John McMullen and James McGloin established an Irish community at nearby San Patricio de Hibernia.

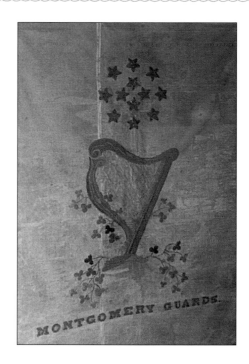

Irish military societies In the 1840s and 1850s, Irish militia units became popular. Many were named after heroes of Irish history, such as Patrick Sarsfield and Robert Emmet. General Richard Montgomery, the Irish general killed during the American Revolution, was a particular favorite. Montgomery Guard units were formed in Boston, New York, and Louisiana. The militiamen initially met for camaraderie and for the chance to parade in military finery. But as anti-Catholic sentiment escalated, they often were called upon to defend against nativist violence.

Paddy wagons The term paddy wagons, which came into usage in America in the latter half of the 19th century, refers to the enclosed wagons used by police to haul away lawbreakers. There are two theories about the origin of the term, both based on the common nickname "Paddy" for Irishmen. One theory holds that the wagons got their name because so many drunken Irishmen were taken into custody in them. The other says quite the contrary: that the name came from the fact that so many arresting police officers were Irish. Either explanation is plausible.

Boxing champ and U.S. congressman Known as "Old Smoke" because of a serious burn suffered during a gang fight, Tipperary native John Morrissey was one of America's great bare-knuckle boxers. On October 12, 1853, he defeated Yankee Sullivan in front of 3,000 riotous fans to capture the heavyweight championship. Following his boxing days, he operated a lucrative racecourse and casino in Saratoga, New York. In addition, with the backing of Tammany Hall, he was twice elected to the U.S. House of Representatives. Eventually, however, he turned against Tammany because of its corrupt dealings and helped put Boss Tweed in jail. He ended his days as a New York state senator.

1845-60

1857: During a seven-year residence in the United States, Irish playwright Dion Boucicault premieres his hit play *The Poor of New York*.

March 4, 1857: James Buchanan, a son of Scots-Irish immigrants, is sworn in as the 15th president of the United States.

July 4, 1857: A rumble between Irish street gangs—including the Dead Rabbits, Plug Uglies, and others—versus the nativist Bowery Boys gang erupts in violence that rocks New York's Five Points neighborhood. Police secure the streets, but not before nearly a dozen people are killed and many more wounded.

November 1857: Hungry immigrants in New York's Five Points ghetto riot in protest of inflated bread prices.

1858: Irish immigrant Michael Phelan, whose role in popularizing his sport will earn him the title "Father of American Billiards," wins the unofficial American championship by besting Philadelphia billiards star Ralph Benjamin.

March 17, 1858: Irish patriot James Stephens founds the Irish Republican Brotherhood in Dublin. Drawing many of its members from the Young Ireland movement, the IRB also seeks to effect change through armed rebellion. Later in the year, John O'Mahoney, a highly educated Irish patriot and a recent immigrant to New York, will found the Fenian Brotherhood. This will be the American arm of the IRB.

August 15, 1858: Before a crowd of some 100,000 people, Bishop John Hughes lays the cornerstone for New York's Saint Patrick's Cathedral. When completed, it will be the largest Catholic cathedral in the United States.

The post-famine Irish
Irish tenant farmers pose in a photographer's studio in 1853. The loss of two million people through death and emigration dramatically changed Ireland and the Irish. Farms decreased in number but increased in size. Fear of being unable to support a family led to a sharp increase in the ages at which Irish people married. Some, knowing their chances of having a patch of land to farm were nil, never married at all. The bleak conditions prompted many young people to leave Ireland. In addition, resentment toward England reached heights not known before the famine. This bitterness led to widespread agrarian protests and political agitation.

Children's Aid Society Appalled by the vast numbers of (mainly) Irish homeless and orphaned children living in the streets of New York's Five Points neighborhood, Methodist minister Charles Loring Brace in 1853 established the Children's Aid Society. He believed that by removing children from slums and sending them by train to pioneering families in the West (as illustrated in these images), they would be raised in a healthy environment while learning how to lead productive lives. However, critics charged that these children were often exploited and kept virtually as slaves. Many Irish cried that Protestants were "kidnapping" their community's children, some of whom were not orphans but instead children of destitute parents.

Sisters to the Rescue

In a callous age, when society often ignored the sufferings of the destitute, poor, and sick, Catholic nuns provided badly needed services. Two of the religious orders most active in working with Irish immigrants were themselves from Ireland: the Sisters of the Presentation of the Blessed Virgin Mary and the Sisters of Mercy.

The Presentation Sisters, founded by Honoria "Nano" Nagle in Cork in 1775, were dedicated to the Catholic and moral education of the young. By 1833 Nagle's followers leapfrogged the Atlantic to open a school in Newfoundland. In 1854 they took another huge step, establishing a school in San Francisco to work with the children of Irish gold miners.

The Sisters of Mercy, founded in Dublin in 1831 by Catherine McAuley, strived to alleviate the suffering of the aged and the infirm. They particularly sought to help women, who without the sisters' support might fall into dissolute ways. By 1843 the Mercyites had established

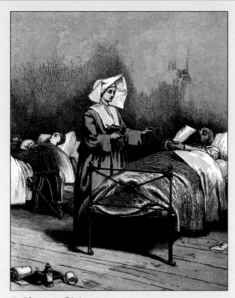

A Sister of Mercy

themselves in the United States. Wherever they settled, they opened Mercy Houses in which women in dire straits could seek refuge and learn a skill. Eventually, the sisters' work led them to open schools across the country. Girls received an education and acquired the means to support themselves.

Other religious orders, while not founded in Ireland, frequently found themselves in America ministering to the Irish. The Sisters of the Good Shepherd were a French order concerned with the rehabilitation and education of women who had fallen into immoral living. The Sisters of Notre Dame operated industrial schools, such as the one they opened in Boston in 1853 to teach young women marketable skills. The Sisters of Charity, founded by American-born Elizabeth Ann Seton, worked with the sick. It was the Sisters of Charity who opened St. Vincent's Hospital in New York in 1849 to care for poor—primarily Irish—immigrants.

Foster writes the classics

Pennsylvania-born Stephen Collins Foster penned songs for the ages during his brief lifetime. Classics such as "Oh! Susanna," "Beautiful Dreamer," "My Old Kentucky Home," and "Jeanie with the Light Brown Hair" (*far right*) ensured that Foster stood tallest among his peers during the mid-19th century peak years of music hall and minstrel shows. Foster's marriage to Jane McDowell, however, was less durable than his works. Such personal troubles, combined with a faltering muse and alcoholism, led to his penniless and lonely death at just 37 in 1864.

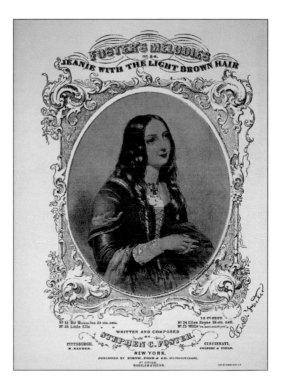

September 1, 1858: An angry mob sets fire to the Marine Hospital on Staten Island, long used as a quarantine facility for ill immigrants. Fortunately, only about 100 patients are housed there, and neither of the two deaths that occur this evening is due to fire.

1859: Irish American philanthropist William Corcoran hires famed architect James Renwick to design an art gallery at 17th and Pennsylvania in Washington, D.C. The federal government will seize the building during the Civil War, and it will ultimately house a collection of fine art. • Roach's Shipyard, which will grow to become one of the nation's largest shipyards, is established at Chester, Pennsylvania, by Irish American John Roach.

1860: In the past decade, more than a million Irish citizens have emigrated, with most going to North America. • With more than 200,000 of its citizens born in Ireland, New York becomes the world's largest "Irish" city. • Irish-born U.S. Army colonel Michael Corcoran faces a court-martial for refusing to lead his regiment, the 69th New York Militia, in a parade in honor of a state visit by the prince of Wales.

January 14, 1860: John Downey, an Irish immigrant and successful businessman who was lured west by the Gold Rush, is named governor of California.

September 19, 1860: Thomas Dartmouth Rice, an Irish American performer who popularized the minstrel show, dies in New York City. Peaking in the 1850s, minstrelsy featured white men with blackened faces imitating African American song and dance. The popularity of Rice's signature piece, *Jump Jim Crow,* earned him the sobriquet "Father of American Minstrelsy."

"Cleanliness" ad excludes Irish

In this 1854 ad, a Boston soap company appeals to the nativist sentiments of many Americans concerned with the large number of foreigners, particularly Irish, entering the country. The purity supplied by the soap is equated with an American purity, as symbolized by the two Native Americans holding the national flag. In case this subtle message was lost on the consumer, the words "Know Nothing Soap" are emblazoned across the Stars and Stripes. This relates to the nativist and "patriotic" "Know-Nothing" party.

Catholics respond to "Know-Nothing" attacks

One of the principal charges made by Protestant Americans against Irish Catholics was that as members of an authoritarian church, they were subject to the dictates of their clergy and therefore inimical to American democracy. Catholics were quick to refute this charge, pointing out that republics had once existed in the Catholic city-states of the Italian peninsula. In this broadside, Catholics in Washington, D.C., feel compelled to answer "Know-Nothing" party claims that Archbishop John Hughes of New York was in the nation's capitol to influence their vote.

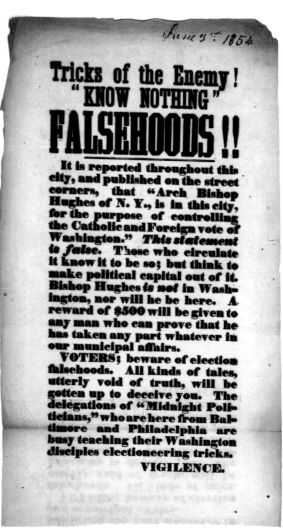

June 3rd 1854

**Tricks of the Enemy!
"KNOW NOTHING"
FALSEHOODS !!**

It is reported throughout this city, and published on the street corners, that "Arch Bishop Hughes of N. Y., is in this city, for the purpose of controlling the Catholic and Foreign vote of Washington." *This statement is false.* Those who circulate it know it to be so; but think to make political capital out of it. Bishop Hughes *is not* in Washington, nor will he be here. A reward of $500 will be given to any man who can prove that he has taken any part whatever in our municipal affairs.

VOTERS; beware of election falsehoods. All kinds of tales, utterly void of truth, will be gotten up to deceive you. The delegations of "Midnight Politicians," who are here from Baltimore and Philadelphia are busy teaching their Washington disciples electioneering tricks.

VIGILENCE.

Hoping for better in the USA In this cartoon from 1855, a swarm of people goes down to the docks to board ships destined for America. A sign on the U.S. shore states the need for one million men and promises good wages for all. Tales of "streets paved with gold" enticed many to try their luck at a better life, even if it meant leaving everything behind. Not only the Irish pinned their hopes on America; 53,000 German immigrants landed in New York in 1847.

"Pathfinder of the Seas"

Matthew Fontaine Maury has been called the "Pathfinder of the Seas" for his pioneering work in oceanography and meteorology. A Virginia-born grandson of French-Irish immigrants, Maury became interested in the study of the oceans while on extended voyages with the U.S. Navy from 1825 to 1834. His research on the subject was published in 1855 as the *Physical Geography of the Sea,* considered the first textbook on modern oceanography. During the Civil War, he was a commander in the Confederate Navy. After the war, he served as professor of meteorology at Virginia Military Institute.

Anti-Catholic fervor The illustrators of Currier & Ives were among the many artists who captured the anti-Catholic spirit of 19th century America. In this drawing from 1855, two noble Americans stand ready to defend the United States against what many saw as an invading force of Irish Catholics. (Note the shamrock that the bishop is grabbing to anchor himself to U.S. soil.) Bearing a sword and crucifix, Pope Pius IX demands "submission." However, Brother Jonathan says the clergymen will not be allowed to place "the mark of the Beast" on Americans.

Drew stars on Philly stage John Drew, born to a poor Dublin family in 1827, was one of the great stage actors of his day. Drew is seen here as Handy Andy, a character created by novelist Samuel Lover, who explored Irish life in comic yet complex ways. Drew made a name for himself on the stages of Philadelphia and New York but died when he was just 34, after a fall.

One of his daughters married into the Barrymore family, making Drew an ancestor of actress Drew Barrymore.

"[T]hese ruffians emerged from their dens like a
horde of wild beasts and disgraced our city."

—*THE NEW YORK TIMES,* COMMENTING ON SPREADING GANG VIOLENCE, 1857

Irish Gangs

Prior to the Civil War, Irish gangs existed in all major cities in the East. Penniless, frequently unemployed, and despised by Yankee Americans, young Irish immigrants often grouped in gangs to survive in the New World. A recent popular image of these gangs was created in the Martin Scorsese film *The Gangs of New York* (2002), which was based on Herbert Asbury's 1927 book of the same name. Unfortunately, both Asbury and Scorsese were loose with the facts.

Scorsese's film centers on a conflict between an Irish gang based in Lower Manhattan's Five Points neighborhood—a slum that Charles Dickens described after an 1842 visit as a "world of vice and misery"—and a group of Protestant nativist thugs bent on keeping the Irish in their place. In this cinematic recreation of 19th century street warfare, the violence is frequent, brutal, and lethal.

The reality was somewhat different. Irish gangs with such colorful names as the Five Pointers, the Swamp

Dead Rabbit gang member

Angels, and the Dead Rabbits (from the Gaelic *Dead Raibéad,* meaning a man to be feared) were more concerned with controlling local jobs and winning elections than with fighting nativist outsiders. Their opponents were usually other Irish gangs vying for the same jobs and political positions. They did resort to violence, but it was usually of the pushing, shoving, fisticuffs variety rather than the butchering depicted in the Scorsese film.

The career of one Irish gang leader in this period is instructive. In the 1840s and 1850s, Irish-born Mike Walsh led a Five Points gang known as the Spartan Band. At a time when politics was rough and tumble, the Band was Walsh's "muscle," ensuring that his voice was heard—a voice that articulated the grievances of Irish laborers. He called for shorter hours for working men, the right to strike, and the abolition of child labor. His admiring constituents elected him to the New York state assembly and later to Congress. He was at once gang leader, social reformer, and politician.

Dead Rabbits, Bowery Boys go at it Two Irish gangs, the Dead Rabbits and the Bowery Boys, are depicted in this recreation of their battle on July 4, 1857. Lower Manhattan in the mid-19th century was a hard place for the timid. Its demographic landscape changed virtually every day, with the post-famine Irish immigrants forcing most of the pace. Political fiefdoms were carved out with immigrant muscle and sometimes blood. The Irish were not alone in forming gangs to defend neighborhoods, but their numerical dominance ensured top historical billing.

Buchanan goes it alone As American president in the years just prior to the Civil War, James Buchanan was widely criticized. While he viewed the secession of southern states as illegal, so too, he argued, was fighting to turn back the secessionist tide.

In an era of militarism inspired by Manifest Destiny, Buchanan's legalistic pacifism cut little ice with his peers. Moreover, historians have generally given this president, whose father was from Donegal, a thumbs-down on decisive and effective leadership. Perhaps he lacked for a woman at his side; Buchanan remains the only unmarried president in the nation's history.

Votes cast in Irish saloons Just as schools and community centers might be used as voting centers today, it was very often the local saloon that was the assigned place to cast votes in the districts and wards of 19th century American cities, which were dominated by Irish immigrants and their emerging political leaders. The saloons themselves frequently doubled as political clubhouses, and there was little problem in attracting men to vote in them on election day. That was particularly true if the candidate, who might be the actual saloonkeeper, fueled his support by offering drinks on the house.

St. Patrick's Day parades Since colonial times, St. Patrick's Day parades have been staged in America. Prior to the Revolution, they were comprised primarily of Irish soldiers serving in the British Army. After independence, the tradition continued with Irish American soldiers. By the 1840s, parades were held wherever large Irish communities existed—from New York (pictured in 1860) and Boston all the way to Chicago. In 1853 San Francisco held its first St. Patrick's Day parade. Usually organized by Irish aid societies, the parades expressed the pride, sense of community, and homesickness of the exiled Irish.

Success in California When 15-year-old John Downey left County Roscommon in 1842, he could not have imagined the life that lay before him. After being educated as a pharmacist in Maryland, Downey went west in 1849 in search of California gold. He found not gold but riches after opening the first drugstore in Los Angeles. Entering politics in 1856, he was elected to the state legislature and then became governor of California four years later. Out of office in 1862, Downey returned to Los Angeles, where he proceeded to build a real estate empire.

Douglas "courts the Paddies" This satirical cartoon depicts the leading presidential candidates and their alleged supporters in the election of 1860. The central figure of Dred Scott calling the tune on his fiddle represents the issue of slavery as the dominant question of the day. Republican Abraham Lincoln (*upper right*), southern Democrat John C. Breckinridge (*upper left*), and Constitutional Unionist John Bell (*lower right*) dance with their constituencies. In the lower left, Democrat Stephen Douglas jigs with "Paddy," suggesting his courting of the Irish vote. The cross that dangles from the Irishman's neck was to remind voters of Douglas's alleged Catholicism.

Letters home Leaving Ireland for America in the 19th century was more often than not a one-way journey, with family members parting for life. What held the family narrative together was the emigrant's letters from New York, Boston, or elsewhere, a correspondence frequently accompanied by American dollars to help support relatives back in Ireland. The letter might also include an invitation to a sibling to make the same transatlantic voyage, especially when work in America was plentiful.

VIEW OF THE NEW CATHEDRAL OF ST. JOHN, NEWFOUNDLAND.

The Irish who settled in Canada In 1806 the Benevolent Irish Society was formed in Newfoundland. But it was five decades later—around the time that Newfoundland's Cathedral of St. John the Baptist (*pictured*) was constructed—that the Irish came to Canada in great numbers. During and after the famine, the trip to Canada was generally cheaper than the journey to the States, but also more dangerous. Roughly 3,000 immigrants may have perished at the Canadian port of Grosse Isle. The Irish who remained in Canada generally became laborers and settled in more rural areas, as opposed to the urban Irish in the U.S.

Irish Ghettos

In the 1840s, French bishop Louis Amadeus Rappe worked diligently among the poor of Cleveland, a city experiencing rapid growth because of immigrants fleeing the Irish famine. Inevitably, squalid ghettoes formed in that city, including Irishtown Bend on the banks of the Cuyahoga River. The famine Irish fortunate enough to survive the trip to America had little choice but to pack themselves into poor districts in Cleveland as well as New York, Boston, Chicago, and Philadelphia.

These ghettos were, first and foremost, unhealthy places to live. A Boston health commission formed in 1849 found immigrants "huddled together like brutes, without regard to sex or age, or sense of decency." Crime also flourished in this environment. Irish immigrants were swiftly stereotyped as both violent and shiftless.

"Who does not know that the most depraved, debased, worthless and irredeemable drunkards and sots which curse the community are Irish Catholics?" the *Chicago Tribune* wondered. Ironically, while enduring such heartless criticism, Irish workers labored to complete the stately St. Patrick's Church in the mid-1850s. (It remains the oldest public building still standing in Chicago.)

The most infamous of the Irish ghettos was New York's Five Points district. Amid the crime and vice, nine-year-old orphan Mary Mullen was regularly seen sweeping the streets while dressed in rags. Prostitution was pervasive. Tipperary native Bridget McCarthy prostituted her teen-aged niece, according to one study of the Five Points.

Still, life in the ghetto was an improvement over life in famine-scarred Ireland. A recent archaeological dig at the Five Points site confirmed that Irish immigrants lived more comfortably than had previously been believed. Urban ghettos ultimately gave Irish immigrants a chance to organize. Vital new forms of business, song, language, and theater also emerged. Consider William Henry Lane, later known as "Master Juba." He blended Irish and African dance to create today's tap dancing. Unwittingly, immigrants in big cities recreated the supportive *clachans* (small villages), around which their lives had revolved in Ireland.

Factory workers stir up trouble The pre-Civil War years witnessed dramatic industrial expansion in northeastern states, such as Massachusetts, Connecticut, and New York. The Irish happened to be on hand in huge numbers to fill the labor rolls—but at low wages. It wasn't surprising, then, that the Irish began to agitate and organize. They found themselves at the head of industrial disputes, such as the 1860 shoemakers strike in Lynn, Massachusetts. That stoppage spawned tensions (*pictured*), which reflected a growing pan-ethnic restiveness among the ranks of underpaid factory workers.

The Irish laborer He was rough-looking, poorly dressed, prone to despair and its companion, drink, and looked down upon by respectable society. But the Irish laborer in the post-famine years would break his bones and possibly give his life to lay the foundations of a greater and more widely shared American economic prosperity. Whether by digging canals, laying roads and railroad ties, or constructing buildings and bridges, the Irish worker forged a future for his American children and their children that would be a cause of lasting pride for Irish America.

Blue, Gray, and Green

1861–1870

In the fall of 1860, as the United States moved closer to the catastrophe of civil war, an Irish-born officer in the 69th Regiment of the New York State Militia was placed under arrest for disobeying orders. That man was Colonel Michael Corcoran, who had fled famine-ravaged County Sligo in 1849 and became commanding officer of the 69th. Corcoran's troops were almost exclusively Irish natives or first-generation Irish Americans.

The 69th had been scheduled to take part in a military parade in honor of Britain's prince of Wales, who was visiting New York and other American cities in October 1860. Corcoran refused to allow his men to participate in the festivities. "Although I am a citizen of America, I am a native of Ireland," Corcoran said. For the men of the 69th, the prince of Wales was "the representative of my country's oppressors."

Corcoran was relieved of command, but not for long. When the federal garrison at Fort Sumter fell to rebel soldiers in South Carolina in April 1861, Corcoran's sins were forgiven and his court-martial adjourned. He was invited back to lead the 69th Regiment.

The embattled United States needed Michael Corcoran and thousands more like him—natives of Ireland and their children—to preserve the Union.

> ## "You have fought nobly for the Harp and Shamrock, fight now for the Stars and Stripes.... Your adopted country wants you."
>
> —ADVERTISEMENT IN THE NORTH DURING THE EARLY DAYS OF THE CIVIL WAR

Fighting for the North in the Civil War, the Irish Brigade was comprised of 2,000 Irish Catholic volunteers (as depicted in this Mort Künstler painting). Led most famously by General Thomas Meagher, the brigade fought gallantly at the Battle of Fredericksburg, where it lost nearly half of its men.

Abraham Lincoln, the new president who had inspired little support among Irish Americans in the 1860 election, put out a call for volunteers to crush the rebellion in the South. Thousands of Irish Americans responded—including the men of the 69th—and thousands continued to respond throughout the horrific conflict. During the Civil War, some 150,000 Irish Americans wore Union blue. Corcoran was among the thousands of Irish Americans who sacrificed his life for the Union. He died in 1863, at age 36, in a war-related accident.

Why did so many Irish Americans respond to the call of a nation that had not been particularly eager to embrace them? Some, enlisting as substitutes, fought for money. Others saw the war as a chance to prove the nativists wrong about their loyalties, their courage, and their commitment to the ideals of their adopted country. Then again, in the 1864 presidential election, many Irish Americans rejected Lincoln—for a second time—in favor of George McClellan, the onetime Union general who had campaigned as a peace-now candidate. Despite their conspicuous presence in Lincoln's army, Irish Americans were hardly enthusiastic abolitionists. What's more, when the Union—desperate for manpower—imposed a draft in 1863, the Irish in New York revolted and took out their frustrations on the city's black population.

Suffice it to say, the story of the Irish and the American Civil War is complex. And that's just from the Union perspective, for not all of the fighting Irish wore blue. About 30,000 fought for the Confederacy. While most Irish immigrants lived in the industrialized cities of the North, some 85,000 residents of the Confederate States of America were natives of Ireland. Like the Union, the Confederacy fielded several all-Irish units, including the Sixth Louisiana Volunteers, half of whom were Irish immigrants.

Whether they fought for North or South, some of the Irishmen in arms had another cause in mind—that of Ireland itself. Within the ranks of both blue and gray existed an open conspiracy of Irish soldiers known as the Fenian Brotherhood. Named for a mythical Irish warrior named Finn Mac-Cool, the Fenian Brotherhood was the American wing of the Irish Republican Brotherhood (IRB), a new revolutionary organization in Ireland that

Colonel Michael Corcoran was an early hero of the Union Army, leading the 69th regiment into action at the First Battle of Bull Run in 1861. After being captured and released, he raised a group of Irish volunteers known as the Corcoran Legion.

was planning a revolt against British rule. The IRB was recruiting thousands of Irish-born British soldiers into its conspiracy, hoping that these troops would abandon the Queen's colors when the time came to free Ireland.

By 1863 Irish American soldiers had distinguished themselves at Bull Run, Antietam, Fredericksburg (where Irish Confederate troops fired on the Union's Irish Brigade at Marye's Heights), and Gettysburg. Union general George McClellan singled out the Irish Brigade, commanded by Irish immigrant Thomas Francis Meagher, for its "gallantry" and "superb courage" at the bloody Battle of Antietam in the fall of 1862.

Colonel John O'Mahony of the 99th New York Regiment was the founder and head of the Fenian Brotherhood. In conjunction with his IRB allies across the Atlantic, he believed it was time to prepare for a day when these seasoned, well-trained Irish American soldiers would fight not for North or South, but for Ireland.

O'Mahony convened a meeting of Irish American Union officers in Chicago in November 1863 to begin plans for war in Ireland once the American war was over. James Stephens, the founder and leader of the IRB, visited Union armies in 1864 to recruit more Irish Americans to the coming rebellion in Ireland.

Stephens was a superb organizer, but he underestimated the power of British intelligence. His dangerous conspiracy was broken up in Ireland just as the American Civil War ended. However, the American Fenians continued to pursue the goal of an independent Irish Republic. The more militant American Fenians wanted to use Irish Civil War veterans to invade Canada and hold the dominion hostage—with the freedom of Ireland as ransom.

With tacit support from U.S. secretary of state William Seward (who remained bitter toward Britain for its neutrality during the Civil War—and for supplying the Confederates with the warship *Alabama*), the Fenians sent some 7,000 troops to the Canadian border in 1866. But after the Fenians routed the Canadians in their initial conflict, the U.S. government ended the fighting. American soldiers arrested the Fenian generals and seized the weapons of the Fenian soldiers.

Later Fenian invasions of Canada, in 1867 and 1870, fared even worse. But the Irish learned that they were not without allies. After returning from Canada, many of the Irish American troops were given free train transportation back home to New York. The man who picked up the tab was a prominent resident of that city: William Tweed, the boss of Tammany Hall.

The Fenians were Irish Catholic Union veterans who conspired to use their military skills to capture Canada, hoping to exchange it for a free Ireland. The U.S. government, angry at British aid to the Confederacy, initially looked the other way. However, the Fenians—who lost U.S. support in 1866—were easily defeated.

1861-70

1861: Bandleader and composer Patrick Gilmore, an Irish immigrant, enlists with the Union Army, joining the 24th Massachusetts Volunteers along with his band. They will entertain troops and assist on the battlefield for much of the war. Gilmore will ultimately rise to the post of bandmaster general and, during his deployment, compose the Civil War classic "When Johnny Comes Marching Home."

April 12, 1861: The American Civil War begins with a Confederate attack on Fort Sumter, South Carolina. Over the next four years, more than 150,000 Irish-born Americans will serve in the Union Army.

May 1861: With her husband's rise to the presidency of the Confederacy, Irish American Varina Howell Davis sets up house at the Executive Mansion of the Confederate States of America in Richmond, Virginia.

July 2, 1861: Irish American businessman Edward Creighton plants the first post of the Nebraska-to-California transcontinental telegraph line.

July 21, 1861: Irish American colonel Michael Corcoran of the 69th Regiment, New York Militia, is badly wounded at the Battle of Bull Run. Captured by Confederates, he will be incarcerated at Libby Prison until his release in August 1862.

1862: Irish-born businessman Alexander T. Stewart opens the doors of his "Iron Palace," a massive department store with as many as 2,000 employees, at 9th and Broadway in New York City.

July 1, 1862: Philip Sheridan, a son of Irish immigrants and a West Point graduate, is promoted to the rank of general in the Union Army. Sheridan will pursue and then block the retreat of Robert E. Lee at Appomattox, forcing a Confederate surrender.

Fighting Irish The 37th New York Volunteer Infantry, or Irish Rifles, was among the dozens of Civil War units on both sides whose ranks were filled with Irish Americans. Besides the Irish Brigade—comprised of New York's "Fighting 69th," 63rd, and 88th regiments, the 28th Massachusetts, and the 116th Pennsylvania—notable outfits that were all or heavily Irish included the 23rd Illinois, the Ninth Massachusetts, the 17th Wisconsin, the Sixth Louisiana, the 10th Tennessee, and the 24th Georgia. The Irishmen of the 69th Pennsylvania gained a special place in the war's annals for their role in repulsing Pickett's Charge at Gettysburg.

Civil War chaplains Reverend Thomas Mooney says Sunday Mass near Washington, D.C., for the 69th New York State Militia in 1861. Father Mooney served as chaplain for the 69th but was replaced after "baptizing" one of the regiment's cannons, an action that his archbishop considered sacrilegious. The incident illustrates the important role the Roman Catholic chaplain played for Irish American troops in the Civil War. The priest not only represented an important link to home and tradition, but he also provided crucial physical, moral, and spiritual support for troops who faced the constant possibility of death.

Irish Gray

The Irish in blue is a familiar story, but many Irish fought in gray. The internecine aspect of the Civil War was never so starkly played out than at the Battle of Fredericksburg in December 1862.

It was at the epicenter of the struggle, at Marye's Heights, that General Thomas Francis Meagher's Irish Brigade of the Union Army went musket to musket with Georgia men defending a sunken road. These Georgians have been singled out by historian Shelby Foote for being, above all else, "Irish too."

The Irish fought for the South in every major battle of the conflict. In large numbers, they represented the Army of Northern Virginia and regiments from Louisiana, where New Orleans ranked as the second largest entry port for Irish immigrants during the 19th century. The Sixth Louisiana Volunteer Infantry spawned such fighting units as the First Louisiana, which was commanded by Lieutenant Colonel Michael Nolan, a native of Tipperary. It was Nolan's men who held the Federals at bay at Second Manassas by throwing rocks after running out of ammunition. Formations in the Bayou State became collectively known as Louisiana Tiger regiments.

The gray Irish were not confined to Virginia and Louisiana forces. The South's most famous Irish general, Cork-

Rebel Sons of Erin by Mort Künstler

born Patrick Ronayne Cleburne, commanded the 15th Arkansas. Cleburne, known as the "Stonewall Jackson of the West," led his men at Franklin, Tennessee, in November 1864. After having two horses shot from under him, Cleyburne, waving his sword, led his troops on foot. He was mortally wounded just yards from the Union line.

Seven score years after Appomattox, the descendants of men who had fought for union and secession mustered under one flag in Iraq. There, the famed Fighting 69th Regiment out of New York was teamed with the Louisiana National Guard, descendents of the Louisiana Tigers.

Irish slaughtered at Fredericksburg "What a pity—here comes Meagher's fellows." Those words are attributed to Confederate soldiers, Irishmen themselves, as they watched the Irish Brigade advance on an impregnable Confederate position at Fredericksburg in December 1862. Charging into what someone called "a slaughter pen," the Irish troops from New York, Massachusetts, and Pennsylvania struggled to within 30 paces of the enemy line before a torrent of rifle and artillery fire stopped them. Nearly half of the brigade's soldiers were killed or wounded, leading an officer to write, "Irish bones and Irish blood cover that terrible field to-day."

July 1, 1862: President Lincoln signs the Pacific Railroad Act, which calls for the construction of a transcontinental railroad. Though Chinese immigrants will construct much of the railroad in the West, the transcontinental initially will be built mostly by immigrant Irish laborers.

September 17, 1862: The Battle of Antietam, the bloodiest single-day battle in American history, is fought near Sharpsburg, Maryland. Present on this day is Mathew Brady, an Irish American photographer, and his cadre of assistants. Brady's photographs of the carnage will bring the war home to Americans in a way that has never been done before.

October 1862: Thomas Francis Meagher's Irish Brigade is complete with the addition of the 116th Pennsylvania Infantry. During the war, the Irish Brigade will suffer heavy casualties in many major battles.

December 1862: The Union Army's Irish Brigade is overwhelmed by a regiment of Irish Confederates at Marye's Heights during the Battle of Fredericksburg. The Irish Brigade loses approximately 500 of its 1,200 troops.

1863: William "Boss" Tweed wrests control of New York City's Tammany Hall political machine from previous leader Fernando Wood. • "Buffalo" Bill Cody, an American legend of Irish ancestry, joins the Union Army with the Seventh Kansas Cavalry Regiment.

March 3, 1863: For the first time in American history, Congress passes a conscription act to draft soldiers for the Union Army. The Confederate states had enacted their own draft in April 1862.

Mulholland earns Medal of Honor The commander of the 116th Pennsylvania Infantry, St. Clair Augustin Mulholland was wounded four times and eventually received the Medal of Honor. He helped recruit the mostly Irish regiment in 1862 and led it into its first major battle, at Fredericksburg. Mulholland was born in Lisburn, County Antrim, in 1839. A painter before and after the war, he penned an influential history of his regiment. Of the Irish troops' doomed charge at Fredericksburg, he wrote: "They were not there to fight, only to die."

The Fighting 69th The 69th Regiment of the New York State Militia is the best known of a host of Irish volunteer units that served in the Civil War. As the first regiment of the Union Army's Irish Brigade, the 69th fought ferociously—and suffered terrible casualties—at Antietam, Fredericksburg, Gettysburg, and many other battles. Confederate General Robert E. Lee reportedly dubbed the regiment the "Fighting 69th" after learning that the unit had routed his own troops in an 1862 engagement.

Irish Women at War

The Irish were at the forefront of an unsung corps of Civil War volunteers: women who endured the hardships of the battlefield. Bridget Divers rode with her husband's regiment, the First Michigan Cavalry, and gained fame as a bold, tireless, and resourceful presence. Her most celebrated exploit: riding 15 miles behind enemy lines to retrieve the body of a slain First Michigan captain.

According to a witness quoted in Elizabeth D. Leonard's *All the Daring of the Soldier: Women of the Civil War Armies*, Divers rallied reluctant troops at the 1862 battle of Fair Oaks, Virginia, by swinging her soldier's cap in the air and crying, "Go in Boys and bate [beat] hell out of them and rivinge me Husband. God be wid ye."

Jennie Hodgers

Another immigrant Irish woman, Jennie Hodgers, made her mark in an even less conventional way. In 1862 Hodgers enlisted in the 95th Illinois Infantry under a man's name, Albert D. J. Cashier. Her comrades much later remarked that Private Cashier was small, almost petite, and seemed unusually reserved. Those qualities aside, Cashier was the model soldier. "He kept up on the hardest marches, skillfully handled a rifle, and never shirked duty," remembered one compatriot.

It wasn't until the early 1900s that Cashier's true gender was discovered. Her last days were lived out in an insane asylum, but the soldier who had marched 10,000 miles and survived scores of engagements was accorded a burial with full military honors.

Bridget Divers joins the fight Little is known about Bridget Divers's life before or after the Civil War—except that she was a native of Ireland. During the conflict, Divers (*holding flag*) was a larger-than-life figure who impressed everyone she met. When her husband joined the Michigan Cavalry, Divers went with the regiment to Virginia. She distinguished herself in camp, where she worked as a nurse, and in battle. In the 1862 incident depicted here, she rallied wavering Union troops. On many other occasions, she braved the thick of the fighting, often on horseback, to rescue wounded soldiers.

March 17, 1863: The USS *Shamrock*, a 240-foot, steam-powered man-of-war built in the Brooklyn Navy Yard, is christened with a bottle of Irish whiskey.

April 1863: The Society for the Protection of Destitute Roman Catholic Children is established in New York City. The Catholic Protectory, as it is commonly known, eventually will shelter some 100,000 impoverished street children before closing its doors in 1938.

May 10, 1863: Thomas "Stonewall" Jackson, Irish American hero of the Confederacy, dies in Virginia of complications from pneumonia after being injured by friendly fire during the Battle of Chancellorsville.

May 18, 1863: Jennie Hodgers, an Irish immigrant who disguised herself as a man and served the Union as Private Albert Cashier, evades capture during the Battle of Vicksburg by disarming a Confederate soldier.

July 1863: Thousands of New Yorkers, mostly Irish Americans, rock the city in four days of riots in protest of the new military draft. President Lincoln sends in federal troops to quell the violence. • Irish American Union Army general George G. Meade defeats Confederate general Robert E. Lee at Gettysburg, Pennsylvania, the effective turning point of the Civil War.

1864: Irish American Isaac Murphy, the only delegate at Arkansas's secession convention to vote to remain in the Union, is named governor of the state. • Irish-born journalist and U.S. Army officer Charles Graham Halpine publishes *Miles O'Reilly: His Book*. This collection of writings about the war is ostensibly created by the fictional O'Reilly, an Irish immigrant Army private of very modest means.

"**Never were men so brave.... Though totally routed, they reaped a harvest of glory. Their brilliant, though hopeless, assaults on our lines excited the hearty applause of our officers and men.**"

—CONFEDERATE GENERAL ROBERT E. LEE, ON THE UNION ARMY'S IRISH BRIGADE AFTER THE BATTLE OF FREDERICKSBURG

Meagher commands the Irish Brigade By the time of the Civil War, Thomas Francis Meagher had already lived a remarkable life. A Waterford native, he was a leading revolutionary in 1848, credited with devising the Irish tricolor. Found guilty of treason and transported to Tasmania, he escaped to the United States. When the war began in 1861, Meagher first raised a company for the 69th New York Regiment, then organized and commanded the Irish Brigade. He led his troops in 18 months of savage fighting. He resigned after his superiors denied him permission to recruit new troops.

IT IS OUR DUTY

Duty and patriotism prompt me to [support the Union]. The Republic, that gave us asylum and an honorable career...is threatened with disruption. It is the duty of every liberty-loving citizen to prevent such a calamity at all hazards. Above all it is the duty of us Irish citizens, who aspire to establish a similar form of government in our native land. It is not only our duty to America, but also to Ireland. We could not hope to succeed in our effort to make Ireland a Republic without the moral and material aid of the liberty-loving citizens of these United States.

—GENERAL THOMAS FRANCIS MEAGHER, COMMANDER OF THE UNION ARMY'S IRISH BRIGADE, 1861

The Irish Brigade at Gettysburg After more than a year of bloody fighting, the Irish Brigade arrived at Gettysburg with 530 men, only one-fifth its original complement. On July 2, 1863, the midpoint of the three-day battle, the brigade was ordered to attack Confederates who had taken a rocky hill near part of the battleground called the Wheatfield. After receiving a general absolution from their Roman Catholic chaplain, the Irish troops advanced. They forced the Southerners to retreat, but they soon found themselves about to be surrounded and captured. The brigade escaped, but it suffered nearly 200 more casualties.

Meade prevails at Gettysburg

George Gordon Meade was the great-grandson of an Irishman who arrived in Philadelphia from County Limerick in the 1700s. A career soldier, Meade was serving in the North's Army of the Potomac in 1863 when his moment arrived. Meade was abruptly appointed commander of the army as it pursued Robert E. Lee's Confederates into Pennsylvania. The armies collided at Gettysburg, and Meade chose to dig in and defend the strong position that his troops had seized early in the three-day battle. His tough, unyielding leadership was vital to the Union victory.

Gilmore's Civil War classic Perhaps the best-known song to emerge from the Civil War was "When Johnny Comes Marching Home," a work by County Galway native Patrick Sarsfield Gilmore. A close cousin to the bitter Irish ballad "Johnny I Hardly Knew Ye," Gilmore's song—which celebrated the service of Northern soldiers and sailors—became popular in the South, too. Beyond the creation of a single memorable song, Gilmore was renowned as a bandleader, showman, and musical innovator.

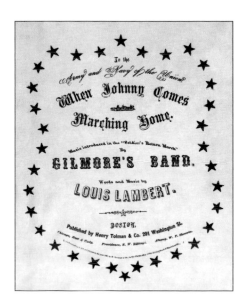

The Draft Riots

The New York City draft riots stand as one of the darkest chapters in Irish American history. For four days during the summer of 1863, Irish men and women took to the streets. They burned large sections of the city to the ground and killed more than 100 people. Although the Irish American rioters despised Republican politicians, Protestant reformers, and Federal officials, they targeted another group on their hate list: African Americans. And when the dust cleared, it was largely New York's black residents who had borne the brunt of the explosive violence that gripped the city.

Ever since the 1840s, when the Irish became a significant portion of the population in the U.S., relations between the new immigrants and African Americans had been strained at best. Despite the fact that both groups suffered from racial or ethnic oppression and discrimination, many Irish laborers blamed their black counterparts for lowering wages and breaking strikes. In the industrial centers of the Northeast, such friction between these minority communities at times resulted in racial violence. New York City proved to be a focal point of racial tension, as the Irish forced African Americans out of the Five Points area and often used physical force to keep them out of factory jobs.

During the Civil War, these tensions again rose to the fore. On January 1, 1863, President Abraham Lincoln officially issued the Emancipation Proclamation, which effectively changed the focus of the war from one of preserving the Union to eliminating slavery. Many Irish opposed the emancipation and the abolition of slavery, fearing it would result in black migration to the North and further competition for jobs.

As the war dragged on and the casualties mounted, many Northerners lost faith in the war, resulting in a decline in enlistments. The Federal government responded by passing the nation's first conscription law, requiring that all men ages 18 to 35 enlist their names in the draft lottery. Only those holding high political office—and the few who could find a suitable replacement or pay $300—were eligible for deferments.

When authorities in New York implemented the law in July 1863, working-class men and women—a large portion of whom were Irish—revolted. Initially, they targeted Federal officials and ranking Republican politicians. Soon, however, rioting mobs descended on the city's African American population, whom they blamed for the war and the hated conscription law.

Irish Americans burned blocks of buildings and entire neighborhoods, targeting black-owned businesses and homes. Even the city's Colored Orphan Asylum was looted and torched. Those who attempted to flee the melee were hunted down. Irish American rioters stoned dozens of black people to death and lynched others from lampposts. Some even proceeded to mutilate the dead, cutting off fingers, toes, and other body parts, which they kept as souvenirs.

After four days of virtual anarchy and lawless destruction, Federal troops—many of whom were also Irish American—quelled the rioting. Official counts recorded approximately 100 deaths, but most historians believe that the true figure was much higher. Whatever the body count, the New York City draft riots would prove to be among the worst, most ferocious race riots in American history.

NEW YORK RIOTERS HANGING A NEGRO.

Draft riot lynchings The August 1, 1863, edition of *Harper's Weekly* depicts the lynching of a black laborer by a mob at the outset of the draft riots. An unknown number of African Americans perished in the violence, and many were forced from their homes or fled the city altogether. Irish American rioters lynched many black New Yorkers. *Harper's Weekly* said of the murder pictured here that the mob "danced round their victim, setting fire to his clothes . . . burning him almost to a cinder."

IRISH FURY

At one time there lay at the corner of Twenty Seventh-Street and Seventh Avenue the dead body of a Negro, stripped nearly naked, and around it a collection of Irishmen, absolutely dancing or shouting like wild Indians. Sullivan and Roosevelt Streets are great Negro quarters, and here a Negro was afraid to be seen in the street. . . . Two boarding-houses here were surrounded by a mob, but the lodgers, seeing the coming storm, fled. The desperadoes, finding only the owner left behind, wreaked their vengeance on him, and after beating him unmercifully, broke up the furniture, and then fired the buildings. A German store near by, because it was patronized extensively by Negroes, shared the same fate, after its contents had been distributed among themselves. A Negro barber's shop was next attacked, and the torch applied to it. A Negro lodging-house in the same street next received the visit of these furies, and was soon a mass of ruins. Old men, seventy years of age, and young children, too young to comprehend what it all meant, were cruelly beaten and killed.

—HISTORIAN JOEL TYLER HEADLEY,
ON THE 1863 NEW YORK DRAFT RIOTS

The death of Henry O'Brien At the height of the draft riots, a predominantly Irish American mob set upon Colonel Henry O'Brien (*in dark clothes*), the Irish American commander of a largely Irish regiment that was sent to help put down the violence. At one point, O'Brien ordered his troops to fire artillery into a crowd, and a female bystander and her child were killed. Later, as he returned unaccompanied to his home in uniform, the mob attacked him, beat him to death over a period of several hours, and mutilated his body.

1864: The Collar Laundry Union, the first all-female labor union in the United States, is formed by Kate Mullaney, a young Irish immigrant employed by a Troy, New York, commercial laundry.

May 1864: St. Clair Augustin Mulholland, a County Antrim-born officer with the Irish Brigade, is wounded in battle. He will survive the war with a general's rank and a Congressional Medal of Honor in recognition of his skills on the battlefield.

August 20, 1864: The long-running British satire magazine *Punch* publishes "Something for Paddy," by renowned cartoonist Sir John Tenniel (Lewis Carroll's illustrator). Featuring a statue of Daniel O'Connell telling an Irish migrant that he will "die for the Union," the cartoon is one of several representations of Paddy that Tenniel will create for *Punch*.

October 19, 1864: At the Battle of Cedar Creek, Virginia, Bridget Divers, also known as the "Irish Biddy," manages to evade capture despite finding herself surrounded by Confederates. Bridget is a rare vivandiere, or "Daughter of the Regiment"—a woman who serves alongside men in the war.

November 30, 1864: Confederate major general Patrick Cleburne dies behind enemy lines at the Battle of Franklin. Born in County Cork, Cleburne's battlefield skills earned him the nickname "Stonewall of the West." However, his ethnicity and willingness to emancipate slaves to serve in the Confederate Army hampered his career.

January 1865: With a relatively anemic labor force of just a few hundred Irish, Central Pacific Railroad officials decide to use Chinese immigrants to help speed construction on the transcontinental railroad.

PROVOST GUARD ATTACKING THE RIOTERS

Union troops quell the rioters The draft riots pitted mostly Irish American mobs wielding guns, knives, clubs, and paving stones against New York's small police force and a smattering of soldiers stationed in the city. The authorities' initial response was disorganized, but as the violence intensified, troops were dispatched from the war front in Pennsylvania. In the words of historian James M. McPherson, the Army units "poured volleys into the ranks of the rioters with the same deadly effect they had produced against rebels at Gettysburg." After four days of mayhem, the mobs dispersed.

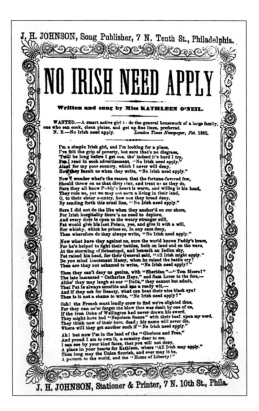

Anti-Irish bigotry Historians disagree about the pervasiveness of "No Irish Need Apply" signs. What can't be denied is the existence of a song by that title. Seeking work, the Irish American immigrant (female in some versions, male in others) comes across the bigoted sign. In the version printed here, the singer notes the absurdity of anti-Irish bigotry, given the "genius" evident in Irish writers such as Samuel Lover. She notes other Irish accomplishments, and she closes with doubts that such bigotry could persist in America, "land of the 'Glorious and Free.'"

The man who wrote "Dixie"

Daniel Decatur Emmett, an Ohio native whose Irish forebearers settled in Virginia before the American Revolution, composed "Dixie" and was a pioneer of minstrel theater. Emmett started his first minstrel troupe in the early 1840s and introduced his most famous song, first titled "I Wish I Was in Dixie's Land," in 1859. The song was popular nationwide, but during the Civil War the South adopted it as an anthem. Emmett wrote many popular songs, including "Old Dan Tucker" and "The Blue-Tail Fly" (also known as "Jimmy Crack Corn"). He also penned poems on Irish themes.

Another round... Part stereotype, part uncomfortable truth, the Irish were associated with drink. This engraving of distinctively Irish characters celebrating St. Patrick's Day in the mid-19th century shows conviviality, not debauchery. Before the famine, Irish temperance crusader Father Theobald Mathew visited the United States to preach the gospel of abstinence to Ireland's exiles. Though he made thousands of converts, immigrants after the famine who were living and working in wretched conditions often embraced what little comforts were available to them.

Stewart's stores make millions Alexander Stewart is considered the father of the modern department store. Born in Northern Ireland, Stewart arrived in New York City in 1823. He used his grandfather's inheritance to invest in a New York City dry goods store. Soon, Stewart's Broadway business was the largest retail store in America. A. T. Stewart and Company branched out to the rest of the country, then the world, opening stores as well as factories and importing operations. It is believed that Stewart earned $1 million a year in the late 1860s.

Notre Dame's Irish connections Although established in 1842 by a French religious community called the Congregation of Holy Cross, the University of Notre Dame du Lac quickly took on an Irish complexion. Many of those who initially joined the order as priests, brothers, and nuns were Irish. Every president of Notre Dame from 1865 to the present has been at least part Irish. Moreover, in its early years, its student body drew heavily from Irish communities in Chicago and northern Indiana. By 1877 most Notre Dame students were the sons of Irish immigrants.

1861-70

March 25, 1865: Confederate spy Robert Kennedy is hanged. He was the ringleader of a November 1864 plot to burn New York to the ground by setting several simultaneous fires in city hotels.

April 9, 1865: Irish American Union general Ulysses S. Grant accepts the surrender of Confederate general Robert E. Lee at Appomattox Courthouse.

April 14, 1865: John Wilkes Booth, an actor and former member of the anti-immigrant "Know-Nothing" party, mortally shoots Abraham Lincoln while the president and his wife watch a production of *Our American Cousin* at Washington, D.C.'s Ford's Theatre.

April 19, 1865: John Conness, an Irish immigrant who ran a successful business purveying dry goods during the California Gold Rush and was appointed to the U.S. Senate in 1863, serves as a pallbearer at the funeral of assassinated president Abraham Lincoln.

June 24, 1865: Father Abram Ryan, a Confederate chaplain for the duration of the Civil War and a son of Irish immigrants, publishes his poem *The Conquered Banner*, which will become an anthem of sorts for the defeated South.

June 30, 1865: Michael O'Laughlin, an Irish American clerk and Confederate veteran, is convicted of conspiracy to assassinate President Lincoln. He will be incarcerated at Fort Jefferson until his death from yellow fever in 1867.

September 15, 1865: With advance notice of a planned insurrection, authorities in Dublin arrest several members of the Fenian Brotherhood, including Jeremiah O'Donovan Rossa, the editor of the nationalist paper *The Irish People*.

A Confederate hero The Civil War transformed Thomas Jonathan Jackson from obscure professor to military legend. The great-grandson of an Ulsterman, Jackson grew up in Virginia, went to West Point, and served in the Mexican-American War. Afterward, he taught science and military strategy at Virginia Military Institute. He joined the Confederate Army in 1861 and earned the sobriquet "Stonewall" at his first engagement, Bull Run. The general is still celebrated for his tactical brilliance, aggressiveness, and ability to inspire his men to astonishing feats of marching and fighting. He died in 1863 when he was shot accidentally by his own troops at Chancellorsville.

Dying for the Union In this cartoon, famous "liberator" Daniel O'Connell scolds a simian Irishman. "You're goin' to die for the Union," says O'Connell, referring to the U.S. Civil War, in which so many Irish immigrants fought and died. The figure on the left, wearing a Lincoln mask, is symbolic of death. While Catholics were gaining political rights in mid-19th century Ireland, they still migrated to the United States.

Economic well-being was more important than political rights. Many Irish Catholics simply believed they could earn higher wages in America.

The Photos of Mathew Brady

In 1862 the U.S. Civil War had entered its second year. However, to residents of bustling Manhattan, the bloody battlefields of Maryland seemed like a world far away.

That changed when acclaimed New York photographer Mathew Brady opened his exhibit "The Dead of Antietem" in his Manhattan studio. The portraits from the battle-front shocked viewers, revolutionized photography, and forever changed the way citizens would experience war.

Brady was born in upstate New York in 1823. He claimed his parents, Andrew and Julia, were Irish immigrants, though official family records are sketchy. After relocating to Manhattan, Brady became a student of Samuel Morse, the telegraph inventor who was also a pioneer in the fledgling field of photography.

By the 1850s, Brady was recognized as a master photographer. Senators, writers, and presidents flocked to his Manhattan studio. When the Civil War broke out, Brady was compelled to document it. "A spirit in my feet said 'go,' and I went," he said.

Brady and a team of about 20 photographers captured gruesome, and mundane, images of the war. Though now

A Brady photograph of a wounded soldier

considered invaluable, there was not much demand for Brady's shocking photos after the grueling conflict. Brady made only enough money to pay off his considerable debts. He died in 1896, broke and obscure.

Irish fed up with war, Lincoln An election-year brawl in the New York slum neighborhood of Five Points exemplifies the Irish community's loyalty to the Democratic Party and its hostility to President Lincoln and the Republicans as the Civil War dragged on. Irish New Yorkers became disillusioned after the heavy casualties their volunteers had suffered, and they were bitterly opposed to both the draft and Lincoln's Emancipation Proclamation. In the 1864 vote, they supported General George B. McClellan, whom they believed would bring the war to an early end. Some Irish precincts gave McClellan more than 90 percent of the vote.

A Nebraska pioneer Edward Creighton was the son of Irish immigrants and a pioneer in the fields of technology and education. Born in Ohio in 1820, Creighton later settled in Nebraska. He and his brother John oversaw the construction of the first major telegraph system in the American West. Edward later became a top executive with the Pacific Telegraph Company. Creighton's wealth was eventually used to open Creighton University in Omaha, the first free Catholic college in the United States.

Kennedy tries to torch New York Confederate captain Robert Cobb Kennedy is pictured sometime before he was hanged as a spy in March 1865. Kennedy, a former West Pointer from a wealthy Irish American family in Louisiana, was part of a team of southern "incendiaries" who crossed the border from Canada to turn New York City into "a dazzling conflagration." On November 25, 1864, Kennedy set fire to P. T. Barnum's American Museum and several hotels. Those blazes, as well as about 10 set by his cohorts, were quickly doused. Kennedy escaped to Canada but was captured in Detroit a month later.

The wisdom of Private O'Reilly Private Miles O'Reilly of the 47th New York was the creation and alter ego of Charles Halpine, a County Meath native and Dublin newspaperman who immigrated to New York in 1851. Halpine began the Civil War as a member of the Irish American 69th New York State Militia, then joined the regular Army. He created Private O'Reilly to voice both serious and satiric comment on the war. Halpine expanded his dispatches into a best-selling book enjoyed by President Lincoln and thousands of others.

Two Union Heroes

On land and sea, in the ranks and in the officer corps, some 150,000 Irish Americans fought to preserve the Union during the Civil War. Arguably, General Philip "Little Phil" Sheridan was the most distinguished Irish American soldier. He rigorously applied his hard-charging, "smash 'em up" tactics on decisive battlefields, including Cedar Creek, Virginia, on October 19, 1864.

After Federal troops had been pushed back, the 5'5" Sheridan rallied his men at Cedar Creek by riding the lines on his huge horse, Rienzi, while telling them they would be back in their camps by nightfall.

Philip Sheridan

Sheridan's victory proved especially timely for Abraham Lincoln's reelection prospects. The general's performance inspired a poem, "Sheridan's Ride," and landed him on the cover of *Harper's Weekly*.

Little Phil's aggressive tactics came up trumps again on April 1, 1865, when he defeated the Confederates at Five Forks, Virginia. This outcome forced the South's evacuation of Petersburg and Richmond. In later years, when Sheridan himself became a presidential prospect, a question arose over his birthplace. Sheridan claimed he was born in Albany, New York, but others said Ireland. Of course, no foreign-born person could become U.S. president.

Another Irishman, Dublin's Stephen Rowan, rose to prominence in the U.S. Navy. Years earlier, Rowan had led the landing party that captured San Diego in the Mexican-American War. During the Civil War, he spearheaded efforts to relieve Fort Sumter. Commander Rowan's combat achievements were recognized, as he earned simultaneous promotions to captain and commodore in July 1862. Rowan commanded the *New Ironsides* in operations against Charleston, South Carolina, and he also led U.S. naval forces in the North Carolina Sounds.

Irish Americans fought as gallantly as anyone to preserve the Union. Thousands sacrificed their lives, and Congressional Medals of Honor were awarded to more than 120 Irish-born Americans.

Wells's revolting comparisons

Depictions of the Irish as animals were not restricted to nativist political cartoons. Samuel Wells, a then-respected author in the mid-1800s, argued that the physical characteristics of the Irish

could be used to explain their supposed inferiority. In the illustration above we see a haggard Irishwoman contrasting poorly with Anglo-Saxon icon Florence Nightingale. At right, a page from Wells's 1852 book, *Comparative Physiognomy*, which compares "paddies" to dogs, attempted to scientifically outline this anti-Irish theory. "Character is indicated by the features of the face," Wells claimed.

November 11, 1865: James Stephens, founder of the Irish Republican Brotherhood, is arrested for plotting to foment rebellion. He will escape prison within two weeks and remain in exile in Paris until 1891.

1865–90: After the Civil War, Irish county societies develop, changing the social landscape for Irish immigrants and Americans in larger U.S. cities. Such clubs as the Sligo Men and the County Longford Men provide both a connection to the homeland as well as a ready-made social network in the United States.

April–July 1866: Members of the Fenian Brotherhood, a group of Irish nationalists, engage in raids on Canada in an effort to encourage British colonialists to pull out of Ireland. However, the Fenians are turned away by British forces.

July 1866: Irish-born U.S. naval officer Stephen C. Rowan is promoted to rear admiral following his illustrious Civil War service. Rowan patrolled the mid-Atlantic for the Union, engaging in dozens of key operations.

March 5, 1867: Riots in counties Cork and Limerick mark the day of the abortive Fenian Uprising, which ends before it begins because British authorities discover the plot. Some 200 Fenian leaders are arrested.

June 20, 1867: In New York, Irish nationalists found the Napper Tandy Club, a new Irish republican organization created to fill the void left by the defunct Fenians. By 1870 the group will rename itself Clan na Gael.

November 23, 1867: The so-called "Manchester Martyrs" are executed in Manchester, England. These three Fenians were sentenced to death by hanging for killing a police officer. The murder occurred as they were helping two of their Fenian brothers escape prison.

The Irish and mental illness Impoverished Irish immigrants were blamed for many social ills in the mid-19th century, so it should not be surprising that an inordinate number of them were believed to be insane. More than 70 percent of the patients at New York's Blackwell Island asylum were immigrants; two-thirds of these immigrants were from Ireland. Some historians now believe that authorities used dubious evidence to institutionalize the Irish and other poor immigrants. Irish American journalist Nellie Bly eventually exposed poor conditions at Blackwell Island.

Shantytowns in Central Park Seneca Village was a largely Irish and African American settlement in what is today Central Park. Such immigrant shantytowns were not uncommon on the outskirts of cities in the 1850s and 1860s. The residents were often viewed with scorn. In 1856 *The New-York Daily Times* ran an article about a shanty's "Celtic occupants" who resembled "hogs and goats." Some shanties, however, had a distinct social order, complete with places of worship and cemeteries. Future Tammany Hall power brokers George Washington Plunkitt and Richard Croker grew up in shantytowns.

HEAD-QUARTERS OF THE FENIAN BROTHERHOOD, UNION SQUARE, NEW YORK.

Fenian headquarters With New York City's large Irish population, it is fitting that the Fenian movement started there. Founders such as John O'Mahony and Michael Doheny hoped to keep the spirit of the 1848 Young Ireland Rebellion alive. Many Fenians wanted independence from Great Britain by any means necessary. They understood that the Irish in other nations—especially America—could play a key role. Irish immigrants to America had received valuable military training during the U.S. Civil War; the Fenians hoped to use this expertise against Great Britain.

"Freedom to Ireland" Eugène Delacroix's famous painting *Liberty Leading the People* became an icon of the French revolutionary movement. Similarly, the American printmaking firm Currier & Ives (famous for their Christmas pictures) created this strong female character to personify "Freedom to Ireland" (1866). With her dress and crown festooned with shamrocks, the woman brandishes a sword while waving a Fenian flag. This image's accompanying text reads, in part: "From Erin's soil the Saxon foe/In shame shall be forever driven." These words and this image reflected the fierce Fenian opposition to British rule in Ireland.

Leader of American Fenians John O'Mahony was one of the most important Fenian leaders. A native of Limerick, he was involved in the failed uprising of 1848. He escaped Ireland and went to the U.S. in the early 1850s. A Celtic scholar, O'Mahony is credited with naming the Fenians after the warriors of Irish mythology, specifically Finn McCool. Irish revolution seemed to be in O'Mahony's blood: His father and other family members had participated in the Irish Rebellion of 1798. O'Mahony led the Fenians in America while James Stephens organized operations in Ireland.

Fenian rebel Like many other Fenians, John Savage was inspired by the 1848 Young Ireland Rebellion. Savage was a talented writer and artist who had won the silver medal at the Royal Dublin Society Art School. However, his revolutionary writings earned the wrath of British authorities, and he fled to the U.S. He worked at newspapers and magazines in New York and Washington, D.C., and he also wrote plays, history books, and political polemics. During the U.S. Civil War, he joined the 69th Regiment. He later served as a top Fenian officer and fund-raiser.

1868: William Gladstone is named British prime minister. Almost from the beginning, he will work to effect change beneficial to the cause of Irish independence.

April 6, 1868: The Workingmen's Benevolent Association, effectively the first coal miners union, is founded in Schuylkill County, Pennsylvania, under the leadership of Irish-born John Siney.

April 7, 1868: Irish-born nationalist and journalist Thomas D'Arcy McGee is assassinated in Ottawa while serving as a member of the Canadian Parliament.

1869: Political cartoonist Thomas Nast launches his first of many attacks on Tammany chief and political power broker William "Boss" Tweed. • Irish American playwright Augustin Daly takes over management of New York City's Fifth Avenue Theater. • The British Parliament passes an act that disestablishes the Church of Ireland. This act effectively removes the Anglican Church as the official state church of Ireland, and relieves the largely Catholic nation of any obligation to pay tithes for its support.

March 4, 1869: Another Irish American rises to the highest office in the land, as General Ulysses S. Grant delivers his inaugural address on the east front of the United States Capitol.

May 10, 1869: The Union Pacific Railroad and the Central Pacific Railroad are linked together at Promontory Summit, Utah, thus completing the transcontinental railroad.

December 9, 1869: The Knights of Labor, the auspicious labor union that will initiate the Labor Day holiday, is founded by a consortium of nine Philadelphia tailors.

The Fenians' invasion The Fenians' first significant military excursion came in 1866, when soldiers led by Colonel John O'Neill invaded Canada, occupying Fort Erie. Fenian leaders hoped to secure lands in Canada (then a British territory) and inspire other Irish uprisings. Their ultimate goal was an independent Irish Republic. By early June, the Battle of Ridgeway raged, costing the Fenians as well as British Canadian forces fewer than 10 soldiers each. Because the Canadians retreated, the Fenians considered it a victory. But the invasion of Canada ultimately failed. President Andrew Johnson wanted to maintain neutrality, and the U.S. Army seized Fenian weapons and ammunition.

THE FENIAN RAID AT PIGEON HILL

[T]hey at once started for Pigeon Hill. When within half a mile of it, the Fenians were found in considerable numbers. The Rifle Brigade advanced from the North and the Fenians retired toward the border firing a few shots. The half Battery of Armstrong guns unlimbered and prepared for action, the 25th Regiment being held in reserve. The Royal Guides galloped to the lines with a view of cutting them off. In this they were successful, for the Fenians were soon seen in their rear, behind a barricade which the Fenians had erected. The Guides charged toward them, jumped the barricade (many of the troopers being members of the Montreal Hunt), and fell upon them pell-mell, sword in hand, and scattered them in all directions. The Guides captured sixteen prisoners, the rest were chased to the border, when the pursuit ceased. Pigeon Hill, Cook's Corner and Frelighsburg were then occupied by our troops. All the Missisquoi frontier is now clear of Fenians and all important points are strongly held by our troops.

—FRANCIS WAYLAND CAMPBELL, DEPUTY SURGEON GENERAL OF THE ROYAL REGIMENT OF CANADIAN INFANTRY IN 1898, DESCRIBING EVENTS OF JUNE 9, 1866

Money for the Fenian cause In an effort to raise money, the Fenians issued these bonds in the United States in 1865. The money raised through bond sales was used to pay operating expenses and finance planned military actions, such as the invasion of Canada. Funds were also used to carry out smaller-scale attacks on British interests in England and its colonies around the world.

THE FENIAN FOLLY.

The Invasion of Canada an Acknowledged Failure.

Sensation Reports About the Liberation of Fenian Prisoners.

Absurd Rumor that Gen. Sweeney has Captured Kingston.

The press reports on the Fenian "folly" Though it was still a time of deep anti-Irish sentiment in the United States, the Fenian invasion of Canada was generally seen as "folly," rather than symbolic of a larger threat. *The New York Times* report on June 5, 1866, does make reference to "dark hints and surmises of another invasion." But what is most prominent in this and many other press accounts is a barely contained glee that the Fenian invasion did not only fail, but seemed to do so in particularly inglorious fashion.

Seward doesn't stop the plot
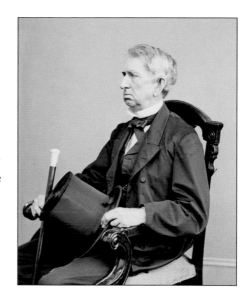
U.S. Secretary of State William Seward initially seemed sympathetic to the Fenians. He did not interfere with their efforts to stockpile weapons, recruit, or even drill in public. Seward, it turned out, had his own agenda. He harbored ill feelings toward the British for their neutral stance during the U.S. Civil War. Following the Fenian invasion of Canada, U.S. officials assisted the British by closing the Canadian border, seizing Fenian weapons, and rounding up their officers. A subsequent Fenian invasion in 1870 was dealt with the same way.

St. Patrick's Day riot The riot on St. Patrick's Day, 1867, drew condemnation of New York's Irish Americans—such as in this Thomas Nast cartoon, which depicts participants as drunken, simian brutes. The riot began after a minor dispute between parade marshals and a teamster escalated into pitched battles with police. Thirty-three officers were injured, including 18 who were seriously hurt. The incident demonstrated the ongoing tension between New York's Irish community and authorities, a tension that flared again in the Orange Day riots of 1870 and '71, in which approximately 70 people were killed.

Mullanphy lends a hand The Mullanphy Emigrant Home in St. Louis was built in 1867 thanks to the generosity of Bryan Mullanphy, an eccentric first-generation Irish American who served as the city's mayor from 1847 to 1848. His father, John, was born in County Fermanagh and made a fortune in the cotton industry during the War of 1812. Although John disinherited his son after a quarrel, Bryan managed to receive a sizable stake in the family fortune, and he endowed a fund to aid immigrants. The Emigrant Home still stands today near the city's famous Gateway Arch.

Large numbers flock to U.S. Despite the Civil War, immigration continued at a high rate in the 1860s, when nearly a half-million Irish migrated to the United States. Economic problems in Ireland were clearly systemic rather than temporary, so immigration seemed the best way to make a better life. Irish immigrants faced brutal conditions in the U.S. Many died in the Civil War, and after the conflict thousands of Irish-born men labored to build the railroads. Immigrants at least felt at home in the big cities, many of which had Irish-born populations in excess of 30 percent.

"Runners" prey on immigrants As soon as they arrived in the United States, immigrants were often exploited by pickpockets and other streetwise criminals. The hustle and bustle of the port as well as the immigrant's desperate state often made them easy prey for so-called "immigrant runners." Some runners affected an Irish accent, spoke Gaelic, or were Irish themselves. Some merely steered immigrants to one business or another, but others outright stole from the newcomers. This was such a problem that at one point New York State officials created the Board of Commissioners of Immigration in an effort to make the city safer for newly arrived immigrants.

Irish, Chinese "devour" Uncle Sam After the Civil War, Chinese immigrants joined the Irish as targets for American nativist fears. The paranoia is made explicit in this caricature from the 1860s. According to the satirist, the Roman Catholic Irish were devouring Protestant America. He also insists that the wave of new Chinese arrivals—who were lured to the U.S. by the California Gold Rush and later by the demand for labor to build the transcontinental railroad—would overwhelm both America and the Irish. The Irish themselves, led by County Cork native Denis Kearney and the Workingmen's Party, later played a central part in agitating for laws to curtail Chinese immigration.

"Paddies" toil on the railroads "Poor Paddy works on the railway" was a famous song lyric that reflected the preponderance of Irish laborers on American rail lines. During and after the U.S. Civil War, there was an explosion of railroad work. Most prominently, construction of America's first transcontinental railroad—the Union Pacific—began. Working alongside Chinese laborers (who were paid the lowest wages of all), the Irish helped build America's first coast-to-coast train line. At one point, Central Pacific laborers laid down 10 miles of track in a single day.

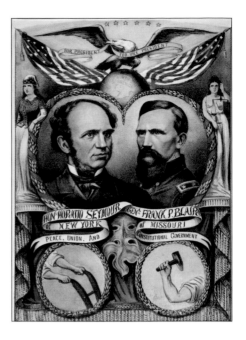

Seymour runs for president New York governor Horatio Seymour was supported by many Irish American political leaders. During the Civil War, Seymour opposed Lincoln's proposed draft, and he teamed with Tammany Hall leader William Tweed to ease tensions following the infamous draft riots of 1863. When Seymour became the Democratic nominee for president in 1868, his enemies painted him as a friend of New York's violent and corrupt Irish community. Seymour and running mate Frank P. Blair eventually lost to Republican Ulysses S. Grant.

Nasty position The racial and ethnic politics of post-Civil War America are illustrated in this 1868 image by cartoonist Thomas Nast. Nast accuses an urban Irishman (*left, with "5 Points" written on his hat*) as well as a capitalist (*right*) and a Confederate (*center*) of uniting to oppress African Americans. Nast's position on African American voting rights was highly progressive. However, his sympathies did not extend to Irish Catholic Democrats. Nast's anti-Catholicism was well known, as was his penchant for depicting the Irish as violent apes.

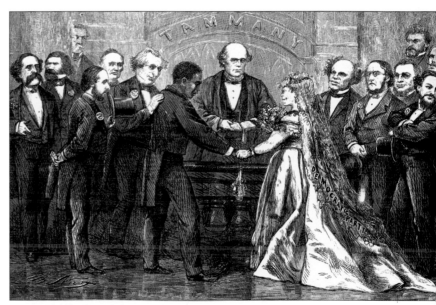

Interracial Marriage In this provocative cartoon, Thomas Nast depicts a symbolic union between a black man and an Irish woman. Presiding over the wedding is Salmon P. Chase, once a prominent Republican who supported the abolition of slavery. In 1868 Chase sought to become president as a Democrat. Nast viewed the Democrats as the party of slavery and simian Irish Catholics. He may not have known that in certain enclaves, such as New York's Five Points, interracial relationships were not uncommon.

1870: The New York City Fire Department, a largely Irish American brotherhood, is reorganized as it exists today—as a professional department under the auspices of the City of New York. • British prime minister William Gladstone's government pushes through a Land Act that seeks to improve the lot of Irish tenant farmers. Though largely weak and irrelevant, the act represents a dramatic shift in Irish landlord-tenant relations and will presage more effective legislation in the 1880s. • Washington, D.C.'s Corcoran Gallery of Art is chartered to house the personal art collection of Irish American financier William Corcoran.

May 14, 1870: Michael Davitt, secretary of the Irish Republican Brotherhood, is arrested in London. He will be tried and sentenced to 15 years in prison for organizing weapons shipments to Ireland. He will serve less than half that time before being granted parole.

May 25, 1870: The Fenian Brotherhood again attempts a Canadian invasion in hopes of swaying British policy in Ireland. However, the Canadians have advance notice of the planned attack, which is easily thwarted.

July 12, 1870: In New York City, a group of Irish Catholics interrupts a Protestant observance of William of Orange's victory at the Battle of the Boyne. The Catholics attack the marchers as they parade up Eighth Avenue. Eight people die in the ensuing riot.

September 1870: Irish-born journalist Patrick Ford founds *The Irish World* in New York City. He will serve as editor of the publication until his death in 1913.

"[The Irish] are mostly found...in the worst portions of the large cities, where they compete with the Negroes—between whom and themselves there is an inveterate dislike—for the most degrading employments."

—REPORT BY THE ASSOCIATION FOR IMPROVING THE CONDITION OF THE POOR, 1860

Living in dark, dirty basements An 1869 engraving highlights the plight of many Irish Americans in New York after the Civil War. Hundreds of thousands of Irish arrived in New York City in the decades following the famine. The influx of new residents, many destitute, into an already crowded city gave rise to notorious slums. The poorest new immigrants settled in shantytowns in the city's rapidly expanding margins or crowded into dark, filthy basements. By the end of the war, 20,000 people lived in cellar quarters like those pictured here.

McGee's rise and fall Thomas D'Arcy McGee, born in Louth in northeastern Ireland in 1825, became a prominent speaker and journalist before he turned 20. Daniel O'Connell referred to McGee's work as "the inspired utterances of a young exiled Irish boy in America." In the late 1850s, McGee settled in Montreal, where he was elected to the Canadian Parliament. His powerful speaking abilities brought him nearly as much attention as the radical shift in his political views. In his final years, he denounced Irish revolution, particularly the Fenian movement. This change cost McGee his life. In 1868 he was assassinated by an Irish former supporter.

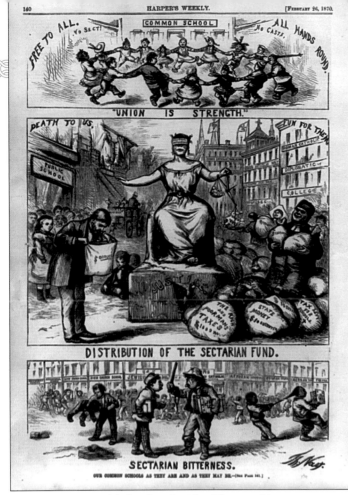

DISTRIBUTION OF THE SECTARIAN FUND.

SECTARIAN BITTERNESS.

OUR COMMON SCHOOLS AS THEY ARE AND AS THEY MAY BE—[See Page 141.]

Public vs. parochial schools The Thomas Nast cartoon "Our Common Schools as They Are and as They May Be" was published in *Harper's Weekly* in 1870. New York City was the focal point of a battle over public funding of parochial schools, and the influential Nast weighed in strongly on the side of denying them government money. The cartoon presents an idealized vision of social harmony in public schools (*top*); vilifies Roman Catholic clergy (*center*); and forecasts sectarian conflict—with Irish Catholics front and center—if religious schools got state support.

Gladstone supports the Irish

As British prime minister (four times from 1868 to 1894), William Gladstone was generally sympathetic to the Irish. He supported laws that protected farmers and Catholics. The main issue during Gladstone's tenure was land rights. He saw the rise of the Fenians and the Land League as signs that the Irish might turn to violence if reforms were not implemented. That's what happened in 1882, when two government officials were killed by a mob in Dublin's Phoenix Park. The incident shocked the British and showed that even sympathetic leaders could not solve the Irish-British conflict over land policy.

A second Fenian invasion *Punch* cartoonist Joseph Swain exploited anti-Fenian sentiment following that organization's attempt to invade Canada in 1870. In this drawing, a brawny Canadian soldier boots an Irish Fenian back to the United States. American sympathy for the Fenians is symbolized by President Ulysses S. Grant (*left*), though in reality the U.S. government actually assisted British efforts to curtail Fenian activity. As was often the case in mid-19th century political cartoons, the Irishman resembles an ape.

Perceived threats on Ireland's farms Throughout the 1870s, tension between farmers and landlords in Ireland led to threats, agitation, and violence. Often, landlords would receive threatening letters signed by "Rory of the Hills." This 1870 cartoon depicts landowners cowering before the Irish agitator, who is fashioned after Caliban, the monstrous slave from Shakespeare's *The Tempest*. "I am in this country observing the conduct and tyranny of agents and landlords," an 1879 letter from Rory to a Sligo land agent reads. "Take heed for yourself on the road . . . for you will be killed."

Machine Politics

1871–1880

The Irish who settled in the great cities of Chicago, Boston, Baltimore, Philadelphia, and San Francisco—along with such smaller cities as Scranton, Pennsylvania, and Butte, Montana—did more than transform the face of urban America. They changed the way these cities governed themselves.

The Irish in America did not invent machine politics, nor did they invent mass democracy. They surely were not the first to recognize the sheer power of numbers in a nation committed to democratic rule. That said, who can deny that the Irish in America saw their opportunities and that they took them? And why wouldn't they?

In the decades just after the Civil War, Irish Americans worked their way up from unskilled labor to crafts and trades. Such projects as the construction of the Brooklyn Bridge in New York and the centennial exhibit in Philadelphia in 1876 attracted a large percentage of Irish American skilled workers. Elsewhere, Irish men worked as carpenters and machinists while Irish women—who came to America in numbers equal to and sometimes surpassing men—found jobs as domestics in upper-middle-class households. Moreover, Irish American professionals were emerging as civic leaders, as was the case with George Galvin, a surgeon who helped found the Boston Emergency Hospital in the late 19th century.

But it was not economic power that defined the Irish American experience after 1865. It was political power—the power of the Irish American vote, courted so assiduously by existing machines and factions. These groups

Thomas Nast, the famous German American cartoonist, depicts the Tammany Hall machine of New York City as a dangerous, untrustworthy jungle beast. According to Nast, Tammany Hall controlled the Democratic Party. In this 1870 cartoon, it devours a Republican lamb that tried to collaborate with it.

cared more about the preservation of power than they did about religious differences or crude bigotry.

The 1870s and 1880s saw Irish American Catholics—only a generation removed from the famine in Ireland and battles with nativists in the New World—gaining high political office. (Of course, political power was nothing new for Irish American Protestants, as the example of Andrew Jackson demonstrates.) In 1880 New York City elected its first Irish Catholic immigrant mayor, William R. Grace, founder of a colossal shipping company. Five years later, Hugh O'Brien became the first Irish immigrant to be elected mayor of Boston.

Then there was the template created by "Honest" John Kelly, who became the first Irish Catholic to lead Tammany Hall, the all-powerful clubhouse that controlled New York City's Democratic Party. Beginning with Kelly, the Irish dominated Tammany for decades, fashioning a legacy of social welfare, political pragmatism, and egregious corruption. Tammany created a model for the urban machines of Kansas City, San Francisco, Chicago, and other cities in the late 19th and early 20th centuries.

Kelly, a onetime congressman, took over Tammany in 1871 in the wake of a historic political corruption scandal. The old boss, William Tweed, was driven from power after press reports revealed that he and his Tammany allies—including Peter Sweeney and Richard Connolly—stole millions through graft and bribery. The collapse of Tweed and his minions created a sensation and, not surprisingly, inspired calls for reform.

According to this Thomas Nast cartoon from 1872, Tammany Hall leader Boss Tweed was a political giant and beyond the reach of the law. In fact, Tweed was convicted and sent to prison. He managed to escape, but he was found in Spain and brought back. He died while incarcerated in 1878.

Honest John Kelly answered the call. During his 15 years as Tammany's leader (he died in 1886), Kelly purged the machine of its excesses and reorganized what was a loose confederacy of allies into a genuine political machine. He developed a network of patronage and a system of outreach that connected voters with their government. Kelly's intentions, of course, were not philanthropic: If the party helped you land a job as a firefighter, or helped your son escape a night in jail, it expected your support on election day. This trade-off horrified reformers, but such pragmatic machine politicians as Kelly—and later bosses such as the Pendergasts of Kansas City, Charlie Buckley of the Bronx, and Frank Hague of Jersey City—thought the arrangement benefited everyone.

Meanwhile, Irish Americans came to dominate the Catholic hierarchy just as surely as they took over urban politics. Not surprisingly, the two fields often intersected. John Kelly, for example, was married to the niece of New York's Cardinal John McCloskey, successor to Archbishop John Hughes and a formidable character in his own right.

Some religious leaders tried to frame political debates within an American Catholic context. Cardinal McCloskey and Bishop Bernard McQuaid of Rochester, New York, were conservative, while Cardinal James Gibbons of Baltimore and Archbishop John Ireland of St. Paul were more progressive. Whatever their disagreements, they all understood that the rise of the Irish to political power had implications for Catholics trying to negotiate a place in American civic life.

As the 20th century approached, Irish Americans were firmly ensconced in city halls from east to west. It was, by any measure, an astonishing and rapid journey from the fetid slums of Philadelphia and Boston to the statehouse and Capitol Hill. How to account for it? There's a lively debate over that question. U.S. senator Daniel Patrick Moynihan, who knew something about politics, suggested that Irish immigrants in the middle of the 19th century carried with them memories of Daniel O'Connell's well-organized mass protest movements. They understood how to organize and how to lead. But novelist and essayist Peter Quinn, whose father was a congressman in the 1940s, disagrees, suggesting that the rise to power took place in an American context. He credits existing machines for their outreach to Irish immigrants and their children.

Whatever the reason for their success, the Irish surely understood a very basic rule of politics: Power is protection. Power can protect a family from starvation and homelessness. Power can protect the unemployed, the widowed, the orphaned.

The Irish had little use for the reformer's concerns about the ways in which power corrupts. They had been powerless once before, and they had starved. They would not allow that to happen again.

After the fall of Boss Tweed, "Honest" John Kelly became the leader of Tammany Hall. In contrast to Tweed, Kelly was a low-key, respectable figure. He ran Tammany as a well-organized hierarchy and had complete control of nominations. It was during his reign that Tammany was labeled a "machine."

January 1871: Irish revolutionary leader John Devoy arrives in America. He was exiled from Ireland following his release from prison, where he had served five years of a 15-year sentence for treason.

July 12, 1871: At least 60 people die when, for the second year in a row, violence breaks out at an Orangemen's rally in New York City.

August 1871: Irish American author Henry James sees the first installment of his first novel, *Watch and Ward*, printed in serial form in the pages of *Atlantic Monthly*.

October 8, 1871: A fire begins in a barn on Chicago's West Side. It will burn for more than a day, scorch about four square miles of the city, and claim the lives of some 300 residents. Though a reporter will blame the conflagration on a cow owned by Irish American Catherine O'Leary, he will later confess to fabricating the story.

October 27, 1871: William "Boss" Tweed, head of Tammany Hall, the New York City Democratic Party power base, is arrested and charged with multiple counts of embezzlement for stealing tens of millions of dollars from the City of New York.

1872: British prime minister William Gladstone ushers the Ballot Act through Parliament. The act, which mandates the secret ballot for both general and local elections, prevents landowners from bullying tenants into voting against their interests. • William James, Irish American physician, pioneer in the field of psychology, and brother of novelist Henry James, joins the faculty at Harvard College. • In a race between two candidates of Irish descent, incumbent Ulysses S. Grant defeats New York Republican and newspaper editor Horace Greeley to earn a second term in the White House.

> **"His untiring activity, his imposing physique and his union of cruelty, shrewdness and audacity had raised him in fifteen years from the position of chair maker to that of multimillionaire dictator of the city."**
>
> —HISTORIAN ALLAN NEVINS, ON BOSS TWEED

The "boss" of New York The most notorious boss of Democratic machine politics was William "Boss" Tweed of New York's Tammany Hall. Of Scots-Irish ancestry, Tweed allied himself with the growing number of Irish immigrants in post-famine New York, and in doing so he controlled that city's politics in the 1860s. His influence rested on three sources: his ability to provide patronage in the form of jobs and money to struggling immigrants; his control of the nomination process, whereby only his men got on the ballot; and a Tammany organization that made sure immigrants voted, whether they were citizens or not. His power enabled him to line his pockets with public money.

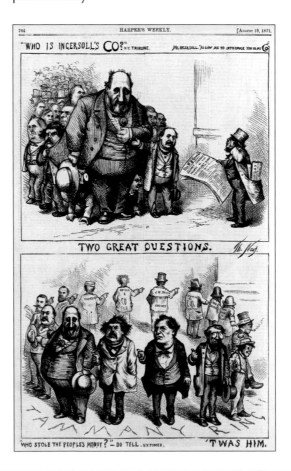

The Tweed scandal Through the 1860s, William "Boss" Tweed and his City Hall henchmen milked the City of New York of anywhere from $30 million to $200 million. In 1871 a disgruntled bookkeeper provided evidence of their fraudulent activities to *The New York Times*, which then exposed the Tweed Ring in a series of articles. Perhaps more devastating to Tweed than the articles were the Thomas Nast cartoons in *Harper's Weekly* (such as this one), which graphically portrayed Tweed's corruption. Tweed himself said, "I don't care so much what the papers say about me. My constituents don't know how to read, but they can't help seeing them damned pictures." Convicted of his crimes, Tweed died in jail in 1878.

The Man Who Slew the Tammany Tiger

Although often caricatured as architects and beneficiaries of corrupt big-city machine politics, Irish Americans played an indispensable part in destroying the most powerful machine chieftain of them all, William "Boss" Tweed of New York's Tammany Hall. Tweed, a chair maker's son who had been apprenticed as a chair maker himself, was a larger-than-life figure who by the late 1860s enjoyed unchallenged control of New York City's governmental institutions. At the same time, his personal fortune had grown to staggering proportions.

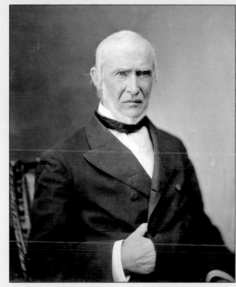

Charles O'Conor

Outrage with Tweed and the corrupt system over which he presided took shape in an 1871 media campaign against the Tammany Hall boss and his cronies. *Harper's Weekly* cartoonist Thomas Nast and *The New York Times* spearheaded the attacks. The crusade made little headway until two Irish American insiders came forward with proof. James O'Brien, a Tweed associate, and Matthew O'Rourke, a newly hired city bookkeeper, each provided details of the colossal scale of the Tweed Ring's thefts. The revelations prompted a committee of leading citizens, joined by the state attorney general, to designate lawyer Charles O'Conor to lead the legal attack on the Tweed Ring.

Charles, the son of the man who had founded New York's first Irish American newspaper, *The Shamrock*, was a vocal apologist for slavery. He was also incorruptible. Stirred by a thirst for "civic vengeance, to punish thieves, and make them suffer visibly for their crimes," O'Conor recruited a panel of judges and attorneys, both Republicans and Democrats, and launched the civil and criminal cases that would smash the Tweed Ring and put its corrupt leader in jail.

Tweed eventually confessed to having engineered a system that siphoned tens and perhaps hundreds of millions of dollars from the public treasury. He died in a New York City jail cell in 1878 at age 55. O'Conor had retired from the case by then, apparently disappointed that the state's effort had failed to bring Tweed's principal lieutenants to justice. He died at his home on Nantucket Island, Massachusetts, in 1884.

Blaming Mrs. O'Leary Within days of the outbreak of the Great Chicago Fire of 1871, stories circulated that it had been started by a cow, owned by Mrs. Catherine O'Leary, that kicked over a kerosene lantern. Though a police and fire department investigation later concluded that the cause of the fire was unknown, prejudice against the Irish at the time made Mrs. O'Leary an easy scapegoat. Illustrations that appeared in the press usually depicted Mrs. O'Leary in an unflattering way. This one gives her the rough, simian-like features that were the staple of anti-Irish illustrators.

1872: *The Catholic Review* rolls off the presses, as it launches its 26-year run as the voice of the Catholic Church in New York.

1873: Hoping to sabotage the Workingmen's Benevolent Association (WBA), Philadelphia & Reading Railroad president Franklin Gowen consults with the legendary Pinkerton Detective Agency. The resulting infiltration of the WBA will uncover the existence of a secretive organization of Irish labor activists that calls itself the Molly Maguires. • Irish American attorney Charles O'Conor serves as prosecutor at William "Boss" Tweed's first embezzlement trial, offering his services *pro bono* to the State of New York. • The Irish American outlaws of the James-Younger Gang, including brothers Jesse and Frank James, commit the first of their storied train robberies.

November 1873: Ireland's Home Government Association, committed to nonviolent, constitutional separation from English rule, gives rise to the Home Rule League political party.

1874: Thanks in no small part to the 1872 Ballot Act, the fledgling Home Rule League gains 60 parliamentary seats in the United Kingdom's general election. • Three years after the Tweed scandal, and under the leadership of "Honest" John Kelly, Tammany Hall regains its relevance on the New York City political scene. • Kate Kennedy, a San Francisco teacher and labor agitator, successfully lobbies for a California state bill that mandates equal pay for women. • At age 22, Thomas Fortune Ryan becomes the youngest-ever member of the New York Stock Exchange. He will become extremely successful in business, at one point holding controlling interest in 30 corporations.

The Irish jig A couple identified as "McCarthy and wife...champion Irish jig dancers" poses in Irish dress. The word *jig* derived from either the Italian *giga* or the French *gigue,* both of which refer to styles of music. But jig is also a type of dance, and the Irish have been performing it for centuries. The lively, joyous Irish version requires a rigid torso but rapid footwork and a stamping of the heels. Since their arrival in the United States, Irish Americans have been performing jigs at festivals, parades, and competitions—or just for fun with friends and family.

Helping the orphans A woman at the Ladies' Mission in Five Points distributes bread to poor children on Christmas. Because of the high mortality rate among Irish immigrants, thousands of orphan and "half-orphan" children roamed the streets of New York, eking out a living by selling newspapers or engaging in petty crime. Charitable organizations developed programs to alleviate the suffering of these "street Arabs." Women of the Methodist Church established a mission to help Five Points's children, and Charles Brace began the "orphan trains" to transport slum children to healthier environments. In 1869 the Sisters of Charity began taking in orphans; this led to the establishment of the New York Foundling Hospital.

The Cuba Five In 1871 the "Cuba Five" sailed into New York Harbor. John Devoy, Charles Underwood O'Connell, Henry Mulleda, Jeremiah O'Donovan Rossa, and John McClure had all spent time in prison for Irish revolutionary activity. As part of an early-release pact, the five (sailing on a ship named *The Cuba*) agreed to live outside of Ireland and Britain. They all moved to New York City, where they spent the next several decades planning, plotting, and fighting for Irish independence.

EFFECT OF THE FIFTEENTH AMENDMENT.
INDIGNANT MOTHER. "Cum in out of dat Mud right straight! Fust ting you'll know you'll be took for Irish Chil'en!" H. May 4. 1871

Archbishop Ireland

Joseph Ireland, who was born in County Kilkenny and immigrated to the United States in 1848, became the first archbishop of St. Paul, Minnesota. A progressive religious and civic leader, Ireland supported reforms in education and the relations between church and state. He is remembered for his firm stance against the use of foreign languages in schools and his support for the "Americanization" of immigrants. Ireland also organized colonization schemes to encourage poor Irish from eastern cities to settle in Minnesota.

General and President U. S. Grant

Ulysses S. Grant, 18th president of the United States (1869–77), was of Scots-Irish ancestry. A graduate of West Point, he was an outstanding Union general in the Civil War. After Grant's capture of Vicksburg in 1863, President Lincoln—frantic to find a winning military leader—named Grant commander of all Federal forces. While in charge, Grant aggressively battled the Army of Northern Virginia and, in April 1865, accepted General Lee's surrender at Appomattox. As president, he supported Radical Reconstruction and civil rights for black Americans. However, his presidency was marred by the dealings of corrupt associates.

The status of blacks and Irish This cartoon aptly underlines the status of Irish Catholics in post-Civil War America. An exasperated African American mother warns her children to get "out of dat Mud right straight" or "Fust ting you'll know you'll be took for Irish Chil'en." In short, the cartoonist's sentiment (facetious or not) is that while the status of blacks was low, that of the Irish was still lower.

January 13, 1874: New York City police violently suppress a demonstration of some 7,000 unemployed, largely immigrant workers who were calling on the mayor to institute a citywide public works program.

January 19, 1874: In Washington, D.C., the Corcoran Gallery opens its doors to the public for the first time. Close to 100 works of art from the private collection of financier William Corcoran go on display in three exhibit rooms.

1875: Irish-born meatpacker Michael Cudahy is named a partner in the Chicago firm of Armour and Company. Cudahy will introduce refrigeration in the packing process, revolutionizing the industry.

April 21, 1875: Irish politician and home rule advocate Charles Stewart Parnell wins election to Parliament as the representative for County Meath.

April 29, 1875: The whaling ship *Catalpa* sails out of New Bedford, Massachusetts, bound for Australia and the planned rescue of six members of the Fenian Brotherhood.

September 1875: After being arrested for theft in Nevada, 15-year-old William Henry Bonney McCarty escapes from jail by wiggling up the chimney. The fugitive will become known as "Billy the Kid."

December 1875: Former Tammany Hall leader Boss Tweed escapes incarceration during a brief furlough. He flees to Cuba and then to Spain. There, he is recaptured due largely to his appearance in many widely publicized Thomas Nast illustrations.

December 5, 1875: Irish nationalist O'Donovan Rossa publishes a letter in *The Irish World* newspaper. He calls for solicitations for a "skirmishing fund" to finance armed rebellion in Ireland.

Dozens killed at Orangemen parade On July 12, 1870, Protestant Orangemen parading in New York were attacked by an Irish Catholic mob, resulting in several dead and many wounded. The following year, fearing another riot, the mayor banned the procession, but he then allowed it to go ahead with a heavy police and military escort. Tensions ran high, and the results were horrific. The troops, who had been sent to protect the public, opened fire on 24th Street and 8th Avenue. All told, at least 60 people were killed and many more injured.

Blaming it on the Irish Famed artist Thomas Nast was noted for depicting Irish Americans as apes intent on destroying American democracy. Here, in a cartoon entitled "Miss Columbia's Public School," Nast portrays an Irish American "orator" calling for the murder of Protestants in the aftermath of the Orange Day riots in New York in 1871. Underneath the words "Hibernian Club," Nast wrote "shillelagh." The speaker's notes contain two talking points: "Our liberty taken away" and "Killing Orangemen."

Irish vs. Irish

After observing a bloody riot on the streets of New York in 1870, famed diarist George Templeton Strong observed that a peaceful parade of Protestants had been interrupted when marchers "were set upon by a swarm of base and brutal Celts." One of the tragic facts of Irish American history is that the Protestant-Catholic divide so prevalent in Ireland was transported to the United States.

Following the American Revolution, Irish Protestants were the dominant immigrant group in the United States. By the 1820s, U.S chapters of the Orange Order were formed "to maintain and uphold the Protestant faith." The organization held annual parades in New York, Philadelphia, and other cities in honor of William III, Prince of Orange, who had defeated Catholic James II at the Battle of the Boyne in Ireland on July 12, 1690.

Violence marked the July 12 (or Boyne Day) parades as early as the 1820s. Exiled United Irishman Thomas Addis Emmet noted that in July 1824, Orange marchers received a "humiliating thrashing" from the "Green Irish." Philadelphia's parade in July 1831 was also marred by a riot after Catholic bystanders began hurling rocks. Animosity increased as Ireland's famine swelled America's Catholic population, which turned to Democratic organizations such as Tammany Hall for assistance. Many Protestant Irish, on the other hand, were more assimilated, affluent, and comfortable with the newly created Republican Party.

The most notorious Protestant-Catholic violence occurred in 1870 and 1871. On July 12, 1870, 2,000 Orangemen gathered in lower Manhattan and marched uptown for a Boyne Day picnic. The march also included the American Protective Association, an anti-immigrant group known for its hostilities toward Catholics. Violence broke out and at least eight people were left dead. The following year was much worse. More than 60 people were officially reported dead, though the number is likely much higher. The city's Republican elites blamed Tammany Hall and its Irish Catholic supporters for the violence.

The Troubles that the Irish thought they had left behind were still haunting them in America.

Irish urged to go west In 1865 the vast American West was largely unpopulated apart from Native American tribes. Just 25 years later, virtually all of the West had been carved into states and territories. By 1890 the frontier had disappeared. The Homestead Act of 1862 granted free farms of 64 hectares to any citizens who would occupy and improve the land. Many Westerners organized meetings in both Ireland and on the East Coast to entice Irish men and women to take up the offer to "unite with a colony." This particular meeting was attended by the commissioner of immigration for Nebraska.

EMIGRATION.
A PUBLIC MEETING
WILL BE HELD IN THE
Market House Rooms, Armagh,
On Wednesday Evening, 20th December, 1871,
AT 7 O'CLOCK,
For the purpose of Organizing a Colony to Emigrate to Nebraska,
UNITED STATES OF AMERICA.
The Meeting will be addressed by
W. D. BLACKBURN, ESQ.,
Commissioner of Immigration for Nebraska.

All those desiring to unite with a Colony to secure FREE Farms and Cheap Homes in the Garden of the Great Free West, are respectfully requested to be present.

Dec. 12, 1871.   Printed at the Armagh Guardian Office.

Siney wins concessions for coal miners In 1868 John Siney helped found the Workingmen's Benevolent Association, which in the early 1870s grew into the influential Miner's National Association. Though born in Ireland, Siney worked as a coal miner in England. In 1863

he brought his organizing skills to the coalfields of Pennsylvania. His miner's union was successful in winning the first safety inspections for mines, the first minimum wage agreement for miners, and the first contract between miners and management. The demise of the union came when it was crushed in the "Long Strike" of 1874–75.

1876: Irish American sculptor Augustus Saint-Gaudens receives his first significant commission: a statue of Admiral David Farragut for New York City's Madison Square. The result will launch the illustrious career of a man whose works will grace public spaces in major cities on both sides of the Atlantic. • Irish-born physician Henry Newell Martin is named the first physiology professor at Baltimore's new Johns Hopkins University. • Irish-born miner Marcus Daly discovers a massive copper lode under the Anaconda silver mine near Butte, Montana. He will buy Anaconda along with several neighboring mines and launch his own mining interest, making a name for himself as America's "Copper King."

April 10, 1876: Irish-born retail magnate Alexander T. Stewart, the "Merchant Prince," dies in New York City as one of the wealthiest men in America.

June 25, 1876: General George Custer begins his ill-fated last stand at Little Bighorn. Though Custer previously charged into battle buoyed by Irish fighting music, this time his Seventh Cavalry band brings up the rear of the column, far from earshot.

1877: Clan na Gael, the secretive Irish nationalist organization, forms the "Revolutionary Directory" with elements of the Irish Republican Brotherhood. Embracing violence as a means to an end, this alliance will launch a terrorist campaign against England in the subsequent decade. • The Compromise of 1877 grants the presidency to Republican Rutherford B. Hayes over Democrat reformer and Tammany Hall foe Samuel Tilden following the contested election of 1876. The unwritten agreement pulls federal troops out of the South and effectively ends Reconstruction.

The poet O'Reilly Irish-born John Boyle O'Reilly was so admired in America that he was the official poet at the 1889 dedication ceremony for the Pilgrim Monument at Plymouth Rock. O'Reilly had a rich background. Due to his Fenian activities in Ireland, he was transported as a convict to Australia. He escaped to America in 1869, wrote poetry and novels, and became editor of *The Pilot*—the largest Irish Catholic newspaper in America. O'Reilly was friendly with writers Oliver Wendell Holmes, Henry Wadsworth Longfellow, and John Greenleaf Whittier.

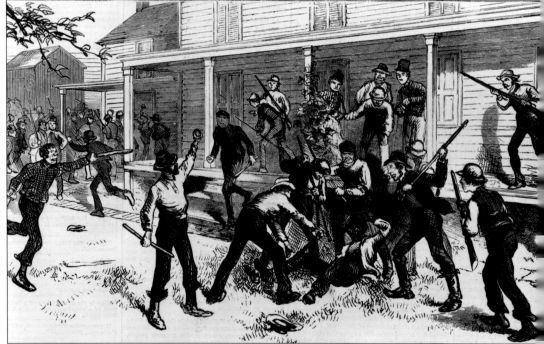

The Patenburg massacre Irish laborers in the small settlement of Patenburg in Hunterdon County, New Jersey, attacked a group of African Americans in a cabin on September 22, 1872. This image from *Harper's Weekly* depicts one of the brutal killings. Overall, three African Americans were murdered. Both Irish and black Americans had been working on a tunnel project in the vicinity. The rampage at the cabin began when the Irishmen heard, perhaps incorrectly, that one of their number had been killed by several black men the day before. The incident reminded *Harper's* readers of the catastrophic draft riots in New York in 1863.

Fire companies become more professional Prior to the Civil War, most fire companies were comprised of volunteers. They functioned more as social and political clubs than as firefighting organizations. Irish engine companies in such cities as New York and Boston often provided organizational muscle in hard-fought elections. By the 1860s, it was clear that volunteer departments were inefficient and, worse, slow to mobilize. What were needed were full-time professionals. Irish volunteers initially resisted the transformation. But once they were guaranteed priority in becoming professional firefighters, they came to constitute the backbone of many urban fire departments.

Fire ravages downtown Boston The fire that swept through Boston in 1872 started on the evening of November 9, in the basement of a warehouse on Summer Street. Twelve hours later, 65 acres of downtown Boston had been reduced to smoking ruins. More than 900 firms were burned out and 776 buildings were destroyed, causing about $75 million worth of damage. At least 20 people lost their lives. To this day, it is one of the most devastating fires in U.S. history.

THE PUBLIC SCHOOLS.

MISTRESS. "Now, Bridget, take the children to School."
BRIDGET. "What, to thim Prodestan Publics? I wouldn't risk me sowl, Ma'am, wid the likes."

Irish Catholics wary of public schools This cartoon conveys a fear of Irish Catholics: that in the public schools, their children would be exposed to Protestant proselytizing. Here, a well-off Irish mother directs Bridget, her Irish servant, to "take the children to School." Concerned, Bridget replies, "What, to thim Prodestan Publics? I wouldn't risk me sowl, Ma'am, wid the likes." There was some basis for Catholic fears, as American schools at the time generally taught from the King James version of the Bible and held to a Protestant interpretation of history.

1871-80

February 12, 1877: The Great Railroad Strike, the first general strike in American history, begins. It is also the first foray into labor activism for iconic labor leader Mary Harris "Mother" Jones, a native of County Cork, Ireland.

April 23, 1877: The first meeting of the Catholic Knights of America is held in Nashville, Tennessee. Both a fraternal organization and a source of life insurance for its members, the Catholic Knights will eventually boast some 20,000 members in 42 states.

June 21, 1877: Ten of 20 condemned Molly Maguires are executed. They were convicted of a series of murders of coal mine bosses on the testimony of a single Pinkerton Agency detective. The remaining 10 will be sent to the gallows over the following two years.

December 1877: Tweed comptroller Richard "Slippery Dick" Connolly is slapped with an $8 million judgment.

December 19, 1877: Michael Davitt, a nationalist and a leader of the Irish Republican Brotherhood, is released from prison. He served half of a 15-year treason sentence for smuggling munitions into Ireland.

1878: Irish American musical theater pioneers Harrigan and Hart debut *The Mulligan Guard Picnic* on Broadway. Their vaudeville-style send-ups of the ethnic immigrant condition will entertain audiences until H & H's 1885 breakup. • Recognizing the expansion of Irish American interests in the United States, Patrick Ford changes the name of his paper from *The Irish World* to *The Irish World and American Industrial Liberator*. • Father Patrick Hennessy of St. Patrick's Church in Jersey City, New Jersey, establishes a Gaelic class in his parish. This allows him to preach to the Gaelic-speaking members of his church while facilitating communication throughout the congregation.

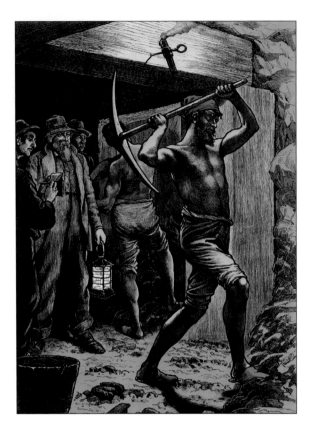

Irish mine silver in Nevada In 1859 two Irishmen, Peter O'Reily and Patrick McLaughlin, discovered silver in the Comstock Lode under present-day Virginia City, Nevada. In the rush that followed, thousands of Irish prospectors from California and Australia, plus new arrivals coming directly from Ireland, poured into the Lode country. By the mid-1870s, approximately one-third of Virginia City's residents were Irish. Four of the greatest fortunes made in the Comstock Lode were made by Irishmen, who came to be known as the "Bonanza Kings": John Mackay, James Flood, James Fair, and William O'Brien.

The Emigrant Savings Bank Irish immigrants withdraw money to send to family back in the home country. The Emigrant Savings Bank was started by an Irish society in 1850 to help newly arrived immigrants save their money, get small loans, and send money home. The bank had a branch in Dublin so that relatives could access funds in Ireland. The Emigrant Bank is still in operation, with 35 branches in the New York metropolitan area. Those searching for Irish ancestors often take advantage of the bank's extensive archives.

The Molly Maguires

During the Civil War era, George K. Smith was not well-liked by the Irish coalfield workers of Carbon County, Pennsylvania. As a mine owner, he had laid off numerous Irishmen and had stonewalled all of their attempts to organize a union. Moreover, Smith also worked with federal officials who attempted to enforce the much-hated Conscription Act, furnishing lists of workers under his employ.

On November 5, 1863, a group of armed men, faces blackened with the coal that they had mined, burst into Smith's home. As the mine owner descended the stairs, one of the intruders raised a pistol and shot him in the head. A moment later, the men were gone.

Smith's murderers were members of a shadowy organization known as the Molly Maguires. During a time when industrialists and government officials conspired to stop all union organizing—using national guardsmen or privately hired armies to break strikes—the Maguires served as the de facto enforcer of Irish miners' rights in the anthracite region of eastern Pennsylvania. The secret society had its roots back in Ireland, where organizations such as the Ribbonmen and Whiteboys used violence against landlords. Those groups attempted to enclose common grazing lands or harass merchants and middlemen who charged unjust prices. Irish workers imported such tactics when they immigrated to the United States.

A meeting of the Molly Maguires

From 1862 to 1875, officials charged the Molly Maguires with 16 killings along with countless beatings and acts of industrial sabotage. Mine owners and railroad operators retaliated by hiring the Pinkerton Detective Agency to break the organization, and in 1873 Pinkerton agent James McParlan successfully infiltrated the Maguires. Within two years, authorities arrested 20 members and promptly charged them with murder. Tried by a court with not one Irishman on the jury, all 20 were found guilty and sentenced to death. McParlan and the Pinkertons had successfully broken the Maguires, leading to the organization's collapse.

Daly's elaborate theaters

Augustin Daly was one of the top theatrical personalities of his day. He wrote and produced plays, but he was best known for the opulent theaters he opened in New York and London. Born in North Carolina, Daly later relocated to Manhattan, where he wrote about theater for newspapers. In 1869 he became manager of the Fifth Avenue Theatre (*pictured*), which he remodeled and unveiled to great fanfare in 1873. Daly worked with the best talent of his day, from Maurice Barrymore to Ada Rehan.

MacSlang

The Irish are noted for their way with the English language. The 1986 PBS series *The Story of English* focused on the critical Irish and Scots-Irish contributions to the emergence of a distinctly American tongue, an English that often bears little resemblance to the Oxford version.

The roots of slang are often harder to classify than diverging dialects. New Yorker Danny Cassidy, however, believes that American slang was largely born from Irish mouths.

Cassidy, the author of *How the Irish Invented Slang*, contends that early Irish immigrants transferred numerous words from their native Gaelic into American street speak. So, for example, the word *baloney*, slang for nonsense or pretentious talk, is—according to Cassidy—not derived from the Italian *bologna* but from the Irish *béal ónna*, with *béal* meaning mouth and *ónna* meaning silly. The word *scram*, Cassidy believes, can be traced to the Irish *scaraim*, which means "I get away."

Cassidy refutes H. L. Mencken's assertion that the Irish gave American English very few new words beyond *speakeasy, shillelagh,* and *smithereens.* Rather, he states, the Irish language in America "is a lost, living tongue, hidden beneath quirky (*corr-chaoí,* odd-mannered, odd-shaped) phonetic orthographic overcoats and mangled American pronunciations." Irish words and phrases, he states, "are scattered all across American language, regional and class dialects, colloquialism, slang, and specialized jargons."

The humor of Harrigan and Hart Before TV, movies, and radio, theater was the entertainment of choice for working-class Americans. For immigrants, the raucous comedies of Harrigan and Hart were particularly popular. Edward Harrigan and Tony Hart began collaborating in the 1870s, producing works that portrayed the hustle and bustle of life among New York's Irish, Jews, Germans, and others who comprised the American melting pot. Some of Harrigan and Hart's more famous works were *The Mulligan Guard* series, *Dan's Tribulations,* and *Cordelia's Aspirations.*

A dramatic Fenian rescue In 1875 men aboard the New England whaling ship *Catalpa* (*pictured*) sailed to western Australia. There, they freed six Irish Fenian convicts who had been imprisoned for life for their activities in the 1860s. John Devoy, a member of the New York-based Clan na Gael (an Irish republican organization) organized the rescue. When a British vessel intercepted the ship, *Catalpa* captain George Smith Anthony declared, "If you fire on this ship, you fire on the American flag!" The ship was allowed to sail back to America.

THE IGNORANT VOTE—HONORS ARE EASY.

Nast weighs in Political cartoonist Thomas Nast, no friend to Irish Catholics, pictured them as on the same social level as black Americans. Given Nast's strong Radical Republican sympathies, this 1876 cartoon probably suggests that Irish support for the Democratic Party was balanced by black support for the Republican Party. Nast was a master at taking a few individual, physical characteristics, exaggerating them, and making them the stereotype for a whole people.

First American cardinal After Patrick McCloskey and his wife, Elizabeth, immigrated to Brooklyn, they became parents of a boy who would become America's first cardinal. John McCloskey studied for the priesthood and graduated in 1834, becoming the first New York-born priest to be ordained. He became a bishop in 1844 and archbishop of New York in 1864, and he served as the first president of St. John's College (Fordham University). Pope Pius IX elevated him to cardinal in 1875. McCloskey, who dedicated the newly finished St. Patrick's Cathedral in 1879, was buried in the cathedral's crypt.

The Irish papers *The Irish-American* was one of the many Irish newspapers that flourished in the late 19th century, each catering to the needs of the increasing Irish population. Many Irish papers carried classified ads of people looking for family members who had emigrated before them. The first known Irish newspaper, *The Shamrock*, was published in New York in 1810. In the 1870s, the *New York Herald* boasted more than 20 Irish immigrants on its staff.

St. Patrick's Cathedral In 1853 Archbishop of New York John Hughes announced that he wanted to build a cathedral. The new church would reflect the growing importance of Catholics in America and the status of New York as the most important city in the New World. Construction on St. Patrick's began in 1858 but was not completed until 1879. (It is pictured here in the mid-1870s.) Critics called it "Hughes's Folly" because it was then situated far outside the city. The visionary Hughes knew that, because of the city's inevitable expansion, the church would one day be in the center of New York.

HOW THE CHINAMAN MIGHT GAIN FAVOR.

Prejudice stronger against Chinese For the Chinese, gaining acceptance into an American society that was strongly racist was no easy matter. They spoke a language vastly different than anything Americans were familiar with. They were not Christians, and they were easily identifiable as different by their features and the color of their skin. In contrast, the Irish—despite the prejudices against them—at least shared in the Western cultural tradition of the vast majority of Americans. For the Irish, assimilation took only a generation or two; for the Chinese, the road was much longer.

The changing face of Five Points Through the 1870s, New York's Five Points remained primarily a working-class Irish neighborhood with a mixture of residences, commercial establishments, and small industries. By day, the streets were crowded with merchants displaying wares under awnings and peddlers hawking goods on the sidewalks. At night, a seedy carnival atmosphere existed with patrons moving in and out of theaters, oyster bars, and saloons. Thievery and murder were still common. One big change from an earlier era was the number of newcomers, mainly Italians and Jews. They replaced the upwardly mobile Irish who had moved out.

Daily life in Five Points Living conditions in New York's Five Points neighborhood were harsh. Most Irish resided in large tenement buildings. The upper floors contained numerous small apartments, while bars and restaurants occupied the lower levels. A single outdoor privy might have to serve the needs of dozens of people. To survive, all family members had to work. Entertainment was found in grog shops, in fraternal and religious gatherings, in volunteer fire companies, and at bare-knuckle matches. If life was harsh in the Five Points, though, it was still better than what many had left behind in Ireland.

HOW TO WIN VOTES AMONG THE POOR

If a family is burned out, I don't ask whether they are Republicans or Democrats, and I don't refer them to the Charity Organization Society, which would investigate their case for a month or two and decide if they were worthy of help about the time they are dead from starvation. I just get quarters for them, buy clothes for them if their clothes were burned up, and fix them up til they get things runnin' again. It's philanthropy, but it's politics, too—mighty good politics. Who can tell how many votes one of these fires brings me? The poor are the most grateful people in the world, and, let me tell you, they have more friends in their neighborhoods than the rich have in theirs.

—GEORGE WASHINGTON PLUNKITT, A TAMMANY HALL LEADER

Power in the Big Cities

Going back to Thomas Dongan's appointment as colonial governor of New York, Irish Catholics had held top offices in government. But famine-era Irish immigrants faced such severe poverty and discrimination that it seemed inconceivable that one of them might someday govern a large city. By the late 1800s, however, the Irish had paid their dues on the lower rungs of the political ladder. Becoming numerous and influential in many cities, they clawed their way to the top.

It is fitting that New York was the first U.S. city to elect an Irish Catholic mayor. William R. Grace was born in County Cork and became a successful businessman before aligning himself with the Tammany Hall Democrats and winning election in 1880. Five years later, Fermanagh-born Hugh O'Brien was elected mayor of Boston. The era of Irish Catholic dominance of urban politics had begun.

New York and Boston were by far the most politically Irish cities. Hugh John Grant, the son of immigrants, won

William R. Grace

New York's election in 1888, while Cork native Patrick Collins won Boston's mayoralty in 1902. Perhaps the most famous of Boston's early Irish mayors was John Francis Fitzgerald. "Honey Fitz" battled the city's Yankee elites, while his daughter married Joseph Kennedy to forge America's most famous political dynasty.

By the early 1900s, heavily Irish machines and their mayors spread all across the United States. Chris Buckley ran San Francisco, William Sheehan ruled Buffalo, Patrick McCabe dominated Albany, and Tom Pendergast became boss of Kansas City. The power brokers were usually Democrats, though Pittsburgh's Chris Magee and "King" James McManes of Philadelphia were notable Republican exceptions.

The Irish became so powerful that, inevitably, they battled each other. In one particularly nasty campaign, John Purroy Mitchel (whose grandfather was a notable Fenian) lost New York's mayoralty in 1917 to John Francis Hylan, whose father hailed from County Cavan.

Irish emigration remains heavy
Though the Great Famine is often thought of as the high point of Irish emigration, citizens continued to flee in large numbers in the second half of the 19th century. From 1851 to 1871, the population dropped by a further one million, an unprecedented decline for any European country. In the 1870s, a half million people emigrated, mainly to the United Kingdom and to North American cities, especially New York (*pictured*). The number of small farms (five to 15 acres) was halved, and the cottier class (those who worked on potato plots) all but vanished. By 1921 five million people had left the island.

Irish-themed plays In the years following the Civil War, Americans flocked to see Irish-themed plays on the American stage. Irish actor and playwright Dion Boucicault appealed to Irish American audiences with his depiction of virtuous Irish maidens and courageous Irish men caught up in struggles against avaricious landlords and oppressive English officials. Other plays, such as *The Limerick Boy* and the Mulligan Guard series, made drinking and social pretensions the stuff of comedy and farce.

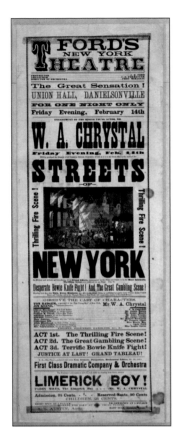

Americans aid Irish farmers In the late 1870s, a succession of crop failures again threatened famine in Ireland. In response, frustrated tenant farmers led by Michael Davitt organized the Land League to protest against unfair rents and heartless evictions. Following American tours by Davitt and Irish parliamentary leader Charles Stewart Parnell, a Relief Fund was established in the United States to support tenant farmers in their "war" against landlords. From 1879 to 1882, the Relief Fund sent approximately 250,000 pounds sterling to Ireland. Pictured is an Irish Relief Fund event in 1880.

Parnell's American tour In January 1880, Charles Stuart Parnell arrived in America to begin a speaking tour. His mission was to raise money for hard-pressed Irish farmers and other Irish nationalist causes. Sometimes called the "Uncrowned King of Ireland," Parnell was an outspoken advocate for Irish independence. To American critics, however, he was a dangerous radical who stirred up Irish Americans, who many nativists believed were already inherently violent. Parnell drew crowds well into the thousands, and he ultimately raised hundreds of thousands of dollars during his three-month tour. Parnell's tour illustrated just how important a role Irish Americans played in the ongoing debate over Irish independence.

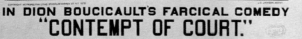

H. J. SARGENTS COMEDY COMPANY.
(ORGANIZATION Nº 4)

IN DION BOUCICAULT'S FARCICAL COMEDY
"CONTEMPT OF COURT."

Boucicault's Irish plays Dion Boucicault was one of the most successful Irish playwrights of the 19th century. His most popular works, such as *Arrah-Na-Pogue*, *Colleen Bawn*, and *The Shaughraun*, mixed comedy and melodrama with elements of Irish life. His play *Contempt of Court* (*pictured*) was a farcical comedy. Boucicault, who was born in Dublin to a French father and Irish mother, also excelled as an actor. His performance as Conn in *The Shaughraun* is considered one of the most memorable "stage Irish" performances of the 19th century.

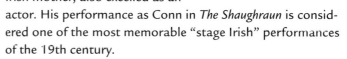

The origin of *boycott* Use of the word *boycott* has its origins in an Irish land feud. In 1879 poor harvests in County Mayo led to near starvation for tenant farmers, who sought relief in the form of lower rents from land owner Lord Erne. Erne's estate manager, a British Army captain named Charles Cunningham Boycott (*pictured*), took the brunt of the blame when relief never came. Local farmers, organized by the Irish Land League, ostracized the estate manager, thus launching the first organized "boycott" in history.

"Workingmen" rail against Chinese In the late 1870s, San Francisco—the West Coast metropolis spawned by the Gold Rush—was one-third Irish. During that time, a radical Workingmen's Party, comprised primarily of Irishmen and led by Irish-born rabble-rouser Denis Kearney—popularly known as "the sandlot orator" for his skills as a speaker—briefly challenged the local Democratic Party for the Irish vote. The Workingmen's Party had a one-issue platform: opposition to the large numbers of Chinese moving to the city after the completion of the transcontinental railroad. Fearful of competition in employment, the party's slogan was "The Chinese must go."

April 12, 1878: Destitute, ill, and unable to repay New York City the massive civil judgment against him, Boss Tweed dies in the Ludlow Street Jail at age 55.

October 27, 1878: The *New York Herald* reports Clan na Gael leader John Devoy's announcement of the "New Departure," a political alliance between home rule leadership and the more radical Fenian and Irish Republican Brotherhood factions.

1879: John Boyle O'Reilly, an Irish revolutionary writer and a member of the Irish Republican Brotherhood, publishes *Moondyne,* a novel drawn from his experience as a convict in an Australian penal camp. • Irish American labor leader Terence Powderly takes the helm of the inclusive Noble Order of the Knights of Labor.

October 21, 1879: The Irish National Land League is founded in County Mayo on the principle that the Irish practice of tenant farming should be abolished in favor of a system in which the farmers own the land on which they work.

1880: Irish-born shipping magnate William Grace is elected mayor of New York City, becoming the first Irish Catholic politician to hold that office. • Though the previous decade saw more than 430,000 Irish immigrants arrive on America's shores, the percentage of all immigrants who are Irish has dropped for the first time, as immigration from Eastern Europe has dramatically increased. • Irish American Joel Chandler Harris authors *Uncle Remus; His Songs and His Sayings: The Folk-Lore of the Old Plantation.*

December 23, 1880: Lincoln County sheriff Pat Garrett and his posse capture Irish American outlaw Billy the Kid at Stinking Springs, New Mexico.

Buffalo Bill and the Wild West "Buffalo Bill" was born William Frederick Cody to Isaac and Mary Ann Cody in LeClaire, Iowa. Though his Irish origins have been contested, his sister, Helen Cody Wetmore, wrote that they descended from Spanish and Irish royalty and claimed that their Irish ancestors had immigrated to the American colonies in 1747. Bill Cody, a soldier, Indian scout, hunter, and showman, was instrumental in creating the myth of the Wild West and the legend of the American cowboy. In the late 19th century and into the 20th century, his Wild West shows toured the world. While in London, he performed for Queen Victoria.

Irish Americans read *The World* *The Irish World* was one of the most influential Irish American newspapers. Founded in 1870 by Galway native Patrick Ford, *The World* aimed to link Irish independence with other global struggles, from the labor movement to racism. (Ford had worked in the printing trade under famous abolitionist William Lloyd Garrison.) This 1880 page depicts the eviction of poor Irish farmers who could no longer pay their rent. At its peak in the late 19th century, *The Irish World* had a circulation of 100,000.

Ford Tough

Patrick Ford

The world according to Patrick Ford needed to be turned on its head. Ford, arguably the most forceful Irish American newspaper editor of the 19th century, championed radical change in his weekly newspaper, known in its founding year of 1870 as *The Irish World*.

Born in County Galway in 1837, Ford and his family immigrated to America to escape the famine. As a boy, he worked as a printer's apprentice in the Boston offices of the abolitionist newspaper *The Liberator*. The title would lodge in Ford's mind. After serving in the Union Army during the Civil War, he settled in New York, where he founded *The Irish World* and unleashed his editorial vitriol against imperialism, aristocracy, and, of course, English rule in Ireland.

Ford, a tub-thumping supporter of Irish land reform, also turned his paper's attention to America's liberal and radical causes. He saw parallels in the struggle for greater freedom in Ireland with campaigns in America for social equality, including suffrage for women. In his radicalism, Ford was a standout in an Irish community that rarely expressed such views, beyond opposing English rule. More typically, they veered toward a conservative, Catholic view of social affairs.

Ford's opinions, however, could not be fully expressed by *The Irish World*'s title. In 1878 he changed it to *The Irish World and American Industrial Liberator*. The paper wasn't shy. On its broadsheet front page, it loudly elevated the cause of Ireland and the Irish. Typical was a front-page attack on the president of Harvard, Charles Eliot, in the October 24, 1896, issue. Eliot had made the mistake of not crediting the Irish with a share of his "Five American Contributions to Civilization."

Patrick Ford's trenchant calls for American change and Ireland's freedom were only partly silenced by his death in 1913. His paper lived on, though it was the lesser for his absence. It ceased publication in 1951.

Billie the Kid, a copy from a very old tin-type.

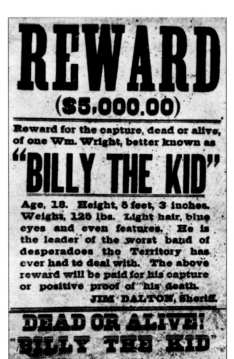

REWARD

($5,000.00)

Reward for the capture, dead or alive, of one Wm. Wright, better known as

"BILLY THE KID"

Age, 18. Height, 5 feet, 3 inches. Weight, 125 lbs. Light hair, blue eyes and even features. He is the leader of the worst band of desperadoes the Territory has ever had to deal with. The above reward will be paid for his capture or positive proof of his death.
JIM DALTON, Sheriff.

DEAD OR ALIVE!
"BILLY THE KID"

Billy the Kid William Henry Bonney McCarty, also known as Henry Antrim and William Bonney and best known as Billy the Kid, is thought to have been born in Manhattan to Irish Catholic parents. He is said to have worn a green band around his hat. Billy the Kid became a symbol of the lawless Old West, apocryphally killing 21 men—one for every year of his life. Historians believe that he probably murdered only nine, but all agree that he was a crack shot. The Kid met his maker on July 14, 1881, when Sheriff Pat Garrett gunned him down in Fort Sumner, New Mexico.

Supporting the Irish Rebellion

1881–1899

"None of us, whether we be in America or in Ireland... will be satisfied until we have destroyed the last link which keeps Ireland bound to England."

—CHARLES STEWART PARNELL

In the spring of 1879, an Irish immigrant named John Devoy left New York City, recrossed the Atlantic Ocean, met with friends in France, sailed to Great Britain, and then crossed the Irish Sea to return to the land of his birth. His journey was prompted not by nostalgia, but by politics: Devoy intended to link the secretive Irish nationalist movement in America to the political and social agitation of Charles Stewart Parnell, an Anglo-Irish member of Parliament. It was an audacious proposal. Devoy was a Fenian through and through, a man who had served time in a British prison for his role in fomenting revolution in Ireland in the 1860s. Parnell was an affluent landlord whose stock in trade was politics, not rebellion.

These unlikely partners, Devoy and Parnell, along with another ex-Fenian named Michael Davitt, put together a political movement in the early 1880s that galvanized Irish Americans by the tens of thousands. In focusing on land reform in Ireland instead of violent rebellion against British rule, Parnell, Devoy, and Davitt created a mass movement of Irish Americans willing to raise money and agitate on behalf of poor Irish tenant farmers. In doing so, however, they earned the enmity of Irish Americans who believed that only violent revolution would resolve Ireland's problems. These determined individuals intended to fire the opening shots of that revolution.

From 1879 to '82, the Land League fought a "land war" against landowners (such as the man in the foreground) in Ireland while demanding the "three Fs" (fair rent, fixity of tenure, and free sale). Charles Parnell and the tenant farmers harassed and boycotted the owners. In 1903 the British bought the land and sold it to the tenant farmers.

The 1880s and 1890s saw Irish Americans assert their newfound political and economic power on behalf of Ireland as never before. Devoy, along with other Irish American nationalists—John Boyle O'Reilly of Boston, Alexander Sullivan of Chicago, William Carroll of Philadelphia, to name a few—created a potent lobby for Irish freedom in American politics. Some of them worked closely with Parnell's sisters, Fanny and Anna Parnell, who raised hundreds of thousands of dollars in America to finance a campaign of agitation for land reform in Ireland. Others raised money for a very different cause—a bombing campaign in Great Britain.

This agitation coincided with Irish Americans' rise to positions of political and economic influence in American society. Irish communities became fund-raising bases for organizations that tried to win independence for Ireland, either through political action or outright rebellion. Some agitators, including Davitt (a freed IRB member who spent a great deal of time in the U.S.) and Patrick Ford (editor of the influential *Irish World* newspaper) tried to link the struggle of Ireland's poor with the plight of the Irish poor in America. Terence V. Powderly of Scranton, Pennsylvania, personified that broad outlook. He was head of a fledgling national labor union, the Knights of Labor, and was active in a secretive nationalist movement called Clan na Gael, or "Family of the Irish."

Clan na Gael was Devoy's power base. Devoy was a disciplined and patient organizer who saw Irish America as the key to ousting the British from Ireland. Although Clan na Gael sought to bring about revolution in Ireland, Devoy saw Parnell's political campaigns as a chance to advance the cause of Irish freedom through reform, not rebellion.

But not all Irish Americans in the growing nationalist movement agreed with Devoy's course of action. Led by Jeremiah O'Donovan Rossa, a group of extreme Irish American nationalists vowed to bring war to Great Britain from American shores. Fueled by O'Donovan Rossa's writings as well as money raised by Alexander Sullivan of Chicago, Irish American radicals sponsored a short-lived "dynamite campaign" in Britain in the mid-1880s.

The radicals took over Clan na Gael from Devoy's allies, and they issued a statement pledging that they would "carry on an incessant and perpetual warfare with the power of England." Explosions soon rocked London's train system, Scotland Yard, Parliament, and the Tower of London. Among the bombers was Thomas J. Clarke, an Irishman who had spent a few years in the United States. He was captured before he could carry out his mission.

John Devoy was a leader of the militant Irish Republican Brotherhood in Ireland. The British imprisoned him for leading a rebellion, and then exiled him to America in 1871. While living in New York, Devoy published a newspaper devoted to Irish freedom and support for Charles Parnell. He also helped finance armed attacks on the British.

British authorities were furious with Washington, accusing the American government of allowing Irish Americans to engage in a form of private warfare. British prime minister William Gladstone told Queen Victoria that "no other civilized country in the world would tolerate the open advocacy of assassination and murder."

Parnell, who was aligned with more moderate Irish Americans like Devoy, was drawn into the controversy when British authorities tried to publicly link him to the bombers and to the murders of two top British officials. But a parliamentary investigation revealed that accusations against Parnell were based on a forged letter. Devoy himself opposed the bombing campaign.

But as the dramatic 1880s drew to a close, divisions in both Ireland and Irish America led to bitter splits that set back the cause of liberty in Ireland. The Irish public turned on Parnell when it was revealed that he had been conducting a years-long affair with Katharine O'Shea, the wife of one of his political colleagues. Parnell was finished, and he died shortly thereafter.

In the United States, different viewpoints regarding the wisdom of the dynamite campaign caused the Clan na Gael to split into two factions. The division turned deadly. One of Devoy's allies, Dr. Patrick Cronin, was murdered in Chicago—presumably by allies of Devoy's rival, Sullivan. The ensuing scandal disgusted many Irish Americans and discredited the movement.

Meanwhile, events closer to home were beginning to change the contours of the Irish immigrant experience. Millions of new immigrants from other parts of the world shared space with the Irish in America's cities. The typical Irish immigrants on the eve of the new century were young women. As Hasia Diner noted in her book *Erin's Daughters in America,* about 53 percent of Irish immigrants were women. Many of these Irish women found work as domestics and contributed mightily to the flow of remittances sent back to Ireland. Other women in the workplace eagerly joined the Knights of Labor, which made a special effort to recruit female Irish workers.

Irish men, in the meantime, found economic security—so prized after the catastrophe of the Great Famine—in urban police forces, fire departments, and other civil service jobs. As the clock ran out on the 19th century, Irish Americans had attained political and economic power that few could have imagined when the first famine immigrants landed on American shores 50 years earlier.

But there was no reason for Irish America to look backward. The 20th century, after all, was filled with possibilities.

By the mid-1870s, the Clan na Gael eclipsed the Fenian movement as the leading Irish nationalist organization in the U.S. Under the leadership of American-born lawyer Alexander Sullivan (*pictured*), the Clan plotted and financed a series of bombing attacks in the 1880s against prominent English landmarks, including Parliament. While generally unsuccessful, the "dynamite campaign" reminded the English of the depths of Irish grievances.

1880s: With Tammany Hall providing social services to New York's Irish immigrant community, many working-class New Yorkers begin to vote a straight Democratic ticket.

1881: Knights of Labor leader Terence Powderly succeeds in abolishing the organization's veil of secrecy, ushering in an era of increased growth within the union. • The *Fenian Ram,* a submarine commissioned by the Irish Republican Brotherhood and funded by the Fenian Skirmishing Fund for action against Britain, is launched in New York. • Irish nationalist terrorists launch a "dynamite campaign" against targets in the English homeland. For the next several years, the British will be terrorized by random, small-scale bombings. • With more and more women joining the workforce, particularly among the less affluent immigrant community, the Children's Aid Society opens New York City's first day-care facility. • County Galway native Michael Logan launches *The Gael.* This monthly magazine, published in both English and Gaelic, celebrates the language and culture of Ireland. • Irish American artist John Mulvaney completes his masterpiece *Custer's Last Rally.* It is considered perhaps the most important artistic rendition of the decimation of Custer's Seventh Cavalry at the Battle of Little Bighorn.

April 28, 1881: While awaiting execution for the murder of a sheriff, Irish American outlaw Billy the Kid escapes from jail. His freedom will be short-lived, as his nemesis, Sheriff Pat Garrett, will find him and shoot him dead in less than three months.

August 8, 1881: Irish American labor leader Peter McGuire forms the United Brotherhood of Carpenters and Joiners of America. In five years, McGuire will join forces with Samuel Gompers and form the American Federation of Labor.

THE MOST RECENTLY DISCOVERED WILD BEAST.

The "dynamite campaign" One of the most controversial episodes in Irish American history was the so-called "dynamite campaign" of the 1880s. The House of Commons, Scotland Yard, Victoria Railway Station, and other prominent landmarks were bombed during the campaign, which was organized by Alexander Sullivan and other Clan na Gael members. When a bomb-making factory for the campaign was discovered in England, police said there were enough explosives to blow up the entire city of London. Rage toward Irish Americans spread throughout England, as seen in this illustration in which a caged beast is labeled "Irish-American Dynamite Skunk." More than two dozen Irish American revolutionaries were ultimately imprisoned for their role in the bombings, which were widely criticized by the vast majority of Irish Americans.

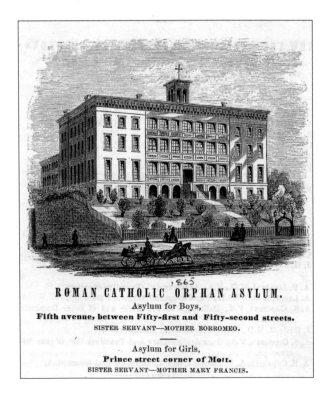

ROMAN CATHOLIC ORPHAN ASYLUM.
Asylum for Boys,
Fifth avenue, between Fifty-first and Fifty-second streets.
SISTER SERVANT—MOTHER BORROMEO.

Asylum for Girls,
Prince street corner of Mott.
SISTER SERVANT—MOTHER MARY FRANCIS.

Homes for the orphans
As a result of poverty, disease, and all-too-frequent industrial accidents, many immigrants died at a young age in the 1800s. As a result, a large number of orphans and half-orphans (those with only one living parent) roamed city streets. Concerned that these children were susceptible to the proselytizing efforts of Protestant missionaries, the Catholic Church responded by opening orphanages staffed by nuns in all major American cities. This one was in New York City.

Fox reinvents the *Police Gazette*

When Richard Kyle Fox took over the moribund *National Police Gazette* in 1876, the 30-year-old newspaper was focusing on stories of highwaymen and outlaws. Fox, who was born in Belfast and immigrated to America in 1874, turned the *Police Gazette* into one of the most successful publications of its day. He introduced sports

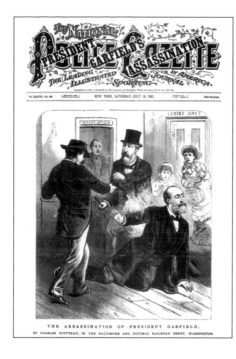

THE ASSASSINATION OF PRESIDENT GARFIELD, BY CHARLES GUITTEAU, IN THE BALTIMORE AND POTOMAC RAILROAD DEPOT, WASHINGTON.

pages, sensational woodcut illustrations, a gossip column, and celebrity features on boxers, chorus girls, and actresses. Fox promoted boxing and is credited with inventing the championship belts awarded in prizefights.

Arthur surprises as president

Chester Arthur, the 21st president of the United States (1881–85), was the son of a Baptist minister from northern Ireland. He rose through the ranks of the Republican Party, and in 1871 he was appointed to the patronage-rich post of collector of customs of the Port of New York. In 1880 he became James Garfield's vice president, then succeeded to the presidency upon Garfield's assassination in 1881. As president, Arthur surprised his critics by turning reformer. He supported the Pendleton Civil Service Reform Act and became known as the "Father of Civil Service."

Ireland's population plummets A personification of Ireland is demoralized by her declining population. The collapse of Ireland's population during and after the potato famine was precipitous. The number of citizens was halved by the end of the 19th century as a result of starvation, disease, and mass flight, particularly from the poverty-stricken west. Only in recent years has the potential for a return to a pre-famine population level become discernible on the island.

The activist priest

Father Edward McGlynn was born in New York City to parents who hailed from County Donegal. McGlynn was acutely aware of the political dimension of a priest's work, and early on he became concerned with the desperate poverty among his parishioners. McGlynn worked tirelessly and donated all his extra money to the poor. A powerful and popular speaker, he campaigned for radical social and economic reformer Henry George and, across the Atlantic, for Ireland's Land League. McGlynn was suspended from the priesthood and then excommunicated from the church for his activism, although he was later reinstated. His career served as an example for later generations of activist priests.

August 16, 1881: Passage of the second Land Act finally grants Irish tenant farmers their long-sought triumvirate: fair rent, a fixed tenure, and freedom to sell their interest in their farm.

September 20, 1881: Chester Arthur, the son of an Irish-born father, is sworn in as the 21st president of the United States following the assassination of his predecessor, James Garfield.

October 13, 1881: Land League leader Charles Stewart Parnell is arrested under the Coercion Acts and thrown into Kilmainham Jail along with other Land League officials.

1882: Irish nationalist Michael Davitt is elected to represent County Meath in Parliament. However, he is incarcerated for an inflammatory speech against British authority and disqualified from serving his term. • Patrick Collins is elected to serve on the Massachusetts delegation to Congress—a first for an Irish-born politician. • Congress passes the Chinese Exclusion Act, due in part to the efforts of Denis Kearney, an Irish activist and head of the Workingmen's Party of California. • Charles Stewart Parnell forms the Irish Parliamentary Party. It will replace the defunct Home Rule Party as the political party of choice for Irish nationalists.

February 2, 1882: In Connecticut, Father Michael McGivney founds the Knights of Columbus, a fraternal organization for Catholic men.

February 7, 1882: Irish American boxing star John L. Sullivan defeats Paddy Ryan, becoming the unofficial heavyweight champion of the world.

April 1882: The Irish American Land League, an adjunct league formed to support the Irish Land League, holds its final convention less than two years after its first was staged at New York City's Trenor Hall.

No good options Members of an Irish family are evicted for failing to pay rent. Perhaps they were victims of exorbitant "rack renting," in which the landlord jacked up the rent after the lease ran out. Once evicted, family members literally had to live by the roadside. Many lost hope of returning to their homes because, as often as not, the structures were destroyed. A workhouse or emigration (if the family was lucky enough to scrape together the sailing fare) were typically the only available prospects.

Farmers retaliate against landlords While the popular image of the "land war" might be that of outraged Irish farmers killing landlords (as this image indicates), murder was in fact quite rare. More common was the destruction of landlords' property. One particularly gruesome tactic was to sever the tendons of cattle. Perhaps more effective, however, was the ostracism of landlords and their agents. When Captain Boycott, a land agent in County Mayo, was shunned by the local community, the incident gave rise to a new word in the English language.

The Irish in the Ring

As champions of boxing's early decades, the Irish literally fought their way out of poverty. Beginning with John L. Sullivan, the Irish ruled boxing until World War II. In fact, they were so closely associated with the sport that heavyweight champs such as Tommy Burns and Jack Sharkey were two of the many fighters who invented Irish names for themselves even though they were not Irish.

John L. Sullivan was born to immigrant parents in Boston in 1858. Sullivan knocked out Tipperary native Paddy Ryan in 1882 and came to be recognized as the first heavyweight champion of the bare-knuckle boxing world. Sullivan was an icon as well as the most prominent athlete of the late 19th century.

Irish American "Gentleman Jim" Corbett finally beat Sullivan in 1892. Both fighters sported five-ounce gloves, ushering in a new boxing era. Like Sullivan, Corbett enjoyed success outside the ring—on stage and screen. He

John L. Sullivan

even wrote a successful autobiography, *The Roar of the Crowd*.

Jack Dempsey was the next great Irish American champion, though his roots were also Scottish and Native American. Dempsey won the heavyweight title in 1919. His toughest opponent was fellow Irish American Gene Tunney, who took the heavyweight crown from Dempsey in 1926 and successfully defended the title before 100,000 raucous fans a year later at Chicago's Soldier Field.

James J. Braddock, the so-called "Cinderella Man," entered the realm of myth in 1935. He returned from boxing obscurity to defeat heavyweight champ Max Baer. In lower weight classes from the 1880s to the 1930s, Jack McAuliffe, Johnny Kilbane, Billy Conn, Mickey Walker, Jimmy McLarnin, and Mike McTigue were some of the great Irish fighters.

In later years, crowd favorites such as Jerry Quarry and Gerry Cooney kept the Irish tradition alive, as Ireland's John Duddy does to this day.

"The Iron Duke" In the 1870s and '80s, William Muldoon emerged as the first wrestling star in American history—then went on to become a boxing trainer and actor. "The Iron Duke" founded the Muldoon Hygienic Institute in Purchase, New York, and he was instrumental in improving sanitary conditions for boxers. He outlawed smoking during matches and attempted to bar drunks and gamblers at fights. Muldoon served as one of the first chairmen of the New York State Athletic Commission. However, he was voted out of that position when he opposed a mixed-race bout between Jack Dempsey (whom he trained) and African American Harry Willis.

Holland designs the submarine Seeking a military advantage over the British, the Irish Republican Brotherhood hired John Philip Holland (*pictured*) to design what eventually would become the U.S. Navy's first commissioned submarine. Holland, born in County Clare in 1841, always had an interest in underwater transportation. He moved to the United States and, in 1879, received financial backing from Irish nationalists who hoped that the underwater vessel might be used to attack the British. Holland's creation was dubbed the *Fenian Ram*, and his submarine design was eventually purchased by the U.S. Navy.

McGuire gives America Labor Day

Peter J. McGuire, born to Irish immigrants in New York City in 1852, is recognized as the father of Labor Day. McGuire, founder of the United Brotherhood of Carpenters and Joiners, quit school at age 11 when his father went off to fight in the Civil War. He became active in radical circles and helped form what would become the American Federation of Labor. During an 1882 meeting, McGuire proposed a "festive parade" in early September. More than 30,000 marchers participated in what would become an annual event and a national holiday.

Wilde's U.S. tour

Ireland's Oscar Wilde, one of the great wits and dramatists of the English language, spent most of 1882 in America lecturing on the Aesthetic Movement in art. The trip, which began well and earned Wilde a good deal of money, was not a success. At his lectures, he appeared in outrageous garb—knee breeches, silk stockings, and a velvet jacket—that flaunted his homosexual orientation. The press crucified him in articles and caricatures. Harvard students mocked him when he spoke in Boston.

The first Labor Day parade America's inaugural Labor Day parade took place in New York on September 5, 1882. With the leadership of the city's labor unions dominated by Irish immigrants and Irish Americans, it was no surprise that the parade's grand marshal was Irishman William McCabe. The march began at City Hall with hundreds of people but ended at Union Square with a much bigger rally, attended by some 30,000 union members and their families. The idea of an annual day honoring American labor took hold, and it was made a federal holiday by an Act of Congress in 1894.

Doomed founder of Clan na Gael A native of Cork, Jerome J. Collins immigrated to the United States in the mid-19th century and became a correspondent and meteorologist for the *New York Herald. Collins,* an ardent Irish nationalist, founded Clan na Gael (Family of the Irish) in 1867 in hopes of creating an Irish American exile group to support revolution in Ireland. In 1879 Collins took part in an expedition, sponsored by the *Herald,* to the Arctic aboard the USS *Jeannette.* In June 1881, the *Jeanette* sank north of Siberia, forcing the crew to split up in search of help. Collins and others died of exposure and starvation in late October.

Murder in Phoenix Park One of the most shocking events in the bloody British-Irish relationship occurred in May 1882, when two high-ranking government officials were murdered. Permanent Undersecretary Thomas Henry Burke and Chief Secretary for Ireland Lord Frederick Cavendish—a nephew of British prime minister William Gladstone—were stabbed while walking in Dublin's Phoenix Park. The killings, which were widely condemned, prompted Charles Stewart Parnell to offer to resign his seat in Parliament. Five men were eventually hanged for the murders.

O'Neil dances the Irish jig The huge numbers of Irish who flooded into American cities in the post-famine years sparked a new genre of stage performer—one who catered specifically to their tastes and sentiment. Kitty O'Neil, born of Irish immigrant parents and pictured here in what passed for sultry dress at the time, was one of the most popular Broadway singers and dancers of the 1870s and '80s. Upon her death in 1893, *The New York Times* claimed she had been the best female jig dancer in the world.

The reign of "Boss" Croker
Cork-born Richard Croker followed in the footsteps of "Boss" Tweed as the leader of Tammany Hall. For 17 years, beginning in 1886, he controlled patronage in New York City and was influential in electing the city's mayors. All the while, he lined his pockets with bribe money from brothels, saloons, and gambling halls. A reform movement, begun in the early 1890s, culminated in the mayoral election of Seth Low—a former president of Columbia University—and ended Croker's reign. "Boss" Croker retired to a palatial estate in Ireland, where he ended his days raising racehorses.

"Ireland Forever" Just as the written word was employed with a vengeance by early Irish immigrants, the skills of illustrators and artists were brought to bear. Many artists portrayed downtrodden Ireland in the best possible light. *Erin Go Bragh*, roughly meaning "Ireland Forever," became a rallying cry for America's Irish, one that has lasted into the 21st century. Today, the saying is more often seen on hats and T-shirts than on fanciful postcards.

April 3, 1882: A few months after his final heist, Irish American outlaw and legendary train robber Jesse James is shot at his home by Bob Ford, a member of his own gang. • A large crowd assembles at New York's Cooper Union to protest the arrest of Irish American citizens in Britain. The Irish Americans were detained without trial under the Coercion Laws.

May 6, 1882: Two Irish civil servants in the employ of the British government are assassinated in Dublin's Phoenix Park. A group calling itself the Irish National Invincibles claims responsibility.

September 5, 1882: New York City's Central Labor Union celebrates the first annual Labor Day. Thousands of workers join a parade from City Hall to Union Square.

1883: Brilliant Brooklyn physician and Irish Nationalist Thomas Gallagher is detained in London, along with three associates, for plotting in the "dynamite campaign." They are captured in part due to the efforts of informer James "Red Jim" McDermott. • Major-league pitcher Tim Keefe, credited with introducing the changeup pitch to baseball, throws 68 complete games—in 68 starts—for the New York Metropolitans. His record on the season is 41–27. • James O'Neill, Irish American actor with the Union Square Theater and father of playwright Eugene O'Neill, portrays Edmund Dantes in *The Count of Monte Cristo* for the first time. It will be the defining role of his career. • Buffalo Bill Cody premieres his quintessentially American variety stage show, *Wild West,* in Omaha, Nebraska. • Irish-born vintner James Concannon begins the cultivation of grapes in California's Livermore Valley. His family winery will continue to produce award-winning vintages into the 21st century.

The two-time president Born in New Jersey, Grover Cleveland was the grandson of an Irish bookseller and the son of a Presbyterian minister. Cleveland not only became president of the United States, but he is the only president ever to be elected to two nonconsecutive terms. The Democrat was first elected in 1884, defeating James Blaine (who was supported by anti-Catholic voters). Four years later, Cleveland won the popular vote but lost the electoral vote to Benjamin Harrison. Cleveland was elected once again in 1892, which means he is technically known as America's 22nd and 24th president.

Blaine goes after Catholic schools James Blaine was an American congressman, senator, and secretary of state who ran for president in 1884. Today, however, Blaine is best remembered for his proposal to add an amendment to the constitution that would ensure that federal money never be used to aid religious schools. The so-called Blaine Amendment failed passage by a narrow margin in 1875. However, more than 30 states individually adopted the measures. They were motivated largely by nativist fears of Catholic schools, which were becoming more and more prominent in American cities.

From Beantown to Greentown

Boston, the city that gave birth to the American Revolution, retained a distinctly English flavor through much of the 1800s. But as post-famine immigrants and their children rose to influential positions, Beantown (Boston) might as well have been called Greentown (Irish).

Martin Lomasney, son of Irish immigrants, was the harbinger of change. He ruled as boss of Boston's Eighth Ward, an incubator for future Irish American political power on a national scale. "Never write if you can speak," Lomasney advised. "Never speak if you can nod. Never nod if you can wink."

Boston in the first half of the 20th century was a political bullring for the upstart Irish. Lomasney, James Michael Curley (the "Rascal King"), John F. "Honey Fitz" Fitzgerald, and Patrick Joseph Kennedy ran fiefdoms in which election results were as predictable as the calendar date for St. Patrick's Day.

Fitzgerald was the city's first mayor born in Boston of immigrant Irish parents. Curley, a populist with scant regard for Yankee convention, served four nonconsecutive terms as mayor and inspired Edwin O'Connor's novel *The Last Hurrah*. The Boston Irish bosses fought and feuded. They formed alliances and fell out of them. Lomasney, known as the "Mayor Maker," didn't get along with Curley. Conversely, Patrick Joseph Kennedy's son married Honey Fitz's daughter, spawning America's most famous family.

Massachusetts's Eighth Congressional District provided a continuous stream of Irish American leaders. Future Speaker of the House Tip O'Neill began his political journey in the Eighth District. Joe Kennedy, son of U.S. senator Robert Kennedy, took over the district by something approaching divine right.

So when, politically speaking, did Greentown revert to being Beantown? Arguably, that day came in September 1998. Boston voters went to the polls in the Eighth Congressional District Democratic primary and decided not to send an Irish American to Congress. It was the final "last hurrah."

Boston becomes more Irish A young man stands in the intersection of Prince and Salem streets in Boston's North End. By the middle of the 1880s, Boston's Irish were well on their way to making Boston Irish. Based on names and accents, a number of the city's political wards were indistinguishable from Ireland itself. In 1884 Hugh O'Brien was elected Boston's first Irish-born Catholic mayor. In the years that followed, the city's Irish expanded their political power as well as their control of jobs—both public and private.

October 25, 1883: Irish American journalist James McClatchy dies, leaving behind a legacy that, under the leadership of his sons, Valentine Stuart and Charles Kenny, will soon grow into the McClatchy Company newspaper empire.

1884: Hugh O'Brien is elected mayor of Boston, thus becoming the first Catholic Irish American to hold that office. • Irish rugby player Michael Cusack founds the Gaelic Athletic Association with a mandate to preserve Irish sports, such as hurling and Gaelic football. • William R. Grace, the first Irish-born mayor of New York City, is elected to a second term in office. • Irish American poet and essayist Louise Imogen Guiney publishes her first collection of poetry.

February 26, 1884: Two people are injured when Irish nationalist terrorists perpetrate a dynamite attack on London's Victoria Railway Station.

May 18, 1884: Irish singer Rose d'Erina, the "prima donna of Erin," marries Vicomte de Ste. Croix at Manhattan's Church of the Holy Innocents.

May 30, 1884: A series of explosions rocks London, as a dynamite attack causes heavy damage to Scotland Yard headquarters. Later in the evening, a cache of unexploded dynamite is discovered under the statue of Lord Nelson in Trafalgar Square.

November 28, 1884: The first opera ever written in Gaelic, translated in English as *The Bard and the Knight*, is performed at New York City's Steinway Hall.

December 13, 1884: Fenian Brotherhood member William Mackay Lomasney dies along with two co-conspirators when the explosives in their rowboat detonate prematurely as they attempt to destroy the London Bridge.

"Is not this country chiefly indebted to her [Ireland] for its faith? There are few churches erected from Maine to California, from Canada to Mexico which Irish hands have not helped to build, which Irish purses have not supported, and in which Irish hearts are not found worshipping."

—JAMES CARDINAL GIBBONS, ST. PATRICK'S DAY, 1870

Archbishop and social activist James Cardinal Gibbons was one of the most influential religious leaders in American Catholic history. His parents, from County Mayo, had settled in Baltimore, the city over which Gibbons presided as archbishop beginning in 1877. Two issues were particularly important to him: labor and assimilation. Gibbons persuaded the Vatican that unions would not undermine Catholic doctrine. He also convinced Pope Leo XIII that American parishes should not be separated by nationality. This helped Catholic immigrants integrate into the broader fabric of American life.

Riley pens "Little Orphant Annie" James Whitcomb Riley (*left*), whose ancestors are thought to have hailed from County Cork, was known as the "Children's Poet." His poetry was humorous and sentimental, and he often wrote in the distinctive dialect of his native Indiana. Riley is best known for his 1885 poem "Little Orphant Annie," which, when republished in 1900, was illustrated by this photograph of a little girl. The poem was the inspiration for Harold Gray's popular 20th century comic strip, *Little Orphan Annie,* which in turn inspired the stage musical and movie.

The Triumphs of Nellie Bly

Elizabeth Jane Cochran was born in 1864 into a comfortable Irish American clan in western Pennsylvania. That easy existence vanished with the early death of her father. She endured a childhood marked by dispossession; a physically abusive, alcoholic stepfather; and the lack of opportunity for intelligent, ambitious girls. But through pluck and daring, Cochran became Nellie Bly, one of the most famous American journalists and the earliest practitioner of investigative reporting.

At age 20, Cochran won a job at the *Pittsburgh Dispatch* when she wrote a letter challenging a male columnist's view that women should stay out of the workplace. She wrote movingly about the lives of working women and about the injustices women faced in divorce courts. After two years at the *Pittsburgh Dispatch*, and after adopting her famous *nom de plume*, she set her sights on working in New York City.

At first unsuccessful at landing a job, she proposed a risky story to Joseph Pulitzer's *New York World*. To expose conditions in the city's insane asylum, she would pose as mentally unbalanced and try to get herself committed. The ploy worked, and the resulting stories were a national sensation. In 1889 Bly set out to beat the fictional record for circumnavigating the globe described in the Jules Verne novel *Around the World in Eighty Days*. She made the trip in 72 days.

Bly published scores of attention-getting stories over the next several years, but she retired from journalism after marrying Robert Seaman, a millionaire manufacturer of steel barrels, in 1895. But here, too, Bly made her mark: She designed and patented the durable 55-gallon steel drum that has remained an industry standard.

Seaman died, and Bly spent part of World War I reporting from the Eastern Front. She resumed her newspaper career upon returning to New York in 1919 and used her position to win attention for neglected and destitute children. Upon her death in 1922, her final editor wrote that she was "the best reporter in America, and that is saying a good deal."

Women as Knights of Labor

The rise of labor unions in 19th century America was never less than a turbulent process. It was Terence Powderly, the son of Irish immigrants, who saw that strength in numbers was best realized when a union was open to people of all races and creeds—and, most crucially, women. Many Knights of Labor were women (including all those pictured), and a significant proportion of the female membership was composed of Irish and Irish American women, many of whom were employed in the garment industry. The most famous female Knight was Cork-born Mary "Mother" Jones.

1885: Irish-born American inventor Patrick Bernard Delaney wins a gold medal at the International Invention Exhibition in London. By the end of his life, he will have filed more than 150 patents, many in the field of telegraphy. • British prime minister William Gladstone proposes an Irish home-rule bill, but it goes down in defeat at the hands of Irish and British members of Parliament. • Tin Pan Alley is born, as several music publishers open their doors in a lower midtown Manhattan neighborhood. It will be the center of American popular music for the next half-century.

December 1885: Elections send 86 members of the fledgling Irish Parliamentary Party to seats in Parliament.

1886: Celebrated Irish American author Henry James publishes his classic novel *The Bostonians*. • James Gibbons, Baltimore's Irish American Roman Catholic archbishop, is named a cardinal, becoming only the second American to rise to that position. • Terence Powderly's Knights of Labor claims a membership of nearly one million workers. • The Statue of Liberty is given to the United States as a gesture of friendship by the French people. Its position at the mouth of New York Harbor will welcome generations of immigrants, many from Ireland. • Near the end of an illustrious career in the U.S. Navy, Irish American sailor Alfred Thayer Mahan is named head of the Naval War College in Newport, Rhode Island.

May 1, 1886: More than 300,000 workers across the U.S. walk off the job, launching a general strike. Workers seek an eight-hour workday.

May 4, 1886: In Chicago, the Haymarket Riot is triggered when someone throws an explosive at a police line in the middle of an otherwise peaceful labor demonstration. At least a dozen people will die.

San Francisco's "Blind Boss"
Never elected to public office, New York-born Irishman Chris Buckley controlled the Democratic Party in San Francisco in the 1880s and early 1890s. Having lost his sight at age 30, he was known as the "Blind Boss." His popular saloon, the Alhambra, was referred to as "Buckley's City Hall." Buckley modeled his political machine on Tammany Hall, and amassed a small fortune through graft and shady dealings with the Southern Pacific Railroad. Only when a grand jury indicted him for corruption did his political influence collapse.

Kicked out of their homes For large numbers of Irish citizens, the 19th century was the age of eviction. Around the time of the Great Hunger, the threat of home loss loomed like a constant storm cloud over just about every sod-roofed hovel. Moreover, the threat didn't dissipate with the end of the potato blight. Because of the prevailing move at the time from tillage to animal grazing, many absentee landlords—by way of their local agents—merged small plots of land, forcing families off their land. This evicted family was forced to live in this tiny hut in Glenbeigh, Ireland.

Nativist Bowers founds the APA In the 1880s and '90s, virulent American nativism again reared its head. In 1887 in Iowa, Henry Francis Bowers founded the American Protective Association (APA), charging that Roman Catholicism and democracy were inimical. Over the next 10 years, the APA was a political force in the Midwest, particularly in local elections. In 1896, when Republican presidential candidate William McKinley declined to subscribe to an anti-Catholic program, the APA charged that he was secretly a Catholic. When McKinley won anyhow, the APA was shown to be toothless on the national level and went into decline.

Working in sweatshops If the vision of men working in deathtrap coal mines during the 19th century has a lasting hold on the Irish American psyche, so too does the image of Irish women working under brutal conditions in clothing factories and laundries. The burdens of working women gave rise to formidable female labor leaders, including Irish-born Mary "Mother" Jones, Leonora Barry, and Kate Kennedy. Kate Mullaney helped form the Collar Laundry Union in Troy, New York, and Philadelphia-born Florence Kelley championed the rights of female and child laborers.

POOR, SHIVERING WRETCHES

I returned to Chicago and went again into the dressmaking business with a partner. We were located on Washington Street near the lake. We worked for the aristocrats of Chicago, and I had ample opportunity to observe the luxury and extravagance of their lives. Often while sewing for the lords and barons who lived in magnificent houses on the Lake Shore Drive, I would look out of the plate glass windows and see the poor, shivering wretches, jobless and hungry, walking along the frozen lake front. The contrast of their condition with that of the tropical comfort of the people for whom I sewed was painful to me. My employers seemed neither to notice nor to care. Summers, too, from the windows of the rich, I used to watch the mothers come from the west side slums, lugging babies and little children, hoping for a breath of cool, fresh air from the lake. At night, when the tenements were stifling hot, men, women and little children slept in the parks. But the rich, having donated to the charity ice fund, had, by the time it was hot in the city, gone to seaside and mountains.

—MOTHER JONES

Irish say good-bye to Five Points Even the toughest 19th century New York City neighborhoods were susceptible to dramatic demographic changes. In 1855 two-thirds of those living in the notorious Five Points district on Manhattan's Lower East Side had been born in Ireland. By the 1870s, the Irish were on the move and being replaced by newcomers, mostly Jewish, Italian, and Chinese immigrants. By 1880 the Irish-born tally was down to one-third, and by the 1890s virtually all of the Five Points Irish had moved on.

August 1886: The Irish National League holds its annual convention in Chicago. One topic of interest is the ongoing "dynamite campaign" in England, to which many of the American convention delegates are strongly opposed.

December 1886: Cigar maker Samuel Gompers is named first president of the American Federation of Labor, a consortium of labor unions, shortly after he cofounds the group with Peter McGuire of the United Order of Carpenters and Joiners.

1887: Leonora Barry, the national women's organizer for the Knights of Labor, visits several textile factories in New Jersey and reports on numerous labor practice violations. • A series of *London Times* articles titled "Parnellism and Crime" accuses Charles Stewart Parnell of sanctioning the Phoenix Park murders and other nationalist terrorist acts. • The Dublinmen, a New York society of Irishmen from Dublin, reorganize themselves to exclude anyone not born in Dublin. The growing popularity of such Irish county societies reflects a stronger connection to the homeland among these most recent immigrants. • Irish American physiologist Henry Newell Martin is named the first secretary-treasurer of the American Physiological Society, an organization he cofounded with four of his colleagues.

March 13, 1887: Iowa attorney Henry Bowers founds the nativist and staunchly anti-Catholic American Protective Association. Though it will enjoy some popularity in the 1890s, it will be irrelevant by the 1900s.

July 4, 1887: Edward McGlynn, a prominent New York Irish American priest, is excommunicated after publicly opposing Archbishop Michael Corrigan, who was in the pocket of Tammany Hall. McGlynn will be reinstated within five years.

The bishops' ultimatum This 1889 cartoon by Louis Dalrymple expresses the belief that Catholic parents must choose between sending their children to parochial schools or excommunication from the Church. During the 1880s, some bishops in what was an increasingly Irish-run U.S. Catholic Church believed that parents who sent their children to public schools should be denied the Church's sacraments. More liberal-leaning bishops opposed this stance and ultimately stymied the idea.

The Irish of New Orleans
Because of its Catholic roots (due to many French and Spanish settlers) and its need for canal workers, New Orleans became an important port of entry for Irish immigrants during and after the famine. But there was an Irish presence in the city even before the mass influx of the 1840s. The first St. Patrick's Day parade in New Orleans took place in 1809, and St. Patrick's Church on Camp Street was founded in 1833. Many Irish laborers found work building the New Basin Canal, and the Hibernia Bank was the city's largest bank for many years. In this picture, Santa Claus distributes gifts to children during the New Orleans exposition of 1885.

Murder in Chicago

On May 22, 1889, ditch cleaners working along Evanston Road on the outskirts of Chicago discovered the body of Dr. Patrick Cronin in a nearby catch basin. Partially decomposed, the corpse was badly bruised and bloated. The subsequent coroner's report stated that the doctor had been stabbed to death. Cronin's friends and family insisted that popular Irish American leader Alexander Sullivan was behind the murder.

The trouble between Cronin and Sullivan had begun four years earlier. Both men were members of the Clan na Gael, a secretive organization dedicated to Irish independence and land reform. In 1883 Sullivan threw all of the Clan's resources behind a controversial "dynamite campaign" intended to bring the British government to its knees. Irish American volunteers planted explosives in the Tower of London, the Houses of Parliament, Westminster Hall, and the London underground. Despite Sullivan's best efforts, the campaign failed to spark a revolution or change British policies. About the only thing it led to was rising turmoil within the Clan na Gael.

Cronin launched an all-out attack on Sullivan, accusing him of misappropriating funds and ordering the dynamite campaign without the consent of the Irish Republican Brotherhood—the forerunner of the modern-day Irish Republican Army. Through a hail of editorials in his newspaper, the *Celto-American*, Cronin denounced Sullivan and

Discovery of Dr. Cronin's body in the catch basin

called for his immediate resignation. Sullivan, in turn, accused Cronin of working as a British spy and fomenting dissent among the Irish American community.

After Cronin's death, Chicago authorities arrested Sullivan and several others. Although charges against the Clan chief were eventually dropped, the ensuing trials of the others implicated in the crime led to a media frenzy. The Clan na Gael came under heavy criticism for its violent actions, and many argued that such Irish nationalism was un-American. As a result, the organization faded into obscurity even while Sullivan remained a force in Chicago politics.

Helen Keller's teacher The popular view of Irish women as outstanding nurses and caregivers owes much to Anne Sullivan (*right*). The daughter of Irish immigrants, Sullivan achieved fame by challenging the dark and silent world of Alabama-born Helen Keller (*left*), who had lost sight and hearing as a young child in 1882. Sullivan's devotion and a unique teaching method—in which she conversed through touch in the hands—helped Keller connect with the world and eventually graduate *magna cum laude* from Radcliffe College. The Sullivan/Keller story was made famous in the 1962 film *The Miracle Worker*.

Critics hail *Myles Aroon* Popular theater enjoyed a golden age in the years immediately preceding motion pictures, and Irish-themed plays rose to the fore on stages from New York to San Francisco. *The New York Times* lauded comedian W. J. Scanlan in an 1889 review of *Myles Aroon,* a play that, according to the *Times,* had some "well-developed ideas in regard to the future of Irish plays." The feature of the play, opined *The Harvard Crimson,* was "the Fair scene which introduced excellent scenery with wonderfully realistic effect. A genuine Irish piper takes part."

OUR DUTY TO THE IMMIGRANT

Every kettle of broth has its scum, and our land, which is the melting pot of humanity, is receiving a larger number and less scum from Europe than ever before, for we subject those who come to a more exacting scrutiny and severer tests than ever before. We can easily judge what environment will do by what we have seen it do. Take two young boys of equal age, place one in the cotton field and the other on the Bowery; one will pick cotton, the other will, in all probability, pick pockets; and they may be equally industrious and proficient in the doing. We admit the immigrant and then abuse him. We expend all our efforts at the point of entry and once we pass him inward we take no more heed of him; leave him to his own resources, to be mocked, reviled and snubbed, cheated or robbed. Our duty to the immigrant is to teach by precept, set a good example for him to follow and guard him in his environment against contaminating influences.

—KNIGHTS OF LABOR LEADER TERENCE POWDERLY

Fear of the Irish As millions of nontraditional immigrants streamed into the United States near the end of the 19th century, the Irish remained—in the view of this editorial cartoonist and others—the one group incapable or unworthy of citizenship. The Irish caricature in this image wields

a knife, symbolizing his physical threat to the nation, and the green flag of Ireland, representing his true loyalty. Well into the 20th century, Anglo-Protestant America feared Irish America's involvement in Ireland's freedom struggle and its defiant Catholicism.

Irish mine for copper in Montana During and after the California Gold Rush, Irish immigrants streamed west to seek their fortunes. Thousands of Irishmen dug for silver in Nevada's Comstock Lode and for silver and gold in Leadville, Colorado. But no place in America had proportionately more Irish than Butte, Montana, where Marcus Daly hired thousands of his countrymen to work at his Anaconda Copper Mining Company (*pictured*). Daly treated his workers well, but after his death in 1900, labor relations soured. Violent strikes in 1914 and 1917 culminated in the lynching of International Workers of the World (IWW) organizer Frank Little.

The Fight for a Living Wage

Terence V. Powderly was one of 12 children born to an Irish immigrant couple during the 1840s and 1850s. The family, however, did not settle in a bustling urban center. They instead lived in Carbondale, Pennsylvania, a region dominated by railroad, factory, and mine workers. Powderly grew up to become, arguably, the most important labor leader of the late 19th century. He also helped permanently change the relationship between workers and the Catholic Church.

Powderly left school at age 13 to work on the railroad. While in his early 20s in 1872, he was elected leader of the Machinists' and Blacksmiths' Union. Yet he still lost his job when America sank deep into depression the next year.

Powderly later became affiliated with a secret labor group that came to be known as the Knights of Labor. Labor unions in Europe had traditionally been secret because they eschewed organized religion. Thus, the Vatican saw unions as a bad influence. The Canadian Catholic Church had even officially condemned the Knights of Labor.

Worker caught between Powderly's "strike" hammer and capital's anvil

However, influential American bishops, such as Cardinal Gibbons of Baltimore, believed unions could combine faith with progress for workers. In 1887 Gibbons prepared a report entitled *The Question of The Knights of Labor*. He eventually persuaded the pope that American unions—especially those led by devout Catholics such as Powderly—were not opposed to the Church.

By then, the Knights of Labor had nearly one million members, thanks to its recruitment of women and African Americans. The peak of its power coincided with the infamous 1886 Haymarket Square Riot in Chicago.

The Knights had always been a moderate union. They opposed strikes and preferred boycotts and negotiations. Following Haymarket, which led to the arrests and executions of labor leaders, workers were increasingly attracted to Powderly's rival union leader, Samuel Gompers, who brought many Knights into the American Federation of Labor by the 1890s. Membership in the Knights declined rapidly. However, Powderly, Gibbons, and the Knights helped make unions a vibrant political force in the United States.

Proud Knights Many members of the (heavily Irish) Knights of Labor, including the men shown here, were skilled workers who proudly thought of themselves as producers of the nation's wealth—as opposed to white-collar middlemen such as brokers and lawyers. In addition to their union membership, many Knights were active in the Land League movement, which financed land reform in Ireland. The Knights also were strong advocates of temperance. The union's founder and guiding light, Terence Powderly, was a member of the Total Abstinence and Benevolent Association.

1888: Workmen finish building the soaring spires of New York City's St. Patrick's Cathedral, the largest Catholic cathedral in the United States. • Irish American track and field star James E. Sullivan establishes the Amateur Athletic Union (AAU) to sponsor America's amateur athletes.

June 3, 1888: Ernest Thayer publishes "Casey at the Bat," his classic comic verse about a fictitious Mudville slugger who fails to save the day when he strikes out in the bottom of the ninth inning.

October 5, 1888: Flame-throwing Pittsburgh Pirates pitcher Pud Galvin notches his 300th win, becoming the first major-league pitcher to reach that milestone.

1889: Irish American physician Charles McBurney discovers a non-invasive method of testing patients for life-threatening appendicitis. • Dr. Howard A. Kelly, an Irish American obstetrician and gynecologist, joins the faculty of the new Johns Hopkins School of Medicine. His many innovations as a teacher and surgeon will include adapting the use of radiation as a treatment for cancer.

Late 1889: More than 650,000 immigrants from Ireland have arrived on America's shores in the past 10 years.

1890: William James, a pioneering Irish American psychologist, releases *Principles of Psychology*, his seminal volume on the study of human behavior. • Charles Stewart Parnell's career begins its freefall when he is named in the divorce proceedings of his married mistress, Katherine O'Shea. He will go on to marry "Kitty," but his reputation will suffer irreparable harm.

Harnett's mass appeal
Born in County Cork during the famine, William Michael Harnett immigrated to Philadelphia as a child. Forsaking an initial career as an engraver, Harnett turned to painting still-life subjects. By his death in 1892, his work had attained popularity on both sides of the Atlantic. Harnett's early subjects were typically everyday items, but he later focused on objects with particularly strong public appeal, such as musical instruments and guns. This painting is entitled *The Faithful Colt*.

Hovenden captures a moment Born in County Cork in 1840, artist Thomas Hovenden moved to New York City in the mid-1860s. One of his most famous paintings is the poignant *Breaking Home Ties* (1890). Capturing a moment of American family life, Hovenden portrays a moving story: a son leaving home, and a mother unable to let him go. Such an image resonated with many Irish, whose children had been leaving Ireland for decades.

Harris's Uncle Remus stories Georgia-born Joel Chandler Harris based his Uncle Remus stories on African American folklore during the era of slavery. A self-described son of a wandering Irishman, Harris himself wandered for much of his youth—on the plantation of a newspaper publisher, who had hired him as a printer's assistant. The stories that Harris heard, and the manner of their telling, found fame beginning in 1879. That year, readers across America were introduced to Brer Rabbit, Brer Fox, and other animal characters who became the voices of the stories' original tellers.

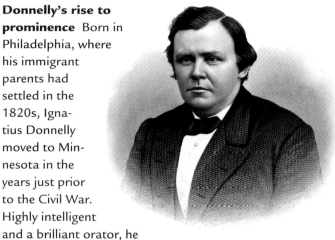

Donnelly's rise to prominence Born in Philadelphia, where his immigrant parents had settled in the 1820s, Ignatius Donnelly moved to Minnesota in the years just prior to the Civil War. Highly intelligent and a brilliant orator, he soon involved himself in politics. At age 28, Donnelly was elected lieutenant governor of the new state of Minnesota, and in the 1860s he sat in the U.S. House of Representatives. Though initially a Republican, he eventually turned reformer and helped found the Populist Party in the early 1890s. Late in life, he became a successful novelist.

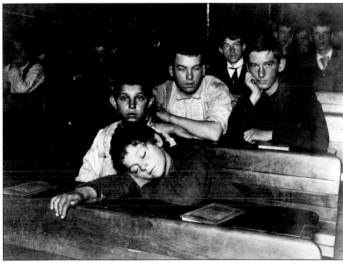

Night school for kids A boy falls asleep at his desk, and others look ready to doze off, during night school at the Seventh Avenue Lodging House in New York City. The school was run by the Children's Aid Society, which provided industrial and night school education to orphaned children and those from the poorest families, especially in East Coast cities. Many kids had to go to school at night because they worked during the day. The photo was taken by journalist Jacob Riis, who aimed to show how miserable conditions were in the poor sections of the city.

Irish steelworkers go on strike In 1892 the contract with the predominantly Irish union workers at Andrew Carnegie's steel mill in Homestead, Pennsylvania, expired. Carnegie and his mill manager, Henry Clay Frick, became determined to break the union. They offered only a decrease in wages. Disgusted, the union men went on strike. Frick tried to bring in strikebreakers, but picketing strikers kept them out. When the company brought in hundreds of Pinkerton detectives to provide security, hostilities erupted. On July 6, nine strikers and three Pinkertons were killed. Eventually, Carnegie crushed the union.

1890: Irish American sculptor James E. Kelly unveils the Soldiers & Sailors Monument in Troy, New York, his first public memorial sculpture. For more than 30 years, Kelly will continue to create public sculptures commemorating American military heroes and significant battles.

January 25, 1890: Intrepid Irish American reporter Nellie Bly returns to a hero's welcome in New York City. Bly recreated Jules Verne's fictional journey around the world in just 72 days—a full week shorter than Phineas Fogg's 80-day trip.

1891: Gaelic scholar Douglas Hyde joins forces with Irish literary giant W. B. Yeats to form the Irish Literary Society.

January 6, 1891: Irish American inventor Thomas E. Murray receives his first patent, for improving the metallic packing on machinery rods. In all, he will hold some 1,100 patents, second only to Thomas Edison.

May 1891: The Irish National Federation of America is formed, with Thomas A. Emmet as its first president.

October 6, 1891: Charles Stewart Parnell, the "uncrowned king of Ireland," dies in England at age 45.

1892: The Populist Party, formed three years earlier by labor interests, holds its first national convention in Omaha, Nebraska. It organizes a slate of candidates for the upcoming federal elections. • Dr. John Murphy invents a device that enables surgeons to suture intestines in a minimally invasive fashion. The device, which he calls the Murphy Button, passes naturally from the body once the intestines have healed. • John Drew, Jr., scion of the famous Irish American acting family, joins the company of renowned theatrical producer Charles Frohman. Drew will work with Frohman for more than two decades.

Irish arrive at Ellis Island
Prior to the famine, Irish immigrants entered the United States via numerous ports on the Atlantic Seaboard and at New Orleans. From 1855 to 1890, the principal port of entry was through a processing center established at Castle Garden on the tip of Manhattan. This was followed in 1892 with the opening of Ellis Island (*pictured*) in New York Harbor. From its beginning until 1924 (when restrictive laws greatly reduced entry into the United States), millions of immigrants passed through Ellis Island—more than 500,000 of them Irish. On the day that Ellis Island opened, January 1, 1892, the first person to register in the new facility was Annie Moore, a teenager from County Cork.

Ellis Island, New York

ELLIS ISLAND'S FIRST ARRIVAL

The new buildings on Ellis Island constructed for the use of the Immigration Bureau were yesterday formally occupied.... There were three big steamships in the harbor waiting to land their passengers, and there was much anxiety among the new-comers to be the first landed at the new station. The honor was reserved for a little rosy-cheeked Irish girl. She was Annie Moore, fifteen years of age, lately a resident of County Cork, and yesterday one of the 148 steerage passengers landed from the Guion steamship *Nevada*. Her name is now distinguished by being the first registered in the book of the new landing bureau.... As soon as the gangplank was run ashore, Annie tripped across it and was hurried into the big building that almost covers the entire island.... When the little voyager had been registered Col. Weber presented her with a ten-dollar gold piece and made a short address of congratulation and welcome. It was the first United States coin she had ever seen and the largest sum of money she had ever possessed. She says she will never part with it, but will always keep it as a pleasant memento of the occasion.

—THE NEW YORK TIMES, JANUARY 2, 1892

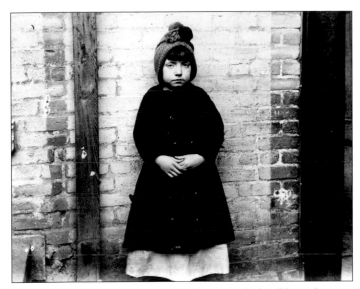

Loss of innocence This little girl, Katie, helped keep house on W. 49th Street in New York during the early 1890s. Childhood innocence was a scarce commodity in 19th century immigrant communities. For most children, education was a luxury superseded by the need to work in factories, as domestic servants, and on the streets. In New York, citizens constantly heard the cries of Irish boys selling newspapers. Gradually, organizations educated and cared for the young. At the West 52nd Street Industrial School, America's first free children's dental clinic opened just a few years after this photograph was taken.

McGivney founds Knights of Columbus Founded in 1882 by Father Michael McGivney, the Knights of Columbus (a member is pictured) had chapters across the United States by 1900. McGivney established the Knights for several reasons: to provide insurance for women and children who had lost their breadwinners through accidents, as a fraternal society to attract young Catholic men who might otherwise be tempted to join secular secret societies, and to act as a Catholic anti-defamation organization. McGivney chose the Columbian name to tie America's origins to a Catholic explorer.

WED !
"DOES OO LOVE OO TIGY-WIGY?"

Yankees resent the Tammany tiger Tammany Hall's most infamous leader was William "Boss" Tweed, who made his entry into New York City politics along with the tiger emblem of the fire company with which he had fought fires and brawled with rival companies. In time, the big cat came to symbolize the very worst of Tammany as far as upper-crust New York was concerned. This 1892 cartoon by Louis Dalrymple depicts an Irish tiger wrapping itself around a maiden. She represents both the city and the presumed purity of the resentful Yankee social class.

The poetry of W. B. Yeats Poet and dramatist William Butler Yeats has been called the greatest literary figure of his age. His poems, which first appeared in the late 1880s, expressed in an Irish context the universal themes of life, drawing heavily on Celtic mythology and folk tales. In "The Lake Isle of Inisfree," for example, he expressed urban man's romantic desire to return to a perceived simpler, rural existence. In 1923 he won the Nobel Prize for Literature, yet some of his best work still lay before him. He twice served as a senator in the Irish Free State.

1892: Bare-knuckle boxer John L. Sullivan loses his heavyweight boxing title to "Gentleman Jim" Corbett after 21 grueling rounds. ● Charles Francis Murphy becomes the head of Tammany Hall's Gas-House district. He ultimately will become the most powerful leader in Tammany history.

January 1, 1892: Annie Moore, an Irish girl celebrating her 15th birthday, steps off the ship *Nevada* and becomes the first immigrant to be processed through Ellis Island.

June 30, 1892: The Homestead Strike begins after contract talks at the Carnegie Steel Company break down. The company locks out its labor force, and union mechanics and transportation workers walk off their jobs in solidarity.

July 6, 1892: Several steelworkers die when agents of the Pinkerton Detective Agency are called in to break up the Homestead Strike and a gunfight ensues.

September 24, 1892: Patrick Gilmore, the celebrated Irish-born Civil War bandleader whose novel arrangements will influence big band orchestration for decades, dies in St. Louis at age 62.

October 29, 1892: Irish-born American artist William Michael Harnett dies in New York. During his lifetime, his remarkably realistic still life paintings appealed to the public but were widely panned by art critics.

1893: A second home-rule bill proposed by British prime minister William Gladstone is defeated in Parliament. ● Thomas Fortune Ryan begins construction on Manhattan's massive streetcar network. ● A run on America's gold supply triggers the Panic of 1893. The United States economy will remain in a state of depression, with more than 10 percent unemployment, until 1897.

Gritty portrayal of Irish slums Though he is best known for his Civil War novel *The Red Badge of Courage*, Stephen Crane's first book-length work was *Maggie: A Girl of the Streets* (1893). Crane, of English and Welsh descent, chronicled the short life of Maggie, a beautiful girl living in the Bowery with her poor and boozy Irish parents. Attempting to escape an intolerable environment, she runs away with an unscrupulous boyfriend who later abandons her. To survive, she turns to prostitution. Crane's *Maggie* was a potent indictment of immigrant life in the slums.

The pioneer "muckraker" A native of County Antrim, Samuel McClure founded *McClure's Magazine* in 1893. He also started the McClure Syndicate—the first newspaper syndicate in the United States. McClure's investigative brand of journalism, which exposed the abuses and corruption of big business and politics, was known as "muckraking" after a reference made by Teddy Roosevelt that compared their methods to "raking the filth." The muckrakers took on business trusts in a number of industries and created a public demand for reform.

Well-to-do Irish choose Nob Hill

When cable cars in the 1870s made it easily accessible, Nob Hill immediately became San Francisco's most prestigious neighborhood. Alongside the mansions built by railroad magnates Leland Stanford, Mark Hopkins, and Collis Huntington were the palatial homes of James Fair and James Flood. Those two Irishmen were among the four "Bonanza Kings" who had made their fortunes in Nevada's Comstock Lode. Flood's impressive residence still stands, although today it is the home of San Francisco's exclusive Pacific-Union Club.

Tammany and President Cleveland

Tammany Hall bowed to the inevitable in 1892 when Democrat Grover Cleveland won his second nonconsecutive presidential term. Tammany's relationship with Cleveland was always uneasy. In 1884 Governor Cleveland had campaigned as a reformer and opponent of the corrupt Tammany Hall Democratic machine. Cleveland's margin of victory over Republican James Blaine that year was small. But after a Blaine supporter, Reverend Samuel Burchard, called the Democrats the party of "rum, Romanism, and rebellion," Tammany's Irish turned out in droves for Cleveland, who won New York by just 1,200 votes.

San Francisco's "Irish" church

Not long after the Gold Rush brought thousands of Irish to San Francisco, Jesuits opened St. Patrick's Church. The small, wood-framed building was located on Market Street, the city's main commercial thoroughfare. By the 1870s, approximately one-third of the city's residents were Irish and many of them lived in The Mission, an area centered on Mission Street, just south of Market. To accommodate this expanded population, a new, grander St. Patrick's opened on Mission Street in 1872. At one time, it was considered the "most Irish" church in America.

Mr. Dooley Tells It Like It Is

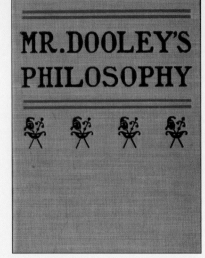

"Th' newspaper does ivrything f'r us. It runs th' polis foorce an' th' banks, commands th' milishy, controls th' ligislachure, baptizes th' young, marries th' foolish, comforts th' afflicted, afflicts th' comfortable, buries th' dead an' roasts thim aftherward."

Americans at the turn of the 20th century would have had no doubt about the source of those words: Mr. Dooley, the creation of Chicago newspaperman Finley Peter Dunne. For three decades, Mr. Dooley spouted his views on the life of his working-class Irish neighborhood, Bridgeport, and on momentous events and personalities in the world beyond.

Dunne was just 26 but already a veteran journalist when he concocted Dooley for the *Chicago Evening Post* in 1893. The character, a skeptical, sharp-eyed observer in the guise of a homespun, bewildered onlooker, was instantly

popular. He had opinions about everything: war and peace, politics and politicians, every social question, and all the fads and fashions of the day. Behind Dooley's nearly impenetrable brogue and humble sayings lay a profound, piercing, and daring eloquence. For example, he defined a fanatic as "a man that does what he thinks th' Lord wud do if He knew th' facts iv th' case." The saloonkeeper also became a source of enduring quotable folk wisdom: "Trust everybody," he said, "but cut the cards."

By 1900 Dunne's work had become a national phenomenon, with Mr. Dooley widely syndicated and the columns collected in book form. Dunne continued writing the Dooley pieces into the 1920s, and several of the Dooley books have been reissued. Dunne died in New York in 1936.

Architect Sullivan breaks new ground The son of an Irish father, Louis Henry Sullivan went on to become the "father of modern architecture." Sullivan shattered architectural conventions by breaking from Greco-Roman models and establishing what came to be viewed as the "modern" style. Sullivan's reputation is particularly linked with the rise of skyscrapers, such as Buffalo's Prudential Building (*pictured*). Legendary architect Frank Lloyd Wright worked for and learned from Sullivan, eventually becoming his chief draftsman.

Sculptor honors American heroes Augustus Saint-Gaudens, who was born in Dublin in 1848 and taken to the United States as an infant, went on to become an acclaimed sculptor. He earned his artistic reputation while designing monuments of American Civil War heroes, such as Robert Gould Shaw (in Boston), John Logan (in Chicago), and William Tecumseh Sherman (in Manhattan). Saint-Gaudens also produced the famous Charles Stewart Parnell monument on O'Connell Street in Dublin.

Hardship and tragedy A New York City journalist and social reformer, James Williams Sullivan exposed the dark side of immigrant life in his writings. In 1895 he published *Tenement Tales of New York*, a series of realistic vignettes of the hardships suffered by New York's poor. One story tells of the life-and-death struggle of young Patrick "Slob" Murphy, who was forced by his neglectful parents to fend for himself on the streets of New York. Murphy's tragic life ends in an accident at age eight.

Hibernians support the Irish The Ancient Order of Hibernians was founded in New York back in 1836, when anti-Irish Catholic bigotry sometimes led to attacks on Catholic churches. The organization became more prominent as the Irish became both more accepted and politically powerful. Today, men's and women's branches of the Ancient Order of Hibernians can be found throughout the United States. The Hibernians bolster the Catholic Church, promote Irish culture, and engage in charitable endeavors.

Celebrating First Communion No matter how poor they might be, the Irish would move Heaven and Earth to dress their children like royalty for their First Holy Communion Day. Early Irish communities in U.S. cities were subdivided into parishes, and members identified themselves first by the names of their churches. For this young lady, who was probably from a relatively well-off family because she was photographed, First Communion was both a profound exercise in embracing her Catholic faith and the first step toward adulthood.

July 31, 1893: The movement to sustain the Gaelic language and culture gets an assist with the founding of the Gaelic League in Dublin.

September 2, 1893: Michael Joseph "King" Kelly, an Irish American major-league baseball legend, plays his last game.

1894: Connie Mack makes his managerial debut with the Pittsburgh Pirates. He will manage for a record 53 years in the major leagues, including 50 with the American League's Philadelphia Athletics.

September 12, 1894: Charles Comiskey plays his final major-league game as a player. He will continue his storied baseball career as a manager for various teams and ultimately as the owner of the Chicago White Sox.

1895: James Buchanan "Diamond Jim" Brady, a multimillionaire Irish American financier and gourmand with a legendary appetite, becomes the first person in New York City to own an automobile. • Cartoonist Robert Outcault introduces *Hogan's Alley*, the first American cartoon strip to enjoy widespread popularity. It stars an Irish kid named Mickey Dugan. • Irish American architect Louis Sullivan, considered the father of the modern steel skyscraper, oversees the creation of his masterpiece, the Prudential (Guaranty) Building in Buffalo.

July 4, 1895: At the height of its short period of influence, the American Protective Association marches in Boston's Fourth of July parade.

August 14, 1895: Irish American artist Thomas Hovenden dies after being critically wounded trying to save a child from being struck by a train. He is perhaps best known for his painting *The Last Moments of John Brown*, which depicts Brown kissing a black baby as he walks to the gallows.

Gilmore and his monster bands

Galway-born Patrick Sarsfield Gilmore fled the famine only to feed his adopted country's insatiable appetite for band music, most especially the martial sort. Gilmore, who served in the Civil War as chief bandmaster for all Massachusetts regiments, became famous after the conflict for his "monster" bands. One such ensemble, which numbered 10,000 vocalists and musicians, made quite a noise at the 1869 National Peace Jubilee in Boston. In subsequent years (until his death in 1892), Gilmore toured with the 22nd New York Regimental Band.

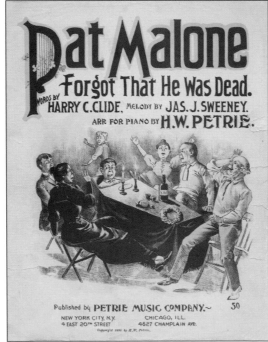

The Irish wake Making light of death is not exclusive to any single group, but the ritual of the wake is most closely associated with Ireland. There, the laying out of the deceased for what could be a lengthy gathering was aided by the island's cool climate. Mourners often traveled long distances for what was as much a celebration of life as it was a marking of death, especially if the departed had attained a good age. A profound belief in an afterlife ensured that even the dead could be the "life" of the party.

The Americanist Controversy

Peter Paul Cahensly was a successful businessmen and founder of the St. Raphael Society, a charitable organization that aided German immigrants. By the late 1880s, the German-born Cahensly was on a collision course with some of Irish America's most prominent citizens—and even the Vatican.

Cahensly was thrust into the spotlight in 1890 when he spoke out publicly against Irish dominance of the American Catholic Church. Since the Great Famine of the 1840s, the Irish had slowly risen from abject poverty. They dominated political machines, police and fire departments, and, as Cahensly noted, the American Catholic hierarchy. This was true even though German Americans also came to the U.S. in great numbers in the mid-19th century.

Yet even in the heavily German Midwest, parish clergy and church leadership were predominately Irish. Around the time that Cahensly spoke out, German Americans comprised about 25 percent of American Catholics but only about 15 percent of bishops. Cahensly argued that German-speaking priests and bishops should serve German American Catholics. Otherwise, Germans would leave the Church and lose touch with their native language and culture. Polish, French, Italian, and other U.S. Catholic groups began to make similar arguments. Eventually, American bishops, and ultimately Pope Leo XIII, were drawn into what came to be called the Americanist controversy.

This debate raised key questions about how immigrants should fit into American society. Should they strive, as Cahensly argued, to maintain close ties to their home land? Or should they assimilate, as James Cardinal Gibbons of Baltimore and Archbishop John Ireland of St. Paul argued?

Cahensly and his supporters may have had legitimate complaints. But Gibbons and others convinced Pope Leo XIII that slicing up American parishes by nationality would splinter the U.S. Church. The victory of Gibbons and the assimilationists helped counter nativist and anti-Catholic charges that these immigrants were loyal only to the Vatican and could never fit into American culture.

"Loyalty to God's church and our country," Gibbons later said. "This is our religious and political faith."

Bryan runs for president

Descended from devout Scots-Irish Presbyterians, William Jennings Bryan was a Nebraska congressman who became the champion of Midwest farmers and the laboring classes. Reacting to the financial panic of 1893, Bryan became a strong advocate of silver-based (and not gold-based) money, which he believed benefited working people. This brilliant orator's "Cross of Gold" speech at the 1896 Democratic National Convention won him the party's presidential nomination. Bryan lost the 1896 race as well as his presidential bids in 1900 and 1908. For his efforts on behalf of poor people, he was known as the "Great Commoner."

McKinley's presidency cut short

A Republican with Scots-Irish ancestors, William McKinley won the 1896 presidential election in a landslide over fellow Irish American William Jennings Bryan. Prior to his presidency, McKinley had served his country

for decades. He fought in the Civil War, sat in the U.S. House for 14 years as a representative from Ohio, and was governor of the Buckeye State for two terms. Though he was reelected president in 1900, his second term was cut short when a deranged anarchist shot him in Buffalo, New York. McKinley's vice president, Theodore Roosevelt, succeeded him.

1896: The United States sends two Irish American athletes, James Brendan Connolly and Thomas Burke, to the first modern Olympic Games in Athens, Greece.

July 13, 1896: Philadelphia Phillies slugger Ed Delahanty belts four inside-the-park home runs in one game.

August 28, 1896: Thirteen years after he is sentenced to life in a British prison for treasonous actions during the "dynamite campaign," Dr. Thomas Gallagher is pardoned and deported. He returns to the United States a broken man.

1897: Fifty Irish American men establish the American Irish Historical Society in Boston in reaction to the pro-nativist political climate. Future president Theodore Roosevelt is among the prominent charter members. • Irish American musician Chauncey Olcott composes his popular ballad "My Wild Irish Rose." • New York Giants slugger Roger Connor retires from the major leagues with 138 home runs—a record that will stand for more than two decades until it is broken by Babe Ruth in 1921.

March 4, 1897: William McKinley, an American of Scots-Irish ancestry, is sworn in as the 25th president of the United States.

June 19, 1897: Captain Charles Boycott dies. His surname became part of the English lexicon in the 1880s, when his efforts to undermine the Irish Land League in County Mayo led to his total ostracism by the local community.

1898: Irish nationalists on both sides of the Atlantic observe the 100-year anniversary of Wolfe Tone's daring, though failed, rebellion and his subsequent execution.

Duryeas create first automobiles Though Henry Ford is viewed as the automobile's top pioneer, Irish American Charles Duryea (*pictured*) and his brother Frank created America's first gasoline-powered cars. Initially bicycle makers, they became fascinated by fuel-propelled vehicles following the Chicago World's Fair in 1886. Seven years later, the brothers successfully drove a gasoline car through the streets of Springfield, Massachusetts. In 1896 the Duryea Motor Wagon Company began selling vehicles, and it remained in business until Ford's Model T revolutionized the industry in 1908.

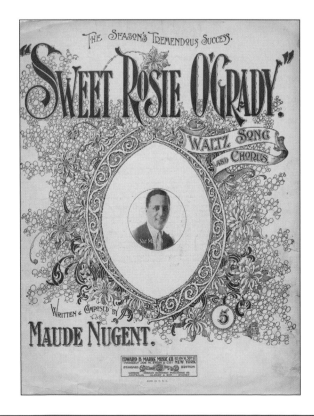

Sentimental Irish music
The Irish appetite for music and song, much of it sentimental, prompted the imaginations of numerous writers and lyricists during the later decades of the 19th century. Thomas Westendorf, an Indiana schoolteacher, penned "I'll Take You Home Again Kathleen" in 1875. Brooklyn-born Maude Nugent added to the growing Irish song catalog with the likes of "Mary From Tipperary," "Mamie Reilly," and her acclaimed 1896 composition "Sweet Rosie O'Grady." This melody wafted its way back across the Atlantic and into the writings of James Joyce.

> "[T]here are no limits to which powers of privilege
> will not go to keep the workers in slavery."
>
> —MOTHER JONES

Women Who Challenged the Capitalists

"Pray for the dead," labor activist Mother Jones once said, "and fight like hell for the living."

Born Mary Harris in County Cork, Mother Jones was one of many Irish women who led America's fledgling labor movement in the late 19th and early 20th century. Jones came from a long line of Irish fighters. Her grandfather was hanged by the British, and her father was forced to flee Ireland. She settled in Memphis and became a schoolteacher, but she lost her husband and four children during a yellow fever epidemic.

Leonora Barry

When Jones also lost her Chicago dressmaking business after the famous city fire of 1871, she became enraged at the gap between rich and poor. She organized coal miners and, in 1903, led the "march of the mill children" from Philadelphia to New York, drawing attention to the plight of underage workers.

Like Jones, Kate Kennedy and Leonora Barry were Irish immigrant schoolteachers whose hardships drove them to action. Kennedy was born in Ireland in 1827 and was active in San Francisco. She demanded equal pay for men and women and ran for public office at a time when most women could not even vote. Barry, born in 1849, toiled for low wages in a factory before joining the Knights of Labor. She eventually became the leader of that union's Committee on Women's Work.

Mary Kenney O'Sullivan was another union trailblazer. In 1892 she became the American Federation of Labor's first female general organizer. Around that time, Kate Mullaney organized female laundry workers in upstate New York.

Perhaps the most famous female labor advocate of the 20th century was Elizabeth Gurley Flynn, a dedicated Marxist whose commitment to both communism and workers landed her in prison. She spoke and wrote often of the revolutionary legacy she inherited from her Irish ancestors.

This cast of strong Irish women lends much credence to Mother Jones's belief that "no nation is greater than its women."

Better jobs for women A larger percentage of Irish immigrants were women, many of whom took jobs as domestic servants and unskilled factory workers. Domestic jobs were usually preferable because of better working conditions and the inclusion of room and board. Many second-generation Irish American women landed better jobs, such as telephone operator (*pictured*), secretary, nurse, and teacher. Though teaching positions were difficult to find, the profession was highly valued by Irish immigrants because it was held in high regard back home.

1898: Joseph McKenna, a former United States congressman and U.S. attorney general, is appointed an associate justice of the Supreme Court. • Industrialist Thomas Fortune Ryan consolidates his tobacco holdings, joins forces with his competition, and establishes the American Tobacco Company.

February 15, 1898: The battleship USS *Maine* is sunk in Havana Harbor, leading to a declaration of war against Spain some two months later. As with every conflict since the Revolution, Irish American soldiers will serve in great numbers and with distinction.

March 17, 1898: John Thomas Ball, lord chancellor of Ireland from 1875 to 1880, dies at age 83.

April 1898: The Spanish-American War erupts as the U.S. confronts Spain over Cuba's ongoing struggle to gain independence from Spain. Though they will be well represented on the battlefield, Irish Americans will generally reject what they perceive as American imperialism.

May 1898: The Rough Riders, the storied volunteer cavalry regiment of the Spanish-American War, is mustered with many Irish Americans—as well as future president Theodore Roosevelt.

July 1, 1898: Rough Riders captain William "Bucky" O'Neill, an American soldier of Irish descent, is killed in action in Cuba.

1899: Irish American author Kate Chopin publishes *The Awakening*, her most famous work of fiction. The book is roundly criticized for its somewhat shocking portrayal of a discontented Victorian housewife. • Gaelic scholar Douglas Hyde successfully crushes an effort to eliminate Irish as a field of study at Dublin's Trinity College.

Hearst builds newspaper empire William Randolph Hearst, the descendant of Scots-Irish immigrants, created the largest newspaper empire in America. His career in journalism began when his wealthy father acquired the *San Francisco Examiner*, which he turned over in 1887 to his 24-year-old son. William bought more newspapers, most importantly the *New York Journal*. Always looking for the sensational in a story, Hearst's *Journal* inspired the term "yellow journalism" from The Yellow Kid, a character in the Hearst comic strip *Hogan's Alley*. In the 1920s, one in four Americans received their news from a Hearst newspaper.

Irish embrace education With so much of Irish societal structure in ruins after the famine, the need for education was never greater. Immigrant Irish communities in the United States vigorously championed the education of their American children, most notably through the network of Catholic Church parochial schools, which would become a crucially important factor in Irish America's ultimate success story. Here, Irish girls in South Boston embrace the gift of reading.

The daughter of Jefferson Davis Varina Anne "Winnie" Davis, youngest child of Confederate president Jefferson Davis and his wife (the Irish-descended Varina Howell Davis), became a celebrity in her own right long after the Civil War. In the 1880s, two decades after the conflict ended, Southern veterans dubbed her "the daughter of the Confederacy." As a young woman, Winnie Davis celebrated her Irish roots by writing a short biography of Robert Emmet, the Irish patriot alongside whom one of her great-grandfathers fought. She died of "malarial gastritis" at age 34.

The James brothers Descendants of Protestant Irish ancestors, Henry James (*left*) and his brother, William (*right*), achieved brilliant careers in the literary and academic worlds, respectively. In 1866 the brothers' wealthy parents moved their family from New York to Cambridge, Massachusetts, to expose their children to the area's intellectual opportunities. The brothers studied at Harvard, but Henry dropped out to pursue a hugely successful career in writing, authoring such classics as *The Turn of the Screw*, *Daisy Miller*, and *The Bostonians*. William took a degree in medicine and became one of the founders of the new field of psychology.

O'Neill and the Rough Riders William "Bucky" O'Neill lived for adventure. Born in St. Louis, where his Irish parents had settled, he studied law in the East, but in the 1880s he moved to Arizona. There he became a newspaperman, and in Tombstone he probably witnessed the famous "Gunfight at the OK Corral." He later moved to Prescott, Arizona, where he became sheriff and eventually mayor. When the Spanish-American War broke out, O'Neill led a band of 300 Arizona militiamen to Texas, where they joined the Rough Riders in the U.S. Volunteer Cavalry. Captain O'Neill was killed in battle in San Juan, Cuba, on July 1, 1898.

"IT'S AWFUL FRESH"

Milder parodies The mid-19th century American Irish were frequently lampooned as being drunken, stupid, and violent. Such popular portrayals softened somewhat by century's end, and a gentler image was propagated—in part by the Irish themselves. In vaudeville acts, such as Gilmore and Leonard's *Hogan's Alley*, creators poked fun at an ethnic group in a way that made its members seem less threatening than outsiders had initially believed. Base fear and loathing was, quite simply, superseded by hokum and high farce.

The Irish in Theatre

Hollywood starlet Drew Barrymore and brooding playwright Eugene O'Neill don't have much in common. However, both can trace their roots to the earliest days of the Irish American theater.

Nineteenth century theater was a diverse mix of high and low, song and dance, minstrelsy and Shakespeare. Crowd passions sometimes led to violence, such as the Astor Place Riots of 1849. More than 20 people died when Irish and other working-class fans protested a performance by actor William Charles Macready, who was beloved by middle-class and British theatergoers.

During this raucous era, an impressive cast of Irish thespians and writers emerged.

Drew Barrymore's great-great-grandfather, John Drew, was born in Dublin in 1827. He later established his theatrical reputation at Philadelphia's Arch Street Theatre, where he worked with his wife, Louisa.

The couple's three children also entered the theater, including John Drew, Jr., an acclaimed New York Shake-

Maurice Barrymore and Georgiana Drew

spearean actor who often shared the stage with Limerick native Ada Rehan. Another Drew, Georgiana, married Maurice Barrymore. Their children—Lionel, Ethel, and John—were among the finest actors of their day.

Cork native Bernard O'Flaherty, under the stage name Barney Williams, began his career performing in blackface. He then starred in numerous Irish roles in New York, London, and Washington during the 1840s and 1850s. Playwright Dion Boucicault, born in Dublin in 1820, popularized the stage Irishman. His plays *The Colleen Bawn*, *The Shaughraun*, and *Arrah-na-Pogue* blend stereotypes and history and are still performed to this day.

James O'Neill, born in Kilkenny in 1847, became famous in the United States for his rousing performance in *The Count of Monte Cristo*. O'Neill was the model for the frugal, haunted father, James Tyrone, in Eugene O'Neill's *Long Day's Journey into Night*. It was not a flattering portrait. Nevertheless, without James O'Neill there would never have been such a masterful play.

Vaudeville's "Irish Queen" As Irish performers laid claim to vaudeville fame, no single voice was as feisty and popular as that of Maggie Cline. A Massachusetts-born daughter of Irish immigrants, Cline quit a job in a shoe factory to embark on a 40-year music hall career. The "Irish Queen" was an energetic performer who enraptured her audiences with a lengthy repertoire of Irish songs. The best known was "Throw Him Down, McCloskey," an 1890 song by John W. Kelly that he sold to Cline for $2.

Vaudeville Irish The Irish played a central role in the late 19th century development of vaudeville, which included a diverse array of music, dance, comedy, melodrama, personalities, and oddities. Vaudeville was particularly popular with ethnic audiences, so the material often dealt with the Irish and other immigrants. The "Vaudeville Irish" (one of whom is pictured) were often stereotypical. But almost as often, stereotypes were undermined—to the delight of the Irish in the crowd.

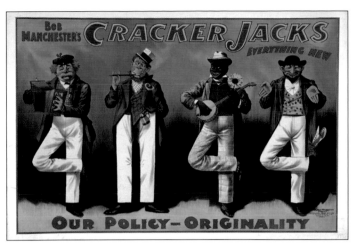

Playing up the stereotypes Though many vaudeville shows portrayed the Irish as amusing and even lovable, some theater producers in the late 1800s relied on blatant bigotry to sell tickets. Many men and women loved to laugh at the other ethnic groups who shared tightly packed city neighborhoods with them. As late as 1899, Bob Manchester's *Cracker Jacks* stereotyped French, Irish, African, and Jewish Americans in a way that would become taboo in the new century.

Irish find work in America As America began building new public works projects for the industrial age, Irish farmers left the forlorn post-famine landscape for wage-paying jobs in the United States. There, they joined second-generation Irish Americans in building projects such as this one: a dam across the Connecticut River in Holyoke, Massachusetts. Ireland continued to lose hundreds of thousands of people to America in the late 19th century as economic opportunities beckoned.

"Mile-a-Minute" Murphy In 1899 Charles Murphy (*left*) of Brooklyn became the first man to ride a bicycle for one mile in under a minute (57.8 seconds). He achieved this extraordinary feat after persuading a railway company to build a two-mile carpet of boards on a railway line so that he could ride in a train's slipstream. He claimed to have invented the concept of streamlining. Throughout his career, "Mile-a-Minute" Murphy broke seven world records in distances up to 10 miles. He was inducted into the U.S. Bicycle Hall of Fame in 1991.

Olcott's weepy ballads "My Wild Irish Rose" was one of Chauncey Olcott's famous Irish ballads of the late 1800s and early 1900s. He also helped pen "Mother Machree," "When Irish Eyes Are Smiling," and "Goodbye, My Emerald Land." "My Wild Irish Rose" is a tribute to "the sweetest flower that grows," and the singer longs for the day when

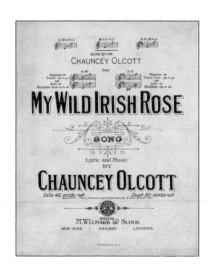

he may "take the bloom from my wild Irish Rose." Olcott's often weepy ballads appealed to American-born Irish who had heard about Ireland in a highly idealized fashion.

Leaders, Rebels, and Soldiers

1900–1918

The travails and tragedies of the Irish experience in America were all too familiar to John Francis Fitzgerald, one of a dozen children born to an immigrant couple in Boston in the late 19th century. Early deaths and alcoholism plagued his family, but young John managed to escape misfortune. Like so many other Irish, he turned to politics as a way out, and in 1906 he was elected mayor of his native city.

Fitzgerald was a popular, charming man, although he never became as powerful a figure as one of his successors, James Michael Curley. His life, however, would become part of the Irish American narrative of the 20th century. His daughter, Rose, married Joseph P. Kennedy, and the achievements of their children would come to symbolize Irish America's rise to power, its apparent assimilation, and its reawakening.

Political leaders like John Fitzgerald were the most conspicuous representatives of Irish America's newfound power and acceptance. But while the Irish surely did dominate urban politics in the early years of the 20th century, other fields were opening to them as well.

Sports, particularly professional baseball, provided another route to achievement. Two Irish Americans, Connie Mack and John McGraw, began legendary careers as full-time managers, Mack with the Philadelphia Athletics

> **"The people not the bosses must rule! Bigger, Better, Busier Boston!"**
> —CAMPAIGN SLOGAN OF JOHN "HONEY FITZ" FITZGERALD, MAYOR OF BOSTON FROM 1906 TO '08 AND 1910 TO '14

President William Howard Taft (*left*) shakes hands with John "Honey Fitz" Fitzgerald, who in 1894 was the only Democrat from New England elected to Congress. Historian Robert Dallek described the Harvard graduate as a "charming, impish, affable lover of people." Later the mayor of Boston, Fitzgerald died in 1950, 10 years before his daughter's son was elected president.

in 1901 and McGraw with the New York Giants the following year. Journalism had attracted male Irish immigrants for decades, but now Irish women were making inroads. Elizabeth Cochran became one of the most famous reporters in the world under the byline of Nellie Bly, and Anne O'Hare McCormick—who began her career at a Catholic newspaper in Cleveland—went on to become the first female journalist to win a Pulitzer Prize.

Less celebrated but just as noteworthy were the achievements of female Irish schoolteachers. Irish nuns were, of course, a mainstay of Catholic education (and of Catholic social services), but in the new century, lay Irish women flocked to education as well. Historian Hasia Diner noted that Irish women comprised a quarter or more of the teachers in Buffalo, New York, and Scranton, Pennsylvania. In Worcester, Massachusetts, just about half of the city's public schoolteachers were Irish in 1908.

The new century, then, saw expanding possibilities for Irish Americans as well as continued economic and political clout. The latter combination attracted Irish nationalists, as Ireland once again began to stir.

The decline and death of Charles Parnell and the scandalous divisions of the Irish nationalist movement in America persuaded many Irish Americans to put aside their hopes for Ireland's independence. But a new political leader, John Redmond, emerged to take up Parnell's cause for Irish home rule—that is, a limited form of independence. Redmond formed relationships with Irish American politicians, business leaders, and ranking clergymen—in other words, the elite of Irish American society. They responded by organizing a group to support and fund Redmond's Irish Parliamentary Party.

Once again, however, some Irish Americans rejected the idea that politics could ever lead to Irish independence from Britain. Furthermore, they refused to accept home rule as the final settlement of Irish national aspirations. With the new century a decade old, Irish American revolutionaries, such as stalwart John Devoy, began making contact with visitors from Ireland. He hooked up with James Connolly, a socialist agitator and union organizer; Maude Gonne, founder of an Irish women's revolutionary organization; and a poet and schoolteacher named Patrick Pearse. These connections revived a dormant Irish American revolutionary movement, and they set in motion a transatlantic conspiracy to bring about, at last, freedom for Ireland.

When Europe's imperial powers marched to war in August 1914, Clan na Gael in America and the Irish Republican Brotherhood in Dublin began preparations for a coordinated rebellion in Ireland with the assistance of

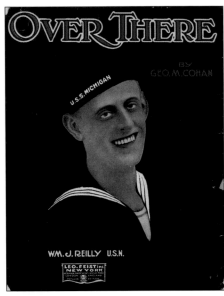

American popular music, based on Tin Pan Alley in New York City, had an increasingly Irish lilt after 1890. The most successful songster was George M. Cohan, a vaudevillian composer and producer whose tunes became American classics. They include "Give My Regards to Broadway" (1904), "You're a Grand Old Flag" (1906), and the wartime showstopper "Over There" (1917).

Britain's bitter enemy, Germany. Devoy served as the rebellion's liaison with the German government, sharing plans for the rebellion with German diplomats in New York and Washington. America, of course, was neutral until 1917, allowing Devoy to plot with the Germans without committing treason.

After months of careful planning, the rebellion was scheduled for Easter 1916. Among its leaders were two men, Connolly and Thomas Clarke, who had lived in the United States for several years. Devoy arranged for a German submarine to bring arms to waiting rebels, while Padraig Pearse made plans to take over several buildings in Dublin, including the General Post Office.

But the Easter Rising, like so many other rebellions in Irish history, was doomed to failure. The German arms shipment never landed because the British intercepted German communications. The rebels were far too few in number—only about 1,500—to pose a serious threat. The rising was put down in less than a week. Pearse, Connolly, Clarke, and other rebel leaders were executed by the British for committing treason, and in the process, they became martyrs for an unfinished cause.

Among the leaders scheduled for execution was a mathematics teacher named Eamon de Valera. He was born in New York City, which presented diplomatic problems for the British at a time when the Allies hoped the United States would enter the war on the side of Britain and France. De Valera's life was spared, but he was sent to prison.

The United States entered the world war in 1917. That same year, Irish American impresario George M. Cohan composed the song "Over There," which accompanied thousands of American doughboys to their troop ships. Among the units dispatched to the Western Front was the traditionally Irish "Fighting 69th" from New York.

The war showed the diversity of Irish America in those early years of the 20th century. While some Irish Americans had worked to bring about Britain's defeat, others—in far larger numbers—crossed the Atlantic to fight on Britain's behalf.

The war ended in 1918 with victory for the Allies. Not long afterward, Eamon de Valera, political leader of a renewed Irish independence movement, escaped from a British jail and fled to the land of his birth. He would rally Irish America's political and economic power as no figure had before—and create bitter enemies in the process.

The Easter Rising was a badly planned uprising of nationalists (*pictured*) in Dublin in April 1916. World War I was underway and Germany tried to send military aid to the nationalists, but it never got through. The British called the revolt treason, and they hurriedly hung the ringleaders. However, those who were executed became martyrs to many Irish, including people who had previously rejected calls for independence.

1900: John Redmond reunites the Irish Parliamentary Party, mending the schism caused by Charles Stewart Parnell's scandalous fall from power. • William Muldoon, perhaps the country's first celebrity personal trainer, opens his Hygienic Institute in Purchase, New York. Muldoon's clients include Theodore Roosevelt and boxer John L. Sullivan, whose drinking Muldoon supposedly curbs "with a baseball bat."

April 2, 1900: Queen Victoria's train departs Windsor en route to Dublin for her first official state visit to Ireland.

1901: Corrupt Tammany boss Richard Croker resigns his post and moves to the Irish countryside.

September 14, 1901: U.S. president William McKinley dies eight days after being gunned down by an anarchist during a public appearance in Buffalo, New York. • Vice President Theodore Roosevelt, whose mother is of Scots-Irish and Huguenot descent, is sworn in as the 26th president after the death of his predecessor. At age 42, he is the youngest man to ever hold the office.

December 4, 1901: The United Irish League of America is established in New York to raise funds and support the efforts of the United Irish League in Ireland, which is pushing for home rule.

1902: Charles Francis Murphy succeeds Richard Croker as the head of Tammany Hall. As straight as his predecessor was crooked, Murphy will become Tammany's most important leader, ensuring the organization's vitality well into the 20th century. • Irish American cartoonist Thomas Aloysius Dorgan creates *Johnny Wise,* his first weekly comic strip, for the *San Francisco Chronicle*.

Irish and the Boer War To Irish nationalists, British oppression of the Boers in southern Africa was analogous to British suppression of the Irish. When the Boer War began in 1899, Irishmen formed the Irish Brigade to fight alongside the Boers. Its commander was Irish American John Blake, a West Point graduate. Despite a U.S. declaration of neutrality, the Irish-influenced Democratic Party openly called for a pro-Boer policy. The Chicago branch of the nationalistic Clan na Gael sent an ambulance brigade to the aid of the Boers. Ironically, with so many Irishmen in the British military (some of whom are pictured during a Boer War battle), the sons of Erin often found themselves facing each other in battle.

Irish on the diamond In the 1880s, one-third to one-half of all professional baseball players were Irish. Some of the late 19th-century Irish stars remain icons of the game. John McGraw (*pictured*), who batted .391 for the Baltimore Orioles in 1899, is best remembered for his 30 years as manager of the New York Giants from 1902 to 1932. Catcher Mike "King" Kelly was baseball's first superstar, playing for Chicago and Boston in the 1880s. Owner Charlie Comiskey was so identified with his Chicago White Sox that the team's ballpark was named after him.

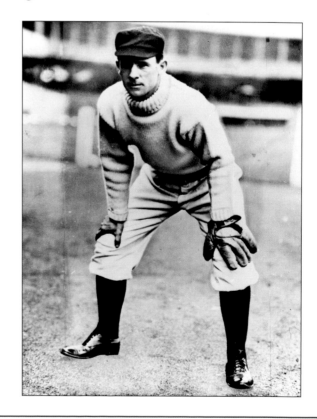

Tammany's questionable wealth

Tammany Hall, as evidenced by its lavish social club, reveled in its own version of the Gilded Age. Though founded as a charitable institution in the late 1700s, Tammany's peak years in the late 19th century were characterized by graft, corruption, and unrestrained pocket lining. Though the early 20th century witnessed a shift toward more progressive politics, the biggest Tammany headline from 1920 concerned the questionable fortune left behind by one of its deceased former bosses, Richard Croker. His estate was estimated at $5 million.

The Three Keatons Irish American vaudevillians Joe and Myra Keaton perform with their son, Buster. The Three Keatons played alongside such legends as W. C. Fields, Eddie Cantor, and Al Jolson. When the family's act broke up, Keaton was in his early 20s. He discovered movies, and his unique combination of talents—unchanging stoicism, extraordinary physical dexterity, and cinematic inventiveness—won him a huge following at the height of the silent era.

Kissing the Blarney stone The Blarney stone, which one kisses by hanging upside down over the battlements of Blarney Castle, has been one of Ireland's most popular tourist attractions for 200 years. It is said to give the gift of eloquence—or gift of gab—and attracts millions of visitors every year. By association, *blarney* has come to mean "flattery designed to gain favor," and a person can be described as being "full of blarney." A pilgrimage to kiss the Blarney Stone is more popular among Irish Americans than among today's native Irish.

1902: Irish American industrialist and philanthropist Andrew Mellon expands the family business into Mellon National Bank, a holding company composed of several smaller banks. • Mark Fagan, a 32-year-old Republican, assumes office as mayor of his native Jersey City, New Jersey. He will serve five nonconsecutive terms.

1903: The Wyndham Act is passed, enabling Irish tenant framers to purchase the land they work. The act effectively ends the practice of landlordism in rural Ireland. • Mary Kenney O'Sullivan, a union organizer and daughter of working-class Irish immigrants, co-founds the National Women's Trade Union League. • American entrepreneur Edward Doheny, son of Irish immigrants, strikes oil in California. Doheny will become one of the biggest oil barons in American history.

March 4, 1903: New York alderman, Tammany figure, and crime boss "Big" Tim Sullivan takes his seat as a member of the U.S. Congress.

April 5, 1903: Irish-born author Mary Anne Sadlier, whose many books reflect the Irish immigrant condition in both the United States and Canada, dies at age 82.

July 2, 1903: Ed Delahanty, whose .346 career batting average ranks fifth best in major-league history, dies after drunkenly falling (or jumping) into the Niagara River and being carried over the Falls.

October 1903: The Royal Rooters, a group of loyal Boston baseball fans that includes John "Honey Fitz" Fitzgerald and is led by bar owner Michael McGreevy, travel to Pittsburgh. Their support helps the Boston Pilgrims defeat the Pirates in the first World Series.

The leprechaun Be wary of leprechauns, for they might be up to mischief. According to Irish folklore, these male fairies spend most of their time making shoes and drinking themselves into a stupor. They also have appointed themselves guardians of ancient treasures (left in Ireland by the Danes), which they have stashed in pots (as in the fabled "pots o' gold"). If captured by a human, a leprechaun will promise to trade great wealth for his freedom. But after he offers a gold coin and subsequently runs away, the coin turns to leaves or ashes. Many Irish citizens could do without the little character, feeling that it represents Ireland about as badly as Mickey Mouse represents the United States.

Tenement living A child bathes in a kitchen sink in a New York City tenement apartment. Even as Irish Americans climbed the social and economic ladders in the first decades of the 20th century, many immigrant descendants or new arrivals from Ireland lived in harsh tenement conditions. Tenement dwellings offered only the barest comforts and rarely included such niceties as bathrooms. Poorly lit and ill-ventilated, they were commonly inhabited by multiple families. Frequently, tenement dwellings served as home sweatshops for women and children working on clothing or other goods.

Hell's Kitchen In the early years of Irish immigration, Hell's Kitchen on Manhattan's West Side earned a reputation as a teeming "sinkhole of despair." By the early 1900s, Irish Americans had begun moving away from the old tenement neighborhoods and into new developments in Queens, Brooklyn, and the Bronx. Yet Hell's Kitchen remained infamous: largely Irish, often crime-ridden, and one of the city's poorest and roughest areas. During Prohibition and beyond, organized crime and gangs infested the area. Many Irish Americans still live in Hell's Kitchen.

Leading apostle of home rule John Redmond (*left, in top hat*), the leader of the Irish Parliamentary Party in the British House of Commons, is pictured in London with fellow nationalist John Dillon. As the leading apostle of home rule, Redmond was an influential figure in Irish American communities. In 1901 Redmond toured the United States and spoke to the newly formed United Irish League of America in New York City. The new organization reciprocated by channeling Irish American cash to the cause of home rule, providing hundreds of thousands of dollars to Redmond's party in just a decade.

Mitchell comes to miners' defense John Mitchell, born to a family of Irish American miners in Illinois, led the United Mine Workers of America (UMWA) in a series of confrontations with mine owners at the turn of the 20th century. He was perhaps best known for leading UMWA strikes in the Pennsylvania anthracite coal industry in 1900 and 1902. In that battle, the union sought recognition from owners as well as better pay and hours for miners. The struggle escalated into a five-month strike. President Theodore Roosevelt intervened to negotiate an end to the work stoppage.

1904: Anne Sullivan, the teacher who educated the deaf and blind Helen Keller, watches Keller graduate from Radcliffe College to become the first deaf and blind person ever to earn a college degree. • Irish American teacher Margaret Haley is named president of the National Federation of Teachers labor union. • James O'Leary, son of Catherine O'Leary (whose cow supposedly started the Great Chicago Fire), begins an illegal gambling operation on a steamship on Lake Michigan. He will make a fortune in gambling.

March 21, 1904: William R. Grace, Irish-born American businessman, philanthropist, and politician who served as the first Catholic mayor of New York City, dies at age 71.

November 8, 1904: Irish American president Theodore Roosevelt is reelected, handily defeating Alton Parker, his Democratic challenger.

December 27, 1904: Thanks to Ireland's recent literary revival, the Abbey Theatre opens in Dublin.

1905: Storefront theaters (nickelodeons) become part of the American landscape, bringing vaudeville acts and the "stage Irish" to motion pictures. • Journalist William Riordan publishes a series of interviews with Tammany sachem George Washington Plunkitt entitled *Plunkitt of Tammany Hall.* The interviews provide keen insight into the mind of a Tammany boss. • Irish-born Ada Rehan, considered one of the finest comedic stars of the American stage, retires.

November 28, 1905: Irish nationalist Arthur Griffith founds Sinn Féin, a political party that seeks to repeal the Act of Union and reestablish a dual monarchy. (Griffith's Sinn Féin bears little resemblance to the radicalized socialist Sinn Féin of the late 20th century.)

Ryan amasses a fortune
Tycoon Thomas Fortune Ryan rose from humble beginnings as a clerk in Baltimore to land a spot on *Forbes*'s first "rich list" in 1902. Starting out as the youngest member to have a seat on the New York Stock Exchange, Ryan built a business empire that included controlling interests in more than 30 companies. When he died, his fortune was estimated at more than $200 million—despite his generous contributions to Catholic charities.

Herbert brings "Babes" to Broadway Born in Dublin, Victor Herbert in 1886 immigrated to America, where he became one of the best-known figures in music. A cellist, conductor, and composer of light opera, he wrote for the Ziegfeld Follies and had a string of hits on Broadway. His *Babes in Toyland,* a musical extravaganza based on Mother Goose nursery rhymes, opened in 1903 and ran for 192 nights. It remains popular to this day. Herbert, along with John Philip Sousa and Irving Berlin, was a founder of the American Society of Composers, Authors and Publishers.

Everybody's Automaker

From 1908 to 1927, Henry Ford made automobile ownership possible for all Americans of average means. In that time span, more than 15 million of his popular Model Ts were sold in the United States. In fact, in 1918 one-half of all cars in America were Model Ts. The popularity of his cars made him one of the wealthiest men in America.

This giant of American industry came from humble Irish roots. His father had left his native County Cork at the height of the famine in 1847. He eventually acquired a farm in Dearborn, Michigan, where he met and married Mary O'Hern, an American-born orphan girl whose adoptive parents also hailed from Cork. Henry was raised to succeed his father on the farm, but early in life he was much more interested in tinkering with mechanical devices.

At age 16, Henry got a job in nearby Detroit as an apprentice machinist. He eventually became an engineer, but he devoted his spare time to building an automobile with an internal combustion engine. He built his first car (though not *the* first car) in 1896. Seven years later, he founded the Ford Motor Company.

Ford's genius was to make his automobiles accessible to a wide market. He did this through efficiency and organization. In 1913 he created the "assembly line" system of manufacturing his Model Ts, whereby his plant turned out a car every 98 minutes. This mass production allowed Ford to profitably sell his cars at an affordable $500 each.

Henry Ford with a Model T, circa 1918

To get his cars to the public, he franchised dealerships in cities across America.

Part of Ford's success was his treatment of his employees. Beginning in 1914, he paid his workers $5 a day, more than double what other workers received. Ford knew that happy workers were good workers. But he also had a dark side. Like many of his generation, he was anti-Semitic. A newspaper that he owned in the 1920s, *The Dearborn Independent*, constantly railed against "international Jewry."

Mother Jones Mary Harris "Mother" Jones marches on behalf of striking miners in Colorado. Born in Cork, Jones became a labor and community organizer in her 50s after her husband and four children died of yellow fever (1867) and her property was destroyed in the Great Chicago Fire (1871). Jones, a white-haired, grandmotherly figure, was known to her supporters as the "Miner's Angel" for her work with the United Mine Workers of America. Often arrested for her activities, she was described by a district attorney as "the most dangerous woman in America." In 1903 she led a Children's Crusade march from Pennsylvania to New York to protest child labor.

1906: John Francis "Honey Fitz" Fitzgerald is elected mayor of Boston, becoming the first Catholic Irish American to hold that office.

August 1906: Irish American surgeon George Washington Crile performs the first successful human-to-human blood transfusion, at Cleveland's St. Alexis Hospital.

December 10, 1906: President Roosevelt becomes the first American to win a Nobel Prize. He wins the Peace Prize for brokering the treaty that ended the Russo-Japanese War.

1907: Philosopher William James, brother of author Henry James, promotes his philosophy of pragmatism in his groundbreaking book of the same name. • Jim Casey, an American teenager of Irish descent, borrows $100 from a friend and launches the American Messenger Company, which will become the United Parcel Service. • Irish American labor leader John Mitchell resigns his post as president of the United Mine Workers of America. Under his leadership, the union experienced dramatic growth and earned a key victory in the Great Anthracite Strike of 1902.

January 26, 1907: J. M. Synge's *The Playboy of the Western World* opens at Dublin's Abbey Theatre. Anger at the play's portrayal of the rural Irish triggers riots in the streets of Dublin.

1908: Johnny Hayes, an Irish-born American, wins the marathon in the third modern Olympic Games. • Socialist labor leader James Larkin founds the Irish Transport and General Workers' Union, serving workers in a variety of trades. • The FBI is born when the U.S. attorney general orders a special investigatory force created under the auspices of the Department of Justice. It initially will be called the Bureau of Investigation, and Irish American agents will play a key role in the agency from its beginning.

The Baltimore Catechism *The Baltimore Catechism* was the mainstay of religious education for generations of Irish American Catholics. In 1829, U.S. bishops called for a new catechism "better adapted to the circumstances" of America. It wasn't until 1885, however, that the American church published *A Catechism of Christian Doctrine, Prepared and Enjoined by Order of the Third Council of Baltimore*—which became known as *The Baltimore Catechism*. Often republished, and revised in 1941, the original catechism consisted of 33 Q&A lessons on the Roman Catholic creed, sacraments, and commandments. The first question and answer: "Q. Who made the world? A. God made the world."

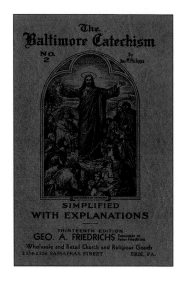

Irish beauty finally recognized
In the middle of the 19th century, such artists as Thomas Nast infamously portrayed the Irish as ape-like creatures. The turn of the century, however, brought a change in America's view of Irish appearance. This young lady's picture adorned a 1906 article entitled "Racial Traits in American Beauty." The woman was described as "Celtic-Anglo-Iberic, with Celtic strain dominant." Cultural blinders came off as the Irish won acceptance in American society.

Gaelic Revival Beginning in the late 1800s, Ireland and America experienced the Gaelic Revival. The crux of the movement was a newfound interest in the Irish language, but people also became more interested in Gaelic music, dance, art, history, and literature. *The Gael,* published in New York, reflected the revival. Stories in this particular issue included "An Irishman's Impressions of a *Feis Ceoil*" and "Irish History in American Schools."

New York's Easter Parade Paraders throng on Fifth Avenue outside New York City's St. Patrick's Cathedral on Easter Sunday, 1904. The Easter Parade began in the late 19th century, when Fifth Avenue was a fashionable address; it was an occasion for the well-to-do to show off their finery. The construction of St. Patrick's, the seat of the New York archdiocese and a focus of Irish American ethnic pride, gave the city's biggest immigrant group a prominent place in the festivities. The parade continues today, mostly as a secular affair.

The legacy of "Honey Fitz" John Francis "Honey Fitz" Fitzgerald, a progenitor of the Kennedy political dynasty, was born in Boston to County Wexford immigrants. Fitzgerald reputedly earned his nickname by singing "Sweet Adeline" during political rallies. He was a fixture in Boston politics for more than three decades, winning election to the city council, the state legislature, and the U.S. Congress. He served three terms as mayor. In 1914, his daughter Rose married Joseph P. Kennedy. Honey Fitz's grandchildren from that union included President John F. Kennedy and U.S. senators Robert and Edward Kennedy.

The Barrymore family John, Ethel, and Lionel Barrymore (*left to right*) continued the acting legacy forged by their parents, Maurice and Georgiana (daughter of Dublin acting great John Drew). Ethel dominated the American stage at the turn of the century and won an Academy Award in 1944. Lionel, who starred in numerous film classics, played Mr. Potter in *It's a Wonderful Life*. John, a prominent silent film actor, is the grandfather of current film star Drew Barrymore.

1908: Irish American athlete John Flanagan wins his third straight Olympic gold medal in the hammer throw.

July 3, 1908: Joel Chandler Harris, Irish American Southerner and author of the racially charged Uncle Remus stories, dies at age 59.

September 27, 1908: The first production Model T rolls out of the Ford Motor Company's Piquette Plant in Detroit.

1909: William Zebulon Foster, the committed Socialist who will serve many years as the general secretary of the Communist Party USA, joins the Industrial Workers of the World labor union. • Newspaper magnate William Randolph Hearst loses his bid to become mayor of New York City. It is his third electoral defeat in five years, as he lost the race for the same office in 1905 as well as New York's gubernatorial race in 1906.

1910: John Fitzgerald is reelected mayor of Boston. He will hold the office for another four years.

1911: Irish American businessman James Augustine Farrell is named president of U.S. Steel. During his two-decade tenure at the helm, the company will become the first billion-dollar business in America. • Irish American John McDermott becomes, at the age of 20, the youngest golfer ever to win the U.S. Open golf tournament.

1912: The musical *The Isle o' Dreams* introduces a timeless Irish ballad, "When Irish Eyes Are Smiling," by Chauncey Olcott and George Graff. • Two Irish-born American Olympic athletes bring home track and field gold—Patrick McDonald for the shot put and Matthew McGrath for the hammer throw.

An exciting adventure For many Irish, immigration to America was an escape from starvation and brutal poverty. But for others, the experience was more of an adventure than a flight from oppression. Economics, marriage prospects, and wanderlust inspired some to cross the Atlantic to start a new life. While most immigrants were single, some arrived with children, whose eyes widened as they glimpsed the exciting cities of the New World for the first time. They saw possibilities, hope, and the chance to fulfill their dreams.

THE IRISH-AMERICAN LINE.

***Puck* and the Irish** *Puck,* a popular humor magazine that flourished from early in the Gilded Age until World War I, often targeted Irish Americans as objects of contempt. This 1907 cartoon suggests a special transatlantic passenger service for Irish immigrants that allowed them to indulge their alleged boorishness. Drawn and published by German Americans, *Puck*'s depiction of Irish Americans in part reflected the tension between the two largest immigrant groups at the turn of the 20th century.

Phelan leads San Francisco revival

Born in San Francisco, James Phelan was the son of an Irish miner who had made his fortune in the Gold Rush. After the 1906 earthquake, he led a citizens committee charged with rebuilding the city. Phelan rose to become a reform-minded mayor of the city and a U.S. senator. He ceaselessly toured the United States, encouraging investors to put their money into the effort. In addition, some historians credit him with creating an architecturally Mediterranean San Francisco. The one blight on his public record was his opposition to Japanese immigration.

Irish and Italians Irish and Italian children read together at a New York library. From 1880 to 1920, four million Italians immigrated to the United States. They had many things in common with the earlier Irish immigrants: They came from poor, rural communities, had a strong sense of family, and were Roman Catholic. However, this did not make them allies with the Irish in their adopted country. Italians' lack of English and tendency to live in closed ethnic enclaves hampered their ability to integrate. They seldom attended the Irish-dominated Catholic churches, and they competed with the Irish for jobs.

TAD's view on sports Judge Rummy was among the many popular dog-headed characters invented by Thomas Aloysius Dorgan—better known to the world as TAD. Dorgan, who drew his first weekly comic strip in San Francisco in 1902, was hired soon after by William Randolph Hearst's *New York Journal*. For more than two decades, he worked as a sports cartoonist, comic-strip artist, and sportswriter. In addition to his cartoon art, Dorgan contributed to American slang with such phrases as "for crying out loud" and "the cat's pajamas."

1900-18

April 1912: A third attempt to pass a home-rule bill through Parliament clears the House of Commons but is once again rejected by the House of Lords.

April 14, 1912: The RMS *Titanic* plows into an iceberg in the North Atlantic. It will sink early the following morning, and 1,500 people will perish. One of the survivors is Margaret Tobin Brown, an Irish American millionaire whose composure and grace will earn her the sobriquet "Unsinkable Molly Brown."

November 5, 1912: Irish American Woodrow Wilson is elected president, as he carries 40 of the 48 U.S. states.

1913: Rose Cecil O'Neill patents the Kewpie doll, a child's doll of her own design. The Kewpie will become an instant and enduring sensation, with millions of dolls sold. • Frank Walsh, a son of Irish immigrants and a staunch supporter of Irish nationalism, is appointed chair of the U.S. Industrial Relations Commission by President Woodrow Wilson.

January 13, 1913: The Ulster Volunteer Force, a unionist militia, is established to resist nationalist efforts to pass home-rule legislation.

August 26, 1913: The Dublin Strike and Lockout begins, as more than 20,000 workers dispute management over their right to unionize.

September 23, 1913: Irish-born journalist Patrick Ford dies in Brooklyn. As editor of *The Irish World,* America's preeminent Irish newspaper, he was the voice of Irish America for more than 40 years.

November 1913: Belfast-born engineer William Mulholland unveils his Los Angeles Aqueduct, a 233-mile marvel that carries water from central to southern California.

Changing collars, from blue to white A woman of Irish descent toils in a factory in Pittsburgh in 1909. From 1890 to 1900, most of the Irish female workforce was employed either in blue-collar jobs or as domestics. However, things changed in the new century, as many American-born Irish women landed white-collar or skilled positions. Twentieth century Irish female immigrants still had to get their starts in factories or as domestics, but at least they had hope that their children would enjoy more fulfilling careers.

On behalf of female workers Established in 1903, the Women's Trade Union League (WTUL; *pictured*) campaigned for better working conditions and fought against the exploitation of female workers. The WTUL was distinctive in the labor movement because it brought together white-collar workers and blue-collar workers. The friendships between early leaders—such as Mary Kenney O'Sullivan, a dressmaker, and Florence Kelley, a U.S. congressman's daughter—helped create the bridge between the class divide. The league supported women's suffrage and counted Eleanor Roosevelt among its members.

Shanty vs. Lace-Curtain Irish

The Irish who came to America in what Daniel Patrick Moynihan called "the green wave" (unleashed by the Great Famine) acted out a cycle that became a template for subsequent immigrants: New arrivals, many penniless, struggled for a social and economic foothold. Many lived in ghettos and were consigned to the toughest, lowest-paying work. Succeeding generations consolidated the immigrants' gains and pushed upward, striving to vault from the rigors of working-class existence into the middle class.

But the Irish experience also contained a unique tension—a clash between poor, working-class immigrants and upwardly mobile Irish Americans who sought to leave the ghettos and their humiliations behind. Bristling with disdain and resentment, they called each other "shanty Irish" and "lace-curtain Irish." That mutual hostility is a recurring theme in James T. Farrell's Studs Lonigan trilogy. A character says, "Why, I knew him when he didn't have a sole on his shoe: and then him stickin' up his nose and actin' like he was highbrow, lace-curtain Irish, born to the purple."

New York labor organizer Elizabeth Gurley Flynn recounted the divide in her own family: "There were tight social lines drawn between the 'lace curtain' Irish of my mother's family and the 'shanty Irish' of my father's.... Neither Gurleys nor Flynns came to their wedding."

Flynn's narrative also touches on a key theme in Irish Americans' climb from the ranks of canal diggers, railroad navvies, slaughterhouse workers, and domestics. Her father, a quarry laborer, studied hard, entered Dartmouth College, and became an engineer. But, Flynn said, the push came from "Mama, who encouraged him in his ambition."

That was a story repeated in every Irish American community, and it emphasizes what social historian Hasia Diner described as "the centrality of Irish women to their families and the strength they demonstrated as they... helped guide the family's journey from Ireland to America, from poverty to comfort, from shanty to lace curtain."

Irish linen and lace
Pure Irish linen and handmade Irish lace were very popular throughout the 20th century. Irish lace was mainly made in the Republic, with Kilkenny lace finding particular favor. Meanwhile, the linen industry was dominated by the mills in the North, particularly in Belfast on the Falls Road. Demand from the growing number of white-collar Irish Americans for Irish linen and lace helped bolster the industry back home, whose workforce was mainly female.

Independent women America opened its doors to thousands of single Irish women who immigrated in search of a better life. Unlike their sisters back home, and their mothers before them, single Irish immigrant women in the early 1900s married by choice rather than succumb to the rural dowry system of arranged marriages. Many married Irish American men whom they sometimes met through small ads or at social gatherings organized to help single immigrants. In America, Irish women became more independent and better educated, and made important economic contributions to the family budget.

November 25, 1913: The Irish Volunteers, a militia of pro-home rule Irish nationalists formed in response to the Ulster Volunteers, hold their first meeting, in Dublin.

1914: Two of Boston's powerful Irish Catholic families merge when John Fitzgerald's daughter Rose marries Patrick Kennedy's son Joe. They will launch America's most enduring political dynasty, which will include their son, U.S. president John F. Kennedy. • The Irish Citizen Army, which developed among union workers as a means of defense during the violent days of the 1913 Dublin lockout, is formally reorganized. Under the leadership of James Connolly, it will evolve from defensive force to revolutionary tool. • The 30-year-old Gaelic Athletic Association establishes a greater New York branch. Their first championships, in hurling and Gaelic football, will be held in 1915, with some 20 clubs competing against each other at Celtic Park in Queens. • Immigration to the Unites States and Canada escalates as war engulfs Europe. • Irish American John Purroy Mitchel is elected mayor of New York at age 34, becoming the youngest person to ever hold that office. • Boston's iconic mayor, James Michael Curley, begins serving the first of his three terms in City Hall.

January 8, 1914: David Ignatius Walsh, the son of poor Irish Catholic immigrants, takes office as the first Catholic governor of Massachusetts.

April 1914: Members of the Ulster Volunteer Force smuggle some 20,000 guns and millions of rounds of ammunition from Germany into Larne, Northern Ireland.

May 16, 1914: A bronze statue of Commodore John Barry, an Irish hero of the Continental Navy, is dedicated in Washington, D.C.'s Franklin Park.

Skilled Irish workers By the first decade of the 20th century, Irish Americans were moving up from the lowest rung of the U.S. workforce to skilled jobs, such as carpentry (*pictured*). Although new Irish immigrants at the turn of the century were concentrated in unskilled jobs—men as laborers, women as domestics—the older immigrant generation had made dramatic progress. At the turn of the century, Irish American men held a large share of jobs in the construction trades and on factory floors. Women were moving into the expanding ranks of clerical workers and schoolteachers.

An Irish American tramp
Happy Hooligan, one of the first widely published American comic strips, was the creation of Frederick Burr Opper, an Ohioan of Austrian extraction. After an early career working for popular publications, including *Puck,* Opper began drawing *Happy Hooligan* for Hearst's *New York Journal* in 1900. The strip, which continued until 1932, affectionately followed the misadventures of Happy, an Irish American tramp who sported a tin-can hat. *Happy Hooligan* has been cited as one of the influences for Charlie Chaplin's "Little Tramp" character.

Riotous theater The audience rioted when John Millington Synge's *The Playboy of the Western World* premiered at Dublin's Abbey Theatre in 1907. The tale, set in the west of Ireland, was decried as vile due to violence and foul language. Synge died in 1909, but the controversy lived on. The Abbey troupe visited New York in 1911, and the Irish American community denounced Synge's play even before it was performed. When the Irish actors took the stage, they were met with cries of "Shame!" and a shower of potatoes and other missiles. The play proceeded, but only after police cleared the most violent protesters from the house.

SHOWERED WITH VEGETABLES

A potato swept through the air from the gallery and smashed against the wings. Then came a shower of vegetables that rattled against the scenery and made the actors duck their heads and fly behind the stage setting for shelter.

A potato struck Miss MaGee, and she, Irish like, drew herself up and glared defiance. Men were rising in the gallery and balcony and crying out to stop the performance. In the orchestra several men stood up and shook their fists.

"Go on with the play," came an order from the stage manager, and the players took their places and began again to speak their lines.

The tumult broke out more violently than before, and more vegetables came sailing through the air and rolled about the stage. Then began the fall of soft cubes that broke as they hit the stage.... They were capsules filled with asafoetida, and their odor was suffocating and most revolting....

The employes [sic] grabbed [protesters] and began hustling them toward the doors. Every one they got there was thrown out and followed until he became a rolling ball that thumped and thumped down the stairs.

—*THE NEW YORK TIMES,* NOVEMBER 28, 1911, DESCRIBING IRISH AMERICANS' PROTEST OF *THE PLAYBOY OF THE WESTERN WORLD* AT NEW YORK'S MAXINE ELLIOTT THEATRE

The unsinkable Molly Brown Margaret "Molly" Tobin, the most famous survivor of the *Titanic,* was one of six children born to Irish immigrant parents. She married miner J. J. Brown in 1886, and they became immensely wealthy after excavating vast amounts of gold and copper. Molly Brown campaigned for women's suffrage and children's rights, and she helped establish the first juvenile court in the United States. She also worked in soup kitchens, and she was awarded the French *Legion d'Honneur* for her work in France during World War I. Her life was made into a film musical, entitled *The Unsinkable Molly Brown* (1964). Kathy Bates played her in the 1997 blockbuster film *Titanic.*

Home work Home-based work was common among Irish American working-class families in the pre-World War I era. Irish labor activist Margaret Hinchey of New York described a typical situation: "Mothers with their small children sitting and standing around them...working by a kerosene lamp and breathing its odors" to make artificial flowers. Here, New York City girls identified as Katie, 13, and Angeline, 11, make cuffs out of Irish lace in 1912. They worked some nights until 8 o'clock, and they earned about $1 per week.

Wilson puts his faith in Walsh St. Louis native Frank P. Walsh was an advocate for labor and the poor. In 1912, during a crucial time for the labor movement, he was selected by President Woodrow Wilson to lead the Industrial Relations Committee. The 1910s were marked by intense clashes between management and labor, with many hoping, and others fearing, that the U.S. was drifting toward socialism. Walsh's passion to help the underprivileged led him to support Irish nationalist causes—much to the chagrin of President Wilson, whose support for ethnic American causes was always weak.

O'Neill creates the kewpie doll A gifted artist as a child, Rose Cecil O'Neill became the highest-paid female illustrator in the United States when she was still just a teenager. In 1909 she had a dream of little cupids dancing around her bed, which became the inspiration for the kewpie (derived from *cupid*) doll. The characters first appeared as illustrations, but demand soon prompted O'Neill to produce porcelain dolls (in Germany) that became a hit all over the world. Known as the "Queen of Bohemia," O'Neill also campaigned for women's rights.

Sports at Celtic Park One of the cultural traditions that the Irish brought with them to America was their love of sports. In 1897 a group of Irishmen founded the Irish American Athletic Club (IAAC) in New York to participate in track and field, bicycle races, handball competitions, Gaelic football, and hurling. Their home field was Celtic Park (*pictured*), a nine-acre athletic complex in Queens. Club members were particularly talented in track and field. In the 1908 Olympic Games in London, eight of the 13 American track and field medal-winners were members of the IAAC.

Sloan and the Ashcan School John Sloan, the Pennsylvania-born grandson of Ulster immigrants, was one of the eight artists who formed the realistic Ashcan School of painting in New York City. The Ashcan painters focused on the life of the city in the first decade of the 20th century—its throngs of immigrants, its tenements, its teeming streets, and all the aspects of its everyday experience. In a 1916 review, *The New York Times* stated that Sloan's *Spring Planting, Greenwich Village* (*pictured*) mysteriously combined images of "the blowsy women, the crooked clothes pole, [and] the dank sod" to convey a sense of "burgeoning Springtime."

Mulholland brings water to L.A. A native of Belfast, William Mulholland became director of the Los Angeles City Water Company in 1902. Mulholland realized that the city's future (and his personal fortune, through land investments) depended on bringing more water into the area. Millions of dollars were procured to bring Owens Valley water to the city. In 1908 work began on the most ambitious engineering project so far undertaken in America, a construction that included 142 tunnels and stretched across more than 200 miles of desert and mountains. Dedicating the Los Angeles Aqueduct on November 5, 1913, Mulholland turned on the water and announced, "There it is. Take it."

June 28, 1914: Austrian archduke Franz Ferdinand is assassinated in Sarajevo along with his wife, Sofia. The killings will set off a sequence of events that launch the First World War.

July 1914: The House of Lords approves the Amending Bill, which would allow for any Ulster county to recuse itself from home rule for up to six years.

1915: Mary Mallon, an Irish cook better known as Typhoid Mary, infects 25 people with typhus at New York's Sloane Hospital. Mary's vehement denials and refusal to change her line of work will lead to her forced quarantine for the remainder of her life.
• New York crime boss Owney Madden, born in England to Irish parents, is sent to New York's Sing Sing Prison after being convicted of manslaughter. • Though essentially defunct since the 1870s, the Ku Klux Klan is reborn in Atlanta. Catholics are the latest target of the white supremacist hate group. • The Gaelic League officially throws its support behind the cause of Irish nationalism. Douglas Hyde, the Protestant academic who founded the organization to promote the survival of Gaelic culture, resigns in protest.

February 18, 1915: Outlaw Frank James, older brother of Jesse, dies at the family farm at age 72 after living out a lengthy retirement in relative obscurity.

March 4, 1915: James Duval Phelan, the son of Irish immigrants and former mayor of San Francisco, takes office as a U.S. senator, representing California.

August 1, 1915: Iconic Fenian leader Jeremiah O'Donovan Rossa is buried in Dublin's Glasnevin Cemetery. The attending masses hear Padraig Pearse deliver his famous eulogy, in which he concludes, "Ireland unfree shall never be at peace."

Irish cool on Wilson As a Democrat, New Jersey governor Woodrow Wilson needed Irish American support to become president in 1912, and he got it. But during Wilson's presidency (1913–21), Irish Americans questioned the devotion to Ireland of a man who was part Scots-Irish, part English. While Irish American nationalists fought to keep the United States from supporting Britain in its World War I struggle with Germany, Wilson took the U.S. to war. Later, Irish American activists joined the successful campaign to block Wilson's League of Nations treaty because Wilson had failed to support Ireland's independence as part of Europe's postwar settlements. For his part, Wilson denounced the more outspoken nationalists as "hyphenated Americans" and questioned their loyalty.

"The Boy Mayor" John Purroy Mitchel, the son and grandson of fighting men, found his own battleground in New York City politics. His grandfather was Irish nationalist hero John Mitchel and his father was James Mitchel, a Confederate Civil War officer. John Purroy Mitchel rose to prominence as an anti-corruption crusader and foe of Tammany Hall. In 1913, at age 34, Mitchel became the youngest candidate ever elected mayor of New York. Dubbed "The Boy Mayor," he lost his reelection bid in 1917. He died the following year in an aviation accident while training to become an Army pilot.

The President's Right-Hand Man

Joseph Patrick Tumulty of Jersey City, New Jersey, was the son of a politically connected Irish American Democrat. He became a lawyer and was elected to the state assembly in 1907. In 1910 Tumulty was captivated by a powerful new presence on the state's political stage: Woodrow Wilson, the Democratic nominee for governor.

Tumulty joined Wilson's campaign and impressed the candidate with his "fine natural instincts...and nice perceptions" on matters of policy and politics. Wilson later wrote that Tumulty could be counted on to tell him "with almost unfailing accuracy what the man on the street—the men on all streets—were thinking."

When Wilson won, Tumulty's reward was appointment as the governor's personal secretary, a role he continued after Wilson captured the presidency in 1912. He advised the president on matters of state and key appointments, organized the first regular presidential press conferences, held daily briefings for reporters, and managed the president's public appearances.

But Tumulty nevertheless found himself under suspicion because of his faith and ethnic background. For decades before and after he served, American Catholics were accused of following the Vatican first, their government second. According to Wilson biographer Phyllis Lee Levin, the Protestant president and some advisers believed that Tumulty's prominence as a Catholic in the administration was a political liability.

Joseph Patrick Tumulty

Beyond this general suspicion, Tumulty was forced to walk a political tightrope over the issue of Irish independence. Wilson became so impatient with Irish American pressure on that issue that he declared he "did not intend to appoint another Irishman to anything...they were untrustworthy and uncertain."

Wilson shoved Tumulty further into the doghouse due to the latter's poor relations with Edith Galt, who married Wilson in 1915. The president dismissed Tumulty, but he relented after an influential reporter interceded on his aide's behalf. Tumulty retired from government service when Wilson left office in 1921, but he maintained a law practice in Washington, D.C., until his death in 1954.

Irish-themed theater The American stage saw a breathtaking range of Irish-themed theater in the first decades of the 20th century. Less and less visible was the simple comic character of the "stage Irishman" (*pictured*), which had been popular during the minstrel and vaudeville eras. Instead, offerings ranged from high drama to lighter and immensely popular fare, such as the works of singer-composer Chauncey Olcott and song-and-dance impresario George M. Cohan.

1916: Playwright Eugene O'Neill's career is launched, as the Provincetown Players premiere *Bound East for Cardiff.*

March 1916: The Friends of Irish Freedom is established in New York City, with composer Victor Herbert serving as the group's first president. In the aftermath of the Easter Rising, the group will raise some $350,000 to help the families of imprisoned rebels.

April 24, 1916: The Easter Rising, the most significant Irish armed rebellion against Britain since Wolfe Tone's failed 1798 plot, breaks out in Dublin. The revolution will be suppressed with relative ease, with fighting concluding by the 30th. Nearly 500 people will die on both sides, and the Irish leadership will be tried and executed in short order.

May 3, 1916: Nationalist Padraig Pearse, a leader of the Easter Rising, is among the first to be executed. Pearse's death, along with that of 14 other Irish leaders, fans the flames of nationalism on both sides of the Atlantic.

August 3, 1916: British diplomat turned Irish nationalist Roger Casement is executed for treason, just five years after his knighthood for meritorious service to the Crown.

October 16, 1916: Irish American birth-control activist Margaret Sanger opens America's first family planning clinic in Brooklyn, New York.

April 1917: Shortly after America enters World War I, Irish American composer George M. Cohan records "Over There." It will prove to be the most popular song of the war.

April 6, 1917: Four days after President Woodrow Wilson outlines the case for war before a joint session of Congress, the United States officially declares war on Germany.

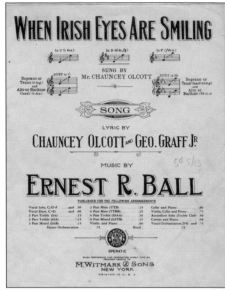

A pair of Irish ballads In 1912 renowned Irish American lyricist and musical star Chauncey Olcott headlined a new show in New York City called "The Isle o' Dreams." The show lasted only 32 performances, but it included the hit song "When Irish Eyes Are Smiling." In later decades, the song became a standard for the likes of John McCormack, Bing Crosby, Lawrence Welk, and Arthur Fiedler's Boston Pops. Ernest R. Ball composed the music for "When Irish Eyes Are Smiling" as well as for the 1915 song "She's the Daughter of Mother Machree," which was about "the fairest of Ireland's fair daughters."

Kelly's Army In the midst of a depression in 1894, an Irish American printer from Oakland, California, named Charles T. Kelly led an "industrial army" of unemployed men on a cross-country journey to demand jobs. Although Kelly's Army, as it was called, never reached its destination of Washington, D.C., he tried the tactic again in 1914. But this time, "General" Kelly's army immediately ran into trouble. Arriving in Sacramento, Kelly was arrested. Police, firefighters, and deputized citizens attacked the army with fire hoses (*pictured*) and pick handles, then burned its camp.

Kelley crusades for workers' rights

The daughter of Congressman William D. Kelley, Florence Kelley studied in Zurich and graduated from Cornell University. While in Europe, she discovered Karl Marx and became a close friend of another Communist philosopher, Friedrich Engels. After returning to the U.S., Kelley became a social and labor reformer. In 1899 she established the National Consumer's League to campaign for a minimum wage and limited working hours for women and children. An ardent supporter of women's suffrage and African American rights, she was a founding member of the National Association for the Advancement of Colored People (1909).

Sinking of the *Empress of Ireland*

EMPRESS OF IRELAND

During the early hours of May 29, 1914, the Canadian ocean liner *Empress of Ireland* was cruising along the St. Lawrence River on its way to Liverpool when it collided with a Norwegian ship, the *Storstad*. Most of the liner's 1,477 passengers and crew were asleep and thus unable to react quickly to the impending disaster. As they tried to flee, they had difficulty negotiating the liner's steeply sloped decks. *Empress of Ireland* turned over and sank just 14 minutes after the collision, carrying 1,012 people to the river bottom.

Hinchey marches for justice

Irish suffragist and union activist Margaret Hinchey marches at the head of a women's delegation in the 1914 Labor Day parade in New York City. Hinchey, who labored as a laundress, subway worker, and elevator operator, was emblematic of Irish American involvement in the movements that sought improved conditions for women in the workplace and on the civic stage. During her activist career, Hinchey became a nationally known figure and met with two presidents—Woodrow Wilson and Calvin Coolidge.

A Great War anthem Jack Judge, a British music hall entertainer and the descendant of Irish immigrants to England, wrote "It's a Long Way to Tipperary" in 1912 and shared credit with a friend, Harry Williams. When World War I broke out, the song became an anthem. In August 1914, the largely Irish Connaught Rangers sang the lively air as they marched through the streets of Boulogne, France. The song caught on with other Allied troops and became popular in Irish communities—and among other audiences—worldwide.

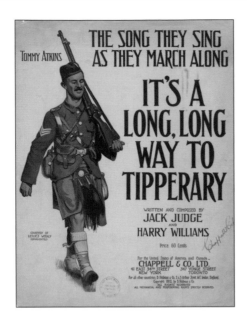

TOMMY ATKINS

THE SONG THEY SING AS THEY MARCH ALONG

IT'S A LONG, LONG WAY TO TIPPERARY

WRITTEN AND COMPOSED BY
JACK JUDGE
AND
HARRY WILLIAMS

Price 60 Cents

For the United States of America and Canada
CHAPPELL & CO. LTD.
41 EAST 34TH STREET   347 YONGE STREET
NEW YORK   TORONTO

Legendary Irish tenor Born in Athlone, John "Count" McCormack became (and still remains) Ireland's most famous tenor. He sang both opera and popular songs, particularly Irish ballads. In 1914 he became the first person to record the World War I song "It's a Long Way to Tipperary." McCormack, who became an American citizen in 1919, cemented his success in the United States and even made several films. In 1928 Pope Pius XI bestowed him with the title of papal count.

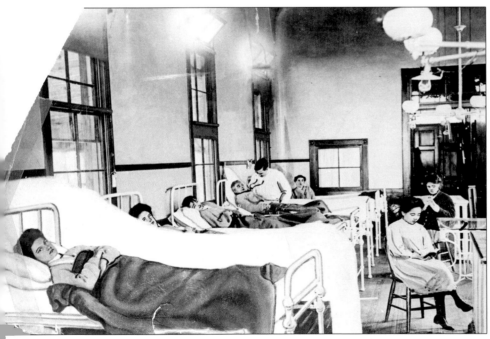

Typhoid Mary Mary Mallon (*foreground*) was the first person ever identified as a healthy carrier of typhoid fever. In 1906 an intense investigation tracked the spread of the disease to her place of employment in New York, where she worked as a cook. Investigators discovered that Mallon had cooked at many places over the years and had infected dozens of people, several of whom died. Police took "Typhoid Mary" into custody. She was institutionalized on New York's North Brother Island, where she stayed for most of her life. She died there in 1938.

U.S. deports socialist agitator Socialist James Larkin was an Irish trade union leader and founder of the Irish Independent Labour Party. In 1914 Larkin went to America to raise funds for the union, and he stayed to help organize U.S. workers. He joined the Socialist Party of America, but he was expelled in 1919 for his support of Russian Bolsheviks. Larkin's incendiary speeches and involvement with the Communist Party made him a target during the "Red Scare." He was jailed in 1920 for "criminal anarchy" and deported in 1923.

Collins cranks out the hits Second baseman Eddie Collins didn't just have the luck of the Irish on his side. He also kept a wad of bubblegum on the button of his cap for good luck. Of course, with his talent, he didn't need it. In his 25 seasons with the Philadelphia Athletics and Chicago White Sox, Collins batted .333 while amassing 3,315 hits and 744 stolen bases. Also a brilliant bunter, he totaled 512 sacrifice hits—a still-standing big-league record. Some baseball historians consider him the greatest second baseman of all time.

70,000 mourn Irish nationalist
Jeremiah O'Donovan Rossa was an architect of the violent Fenian campaign to free Ireland from British rule in the 1860s. The Cork native was arrested, sentenced to life imprisonment, and eventually exiled to the United States. Rossa remained active in the campaign for Irish independence until his death in New York in 1915. Nationalists returned his body to Ireland and planned a hero's rites, and Republican leader Padraig Pearse gave the funeral oration to a crowd of more than

70,000 at Dublin's Glasnevin Cemetery. He concluded: "While Ireland holds these graves, Ireland unfree shall never be at peace." Pearse led the Easter Rising just eight months later.

"The Rebel Girl" Born to an activist father and a feminist, Irish nationalist Elizabeth Gurley Flynn delivered a speech entitled "What Socialism Will Do for Women" at age 15. Flynn became a labor leader and a founding member of the American Civil Liberties Union, and she served as the chairperson of the American Communist Party. Flynn was active in the campaign against the murder convictions of anarchists Sacco and Vanzetti, and she played a leading role in the Industrial Workers of the World. Flynn inspired labor martyr Joe Hill to write the song "The Rebel Girl" while he was in prison awaiting execution.

The "Lady Labor Slugger" Beginning in 1878, Margaret Haley taught sixth grade in one of Chicago's poorest districts. She remained on the job for 16 years before becoming a full-time union leader and activist. In her 40 years of leadership, Haley campaigned for teachers' rights and advocated progressive "child-centered" educational practices. Nicknamed the "Lady Labor Slugger," Haley was a founding member of the Women's Trade Union League (1903). As president of the National Federation of Teachers, she won state pensions for teachers as a basic right.

"Diamond Jim" Brady Born of modest means in New York City, James Brady went to work early in life with the New York Central Railroad. Later, he was involved in the selling of railroad supplies, the manufacture of railroad cars, and securities investment. He was successful in all. With a penchant for fine jewelry, he acquired precious gems worth more than $2 million, earning the nickname "Diamond Jim." The rotund Brady was also famous for the amount of food he could consume at one sitting. One restaurateur said Brady was the best 25 customers he had.

Irish support Britain in WWI A British government poster promotes Irish enlistment during World War I. Although militant nationalists in Ireland and Irish America opposed Great Britain, the mass opinion in both communities backed the British against Germany. Ireland was not subject to military conscription during the Great War, but Irish Parliamentary Party leader John Redmond was foremost among the public figures who urged his countrymen to sign up and fight. Approximately 200,000 Irish soldiers served in the British Army during the war, of whom 30,000 lost their lives.

WHAT GERMANY COULD DO FOR IRELAND

McGuire backs the Germans This illustration appeared in James K. McGuire's 1916 book *What Could Germany Do for Ireland?* McGuire, the former mayor of Syracuse, New York, was a prominent Irish American voice for total U.S. neutrality in World War I and for Irish support of Germany. McGuire argued that Germany was more humane than Britain in its treatment of smaller countries and that Ireland would flourish if it were able to forge an economic and political alliance with the Germans—whom he believed to be the inevitable victors in the war.

Utah's Kearns rails against Mormons
Thomas Kearns was one of the most influential non-Mormons in Utah history. Born in Ontario in 1862 to Irish Catholic immigrants, Kearns was raised in Nebraska. Moving on to Utah as a young man, he made his fortune in mining. He was elected to the U.S. Senate in 1900, but he blamed the state's Mormon establishment for his failure to win reelection. After resuming his mining business, Kearns became owner and publisher of two Salt Lake City newspapers, which he used to assail Mormon domination of state politics.

> **"Self-government is our right, a thing born in us at birth, a thing no more to be doled out to us or withheld from us by another people than the right to life itself—the right to feel the sun or smell the flowers, or love our kind."**
> —IRELAND'S ROGER CASEMENT, JUST BEFORE BEING HANGED FOR TREASON FOR HIS ROLE IN THE EASTER RISING

The Easter Rising Much of Dublin was devastated by fighting during the 1916 Easter Rising. The insurrection began when rebels seized positions around the city on April 24, the day after Easter. But the rebels were outgunned and outmanned, and the Irish public greeted the uprising with hostility. The rebels inflicted heavy casualties on British forces, who responded with an artillery attack that ravaged central Dublin and forced the rebels to surrender. In five days of fighting, 450 people were killed and some 2,600 were injured. The British victory appeared decisive—until the summary executions of the Easter Rising's leaders, an act that provoked outrage in both Ireland and Irish America.

Showdown at the post office British troops fire on rebel positions in Dublin during the Easter Rising. The insurrection surprised British commanders. Their first response, in which they attempted to dislodge rebels using frontal attacks on their positions, proved both ineffective and costly. As the week of the Easter Rising progressed, British commanders decided to bombard rebel positions at Dublin's General Post Office. That tactic overwhelmed the rebels, but it left the downtown in ruins and led to high civilian casualties. In fact, more than half of the 450 killed were noncombatants. Among British forces, 116 died; among the rebels, 64.

Casement hanged for role in Rising Sir Roger Casement walks to the gallows in London in August 1916—an execution that stirred outrage in Irish America. He had been convicted of treason for trying to secure German aid for an Irish uprising. Casement, who had helped organize the Irish Volunteer Force, traveled to Germany after the outbreak of World War I. He won modest material aid for a rebellion, but he was convinced it would fail and tried to head it off. The British captured Casement days before the Easter Rising and sent him to England for trial.

De Valera vs. Devoy

Eamon de Valera's owlish countenance is an enduring image of Irish nationalism. Ironically, his American citizenship (he was born in New York) saved him from a British firing squad after the collapse of the 1916 Easter Rising. De Valera not only survived, but he rose to the leadership of the Irish Republican cause.

In 1919 de Valera returned to the United States to mine the sympathetic vein that was Irish America. Even as he collected large sums of money, de Valera clashed with Irish American leaders, most notably Irish-born Fenian John Devoy and Judge Daniel Cohalan of New York—the most prominent names associated with the Irish American organizations Clan na Gael and Friends of Irish Freedom. De Valera saw the League of Nations, raised from the ashes of World War I, as a forum for securing Irish independence. Devoy and Cohalan saw it as a trap that would bind America into an alliance with Great Britain.

Eamon de Valera

In his book *Irish-American Diaspora Nationalism: The Friends of Irish Freedom, 1916–1935,* Michael Doorley contends that Irish American nationalism had a separate agenda from the Irish version in the years after 1916. De Valera's rift with Devoy and Cohalan seems proof of this. It prompted him to form the American Association for the Recognition of the Irish Republic. This group triumphed by raising millions of dollars. But the tables were turned when Devoy and Cohalan secured most of Irish American opinion after the 1921 Anglo-Irish Treaty plunged partitioned Ireland into civil war.

Devoy and Cohalan backed the new Free State, while Devoy labeled IRA backer de Valera as the "most malignant man in all Irish history." It was a harsh judgment, one that would not stick with those Irish voters who would repeatedly elect "Dev" in the following years as prime minister, and ultimately president, of the long-desired Republic.

Connolly goes down fighting James Connolly is best known as the Irish labor leader executed in 1916 for his role in the Easter Rising. Before that, though, he was a noted socialist in Scotland, Ireland, and the United States. In New York from 1903 through 1910, Connolly tried, with limited success, to get Irish American workers to join the movement. Returning to Ireland, he founded the Irish Citizen Army and allied himself with militant nationalists. During the Easter rebellion, Connolly led the defense of Dublin's General Post Office against British troops. After surrendering, Connolly and his fellow rebel leaders were put to death by firing squad.

"A protest against a barbarity" County Sligo native William Bourke Cockran was a teacher, lawyer, congressman (serving sporadically from 1887 through 1923), and committed Irish nationalist. He declared support for the English cause against Germany in World War I. But when Britain executed Padraig Pearse and the other leaders of the Easter Rising in 1916, Cockran voiced Irish America's outrage in a speech to a mass meeting at Madison Square Garden. "This meeting is a protest against a barbarity without parallel in the history of civilization," he said.

Cohalan rails against British rule

Daniel Cohalan was a Tammany Hall politician and state judge who became a key leader in the campaign to end British rule in Ireland. Cohalan was a close ally of nationalist patriarch John Devoy in the militant Clan na Gael. After the Easter Rising in 1916, Cohalan helped guide the popular Friends of Irish Freedom in raising political and financial support for the Republican cause. Cohalan and his movement, which was critical of Woodrow Wilson's lack of action to support Irish independence, fought the president's foreign policy both during and after World War I.

Boy laborers This teenager, James Donovan, worked as a sweeper in a Fall River, Massachusetts, iron foundry. Photographer Lewis W. Hine snapped the portrait in 1916 as part of a project documenting child labor. The face of the Irish American workforce was changing in the early 20th century, with the children and grandchildren of immigrants moving in large numbers into skilled trades and even white-collar jobs. But many Irish American families, especially those of newer immigrants, depended on the employment of multiple family members in order to make ends meet.

The flag of Ireland Ireland's tricolor flag, inspired by the French banner, was carried from France to Ireland by Young Ireland leader Thomas Francis Meagher. It was first seen during the Young Ireland Rebellion of 1848, yet it was still unfamiliar to many Irish when it was raised over Dublin's General Post Office during the 1916 Rising. The early version had orange closest to the staff, but the later and now official tricolor is ordered green, white, and orange. The colors represent Gaelic Catholic Ireland (green), later Protestant settlers from Britain (orange), and peace between both (white).

Girl domestics In 1916 Evelyn Casey, age 14, was looking for work in Massachusetts. Many Irish girls her age found jobs working in people's homes. One historian stated flatly in 1983, "Domestic work was the Irish female immigrant's preferred job." Domestic employment gave unskilled young women an opportunity to play a key role in the rise of the Irish American community. Jobs in service offered relatively high wages, and Irish domestics earned a reputation as thrifty household managers. They used their savings to help bring over relatives from Ireland and help their families gain an economic foothold in the United States.

Hollywood's first cowboy Nicknamed "Two-Gun Bill," William S. Hart was the original screen cowboy and one of the first silent screen stars. After 20 years on the stage, Hart moved to Hollywood and made his first movie at age 49. Over the next 11 years, he appeared in more than 65 films, earning $150,000 for *The Narrow Trail* in 1917. Hart embodied the honest, brave, and righteous hero we have come to associate with cowboys. He was a collector of western art and a close friend of Wyatt Earp.

Teachers help Irish integrate Irish American female teachers helped Irish immigrants integrate into the mainstream of American society. Their profession allowed them entry into the lower middle class, which garnered respect for their families and Irish Americans in general. Though anti-Catholic "quotas" had been imposed to limit their numbers, by the early 20th century many urban public schoolteachers were Irish American women. As educators, they were instrumental in the "Americanization" of the new immigrants, most of whom hailed from Southern Europe.

O'Leary charged with treason The son of a family that hailed from Cork and Kerry, Jeremiah O'Leary (*center*) was Irish America's most outspoken anti-British activist during World War I. O'Leary's American Truth Society and its magazine, *Bull*, sought to debunk Britain's war propaganda and agitated for Irish independence. O'Leary's efforts, which included personal contacts with German agents, made him a target for prosecution when the United States entered the war in 1917. *Bull* was banned from the mails, and O'Leary himself was charged with treason and interfering with the military draft. He was acquitted on all charges.

A DEMAND FOR IRISH INDEPENDENCE

Resolved, that this assemblage of American citizens of Irish blood, loyal to the United States, and ready to defend her honor and interests, and recognizing that our Government is entitled to the best advice that Irishmen who understand the situation can give, urgently request the President and Congress to demand that England make good her promises in the only way possible in regard to Ireland, namely by according to the Irish people their indubitable right to be regarded as a sovereign people, and by granting to Ireland full national independence... and be it

Resolved, that we therefore submit to the President and Congress that America's entry into the war for democracy and civilization gives our government the right, and imposes upon it the duty, to demand from England that she settle the Irish Question permanently and finally....

—RESOLUTION OF THE IRISH AMERICAN CONVENTION, NEW YORK CITY, MAY 14, 1917

Friends of Irish Freedom

On April 24, 1916, armed Irish nationalists stormed Dublin buildings, such as the General Post Office, and declared the existence of an Irish Republic. The Easter Rising, however, was just one aspect of a broader effort on the part of Irish nationalists to win independence from Britain. Recruiting Irish Americans for this cause was also crucial.

A month before the Easter Rising, a new group called the Friends of Irish Freedom (FOIF) was created in New York City. FOIF would swiftly become America's most prominent Irish independence organization, with more than 250,000 affiliated members. FOIF's high point was probably the February 1919 Irish Race Convention in Philadelphia. Thousands of Irish Americans attended, including politicians, bishops, and even Cardinal James Gibbons of Baltimore.

Irish Republic supporters in San Francisco, 1920

Political unity among Irish Americans seemed indisputable. Just a few years later, however, FOIF's influence more or less vanished. Its rise and fall captures the complexity of Irish American nationalism as well as the differing tactics and goals nationalists were pursuing.

FOIF's roots stretch back to the 1860s and the creation of Clan na Gael (roughly translated as "Family of Gaels"). That organization was part of the Fenian movement that launched an infamous invasion of British lands in Canada.

For 40 years, Kildare native John Devoy was among the most prominent Clan na Gael figures. By 1916 Devoy and others argued for the creation of a broader, more inclusive Irish freedom organization. They wanted to attract Irish Americans who remained skeptical of violence against the British and other more controversial tactics. At an Irish Race Convention in New York in 1916, FOIF was formed "to encourage and assist any movement that would tend to bring about the national independence of Ireland." The group's first president was Dublin-born composer Victor Herbert.

FOIF was an immediate success. In the wake of the Easter Rising and the proposed execution of its planners by the British, FOIF raised $350,000 to assist Irish prisoners.

In 1918 Cardinal William O'Connell of Boston addressed a FOIF meeting at Madison Square Garden. He said that Irish independence should be part of the wave of democracy that was expected to sweep the globe in the wake of World War I.

Though moderate on the surface, FOIF was heavily influenced by more radical Clan na Gael members. A majority of FOIF's trustees, including Devoy, were also Clan na Gael members. Still, by the 1919 Irish Race Convention in Philadelphia, it seemed that FOIF would be a powerhouse for years to come. But President Woodrow Wilson—known for scorning ethnic, or "hyphenated," Americans—expressed little interest in FOIF's calls for Irish independence.

The fatal blow for FOIF was the Anglo-Irish Treaty of 1921, which created the Irish Free State but left Northern Ireland under British rule. Charismatic Irish leader Eamon de Valera had already siphoned off many FOIF supporters by creating his own Irish freedom group. FOIF could not survive the ensuing Irish civil war, which pitted Free Staters against de Valera and others who supported a united island of Ireland.

Despite its swift decline, FOIF played a central role in voicing broad Irish American support for Ireland's independence. A newly reorganized FOIF was introduced in 1989, mainly to assist political prisoners and others still plagued by "The Troubles."

1900-18

May 15, 1917: Frank Hague, arguably the most powerful mayor in the history of Jersey City, takes office. He will hold the post for 30 years.

July 1917: British prime minister Lloyd George calls the Irish Convention to order. Boycotted by Sinn Féin, the moderate delegation makes only nominal headway in the push for home rule.

July 10, 1917: Eamon de Valera, imprisoned for his involvement in the 1916 Easter Rising, is elected to the House of Commons one month after his release.

December 12, 1917: Irish American priest Father Edward Flanagan opens Boys Town in Omaha, Nebraska, with $90, a rented house, and five homeless, neglected boys.

1918: Irish Catholic Al Smith is elected governor of New York. He will win reelection three times, serving four terms. • Nearly 65 percent of Irish farmers now own the land on which they work, a 35 percent increase in little more than a decade. • John Purroy Mitchel dies in a flying accident after losing his bid for another term as New York City mayor. • The 69th New York Regiment is sent to France with the American Expeditionary Force.

June 1918: Mary McWhorter, president of the 75,000-member Ladies Auxiliary of the Ancient Order of Hibernians, delivers a 600,000-signature petition to the White House, calling for President Woodrow Wilson to pressure British allies to grant Ireland its independence.

December 1918: The radical Sinn Féin party trounces the moderate Irish Parliamentary Party in the Irish general elections, securing 73 of a possible 105 seats in Parliament.

A progressive Tammany boss Charles Francis Murphy, pictured here on the Atlantic City boardwalk in 1917, was a saloonkeeper who went on to lead New York City's Tammany Hall for more than two decades. Murphy was a different kind of boss. He was noted for backing progressive causes and progressive candidates as a way of maintaining Tammany's support among working-class voters. He pushed for the reform of labor and workplace laws, and he was the patron of the Irish American progressive Al Smith, who became governor of New York and a Democratic presidential candidate.

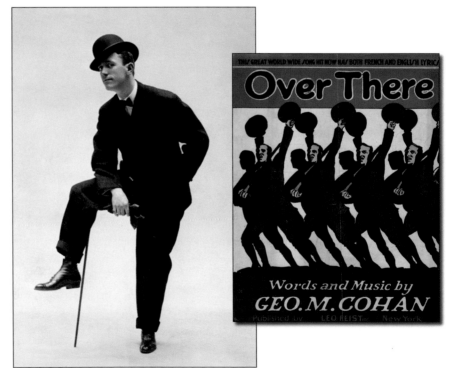

Cohan writes American classics Born to Irish American vaudevillians in 1878, George M. Cohan was on the stage from infancy. As a teenager, he sang and danced in his family's show, wrote and published his own songs, and managed the family's act. After moving to New York in 1900, Cohan quickly established himself as Broadway's most prolific star, composer, and producer. Cohan's hit songs included such classics as "Give My Regards to Broadway," "Yankee Doodle Dandy," and "You're a Grand Old Flag." All that was a prelude to "Over There," which Cohan wrote when the United States entered World War I. An immediate sensation, "Over There" remains a stirring anthem of American patriotism and resolve.

> **"It was desired to enlist strong, intelligent, decent living men, men whose sturdy Americanism was strengthened and vivified by their Celtic blood, men who would be worthy successors to their forgotten patriots who at Bloody Lane and Marye's Heights earned the title 'The Fighting Irish.'"**
> —POET JOYCE KILMER

A wild ride For "Wild Bill" Donovan, life was a string of adventures. Early in his military career, he led a cavalry troop of the New York state militia to the U.S.-Mexico border during the Pancho Villa campaign. In World War I, he led the 165th Regiment of the 42nd Division and was awarded the Congressional Medal of Honor. Between the wars, Donovan became a successful lawyer in and out of government. In 1941 he was appointed chief of the U.S. intelligence community. He founded the Office of Strategic Services, which later became the CIA.

Quinn: Don't back Germany John Quinn was a New York corporate lawyer, noted collector of paintings and books, leading supporter of Irish culture, and confidant of poet William Butler Yeats. Quinn was a strong proponent of home rule for Ireland, but he was also an ardent supporter of the war against Germany. He mocked Irish American nationalists who believed support for Germany would lead to freedom for Ireland. If the Germans prevailed, Quinn wrote in 1917, the Irish "would look back to conditions in Ireland before the war as heaven itself."

Bringing up Father Appearing in newspapers across America from 1913 to 2000, *Bringing Up Father* was the longest running daily comic strip ever. George McManus's strip depicts the foibles of an Irish family—Maggie and Jiggs and their daughter, Nora—after they become instantly wealthy by winning the Irish Sweepstakes. Despite his riches, Jiggs wants nothing more than to spend time with his Irish cronies, particularly his tavern-owning friend, Dinty Moore. Maggie and Nora have loftier social ambitions. Viewers of the TV sitcom *The Beverly Hillbillies* will recognize similarities.

Father Duffy boosts morale In New York City, Father Francis Duffy's statue dominates the north end of Times Square. Duffy first served as a regimental chaplain in the Spanish-American War (1898) and then in Europe during World War I. The New York 69th was mainly comprised of New York Irish immigrants and their sons, and Duffy played a crucial role in keeping up their morale, in spite of heavy casualties. Father Duffy was immortalized by Pat O'Brien in the 1940 film *The Fighting 69th*.

Happy Days
1919–1932

"He helped raise the pay of teachers.... He is an enemy of child labor. ... He wants to make it impossible for women to be employed at less than a living wage."

—CAMPAIGN LITERATURE FOR PROGRESSIVE NEW YORK GOVERNOR AND THREE-TIME PRESIDENTIAL CANDIDATE AL SMITH, AN IRISH CATHOLIC

As he looked out on a raucous crowd that was turning New York's Madison Square Garden into a sweaty, disorderly temple of democracy, William Jennings Bryan could not contain his anger. Jeers and shouts from the Tammany Hall contingent had turned the climax of the 1924 Democratic National Convention into a chaotic and frightening spectacle. These Irish Catholics were on the verge of taking power, and Bryan—an old man who had carried the Democratic Party's banner three times to no avail—could take it no longer.

From his place on the stage, the great orator aimed his glare at the Irish Americans who supported Al Smith for president—Al Smith, a Catholic, the symbol of urban immigrant life, a man who opposed the noble cause of Prohibition. "You," Bryan spat out, "do not represent the future of this country!"

How wrong he proved to be. The 1924 Democratic National Convention was one of those rare moments when politics and culture joined forces to produce historic change. Smith, the Irish Catholic governor of New York, did not win the nomination. Instead, after 102 exhausting ballots, the convention chose former solicitor general John Davis as its presidential candidate. But the future belonged to Smith and to millions of Irish Americans like him. Politically, culturally, and economically, they were on the threshold of power. And no force on earth, not even the formidable force of Bryan's oratory, would block them from taking the next step.

Alfred Emanuel Smith personified the coming of age of Irish America, even if he was also Italian and German. Raised on Manhattan's Lower East

Presidential candidate Al Smith represented New York City and Irish Catholicism to the nation in 1928. He rallied the Catholic voters, including women (who were allowed to vote in 1920), but much of the nation wasn't ready to elect a Catholic president. Smith lost heavily in rural and small-town America, and he lost half the South to dour Quaker candidate Herbert Hoover, who won 40 states overall.

Side and educated, as he liked to say, at the Fulton Fish Market, Smith was a master politician who put in place social welfare reforms that another New Yorker, Franklin D. Roosevelt, would use as a model for the New Deal.

Smith was elected governor of New York in 1918. He lost his first bid for reelection in 1920, but he reclaimed the job in 1922. By the time the Democrats assembled in New York in 1924, he was a legitimate presidential aspirant—even though the nation had never come close to electing a Catholic president.

Smith could harbor historic ambitions because so many Irish Americans were at or near the pinnacles of American society. Joseph P. Kennedy, the son of a saloon owner and grandson of Irish immigrants, already had made millions in the banking business and was about to go west to help reorganize the fledgling film industry in Hollywood. F. Scott Fitzgerald was emerging as one of the nation's great novelists, publishing *The Great Gatsby* in 1925. Eugene O'Neill's plays dominated the American stage, while another Irishman, George M. Cohan, was the darling of Broadway. A young actress named Helen Hayes was about to become one of the American stage's leading lights. Jack Dempsey won the heavyweight championship of the world in 1919, and Georgia O'Keeffe's semi-abstract flowers and landscapes were winning critical and popular acclaim.

If the Irish in America seemed confident in themselves and in their place in the world during the 1920s, surely events overseas had something to do with it. After hundreds of years of British rule, Ireland—most of it, anyway—was, at long last, a nation once again. The Irish Free State, consisting of 26 of the island's 32 counties, won independence in 1921. A bloody civil war followed between the new government and those who opposed the island's partition. The government prevailed, and Ireland had a place among the world's nations. Irish Americans, so intimately connected with their homeland's struggle for independence, rejoiced.

Although Al Smith could not persuade his fellow Democrats to give him their nomination in 1924, the future looked bright, not only for Smith but for Irish America and the nation in general. The 1920s brought prosperity and peace after war and turmoil. And it was a useful, productive peace. In Albany, Smith continued to press for reforms on behalf of working men and women, the kind of people he had grown up with on the Lower East Side. He enjoyed the give-and-take of politics, leading one of his protégés, Franklin Roosevelt, to call him the "Happy Warrior."

During the 1928 presidential campaign, Irving Berlin wrote a song called "Good Times with Hoover, Better Times with Al." Voters didn't see it that way. Smith lost the election due to "the three Ps": prejudice (he was Catholic), prosperity (the economy was booming), and Prohibition (which Smith opposed but rural America supported).

Civil war broke out in Ireland in 1922–23 when Britain's offer of independence was rejected by a minority of militants, led by Eamon de Valera. Michael Collins defeated the insurgents and created the new independent nation called the Irish Free State, but he was assassinated in 1922. De Valera ascended to power in 1932.

By 1928 William Jennings Bryan was dead and the forces that had opposed Smith in 1924 were in retreat, or so it seemed. Smith was practically handed the party's presidential nomination that year, and so he became the first Catholic to run for president on behalf of a major party. The accomplishment was a milestone—and an illusion. As Smith campaigned around the nation that year, his religion, ethnicity, urban attitudes, and distaste for Prohibition inspired an anti-Catholic backlash that stunned him and many of his supporters. He lost in a landslide to Herbert Hoover. Smith never got over the hatred he saw on the campaign trail.

While Smith was going down to defeat, Roosevelt was winning a close race to succeed him as governor. Roosevelt, a WASP patrician from the Hudson Valley, had entered politics as an anti-Tammany crusader. But over the years, he learned much from the Irish, who dominated machine politics and who had turned many of the nation's cities into Democratic strongholds. Roosevelt cultivated relationships with such Irish politicians as James Farley, Edward J. Flynn, and Thomas Corcoran, and he built on Smith's legacy of reform in New York.

In 1932, with the nation in the throes of a catastrophic depression, Smith thought he ought to be given another chance at the presidency. He found himself opposed not only by Roosevelt but by such Irish American power brokers as Flynn and Farley. They helped to engineer Roosevelt's victory—and a bitter defeat for the Happy Warrior.

Al Smith no longer represented the nation's future. But for Irish America, even greater successes were beckoning.

1919: Boston's John Francis "Honey Fitz" Fitzgerald is elected to the U.S. House of Representatives, where he will serve until 1921. • The Irish Volunteers, the Catholic militia created during the heated political battle for home rule, rechristens itself the Irish Republican Army (IRA). The IRA's terrorist campaign will figure prominently in Anglo-Irish relations through much of the 20th century. • Former Massachusetts governor David Ignatius Walsh, who was the first Catholic to serve in the state's highest office, is elected to his first term in the U.S. Senate. • President Woodrow Wilson is awarded the Nobel Peace Prize for spearheading the creation of the League of Nations. • The American Messenger Company, founded by an Irish American teenager named Jim Casey, changes its name to the United Parcel Service.

January 21, 1919: The First Dáil Éireann, or Irish Parliament, is convened. It is comprised of victorious Sinn Féin parliamentary candidates who refuse to take their seats in the British Parliament. Irish revolutionary Michael Collins will be named finance minister of the First Dáil Éireann. • The Irish War of Independence begins when two officers of the Royal Irish Constabulary are murdered in County Tipperary by members of the Irish Republican Army.

February 3, 1919: With the assistance of Michael Collins, with whom he will have a falling out over the 1921 Anglo-Irish Treaty, Eamon de Valera escapes from Lincoln Jail in England.

June 1919: Eamon de Valera begins an 18-month tour of the United States in an effort to secure financial support for the Irish Republic from the American people. He also seeks official recognition for the Irish Republic from the U.S. government.

The "King of Comedy"

Mack Sennett, the son of Irish immigrants, infused humor into silent films. In 1912 he founded Keystone Studios, which specialized in the making of comedies. Such stars as Charlie Chaplin and Fatty Arbuckle appeared in his early movies. Sennett once said that his films were a madcap series of slapstick routines that always ended in a great chase. This was exemplified in his popular Keystone Kops series. After making more than 1,000 silent films and dozens of talkies, the "King of Comedy" retired in 1935 at age 55.

The Bowery as a watering-place

Life in the Bowery A mythic avenue long associated with ribald entertainment, ethnic gangs, and vice, Manhattan's Bowery was also home to everyday people, as seen in this image of boys cooling off on a summer day in 1919. In the mid-19th century, the Bowery was lined with beer gardens and music halls, but it began to slide toward a more bleak kind of poverty at the end of the 19th century. It became noted for its vagrant men and flophouses. The Great Depression of the 1930s only worsened harsh conditions along the Bowery.

> **"Armed and uniformed men were seen entering the field, and immediately after the firing broke out scenes of the wildest confusion took place. The spectators made a rush for the far side of Croke Park and shots were fired over their heads and into the crowd."**
>
> —IRELAND'S *FREEMAN'S JOURNAL,* DESCRIBING BLOODY SUNDAY

Valera tours America Eamon de Valera's tour of the United States in 1919 came during a hectic time in Ireland. Months earlier, as leader of the Sinn Féin political party, de Valera helped establish the First Dáil Éireann (Irish Parliament). Also that year, the Irish War of Independence erupted. While touring the U.S., de Valera raised substantial amounts of money among influential Irish Americans. This was also a homecoming of sorts for "Dev," who had been born in the U.S. After de Valera returned to Ireland in 1920, he sided with the IRA. He became president of Ireland in 1959.

Bloody Sunday One of the most ghastly days of the Irish War of Independence was Sunday, November 21, 1920. IRA squads killed more than a dozen British agents in Ireland as part of Michael Collins's famous guerrilla war strategy. The British response was swift. Members of the infamous Black and Tans entered Dublin's Croke Park during a Gaelic football match and killed 14 spectators. The day came to be called "Bloody Sunday." Irish sympathizers in the United States saw this as another example of British ruthlessness, and even neutral observers were shocked by the brutality of the killings.

A champion for steelworkers Irish immigrant John Fitzpatrick (*far left*), along with labor organizer William Z. Foster (*second from left*), won a major victory for meatpackers in Chicago. Afterward, in 1919, they assisted Pittsburgh steelworkers before and during the massive strike of 1919. Prior to the unionization drive led by Foster and Fitzpatrick, Pittsburgh steel laborers had to work 12-hour days, six days a week. They saw little of the monumental profits reaped by the booming steel industry. The 1919 strike ultimately led to higher wages and better working conditions.

MacSwiney's hunger strike

Hunger strikes have long been a tool used by Irish nationalists to gain public sympathy. In one of the most publicized cases, Lord Mayor of Cork Terence MacSwiney refused all nourishment in 1920. After being arrested because of his involvement with the IRA,

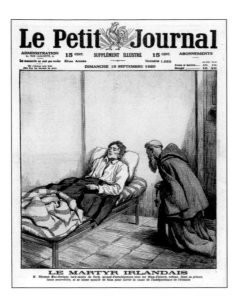

MacSwiney argued that the British had no legal authority in Ireland. MacSwiney's hunger strike gripped the public and the media. Some saw his act as suicidal and thus morally wrong (MacSwiney did die), but many others saw him as a noble figure who fought British tyranny in Ireland.

The Black and Tans In 1919 the British government began recruiting soldiers to assist the Royal Irish Constabulary (RIC) in efforts to beat the IRA during the Irish War of Independence. The soldiers came to be called Black and Tans because of their black and khaki uniforms. But it was their reputation for brutality that made the Black and Tans infamous. Theft, harassment of civilians (as seen in this image), and even murder were not discouraged. In the end, many Irish joined or came to sympathize with the IRA in the face of Black and Tan intimidation.

British execute Irish POWs As dawn broke in Dublin on March 14, 1921, a procession of women carrying a banner that read "England Executes Prisoners of War" made its way to Mountjoy Prison to protest the execution of six Irishmen. The men had been convicted in an IRA assassination plot, and they were hanged on March 14. The executions took place despite international opposition, which included a plea from the Vatican. Irish nationalists saw this as yet another example of excessive British force.

WAR RAGES IN IRELAND

Following another attack by civilians on the police, three more small towns and villages were sacked last night by men in uniform. These places, which are all situated on or near the coast of County Clare, are Milltown-Malbay, Ennistymon and Lahinch. In all, eighteen houses were burned down, seven in Milltown-Malbay, six in Lahinch, and five at Ennistymon. At the last named place two civilians were shot dead and one man was killed at Lahinch. Whole families are reported to have left the neighborhood in fear of further outbursts. Only meagre accounts of the affair have come to hand as yet. The attacks by uniformed men were in revenge for the ambushing of a motor lorry near Ennistymon on Wednesday, when six policemen were killed. In the fight four of the assailants were also seen to fall. Thirty-six arrests were made of people suspected of being implicated in the attack and great military activity now prevails in the locality. All the roads are commanded by machine guns and approach to the spot is impossible.

—*THE NEW YORK TIMES*, SEPTEMBER 24, 1920

Irish Presence in Philadelphia

The Irish Press, an important journal of Irish American opinion, was published in Philadelphia by Joseph McGarrity, a native of County Tyrone and a strong ally of Irish leader Eamon de Valera. This headline reflects the anger of Irish nationalists over the recently signed Anglo-Irish Treaty. Philadelphia looms large in the history of Irish America. It was the site of anti-Irish riots in 1844, and it became the place of exile for thousands of famine immigrants. By the 1870s, St. Patrick's Day was a huge event in the city, attracting up to 6,000 marchers. In a historical twist, Irish Americans tended to support the city's Republican machine rather than its local Democratic Party.

Anglo-Irish Treaty

In July 1921, representatives of Great Britain and the Irish Republic negotiated the Anglo-Irish Treaty. Irish reps included (*left to right*) Gavin Duffy, Michael Collins, and Arthur Griffith. The peace agreement ended the Irish War of Independence (in which more than a thousand people had been killed) and created the Irish Free State (within the British Empire). It also gave six-county Northern Ireland, which had been established by the 1920 Government of Ireland Act, the option to opt out of the Irish Free State—which it did. Many Irish nationalists saw this as a betrayal, but British leader Lloyd George said the only other option was a long war with Britain.

New map of Ireland

The Anglo-Irish Treaty of 1921 called for the partition of Ireland into two entities, the Irish Free State, which would consist of 26 of the island's 32 counties, and Northern Ireland, composed of six counties. Northern Ireland was overwhelmingly Protestant and remained part of the United Kingdom. The Free State, overwhelmingly Catholic, was given the freedom to govern its domestic affairs. But the Free State was not a republic; instead, it was a dominion within the British Empire, like Canada. Politicians in the Free State were required to swear loyalty to the British crown. It was a bitter compromise, but one that the majority of Irish accepted. The pro-treaty government fought a civil war against former comrades who opposed the treaty. The anti-treaty side lost the war.

Collins fights for independence

After spending time among Irish nationalist exiles in London as a teenager, Michael Collins returned to Ireland in 1916 and emerged as a leader of the Easter Rising. After his release from prison, he became an ally of Eamon de Valera and Sinn Féin. During the Irish War of Independence, Collins developed a highly successful guerilla warfare strategy, thus becoming Britain's most wanted enemy. In July 1921, Collins led the Irish team of peace negotiators, which accepted peace with the British and the partition of Ireland. Eamon de Valera and others vehemently opposed the treaty, which led to the Irish Civil War and, ultimately, Collins's death in 1922.

June 28, 1919: The First World War is officially over, as Germany and the Allies sign the Treaty of Versailles.

July 1919: Former Secret Service chief William J. Flynn is tapped to lead the Bureau of Investigation, the predecessor of the FBI. Another Irish American detective, William J. Burns, will succeed Flynn in 1921.

September 12, 1919: Britain prohibits the Dáil Éireann, asserting that it is an illegal institution. Its members will continue to meet in secret.

1920: British Parliament passes the Government of Ireland Act, which partitions Ireland into a North and South in an effort to enact home rule. • The Royal Irish Constabulary Reserve Force is established to counter IRA terrorist activity. Also known as the "Black and Tans" for their uniform colors, the force will prove to be unconcerned with collateral damage suffered by Irish civilians. • Mary Louise Cecilia Guinian, known as "Texas," opens the 300 Club in Manhattan. • *Beyond the Horizon,* Eugene O'Neill's first play, opens on Broadway. It will earn the Irish American playwright a Pulitzer Prize.

January 16, 1920: Prohibition goes into effect, making illegal the consumption and sale of alcohol throughout the United States. Bootlegging (unlawful selling of alcohol during Prohibition) will birth the criminal careers of many notable Irish American gangsters, including Chicagoans George "Bugs" Moran and Dion O'Banion.

March 20, 1920: Royal Irish Constabulary officers murder Thomas MacCurtain, the lord mayor of Cork. His successor, Terence MacSwiney, will be imprisoned for treason in August and will die of starvation from a hunger strike in October.

Civil War rages in Ireland Liam O'Flaherty's chilling 1923 story, "The Sniper"—in which one brother unknowingly kills another—captures the heartbreaking nature of the Irish Civil War. Following the Anglo-Irish Treaty, six counties of Northern Ireland were left under British rule. Supporters of peace negotiator Michael Collins believed the treaty terms were the best deal the Irish could get. But Eamon de Valera's staunch allies saw the treaty as a betrayal. The two sides waged bloody war, with a 55,000-man National Army facing 15,000 anti-treaty IRA volunteers (*pictured*). Some 3,000 people were killed, with the IRA suffering most of the losses. A cease-fire was finally called in the spring of 1923.

"Texas" lights up New York Mary Louise Cecilia "Texas" Guinan was a singer, movie star, and nightlife fixture of Prohibition-era New York. Born in Texas to Irish and Canadian parents, Guinan became a dancer before appearing in silent films, such as 1920's *The Wildcat.* After moving to New York, Guinan opened the 300 Club, a speakeasy famous for its dancing girls and illegal booze. She continued to make movies before dying at age 49 in 1933. Many say that Mae West's screen persona was based on Guinan.

Irish Prince of Broadway

Eugene Gladstone O'Neill's fate as the haunted, preeminent playwright of Irish America was cast on October 16, 1888. On that day, he was born in a hotel room just off of Broadway, New York's famed theater district.

Eugene's father, James, was one of the most successful stage actors of his day. But James O'Neill was also an Irish immigrant scarred by the past—specifically the Irish famine, which bred in him a lifelong fear of poverty. Eugene O'Neill once said that "the most important thing about me and my work [is] the fact that I am Irish." Following Eugene's birth, his mother was given a prescription for morphine. She developed an addiction that loomed large in the O'Neill family.

Eugene briefly attended Princeton, but the sickly writer's real education came when he read voraciously while recuperating from various ailments. O'Neill's first Broadway play, *Beyond the Horizon,* was produced in 1920. It won a

Eugene O' Neill with wife Carlotta Monterey

Pulitzer Prize, as did *Anna Christie* and *Strange Interlude. The Emperor Jones, The Hairy Ape, Desire Under the Elms,* and *Mourning Becomes Electra* were other plays that cemented O'Neill's reputation.

O'Neill won the Nobel Prize in 1936. For the final, brilliant phase of his career, he turned to his family and the Irish American experience. *A Touch of the Poet,* set in 1820s Boston, explores the delusions of an Irish immigrant tavern keeper. *The Iceman Cometh* is an epic set among dreamers and schemers in a grimy New York bar. And *A Moon for the Misbegotten* revolves around a Connecticut Irish farmer and his doomed efforts to marry off his daughter to a romantic boozer.

Three years after O'Neill's death in 1953, *A Long Day's Journey into Night* opened. It was a sensation, an epic clearly based on O'Neill's own family. In the play, one character says, "Keep your dirty tongue off Ireland." It turns out that it was O'Neill who could not stop talking about the Irish.

Irish feel targeted by prohibitionists

Prohibition, meaning the ban of alcohol in America from 1920 to '33, was part of a much larger urban-rural conflict in the United States. Supporters of Prohibition often linked the ills of alcohol with other supposed urban problems: ethnic neighborhoods, Democratic political machines, and the Catholic Church. These institutions, along with the saloon, were integral to the urban Irish, who felt culturally attacked by the largely rural and Protestant prohibitionists. One Irish group did thrive under Prohibition. Gangsters Bugs Moran, Dion O'Banion, Owney "The Killer" Madden, and "Mad Dog" Coll all rose to prominence selling illegal booze.

Gallagher and Shean In 1912 Irish American comedian Ed Gallagher joined with Albert Schoenberg to form the team of Gallagher and Shean. Though they enjoyed success on stage, they broke up in 1914 because of personal friction, and they did not appear together again until 1920. Performing in outlandish costumes—Gallagher as a well-heeled tourist and Shean in a fez and skirted jacket—the duo was a mainstay of the Ziegfeld Follies in the early 1920s. Their popular theme song, "Mister Gallagher and Mister Shean," was repartee set to music.

Effects of the 19th Amendment This 1920 cartoon reflected the hope of many reformers that the passage of the 19th Amendment—which gave women the vote—would reduce the corrupt practices of the urban political machines. Their hopes were unfounded, however, because they failed to understand the culture of the Irish American family at that time. Many Irish women, while a strong force in the home, deferred to their men when it came to politics. Through the "Roaring '20s," the political machines continued on their merry way.

From bricklayer to Olympic hero The youngest of 10 children from County Mayo, John Kelly worked as a bricklayer's apprentice in Philadelphia before serving in World War I. Though outstanding in the sport of rowing, he was refused entry to the Henley Royal Regatta in England because of his low social standing. Kelly responded by winning three Olympic gold medals when he rowed for America in 1920 and 1924. The handsome athlete became a media celebrity, which helped him turn his brick-works into a million-dollar business. Kelly was the father of actress Grace Kelly and grandfather of Prince Albert II of Monaco.

Superstar of the silent screen In the 1920s, filmgoers across America recognized Joseph "Buster" Keaton's dead-pan expression and straw boater hat. He is considered one of the greatest comedy actors and filmmakers of the silent movie era. His Irish American parents, both of whom were vaude-villians, introduced their son to the stage. In 1917, at age 22, Keaton made the switch from the stage to the movie set, and his career took off. *The General* (1927), which he co-directed and starred in, ranks among the greatest silent films of all time. Here he's pictured in the 1921 film *The Goat*.

The hunt for a cop killer On December 11, 1921, convicted murderer Tommy O'Connor (*pictured*) escaped from the Cook County jail in Chicago just a few days before he was to be hanged for killing Sergeant Patrick O'Neill of the city's police department. Within hours, 5,000 police officers were searching the city with orders to shoot O'Connor on sight. But O'Connor was

never found. Cook County officials refused to discard the jail's gallows until 1977. O'Connor's victim, O'Neill, was one of thousands of Irish American police officers in the Windy City.

Donahey's fanciful creations "Old Mother Hubbard and Her Dog" represents but a fragment of the output of illustrator and cartoonist William Donahey. Donahey came from an old Ohio family; one brother became governor and a U.S. senator. Donahey's art was rich and realistically detailed, but it was always touched by the fanciful. He is best known for *The Teenie Weenies,* a

comic strip that details the intricate life of a society of tiny beings. The strip premiered in the *Chicago Tribune* in 1912 and ran almost continuously from 1914 until a few months before Donahey's death in 1970.

A more comfortable living Mary and Kathryn Cottrell enjoy a pleasant day in Hot Springs, Virginia. By the 1920s, many Irish Americans had moved into the middle and upper classes. Greater access to both Catholic and public education (including colleges, even Ivy League universities) led to new opportunities in business and law. Every day, Irish Americans left poor urban parishes for more respectable neighborhoods. Joseph Kennedy and Henry Ford were just two of the Irish Americans who had become millionaires by the 1920s.

U.S. restricts immigration Following World War I, Congress placed restrictions on the number of immigrants allowed annually into the United States. This reversal of America's long-standing open-door policy resulted from two factors. First was labor's fear that an influx of unskilled workers would drive down wage gains made during the war. Secondly, many Americans believed that the Eastern Europeans then streaming into the country were degenerate and "red" in their politics. The immigration acts established quotas based on the number of natives of each foreign country already residing in the U.S.

November 21, 1920: More than 30 people die in Dublin when an attack on British intelligence officers is answered by a mass murder of civilians at a Gaelic football match. The day will become known as "Bloody Sunday."

May 19, 1921: Congress passes the first of a series of immigration restriction acts (others will follow in 1924 and 1929). The Irish are so entrenched in America that these laws are not meant to limit immigrants from Ireland but, instead, those of other nations.

October 25, 1921: William Barclay "Bat" Masterson—journalist, army scout, outdoorsman, U.S. marshal, and Irish American icon of the Old West—dies at age 67 in New York City.

December 6, 1921: Representatives of the Irish Republic and British leadership sign the Anglo-Irish Treaty, bringing an end to the Irish War of Independence.

April 1922: Ten Irish civilians are killed in Dunmanaway, County Cork, by members of the Irish Republican Army.

June 28, 1922: The Irish Civil War breaks out over the controversial Anglo-Irish Treaty, as Irish nationalist Michael Collins opens fire on the Four Courts building in Dublin.

August 22, 1922: Irish National Army Commander and former IRA intelligence director Michael Collins is shot and killed in an ambush by IRA forces. It remains unclear if Collins was a victim of assassination (targeted for his support of the Anglo-Irish Treaty) or if he was simply in the wrong place at the wrong time.

November 23, 1922: President Warren Harding nominates Irish American justice Pierce Butler to the U.S. Supreme Court.

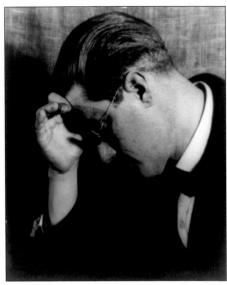

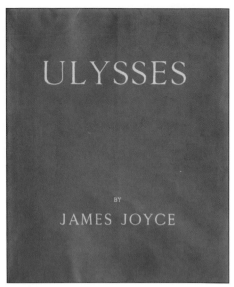

U.S. bans Joyce's *Ulysses* Beginning with the short story collection *Dubliners* (1914) and *Portrait of the Artist as a Young Man* (1916), Ireland's James Joyce portrayed his country and Irish Catholic society in a critical light. His masterpiece, *Ulysses* (1922), added a new dimension of discomfort for many Irish Americans. Decrying its purported obscenity, the Roman Catholic Church added *Ulysses* to its index of banned books. Moreover, the U.S. government blocked the book from being imported or published. Dr. Joseph Collins, an Irish American neurologist, wrote in *The New York Times* that the "average, intelligent reader" of *Ulysses* "will glean little or nothing from it . . . save bewilderment and a sense of disgust."

A Hollywood murder
William Desmond Taylor (*right*), who immigrated to the United States from County Carlow in 1890, was one of Hollywood's most prolific directors during the silent film era. On February 1, 1922, Taylor was fatally shot in the back in his Hollywood home. News of the murder became more salacious after police found love letters to Taylor from 19-year-old actress Mary Miles Minter (*left*). Police identified numerous suspects but never made an arrest. Taylor's murder, along with the sensational rape trial of actor Fatty Arbuckle at around the same time, scandalized Hollywood.

> **"The comic-strip farce of the Levys' and the Murphys' painful accep-tance of their children's marriage had played all over the U.S. (once 16 road companies were hard at it) and throughout most of the civilized world. It had even lasted eight months in Berlin just before Hitler."**
>
> —*TIME* MAGAZINE, MAY 3, 1943, ON *ABIE'S IRISH ROSE*

Abie's Irish Rose

The play *Abie's Irish Rose* was one of the most popu-lar theatrical productions of the 1920s, playing to packed houses during a five-year run on Broadway. Critics generally loathed Anne Nichols's melodrama of Irish-Jew-ish intermarriage. Nevertheless, *Abie's Irish Rose* captivated audiences with its mix of comedy, romance, and religious tension. It was performed more than 2,300 times from 1922 to 1927, and was adapted for film in 1928.

The play's main characters are Abie Levy and Rose Murphy. "Abie was a Romeo, heir to riches in New York, but with the ghetto in his blood," a *New York Times* review noted. Rose, meanwhile, "was a Juliet, with the blarney." The two marry, yet they conceal the marriage from their respective widower fathers. The rest of the play consists of culture-clash comedy, the revelation of the forbidden mar-riage, and a reluctant reconciliation.

The success of *Abie's Irish Rose* indicated a growing audi-ence for theater that reflected the lives of working-class ethnic Americans. It also sent a clear message of American assimilation. The angry fathers in the play represent Old World intolerance. Abie and Rose are New World Ameri-cans, and their children are even more so.

Abie's Irish Rose inspired dozens of movies, books, radio programs, and plays about mixed Irish marriages. The crit-ics generally dismissed such efforts, but Irish audiences embraced these works. Not only were they entertaining, but they helped nudge the Irish and others toward accep-tance in the U.S.

The "Irish Riviera" The term "Irish Riviera" has been applied to several oceanfront enclaves that are cozy but a little rough around the edges. That's not the case with Spring Lake, New Jersey. As early as the 1860s, wealthy New Yorkers and Philadelphians flocked to the picturesque town. When Irish Americans began entering the upper middle class, they were particu-larly attracted to Spring Lake's Victo-rian cottages, boardwalk, shops, and, of course, the body of water that gave the town its name.

December 6, 1922: The Irish Free State is created. It is comprised of the 26 counties of predominately Catholic southern Ireland, and it excludes the six Protestant counties in Northern Ireland.

1923: Irish gangster Owney Madden opens the Cotton Club in Harlem. The storied nightclub will launch the careers of such musical greats as Duke Ellington and Louis Armstrong. • The renowned Lahey Clinic in Boston is founded by Irish American physician Frank H. Lahey.

April 1923: The Anti-Treaty IRA faction calls for a cease-fire in the Irish Civil War, leaving the National Army of the Irish Free State victorious.

September 1923: Irish American boxer Jack Dempsey successfully defends his heavyweight title for the last time, defeating Argentinian fighter Luis Angel Firpo at New York's Polo Grounds.

1924: Irish American stuntman Alvin "Shipwreck" Kelly launches the fad of pole-sitting when he perches on a flagpole for 13 hours and 13 minutes. He eventually will outdo himself with a 49-day effort.

November 10, 1924: A five-year war between rival Irish and Italian Chicago gangs is launched when members of Al Capone's crime family whack Irish mobster Dion O'Banion while O'Banion clips chrysanthemums in his flower shop.

April 10, 1925: *The Great Gatsby,* F. Scott Fitzgerald's brilliant novel about love and loss amid the prosperity of the Roaring '20s, is released.

October 11, 1925: Special Agent Edwin C. Shanahan is gunned down by a Chicago car thief, becoming the first member of the FBI to die in the line of duty.

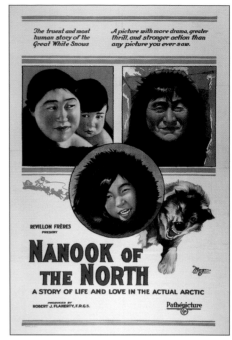

Filmmaking pioneer Film historians consider Robert Flaherty the "father of documentary filmmaking." Born in Michigan to an Irish father and German mother, Robert and his family moved to Canada, where he became intrigued with Inuit culture. Flaherty's documentary on Inuit life, *Nanook of the North,* appeared in 1922. Its success was followed by *Moana,* about life in Samoa, and *Man of Aran,* which depicted the daily struggles of people living on an Irish island. Because Flaherty staged many scenes in his movies, some critics have said his films are not true documentaries.

Irish gangster opens Cotton Club Owney "The Killer" Madden was a gangster who grew tired of the outlaw life and who, uncharacteristically for the breed, lived past 70. A native of Liverpool, England, Madden set his lethal seal on Irish New York during the peak years of incorporated crime. Linked to such Irish gangs as the Gophers and Westies, he wound up serving time for murder in Sing Sing. But Madden was smart enough to make seemingly legitimate money. In 1923 in Harlem, he opened the Cotton Club, which became a cultural Mecca for African American jazz musicians. He retired to Hot Springs, Arkansas, 12 years later.

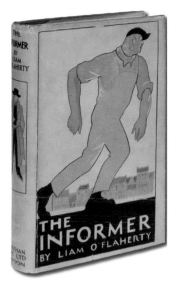

O'Flaherty's harrowing tale *The Informer,* a novel by Liam O'Flaherty later made into a haunting 1935 film by John Ford, tells the story of an Irish rebel with dreams of leaving Ireland for the United States. All he needs is money. Opportunity strikes when he learns that he can turn over one of his former comrades to the British. Echoing classic horror tales such as Poe's "The Tell-Tale Heart"—not to mention the biblical story of Judas—O'Flaherty created a riveting tale that highlighted the Irish hatred of "informers."

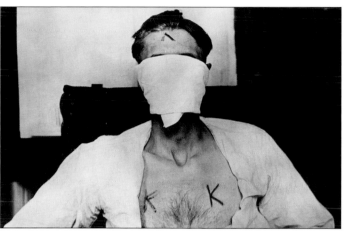

The KKK targets Catholics In 1924 Ku Klux Klansmen abducted Nelson Burroughs (*pictured*) in Massachusetts and tried to force him to renounce the Catholic Church. On May 17, 1924, Notre Dame students stood up to Klan members who had gathered in South Bend to rally against their university—in Klan eyes a symbol of unacceptable Catholic influence in America. The 20th century KKK targeted African Americans, Catholics, and Jews. Fifty years later, its effort to insert itself into the Boston busing crisis resulted, somewhat ironically, in a pummeling by vengeful Irish Catholics.

"Booze war" murders Police and civilians on the South Side of Chicago examine the car of William H. McSwiggin after he was gunned down on April 27, 1926. As a 26-year-old prosecutor in the state's attorney's office, McSwiggin had sent seven criminals to death row in the previous eight months. Evidence suggested that Chicago mob boss Al Capone was behind the attack, but six grand juries failed to indict him or anyone else. Some speculated that Capone had killed McSwiggin by mistake, intending instead to knock off Jewish crime boss Earl "Hymie" Weiss. The murder was one of numerous "booze war" killings in Chicago during the Prohibition era. In a complicated landscape, Capone's Italian gang controlled the South Side, while Irish and Jewish mobsters battled for control of North Side territory.

Crowe prosecutes Leopold and Loeb Irish American Robert Crowe (*left;* pictured with investigators) was the district attorney for Cook County in 1924 when two University of Chicago students, Nathan Leopold, Jr., and Richard Loeb, were indicted for the murder of a 14-year-old boy named Bobby Franks. The two men killed Franks, the government charged, simply because they sought to commit a perfect crime. Crowe, a Yale Law School graduate described as a "jut-jawed Irishman," was the chief prosecutor in the case. The men eventually admitted their guilt, but their defense attorney, the famed Clarence Darrow, persuaded a judge to send them to prison rather than order their execution.

1926: Irish leader and Dáil Éireann president Eamon de Valera severs ties with Sinn Féin and forms a new political party, Fianna Fáil. • Anti-Communist activist Father Charles Coughlin launches the radio show *Golden Hour of the Little Flower*. A champion of Franklin Roosevelt in the 1932 election, Coughlin will vigorously oppose the president's 1936 reelection bid.

February 1, 1926: Irish American Brigadier General William "Billy" Mitchell, the "father of the U.S. Air Force," resigns from the U.S. Army Air Service rather than accept a court-martial conviction for insubordination.

1927: The University of Notre Dame officially nicknames its sports teams the Fighting Irish.

July 15, 1927: Irish nationalist politician Countess Markiewicz dies only five weeks after her successful bid for reelection to the Dáil Éireann.

October 1, 1927: *Abie's Irish Rose* closes on Broadway after a run of more than five years and 2,327 performances. The story about the marriage of an Irish Catholic woman and a Jewish man was extremely popular with theater audiences.

1928: Gaelic Park, in the Bronx borough of New York City, is established. It will thrive as a center for Irish sports, such as hurling and Gaelic football, well into the 21st century. • Popular Irish American Democrat Huey Long wins Louisiana's gubernatorial contest with his catchphrase "Every man a king."

March 12, 1928: Hundreds of people lose their lives when the St. Francis Dam, part of the Los Angeles Aqueduct, fails. Irish-born engineer William Mulholland accepts blame for the tragedy. He will retreat from the public eye until his death in 1935.

Democrats sink their own ship The 1924 presidential election was a disaster for the Democrats. Their convention was split between those who favored Al Smith (mainly Catholic, anti-Prohibition urban Northerners) and those who supported William McAdoo (rural Protestant Southerners and Midwesterners). Deadlocked after more than 100 ballots, the convention chose a conservative compromise candidate, lackluster John Davis of West Virginia. Robert La Follette of Wisconsin further muddied the waters when he ran as the candidate of the Progressive Party. The Irish vote split. In November, Republican Calvin Coolidge easily won.

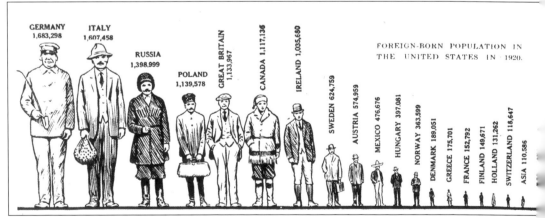

Immigration laws don't affect Irish Under the most extreme of the Immigration Acts—the Johnson Act (1924)—annual immigration was limited to just two percent of America's foreign born, based on the 1890 census. Because there had been few Eastern Europeans in the United States prior to the 1890s, their annual allotment was greatly reduced. The Irish were hardly affected at all. Through the 1920s, they did not fill the quota allotted them. For the Irish, it was the worldwide slump of the Great Depression that greatly curtailed immigration to America.

Fallon's clients get off scot-free William Fallon was a prosecutor's worst nightmare. As a defense attorney in 1920s New York, Fallon earned a reputation as an attorney whose clients walked away from hard time, every time. He notched 126 successive courtroom victories while defending the famous and the infamous, including gangsters. Fallon's clients included mobster Arnold Rothstein (fixer of the 1919 World Series) and New York Giants manager John McGraw. Suspicion fell on Fallon himself when he was charged with jury tampering in 1924, three years before his death.

Dempsey reigns as heavyweight champ This George Bellows painting of Irish American Jack Dempsey and Luis Firpo actually depicts the eventual winner, Dempsey, tumbling through the ropes. A Colorado, native, Dempsey captured the heavyweight championship in 1919. Four years later, he fought the Argentinean-born Firpo at the Polo Grounds. Firpo knocked Dempsey out of the ring in the first round, a scene recreated by Bellows a year later. Dempsey, however, kayoed Firpo in the second round. He held on to the heavyweight title until 1926, when fellow Irishman Gene Tunney beat him in front of 120,000 fans in Philadelphia.

Catholic high schools emerge Cardinal Patrick Hayes lays the cornerstone for New York's first Catholic high school in 1925. The 1920s were a boom time for American Catholic education. More and more high schools opened to serve the growing children of Irish Americans—as well as the Italians, Poles, and newer Irish immigrants who came to the United States at the turn of the century. Tuition-free Catholic high schools for boys began opening in Philadelphia in the 1890s. In the decades that followed, high schools for boys and girls opened at a rapid pace.

Hurling's American heyday Hurling is the world's fastest field game—and one of the oldest. Yet the game has been battling to stay afloat in the United States in recent years because of the fall-off in new players resulting from declining immigration from Ireland. In the 1920s, when this photo was taken, fielding hurling teams was far less a problem. Members of Gaelic athletic clubs also played Gaelic football and camogie, a women's version of hurling. These clubs were a key part of Irish immigrant social and cultural life in America's big cities.

Two Literary Giants

John O'Hara

F. Scott Fitzgerald

John O'Hara and F. Scott Fitzgerald were among the most celebrated Irish American writers in the first half of the 20th century. O'Hara's creative arc reached from the late 1920s through the 1960s. He wrote bushels of short stories and a shelf-full of popular novels. Fitzgerald reached his zenith in 1925 with *The Great Gatsby,* the landmark novel of Jazz Age America. But alcoholism, depression, and a chaotic personal life strangled his talent, and he died at age 44.

Longevity aside, O'Hara and Fitzgerald shared what scholar Charles Fanning calls an "ambivalence" about their ethnic background and social standing that led them to avoid writing in any depth about Irish American life.

O'Hara was born in Pottsville, Pennsylvania, in 1905. He came from a well-off family that was derived on one side from pre-American Revolution settlers and on the other from "black Irish" immigrants. O'Hara's father was Irish, an accomplished doctor, and a surgeon. But the father's early death spoiled the son's dream of attending Yale. For the rest of his life, he yearned for a social status that he could never attain. Critic Edmund Wilson wrote that "the cruel side of social snobbery" was O'Hara's main theme. Fanning says O'Hara shared Fitzgerald's ambivalence toward his Irishness, citing an autobiographical passage from the novel *Butterfield 8:* "I want to tell you something about myself that will help to explain a lot of things about me.... I am a Mick."

Fitzgerald was born in St. Paul, Minnesota, in 1896. From his father's side—a family that traced its roots to colonial Maryland—he inherited pedigree but not wealth. From his mother's family—famine-era immigrants who had succeeded in business—he got money but no standing. The principal theme in his writings was the power of money and social prestige. Fitzgerald's discomfort with his Irishness is evident in a 1922 letter in which he mentions James Joyce's *Ulysses.* He wrote: "There is something about middle-class Ireland that depresses me.... Half of my ancestors came from just such an Irish strata or perhaps a lower one. The book makes me feel appallingly naked."

Mitchell pushes for greater airpower
Billy Mitchell blazed a heroic trail in the skies over World War I's trenches. Mitchell, by war's end a brigadier general, passionately advocated for an air force separate from the Army and Navy. He sank captured German ships to prove that airpower would be decisive in future conflicts, but his dogged criticism of unbending superiors led to his court-martial in 1925. Mitchell, who in a 1924 report predicted a Japanese attack on Pearl Harbor, quit the military in disgust. He died in 1936, five years before his most crucial prophecy came to pass.

Irish land civil service jobs Less visible than their counterparts who worked as police officers, firefighters, and teachers, many Irish Americans were attracted to a wide range of other civil service jobs, such as mail carrier. Since the 1850s, the Irish had used politics and government to advance, so they were well positioned to obtain civil service work. Meanwhile, in the 1920s, the Irish were still heavily clustered in large cities, where civil service jobs were most plentiful. The expansion of the federal government under the New Deal in the 1930s only increased civil service opportunities for Irish Americans.

The first eastern congresswoman The daughter of Irish immigrants, New Jersey's Mary Teresa Norton was the sixth woman elected to the U.S. Congress but the first from an eastern state and the first Democrat. Norton served 13 consecutive terms in the House, representing New Jersey's 12th congressional district from 1925 to 1951. Chairing four committees during her House years, Norton was a vigorous champion of labor and women's rights. She died in 1959 at age 84.

Mellon's money A second-generation Irish American, Andrew Mellon (*right*, with U.S. Congressman Richard Elliott) took over his father's banking firm, T. Mellon and Sons, in 1882. Renamed Mellon National Bank, the firm's investments in such companies as U.S. Steel and Gulf Oil helped make Mellon a very wealthy man. He became involved in Republican Party politics and served as treasury secretary from 1921 to 1932 under three presidents: Warren Harding, Calvin Coolidge, and Herbert Hoover. His policy of increased taxation on the rich and less taxation on the working class led to more tax revenue but stunted economic growth.

Chicago's Irish Catholics As the nation's leading railroad hub in the 19th century, Chicago became the destination for tens of thousands of Irish immigrants who had ventured inland after reaching the eastern shores. By the 1920s, Chicago's Irish Catholics were the city's dominant ethnic group. They, along with the city's large population of Eastern European Catholics, turned out at Soldier Field in 1926 for an International Eucharistic Congress. Among the dignitaries in attendance was the city's beloved cardinal, George Mundelein.

November 1928: In an election marred by rampant anti-Catholic bigotry, Al Smith becomes the first Catholic Irish American representing a contending political party to run for president. Smith is strongly rejected in America's heartland, due largely to his Catholic faith and his opposition to Prohibition.

November 23, 1928: Industrialist and financier Thomas Fortune Ryan dies. This Irish American's legacy of philanthropy includes some $20 million in donations to various Catholic charities.

1929: Irish American artist Georgia O'Keeffe spends the summer in New Mexico for the first time. For the remainder of her career, many of her paintings will clearly reflect a Southwest influence.

February 14, 1929: Members of Al Capone's crime syndicate gun down six members of Irish American Bugs Moran's gang and an unlucky bystander. The murders will come to be known as the St. Valentine's Day Massacre.

October 29, 1929: The Wall Street stock market crashes, kicking America into what will be known as the Great Depression. Joseph Kennedy is one of the relatively few major investors who fortuitously gets out of the market in time to save his fortune.

1930: Mildred Wirt Benson, writing under the pseudonym Carolyn Keene, pens the first of the original Nancy Drew mysteries.

November 30, 1930: Famed Irish-born labor leader Mary Harris "Mother" Jones dies in Maryland. She will be buried in the Union Miners Cemetery in Mount Olive, Illinois, alongside the miners whose rights she worked to secure.

Chicago's shameless aldermen John "Bathhouse" Coughlin (*left*) and Michael "Hinky Dink" Kenna (*right*) epitomized Chicago machine politics from the 1890s to the 1930s. As aldermen, they ran the city's notorious Ward One as their own private fiefdom. Everyone paid Bathhouse and Hinky Dink: brothel owners, saloonkeepers, gamblers, and job seekers. Through favors owed by the police and judges, the two aldermen kept their underworld clients safe from the law. At election time, Coughlin and Kenna rounded up the homeless and destitute, paid them 50 cents, and sent them out to vote with ballots that were already filled out.

An eloquent heavyweight champ Gene Tunney, the son of a longshoreman from County Mayo, stunned the boxing world with his victory over Jack Dempsey in 1926. He defeated Dempsey again the following year in the famous "long count" match, in which he lay on the canvas well past the 10-second limit and then recovered to win the fight. Tunney had grown up in Manhattan's Greenwich Village, where his father idolized John L. Sullivan, the bare-knuckled Boston heavyweight. Gene was not just a great boxer but also a learned man who loved to quote Shakespeare. He retired as champ, served in World War II, and went on to enjoy a successful career in business.

Gentleman Jimmy Runs Wild

James J. Walker, known as "Gentleman Jimmy" to New Yorkers, was the perfect mayor for the Roaring '20s. He loved a night on the town and the company of a pretty woman, even if that woman was not always his wife.

Walker's first career was in show business. He was a songwriter who wrote the hit "Will You Love Me in December as You Do in May?" But Walker's Irish immigrant father—a Tammany Hall loyalist—convinced Jimmy to become a lawyer. Thus began a career that mirrored Walker's native city. It was all glitter and good times during the 1920s before things came crashing down during the Depression-ravaged 1930s.

Born in 1881, Walker was first elected to the New York state assembly in 1909. Later, in the state senate, he made a name for himself as a key ally of fellow Irishman Al Smith. Walker ran for mayor in 1925 with the support of Tammany Hall, which had become more respectable under the guidance of boss "Silent" Charlie Murphy, who died in 1924.

Under Mayor Walker, the Jazz Age was in full swing. Aside from his playful persona, New Yorkers loved him because he preserved the all-important nickel subway fare.

Walker's troubles began after his 1929 reelection. An investigation into court corruption by Judge Samuel Seabury revealed that Walker might have been taking bribes. The mayor's lavish lifestyle only fueled such speculation. Moreover, Walker's adulterous relationship with actress

Jimmy Walker with new bride Betty Compton

Betty Compton became public. Even Walker's former ally, Franklin Roosevelt, turned on him.

Walker obtained a divorce, resigned in 1932, and fled for Europe with Compton. Tammany's reformed image was in ruins. As a result, the machine's mortal enemy, reformer Fiorello LaGuardia, was eventually elected mayor.

For Jimmy Walker, as with many in Jazz Age New York, if the 1920s was like a great party, the 1930s seemed like a severe hangover.

Sullivan chronicles the Irish Mark Sullivan's six-volume history of the early 20th century, *Our Times,* is one of the most comprehensive works of U.S. history ever published. Born into a large Irish immigrant family in Pennsylvania, Sullivan became a journalist and the editor of *Collier's Weekly.* But Sullivan has best been remembered for *Our Times,* published from 1926 to 1935. By analyzing elite and popular American culture (a groundbreaking method at the time), Sullivan charted America from the turn of the century through the Great Depression.

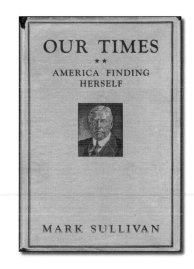

The prolific career of Helen Hayes The "first lady of American theater," Helen Hayes was born in Washington, D.C., in 1900. Her father was a poultry salesman, and one of her mother's aunts was an Irish-born performer—a singer named Catherine Hayes. During her 66-year career on stage, Helen won Tony Awards for best actress in *Happy Birthday* (1946) and *Time Remembered* (1957). She also earned Oscars for her roles in *The Sin of Madelon Claudet* (1931) and *Airport* (1970). Hayes became active in Catholic issues later in life and was awarded the Presidential Medal of Freedom in 1986.

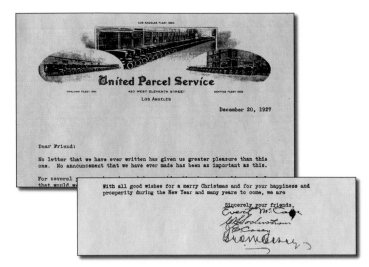

The founders of UPS
The United Parcel Service began as a small, private messenger service in Seattle, founded in 1907 by Irish Americans James E. Casey and Claude Ryan. Casey was just 19 years old at the time. Originally named the American Messenger Company, it took on another partner, Evert McCabe, and began to expand in the years following World War I. Its name was changed to United Parcel Service when it expanded its reach to California in 1919. Today, UPS is a $46 billion business known around the world for its speed and efficiency.

Hoover trounces Smith in '28 While they had little chance of defeating a Republican in the prosperous 1920s, the Democrats nominated Irish Catholic Al Smith for president in 1928. Opponents campaigned against his religion and his anti-Prohibition stance. Smith's support came mainly from the nation's largest cities, where the Irish and immigrant votes were strong. In the end, however, Republican Herbert Hoover won convincingly, with Smith carrying only Massachusetts, Rhode Island, and six southern states—the latter because Hoover was perceived as an anti-segregationist.

Two happy warriors Al Smith and Franklin Roosevelt dine together in happier times. In his early days, FDR admired and supported the progressive governor of New York. Twice, in 1924 and 1928, Roosevelt nominated Smith as the Democratic candidate for president. But when Roosevelt himself was the nominee in 1932, Smith felt betrayed. He turned bitter. Through the 1930s, Smith harshly criticized the New Deal, charging that it was unnecessarily hostile to business. In the elections of 1936 and 1940, Smith supported President Roosevelt's Republican opponents.

Tully's gritty novels James Tully achieved fame after overcoming tremendous odds. Born in Ohio in 1886, Tully was the son of dirt-poor Irish immigrants. His education was more worldly than scholarly, but he nevertheless rose to prominence as a writer—first as a Hollywood reporter, then as author of acclaimed novels. His *Shanty Irish* was inspired by his childhood poverty and years as a drifter. Tully, lauded by H. L.

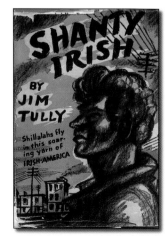

Mencken among others, died in 1947. His legacy was a genre of gritty, pull-no-punches writing that inspired numerous authors and journalists.

The first president After Ireland achieved virtual independence from England in 1922, William T. Cosgrave (*left*) became the first president of the Irish Free State. An early supporter of the separatist Sinn Féin party, W. T. (as he was always known) had participated in the Easter Rising of 1916. Only a general amnesty in 1917 saved him from a life sentence of penal servitude. As president of the Irish Free State, Cosgrove in 1928 visited the United States, where crowds of adoring Irish Americans turned out to see him. Here he shares a ride with Chicago mayor "Big" Bill Haywood.

"Big Tim" runs out of luck Chicago crime and corruption during the early 20th century often came with Irish names attached. One was Timothy "Big Tim" Murphy, a labor leader who was up to his eyeballs in the rackets. Murphy managed not to run afoul of Al Capone, and for a time he lived a charmed existence. Though linked to numerous crimes, he avoided conviction. Eventually he was nailed, and he served seven years for train robbery. Murphy was fatally shot at his home on June 26, 1928. His killer was charmed, too, never answering for the crime.

St. Valentine's Day Massacre There was lead rather than love in the air on February 14, 1929, when Al Capone's men mowed down six of George "Bugs" Moran's outfit (plus a hanger-on) in a garage, where Moran's boys had expected nothing more dramatic than another delivery of illicit whiskey. Moran, head of an Irish mob in Chicago called the North Side Gang, had warred with Capone's Italian-dominated faction. But the St. Valentine's Day Massacre broke Moran, whose roots were Irish and Polish. Moran subsequently left Chicago for a life of bank robbery in the Midwest.

"Bugs" Moran George Clarence "Bugs" Moran, of Irish-Polish descent, was the last captain of a gang of bootleggers, union organizers, and safe-blowers known as the North Side Gang. Moran was also a thorn in the side of Al Capone—his archenemy in the fight to control Chicago's North Side criminal operations. Capone ordered the St. Valentine's Day Massacre in 1929 to wipe out Moran. But although seven members of the gang were killed, Moran did not show up and was unharmed. Moran died in 1957 in Leavenworth Federal Penitentiary, where he was serving time for bank robbery.

> **"You guinea bastards sell the flesh, but leave me out of it. Prostitution is against Our Mother the Church and I'll have nothing to do with the stinking business."**
>
> —CHICAGO GANGSTER DION O'BANION TO AN ITALIAN MOBSTER

Irish Gangsters vs. the Mafia

On the morning of February 14, 1929, four men opened fire on seven others in a garage on Chicago's North Side. The famous massacre was ordered by Al Capone, who was gunning for Bugs Moran. But Moran, the infamous Irish crime boss, was not at the scene.

The St. Valentine's Day Massacre was the culmination of the Irish-Italian turf wars that dominated the 1920s. These wars were fueled by Prohibition and the competition over the sale of illegal booze. Chicago happened to be the center of Irish organized crime, much to the dismay of Italian American criminals such as Capone.

Dion O' Banion

Dion O'Banion was the era's most prominent Irish gangster. He grew up in a Chicago neighborhood known as Little Hell, an altar boy who was also schooled by the mean streets. Even when he became a full-time murderer, O'Banion sported a rosary in his pocket and a carnation in his jacket. In fact, O'Banion loved flowers so much that he opened a flower shop on State Street, which is where he was killed in 1924 after he had swindled members of Capone's crew.

Moran, who inherited O'Banion's North Side operation, tried to eliminate Capone numerous times. He failed, just as Capone failed to hit Moran on Valentine's Day. Still, by the 1930s, it was clear that the Italians (with numerous Irish underlings) had won the Chicago War.

In New York, the West Side Gophers gang was headed by Owney "The Killer" Madden. Madden, who ran the famous Cotton Club, struck deals with Italian and Jewish gangsters. Though of Irish ancestry, he did not have a problem targeting fellow Irish gangsters.

Consider Vincent "Mad Dog" Coll, a native of County Kildare. He began his criminal career as a hitman for Dutch Schultz. Coll, however, began to make waves as he demanded more money. In 1932 Madden was among those who approved a hit on Coll.

For most Irish gangsters, business was more important than ancestral roots.

The pioneering work of Dr. Crile
Born on a farm in Ohio to a Scots-Irish family, George Crile went on to become a pioneering doctor and humanitarian. He performed groundbreaking medical work related to blood pressure, shock, and various surgical methods. He also performed the first successful blood transfusion, in 1906, and founded the revered Cleveland Clinic. He is pictured here in 1929 during a horrific fire at the clinic. More than 120 people lost their lives.

Big Irish families When the Casey family arrived in the United States in 1929, they seemed like a parade unto themselves. There were 10 of them in all, and the Caseys were just one of many very large Irish American families. One key reason for the large families was the Irish devotion to the Catholic Church, which not only prohibited the use of any contraceptive method but also wanted devout children to secure the future of the American Catholic Church. Expanding Catholic social services helped to ease the burden placed upon the heads of large families.

The fabulous Rooney family

The Rooney family (*left to right*, Pat Rooney III, mother Marion, father Pat) was one of the top song and dance families in show business. Pat Rooney became famous for dancing in theater shows, such as *Daughter of Rosie O'Grady*, and early sound films, such as *Night Club*. Rooney's son, Pat III, later joined the family on tour. The younger Pat later played the part of Arvide Abernathy in the original Broadway play *Guys and Dolls*. He performed on television, stage, and screen until his death in 1962.

Carmichael's classic melodies The popularity of Irish-themed songs and the prolific output of Irish American songwriters flowed from the 19th century into the 20th. It reached new heights in the works of Hoagland Howard "Hoagy" Carmichael, composer of "Stardust" (1929)—to this day one of the most popular melodies ever recorded. Born in Indiana in 1899, Carmichael was a lawyer before turning to composing, arranging, and band leading. His many classics include "Georgia on My Mind" (1930) and "Heart and Soul" (1938). Carmichael also acted in movies and hosted radio and television shows.

Kelly is tops at pole sitting Ancient Christian seers sat meditating atop poles. However, Alvin "Shipwreck" Kelly sought not spiritual elevation but fame and notoriety. A Hollywood stuntman, Kelly sparked a national craze in 1924 when, responding to a dare, he perched atop a pole for 13 hours and 13 minutes. Many imitators followed, but Kelly was not to be overshadowed. He is pictured in Union City, New Jersey, in 1929, but it was in Atlantic City a year later that Kelly set a world record by spending 49 days at the pinnacle of a pole.

O'Connell rules in Albany Daniel P. O'Connell (*left, with his attorney*) was the leader of the Democratic Party political machine in Albany, New York, from 1919 until his death in 1977. Although he never held office and was rarely seen in public, O'Connell's machine controlled nearly 100 percent of all city and county offices. It controlled the Albany police force and all local seats in the state senate and assembly. This from a man who had only a fifth-grade education. His machine was so powerful, it influenced politics in Albany for two decades after he died.

Giant of the hardwood At 6'6", Charles "Stretch" Murphy is considered basketball's first big man. The man in the middle for Purdue University, Murphy dominated the boards while smashing Big Ten scoring records. A three-time All-American, he led the Boilermakers to the Big Ten championship in 1930. His teammate was a scrappy guard named John Wooden, who would coach UCLA to 10 NCAA championships. After college, Murphy played professionally but to little fanfare, as the NBA had yet to be established.

The Stooges and beyond Ted Healy was a quick-witted, highly urban comic who accomplished the leap from vaudeville stardom to a prolific Hollywood career. Healy's early fame was as leader of "Ted Healy and His Stooges," who were Larry Fine and Moe and Shemp Howard (and

later Curly Howard). The four went to Hollywood together in the early 1930s. The Stooges soon split from Healy to sign with Columbia; Healy was snapped up by MGM, where he enjoyed juicy supporting parts as hardboiled reporters, tough cops, and other wiseacres. He was especially funny as Jean Harlow's sponging brother in a 1933 comedy, *Bombshell*. Healy was killed at a Hollywood nightclub in 1937.

Jones cops the grand slam Born on St. Patrick's Day in 1902, Bobby Jones was one of the towering figures in American sports during the 1920s. The Atlanta-born Jones captivated the golf world in 1930 when he accomplished a feat never matched

before or since: Jones won the British Amateur, British Open, U.S. Amateur, and U.S. Open to capture golf's Grand Slam. (That term, incidentally, was applied to golf by Jones's close friend, sportswriter O. B. Keeler.) In his prime, Jones was on par with Babe Ruth and Jack Dempsey in the sporting world.

Cochrane stars behind the plate

Mickey Cochrane, of Scots-Irish descent, ranks among the greatest catchers who ever lived. A five-sport letterman at Boston University, Cochrane forged a 13-year Hall of Fame career with the Philadelphia Athletics and Detroit Tigers. He ripped .357 for the world champion A's in 1930, and his .320 career average remains the best in history by a catcher. "Black Mike's" playing career ended in 1937 after he was hit in the head by a ball. Mickey Mantle was named after him.

The Pendergast machine

In the 1920s and 1930s, "Boss" Tom Pendergast—like his brother "Big" Jim Pendergast before him—controlled politics in Kansas City, Missouri. "Boss" Pendergast's Jackson County Democratic Club was known as "Little Tammany." Through graft and corruption, it controlled state and local elections. Pendergast himself grew rich through government construction contracts. At one time, he owned speakeasies, brothels, gambling dens, and racehorses. Harry S. Truman got his start in politics through the Pendergast machine, though he never participated in its shady practices.

Irish Sweepstakes

From 1930 to 1987, in every Irish tavern in America, one could purchase tickets in the Irish Sweepstakes. Each ticket gave its holder a chance to win a sizeable amount of money based on the results of key horse races held in the British Isles. The Sweeps began when the newly formed but impoverished Irish Free State sought a means to build and support Irish hospitals. Given the Irish love for horses, and a worldwide Irish community, the sale of lottery tickets based on horse racing was a natural. When the Sweeps ended in 1987, it had netted more than 135 million pounds sterling for Irish hospitals.

Tarzan's beloved Jane

Maureen O'Sullivan's screen career spanned more than 60 years, but the Roscommon-born actress is best remembered for her role as Jane in six Tarzan movies alongside Johnny Weissmuller (*pictured*). Playing Jane made O'Sullivan a star, but she had her sights on more challenging roles, and she duly secured them opposite such acting greats as Greta Garbo, Myrna Loy, and Laurence Olivier. O'Sullivan had seven children during her marriage to Australian writer John Farrow, one of them being actress Mia Farrow.

1931: Irish American actor Lionel Barrymore wins the Academy Award for best actor for his performance in *A Free Soul.* • James Cagney stars in *Public Enemy,* a classic gangster film based in part on the life and crimes of Irish mobster Dion O'Banion.

1932: Nevada politician Patrick McCarran is elected to serve in the U.S. Senate. Ironically, this Irish American is elected, and will make his most notable achievements, on an anti-immigration platform. • Father Francis Patrick Duffy, the "Fighting Chaplain" who was a decorated (though unarmed) member of the Irish Brigade during the First World War, dies in New York City. • Helen Hayes, the legendary actress known as the "first lady of American theater," is awarded the best actress Academy Award for her work in *The Sin of Madelon Claudet.* • James Aloysius Farley is tapped to head the Democratic National Committee. As DNC chief from 1932 to 1940, he will help lead President Franklin Roosevelt to two of his four successful presidential election victories. • Eamon de Valera emerges as the prime minister of the Irish Republic, as his Fianna Fáil party wins a plurality in Ireland's general elections. • Irish American crooner Bing Crosby's star rises with the release of Paramount's *The Big Broadcast.* • President Herbert Hoover appoints Irish American attorney Thomas Gardiner Corcoran to the Reconstruction Finance Corporation, a government agency that provides loans to businesses, banks, and public utilities in an effort to lift the economy out of depression.

September 1, 1932: New York City mayor James John "Jimmy" Walker resigns from office under a cloud of corruption. He will flee to Europe for three years of self-imposed exile with his mistress, showgirl Betty Compton.

Building skyscrapers As America's cities expanded into the skies, the construction trades offered jobs to countless working-class Irish. The work was not for the faint of heart, as this image of the Empire State Building indicates. The building trades were well organized and often tied into heavily Irish political machines, which regulated the nuts and bolts of new construction. Not coincidentally, construction of the Empire State Building began on March 17, 1930—St. Patrick's Day.

Hague rules in Jersey City Growing up poor in the tenements of the Horseshoe section of Jersey City, New Jersey, Frank Hague—the son of Irish immigrants—determined that his life would be better. Hague (seen here shaking hands with Franklin Roosevelt) entered politics as a Democratic ward organizer. He worked his way up the ranks and, in 1917, became mayor of Jersey City—a position he held for the next 30 years. While responsible for many civic reforms, he also financed a lavish lifestyle from kickbacks (known as "rice pudding") from the salaries of Democratic appointees. Hague became an avid supporter of Roosevelt in 1932 after Al Smith lost the Democratic nomination.

The President Maker

James Aloysius Farley reached the heights of political power in the 1930s as one of President Franklin Roosevelt's closest advisers. But it was a long struggle to the top for the New York State native.

Farley was just 10 years old when his Irish immigrant father died after being kicked by a horse. James and his four brothers all worked summers to help the family make ends meet.

According to his 1938 autobiography, Farley always had a passion for politics. He became a town clerk and later was elected to the state assembly. Farley impressed New York Democratic officials, including Bronx boss Ed Flynn, so much that he was introduced to 1928 gubernatorial candidate Franklin Roosevelt. Farley ended up running both of Roosevelt's gubernatorial campaigns. When FDR ran for president in 1932, Farley lined up crucial support for his nomination.

President Roosevelt rewarded Farley by naming him postmaster general and Democratic Party chairman. A loyal supporter of FDR's New Deal, Farley became a national power broker and key strategist for both Roosevelt and the Democrats. By 1940 tensions mounted

James Farley (*left*) with President Roosevelt

between FDR and Farley, partly because of the latter's own presidential ambitions.

Farley ultimately returned to the private sector, where he worked until the early 1970s. He died in 1976. The main branch of the U.S. Postal Service in midtown Manhattan bears his name.

Irish switch allegiance to FDR Once the 1932 Democratic National Convention nominated Franklin D. Roosevelt over Al Smith, the American Irish—more out of party loyalty than any great love for FDR—moved solidly behind the aristocrat from Hyde Park. More than 70 percent of the New York Irish vote went to Roosevelt, and the percentage was even higher in Massachusetts. In the general election, Roosevelt and his party forged a coalition of Irish, Italians, Germans, Jews, blue-collar workers, and intellectuals, which would be the core of the party for the next 40 years.

Hard Times

1933–1945

The Great Depression and the New Deal were transforming events in U.S. history. During these difficult years, millions of unemployed Americans worried about feeding their families, as a plethora of new government programs took the place of the old, Irish-led political machines.

For many Irish Americans, hard times were a reminder of why they so valued the economic safety net of civil service over the riskier business of private enterprise. That is not to say that Irish Americans were less affected by the calamity that followed the stock market crash in 1929. Indeed, the bread lines were no shorter in Irish neighborhoods than they were elsewhere. But the Irish knack for politics and their preference for economic security over risk management helped at least some to put food on the table during the worst economic decline in the nation's history.

In fact, for Irish America, hard times coincided with a golden age of power, art, culture, and influence. The nation at large might have rejected Al Smith's presidential bid in 1928, but Irish America was not content to wallow in despair. Other avenues remained open and new ones emerged, even if the White House seemed temporarily out of reach—for an Irish Catholic, anyway.

The 1930s saw the rise of a generation of Irish American entertainers: stage actress Helen Hayes, crooner Bing Crosby, actor Jimmy Cagney, comedian Gracie Allen, director John Ford, and humorist Fred Allen. Playwright Eugene O'Neill continued to explore the human condition on Broadway,

Of Irish descent, Colin P. Kelly, Jr., was arguably the first American hero of World War II. Three days after the assault on Pearl Harbor, the B-17 bomber that he was piloting attacked Japanese warships but was hit by a Japanese Zero fighter. Kelly stayed at the controls long enough for the crewmembers to bail out; then his plane exploded.

while author James T. Farrell emerged with his brilliant, evocative, and controversial trilogy of novels set in Irish Chicago that focused on the life and tragedies of Studs Lonigan.

Farrell wrote about the ethnic ghetto from which he himself had emerged, a place he associated with a deep and abiding poverty of the spirit. O'Neill and Ford consciously explored universal experience through their Irish American sensibility. O'Neill once said that critics had "missed the most important thing about me and my work, the fact that I am Irish." While John Ford made several movies about Ireland and Irish America later in his career, many observers believe his most Irish film was an adaptation of John Steinbeck's novel, *The Grapes of Wrath*, released in 1940. The Depression-era story of Americans who leave behind despair and poverty is, Ford noted, a story "similar to the famine in Ireland."

Through the 1930s and into the war years of the 1940s, Irish American cultural figures continued their rise to prominence. But it was in the more traditional field of politics where Irish Americans exercised their greatest influence. And the man who helped make it possible was a Hudson Valley patrician named Franklin D. Roosevelt.

Roosevelt was elected president in 1932, defeating Herbert Hoover, the man who had beaten Al Smith in 1928. But before FDR took on Hoover, he was forced to contend with Smith for the 1932 Democratic Party nomination, which caused a tragic split between the two old friends and allies. Roosevelt had on his side an impressive collection of Irish American political talent, including Edward J. Flynn, the boss of the Bronx; Frank Murphy of Michigan; and a Harvard-educated lawyer from Rhode Island named Thomas Corcoran. In addition, Roosevelt managed to transform himself from a reformer who disdained old-fashioned political leaders early in his career to a pragmatic dealmaker who built bridges to Irish American bosses, such as Frank Hague in Jersey City and James Michael Curley in Boston.

Roosevelt's New Deal program attracted Irish American voters by the millions, and they became a key ingredient in an electoral coalition that would define American politics until the late 1960s. It also attracted a famous Irish American opponent, Father Charles Coughlin, as well as the support of a lesser known but remarkably influential priest, Monsignor John A. Ryan.

When the Great Depression hit in the early 1930s, local volunteers collected food and clothing for relief. As unemployment soared to 25 percent, the local efforts collapsed and the federal government stepped in. The WPA was the largest relief works program. It provided jobs for millions of Americans, including Jack Reagan—Ronald Reagan's Irish American father.

Coughlin gained fame and enormous power as a virulent critic of Roosevelt with anti-Semitic radio sermons that exploited hate to prey on the economic frustrations of Depression-era America. Ryan did not have Coughlin's access to the airwaves, but in his writing he laid out a progressive Catholic position on social justice, ecumenism, and outright support for the New Deal. Not coincidentally, Monsignor Ryan in 1941 became the first Catholic clergyman to offer a prayer at a presidential inauguration, at the invitation of Roosevelt himself.

When war came to America in 1941, Irish America was far less divided on the subject than it had been in 1917, when Ireland still was under British rule and Germany was seen, at least by some Irish Americans, as a potential ally in the cause of Irish freedom. As before, Irish Americans rallied to the armed services, including five brothers named Sullivan from Iowa who joined the Navy and were assigned to the light cruiser USS *Juneau*. When the ship was torpedoed in the South Pacific in November 1942, all five Sullivan brothers were aboard, and all five died. In a time of terrible tragedies around the world, the fate of the Sullivan brothers pierced the hearts of a nation grown accustomed to extraordinary sacrifice.

Red-haired, short, and muscular, Jimmy Cagney was a scrappy street fighter. His tough Bronx neighborhood taught him the gestures, speech mannerisms, and staccato delivery that made him a Hollywood star of the 1930s. His role as George M. Cohan in *Yankee Doodle Dandy* (1942; *pictured*) raised wartime morale and illustrated that the Irish had achieved acceptance as loyal Americans.

In 1944, as an ailing Franklin Roosevelt prepared for an unprecedented fourth term as president, it was Democratic National Committee chair Robert Hannegan, one of the president's closest political advisers, who believed that Vice President Henry Wallace ought to be dumped from the national ticket in place of a Missouri senator named Harry Truman. FDR took Hannegan's advice. It is hard to imagine the fate of postwar America—indeed, the entire world—had Roosevelt decided otherwise.

There was no small irony in Irish America's support for the New Deal, as the expansion of federal programs hastened the end of the old machines that had done so much to propel the Irish into positions of power. With the close of the war, however, many other changes were coming. The face of Irish America would change, too, and then change again, in the coming decade and a half.

1933: Irish American brothers and musicians Jimmy and Tommy Dorsey form the Dorsey Brothers Orchestra. They will go their separate ways two years later but reunite in 1953. • Dorothy Day and Peter Maurin establish both *The Catholic Worker* newspaper and the Catholic Worker Movement, an organization of antiwar Socialist Catholics that provides food, clothing, and shelter to the needy. • Willis O'Brien, Irish American stop-motion animator and legendary cinematic special effects master, animates the star of the classic *King Kong*. • Cincinnati archbishop John McNicholas founds the Catholic Legion of Decency to police the content of motion pictures in America.

March 4, 1933: Franklin Delano Roosevelt (of Dutch and French descent) is sworn into office on the U.S. Capitol steps, the first of his four presidential inaugurations. He will soon launch the New Deal, a series of legislative initiatives aimed at pulling the United States out of the Great Depression.

April 8, 1933: Irish American Democrat Ed Kelly takes office in what will be a 14-year reign as mayor of Chicago. He calls his standard campaign speech "Roosevelt Is My Religion."

1934: Activist Catholic priest Father Charles Coughlin vocally criticizes President Roosevelt's New Deal on his radio show, reaching an audience of millions. • William Murphy, an Irish American physician, wins the Nobel Prize for Medicine with his codiscovery of the remedy for pernicious anemia.

January 1, 1934: Republican Fiorello LaGuardia takes office as mayor of New York City. A staunch reformer and anti-corruption candidate, he will oversee the dismantling of the Tammany political machine.

Quill heads the TWU One of eight children born on a Kerry farm, Mike Quill arrived in the United States in the tumultuous late 1920s. Ireland had been ravaged by civil war, and the U.S. was on the brink of depression. Quill began working in New York's subway system and helped form the Transit Workers Union (TWU), which was created in 1934 by veterans of the Irish Civil War. Quill became leader of the TWU that

year. In 1966 he spearheaded a much-publicized transit strike, which crippled New York City. To this day, Quill remains a hero to many New York labor leaders.

O'Brien brings King Kong to life Movie special effects technician Willis O'Brien was a cartoonist and sculptor who became a master of stop-motion animation, by which articulated puppets are painstakingly moved, one frame at a time, to simulate life and movement. He is best remembered for his remarkable work on the 1933 epic *King Kong*. O'Brien had further success with *Son of Kong* (1933), *Mighty Joe Young* (1949), *The Black Scorpion* (1957), and others. This photo of the animator at work on *Son of Kong* was snapped not long after O'Brien's ex-wife murdered their sons and then shot herself. When O'Brien saw the photo later, he tore it in half.

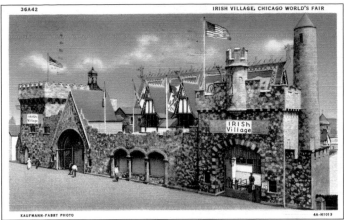

Irish village at Chicago's fair The Chicago World's Fair of 1933–34, held in celebration of the city's centennial, featured a faux Irish village exhibit complete with a round tower (*right*). The U.S. flags flying from the "village" were a tribute to the strong transatlantic bond between America and Ireland. Chicago, of course, had a strong Irish presence, and was home to two of Irish America's great fictional characters: Mr. Dooley, created by journalist Peter Finley Dunne, and Studs Lonigan, the central figure in novelist James T. Farrell's trilogy.

Ford directs Irish-themed films A towering figure of American cinema, director John Ford mined his Irish American heritage in many films, most famously *The Quiet Man* (1952). Ford, whose father was an Irish immigrant, often claimed that his birth name was Sean Aloysius O'Feeney. His first great film (and one of many collaborations with fellow Irish American John Wayne) was *Stagecoach* (1939). Among Ford's many Irish movies were *The Informer* (1935), *The Rising of the Moon* (1957), and *The Last Hurrah* (1958). He is also considered the master of the American western. Ford won four Oscars for best director, a record that has yet to be matched.

Ford's English Irishman Though long associated with the Irish films of John Ford (such as *The Quiet Man*), actor Victor McLaglen was actually born in England. After service in the British Army (including, he claimed, a stint with the Royal Irish Fusiliers), McLaglen went to Hollywood. One of his early starring roles was in *The Informer* (1935; *pictured*), Ford's adaptation of Liam O'Flaherty's Irish Civil War novel. The book and film captured the deep Irish hatred for traitors who undermined the struggle against the British.

Murray forms the CIO Born in Scotland to an Irish Catholic father and Scottish mother, Philip Murray became one of the most important labor leaders in 20th century America. As a young man, Murray went to work in Pennsylvania's coal mines and quickly became involved in union work, where he was a close associate of John L. Lewis. After the American Federation of Labor rejected membership to unions of unskilled workers, Murray and others, in 1935, formed the Congress of Industrial Organizations (CIO). Murray served as its president until his death in 1952.

1935: After a brief foray into film, "first lady of American theater" Helen Hayes returns to Broadway. • Errol Flynn, the swashbuckling Irish American playboy of Hollywood's golden age, sees his star rise with the release of *Captain Blood*.

January 3, 1935: Longtime mayor of Boston James Michael Curley takes office as governor of Massachusetts, though his scandal-ridden tenure in the state's highest office will be brief.

September 10, 1935: Celebrated Louisiana governor Huey Long dies two days after he is felled by an assassin's bullet at the capitol building in Baton Rouge.

1936: On the heels of a series of murders committed by members of the Irish Republican Army, Eamon de Valera outlaws the terrorist group.

March 5, 1936: Two Irish American entertainers win Academy Awards for their work in the 1935 film *The Informer:* best actor Victor McLaglen and best director John Ford.

April 24, 1936: Irish American writer Finley Peter Dunne dies in New York. A popular humorist in his day, Dunne is famous for his syndicated tales of "Mr. Dooley," a fictionalized, stereotypical Irish pub owner from Chicago's South Side.

October 8, 1936: Irish American Monsignor John Ryan delivers an address on his radio show entitled "Roosevelt Safeguards America." The speech is an effort to counter the anti-Roosevelt broadcasts of Father Charles Coughlin, another Irish Catholic radio personality.

1937: Irish American author Margaret Mitchell is awarded the Pulitzer Prize for her Civil War novel *Gone with the Wind*. It will become one of the best selling books of all time and inspire an enormously successful film adaptation two years later.

Best in the long run
In 2000 *Runner's World* magazine named him "Runner of the Century," and indeed Johnny Kelley's accomplishments in marathon running are unparalleled. From 1928 to 1992, Kelley ran in 61 Boston Marathons—the last when he was 84 years old. He won twice, in 1935 and 1945, and finished second seven times. Bill Rogers, another Boston winner, once said that Kelley "was the Boston Marathon." In this photo, taken after the 1935 race, he is crowned with

the victor's laurel wreath. Kelley was always a fan favorite in the Boston Marathon because he was a local Irish boy.

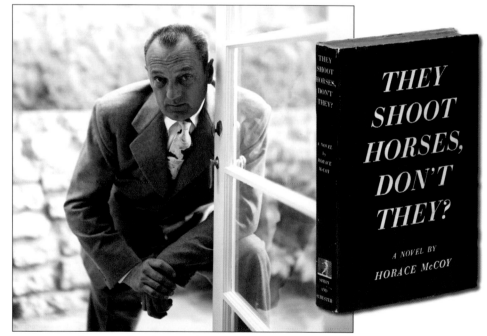

McCoy authors a classic Best known for writing the tragic Depression-era novel *They Shoot Horses, Don't They?,* Horace McCoy was born in Tennessee and served in World War I before becoming a journalist. In the 1930s, he began publishing crime stories and novels. Published in 1935, *They Shoot Horses, Don't They?* is a bleak exploration of the Great Depression and the gruesome toll it took on Americans. The book focuses on a marathon dance contest that pushes desperate participants to exhaustion—and even death. The book was made into a classic film starring Jane Fonda in 1969.

Studs Lonigan

Drunkenness. Violence. Sin. Hypocrisy. Bigotry.

At times, the greatest work of Irish American fiction seems as if it were written by an anti-Irish nativist. The characters border on despicable, and their flaws are distinctly Irish Catholic. Still, the Studs Lonigan trilogy, by James T. Farrell, is an epic achievement of realism. In the three books (*Young Lonigan, The Young Manhood of Studs Lonigan,* and *Judgment Day*), Farrell seemingly has little affection for his subjects. But he certainly knew the Chicago Irish and their environment.

As depicted by Farrell, Irish Americans were no longer slum dwellers by the 1930s, but they weren't quite respectable. According to Farrell, they were provincial and bigoted. They were religious, but just as often they were sinful. They waxed nostalgic about "the old country," yet they looked down upon the Eastern European immigrants who were replacing the Irish in Chicago's ghettoes.

Farrell himself was born in a four-story flat on Archer Avenue in 1904. His grandfather (also James) had left Tipperary around the time of the Irish famine. Farrell was a prolific writer, authoring more than 50 books, but Studs Lonigan is by far his most memorable creation.

According to biographer Robert Landers, Farrell's tragic protagonist was a "victim of what Farrell often called the 'spiritual poverty' that surrounded him." The bleakness of Studs's world is overwhelming. The overall message seems to be that a Chicago Irish kid must escape his neighborhood or die. However, the Lonigan trilogy features some sympathetic characters, particularly budding writer Danny O'Neill. (Farrell wrote five novels about O'Neill, who seemed to be his alter ego.)

The Lonigan books remain critical favorites. In 1999 the Modern Library ranked the Studs Lonigan trilogy No. 29 on its list of the top 100 English-language novels of the 20th century.

Brennan strums along
Of humble beginnings, Walter Brennan went on to play down-home characters in Hollywood movies. Born in Massachusetts to Irish immigrant parents, Brennan began his Hollywood career with work as an extra. In a career that spanned 50 years—in some of the biggest films of the mid-20th century—Brennan won three Academy Awards for best supporting actor. Here he strums for Barbara Stanwyck in the 1936 film *Banjo on My Knee.*

1937: Anne O'Hare McCormick of *The New York Times* wins the Pulitzer Prize for her foreign correspondence.

March 4, 1937: Irish American Walter Brennan receives the best supporting actor Oscar (his first of three) for his work in *Come and Get It.*

June 14, 1937: The Dáil Éireann passes a new constitution, which establishes Ireland as an independent representative democracy.

August 26, 1937: Andrew Mellon, Irish American financier and philanthropist, dies. He bequeaths his priceless art collection to the U.S. government for the establishment of the National Gallery of Art.

1938: President Roosevelt appoints prominent Irish American Bostonian Joseph Kennedy to the post of U.S. ambassador to Britain. • Britain and Ireland end their economic war, which began in 1932 when Eamon de Valera's Fianna Fáil party enacted a series of protective trade tariffs. • James Cagney and Pat O'Brien star in *Angels with Dirty Faces,* a film about the underbelly of New York's Irish American community in the early decades of the 20th century.

March 10, 1938: Irish American stars collect accolades in several Academy Award categories, including a best actor nod for Spencer Tracy in *Captains Courageous.*

July 17, 1938: After being denied permission to make a transatlantic flight in his single-engine plane, Douglas Corrigan takes off from Brooklyn, ostensibly on a trip to California. His arrival in Ireland some hours later captures the public's imagination.

September 9, 1938: Metro-Goldwyn-Mayer Pictures releases *Boys Town,* a film based on the true story of Father Edward Flanagan and the orphanage of the same name that he founded in 1917.

Kelly's Weary Willie In the early 1920s, Emmett Kelly drew the character he would later turn into a famous clown. Kansas-born Kelly was a cartoonist whose creation, Weary Willie, would spark his career as one of America's most popular clowns during the Depression years. Weary Willie had circus audiences howling with laughter so much that Kelly was recruited by Ringling Bros. and Barnum & Bailey Circus. He even made an appearance in the acclaimed 1952 film *The Greatest Show on Earth.*

Hughes boots the AAA Charles Evans Hughes, Irish on his mother's side, was nominated to be chief justice of the Supreme Court by President Herbert Hoover in 1930. He already had enjoyed a brilliant career, having served as governor of New York, secretary of state under Warren Harding, and a justice of the U.S. Supreme Court. Though a Republican chief justice, he supported many of President

Franklin Roosevelt's New Deal programs. But when the president pushed through the Agricultural Adjustment Act, which subsidized farmers who took acreage out of production, the Hughes court declared many of its provisions unconstitutional. In this Willard Combes editorial cartoon, Hughes kicks the Agricultural Adjustment Administration to pieces.

Author Cain dabbles in crime Though James Cain disliked being labeled, he is regarded as one of America's foremost crime fiction writers. Three of his novels—*The Postman Always Rings Twice* (1934), *Double Indemnity* (1936), and *Mildred Pierce* (1941)—are considered American classics, and were all made into notable film noir movies in Hollywood. Born in Maryland of Irish American parents, Cain moved to Hollywood to continue his career as a journalist, screenwriter, and novelist. Of all the crime novelists of his era who trafficked in stories of weak men undone by strong, duplicitous women, Cain achieved a particularly high level of sophistication and ferocity.

Mitchell pens a Civil War classic Margaret Mitchell was born in Atlanta into an Irish American family—not unlike the one portrayed in her Pulitzer prize-winning novel, *Gone with the Wind* (1936). Mitchell was working as a writer for the *Atlanta Journal* when a series of injuries forced her to quit her job. She wrote her novel while convalescing, using her childhood memories as a backdrop for her sweeping southern saga. The book went on to become one of the best-selling books of all time. The 1939 movie adaptation won eight Academy Awards.

"Cinderella Man" James Braddock was arguably the nearest thing to a real-life Rocky Balboa—although he was Irish and hailed from New Jersey. Braddock's mediocre career looked done when he broke his hand in a 1933 bout, but he scrapped back to score a shocking victory over Max Baer in a 1935 world heavyweight title fight. Braddock, dubbed "Cinderella Man" by Damon Runyon, lost his title to Joe Louis two years later (*pictured*) despite knocking Louis to the canvas early on. Braddock's big heart finally gave out in 1974.

Swashbuckling Errol Flynn Irish Americans embraced early Hollywood actors who exhibited certain virtues: courage, humor, rebelliousness, and rascally roguishness. Errol Flynn fit the profile. The Australian-born Flynn was famous for his smile, swagger, looks, and swashbuckling screen roles, most notably in *The Adventures of Robin Hood* (1938; *pictured*). Though a hero on screen, Flynn was no role model in real life. Alcohol, a reputation as a womanizer, and charges of statutory rape—for which he was acquitted—put an early end to Flynn's Hollywood career. He died in 1959 at age 50.

Cagney plays Irish gangsters James Cagney (*left*) and Humphrey Bogart (*right*) were a formidable team in *Angels With Dirty Faces,* a movie in which Cagney's character was torn between church and crime, faith and profit. Cagney's edgy portrayals were frequently of streetwise Irish gangsters. The son of a barkeep, Cagney may well have seen Irish mobsters on Manhattan's Lower East Side. His career began with a vaudeville song and dance act, but he went on to become a versatile Hollywood star. He headlined such films as *Yankee Doodle Dandy* and *The Public Enemy.*

"Wrong Way" Corrigan He flew the wrong way right into the history books. Douglas Corrigan was a man who could assemble things but not chart a course—or so he led everyone to believe. Determined to recreate his hero Charles Lindbergh's 1927 flight across the Atlantic, the Texas-born Corrigan purchased an old Curtiss Robin plane and sought federal permission to fly east. He was denied, but in July 1938 he flew anyway. He landed in Ireland and told astonished greeters that he thought he was in California. Thus was born the legend of "Wrong Way" Corrigan.

Cinnamon Bear During Thanksgiving Week in 1937, youthful radio listeners met "a little teddy bear with a green ribbon around his neck . . . not more than four inches high." It was *The Cinnamon Bear,* created for a Christmas season radio series by California writer Glanville Heisch. The adventurous bear, named Paddy O'Cinnamon, spoke with an Irish brogue. For 26 evenings, he led his twin companions, Judy and Jimmy Barton, on a magical quest to find a silver Christmas star that had been purloined by the nefarious Crazy Quilt dragon. The show, aired in 15-minute episodes, won a devoted following and was re-aired each Christmas season for more than half a century. The series proved particularly popular in Chicago and Portland, Oregon.

The Polarizing Radio Priest

During the heyday of radio in the 1930s, one of the most popular voices on the airwaves was that of Father Charles Coughlin, the "radio priest." From the Shrine of the Little Flower, which he had established in a Detroit suburb in the 1920s, Coughlin broadcast a weekly program that during the Depression attracted an audience of some 30 million. From simple religious homilies, Coughlin gradually expanded his radio themes until they touched upon the great issues of the day: the causes of the Depression, the redistribution of wealth, the rise of communism, and the American political system.

As his popularity grew, he became increasingly anti-Semitic and a strong opponent of President Roosevelt. He branded Roosevelt's New Deal programs communistic and called the president a "liar" and "anti-God." In his anti-Semitism, he frequently linked Judaism to communism and became an admirer of Italian and German fascism. In 1938 his lukewarm criticism

Father Charles Coughlin speaking from Cleveland

of Nazi actions against German Jews led to an outcry of protest, and his popularity began to diminish. His superior in Detroit, Archbishop Edward Mooney, admonished him for his anti-Jewish diatribes and ordered him to cease. In 1940 Coughlin's program went off the air, and he returned to pastoral obscurity.

Coughlin's reactionary views were out of keeping with his church. On social issues, the Catholic Church in America inclined to the positions espoused in the writings of Father John Augustine Ryan, a professor at Catholic University. In two works, *A Living Wage: Its Ethical and Economic Aspects* (1906) and *Distributive Justice: The Right and Wrong of Our Present Distribution of Wealth* (1916), Ryan advocated policies later embodied in the New Deal. For a time, Ryan served on the Industrial Appeals Board of Roosevelt's National Recovery Administration. Throughout the 1930s, he defended the president from Coughlin's radio attacks.

Bergen's Irish dummy

Chicago-born Edgar Bergen achieved fame as a ventriloquist, but it was his sidekick, Charlie McCarthy, whose voice turned the duo into show business legends. Bergen's wise-cracking partner was based on a real-life Irish newspaper boy in Chicago. For nearly 20 years, from 1937 to 1956, Bergen and McCarthy had their own radio show. Their many listeners either believed that Bergen was working as a ventriloquist or that the rascally McCarthy was, in fact, a real person.

"There is no such thing as a bad boy."

—SPENCER TRACY AS FATHER EDWARD J. FLANAGAN IN *BOYS TOWN*, 1938

Father Flanagan and Boys Town Father Edward J. Flanagan and his work were made famous by the 1938 film *Boys Town* (*left photo*), starring Irish American Spencer Tracy (*left*), who won an Oscar for the role, and the non-Irish Mickey Rooney (*right*). The real Father Flanagan (*right photo*) was born in County Roscommon and immigrated to the U.S. in 1904. After his ordination, he was sent to his first parish, in Nebraska. He opened a home for boys in a rundown Victorian house in Omaha in 1917. The real Boys Town, which has grown into a national organization in 14 states, helps more than 47,000 children a year.

Blue...yet romantic Bunny Berigan, a trumpeter of the big band/swing era, became a jazz legend despite a life cut tragically short by alcoholism. Born in 1908, Berigan hailed from an Irish German family in small-town Wisconsin.

He starred in the bands of Benny Goodman and Tommy Dorsey and formed his own orchestra in 1937. His signature tune, on which he both played and sang, was "I Can't Get Started." A 1982 *New Yorker* review observed that Berigan's playing was "blue, emotional, down, funky," yet "lyrical, romantic, melodramatic, and garrulous. It had a kind of Irish cast." Excessive drinking caused Berigan to develop cirrhosis of the liver by his early 30s. He ignored doctors' pleas to quit drinking, and he died at age 33.

Disney's Irish roots Even Walt Disney, the "Father of Animation," had Irish blood in his veins. The native Chicagoan's father was of Irish Canadian descent and his mother was German American. Family members said that Disney's Irish roots were not a common household topic. Moreover, films

such as *Darby O'Gill and the Little People* (in which King Brian is a 21-inch leprechaun), as well as Disney's clashes with unions, didn't exactly strengthen his Irish credentials. Still, in the 1960s, a Disney company archivist traced the family's Irish roots back 15 generations. Walt's nephew Roy and his Irish American wife later bought a castle in County Cork.

The middle-class Irish In the pre-World War II years, a growing Irish American middle class emerged. Some lived in houses such as those seen here in this Irish neighborhood in Boston. The Irish American middle class was largely urban and Catholic. Men worked in the building trades or as policemen and firemen. The few lucky enough to receive a college education went to such schools as Fordham in New York and Loyola in Chicago. The preferred professions were law and medicine. Women, if they worked outside the home at all, found meaningful vocations as teachers and nurses. The center of social life was the parish church, where young Irish American couples often met—and married.

Roach makes America laugh In 1984 Hal Roach accepted an honorary Oscar that recognized his enormous contribution to American entertainment. This son of Irish immigrants established his own movie studio in 1915. He went on to produce (and occasionally direct) shorts and features starring Harold Lloyd, Our Gang, Charley Chase, and the most beloved comedy duo of all time, Laurel and Hardy. Popular Roach Studios features that came later included *Of Mice and Men* and *Topper*. Roach retired in 1955 after moving into TV production. He remained a public figure until his death, at 100, in 1992.

HIDING HER IRISH IDENTITY

She worked for prestigious law offices.... And she was a great...a great legal stenographer because when she went freelance the agencies were always calling her.... In many places she found that being Irish was a hindrance. They would question twice—if there were two people ready for a job...the Irish person wouldn't get it. And this...would have been when we came over here... in the '30s, going right up to close to the '40s.... So she knew she's going to change her name from Bridget. But would you believe it, she changed her name to Iolanthe. And we said, "Where did you get that name?" And it was from Gilbert and Sullivan's *Iolanthe*. She took that name, Iolanthe!...I used to hear people call her "Lanthe".... I'm sure my dad knew about the fact that she was now Iolanthe. But of course she was still Bridget to him. But that shows one of the negative aspects that I was not aware of.

—JOHN J. FALLON, A COUNTY GALWAY NATIVE,
ON HIS MOTHER'S USE OF A NON-IRISH NAME
TO GAIN EMPLOYMENT IN NEW YORK

November 11, 1938: Mary Mallon, the Irish American cook better known as "Typhoid Mary," dies of pneumonia while serving a life sentence in quarantine for spreading the deadly typhus bacteria to her New York clients.

1939: William Patrick Hitler, Adolf's nephew, is stranded in the United States along with his Irish mother when World War II breaks out in Europe. • With the outbreak of war in Europe, Eamon de Valera's government continues with the tradition of neutrality that Ireland has followed since the 1922 break with Britain. In practice, the Irish will tend to be more helpful to the Allied cause. • John Steinbeck publishes *The Grapes of Wrath,* perhaps his most celebrated novel. Steinbeck's work is known for its rich characterizations of the working poor and the immigrant condition in America. • Herbert Romulus O'Conor takes his seat as Maryland's governor, becoming the first Catholic Irish American to hold that office. • Tom Pendergast, the Irish American boss of the Kansas City, Missouri, Democratic political machine, is sent to Leavenworth Penitentiary on tax evasion charges. • Crime novelist Raymond Chandler, the American-born son of an Irish mother, publishes *The Big Sleep,* his debut novel.

October 1939: The National Association of Broadcasters enacts strict new rules that limit the airtime of politically polarizing radio personalities. The rules effectively silence Father Charles Coughlin's isolationist and anti-Roosevelt rhetoric.

1940: President Roosevelt taps Bronx political boss Ed Flynn to head the Democratic National Committee. • *Knute Rockne, All American,* the classic film about the iconic Notre Dame football coach starring Pat O'Brien and Ronald Reagan, is released.

Sturges spoofs the well-to-do In his best movies, writer-director Preston Sturges combined screwball comedy and social consciousness. Sturges's mother, Mary, was an Irish immigrant who sought her own career in show business. In fact, his early exposure to artists and high society might have inspired later spoofs of the upper crust. Sturges's breakthrough film was 1939's *The Great McGinty,* and two of his best were released in 1941—*The Lady Eve* (with Barbara Stanwyck and Henry Fonda) and *Sullivan's Travels* (with Joel McCrea and Veronica Lake).

The Tin Man Irish American Jack Haley started out as a vaudeville performer and went on to star in more than 30 movies. Undoubtedly, he is best remembered for his 1939 role as the Tin Man in *The Wizard of Oz* (*pictured*). Buddy Ebsen was first given the role, but he had to drop out because of an allergic reaction to the aluminum-based makeup. Haley's son, Jack Jr., a successful Hollywood producer, was briefly married to entertainer Liza Minnelli.

The Saga of Eddie O'Hare

Eddie O'Hare was an Irish American lawyer who loved the fast life. Not surprisingly, then, he made his first bundle of money in partnership with Owen P. Smith, who had invented the mechanical rabbit used at dog tracks.

O'Hare managed to grab his partner's money when Smith died in 1927. O'Hare left his wife and moved with his kids to Chicago, where he hit the big time as a confidant of Al Capone. Through Capone, O'Hare became a partner in a dog track (which later would become Sportsman's Park Race Track). O'Hare fixed races by offering hamburgers to competing hounds just before race time. The one dog that didn't get the greasy meat would win the race. O'Hare's friends in the mob were grateful, but he eventually put his life at risk by ratting on Capone. It was rumored that officials helped O'Hare's son, Butch, get into the Naval Academy

O'Hare's murder

in exchange for information on the mob boss. Even if that wasn't true, O'Hare's testimony helped put Capone in prison.

O'Hare fell in love with Ursula Sue Granata, but because he was divorced, he couldn't arrange for the Catholic Church wedding she wanted. They were engaged for years. All the while, O'Hare continued to tip off the government about his mob associates until one of them ordered his murder in 1939. O'Hare was killed in his car. In his pockets were a rosary, a crucifix, and a poem ending with the line, "For the clock may soon be still." As for the mobster who ordered the hit, Frank Nitti, he wound up marrying Ursula!

O'Hare's son went on to become a Navy pilot and its first ace of World War II, but he was shot down and killed in 1943. Chicago's O'Hare International Airport is named for him.

Irish gives hoops a boost Edward S. Irish—known to all as "Ned"—is recognized as the "Father of Big Time Basketball." Born in Lake George, New York, Irish served as basketball director for New York's Madison Square Garden as that venue became a magnet for top collegiate basketball games throughout the 1930s and '40s. Irish also founded the New York Knickerbockers, and he was integral in creating the Basketball Association of America—the forerunner to today's NBA.

Barry's theatrical success Philip Barry was an acclaimed playwright whose credits include *The Philadelphia Story* and *Here Come the Clowns*. Born in Rochester, New York, Barry graduated from Yale and wrote his first prominent play, *Holiday*, in 1928. This was followed by *Tomorrow and Tomorrow* and *The Animal Kingdom*. Barry's 1939 play *The Philadelphia Story* was a screwball romantic comedy about a bride torn between a dashing journalist and her ex-husband, neither of whom were the groom. The play was made into a successful 1940 film starring Katharine Hepburn, Cary Grant, and James Stewart.

TIME
The Weekly Newsmagazine

PHILIP BARRY

1940: Robert Foster Kennedy, an Irish American neurology pioneer who was educated at Dublin's Royal University of Ireland, is named head of the American Neurological Association. • William Francis Murphy, a Catholic Irish American jurist, a former Michigan governor, and the U.S. attorney general, is named an associate justice of the U.S. Supreme Court.

May 15, 1940: Brothers Dick and Mac McDonald open the first McDonald's restaurant, in San Bernardino, California.

July 1940: With plenty of assistance from Chicago's Irish American political machine, President Roosevelt orchestrates an unprecedented third nomination as the Democratic candidate.

July 13, 1940: Monsignor Fulton Sheen presides at the "wedding of the century" between Henry Ford II and Anne McDonnell.

October 29, 1940: The United States holds its first peacetime draft, with War Secretary Henry Stimson drawing the first number: 158. Some 75,000 men will be called up within two weeks.

December 1940: At the end of a year that sees Joseph Kennedy attempting to meet with Hitler and declaring that "democracy is finished in England," the Roosevelt administration accepts the resignation of the errant ambassador and brings him back to the U.S.

1941: Irish-born American Paul O'Dwyer, a vehement opponent of the war, travels the United States speaking to pro-neutrality (particularly Irish American) groups. • Charles Evans Hughes, a Republican politician of Irish ancestry who lost a bid for the presidency, resigns as the chief justice of the U.S. Supreme Court.

Steinbeck's "Irish" themes "I am half Irish," Nobel Prize-winning author John Steinbeck once said. "The rest of my blood being watered down with German and Massachusetts English. But Irish blood doesn't water down very well." Though he didn't write directly about the Irish in such classics as *East of Eden* (1952), some critics believe that the themes of migration and starvation that Steinbeck explored in *Of Mice and Men* (1937) and *The Grapes of Wrath* (1939) were the result of his Irish heritage. The latter novel was later made into a brilliant film directed by fellow Irish American John Ford.

The Irish Zorro With an Irish surname, and a first name that matched that of an Irish county, there was little doubting Tyrone Power's Irish roots. But Ohio-born Power is best remembered for playing the Mexican hero Zorro as well as other swashbuckling characters. Here he embraces Linda Darnell in *The Mark of Zorro* (1940). With his family involved in theater, Power's choice of work was not entirely a surprise, but it took a different turn in World War II when he joined the Marines. Power's acting career accelerated after the war, and he earned critical acclaim for his performance in the 1946 film *The Razor's Edge*.

Fibber McGee and Molly As Irishness became more accepted in America, Irish American characters became sympathetic figures in popular entertainment. *Fibber McGee and Molly* was created in 1935 by writer Don Quinn and radio actors Jim Jordan and his wife, Marian Driscoll Jordan. From their fictional home at 79 Wistful Vista, Fibber and Molly laughingly endured the funny, often absurd situations of everyday middle-class life. Molly was ever-patient with Fibber's harmless boasting and occasional cockeyed ideas, and radio audiences waited each week for the moment when Fibber—despite Molly's warning—would open the door to the dangerously overstuffed hall closet. *Fibber McGee and Molly* remained on the airwaves until 1959.

Mayor Kelly's volatile reign Like many other big-city Democratic mayors, Chicago's Ed Kelly (*right*) claimed great achievements and popularity but left office under a cloud of corruption. Kelly became mayor in 1933 under tragic circumstances. Previous mayor Anton Cermak had been assassinated in Florida by a bullet intended for President Franklin Roosevelt. Chicago boss Patrick Nash selected Kelly to replace Cermak. Serving as mayor until 1947, Kelly adeptly managed Chicago's economy during the Depression and took a progressive stance on integration. By the 1940s, however, the so-called "Kelly-Nash" machine was shaken by numerous scandals.

Rise and fall of Howard Hughes

He blazed a trail across the skies and imagination of 20th century America...then flamed out, becoming a reclusive exile. Hughes turned his family's tool company into Hughes Aircraft Company at a

time when the aviation business was taking off in a vertical climb. In the years before World War II, the hard-driving Texan set several records for long distance flights. He also became a movie mogul and one of America's wealthiest men. His withdrawal from America, and many would say from reality, began after the war.

Ireland stays neutral This editorial cartoon by Herblock (Herbert Block) highlights Ireland's controversial stance of neutrality during World War II. Prime Minister Eamon de Valera sits in front of tombstones depicting other neutral nations that were invaded by the Germans.

"THE DON'T-DO-ANYTHING-THAT-MIGHT-OFFEND-HITLER CLUB"
—A Herblock Cartoon, copyright by *The Herb Block Foundation*

The cartoon implies that neutrality does not ensure security. Nevertheless, many Irish would have been horrified to fight on the same side as the British, and de Valera believed that neutrality was necessary to preserve the unity of the Irish Free State. Neutrality did result in regrettable episodes. Most infamously, de Valera offered condolences to the German ambassador in Dublin upon the death of Adolf Hitler.

Irish join the fight Though Ireland was neutral during World War II, many Irish-born soldiers joined British, American, and other military forces. Meanwhile, Northern Ireland—as part of Great Britain—contributed greatly to the war effort. Northern Ireland's Royal Ulster Rifles (*pictured*) took part in the invasion of France. The London Irish were a collection of soldiers with a strong Irish tradition who fought for Britain. Battalions of the London Irish saw action in Sicily and Tunisia, among other places.

Arming the Allies Many shells destined for detonation against Germany were produced in Northern Ireland, as evidenced in this image from April 1940. Once World War II began, factories in Northern Ireland produced everything from bullets and weapons to battleships and aircraft. Belfast already had a strong shipmaking tradition, signified by the famous Harland and Wolff shipyard. Northern Ireland also had a large number of residents desperate for work. As the war progressed, ships damaged during battles in the Atlantic were repaired in Derry. An estimated 700 warships were built in Belfast during the war.

Nazi air raids Irish soldiers in County Wexford, Ireland, examine the effects of a German air raid in August 1940. Though the Irish Free State was neutral, the Nazis did bomb the country several times—including two attacks on Dublin in 1941 that killed more than 50 people. As part of Britain, Northern Ireland faced many deadly German attacks. In April 1941, Belfast endured air raids that inflicted serious damage on the city's vital shipyards as well as its residential sections. As many as 1,000 residents of Northern Ireland were killed by Nazi air raids. German officials also considered an invasion of Northern Ireland—and even the Irish Free State—in order to invade England at a later date.

Notre Dame's Fighting Irish

The University of Notre Dame did not invent college football. To millions of Irish Americans, however, it probably seems that way.

It was actually a stocky and fiery Norwegian named Knute Rockne whose coaching and marketing, from 1918 to 1930, put the Fighting Irish on the national map. Their willingness to travel from coast to coast to battle the best college teams in the land, and their amazing success rate against those schools, inspired an unparalleled following. Under Rockne, Notre Dame won more than 88 percent of its games and earned some form of national championship status six times.

Though Rockne was killed in a 1931 plane crash, his winning legacy lived on at the South Bend, Indiana, school. Beginning in 1935, the Fighting Irish began a string of 15 consecutive seasons in which they lost no more than two games.

Notre Dame's second great coach, Frank Leahy, took the reins in 1941. Six of his 11 teams completed unbeaten seasons, and five were named national champions by at least one publication or wire service. By this time, Irish Americans all across the country could sing Notre Dame's "Victory March" or recite tales and statistics chronicling ND football glory.

Great coaches such as Rockne, Leahy, Ara Parseghian, and Lou Holtz have crafted the winning tradition of Fight-

Notre Dame running back Creighton Miller

ing Irish football. Fabled players, including George Gipp, "The Four Horsemen," Johnny Lujack, Paul Hornung, Joe Montana, and Tim Brown, have carried that tradition through the generations.

Since the Associated Press began awarding national championships in 1936, no college football program in the nation has produced more than Notre Dame's eight such titles. Seven Notre Dame standouts have earned Heisman Trophies as the best college players in the land—another distinction no school can top.

O'Brien's "Irish" roles Pat O'Brien was one of the Irish American giants of the big screen. The Milwaukee native's many credits include *Boys Town, Angels with Dirty Faces,* and *The Last Hurrah.* One of his most famous "Irish" roles, however, was his portrayal of Norwegian American Knute Rockne (*pictured*) in 1940's *Knute Rockne, All American.* The film, which also starred Ronald Reagan as George Gipp, was about the legendary Notre Dame Fighting Irish coach. The film made that school's football program more popular than ever.

PAT O'BRIEN

The senior Kennedy

The patriarch of America's greatest political dynasty, Joseph Patrick Kennedy was born in 1888 into a prosperous Boston family. A successful banker and later movie producer, Kennedy married Rose Fitzgerald, daughter of Boston mayor John Fitzgerald. By the 1930s, Kennedy himself was a political power broker. A key aide to Franklin Roosevelt (and the ambassador to Britain), he hoped

to succeed FDR as president, but Kennedy's isolationist views proved too controversial. When his son Joseph Jr. was killed in World War II, Kennedy worked to make his son John a senator, then president. Joseph Kennedy lived to see JFK's election as the first Irish Catholic president, but he also witnessed the assassinations of sons John and Bobby.

Master of pulp fiction Born in Chicago, Raymond Chandler moved to Britain in 1895 with his Irish-born mother after his father had deserted them. After returning to the United States in 1912, he held down a number of jobs while writing pulp fiction. Chandler's best-known protagonist, Philip Marlowe (*The Big Sleep,* 1939; *Farewell, My Lovely,* 1940), became synonymous with the hard-boiled private eye genre and was featured in a number of movies, most famously brought to life by actor Humphrey Bogart. Chandler himself became a screenwriter, collaborating with such noted directors as Billy Wilder and Alfred Hitchcock.

"Tommy the Cork" Thomas Corcoran was one of the first true Irish American power brokers in Washington, D.C. One biography referred to him as "Washington's ultimate insider." "Tommy the Cork" grew up in Pawtucket, Rhode Island, where his father was a prominent lawyer. After attending Harvard, he was recruited by former professor Felix Frankfurter, himself a top FDR adviser. Corcoran is credited with guiding much of FDR's vaunted New Deal legislation through Congress. One biographer credited Corcoran—for better or worse—with creating modern political lobbying. Here he testifies before Congress regarding defense contracts.

Soft-hearted tough guy An accomplished playwright and screenwriter, James Gleason rose to fame as an actor. The New York–born Gleason usually played hard-boiled characters who were actually softhearted. He often played cops, including inspector Oscar Piper in the Hildegarde Withers mysteries and Lieutenant Rooney in the 1944

film *Arsenic and Old Lace.* Gleason was nominated for a supporting actor Oscar for his performance as boxing manager Max Corkle in the 1941 film *Here Comes Mr. Jordan,* and he played politico "Cuke" Gillen in *The Last Hurrah* (1958).

Murphy's rise to the Supreme Court Michigan native Frank Murphy was elected mayor of Detroit in 1930 before moving on to several other high-profile political jobs. After helping Detroit avoid bankruptcy at the start of the Great Depression, Murphy was elected the governor of Michigan in 1937. Two years later he became U.S. attorney general, and Franklin Roosevelt appointed him to the U.S. Supreme Court in 1940. Murphy famously opposed the imprisoning of Japanese Americans during World War II.

Wedding of the century On July 13, 1940, Henry Ford II (grandson of automotive pioneer Henry Ford) married Anne McDonnell in Southampton, New York, in what was described as the "wedding of the century." McDonnell was the daughter of a large and prominent Irish family that lived in a 29-room apartment in the winter and a 50-room home in Southampton in the summer. More than 1,100 guests attended the wedding, and 16 guards were employed to protect the wedding presents. Henry Ford gave the newlyweds a custom-built Ford car.

The adventures of Dixie Dugan In 1929 writer J. P. McEvoy and artist John H. Striebel unveiled a new comic strip about an Irish American showgirl named Dixie Dugan. The strip ran in newspapers for nearly 40 years and was spun off into books, movies, and songs. Initially a glamorous, even risqué, look at show business, Dixie became just another hard-working city woman following the Great Depression. She was a strong-minded, independent character whose adventures often reflected the current events of the day, from the Depression to World War II.

1933-45

February 27, 1941: In Hollywood, Walter Brennan wins his third best supporting actor Oscar in six years for his work in *The Westerner*, while John Ford is honored for his direction of *The Grapes of Wrath*.

April 7, 1941: Belfast is bombed for the first time during the Second World War. As an important Allied shipbuilding center, the city will be targeted by German bombers two more times in the coming months, and nearly 1,000 residents will lose their lives.

May 31, 1941: German bombers mistakenly attack Dublin, capital of the neutral Republic of Ireland, killing some 30 civilians.

July 1941: Roosevelt taps William Donovan as America's top spy when he names him Coordinator of Information. His office will be renamed Office of Strategic Services the following year, and will ultimately become the Central Intelligence Agency.
• Army construction chief Brehon B. Somervell orders the design of a massive building to house the War Department. Crews will break ground on the Pentagon in September.

December 7, 1941: The Japanese attack the Navy base at Pearl Harbor, Hawaii, dragging the United States into war. The massive mobilization necessitated by the war will effectively eliminate prejudice against Catholics, as American men from all cultures and walks of life will come to depend on each other on the battlefield.

December 10, 1941: Irish American aviator Colin Kelly dies when his bomber is shot down by Japanese Zeros. Credited as the first American aviation hero of the war, Kelly maintained control of his dying aircraft, allowing most of his crew to escape. The bomber exploded before Kelly could save himself.

Creepy moment for Gorcey The son of a vaudevillian, Leo Gorcey (*left*) made a splash in the 1935 Broadway production of Sidney Kingsley's *Dead End*. With others from the original cast, Gorcey went to Hollywood in 1937 to recreate his *Dead End* role, and for the next 20 years he starred in about 70 movies as the on-screen leader of the Dead End Kids, the East Side Kids, and the Bowery Boys. Gorcey's wisecracking, streetwise Irish persona, and his flair for physical comedy and malapropisms, made him a box office favorite. In this scene from the 1941 East Side Kids comedy *Spooks Run Wild*, Leo has a startling encounter with Bela Lugosi.

Breen brings "decency" to Hollywood In the early 1930s, Hollywood was under attack for producing glamorous gangster movies, such as *The Public Enemy*. Many Catholics joined the Legion of Decency, a church-supported group that often boycotted movies. Producers, forced to clean up movies, hired devout Catholic Joseph Breen to oversee "the code." Breen ultimately wielded nearly as much influence as Hollywood's producers. Some saw this as censorship, but not Breen, who—during Hollywood's Golden Age—often encouraged filmmakers to be subtle rather than explicit. Here, Breen makes sure that these actresses' harem dresses are not too revealing.

Hollywood's Green Age

Hollywood's Golden Age had a green hue. Director John Ford and such actors as James Cagney, Spencer Tracy, and Maureen O'Hara gave a distinct Irish flavor to movies before, during, and after World War II.

Many of Ford's 100-plus movies were filmed on the vast stage of the American West. Ford, the son of Irish immigrants, rolled out such classics as *Stagecoach* and *The Grapes of Wrath*. In *The Quiet Man*, he made famous the screen duo of Dublin-born O'Hara and John Wayne, who had ancestral ties to County Mayo, the setting for the film. The careers of Bing Crosby, Grace Kelly, Gene Kelly, Ronald Reagan—along with Barry Fitzgerald and Victor McLaglan, Wayne's partner and protagonist, respectively, in Ford movies—further projected the Irish Hollywood.

James Cagney, the son of an Irish bartender, was the perfect choice to portray Irish American composer George Michael Cohan in the 1942 musical *Yankee Doodle Dandy*.

Cagney won an Oscar for the role, which was a break from his more typical image—that of the streetwise Irish gangster.

Irish screen stereotypes softened during the war, as the film industry was urged to portray a more homogenous America. Before and after the war, the Irish Catholic priest took on a whole new image. Long the symbol of a foreign, un-American culture, he was portrayed as the essence of American virtue. Spencer Tracy was a natural to play Father Flanagan in the 1938 *Boys Town*. In fact, he earned an Academy Award for best actor. The 1944 film *Going My Way* won seven Oscars, including best actor for the Roman-collared Crosby.

A crowning moment for the Hollywood Irish, one rooted in that green Golden Age, came in 1984, when President Ronald Reagan presented Cagney with the U.S. Medal of Freedom.

Perennial Oscar contender James Cagney plants a congratulatory kiss on fellow Irish American actor Greer Garson at the Academy Awards ceremonies in March 1943. Garson had just won the best actress Oscar for *Mrs. Miniver*. Born in England in 1904, Garson was the daughter of an English father and an Irish mother. She made her film debut in the 1939 classic *Goodbye, Mr. Chips*, which earned her the first of her seven Oscar nominations. She was one of Hollywood's most accomplished stars during World War II, earning nominations each year from 1942 through 1945. She won a Golden Globe, and another Oscar nomination, in 1960, when she played Eleanor Roosevelt in *Sunrise at Campobello*.

A zealous attorney Brooklyn-born Irish American William Power Maloney was one of the most flamboyant celebrity lawyers of his day. On the eve of World War II, U.S. attorney general Francis Biddle hired Maloney as a special assistant to investigate treasonous activities. In 1942 the zealous Maloney brought charges of sedition against 28 individuals, but the evidence was flimsy. A cautious Biddle took Maloney off the case and assigned him to administrative work. The charges against those indicted were later dismissed. While in private practice after the war, the dapper Maloney represented mobster Joe "Bananas" Bonanno.

February 20, 1942: Irish American Lieutenant Commander Edward "Butch" O'Hare is named the first Navy flying ace of World War II.

February 26, 1942: For the second consecutive year, Irish American director John Ford picks up the Academy Award for best director, this time for his work on *How Green Was My Valley*.

November 13, 1942: The USS *Juneau* is torpedoed by a Japanese submarine off San Cristobal in the Solomon Islands, claiming the lives of the five Sullivan brothers of Waterloo, Iowa.
• Irish American Rear Admiral Daniel Callaghan is killed on the bridge of his flagship while directing an assault against a greatly superior Japanese force off Guadalcanal. For his heroism, he will be posthumously awarded the Congressional Medal of Honor.

1943: Lloyd Wendt and Herman Kogan publish *Lords of the Levee*, their exposé about the corrupt world of Irish American political bosses in Chicago: "Hinky Dink" Kenna and "Bathhouse" John Coughlin.

February 3, 1943: Navy chaplain Father John Washington, a son of Irish immigrants, dies along with 700 others when the USS *Dorchester* is torpedoed by a U-boat off the coast of Greenland. Washington and three colleagues who also die will collectively be honored for their selflessness as the "four immortal chaplains."

March 4, 1943: Irish American stars capture both best actor and best actress Academy Awards: James Cagney for *Yankee Doodle Dandy* and Greer Garson for *Mrs. Miniver*.

November 20, 1943: The 69th New York ("Fighting Irish"), renamed the 165th Infantry Regiment, joins the battle for the Pacific, landing on Butaritari on the Makin Atoll.

U.S. troops in Northern Ireland American soldiers based in Northern Ireland receive their rations in August 1942. Northern Ireland played an important strategic role in World War II, as large numbers of American and British troops served there. In fact, the Allied presence was so strong that leaders of the Irish Free State to the south feared that Allied troops might actually invade Ireland. They understood that control of Ireland's ports would have been a great advantage for the Allies.

The selfless work of Irish nuns The number of people seeking to enroll in religious orders in Ireland rose rapidly at the end of the 19th century, so much so that Ireland was able to "export" priests and nuns to America throughout the 20th century. These men and women of God cemented the Irish presence in the American Catholic Church, both in the hierarchy and on a grassroots level. Irish nuns made an important contribution to education as teachers, to the health services as nurses, and to social reform in their work for the poor.

O'Neill marries Charlie Chaplin
Oona O'Neill's life was defined by genius. Her father was legendary Irish American playwright Eugene O'Neill, whom she rarely saw after his bitter divorce from her mother when Oona was two years old. Then, at the age of 18, Oona married comedic legend Charlie Chaplin,

who was 54. Eugene O'Neill vehemently opposed the marriage, but Oona was not swayed by her father and ended up having eight children with Chaplin. They lived in Switzerland, where Oona died at age 66 in 1991.

Outstanding child actress
One of the most highly regarded child actors in movie history, Margaret O'Brien made her first film appearance at the age of four, in MGM's *Babes on Broadway* (1941). The daughter of an Irish circus performer and a Spanish

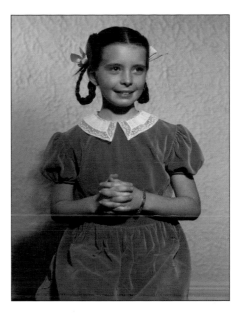

flamenco dancer, she is best known for her portrayal of "Tootsie" in Vincent Minnelli's 1944 movie *Meet Me in St Louis* (starring Judy Garland), for which she won a special Academy Award for "outstanding child actress."

McSorley's Ale House Long ago, Irish pubs were a last-resort refuge for immigrants battling grinding poverty as well as places to do business and plot politics. The pubs evolved into an intrinsic part of broader American culture, most especially in big cities. In Lower Manhattan, McSorley's Ale House (*pictured*) ranks as one of the most historical and revered "public houses." A woman founded the ale house in 1854, but it served men only until a lawsuit was filed in 1970. McSorley's, which brews its own beer, remains a hot spot in the 21st century.

The big jobs go to Crowley A prominent Catholic, Democrat, and financier, Leo Crowley in 1934 was appointed head of the newly created Federal Deposit Insurance Corporation (FDIC) to protect people's savings during the Depression. As World War II approached, Crowley was instrumental, at President Roosevelt's request, in persuading Archbishop Edward Mooney of Detroit to silence pro-fascist "radio priest" Father Charles Coughlin. In 1943, while still serving as head of the FDIC, Crowley also directed the Foreign Economic Administration, which was responsible for the war's Lend-Lease program.

1933–45

November 26, 1943: Flying ace and Medal of Honor recipient Edward "Butch" O'Hare is lost when he is shot down by the Japanese near the Gilbert Islands in the Navy's first carrier-based nighttime air raid.

1944: After several requests, William Patrick Hitler, son of Adolf Hitler's half brother and his Irish wife, is cleared to serve in the U.S. Navy during World War II.

June 4, 1944: With the capture of Germany's *U-505* and its Enigma cipher machine, Irish American Daniel Gallery becomes the first U.S. Navy captain to capture a foreign warship since the War of 1812.

June 6, 1944: The Allies land on the beaches of Normandy, France, in one of the largest amphibious assaults in world history. The D-Day invasions would not have been possible without the landing craft known as the Higgins boat, designed by Irish American Andrew Higgins.

June 17, 1944: The 165th Infantry Regiment lands on Saipan. By the end of the summer, the "Fighting Irish" will have completely subdued all enemy resistance.

July 6, 1944: Irish American clown Emmett Kelly is among the Ringling Bros. and Barnum & Bailey performers who attempt to quell the flames of the Hartford (Connecticut) Circus Fire on a day when 167 people will perish.

August 12, 1944: Joseph Kennedy, Jr., scion of the fledgling Irish Catholic Kennedy political dynasty, dies during a special operations mission in the skies over Britain.

December 1944: Irish American General Anthony McAuliffe delivers his one-word response to a German surrender demand at Bastogne: "Nuts." When the smoke clears the following month, McAuliffe's 101st Airborne Division will emerge victorious.

JFK and Joseph Jr. Joseph Kennedy, Jr. (*right*), took leave from Harvard Law School in 1941 to enlist in the Navy as a pilot. He served two tours, in 1943 and 1944, and became eligible to leave the service. Instead, he volunteered for an additional mission and was killed on August 12, 1944. His brother John (*left*) nearly met a similar fate. JFK also enlisted in the Navy. Serving in the Pacific, he commanded a patrol boat, the *PT-109,* which was rammed by a Japanese ship in August 1943. He severely injured his back but saved 10 crew members. A book and movie were made about the *PT-109* episode, making Kennedy a hero—and a rising political star.

Byrnes wields political clout The grandson of Irish famine immigrants, James Francis "Jimmy" Byrnes rose to South Carolina's highest offices. He served in the U.S. House of Representatives (1911–25), in the Senate (1931–41), and as governor (1951–55). After two years as a justice of the U.S. Supreme Court (1941–42), Byrnes was appointed director of war mobilization during World War II. President Roosevelt considered him as a running mate in 1940 and 1944, but ultimately rejected him for his segregationist views and his unpopularity among Irish Catholics over his conversion to Protestantism. Byrnes served as America's secretary of state from 1945 to '47.

"I could tell he was a policeman—he had his hat off and the woodpeckers were starting to congregate."

—FRED ALLEN

Radio's Favorite Irishman

Opined writer James Thurber, "You can count on the thumb of one hand the American who is at once a comedian, a humorist, a wit, and a satirist, and his name is Fred Allen."

The man so warmly hailed by Thurber is no longer a household name. But in the 1930s and 1940s, Allen was one of the great stars of America's radio age. His brilliantly crafted, acid-tinged, and sometimes subversive humor is still an influence on the American entertainment scene.

Allen was born just outside Boston in 1894 and was raised by an aunt. He got his start performing as a juggler in vaudeville. Beginning in 1932, Allen became a network radio fixture. A perfectionist and workaholic, he crafted a satiric style and exhibited a talent for commentary and sketch comedy that still serves as a model for TV's late-night luminaries. One of his show's hallmark features was "Allen's Alley," peopled by a cast of

Fred Allen

oddballs and blowhards, including one Ajax Cassidy, a comically pugnacious Irish tippler. The character, devised to appeal to "the Irish with a sense of humor," was typically featured in exchanges like this:

FRED: Mr. Cassidy, you have a black eye.

AJAX: I have that....I look as though me eyeball is passin' through a total eclipse.

FRED: Tell me, who gave you the peeper?

AJAX: Shoot, nobody gave it to me. I had to fight half an hour to get it.

Many Irish Americans hated the depiction; some even threatened boycotts. Allen, true to his nature, kept the character in the act until the end. And that end came in 1949, with the arrival of television. Allen gave TV a try, but he was never happy or sure of himself in the medium. He was in the midst of writing his memoir, *Much Ado About Me*, when he died on St. Patrick's Day, 1956.

Irish shine in *Going My Way* The 1940s turned into something of a golden era for America's Hollywood Irish, with the 1944 classic *Going My Way* earning much of the critical acclaim and box office success. The movie was fronted by two Irish American actors, Bing Crosby (*left*) and Pennsylvania-born Frank McHugh (*center*), who enjoyed a lengthy career in both lead and supporting roles. *Going My Way* is particularly remembered for providing Barry Fitzgerald (*right*)—the hugely popular former Abbey Theatre player—with an Oscar for best supporting actor. The film won seven Oscars altogether.

War Heroes

Irish America's finest word during World War II was expressed just before Christmas 1944. It came after Germany had demanded the surrender of American troops in Bastogne at the height of the Battle of the Bulge. The American commander in the Belgian town, Brigadier General Anthony McAuliffe, responded thus:

> To the German Commander:
>   "Nuts!"
> —The American Commander

McAuliffe was just one of countless Irish American heroes during the Second World War. On December 10, 1941, Captain Colin Kelly took off from Manila in his B-17 bomber without fighter escort. Kelly spotted Japanese naval ships. His B-17 dropped bombs but was attacked by enemy fighters. With the plane ablaze, Kelly ordered his surviving crew to bail out. Moments after the last man did, the plane exploded with Kelly still at the controls. America, still reeling from Pearl Harbor, had its first war hero.

Serving beyond the call of duty was not confined to fighting men. Father Joseph O'Callahan served as chaplain on the USS *Franklin* when it was bombed on March 19, 1945. Though wounded, O'Callahan administered last rites, organized damage control, and, incredibly, led some 700 men to safety. He won the Congressional Medal of Honor.

While the future President Kennedy survived the sinking of his *PT-109*, the Sullivan brothers would not be so

Sullivan brothers

fortunate. On November 12, 1942, the cruiser *Juneau* was sunk off the Solomon Islands. The five Sullivan brothers from Iowa—Albert, Francis, George, Joseph, and Madison—all perished. President Roosevelt described this as "one of the most extraordinary tragedies" met by one family. The Navy would change regulations to keep brothers apart and, before war's end, name a destroyer after the brothers.

A second USS *The Sullivans* was commissioned in 1997. Said Albert's granddaughter, Kelly Sullivan Loughren, in launching the ship, "In honor of my grandfather and his brothers...may the luck of the Irish always be with you and your crew."

New York's Irish fight together

With its origin dating back to the Revolutionary War, it's not surprising that the 69th New York Infantry—the so-called "Fighting Irish"—played a key role in World War II. By then, the unit—recruited entirely from New York City—had been renamed the 165th Infantry Regiment. As seen in this image, the 165th landed on Butaritari, an island in the Makin Atoll, in November 1943. Later, the 165th saw fierce fighting in Saipan and Okinawa in the closing days of the war.

A hero in the sky O'Hare International Airport in Chicago is named after Lieutenant Commander Edward Henry "Butch" O'Hare. The U.S. Navy's first flying ace of World War II, O'Hare was posthumously awarded the Congressional Medal of Honor for his service in the Pacific during World War II. On November 26, 1943, O'Hare participated in the first carrier-based night attack on Japanese forces. The 29-year-old's F6F Hellcat fighter plane was shot down and never recovered. After the war, *Chicago Tribune* publisher Colonel Robert McCormick suggested changing the name of Chicago's Orchard Depot Airport in honor of O'Hare.

Hannegan vaults Truman to power The man most responsible for Harry Truman becoming president upon the 1945 death of Franklin Roosevelt was Robert E. Hannegan. Hannegan (*left*) and Truman (*right*) were old friends. Hannegan's political background was the St. Louis Democratic machine. When he was just 31, he helped Truman get elected senator in 1934—and did it again in 1940. Truman returned the favor by helping Hannegan to get appointed commissioner of the Internal Revenue in 1943. As chair of the Democratic National Committee in 1944, Hannegan persuaded Roosevelt to drop incumbent Henry Wallace from the ticket and name Truman his running mate.

Higgins boats "win the war" Dwight D. Eisenhower once said that Andrew Jackson Higgins (*left photo, in tie*) "won the war for us." Higgins designed the boats (*right photo, at Guadalcanal*) used to land at Normandy in June 1944, on D-Day, the turning point of World War II. The so-called Higgins boats were small craft that were loaded onto large ships. Once the soldiers were in sight of their destination, the Higgins boats took them ashore much more easily than the larger boats could have. Ultimately, more than 20,000 Higgins boats were built and used in the invasions of Normandy as well as in Sicily, North Africa, and the Pacific Islands.

December 15, 1944: William Leahy is named the first U.S. Fleet admiral, becoming the first senior officer of any branch of the U.S. military to earn a five-star rank.

January 7, 1945: Irish American ace pilot Thomas McGuire, whose 38 kills are only two shy of top ace Richard Bong, is killed in a dogfight with a Japanese fighter pilot over the Philippines.

March 15, 1945: A trio of Irish Americans receive Academy Awards for *Going My Way,* including Leo McCarey (best director), Bing Crosby (best actor), and Barry Fitzgerald (best supporting actor).

April 1945: Upon learning of the death of Adolf Hitler, Irish leader Eamon de Valera inexplicably sends his condolences to the German ambassador. He is the only leader of a neutral nation to do so.

April 9, 1945: The 165th Infantry Regiment lands on Okinawa to capture the heavily defended airfield in what will prove to be one of the bloodiest battles in the Pacific.

April 12, 1945: President Franklin Roosevelt dies of a cerebral hemorrhage at his resort in Warm Springs, Georgia. Vice President Harry S. Truman, who is part Scots-Irish, is sworn in as the new president later in the day.

April 30, 1945: Half-Irish William Joyce, the American-born Nazi propagandist known as Lord Haw Haw, records his final broadcast during the Battle of Berlin. The Allies will overrun his studio the following day.

June 2, 1945: Audie Murphy, an Irish American U.S. Army infantry lieutenant, short of stature but tremendously brave and highly skilled on the battlefield, is awarded the Medal of Honor.

A pioneer journalist Born in New York to a Jewish father and an Irish mother, Margaret Bourke-White became a world-famous photographer, photojournalist, and writer. She was the first Western photographer to enter the Soviet Union, the first female photographer for *Life* magazine, and the first female war correspondent during World War II, when she documented the collapse of Germany while following Patton's army. Bourke-White photographed Gandhi hours before his assassination, and she later covered the Korean War.

The bravest of all Irish American Audie Murphy was the most decorated U.S. combat soldier of World War II—and perhaps the bravest. In his most daring venture, in the woods of France on January 26, 1945, Murphy mounted a burning tank destroyer. Though the tank could have exploded at any moment, he employed its machine gun for an hour, killing or wounding 50 to 100 German soldiers. All told during the war, Murphy killed some 240 Germans. Honored with 28 U.S. medals, Murphy parlayed his fame into a 44-film acting career. He played himself in the 1955 war movie *To Hell and Back*. Murphy, who suffered from what we now call post-traumatic stress disorder, died in a plane crash at age 46.

McAuliffe defies the Germans In December 1944, General Anthony McAuliffe served as acting commander of the 101st Airborne Division, which was surrounded by German troops in the Belgian town of Bastogne. The Germans demanded that the Allied troops surrender, but General McAulliffe entered military lore when he sent a one-word reply: "Nuts." General McAul-

liffe and his troops held off the Germans for six days before General George Patton was able to send additional troops to secure the safety of McAulliffe's 101st.

McGuire fights to the death McGuire Air Force base in New Jersey is named for Major Thomas McGuire, Jr., one of America's most distinguished airmen. Born in 1920 in Ridgewood, New Jersey, McGuire attended Georgia Tech but left to join the Army Air Corps in 1941. McGuire was ultimately awarded the Congressional Medal of Honor, the Distinguished Service Cross, three Silver Stars, and three Purple Hearts for his service in the Pacific. He died as the war was ending, in January 1945, after crashing following a fierce air fight. McGuire was posthumously awarded the Medal of Honor.

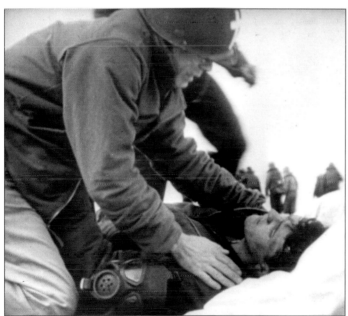

Irish chaplains prove heroic During World War II, hundreds of Irish Catholic priests served as chaplains in the armed forces, and many of them made the supreme sacrifice while ministering to the wounded and dying. One Navy chaplain, Father Joseph T. O'Callaghan (*pictured*), received the Congressional Medal of Honor for his actions on March 19, 1945. On that day, a Japanese plane scored two direct hits on the aircraft carrier USS *Franklin*, incapacitating the ship and killing 724 seamen. While fires raged and secondary explosions shook the deck, O'Callaghan administered last rites, led rescue parties, and organized and directed firefighting. In 1965 the Navy named a ship in his honor.

FIGHTING IRISH PREVAIL AT SAIPAN

The [165th infantry] regiment left Hawaii on May 31st 1944 with the 105th Infantry and landed on Saipan on June 17th 1944. The 165th immediately assaulted Saipan's airstrip, known locally as Aslito Field, pushing over the tarmac and attacking the prime Japanese defensive works on Ryan's Ridge to the South East of the field. The 165th broke the defenses on the ridge on the 18th after a day of brutal and confused fighting, allowing the capture of Aslito Field. Following the capture of the airfield the 165th, after a brief attack on Nafutan Point, was sent to bolster the line of the 4th Marine Division. The 165th was involved in bitter fighting around Mount Tapotchau, Purple Heart Ridge, and Death Valley, fighting with the 106th Infantry in an attempt to break these, the island's last and strongest defensive positions. The 165th eventually finished off the last organized resistance on Saipan, effectively ending the battle.

—UNIT HISTORY PROJECT, NEW YORK STATE MILITARY MUSEUM, ON A REGIMENT KNOWN AS THE "FIGHTING IRISH" DUE TO ITS LARGELY IRISH AMERICAN MAKEUP

Catholics contribute, celebrate World War II was another opportunity for Irish Americans and other Roman Catholics to prove they could be patriotic American citizens. With so many Catholics serving in the military, most servicemen were remembered at weekly Mass. In addition, parishes regularly held food drives or other events aimed at boosting morale at home and on the front lines. Here, a priest and parishioners celebrate the surrender of Germany in May 1945. Families of Pacific Theater soldiers would rejoice three months later.

Truman's trusted aide From an Irish family in Massachusetts, Matt Connelly rose to become President Harry Truman's appointments secretary. He first came to Truman's notice in 1938, when he worked as a special investigator for the Works Progress Administration (WPA). When then-senator Truman formed a committee to look into U.S. war spending, he appointed Connelly chief of staff. He then brought him along to the White House in 1945. Connelly's illustrious career was blemished in 1955 when he fell victim to political persecution, was indicted, and was later convicted of taking a bribe. President Kennedy pardoned him in 1962.

Positive programs for Catholic youth Bishop Bernard J. Sheil knew that the streets of Chicago's West Side could be mean. So in 1930, he proposed the formation of the Catholic Youth Organization (CYO). These parish-based groups sponsored athletic clubs, activities, and other social events. CYO groups, which eventually spread across the United States and the world, were consistent with the Catholic Church's message of social justice, which advocated assisting the underprivileged. Parish-based Holy Name societies helped the poor and unemployed. Here, former middleweight boxer Charlie White instructs boys in Chicago.

Crosby returns as Father O'Malley

In addition to his legendary screen partnership with Bob Hope and Dorothy Lamour in the "Road" films, crooner Bing Crosby starred alongside many other Hollywood greats. Included was Ingrid Bergman, seen here in a nun's habit beside Crosby's Father Chuck O'Malley in the 1945 hit *The Bells of St. Mary's.* In the Leo McCarey-directed film, Crosby reprised a role he had first played, and won an Oscar for, in *Going My Way* (1944). Crosby's portrayal of the unquestionably virtuous Catholic priest came at a time when Catholicism was achieving a broad level of familiarity and acceptance in general American culture.

McCarthy's golden voice Clem McCarthy called America's biggest sporting moments during radio's golden era. Born in Rochester, New York, McCarthy achieved fame for his singular boxing and horse racing commentaries during the 1930s and '40s. His call of the 1938 Joe Louis-Max Schmeling rematch at Yankee Stadium remains a classic: "Louis measures him. Right to the body, a left up to the jaw, and Schmeling is down! The count is five! Five, six, seven, eight, the men are in the ring! The fight is over, on a technical knockout."

The Irish cop These Irish police officers, who served the citizens of Boston, reflected a cultural phenomenon. The Irish cop was on the beat in the very earliest days of organized policing—not just in the nation's major cities, but also in smaller cities, in suburbs, and in rural America. The Irish got started in police work because in so many city neighborhoods they were the citizens who either needed a police service or needed a little policing. Serving in uniform became family tradition and ensured a place for the Irish cop in American history and popular lore.

Rise to Prominence

1946–1963

The 1950s are often recalled as a time of gray conformity and sleepy satisfaction in the United States, but for Irish America, the decade is known as a time of mobility, prominence, and—at long last—hard-won economic security. Like other white ethnics in the '50s, millions of Irish moved from city to suburb, abandoning the neighborhoods and parishes of their parents and grandparents. Whether their collars were white or blue, whether they worked outside the home or were homemakers, they shared in the wondrous prosperity of the age. They also continued to move through the ranks of one of their notable chosen professions, politics.

What's more, the decade's heavy lean toward anticommunism, caricatured by Senator Joseph McCarthy of Wisconsin, offered Irish Americans a chance to prove themselves one final, decisive time to mainstream Protestant America. Daniel Patrick Moynihan, a young professor and political aide at the time, took note of the way the 1950s turned American culture on its head. Nobody questioned the loyalty of Irish Catholics during the Red Scare of the Eisenhower years, Moynihan wrote, because Irish loathing of communism was so evident. As the government looked to root out potential

Glamorous, handsome, smart, and rich, and with a winning personality, John F. Kennedy kept secret his serious illnesses and his multiple sexual affairs. Catholics not only loved him but they voted for him 3–1. Partly because there were more Catholics than in Al Smith's day, JFK won a squeaker against Richard Nixon in the 1960 presidential race.

security checks, Moynihan wrote, "Harvard men were to be checked; Fordham men would do the checking."

There was at least one Harvard man whose loyalty was without question. Coincidentally or not, he happened to be Irish Catholic. His name was John F. Kennedy.

Like writer Mary McCarthy, a Vassar graduate and child of privilege, and actress Grace Kelly, daughter of a prosperous Philadelphia Irish family, Kennedy exuded sophistication, polish, and assimilation. Kennedy, McCarthy, and Kelly represented a new chapter in the Irish American journey. They were very different than the familiar brawling Irishman played by John Wayne in the 1952 classic *The Quiet Man* (directed by the Irish American John Ford), or the meaty-faced hacks who populated the book and film versions of Edwin O'Connor's classic Irish American story, *The Last Hurrah.* Mary McCarthy had little in common with Senator McCarthy; John Kennedy lived in a political universe different than that of Chicago's Richard J. Daley; and Grace Kelly's world was far removed from Gracie Allen's.

The Last Hurrah, published to great acclaim in 1956, captured the sense that something was coming to an end in the 1950s—and something new was beginning. In the book, charming rogue Frank Skeffington loses his big-city mayor job to a soft, ambitious lightweight. Skeffington represents older Irish Americans whose children went to college, owned homes, and celebrated their newfound affluence and power.

Of course, not every Irish American fled to the burbs, went to Fordham, and wore well-pressed suits to work in the 1950s. The stories of blue-collar Irish Americans found artistic expression in the comedy of Jackie Gleason and Art Carney, the male leads of the classic 1950s TV comedy *The Honeymooners.* With Gleason playing a bus driver and Carney a sewer worker, *The Honeymooners* humanized urban, working-class America at a time when Irish America was moving out of the cities and into the middle class.

Whether they were carrying briefcases to downtown office buildings or lunch buckets to construction jobs, many—although surely not all—Irish Americans were excited about the presidential campaign of John F. Kennedy in 1960. Urbane, intelligent, and charismatic, Kennedy seemed to be the culmination of Irish America's rise to power and prominence, the symbol of Irish Catholics' yearning for acceptance of their religion, culture, and values.

Of course, while Kennedy may have represented so much to Irish Americans, he was hardly representative *of* Irish Americans. He was wealthy, had

There have been many famous and powerful Irish Catholic Democrats, but Senator Joe McCarthy was one of the few Irish Catholic Republicans to seize the national spotlight. Through the early 1950s, McCarthy made reckless accusations that the federal government was riddled with Communists. His rhetoric inflamed the anti-Red paranoia that swept across the United States.

attended prep schools and Harvard, and was a member in good standing of Washington's social elite. And yet, as author William Shannon noted in his book *The American Irish,* Kennedy "personified political traditions that were specifically Irish and Catholic." The old machines were built on "pragmatic insights and intuitions about human nature," Shannon noted. Machine candidates, for example, never lost an election for the sake of an abstract principle. Kennedy was very much a product of this non-ideological, loyalty-based political ethic.

Kennedy's victory over Richard Nixon in 1960 was a milestone in American history. He was the first non-Anglo-Saxon Protestant to win the nation's highest office. For Irish Americans, Kennedy's victory was sweet vindication and a cause for celebration. They had suffered the violent bigotry of the nativists and Know-Nothings in the 19th century and the subtle but palpable hostility of polite society in the 20th century. But in 1960 they prevailed, at last.

The first Irish Catholic president was very much at home with the country's Anglo-Saxon establishment. Though Irish American political operatives were part of the court at Camelot, important policy decisions were in the hands of the WASPs who were Kennedy's most important advisers.

In June 1963, Kennedy insisted on including a stop in Ireland during the same European tour that took him to the Berlin Wall. He visited Dunganstown in County Wexford, birthplace of his immigrant grandfather, Patrick Kennedy. He spoke eloquently to the Irish Parliament, and was welcomed as the greatest son of a storied diaspora.

Kennedy was assassinated just a few months later, on November 22, 1963. The sorrow was global; the tragedy was not Irish American, but human. No president since, with the possible exception of another Irish American, Ronald Reagan, has captured the nation's imagination like Kennedy did.

The day of his death also marked the climax of Irish American political power in the 20th century. Moynihan noted that on November 22, 1963, the president, the speaker of the house (John McCormick of Massachusetts), the majority leader of the U.S. Senate (Mike Mansfield of Montana), and the chairman of the Democratic National Committee (John Moran Bailey of Connecticut) were all Irish Catholics.

"It will not come again," Moynihan wrote.

It likely will not, not in the more diverse American society of the 21st century. But that only makes the achievement all the more remarkable.

Though one of television's classic sitcoms, *The Honeymooners* lasted for only two seasons (1955–56) and 39 episodes. Afterward, Jackie Gleason (*right*) became a star in Hollywood and on Broadway, winning a Tony in 1960. Art Carney (*left*) worked in TV and movies, winning an Oscar in 1974. The limp of his "Ed Norton" character came from a real shrapnel wound that he suffered at Normandy in 1944.

1946: The University of Notre Dame Fighting Irish win the first of three national football titles they will capture under head coach Frank Leahy.

January 1, 1946: Irish-born judge and politician William O'Dwyer is sworn in as the 100th mayor of New York City. The ceremony's festivities include the singing of the 1940 show tune "It's a Great Day for the Irish."

February 18, 1946: Francis Joseph Spellman, archbishop of New York, is elevated to cardinal.

March 7, 1946: James Dunn earns best supporting actor honors for his work in *A Tree Grows in Brooklyn*.

November 1946: Joseph McCarthy wins election to the U.S. Senate, representing Wisconsin.

1947: Thanks to the Servicemen's Readjustment Act of 1944, known as the GI Bill, nearly half of all college admissions this year are World War II veterans. • Kathleen McCormick wins control of her late husband's International Harvester fortune. She will devote much of the money to promote legalized contraception and abortion.

July 1947: Writing under the pseudonym "Mr. X," George Kennan publishes an article in *Foreign Affairs* magazine in which he advocates "containment," the eventual centerpiece of President Harry Truman's Soviet policy.

1948: Irish American mathematician Claude Shannon, regarded as the father of information theory, publishes his groundbreaking paper, "A Mathematical Theory of Communication," in the *Bell System Technical Journal*. • Inspired by the efficiency of Henry Ford's assembly line, Dick and Mac McDonald apply what they call the "Speedee Service System" to their San Bernardino, California, hamburger restaurant.

New York's Irish-born mayor William O'Dwyer holds the distinction of being the last mayor of New York to be born in Ireland. He came up through the ranks, working as a policeman and putting himself through law school. Then, as Brooklyn's district attorney, he achieved fame for his efforts against organized crime. O'Dwyer became mayor in 1946 and was reelected in 1949. Although he was popular, allegations of corruption within his administration forced him to resign in 1950. That year, he accepted President Truman's offer of an ambassadorship.

The "Pittsburgh Kid" Pittsburgh's Billy Conn (*left*) was one of the fiercest boxers of the 1930s and '40s. By age 21, the "Pittsburgh Kid" had defeated nine current or former world champions. Though he often fought in lower weight classes, he lost to just one heavyweight, Joe Louis, seen in this photo from their 1946 match. Conn's most famous match against Louis was in 1941. Despite weighing 30 pounds less, Conn nearly beat Louis, who later called Conn his toughest opponent.

Leahy wins 39 straight for ND After a successful playing career under legendary coach Knute Rockne, Frank Leahy returned to Notre Dame as the team's head coach in 1941. He went undefeated that year and won the national championship in 1943. After a stint in the military, he built a dynasty in South Bend, compiling five undefeated seasons and winning three

national titles from 1946 to '53. At one point, his teams won 39 straight games. Leahy was known for his intense practices, and his teams were almost always better conditioned and better prepared than their opponents.

The fiction of J. F. Powers Irish American writer J. F. Powers liked to write about the Catholic Church. Born in Illinois in 1917, the same year as John F. Kennedy, Powers drew on his experiences in the Church while penning his acclaimed short stories. Powers became the keen-eyed chronicler of the changes that blew through his Church in the baby boom years after World War II. His short story collection *Prince of Darkness and Other Stories* was published in 1947. *Morte d'Urban*, his first novel, won the National Book Award for fiction in 1963.

A leading voice in Washington Columnist Mary McGrory chronicled Washington, D.C., for 50 years, from the Army-McCarthy hearings to the war in Iraq. According to *The New York Times,* she had a "profoundly Irish love" of politics. McGrory wrote for *The Washington Star* and then *The Washington Post*

from 1947 until her death in 2004. Her tenacious reporting skills and exquisite writing earned her a Pulitzer Prize for commentary in 1975. *New York Times* columnist Maureen Dowd called her the "most luminous writer and clearest thinker in the business."

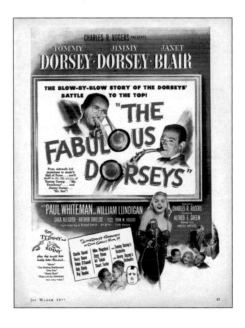

The Dorsey brothers The 1947 film *The Fabulous Dorseys* told the tumultuous family story of Tommy and Jimmy Dorsey, who starred in the film and were two of the most popular musicians of their era. The sons of a music teacher from Shenandoah, Pennsylvania, Thomas Francis Dorsey and James Dorsey began performing in bands in the 1920s before forming the Dorsey Brothers Orchestra in 1934. The duo, however, often fought with each other. Tommy, the younger brother, formed his own band in 1935 and had a highly successful career. Tragically, both brothers died in their early 50s.

1948: Irish American illustrator Walt Kelly, art director for the *New York Star,* introduces his comic strip character Pogo. Kelly and Pogo will enjoy a 26-year run in syndication.

January 7, 1948: *The Treasure of Sierra Madre* premieres. It will earn Oscars for director John Huston and his father, actor Walter Huston.

1949: Boston mayor James Curley is defeated by his former protégé as he attempts to win a fifth term. Winning candidate John Hynes had been a loyal aide, but a careless, insulting statement by Curley led Hynes to vow to defeat him. • "Murphy's Law," named for McDonnell-Douglas engineer Edward Murphy, Jr., enters the lexicon at an Edwards Air Force Base press conference following a series of flawed human acceleration tolerance tests.

February 2, 1949: Golfing great Ben Hogan survives a catastrophic car accident. Despite multiple severe injuries and nearly two months in the hospital, Hogan will be back to championship form in 1950.

April 18, 1949: The Republic of Ireland Act comes into effect. The act abolishes Britain's monarchial rule over Ireland and makes Ireland a republic.

June 1949: The British Parliament passes the Ireland Act, reasserting that Northern Ireland is still part of the United Kingdom.

1950: The McCarran Internal Security Act passes when a Democratic Senate overrides President Truman's veto. Truman believed that the act—which called variously for registration, deportation, and incarceration of subversives—was a threat to America's essential freedoms. • Bishop Fulton Sheen is named national director of the Society for the Propagation of the Faith.

Huston's classic films From Scots-Irish ancestry, John Huston was one of the most important film directors of the 20th century. After bouncing around in his early life as an actor, writer, and painter, he took up film directing with Warner Brothers in the late 1930s. His 1941 film *The Maltese Falcon* met with critical success. That film, along with *The Treasure of Sierra Madre* (1948), are considered classics of American filmmaking. Huston's father was well-known actor Walter Huston, and his daughter is Oscar-winning actress Angelica Huston.

A tribute to Father Dunne The 1948 film *Fighting Father Dunne* capitalized on the popular WWII era theme of the Irish American priest as mentor to poor urban boys in danger of going astray. The highly sentimental story of a priest establishing a home for wayward newspaper boys was loosely based on the life and work of Father Peter Dunne in St. Louis. For more than 30 years, Dunne's shelter provided a home for up to 200 boys. In the film, he was played by Pat O'Brien.

Champion of Birth Control

"**N**o woman can call herself free until she can choose consciously whether she will or will not be a mother." These were the radical words of Irish American Margaret Sanger, founder of the National Birth Control League and the newsletter *Woman Rebel*. Through much of the 20th century, Sanger traveled the world, advocating contraception and female hygiene. Her crusade landed her in jail and brought harsh criticism from the Catholic Church and the American political establishment.

One of 11 children, Sanger said that her mother had died young (at age 50) due to her multiple pregnancies. Margaret's first job, as a maternity nurse in New York City, only strengthened her advocacy of birth control. There

Margaret Sanger

she witnessed poverty-stricken young women die after trying to self-abort unwanted pregnancies, using everything from coat hangers to turpentine. Sanger believed that to avoid such tragedies, women needed to take preemptive measures. She therefore dedicated her life to educating the public on contraception.

By midcentury, Sanger had spread her gospel to Russia, India, China, Japan, Malaysia, and Europe. Her travels led her to establish a new organization, the International Planned Parenthood Federation. Through this new vehicle, Sanger proclaimed that the world's conflicts and its poverty resulted from overpopulation. She continued to actively espouse birth control until her death in 1966.

Everyone loves Dennis Day

Always grinning from ear to ear, Irish tenor Dennis Day was an extremely popular singer as well as a radio and television personality. He was much loved for his impersonations of famous celebrities, such as Jimmy Durante and Jimmy Stewart, on the radio and

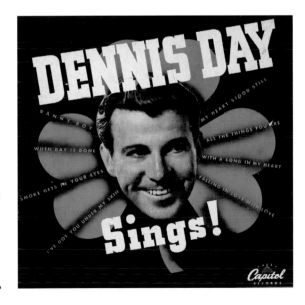

television programs of Jack Benny, with whom he was associated from 1939 until Benny's death in 1974. Born Owen Patrick Eugene McNulty, Day was the son of Irish-born immigrant parents. Besides his work on Benny's programs, Day starred in radio's *The Dennis Day Show* and appeared on such TV programs as *The Lucy Show* and *The Bing Crosby Show*.

From a woman's perspective

First published in 1948, Mary Doyle Curran's *The Parish and the Hill* was a controversial look at the "lace curtain" and "shanty" Irish of a New England mill town. Set during the 1920s in Curran's native Holyoke, Massachusetts, the

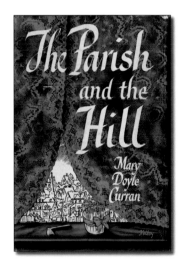

novel explores conflicts among three generations of Irish Americans. Through its central character, Mary O'Connor, *The Parish and the Hill* was one of the first novels to explore Irish American life from a woman's perspective.

1950: Golfer Sam Snead wins 11 PGA events.

1950–53: Thousands of Irish Americans fight for their country in the Korean War. Irish American Medal of Honor winners include Henry Commiskey, Lloyd Burke, John D. Kelly, and Richard Thomas Shea.

February 9, 1950: Speaking to an audience in Wheeling, West Virginia, Senator Joseph McCarthy launches his anti-Communist crusade. He claims to have a list of 205 Communists working for the federal government.

March 20, 1950: Irish American bank robber Willie Sutton makes the FBI's second "Ten Most Wanted Fugitives" list. He will be captured in 1952.

1951: New York's Bishop Fulton Sheen begins broadcasting his weekly television series *Life Is Worth Living.*

1952: Colorado housewife Virginia Tighe causes a sensation when she allegedly recalls her previous life as an Irishwoman named Bridey Murphy while under hypnosis. Subsequent research into Tighe's claims reveals a childhood neighbor as the likely source of the "memories." • Labor leader George Meany is named president of the American Federation of Labor.

February 6, 1952: Britain's King George VI dies of lung cancer, leaving the throne to his daughter Elizabeth.

August 14, 1952: *The Quiet Man,* a film about an Irish American boxer who settles in Ireland, premieres in the United States. The film, which stars John Wayne and Maureen O'Hara, will earn director John Ford an Oscar.

1953: The McDonald brothers begin to franchise their hamburger restaurant and its revolutionary service system. They will partner with salesman and visionary businessman Ray Kroc the following year.

A parade of sisters The O'Neil sisters of Boston (pictured in 1952) were a parade unto themselves. In the 1940s and '50s, the sisters dressed in matching outfits and marched in the city's annual Easter parade. Wearing clothes made by their mother, Julia, a talented seamstress, the sisters were an instant hit with both the press and the public. As they grew in number over the years, the O'Neils seemed to perfectly dovetail with the postwar baby boom, which was spreading well beyond its popularly conceived Irish and Catholic confines.

YOU DIDN'T CURSE AROUND A GIRL

And the girls were treated with respect then, too, even in a tough neighborhood. You didn't dare curse around a girl, just an unwritten rule—if you did that, you know, you were gonna have a little facial. Basically, the girls that were carrying the books across the street for the nuns, see, they had the Monday night novena. When it was snowing out, we used to ambush them from the roof with snowballs and all that. Turn the corner right past the M&M Dairy, went up on the roof across the street. And that was kind of fun. And they're holding their hats running down the street, throw snowballs down and all that kind of stuff. Just raising hell, if you could; there was certain lines to it. We were mischief-oriented, the guys were. You had energy and you were doing these things. But the borderline, you stopped—you always respected the girls. But that was something that they expected, the snowballs. And different weather, guys would go up with water balloons.

—DONALD A. KELLY, A FORMER SENIOR VICE PRESIDENT OF THE EMIGRANT SAVINGS BANK, ABOUT HIS YOUTH ON MANHATTAN'S UPPER WEST WIDE IN THE 1940s AND '50s

What the Irish should speak The language conflict in Ireland has always been heated. Irish nationalists believe the English language is a product of British tyranny and argue that only the Irish Gaelic language should be used. These posters, from 1949, represent the view that English language magazines and newspapers should be abolished in Ireland. Nevertheless, even as Ireland achieved independence and the Irish language was taught to schoolchildren, English remained the country's dominant language.

Cannon's take on sports The son of a Tammany Hall politician, Jimmy Cannon dropped out of high school but went on to become one of the greatest sportswriters ever to drop ink onto an American newspaper page. During his career with a string of New York dailies, Cannon

reminded readers that their sports heroes were also human and vulnerable. He described Joe Louis as "a credit to his race, the human race" and Babe Ruth as "a parade all by himself, a burst of dazzle and jingle."

Birth of the Irish Republic In 1949 independent Ireland unilaterally declared that it would become a republic and, as such, would fulfill the dreams of Irish nationalists since the late 18th century. From 1921 until 1949, the Irish Free State technically remained part of the British Commonwealth, which meant that the British monarch was its putative head of state. Beginning on April 18, 1949, however, Ireland cut its final connection to the British crown. Crowds, dignitaries, and military units gathered in front of the General Post Office on O'Connell Street in Dublin to celebrate the milestone. The change did little to spur the Irish economy, but it was a source of great pride for the many Irish nationalists who loathed any formal connection to Britain's monarchy.

Can Catholics be trusted?
The raw religious bias against
Catholics in 19th century
America changed by the mid-
20th century. Postwar American
politics witnessed the steady rise
of Catholic politicians, but the
emergence of the Kennedy family as a national political force
provoked a special response.
Paul Blanshard's 1949 book,
*American Freedom and Catholic
Power,* a compilation of articles,
pressed the view that Catholics
could not be trusted with power in American democracy.
Blanshard, in fact, compared the Vatican to the Kremlin.
While many concurred, most Americans did not—as demonstrated by the 1960 presidential election result.

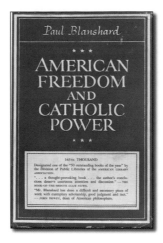

**"Slammin'
Sammy"** The
folksy Sam Snead,
the descendant
of Scots-Irish set-
tlers in Virginia's
backcountry, was
for four decades
(1930s to '70s)
one of the top
professional golf-
ers in the world.
During his career,
he won seven
majors: three Mas-
ters, three PGA
Championships,
and one British
Open. Moreover,
he amassed 82
PGA Tour vic-
tories, more than anyone else in the 20th century. Snead's
graceful swing and lengthy drives earned him the nickname
"Slammin' Sammy."

O'Keefe plays the tough guy Born in 1908 as Edward
Flanagan to a pair of Irish immigrant actors, Dennis O'Keefe
gained steady work in Hollywood after he changed his name
in 1937. He played many roles as tough heroes, mostly in
small-budget crime dramas such as the 1949 film *Abandoned*
(*pictured*). O'Keefe worked alongside fellow Irish American
actor John Wayne in the World War II action movie *The Fighting Seabees* (1944). As his film career wound down, he starred
in his own television show in the 1950s. He died in 1968.

O'Malley brings baseball to L.A. Dodgers owner Walter
O'Malley, pictured with manager Charlie Dressen in 1950,
was both praised and scorned for the innovations he
brought to the game of baseball. Born in the Bronx, O'Malley
was an executive with the Dodgers when Branch Rickey signed
Jackie Robinson. O'Malley's most controversial decision was to
move Brooklyn's beloved Dodgers to Los Angeles, paving the
way for West Coast baseball. He also built Dodger Stadium
in the Chavez Ravine area of Los Angeles, which forced the
destruction of a Mexican American community.

Irish in the suburbs Like many other Americans from all walks of life, the Irish left their old urban neighborhoods after World War II. Lured by new highways, government incentives such as the GI Bill, and the chance to own their own homes, they flocked to the suburbs. They built churches and schools and created new chapters of traditional Irish organizations. Tract housing broke down old barriers between the Irish and other white ethnic groups. But as the fiction of acclaimed novelist Alice McDermott illustrates, the Irish managed to hold on to a separate identity.

Curran battles for maritime workers Joe Curran rose from the streets of the Lower East Side in Manhattan to become one of the country's most powerful labor leaders during the 1940s and '50s. As a young seaman, he was among the leaders of a strike aboard the USS *California* in 1936. The following year, Curran helped organize the National Maritime Union, which he led for nearly 40 years. Under his direction, the country's maritime workers won a succession of battles for higher wages and better benefits. He retired in 1973 and died in 1981.

Korean War heroes All four of these Irish American soldiers were awarded the Medal of Honor for their bravery during the Korean War. *Left to right:* Marine First Lieutenant Henry Commiskey killed seven enemy soldiers in hand-to-hand combat in September 1950. Marine Private First Class John D. Kelly died on May 28, 1952, while single-handedly assaulting a North Korean machine gun bunker, as part of a larger charge led against overwhelming odds. In October 1951, while leading his 35-man company on a daring assault against three North Korean bunkers, Army First Lieutenant Lloyd Burke killed more than 100 North Koreans without a single American casualty. And Army First Lieutenant Richard Thomas Shea fought to the death while exhibiting extraordinary leadership on Pork Chop Hill in July 1953.

1953: Maureen "Little Mo" Connolly, an Irish American tennis sensation, becomes the first woman to win all four Grand Slam competitions in a single year.

January 3, 1953: Representing Massachusetts's 11th district (Boston), Thomas "Tip" O'Neill takes his seat in the U.S. House of Representatives. He will retain the office for more than 30 years.

March 19, 1953: Anthony Quinn captures best supporting actor honors for his work in *Viva Zapata!*

June 2, 1953: Elizabeth Alexandra Mary, heir to the British throne, is officially crowned Queen Elizabeth II in an elaborate ceremony at London's Westminster Abbey.

August 1953: The American Federation of Labor suspends the membership of the corruption-plagued International Longshoreman's Association.

September 12, 1953: Boston's Cardinal Cushing officiates at the wedding of Jacqueline Bouvier and John F. Kennedy at St. Mary's Church in Newport, Rhode Island.

1954: Physician Joseph E. Murray performs the world's first kidney transplant. He removes a kidney from Ronald Herrick and transplants the organ to Herrick's ailing twin brother, Richard.

April 12, 1954: Bill Haley and His Comets record "Rock Around the Clock," the song that will bring rock 'n' roll into the American mainstream.

April 22, 1954: The televised Army-McCarthy hearings begin. Accused of pressuring the Army for special treatment for a former aide, McCarthy is vindicated, but his bombastic public persona irreparably damages his approval ratings.

A different beat The Irish began their trademark service to law enforcement by policing city neighborhoods that were white and, often, Irish. Serving in police departments became a tried and tested route to a secure future—virtually a family business for countless Irish Americans. As the 20th century brought dramatic changes to large cities, Irish American cops frequently policed streets in neighborhoods of African Americans or non-European immigrants. Racial tension became increasingly evident during the turbulent 1960s, with Irish cops (often unfairly) being tagged as the unsympathetic enforcers of unjust laws.

Leading conservative The son of a large, wealthy Catholic family of Irish descent, William F. Buckley became America's most prominent conservative. He founded *National Review* magazine and, for decades, was the host of the combative TV show *Firing Line*. Buckley shot to fame after writing *God and Man at Yale* (1951), a critique of elite institutions and their attitudes toward religion. A fierce anti-Communist throughout the 1950s and '60s, Buckley is often credited with creating the modern conservative movement, which culminated in the election of fellow Irish American Ronald Reagan as president in 1980.

Clooney rockets to fame An acclaimed singer and actress, Rosemary Clooney was born in Kentucky to Irish Catholic parents, Andrew Joseph Clooney and Frances Marie Guilfoyle. As a young teenager, Clooney began performing and recording songs with her sister, Betty. By the 1950s, she was recording hit songs (including four No. 1s) and starring in Hollywood musicals, such as

White Christmas. Despite struggling with numerous personal problems, Clooney had a long, distinguished career. Her brother, Nick, was a broadcast journalist and TV host. Nick's son—Rosemary's nephew—is actor George Clooney.

The real *Waterfront* hero Movie fans might not realize it, but the heroic priest character played by actor Karl Malden in the Oscar-winning film *On the Waterfront* was based on an Irish American Jesuit named John M. Corridan (*left*). He is pictured here during a strike on the New York waterfront in 1951. Father Corridan, who helped run the Xavier Institute of Industrial Relations, sympathized with waterfront workers in their battles with management and organized crime. The film drew attention not only to waterfront corruption, but to Father Corridan's crusade for justice on the docks.

An Irish classic The 1952 film *The Quiet Man* was the first American feature film shot in Ireland. Though it was a bit of a misty-eyed yarn, American audiences loved it. The star power brought to the big screen by director John Ford included the legendary team of John Wayne and Maureen O'Hara. The puckish Barry Fitzgerald was a familiar face at this point to

American audiences, as were those of Ward Bond and Victor McLaglen—both stalwarts in Ford's westerns. Wayne and O'Hara's personal chemistry sparked the romantic story line, underlining sly innuendo and highlighting moments of broad comedy. The movie won two Oscars and became an annual staple on television around St. Patrick's Day.

McCarran restricts immigration Senator Patrick McCarran (D-NV) dangles a toy leprechaun that he bought in Ireland, home of his emigrant parents. The senator was not so sentimental when it came to debating immigration. Elected to the U.S. Senate as a Democrat in 1932, McCarran cleaved to the right of his

party and coauthored the McCarran-Walter Act. The law, passed by Congress in 1952, further restricted immigration to the United States. McCarran also cowrote the McCarran-Wood Act, which required American Communists to register with the government.

The Superstar Bishop

A longside Jackie Gleason and Lucille Ball, one of television's first superstars was an Irish American priest from Illinois. Bishop Fulton Sheen attracted as many as 30 million viewers every Tuesday evening with his show *Life Is Worth Living*. The set consisted only of Sheen and a blackboard, but the genial priest captivated audiences with humorous, inspirational, and spiritual talks.

As Bing Crosby did in Hollywood films, Sheen helped make Irish Catholicism seem less alien at a time when significant vestiges of anti-Catholicism remained. The Catholic weekly magazine *America* called Sheen "the greatest evangelizer [sic] in the history of the Catholic Church in the United States."

Born in El Paso, Illinois, in 1895, Sheen became a radio star in the 1930s. *Life Is Worth Living* premiered on the Dumont TV network in 1951 and later moved to ABC. Sheen won an Emmy in 1952 and, calling on his famous sense of humor, thanked his writers: "Matthew, Mark, Luke, and John."

Sheen did not shy away from the more serious issues of the day. On television as well as on radio, in books, and

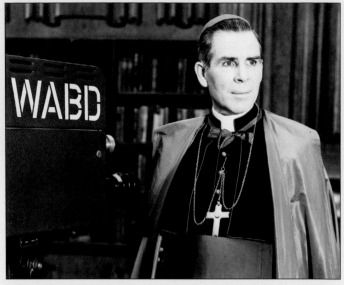

Bishop Fulton Sheen

in newspaper columns, he was a fierce opponent of communism. In September 2002, 23 years after his death, the Catholic Church began the process that may lead to sainthood for the famous bishop.

The McGuire Sisters Christine, Phyllis, and Dorothy McGuire (*left to right*) began performing in their Middletown, Ohio, church, where their mother served as an ordained minister. Known for their beautiful harmonies, the sisters were introduced to the public in 1952 on *Arthur Godfrey's Talent Scouts*. They

went on to record such hits as "Something's Gotta Give" and "Goodnight, Sweetheart, Goodnight." The McGuire Sisters were one of America's top musical acts until the late 1960s, when they stepped back from the spotlight. Three decades later, they reunited for public performances.

Kelly dances to fame Gene Kelly dances on in the memories of millions. Emerging from the Pittsburgh-based family act known as "The Five Kellys," Gene took his talents as a singer, dancer, and actor to Broadway and later Hollywood. His ability to blend dance styles made him a huge hit with Ameri-

can and worldwide moviegoers. Kelly's signature "Singin' in the Rain" performance, in the 1952 film of the same name, attained iconic status. Kelly's other screen hits include *For Me and My Gal* (1942) and *An American in Paris* (1951).

Architect of America's Cold War policy Of Scots-Irish ancestry, George F. Kennan was the key architect of America's foreign policy toward the Soviet Union following World War II. Kennan gained valuable insights while serving in the American Embassy in Moscow during World War II. His warnings of the Soviet Union's expansionist designs led to the U.S. adopting a policy of containment during the Cold War. Later, he served as U.S. ambassador to the Soviet Union. After retirement from the State Department, he taught courses on foreign policy at Harvard, Oxford, and the University of Chicago. Kennan also was a prolific writer, twice winning Pulitzer Prizes.

Spillane books fly off the shelves Thanks to bestsellers such as *I, the Jury* and *Kiss Me, Deadly*, Mickey Spillane became the most popular detective novelist of the 1940s and '50s. When critics mocked his plots, Spillane shot back: "I'm not writing for the critics." Born in Brooklyn, Spillane joined the Army right after the attack on Pearl Harbor. He honed a tough-guy writing style and created the famous detective Mike Hammer. Many of Spillane's bestsellers were made into movies—and spawned countless imitators. Publishers have sold more than 220 million copies of his books worldwide.

The Teamsters' longtime leader Daniel J. Tobin (*right*) led the International Brotherhood of Teamsters for decades. An influential voice for labor, Tobin oversaw the rapid expansion of his union before facing a storm of controversy. A native of County Clare, Tobin moved to Boston in 1890 and became Teamsters president in 1907. The union experienced rapid growth in the 1910s and 1920s. Tobin became a close aide to Franklin Roosevelt, but by the 1940s the Teamsters became synonymous with corruption. He stepped down as president in 1952.

America loves Lucy As television found a place in American living rooms in the 1950s, two Irish American entertainers were part of what became one of the era's classic pioneering shows. Lucille Ball, whose mother was part Irish, and William Frawley, an accomplished Irish American film actor, were part

of an ensemble that made *I Love Lucy* must-see TV in the era of black-and-white shows. In this 1953 image, the two stars embrace at a party celebrating the 13th anniversary of Ball's marriage to co-star Desi Arnaz.

June 24, 1954: The Oscar-winning film *On The Waterfront* is released. It stars Marlon Brando as Terry Malloy and Karl Malden as Father Barry, whose character was inspired by real-life crime-busting priest John Corridan.

July 20, 1954: Maureen Connolly's tennis career comes to a sudden end when she is hit by a truck while horseback riding.

December 2, 1954: The Senate passes an official condemnation of Senator Joseph McCarthy, with a split vote on the Republican side of the aisle and unanimity from the Democrats.

1955: The American Federation of Labor merges with the Congress of Industrial Organizations to create the AFL-CIO. AFL president George Meany becomes president of the new mega-union.

July 17, 1955: Irish American producer, animator, and entrepreneur Walt Disney opens Disneyland in Anaheim, California.

October 1, 1955: The television comedy *The Honeymooners* premieres, starring Irish Americans Jackie Gleason (as Ralph Kramden) and Art Carney (as Kramden's friend and sidekick, Ed Norton).

November 19, 1955: Right-wing icon William F. Buckley, Jr., launches *National Review,* America's preeminent conservative political journal.

February 8, 1956: Connie Mack, who as a player, manager, and owner was a mainstay of Major League Baseball for more than six decades, dies at age 93.

March 1956: A machinery accident in a Dover, New Hampshire, factory leaves Irish folk singer Tommy Makem out of work, inspiring him to join musical forces with his friends the Clancy Brothers.

Golf's dominant player The normally stoic Ben Hogan breaks character while teaching Madelon Leonard how to handle an iron. Despite a horrific car accident in 1949, which nearly killed him and his wife, Valerie, Ben Hogan was the dominant golfer of his era. Raised in Dublin, Texas, Hogan won more than 60 PGA tournaments, including a stirring victory in the 1950 U.S. Open after recovering from his accident. His best year was 1953, when he won all three major tournaments he entered—a feat that has come to be called the "Hogan Slam." Hogan's life was turned into a movie two years earlier in *Follow the Sun,* starring Glenn Ford.

JFK, Jackie tie the knot U.S. congressman John F. Kennedy, the son of former U.S. ambassador Joseph Kennedy, began dating reporter Jacqueline Bouvier in 1952. Jackie had been engaged until then, while Jack was pursuing bachelorhood with a vengeance. Nonetheless, the ambitious Massachusetts politician was drawn to the cultured, intellectual beauty. Since they shared many interests, it was only a matter of time before the newly elected senator proposed. On September 12, 1953, 750 guests gathered in Newport, Rhode Island, to witness what the press dubbed "the wedding of the year," which rivaled anything in Hollywood for glamour and star appeal.

"Little Mo" wins the Grand Slam

Born in 1934, Maureen "Little Mo" Connolly became one of the first super-stars of women's tennis. Raised in San Diego, she was encouraged by her mother to take up the sport, and in 1947 she won the Southern California Invitational Tennis Championship.

Other championships quickly followed. The apex of her career came in 1953, when she won the Grand Slam of tennis: Wimbledon and the U.S., Australian, and French Opens. Fame was fleeting, however. The next year, a horseback riding accident ended her athletic career.

Masculine hero In the middle decades of the 20th century, Burt Lancaster was Hollywood's version of the masculine hero: ruggedly handsome, supremely confident, intense, and tough. Perhaps his upbringing in a poor, working-class family with Protestant Irish roots in East Harlem—and his later professional work as an acrobat—molded him that way. Lancaster is best remembered for his iconic beach love scene with Deborah Kerr (*pictured*) in *From Here to Eternity* (1953). He also won a best actor Oscar for his role in *Elmer Gantry* (1960).

Considine pens the big stories Bob Considine ranked among the premier Irish American newspaper reporters and columnists of the mid-20th century. Working for Hearst newspapers, Considine earned a reputation for the classic big story, often comprised of seemingly small details. Considine wrote more than two dozen books and movie screenplays, covering everything from war to sports. His works included a biography of Babe Ruth, published just before the baseball legend's death. Considine, who once said that he would grope for the nearest open grave if he had no newspaper to work for, died in 1975 at age 68.

An expert on schizophrenia Harry Stack Sullivan was a pioneer in the study of schizophrenia. He also authored a book on the interpersonal theory of psychiatry (*pictured*), which focused on relationships rather than on patients as individuals. He believed that patients suffering from schizophrenia were not incurable, and that the cure might be found in cultural forces that shaped the patients' relationships. Sullivan, a graduate of the Chicago School of Medicine and Surgery, died in 1949 at age 56.

March 1956: Thomas Dooley, a Navy physician and prominent Catholic, is forced to resign from the service for allegedly engaging in a homosexual act while touring to promote his new anti-Communist tome, *Deliver Us from Evil*.

July 25, 1956: The original GI Bill expires after sending nearly eight million war veterans to college and into other educational and training programs.

September 30, 1956: President Dwight Eisenhower nominates Irish American jurist William Brennan to the U.S. Supreme Court.

December 11, 1956: The Irish Republican Army (IRA) launches Operation Harvest, an effort to capture British Northern Ireland with a campaign against military and infrastructure targets.

1957: Father John Corridan, an Irish American priest, accepts a teaching position in upstate New York after more than a decade battling corruption on Manhattan's waterfront.
• Former Boston mayor James Curley pens his autobiography, *I'd Do It Again*. • Irish American playwright Eugene O'Neill wins a Pulitzer Prize for Drama for his play *A Long Day's Journey into Night*. • After six years in production and boasting some 30 million weekly TV viewers, Bishop Fulton Sheen's *Life Is Worth Living* is discontinued.

January 10, 1957: Harold Macmillan takes office as Britain's prime minister, replacing the outgoing Anthony Eden.

January 30, 1957: Senator John McClellan forms a committee to investigate the symbiotic relationship between labor unions and organized crime.

May 2, 1957: Senator Joseph McCarthy dies of complications from cirrhosis of the liver.

O'Neill's journey When Irish American playwright Eugene O'Neill finished writing *A Long Day's Journey into Night* in 1942, he stated that he didn't want it published until 25 years after his death. The play was based on his troubled family, whom he didn't want to disparage. Yet three years after O'Neill's 1953 death, the play premiered on Broadway. It was dubbed a masterpiece. Fredric March (*right*) played James Tyrone, Sr., an Irish actor based on Eugene's father, James O'Neill. Florence Eldridge (*left*) played Mary Cavan Tyrone, who, like Eugene's mother, was addicted to morphine. The play won a Tony Award for the best play of 1956.

Kilgallen's gossip Film and later television spawned a new generation of gossip and social writers. In Dorothy Kilgallen, the newspaper business had a social columnist who could keep up with all that was news, gossip, and in between. Her syndicated newspaper column, *The Voice of Broadway*, ran for 27 years. The Chicago-born Kilgallen herself moved through the media's expanding outlets, starring on a radio show with her husband, Richard Tollmar, and later as a fixture on the hugely popular 1960s television show *What's My Line?*. Tragically, Kilgallen died from a drug overdose at age 52 in 1965.

Moving On Up

Irish America changed tremendously in the years following World War II. Much of this change was due to the educational benefits offered by the GI Bill. In unprecedented numbers, young Irish Americans received a college education and became professors, physicians, lawyers, and accountants. Where their parents had been working-class, they were now professionals.

With their newfound affluence, coupled with the postwar boom in housing construction, the Irish were able to move out of the crowded tenements and row houses of their old ethnic neighborhoods and into the single-family homes of the suburbs. In San Francisco, the Irish in the Mission District gradually

Irish in business, civil service, and the Church

moved to more comfortable homes in Marin County and on the Peninsula. Similar migratory changes took place in Chicago, Boston, and New York City. In moving up, the Irish also moved out.

Their emergence in positions of business leadership reflected their changed circumstances. Michael Flatley, a young Irishman who fought in the Korean War, received an education at Northeastern University and Boston College through the GI Bill, and in 1958 he founded a development company. By 1990 the company owned more than 75 properties in New England, mainly shopping malls, hotels, and residential complexes. New Jersey-born Charles Feeney, who was educated at Cornell in the early 1950s, made a fortune in real estate, hotels, energy, and information technology. In the 1990s, *Forbes* magazine described him as one of the 400 richest individuals in America.

In the field of law, success stories abound. In 1956 William Brennan, from a working-class Irish family in New-

ark, New Jersey, was appointed to the Supreme Court. At the end of the century, Kathleen Sullivan, a brilliant Harvard-educated lawyer, was named dean of Stanford's prestigious law school.

As the Irish became more affluent and moved to the suburbs, they left some of the patterns of their old lives behind. Because political patronage had little meaning in well-off middle-class communities, the suburban Irish were less interested in old-style ward politics.

Despite the obvious success of the Curleys in Boston and the Daleys in Chicago, the days of the urban Irish boss—so well described in the Edwin O'Connor novel, *The Last Hurrah*—had passed. Other institutions once strongly entrenched in urban Irish America also had trouble making the transition to suburbia. For example, such fraternal organizations as the Knights of Columbus and the Ancient Order of Hibernians gained little membership in the growing suburbs. Increasingly, transplanted city dwellers sent their children to public rather than parochial schools.

Although Irish America changed, Irish identity remained strong. Irishness had always existed more in intangibles than in the easily observed. A sense of humor and the ability to laugh at oneself remained characteristically Irish, as did contempt for any form of pretension. Too great an emphasis on material possessions was looked on as a fault, and helping one's fellow man was the greatest virtue. Charles Feeney, in giving away millions of dollars of his fortune, once expressed his Irish disdain for material possessions in saying, "You can only wear one pair of shoes at a time."

The premier broadcast journalist
Edward R. Murrow's journey from a log cabin in North Carolina to world fame echoed that of earlier Scots-Irish groundbreakers. He initially ascended to the very top echelon of American journalism through the medium of radio. His CBS broadcasts during World War II brought the European conflict into the homes of otherwise isolated Americans. Murrow's reports, rounded off with his signature "Good night and good luck," included firsthand accounts of bombing raids over London. When Murrow moved into television in the 1950s, he used his reach and influence to combat McCarthyism. He died in 1965.

The original McDonalds Billions and billions have been served thanks to the brothers McDonald. Maurice and Richard opened their first restaurant in San Bernadino, California, in 1948. Maurice "Mac" McDonald and Richard were, however, a pop and pop duo until they teamed with Chicago-born Ray Kroc, who initially saw the small McDonald's chain as an outlet for his milk shake machines. Kroc and the McDonalds reached a sale deal in 1954 that included royalties for the brothers based on future revenue. But Kroc rescinded on royalties when the McDonalds declined to sell him their original restaurant. The brothers came away with about $2 million, but lost out on all those future burger sales because the royalty agreement had not been in writing.

"McCarthyism is Americanism with its sleeves rolled."

—U.S. SENATOR JOSEPH McCARTHY

McCarthy and the Red scare Wisconsin senator Joseph McCarthy (*left*) sits through the infamous Army-McCarthy hearings of 1954. McCarthy, whose Irish Catholic parents raised him in rural Wisconsin, rose to national prominence by arguing that Communists were infiltrating every level of the U.S. government. McCarthy's apparent patriotism and anti-communism struck a chord with many Catholic Americans, who despised the anti-religious nature of communism and who were still looking to assimilate into the American mainstream. McCarthy, however, quickly became a demagogue. He lost whatever credibility he had when he claimed that even the military was rife with Communists.

Hollywood's handsome star Gregory Peck was one of Hollywood's most handsome and durable leading men, starring in classics from the 1940s (*Gentlemen's Agreement*) through the 1990s (*Other People's Money*). In between, he was nominated for five Academy Awards, including a win as best actor in 1963 for *To Kill a Mockingbird*. Born in San Diego, Peck was the grandson of Catherine Ashe, who was related to Easter Rising figure Thomas Ashe. In 1997 *Irish America* magazine named Peck its Irish American of the year. He later became a founding patron of the University College Dublin School of Film.

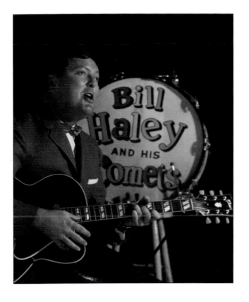

Haley rocks around the clock Bill Haley and His Comets helped spark a revolution in 1954. Their hit single "Rock Around the Clock" jumped to the top of the charts that year and helped make rock 'n' roll popular and acceptable to white audiences. Haley had begun as a country performer, but after an early hit in 1951 with "Rocket 88," he turned his attention to rock 'n' roll. He and his bandmates captivated audiences with their matching plaid jackets and swinging stage presence. "Rock Around the Clock," released on May 10, 1954, eventually sold more than 25 million copies.

The Life of Riley A popular radio program in the 1940s, and then an equally popular TV show in the 1950s, *The Life of Riley* starred William Bendix (seen with Lugene Sanders) as affable but bumbling blue-collar worker Chester Riley. The title for the show came from the well-known phrase that implied a life of ease and contentment. The origins of the term are obscure. One source suggests it may have come from the 1880s song "The Best in the House Is None Too Good for Riley." A more likely origin was the late 19th century poems of James Riley, which featured barefoot boys loafing and enjoying life.

The Irish of Dearborn Mickey Conner sets up for an inside pitch to Mother Claudia at St. Bernadette's School in Dearborn, Michigan. Throughout the 20th century, this Detroit suburb was a classic ethnic community with a large concentration of American Irish. Social life for Irish Catholics centered around the parish church and parochial school. Besides being the headquarters of the Ford Motor Company, Dearborn's chief claim to fame from 1942 until 1978 was that its mayor—Orville Hubbard—was one of the most outspoken segregationists north of the Mason-Dixon Line. Ironically, Hubbard had little use for the Irish, but they kept him in office because of his commitment to keep Dearborn white.

October 8, 1957: Dodgers team owner Walter O'Malley announces that his baseball club will leave Brooklyn and begin the 1958 season in Los Angeles.

November 27, 1957: A daughter, Caroline, is born in New York City to Jacqueline and Senator John F. Kennedy.

1958: Cardinal Spellman, archbishop of New York, serves as a cardinal elector in the papal conclave that names the new Pope, John XXIII. ● Irish American rocker Eddie Cochran shoots to stardom on the beat of his chart-topping hit, "Summertime Blues."

November 1958: Edmund Gerald Brown, Sr., known as "Pat," is elected the 32nd governor of California. His son, Jerry, will follow in his footsteps in 1974.

November 12, 1958: Iconic Boston politician James Michael Curley dies. He will be buried in New Calvary Cemetery following the largest funeral in Boston's history.

1959: Eamon de Valera is elected president of Ireland, an office he will hold for two full, seven-year terms.

April 1959: NASA announces the final selection of Astronaut Group 1, more commonly known as the Mercury Seven. The storied group includes Irish American astronaut John Glenn.

October 14, 1959: Years of self-abuse catch up with former Hollywood heart-throb Errol Flynn, who dies at age 50.

May 1, 1960: An American U-2 spy plane piloted by CIA flyer Francis Gary Powers (an Irish American) is shot down over Sverdlovsk in the Soviet Union, further chilling relations between the two nations. Powers will be detained by the Soviets for 21 months before being returned to the U.S. in a spy swap.

Unemployment plagues Northern Ireland Prior to the outbreak of the violent "Troubles" in the 1960s, Northern Ireland still had many problems. Though industry in the region had boomed during the war years, unemployment rose sharply as the war economy came to a close. Changes in agricultural technology also hurt farmers. By the mid-1950s, as many as 30,000 Northern Irish were unemployed. Derry had a 20 percent unemployment rate. Such economic hardships were typically worse in Catholic neighborhoods, where discrimination remained a fact of life.

Immigrants of the '50s Irish immigration to the United States during the 20th century was marked by roughly 30-year intervals. The 1950s witnessed one such spurt, with tens of thousands making the trip across the Atlantic. They arrived via ship at Ellis Island and other ports in the early part of the decade, then came largely by plane at decade's end. Many of these immigrants entered the military and public service. At a time when Irish Americans were assimilating into mainstream society—especially in the burgeoning suburbs—the new immigrants ensured the survival of Irish culture.

Labor's Powerful Leader

William George Meany, one of the foremost labor leaders in American history, embodied the American dream. His grandparents migrated from Ireland to America in the 1850s and settled in New York City, where they hoped to build a better life for their children. His father, Michael, worked long hours as a plumber in the Bronx. Born in 1894, young George followed in his father's footsteps. He dropped out of school at age 14 and joined his father in the plumbing trade. The younger Meany was both bright and ambitious. He was elected to the executive board of the United Association of Plumbers and Steam Fitters at age 24 before becoming president of the New York State Federation of Labor in 1934.

George Meany

In 1939 Meany became secretary-treasurer of the powerful American Federation of Labor (AFL). During World War II, he served on the War Labor Board and expanded the AFL's membership base. The subsequent Cold War brought the wrath of many anti-Communist congressmen who began accusing the labor movement of harboring socialists and other political subversives. After the passage of the anti-union Taft-Hartley Act in 1947, Meany leapt into action. He took a hard-line stance against far-left politics, warning fellow union members of Moscow's attempt to "dominate the entire world with their godless ideology of communism."

In 1952 Meany ascended to the presidency of the AFL and merged his union with the CIO. Meany converted the AFL-CIO into a powerful lobbying force in Washington, and he was instrumental in electing Harry Truman, John Kennedy, and Lyndon Johnson to the presidency.

Throughout the 1960s, Meany strongly supported the war effort in Vietnam while also supporting the civil rights movement and the largely Hispanic United Farm Workers. Until his death in 1980, Meany held true to the union, stating, "The basic goal of labor will not change. It is . . . to better the standards of life for all who work for wages and to seek decency and justice and dignity for all Americans."

Daley rules Chicago Richard J. Daley was one of the most powerful Irish American mayors ever. He ruled Chicago for more than 20 years, beginning with his 1955 election (*pictured*). A devout Catholic, Daley lived most of his life in the South Side Irish enclave where he had grown up. Daley became known as a "president maker" within Democratic circles. His image was tarnished by the violent events of the 1968 Chicago Democratic convention. Still, in his last election he received nearly 60 percent of the vote. Daley died while still in office in 1976. His son, Richard M. Daley, was elected mayor in 1989 and remained in office well into the 21st century.

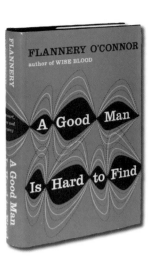

Kelly's political satire It's not easy to blacklist a cartoon character, so Senator Joseph McCarthy was stuck with wildcat Simple J. Malarkey, an inhabitant of Okefenokee Swamp in Walt Kelly's daily strip *Pogo*. Beginning in 1948, *Pogo* delivered to newspaper readers across America a cast of animal characters that uproariously parodied politicians and political and social issues. Philadelphia-born Kelly proposed the strip's central character, Pogo the Possum, for the presidency every four years. The strip's most famous line, "We have met the enemy and he is us," was first used on a Pogo poster for Earth Day in 1970.

Purveyor of southern Gothicism A devout Roman Catholic from the South, Flannery O'Connor was one of America's most powerfully unique, and deeply religious, writers. Her stories are laced with ghosts, freaks, dread, and other Gothic elements. Yet there is also a powerful sense of Christian redemption. In the title story of her 1955 collection, *A Good Man Is Hard to Find,* a character called the "Misfit" murders a woman, yet O'Connor forces readers to reexamine their notions of good and evil. O'Connor died at age 39 after living with lupus for more than a decade.

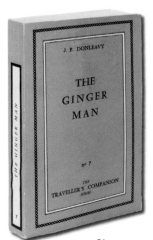

Donleavy's Dangerfield In his novel *The Ginger Man* (1955), J. P. Donleavy created one of the most lovable rogues in American literature, Sebastian Dangerfield, who carouses and drinks his way through postwar Dublin. To an extent, Dangerfield's escapades reflected Donleavy's own experiences while a student at Dublin's Trinity College following World War II. Rejected by American publishers because of its racy content, *The Ginger Man* was first published by Paris's Olympia Press, which was known for its interest in erotica. None of Donleavy's succeeding novels met with the success of *The Ginger Man.*

"Queen of the Jungle" Tall, blonde, and buxom, Nellie "Irish" McCalla starred in the TV series *Sheena, Queen of the Jungle,* which aired in 1955–56. Of Irish and Franco-Swiss ancestry, McCalla first caught people's attention as a model for pinup artist Alberto Vargas. As Sheena, McCalla was required to do little more than swing on vines. Though remembered by fans for her gentle nature on the show, she never developed as an actress. She later became an artist, completing more than 1,000 paintings.

A cool jazz musician Jazz musician Gerry Mulligan and his baritone saxophone were the very definition of "cool" from the 1940s until his death in 1996. The New York native began his career while still a teenager in 1944. He quickly captured the attention of the

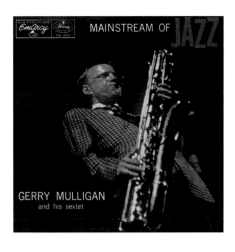

notable jazz artists Charlie Parker and Miles Davis. Mulligan collaborated with Davis on the album *Birth of the Cool,* which launched both men as jazz superstars. Mulligan wrote and composed in addition to playing the saxophone, and he jammed with the likes of Stan Getz, Thelonious Monk, and Dave Brubeck.

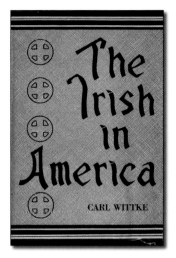

Groundbreaking history
In 1956 Carl Wittke published *The Irish in America,* the first attempt by an academic historian to document the story of the Irish in the United States. Prior to Wittke's book, some work had been done on the Scots-Irish, but very little had been written about the massive numbers of Irish Catholics who had entered the United States beginning in the 1840s. Wittke's work, along with the election of John F. Kennedy as president, changed that: In the second half of the 20th century, hundreds of books explored every facet of the Irish American experience.

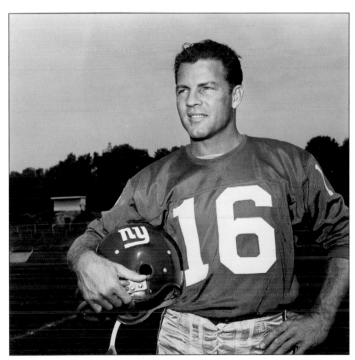

A Giant superstar A golden boy from the University of Southern California, Frank Gifford enjoyed a legendary career with the New York Giants. Gifford starred as a running back, receiver, and defensive back—and on occasion passed and kicked the pigskin. The eight-time Pro Bowler led the Giants to five NFL Championship Games. In 1956 he won the league MVP Award as well as the NFL title. Gifford remained a household name throughout the century, first as the play-by-play announcer for *Monday Night Football* and then as the husband of talk show celebrity Kathie Lee Gifford.

Mills's views influence the New Left Columbia University sociologist and Irish American C. Wright Mills published his influential *The Power Elite* in 1956. Mills argued that in spite of the alleged power of public opinion and democratic institutions, America had come to be dominated by a small group of powerful, loosely connected elites from government, the corporate world, the military, the media, and higher education—often referred to as "the establishment." Although representatives from these groups were not formally organized, they often knew each other, possessed shared interests, and tended to build consensuses, thus bypassing regular governmental channels in shaping public opinion. Mills's work profoundly influenced the anti-establishment New Left of the 1960s.

Irish American Princess

When Grace Kelly died after a car crash in Monaco in September 1982, it was as if both Ireland and Irish America had lost a princess. Kelly, the daughter of a Philadelphia construction magnate, had been a great source of pride for Irish Americans, a pride matched only by John F. Kennedy's rise to the White House. Both Kelly and Kennedy had provided a mid-20th century version of Camelot—each, interestingly, with spousal ties to French soil.

Grace Patricia Kelly achieved fame with her beauty and acting skills. She made her screen debut in 1951, and before long she was a Hollywood star thanks to performances alongside Gary Cooper in *High Noon* and Clark Gable in *Mogambo*—as well as leading roles in three Hitchcock classics, *Dial M for Murder* (1954), *Rear Window* (1954), and *To Catch a Thief* (1955). However, it was her fairytale April 1956 marriage to Prince Rainier III of Monaco that elevated her to popular culture's pantheon.

Kelly met Rainier at the 1955 Cannes Film Festival, and they were married within a year. The marriage gave the couple three children and lasted until Grace's death at just 53. As princess, Grace visited Ireland. Like so many Irish Americans, she was drawn to the country because of her family roots. Throughout her life, she collected a considerable number of Irish books and pieces of music. Today, her collection lies at the heart of Monaco's Princess Grace Irish Library.

Grace Kelly

The Bridey Murphy craze

In 1956 Morey Bernstein's *The Search for Bridey Murphy* ignited interest in the notion of reincarnation. In his book, therapist Bernstein recounted how while using hypnosis on one of his subjects—a woman he called Ruth Simmons—she revealed her former life as an Irish woman in 19th century County Cork, complete with Irish brogue and details of her Irish life. The book was an international bestseller. Later investigations showed no evidence of a Bridey Murphy in Ireland and attributed Simmons's stories to youthful imaginings.

TRUE STORIES OF THE STRANGE AND THE UNKNOWN

November 1956

35¢

BRIDEY MURPHY IN IRELAND

A Personal Investigation

By WILLIAM J. BARKER

Square but hip

Decades after *The Ed Sullivan Show* ended, millions of Americans can still hear in their minds the distinctive voice of Ed Sullivan introducing the likes of Elvis Presley and the Beatles. Sullivan, a former boxer and New York entertainment columnist, made the move to television at the point when audiences were becoming truly mass. From 1948 to '71, his variety show featured everything from opera singers to circus performers. Sullivan, who came off as something of a square, was—more than any broadcaster of his era—responsible for putting the "hip" into America's homes.

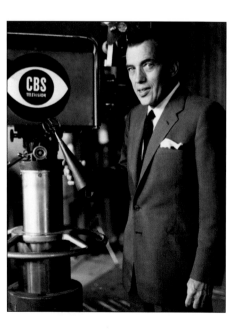

The Border War The 1950s were a tense but generally peaceful time in Northern Ireland, especially when compared to the unrest that would engulf the region in the 1960s. Still, tension existed between Catholics and Protestants. Most notoriously, the IRA waged what came to be called the Border War, setting off bombs that resulted in numerous deaths on both sides of the conflict. Though Catholics remained second-class citizens, the Border War had little support among the broader Catholic population.

Sixty years with *The New Yorker* For a magazine that for so long published with minimal colorful illustration, *The New Yorker* has not lacked for colorful characters in its stable of writers. Foremost among them was Brendan Gill. The Connecticut-born Yale graduate was a 60-year fixture at the magazine, beginning in 1936. The author of 15 books, Gill is considered one of America's most influential writers of the period. He drew acclaim while raising eyebrows and hackles, particularly with his book *Here at the New Yorker*, which gave outsiders a peek into the weekly's inner sanctum.

McCarthy's heavy themes A prolific writer of novels, essays, and literary criticism, Mary McCarthy is best known for her novel *The Group* (1963) and her autobiographical *Memoirs of a Catholic Girlhood* (1957). Born in Seattle in 1912, McCarthy mourned the death of her parents during the flu epidemic of 1918. In *Memoirs*, she described her upbringing by a stern aunt and uncle as well as the loss of her Catholic faith. She also explored the divergence of memory from reality. *The Group*, loosely based on the lives of McCarthy's undergraduate friends at Vassar, satirized the ideals of upper-class society and the vacuity of women's lives.

A leading actress Shirley MacLaine, Warren Beatty's older sister, was one of America's leading actresses in the latter half of the 20th century. Hollywood scouts discovered her as she performed as an understudy in the Broadway production of *Pajama Game*. MacLaine's first film success came at age 21 in Alfred Hitchcock's *The Trouble With Harry* (1955). Dozens of films and five acting Oscar nominations followed. She won once, for best actress in the 1983 tearjerker *Terms of Endearment*. MacLaine's views on reincarnation garnered much press coverage in the 1980s.

May 11, 1960: The Food and Drug Administration approves the first birth control pill, due largely to efforts by Irish American physician and medical researcher Dr. John Rock.

November 8, 1960: Massachusetts senator John F. Kennedy wins a close presidential race over challenger Richard Nixon. Kennedy gets invaluable help from Chicago mayor Richard Daley's Democratic political machine.

December 17, 1960: Benjamin Smith, John Kennedy's Harvard roommate, is appointed to fill Kennedy's vacated Senate seat until Ted Kennedy is old enough to run for Senate and claim the seat himself. Accordingly, Smith agrees to not run for reelection.

1961: Bishop Sheen launches *The Fulton Sheen Program,* similar in style and content to his earlier television series. It will enjoy a seven-year, nationally syndicated run. • Ray Kroc purchases the McDonald's restaurant brand from Dick and Mac McDonald. • Veteran television journalist Edward R. Murrow ends his long tenure with CBS to take the helm of the United States Information Agency.

January 20, 1961: John F. Kennedy is sworn in as the 35th president of the United States.

March 1961: The Irish folk quartet the Clancy Brothers & Tommy Makem are signed by Columbia Records following their impressive national debut on *The Ed Sullivan Show.*

April 12, 1961: Shortly before America's Bay of Pigs invasion of Cuba, President Kennedy makes a critical decision to withhold U.S. troops from the assault orchestrated by his own CIA, forcing the Cuban expatriates to go in without military support.

A traditional *Feis* Young women of Chicago compete in a dance competition in the 1958 Pilsen Park *Feis*. A *Feis* is a traditional Gaelic arts and cultural festival, the origins of which date back to Ancient Ireland. Back then, Gaels celebrated with music, dance, sports, and theater. In modern times, dance competitions are often the highlight of these festivals. Halifax, Nova Scotia, currently boasts the largest annual *Feis* in North America.

Clancy Brothers & Tommy Makem The Irish were destined to be on board the folk music train when it hit top speed in the 1950s. At decade's end, it was the Aran-sweatered Clancy Brothers & Tommy Makem who flew the Irish flag highest in folk central, Greenwich Village in New York City. The group (Makem is second from the left) popularized traditional Irish music for American audiences. Their 1959 album, *Come Fill Your Glass with Us*—packed with Irish drinking songs—sparked their success.

The Last Hurrah

At the opening of *The Last Hurrah*, Edwin O'Connor's 1956 novel about the passing of a big-city boss, the author assures that any resemblance the story bears to real people or events is "purely coincidental." As historian James J. Connolly notes, "These are perhaps the only lines in the book that no reader believed true." The universal assumption was that O'Connor modeled his main character, Frank Skeffington, on Boston's James Michael Curley, who was at the center of Boston politics for half a century.

James Curley

Born in 1874 to County Galway immigrants, Curley lost his father at age 10. He entered politics in his early 20s and won positions in city government and the Massachusetts legislature. Curley beat a Democratic machine veteran, John "Honey Fitz" Fitzgerald, in 1914 to win his first of four terms as Boston's mayor. He eventually served four terms in Congress and one as Massachusett's governor. His electoral success was blemished by two jail terms for fraud—once while he was Boston's sitting mayor.

Curley was both celebrated and infamous for his mastery of patronage and his manipulation of the public treasury. His financial policies were blamed, in part, for Boston's steep economic decline in the 1940s and 1950s.

A magnificent speaker with a devastating wit, he was also a scheming trickster. For example, in his 1924 race for governor, during which the Ku Klux Klan was in the midst of a national resurgence, Curley created incidents by getting workers to set crosses ablaze outside his campaign rallies.

In *The Last Hurrah*, stated historian John V. Kelleher, O'Connor was trying to capture the passing of an age, "the end of Irish-American individuality and wild vigor." The figure that emerged—Skeffington—was brilliant, raffish, and perhaps a bit disreputable, but noble all the same.

The parallels between the fictional mayor and the real one were evident to most readers, including Curley. The ancient politician spent his last years basking in the novel's glow. As biographer Jack Beatty wrote in *The Rascal King*, O'Connor's novel helped shift Curley's reputation from scoundrel to character, a transformation he clearly enjoyed before his death in 1958.

A rock sensation Though just 21 when he died, Minnesota native Eddie Cochran changed the face of rock 'n' roll. With such hits as "Summertime Blues," "C'mon Everybody," and "Twenty Flight Rock," he captured the teen experience with humor and panache. Cochran inspired a diverse range of rock pioneers, from the Beatles to the Sex Pistols. He was a groundbreaking guitarist whose influence could be heard in the Who's Pete Townsend as well as Jimi Hendrix. In April 1960, Cochran died in a car crash. He was inducted into the Rock and Roll Hall of Fame in 1987.

Williams hangs with mixed company Politi-cal controversy can be lucrative. A graduate of Georgetown, attorney Edward Bennett Williams made his repu-

tation defending such divisive figures as U.S. senator Joe McCarthy and union boss Jimmy Hoffa. Here he testifies at a Rackets Committee hearing in 1958. A staunch Catholic, Williams served as a confidant of presidents, from Kennedy to Reagan. Later in life, he became a philanthropist. As a leader of the Knights of Malta, he was a key supporter of Mother Teresa—even as he devoted time to the sports teams that he partly owned, the NFL's Washington Redskins and MLB's Baltimore Orioles.

Touhy's downfall Roger Touhy was the son of a widowed Irish-born Chicago cop. Along with four of his brothers, Roger chose a life of crime over the law. During Prohibition, he became one of Chicago's biggest beer distributors, thus prompting takeover bids by Al Capone that spiraled into violence. Capone couldn't outgun Touhy's gang, but he succeeded in framing him for the 1933 kidnapping of John Factor—brother of cosmetics king Max Factor. Touhy went to jail in 1934, was paroled in 1959, and was shot dead within a month.

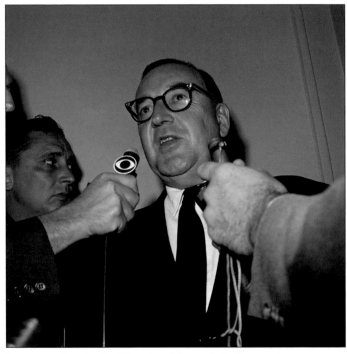

Brown rules in California Edmund G. Brown, better known as "Pat," was an Irish American politician in Califor-nia who served two terms as the state's governor (1959 to 1967). Brown, a liberal Democrat, helped build California's massive higher-education system. He famously defeated former vice president Richard Nixon in 1962 when Nixon tried a political comeback after losing the presidency to John Kennedy in 1960. But four years later, in 1966, Brown lost to another future president, Ronald Reagan. Brown's son, Jerry, succeeded Reagan as governor. Pat Brown died in 1996 at the age of 90.

Ryan chronicles World War II Dublin-born Cornelius Ryan was one of the great chroniclers of the Second World War. His three most important books— *The Longest Day, The Last Battle,* and *A Bridge Too Far*—described the war not simply in terms of statistics and grand strat-egy, but in the experiences of common soldiers and everyday people. Ryan began his career as a journalist in London dur-ing WWII, then moved to the United States in 1947. He had

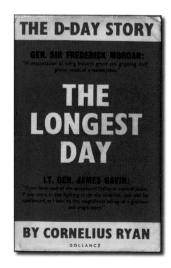

THE D-DAY STORY

GEN. SIR FREDERICK MORGAN:

THE
LONGEST
DAY

LT. GEN. JAMES GAVIN:

BY CORNELIUS RYAN
GOLLANCZ

a long and distinguished career as an editor, first at *Collier's* magazine and then with *Reader's Digest*.

Support for a Catholic president Jesuit priest John Courtney Murray countered those who virulently opposed a Catholic presidency. Murray was born during the Teddy Roosevelt administration at a time when the presidency was the preserve of Protestants of various denominations. Murray's 1960 book, *We Hold These Truths: Catholic*

Reflections on the American Proposition, defended the idea that a Catholic could lead his country without running afoul of faith. Religion was certainly an issue in the 1960 election: John Kennedy was a Catholic and Richard Nixon a Quaker.

The art of Georgia O'Keeffe Georgia O'Keeffe ranks among America's preeminent modern artists. O'Keeffe's paternal grandparents emigrated from Ireland in the 1840s and settled in Wisconsin, where she was born and raised. After studying art at a convent school in Madison and at the Art Institute of Chicago, she moved in 1918 to New York, where she later married photographer Alfred Stieglitz. After her husband died in 1946, O'Keeffe moved permanently to New Mexico, an area she had been visiting since the 1920s. O'Keeffe's imagery reflected dramatic desert landscapes, stark animal bones, and colorful close-ups of flowers—images now famously associated with the Southwest, and with O'Keeffe.

"The jungle doctor" Dr. Tom Dooley's crusades against disease and communism in Southeast Asia made him a popular hero. As a naval officer in 1954, Dooley witnessed the flight of refugees from Communist North Vietnam. Not content with writing a best-selling book, *Deliver Us from Evil,* Dooley plunged back into a corner of the world that was on the verge of even greater conflict. He founded St. Patrick's Hospital in Laos, established the Medical International Cooperation Organization, and became known as "the jungle doctor." He died from cancer at age 34 in 1961.

Rock supports "the pill" One of the inventors of the oral method of contraception—"the pill"—was Dr. John Rock, a devout Irish Catholic from Massachusetts and a longtime professor of obstetrics and gynecology at Harvard Medical School. His concern for the health and safety of women initially led him to advocate the rhythm method of contraception, which the Catholic Church advocated. He later vigorously defended use of the pill, which he believed, like the rhythm method, worked naturally with a woman's physiology. The Church took a different view, and in the 1968 encyclical *Humanae Vitae* it declared the use of oral contraceptives immoral.

1946-63

April 17, 1961: Burt Lancaster wins a best actor Oscar for his work in *Elmer Gantry*.

April 17–19, 1961: The U.S.-planned Bay of Pigs invasion fails dramatically, as Castro's military handily defeats a 1,300-man attack force of Cuban exiles. More than 200 die, while nearly 2,000 others are captured and imprisoned. The fiasco is considered John F. Kennedy's greatest failing as president.

1962: Concerned with the proliferation of dangerous agricultural pesticides, ecologist Rachel Carson releases *Silent Spring*, a call for people to live in harmony with the Earth. Carson's book is widely credited with launching the modern environmental movement.
• John McCormack, an Irish American Bostonian, is named 53rd speaker of the U.S. House of Representatives.
• Michael Harrington publishes *The Other America*, a far-reaching exposé of poverty in America. Years later, President Lyndon Johnson will invite Harrington to sit on a planning board as Johnson crafts his administration's "War on Poverty."

February 20, 1962: Irish American astronaut John Glenn becomes the first American to orbit the Earth, aboard the NASA spacecraft *Friendship 7*.

February 26, 1962: The Irish Republican Army officially declares an end to its disastrous Border Campaign, code-named Operation Harvest.

April 11, 1962: The New York Mets, a National League expansion team brought to the city thanks to the efforts of William Shea, play their first game. The team's home ballpark, Shea Stadium, will be named for their benefactor.

October 14, 1962: The Kennedy administration gains solid evidence of Soviet missile installations in Cuba when an American U-2 spy plane returns with aerial photographs.

The baby boom As millions of Americans returned home after World War II, families were reunited or newly created. And then came children, by the millions. Irish Americans were eager participants in the 1946–64 baby boom, as this picture of an extended-family gathering suggests. The Irish shared with their fellow Americans a sense of optimism thanks to the nation's soaring postwar economy. Good jobs and affordable housing allowed the Irish to feed more mouths than ever before.

The Catholic faith Even in the midst of dizzying changes after World War II, the rituals of Catholicism—the dominant religious tradition of Irish America—remained very much the same. Irish Catholics abstained from meat on Friday, often went to confession on Saturday afternoon, and murmured responses in Latin during Sunday morning Mass. Irish clergy remained firmly in charge of the Church in America, most prominently Cardinal Francis Spellman of New York. All the while, Irish American nuns educated generations of schoolchildren and cared for the sick in the Church's sprawling health care network.

> "Mr. President, with a bit of luck and the help of a few close friends, you're going to carry Illinois."
> —CHICAGO MAYOR RICHARD J. DALEY TO JOHN KENNEDY ON ELECTION NIGHT, 1960

The "American pope" A towering figure in American Catholicism, Francis Cardinal Spellman was New York's archbishop for nearly 30 years. Seen here in 1960 with presidential candidates Richard Nixon and John F. Kennedy, Spellman was referred to by biographer John Cooney as the "American pope." Born in Massachusetts, Spellman became New York's spiritual leader in 1939. During World War II, he became a close adviser to President Roosevelt, and after the war he was an outspoken anti-Communist. This led to controversy when he became an ally of Senator Joseph McCarthy and, later, publicly supported the Vietnam War.

JFK's rise to the White House When he was a young man, John Fitzgerald Kennedy thought he would pursue a career in journalism. Politics was to be the profession of his older brother, Joseph Kennedy, Jr. But when Joseph was killed during World War II, the burden of expectations fell on young Jack's narrow shoulders. He won election to the House of Representatives from Boston in 1946, and he served in the U.S. Senate from 1953 to '60. Although his record was not especially sparkling, Kennedy was smart, movie-star handsome, and very much a centrist Democrat. In the 1960 presidential primaries, he defeated such notables as Adlai Stevenson, Texas senator Lyndon Johnson, and Minnesota senator Hubert Humphrey. He then narrowly defeated Vice President Richard Nixon in November, and became the nation's first Catholic president.

JFK ADDRESSES IOWA "FAH-MAHS"

One night during the 1960 campaign he was speaking to a crowd of farmers in Sioux City, Iowa, where his clipped Cape Cod accent, with its broad and flat *a* sounds and no rolling *r*'s, seemed comically out of place. He reached a climax in his oration on agricultural depression with a shouted question, "What's wrong with the American fah-mah today?" He stopped for a momentary dramatic pause, and down from the balcony loud and clear came a reply from a comical listener in a perfect imitation of the New England accent, "He's *stah*-ving!" The hall rocked with laughter, but nobody in the crowd was laughing harder than Jack Kennedy himself. He was doubled up and stamping around on the platform.

—KEN O'DONNELL, KENNEDY AIDE

O'Hara sings Irish songs As a girl, Maureen O'Hara aspired to sing opera. In the late 1950s, during a momentary lull in her screen career, the red-haired actress turned her pleasing soprano to well-received albums released by RCA

and Columbia Records. A 1958 LP, *Love Letters from Maureen O'Hara*, featured "I Only Have Eyes for You" and other standards from the Great American Songbook. With the 1961 album pictured here, O'Hara revisited her roots. She sang with all the warmth and conviction one would expect from a woman with dual Irish and American citizenship—and a keen love of Ireland.

Pulitzer-winning poet Phyllis McGinley was an acclaimed writer of children's books, poetry, songs, and more. Born in Oregon in 1905, she attended the University of Southern California. After marrying in 1937, she settled in Larchmont, New York. Critics suggest that the suburban, domestic setting inspired some of her best work, such as *Stones from a Glass House* and *A Pocketful of Wry*. In 1961 McGinley won the Pulitzer Prize for her collection of light verse *Times Three: Selected Verse from Three Decades with Seventy New Poems*.

Speaker of the House A Boston politician, John McCormack became one of the most powerful men in America when he became speaker of the U.S. House of Representatives in 1962, a position he held for nine years. Forced to drop out of school at age 13 after his father's death, McCormack was admitted to the Massachusetts bar after clerking in a law office. He was elected to the U.S. House in 1928. A progressive Democrat, he vigorously supported FDR's New Deal. Known for his integrity, McCormack was often referred to as "The Archbishop."

A priest on edge Though Edwin O'Connor's *The Last Hurrah* ranks among the most famous Irish American novels, his 1961 book, *The Edge of Sadness,* may be an even greater piece of literature. O'Connor's Pulitzer Prize-winning story centers on Father Hugh Kennedy, a doubt-ridden Catholic priest in a hard-pressed city neighborhood and his relationship with a large Irish American family of parishioners. The narrative serves as an edgy counter to the Hollywood depictions of jolly, self-assured Irish American clergy, which had been popular in preceding decades.

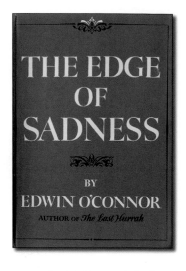

Fighter for the Underdog

A proponent of free speech, civil rights for all, and a woman's right to an abortion, Supreme Court Justice William Brennan, Jr., stands as one of the most progressive justices of the 20th century.

Brennan was born in 1906, the son of Irish immigrants from County Roscommon. He attended the University of Pennsylvania and Harvard Law School, where he studied under future Supreme Court Justice Felix Frankfurter. Although he never ranked at the very top of his class, Brennan worked hard, studying day and night. He initially worked as a private practice attorney and, during World War II, served in the Army Ordinance Department. His diligence and dedication eventually led to his appointment as a superior court judge and, later, earned him a seat on the New Jersey Supreme Court. It was during this time that Brennan began his long career of fighting for the underdog.

Brennan quickly gained a reputation for his liberal outlook, social conscience, and adherence to due process. In the case *State* v. *Midgely,* for example, he voted to free a convicted criminal because of a court irregularity, writing, "The plea of double jeopardy must be honored though a regrettable defeat of justice may result." During the election year of 1956, President Dwight Eisenhower hoped to gain support among Democrats by appointing Brennan to the Supreme Court. Over the next 34 years, Brennan emerged as the foremost defender of the Bill of Rights.

William Brennan, Jr.

In 1962 Brennan struck down southern states' attempts to undermine African American voter strength by gerrymandering legislative districts. Eleven years later, he stood firmly with the majority in the landmark decision *Roe* v. *Wade,* which deemed it unconstitutional for a state to place restrictions on abortion. In the case *Paris Adult Theater* v. *Slaton,* Brennan argued that the first amendment prohibited state and federal governments from suppressing "sexually oriented materials on the basis of their allegedly 'obscene' contents." On July 20, 1990, Brennan retired his seat, leaving a legacy that fundamentally shaped American political culture.

Kennedy's trusted aide Kenneth O'Donnell went to Harvard University with Robert Kennedy after flying 30 bombing missions over Europe during World War II. When John Kennedy won the presidency, he made O'Donnell his appointments secretary—a nondescript title that masked the power O'Donnell wielded over White House staff. He was the president's gatekeeper and confidant. Ironically, although one of several Irish American aides on the White House staff, O'Donnell originally opposed Kennedy's wish to visit Ireland in 1963. He thought it would be a waste of valuable presidential time. O'Donnell died in 1977 at age 55.

O'Hara's vibrant poems Long associated with his freewheeling poems that explore the frenetic pace of New York City, Frank O'Hara was actually born in Baltimore and grew up in Grafton, Massachusetts. O'Hara served in the Pacific during World War II before attending Harvard on the GI Bill. Once in New York, he fell in with painters, jazz musicians, and other artists. They influenced the vibrant nature of his poems, such as "The Day Lady Died" and "Ave Maria." O'Hara was just 40 when he died after being struck by a vehicle on New York's Fire Island.

Fleming explores the Jersey City machine Few writers were better positioned than Thomas Fleming to chronicle the collapse of an Irish political machine. Fleming's father was part of the Frank Hague machine in Jersey City, New Jersey, and the fall of that legendary character formed the backdrop of Fleming's first novel, *All Good Men,* published in 1961. A prolific author of both fiction and nonfiction, Fleming wrote a touching memoir in 2005 entitled *Mysteries of My Father.*

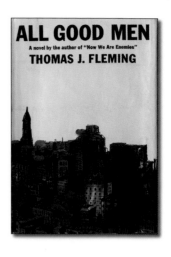

Examining his presidency Quick-witted, intellectually curious, and tremendously competitive, John F. Kennedy was a memorable president even if his short tenure prevents historians from considering him among the nation's greatest chief executives. Failure, in the form of a botched invasion of Cuba and a disastrous summit meeting with Soviet leader Nikita Khrushchev, haunted his first year in office. But his handling of the Cuban Missile Crisis, his belated recognition of the civil rights movement, his management of the nation's economy, and his determination to put an American on the moon by 1969 were all historic successes.

Glenn orbits the planet Irish, Scottish, and Americans all could beam with pride on February 20, 1962. That day, John Glenn, of Scots-Irish descent, became the first American to orbit Earth. Glenn, a fighter ace in World War II and Korea, never reached the moon. He turned his attention to politics and became a Democratic U.S. senator from Ohio in 1974. However, he donned a spacesuit again in 1998 in the Space Shuttle *Discovery,* thus becoming, at age 77, the oldest man to fly in space.

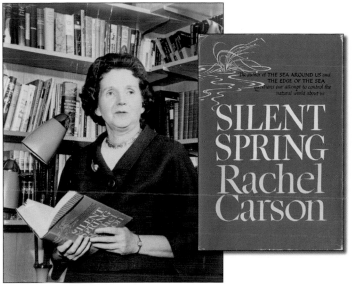

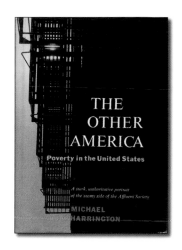

A study of American poverty Michael Harrington's 1962 book *The Other America* jarred Americans with its revelations about the extent and depth of poverty in their "affluent" country. President Kennedy was impressed enough with Harrington's analysis that he made the elimination of poverty a high priority in his administration—a goal adopted by his successor, Lyndon Johnson. Harrington himself had grown up in a middle-class Irish Catholic family during the Depression and World War II. He received a first-rate education at Holy Cross and the University of Chicago, and he spent his adult life advocating for the poor.

Carson's eye-opening book One of the founders of the environmental movement, Rachel Carson had Irish roots on both sides of her family. After receiving an M.S. in zoology from Johns Hopkins in the 1930s, she went to work for the U.S. Department of Fisheries as a marine biologist. In the 1940s and '50s, she wrote three books that became best-sellers: *Under the Sea Wind, The Sea Around Us,* and *The Edge of the Sea.* Her 1962 effort, *Silent Spring,* changed the nation. The book exposed the deleterious effects of the pesticide DDT, and it raised awareness of humans' assault on the environment.

A liberal lawyer Born in San Francisco to poor Irish immigrant parents, Vincent Hallinan became one of the city's most controversial lawyers. Along with his wife, Vivian, he supported the right of workers to unionize, fought for civil rights, and opposed the Vietnam War. In the late 1940s, he defended labor leader Harry Bridges in a celebrated trial. He once even sued the Catholic Church for fraud, demanding that it prove the existence of heaven and hell. Twice he spent time in federal prisons, once for contempt of court and once for income tax evasion. Hallinan recounted his activist legal career in his 1963 memoir, *A Lion in Court.*

The changes of Vatican II The Second Vatican Council convenes in Rome in 1962. The council, summoned by Pope John XXIII to address the Roman Catholic Church's role in the modern world, unleashed an era of change. For Irish American Catholics, the transformation affected a wide range of everyday practices. The Mass changed from Latin to English and, to the dismay of more traditional Catholics, became less formal. Vatican II relaxed the rules for fasting before taking Communion, and it opened up the Church to an expanded role for women and lay people. The council's legacy is still a subject of debate within the Church.

October 22, 1962: In a televised address to the American people, President Kennedy announces the presence of Soviet missiles in Cuba. He orders that a naval blockade of the island be enacted the following day.

October 28, 1962: Soviet premier Nikita Khrushchev delivers a radio address to Moscow announcing the withdrawal of Soviet missiles from Cuba. The move averts war and ends the Cuban Missile Crisis, the predominant event of the Kennedy administration.

November 6, 1962: Senator Ted Kennedy assumes office, taking over the Senate seat that his brother John had held before his successful presidential bid.

1963: The Chieftains, a traditional Irish music group, is founded in Dublin. They will go on to win six Grammy Awards.

April 8, 1963: Gregory Peck earns best actor honors for his work in *To Kill a Mockingbird*.

June 1963: The Papal Conclave convenes at the Vatican and names Pope Paul VI head of the Catholic Church. Cardinal Cushing of Boston serves as one of the cardinal electors, along with Cardinal Spellman of New York.

June 27, 1963: President Kennedy, arriving in Ireland on an official state visit, is given a hero's welcome by throngs of admirers.

November 22, 1963: President Kennedy is assassinated in Dallas.

November 25, 1963: President Kennedy's body is buried at Arlington National Cemetery. The elaborate state funeral ends with the first lady lighting the eternal flame at the Kennedy grave site.

The Cuban Missile Crisis John Kennedy presided over the gravest crisis of the Cold War, the Cuban Missile Crisis of October 1962. It began when Kennedy received evidence that the Soviets were building missile sites in Cuba, from which they could threaten the entire western hemisphere. While some military advisers urged him to launch an immediate air strike to destroy the sites, Kennedy chose to impose a naval quarantine of Cuba to prevent further shipments. Throughout the crisis, he relied heavily on the advice of his brother, Attorney General Robert Kennedy (*left*). The crisis ended when the Soviets agreed to dismantle the sites.

America loves the Kennedys At a time when millions of young American couples were rearing children in their new suburban homes, the Kennedys were seen as the nation's "first family." The public and media never tired of images of the attractive couple and their adorable children, Caroline (born in 1957) and John Jr. (1960). The public, of course, was unaware that President Kennedy was hardly a model husband. They saw a doting father who also happened to be leader of the free world.

Kennedy visits Ireland As his aides planned a tour of Europe in mid-1963, John Kennedy insisted that they include Ireland on the itinerary. He had been to the land of his ancestors twice before, in 1945 and 1947, but this time he would return as Ireland's conquering hero. He landed in Ireland after delivering his famous speech at the Berlin Wall, and he was welcomed as Ireland's favorite son everywhere he went—including Cork (*pictured*). Robert Kennedy later said that the Irish trip was the "happiest time" of his brother's administration. JFK promised to return in the spring of 1964.

America mourns As a shocked nation mourned its fallen leader, *Washington Post* writer Mary McGrory and Kennedy aide Daniel Patrick Moynihan tried to console each other. "We'll never laugh again," said McGrory. "Mary, we'll laugh again," Moynihan said, "but we'll never be young again." That sentiment spoke for a generation of Americans, a generation that never forgot and never will forget hearing the terrible news of November 22, 1963. The turbulence and heartbreak of the 1960s began on that day, and in five years would claim another Kennedy.

The assassination In preparation for his reelection campaign, President Kennedy went to Texas to heal a feud between the state's governor, John Connally, and one of its senators, Ralph Yarborough. On November 22, 1963, he visited Dallas, touring the city with his wife in an open limousine. Lee Harvey Oswald had a view of the presidential motorcade from the sixth floor of the Texas School Book Depository, from which Oswald reportedly fired three shots. The first, called "the magic bullet," allegedly hit Kennedy in the back, exited his throat, then struck Connally in the back and wrist. The third bullet struck the president in the head. John F. Kennedy died at age 46.

The New
Irish
1964–1989

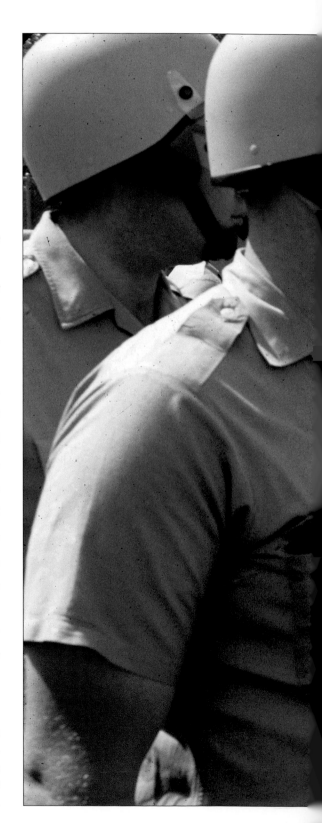

The election of John F. Kennedy seemed to bring the story of the Irish in America to a dramatic and triumphant conclusion. While achievement in politics surely is not the only measure of any group's success, the Irish were heavily invested in the ways and means of government. Kennedy's election, then, symbolized Irish America's acceptance into mainstream American culture.

But after Kennedy's presidency and assassination, the Irish American story continued to unfold. The mid-1960s saw dramatic changes in the country at large and among Irish Americans in particular. The move out of the old neighborhoods and parishes continued in Boston, Philadelphia, New York, Chicago, Baltimore, and other cities. Yet while prosperity and acceptance offered the Irish economic and cultural security, something, it seemed, was lost along the way to assimilation. Daniel Patrick Moynihan noticed the hole in the heart of Irish America when he described the lonely, dusty headquarters of the once-vibrant American Irish Historical Society in Manhattan as a "great tomb."

Suburban and prosperous, Irish Americans in the 1960s seemed less concerned about their ethnicity and more interested in their hard-won accep-

The year 1968 was rough, violent, and bitter for America, and the Irish were in the thick of it. Two Irish Catholics, Eugene McCarthy and Robert Kennedy, fought it out for the Democratic nomination, and then Kennedy was assassinated. At the Democratic National Convention, anti-Establishment youth faced off against Chicago's largely Irish police force (*pictured*).

"[B]eing Irish need not mean identifying with [Irish American authority figures] Cardinal Spellman, "Bull" Connor, Charles Coughlin or Mayor Daley. It could mean being an American rebel...."

—IRISH AMERICAN ANTIWAR ACTIVIST TOM HAYDEN, AFTER OBSERVING CIVIL RIGHTS MARCHERS IN DERRY, NORTHERN IRELAND

tance as Americans. As historian Thomas J. Shelley noted, the era's most notable Irish American cleric, Cardinal Francis Spellman, took dutiful pride in his Irish roots but was far more interested in his American identity. In fact, he chastised a biographer who referred to him as "Irish."

Irish Americans in the 1960s and into the 1970s shared with other Americans a concern that transcended ethnicity: a palpable fear that the American Dream, only recently realized for so many, was coming to an end. Kennedy's assassination in 1963 occurred at the beginning of one of the most tumultuous eras in American history. The Vietnam War, the civil rights movement, and urban rioting tore apart the nation, dividing city and suburb, black and white, young and old. African Americans took to the streets to demand justice, often confronting the police departments that the Irish still dominated.

At the same time, ironically, Catholics in Northern Ireland followed the lead of African Americans. They organized mass protests to demand an end to government-sanctioned discrimination in the British-ruled province. And just as riots in Detroit, Newark, and other U.S. cities required the deployment of federal troops, British soldiers were deployed to Northern Ireland when Catholic protests led to a violent backlash from the province's Protestant majority. Soon, the struggle for Catholic equality in Northern Ireland led to guerrilla war. In response, small groups of Irish Americans offered material and political support to a revived Irish Republican Army, just as they had in the past.

Amid the turmoil of 1968, two Irish American politicians emerged as voices of protest: Senator Robert F. Kennedy of New York, brother of the slain president, and Senator Eugene McCarthy of Minnesota, a witty man who wrote poetry when he wasn't writing laws. But they were by no means the only Irish voices heard in the passionate debates of the 1960s. Tom Hayden led protests in the streets of Chicago during the 1968 Democratic National Convention, and William F. Buckley turned his magazine, *National Review*, into a must-read for an emerging conservative movement. Bernadette Devlin, a leader of the civil rights movement in Northern Ireland, traveled to the U.S. and equated the struggle in her homeland to the struggles of blacks in America. Philip and Daniel Berrigan, Catholic priests, became prominent antiwar activists. And in 1966, a onetime actor confounded political experts by defeating the popular Irish American governor of California, Pat Brown. The actor's name was Ronald Reagan, an Irish Protestant and a Republican.

Historically, Irish agitators had come in two varieties: those who were battlers for labor unions and those who fought for freedom in Ireland. The Berrigan brothers, both Catholic priests, represented a postmodern approach in the 1960s. The Berrigans ignored practical matters like unions and elections and focused on utopian dreams, like ending war and the nuclear arms race.

The diversity of opinion within Irish America in the 1960s and '70s reflected the generational, cultural, religious, and geographic conflicts of those turbulent years. Irish Americans began to drift away from the Democratic Party just as they had drifted away from the cities. By 1980 the Irish were foremost among a voting bloc identified as Reagan Democrats—that is, voters who were registered in the party of their parents but who responded to the conservative message of Ronald Reagan.

Irish Catholics, who had transformed and then dominated the Irish American narrative, experienced another sort of cultural dislocation in the aftermath of the Second Vatican Council in the early 1960s. The council ushered in a series of changes to the liturgy and to the relationship between the American Catholic clergy (dominated by Irish Americans) and the laity. A new generation of Irish American Catholics demanded a greater voice in Church affairs, and was less inclined to accept clerical instruction on matters of personal morality (for example, birth control).

By 1980, when Reagan was elected president with the support of Irish Catholic Democrats, Irish assimilation seemed complete. Actors such as Jack Nicholson and journalists such as Mary McGrory of *The Washington Post* were seen not as ethnics but simply as high-achieving Americans. So when Reagan was wounded by a gunman on March 30, 1981, the Irish dimension to the tragedy was barely noticed. In addition to Reagan, White House Press Secretary James Brady, Secret Service agent Tim McCarthy, and Washington police officer Tom Delehanty were wounded in the attack. The doctor who briefed the press on the condition of the victims was Dennis O'Leary, dean of clinical affairs at George Washington University Hospital.

Few would have guessed on that grim day in 1981 that the next eight years would see a resurgence of Irish American power, a renewed interest in Irish affairs, and a strengthening of the bonds between the United States and Ireland. Not coincidentally, thousands of young Irish made their way to America (beginning in the mid-1980s) in search of work. The Irish Republic's unemployment rate reached 20 percent during the decade, and so, like their cousins before them, the Irish came to the States in hopes of bettering themselves. But unlike their predecessors, many of the new Irish were illegal immigrants.

Legal or not, they helped inspire a revival of Irish culture and influence in the 1990s, a decade that would also see America take the lead in bringing peace to Northern Ireland.

Ronald Reagan, born to an Irish Catholic father but raised as a Protestant, started as a liberal Democrat but became a conservative Republican. He charmed millions of Democrats, sweeping them into his coalition to win landslide elections as governor of California and then as president in 1980 and 1984. The GOP still looks to him as its great role model.

1964-89

June 1964: Ted Kennedy is involved in a plane crash that kills his pilot and an aide and leaves the senator with a broken back.

August 3, 1964: Irish American novelist Flannery O'Connor dies from complications of lupus at age 39.

September 24, 1964: The Warren Commission releases its findings on the assassination of President John F. Kennedy. It determines that Lee Harvey Oswald acted alone. Nevertheless, conspiracy theories will continue into the new millennium.

November 3, 1964: Less than a year after the assassination of his brother, Robert F. Kennedy successfully campaigns to represent New York in the U.S. Senate.

January 14, 1965: Sean Lemass, prime minister of the Republic of Ireland, meets with Terence O'Neill, Northern Ireland's prime minister. It is the first meeting of the divided nation's leaders in more than 40 years.

October 3, 1965: President Lyndon Johnson signs the Immigration Act of 1965, which removes racist policies that were designed to limit the numbers of visas offered to certain ethnic groups.

December 7, 1965: Pope Paul VI promulgates *Dignitatis Humanae Personae*, the Second Vatican Council's groundbreaking assertion of every person's right to religious freedom. It was largely influenced and drafted by Irish American priest John Courtney Murray.

May 21, 1966: The Ulster Volunteer Force (UVF), a loyalist terrorist militia, declares war on the Irish Republican Army (IRA). This declaration is considered by many to be the beginning of the 30-year period of violence known as The Troubles.

The German "Irishman"

Though of German descent, Mathias Bauler exemplified the Irish American style of ward politics, even down to adopting the nickname "Paddy" and using his saloon as his political headquarters. For 34 years, from 1933 to 1967, he served Chicago, and himself, as a Democratic alderman. His favorite method of retaining a support base was through a patronage system known as "ghost payrolling": He put friends on the city's payroll and paid them for little or no work. When the first Richard Daley defeated a reform-minded candidate for mayor, Bauler famously said, "Chicago ain't ready for reform."

McNamara blamed for Vietnam The secretary of defense under presidents Kennedy and Johnson, Robert McNamara was a polarizing figure during the Vietnam War. Some critics believed he was trying to win an unwinnable war. Born in San Francisco in 1916, McNamara earned a graduate degree from Harvard Business School and became president of Ford Motor Company. Tapped as defense secretary in 1960, he was initially a trusted adviser, assisting President Kennedy during the Cuban Missile Crisis. He was similarly confident about successfully managing the Vietnam War, but as the conflict dragged on, he became a lightning rod for criticism. McNamara offered his resignation to President Johnson in 1967, and he later admitted to making poor judgments when it came to Vietnam.

Ryun shatters world records University of Kansas freshman Jim Ryun leaves his competitors in the dust at the 1965 Sugar Bowl Track & Field Classic. At Wichita High School East, Ryun became the first high school runner ever to break the four-minute mile—and he did so as a junior. He went on to set world records in the mile (3:51.1 in 1967), 1,500 meters, and 880 yards. His mile record lasted for eight years. A three-time Olympian, Ryun later excelled in politics, serving in the U.S. House of Representatives for more than a decade.

Lemmon's versatility
One of America's most popular actors, Massachusetts-born Jack Lemmon was a product of Harvard, the United States Navy, and acting school. Not surprisingly, he was an intelligent, disciplined actor with a great range of talents. Twice an Oscar winner, Lemmon could play comic and serious characters with equal skill. His performances in such films as *Some Like It Hot* and *The Odd Couple* proved his comedic talent, while his dramatic ability shone through in such films as *The China Syndrome* and *Missing*.

The majority leader
Mike Mansfield served as Senate majority leader for nearly two decades, spanning the tumultuous civil rights, Vietnam, and Watergate years. Born in 1903 to Irish immigrants in New York City, Mansfield went to live with relatives in Montana after his mother died. He was elected in 1952 to the Senate, where he won many allies with his collegial style. When Lyndon Johnson became vice president in 1961, Mansfield assumed Johnson's post as Senate leader. He served a record 16 years as majority leader before retiring in 1977.

Leary promotes LSD Timothy Leary, son of an Irish American dentist from Massachusetts, became a pop culture sensation in the 1960s because of his advocacy of drug use. As a lecturer in psychology at Harvard in the early 1960s, Leary promoted the use of mind-altering drugs among his students. He was dismissed from Harvard's faculty in 1963. Three years later, he announced the formation of a new religion based on the use of LSD and other drugs. His involvement in the era's counterculture put him in contact with such radical political groups as the Black Panthers and the Weathermen, furthering his image as a '60s rebel. "Turn on, tune in, drop out," was his famous mantra.

Ireland's "33rd county" In the years before transatlantic air travel became routine, the Irish of the Northeast found their "home" in New York's Catskill Mountains. In the villages and hamlets of Greene County, dubbed Ireland's "33rd county," Irish-themed hotels, motels, bars, and restaurants kept Irish visitors feeling that they had winged it back to the Emerald Isle itself. The village of East Durham became the center of affairs, with green-painted shamrocks adorning the main street's center line.

Boston's popular archbishop Cardinal Richard Cushing's tenure as archbishop of Boston spanned 26 years, from 1944 to 1970. As such, Cushing was witness to profound changes, both in broader American society and within the confines of his church. He attracted sustained media attention when John F. Kennedy, a personal friend, became the first Catholic president. Cushing's style was that of a conciliator. Like Kennedy, he worked to improve ties and diminish misunderstandings between Catholics and those of other faiths.

Athlete, scholar, and senator Bill Bradley said that viewing an exhibit on Scots-Irish immigration prompted him to study the lives of his own ancestors in Ireland. Since then, the 2000 U.S. presidential candidate has been outspoken in his support of efforts to end violence and terrorism in Northern Ireland. Before serving as U.S. senator from New Jersey (1979–97), Bradley distinguished himself as a Rhodes Scholar, Sullivan Award winner as the nation's best amateur athlete, 1964 Olympic gold medalist, and star forward who helped the New York Knicks claim two NBA championships.

Left-wing priests Father Philip Berrigan (*center*) and his brother, Father Daniel Berrigan, participate in a 1968 protest against the Vietnam War. The Minnesota-born Berrigans became emblematic of left-wing political activism among Irish American priests during the 1960s and '70s. Arrested repeatedly, the Berrigans and other activist priests posed a challenge to the conservative American Catholic hierarchy on both political issues and on matters of clerical discipline. Philip Berrigan left the priesthood, married, and had three children. Well into the 21st century, Daniel Berrigan remained both a priest and a committed activist.

DIFFERENT VALUES, SAME HERITAGE

Our reaction to John Kennedy's death opened a chasm in the Irish American community. Some chose the security of money and power on a path that led to the Republican Party. Suburban, law-abiding, and prosperous, they were the Catholics who resisted the social changes of Vatican II. They saw themselves, intensely, as patriots in the spirit of the pragmatic Daniel Patrick Moynihan.

Others, and I am one, chose to embrace change and to work for values held by old-line Democrats and socially engaged clergy: civil rights, peace, economic equity. As a teacher, I stressed human rights and the freedom of inquiry to black and Latino students that I likened to the Irish of America 150 years ago. Politically and theologically, I am in spirit with the Catholic Worker and the Berrigans.

However they may diverge, both sides of this divide unite on a crucial point: the importance of Irish heritage. They encourage the study of Irish culture and history, and they are able to go to Ireland, many in search of their roots.

At our best, we Irish in America have compassion for the weak, contempt for oppressors, courage to rebel, and a willingness to forgive. We laugh at our own pretensions and never yield when fighting for the right. We stand always with one foot on either side of the Atlantic: absolutely American and absolutely Irish until we die.

—JIM FLANAGAN, WEST LONG BRANCH, NEW JERSEY

Beatty thrives in Hollywood Warren Beatty took up the stage in the late 1950s at the urging of his older sister, actress Shirley MacLaine. His good looks and acting ability earned him starring roles in Hollywood. Beatty both starred in and produced the 1967 film *Bonnie and Clyde*, earning Oscar nominations for best actor and best picture. The film's success inspired Beatty to produce, direct, and write as well as act. He received Academy Award nominations as an actor, director, and writer for the 1981 film *Reds*.

Fleming wins gold, hearts In 1968, with America mired in war abroad and racial tension at home, figure skater Peggy Fleming's gold medal-winning performance at the Winter Olympics captivated the nation. Born in San Jose, California, Fleming first captured the world's attention at the '64 Olympics. In Grenoble, France, in 1968, she put on a performance for the ages, with all nine judges placing her first. Fleming raised the profile of skating in the United States and went on to become a popular TV personality and commentator.

June 1966: The first and second victims of The Troubles die this month when the UVF claims responsibility for the shooting deaths of John Patrick Scullion, age 28, and Peter Ward, 18, in West Belfast.

August 26, 1966: Chicago mayor Richard J. Daley meets with Dr. Martin Luther King in an effort to diffuse tensions in the city resulting from King's efforts to open "white" neighborhoods to black families.

November 26, 1966: A week after their legendary 10–10 tie against Michigan State, the Notre Dame football team routs Southern California 51–0 to secure the national championship.

January 29, 1967: The Northern Ireland Civil Rights Association (NICRA) is founded in Belfast with a mandate to protect the civil rights of Northern Ireland's Catholic minority.

October 1967: Navy pilot John McCain is shot down over North Vietnam. He will be held as a prisoner of war for more than five years.

October 17, 1967: The "Baltimore Four," a group of renegade war protesters that includes Irish Catholic priest Philip Berrigan, storms into the Baltimore Customs House and dumps blood on draft records.

November 1967: Kevin White is elected mayor of Boston. He will serve four consecutive four-year terms.

December 2, 1967: Cardinal Francis Joseph Spellman, archbishop of New York, dies at age 78.

February 1968: Irish American figure skater Peggy Fleming captures a gold medal at the Olympic Winter Games in Grenoble, France.

February 29, 1968: U.S. defense secretary Robert McNamara, who oversaw the execution of much of the Vietnam War, resigns his post to take over the top spot at the World Bank.

Bobby Kennedy reaches out After his brother's assassination, Robert Kennedy transformed himself from a tough political operative to a politician who reached out to the poor and disenfranchised. Although shy by nature, Kennedy was able to connect with voters in a more intimate way than his older brother did. African American voters, inspired by his appeals for racial harmony and civil rights, supported his candidacy for the U.S. Senate in 1964 and his presidential campaign in 1968.

The nation mourns again Robert Kennedy's assassination in June 1968, just weeks after the murder of Dr. Martin Luther King, Jr., plunged the nation into mourning yet again. His death marked the end of an Irish American dream of another Kennedy in the White House—and of the broad coalition he had put together during his presidential campaign. The quote attributed to Robert Kennedy in this photograph actually originated with the great Irish playwright, George Bernard Shaw. Robert's brother, President Kennedy, also used this quote in his speeches.

RFK, McCarthy Run for President

During the late 1960s, Robert F. Kennedy proved to be one of the most eloquent voices for the disaffected. The younger brother of John F. Kennedy, RFK rose to prominence as a tough law-and-order attorney in the 1950s, when he brought charges of racketeering against Teamsters leader Jimmy Hoffa. Appointed U.S. attorney general after running John's successful presidential campaign, RFK found himself in the middle of the great civil rights struggle in the South. He came to sympathize with African Americans and their fight for voting rights and desegregation. After his brother's assassination, he resigned his post and was elected to the U.S. Senate in 1964. Four years later, RFK stood as one of the most popular liberal leaders in America, calling for relief for the nation's poor and a cease-fire in Vietnam.

McCarthy (*left*) and Kennedy

An even bigger critic of the war in Southeast Asia was U.S. senator Eugene McCarthy of Minnesota, who took great pride in his Irish roots. McCarthy had a firm intellectual background, working as a professor of economics before taking a seat in Congress in the late 1940s. The senator who had once bragged that he was "twice as liberal as [Hubert] Humphrey…and twice as Catholic as Kennedy" entered the presidential race of 1968. Although the odds were stacked against him, McCarthy won both the Wisconsin and New Hampshire primaries. Robert Kennedy took note of McCarthy's success and decided to enter the race just before St. Patrick's Day, 1968.

On June 4, Kennedy took charge, winning the all-important California primary. Shortly after delivering his victory speech, an assassin gunned him down, and within hours he was dead. McCarthy continued to seek the party's nomination, and at the Democratic convention in Chicago he insisted on a withdrawal from Vietnam. To his dismay, party regulars endorsed Vice President Hubert Humphrey and a continuation of President Lyndon Johnson's war policy. Two years later, a discouraged McCarthy gave up his Senate seat. Although he would never again hold political office, he ran for president four more times.

A leader of the New Left Tom Hayden was born in Detroit to the descendants of Ulster immigrants. Reared in a conservative Catholic parish, Hayden became immersed in progressive causes while at the University of Michigan. A founder of the New Left group Students for a Democratic Society, he drafted the 1962 Port Huron Statement, which called for a rebirth of participatory democracy to achieve social change. Hayden, a leading opponent of the Vietnam War, took his campaign for progressive change to the California State Senate, where he served from 1992 to 2000. He remains active on issues ranging from labor reform to environmentalism. In his 2001 book *Irish on the Inside,* Hayden explores his own past and that of liberal Irish America.

1964-89

March 12, 1968: Eugene McCarthy nearly defeats incumbent president Lyndon Johnson in New Hampshire's Democratic primary, prompting Johnson to announce that he will not seek reelection.

April 10, 1968: Irish American actor George Kennedy earns best supporting actor honors for his role in *Cool Hand Luke.*

June 5, 1968: Robert F. Kennedy is shot at the Ambassador Hotel in Los Angeles following a speech celebrating his victory in California's presidential primary. He will die the following day.

July 1968: The first Special Olympics is convened at Chicago's Soldier Field. Eunice Kennedy Shriver, the late president's sister and the organization's founder, will see the Special Olympics grow to nearly a million participants by the end of the century.

July 25, 1968: Pope Paul VI promulgates *Humanae Vitae,* an encyclical detailing the official position of the Roman Catholic Church on birth control.

August 1968: Chicago's Democratic National Convention, held in the epicenter of Democratic politics, is rocked by clashes between city police and antiwar protesters.

August 24, 1968: The Northern Ireland Civil Rights Association (NICRA) and other social justice organizations sponsor Northern Ireland's first march for Catholic civil rights, from Coalisland to Dungannon.

October 5, 1968: NICRA organizes another civil rights march, but the Royal Ulster Constabulary ends it before it can begin, attacking the marchers with batons. The violence is filmed and televised, angering Catholics and touching off two days of rioting in Derry.

Daley erupts at '68 convention
Chicago mayor Richard J. Daley responds furiously to criticism from speakers at the 1968 Democratic National Convention. Daley had ordered a tough response to antiwar demonstrators who had converged on the city, and the result was several days

and nights of increasingly ugly confrontations in which police targeted both protesters and members of the news media. The battles spilled onto the convention floor, where Daley's fellow Democrats denounced the police as "Gestapo" and decried their "mindless brutality." Daley's influence in the national party, which had reached its zenith with the election of John F. Kennedy in 1960, entered a long decline—though Chicagoans elected him to two more terms as mayor.

Clean for Gene A devout Irish German Catholic from small-town Minnesota, Senator Eugene McCarthy ran one of the most unusual campaigns in U.S. history in 1968. A vocal opponent of the Vietnam War, McCarthy challenged President Lyndon Johnson for the Democratic presidential nomination. His candidacy instantly attracted a corps of young volunteers who got "Clean for Gene" by cutting their hair, shaving their beards, and adopting conservative dress for the campaign. McCarthy's early success may have contributed to Johnson's withdrawal from the race, though Vice President Hubert Humphrey won the nomination. Despite this, McCarthy's candidacy launched a new generation into national politics.

Dohrn and the Weathermen In the late 1960s, former cheerleader Bernardine Dohrn became a leader of the radical Weather Underground (*aka* the Weathermen). Born in Milwaukee, Dohrn became attracted to radical causes after graduating with a law degree from the University of Chicago. The Weathermen, a radical offshoot of the Students for a Democratic Society, declared war on the U.S. government. They inflicted large amounts of property damage during their "Days of Rage" in Chicago in 1969, and they bombed numerous buildings, including the Pentagon and U.S. Capitol. Dohrn turned herself in in 1980 and, after a brief prison term, became a law professor at Northwestern University.

Nixon wins the presidency Richard Milhous Nixon, pictured with wife Pat and daughters Tricia (*second from right*) and Julie, was born to a Quaker family in California. His father was Scots-Irish while his mother was of Irish and English descent. Nixon became a congressman in 1946 and cultivated a reputation as a fierce anti-Communist. In 1952 Dwight Eisenhower tapped him as vice president, the first of five presidential tickets on which Nixon would appear. He lost a close race for president to John Kennedy in 1960, but he defeated Hubert Humphrey in 1968 by appealing to America's "silent majority" (which included many working-class Irish Catholics). Nixon was reelected in 1972 but became mired in the Watergate scandal, which forced him to resign in 1974.

War hero and presidential candidate Bob Kerrey's great-grandfather left England in 1851 and changed the spelling of the family's last name from Kerry to Kerrey. Bob Kerrey, a native of Nebraska, won a Medal of Honor as a Navy SEAL during the Vietnam War and lost the lower half of his right leg after being hit with shrapnel. He was elected governor of Nebraska in 1982 and senator in 1988. In 1992 he ran for the Democratic Party's presidential nomination, but he lost to Arkansas governor Bill Clinton. Kerrey retired from the Senate in 2001 to become president of the New School, a university in New York. He also served on the 9/11 Commission.

The hated atheist Once dubbed the "most hated woman in America," Madalyn Murray O'Hair enraged a generation of Irish Catholics and other devout Americans with her crusade against religion. Born Madalyn Mays into a Pittsburgh Presbyterian family, she had an affair with a married Catholic named James Murray. He refused to divorce his wife, but Mays adopted his name anyway. (She later married Richard O'Hair.) In 1960 O'Hair made headlines when she challenged the practice of Bible reading in Baltimore's public schools. She spent the next three decades supporting atheism and the strict separation of church and state. O'Hair disappeared in 1995, and authorities eventually discovered that she had been murdered by former supporters.

November 1968: Eight years after losing a very close contest to John F. Kennedy, Irish American Richard M. Nixon is elected U.S. president.

1969: The IRA splits into two factions: the "originals" and the "provisionals," distinguished mainly by the fact that the "provisionals" are more willing to use terrorist violence as a means to an end. • The Irish Northern Aid Committee (NORAID) is founded. Despite being routinely condemned as the American fundraising arm of the Provisional IRA, it will operate legally in the United States well into the 21st century.

January 1, 1969: The People's Democracy, a socialist civil rights group, stages the "Long March" from Belfast to Derry. While approaching Derry, the marchers are attacked by loyalists. The police observe but fail to intervene.

April 1969: Bernadette Devlin, a socialist political activist from Northern Ireland, becomes the youngest member of Parliament in British history when she is elected at age 21.

July 19, 1969: Ted Kennedy drives off the Dike Street bridge on Chappaquiddick Island and leaves the scene of the accident. His passenger, Mary Jo Kopechne, dies.

July 20, 1969: Astronaut and *Apollo 11* command module pilot Michael Collins steers the spaceship *Columbia* in lunar orbit while fellow *Apollo* astronauts Neil Armstrong and Buzz Aldrin take a walk on the moon. Collins and Armstrong are of Irish descent.

August 1969: In what will become known as the Battle of the Bogside, a crowd of unarmed Derry civilians riots for three days after officers of the Royal Ulster Constabulary attempt to disperse protesters at a loyalist parade.

A leading voice in Washington Daniel Patrick Moynihan was one of Irish America's most gifted public servants. Reared in New York, he was a noted scholar of America's ethnic communities and voiced often-unpopular opinions on how to solve problems of urban poverty and racial discrimination. He served as an adviser to four presidents and won four terms in the U.S. Senate. Moynihan is also remembered for a poignant remark after the assassination of John F. Kennedy in 1963: "I don't think there's any point in being Irish if you don't know that the world is going to break your heart eventually."

Irish Americans on the moon Chicago mayor Richard J. Daley's press secretary once described Daley's limited version of diversity as "nine Irishmen and a Swede." Daley would have felt at home on *Apollo 11*. The first moon-landing crew was comprised of two astronauts with Irish roots, Neil Armstrong (*left*) and Michael Collins (*center*), and one with Swedish ties, Buzz Aldrin (*right*). In the case of Armstrong, the first person to walk on the moon, his family origins were Scots-Irish. Collins, who was born in Italy (where his father was stationed with the U.S. military), took into space the name of one of Ireland's greatest heroes in the struggle for national independence.

"We Shall Overcome"

By the mid-1960s, Northern Ireland was a tinderbox. Since partition, the minority Catholics had suffered injustices similar to those endured by black citizens in the American South: job and housing discrimination, high unemployment, voting irregularities, and abuse by law enforcement. Inspired by the civil rights movement in the United States, Catholics and Protestants who abhorred such inequality rallied together under the umbrella that was the Northern Ireland Civil Rights Association.

NICRA evolved from a series of meetings, particularly a rally held in Belfast in January 1967. Its tactics of marches and sit-downs, according to author Jack Holland in *Hope Against History*, "would be based on the campaign for black civil rights, which at the time was reaching its climax in the United States."

The new group announced five goals that sounded general in their wording but were actually very pointed given the nature of Northern Ireland society. NICRA aimed to defend the basic freedom of all citizens; to protect the rights of the individual; to highlight all possible abuses of power; to demand guarantees for freedom of speech, assembly, and association; and to inform the public of their lawful rights.

NICRA marches were met with banning orders. A march in the city of Derry on October 5, 1968, was violently dispersed by members of the North's armed police, the Royal Ulster Constabulary. To the world watching on television, the scenes were replays of police reaction to Dr. Martin

Marchers honoring one-year anniversary of Bloody Sunday

Luther King, Jr., and his followers in southern U.S. cities. King's nonviolent tactics, right down to the singing of the popular protest song "We Shall Overcome," remained a hallmark of the NICRA campaign even as it was sidelined by The Troubles.

This was later acknowledged by NICRA co-leader and future Nobel Peace Prize winner John Hume. In a 1985 commencement speech at the University of Massachusetts, Hume said that Dr. King's "dream" had been an inspiration for both himself and for NICRA. "The American civil rights movement gave birth to ours," Hume said.

Battle of the Bogside Every year on August 12, Protestants in Northern Ireland marched through the streets of Derry (or Londonderry, as Protestants called the city) to commemorate a Protestant victory over King James II, a Catholic, in 1689. But in 1969, as the march made its way through the Catholic ghetto known as the Bogside, protesters began hurling rocks and other missiles at the marchers. Police responded with tear gas, and over the next few days, six people were killed and hundreds wounded in confrontations between Catholics and the police. The Battle of the Bogside showed that Catholics were fed up with militant Protestant displays of domination in the province.

Breslin's perspectives Born in Queens, Jimmy Breslin became the quintessential Irish newspaperman, finding poetry and tragedy in the ethnic enclaves of New York. The columnist always knew how to find a fresh angle. For example, on the day of John F. Kennedy's funeral, Breslin famously profiled the president's gravedigger. He also became an acclaimed fiction writer, capturing the working-class Irish American experience in such novels as *World Without End, Amen* and *Table Money*. In the former novel, an Irish New York beat cop goes to Northern Ireland and discovers abysmal conditions for Catholics. Breslin ran for public office in 1969 (alongside Norman Mailer) and won the Pulitzer Prize for Commentary in 1986.

Union boss orchestrates murder United Mine Workers President Tony Boyle was at the center of one of America's most notorious episodes of union violence. Born in the heavily Irish mining camps of Butte, Montana, Boyle became president of the mine workers' union in 1963. Six years later, he was challenged by Joseph Yablonski, who lost but demanded an investigation into Boyle's victory. Yablonski was later found murdered. A subsequent investigation determined that Boyle had ordered the killing. He was convicted and sent to prison for life.

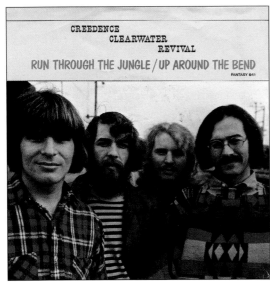

John Fogerty and CCR Best known for combining roots rock with, at times, socially conscious lyrics, Creedence Clearwater Revival was one of the most popular groups of the 1960s and '70s. John Fogerty (*left*) was the group's driving force—its songwriter, vocalist, and lead guitar player. In 2004 an interviewer for *Irish America* magazine called him "probably the best Irish American songwriter." CCR hit the big time with "Proud Mary" and "Down on the Corner," and it gained critical respect for the angry, working-class anthem "Fortunate Son" and the Vietnam-era ballad "Who'll Stop the Rain."

O'Dwyer fights for human rights Paul O'Dwyer, a firebrand liberal New York lawyer and politician, had politics in his blood. His brother William served as mayor of New York in the 1940s. Paul was one of 10 children born to a County Mayo family. As a lawyer, he epitomized Irish liberalism, which associated British oppression in Ireland with all forms of injustice, including civil rights and poverty in the United States. O'Dwyer was elected New York City Council president in 1974, and he remained a crusading lawyer until his death in 1998.

A fortune in showbiz A California-born Irish American, Merv Griffin began his show business career as a singer and actor, but he became best known as the host of *The Merv Griffin Show* (1962–86). The daytime program blended entertainment with guests who were often outspoken and controversial. Here he chats with entertainer Liza Minnelli. Griffin became enormously wealthy thanks to the game shows produced by his company, Merv Griffin Entertainment. *Jeopardy!* and *Wheel of Fortune*—daily staples of American television for decades—were among the company's big hits.

An extraordinary officer The son of an Irish Catholic mother, and descended on his father's side from a long line of American soldiers, Colonel David Hackworth was one of the U.S. Army's most remarkable officers. He joined the service at age 15, achieved the rank of captain at 20, and won 91 medals during a quarter-century in the ranks. In Vietnam, Hackworth was known as a tough commander and an expert on guerrilla warfare. He won lasting notoriety when, in 1971, he publicly criticized the conduct of the war. In retirement, Hackworth achieved distinction as a journalist.

Morrison's music Jim Morrison and his band, the Doors, expanded California rock with Morrison's often-mystical lyrics and smartly fused elements of jazz and folk. The Doors released six studio albums in Morrison's lifetime, reaching an artistic high point with their 1971 LP, *L.A. Woman*. Three months later, Morrison was dead at age 27, victim of a heart attack that probably was brought on by drug and alcohol abuse. Since then, his bohemian outlook and hypnotic melodies have attracted succeeding generations of young people.

O'Connor plays Bunker In the groundbreaking 1970s sitcom *All in the Family,* closed-minded character Archie Bunker mocked the Irish, Catholics, and every other ethnic group. But ironically, Bunker was actually played by a liberal Irish Catholic. Carroll O'Connor was born in New York, but he attended school and began his acting career in Ireland. O'Connor appeared in numerous films in the 1960s, but he achieved enduring fame as Bunker, whom *TV Guide* once named the greatest character in television history. O'Connor later starred as a southern sheriff in TV's *In the Heat of the Night* before his death in 2001.

November 18, 1969: Joseph Kennedy, Sr., former U.S. ambassador to Britain and father of the late president, dies. He is predeceased by four of his nine children, including his three oldest sons.

1970: The Social Democratic and Labour Party (SDLP) is established in Belfast. SDLP's pacifism will soon distinguish it from Sinn Féin, Northern Ireland's other main nationalist political party. • Belfast native George Ivan Morrison, better known as Van Morrison, releases his album *Moondance.* The title track will become one of the Grammy award-winning artist's best-known works.

April 7, 1970: John Wayne's performance in *True Grit* nets him the best actor statuette at this year's Academy Awards.

August 21, 1970: Paramount Pictures releases *The Molly Maguires,* an Oscar-nominated film about the Pinkerton infiltration of the terrorist labor organization, starring Sean Connery.

November 2, 1970: Richard James Cushing, a son of Irish immigrants who served as archbishop of Boston for more than 25 years and was made cardinal in 1958, dies in Boston at age 75.

November 3, 1970: Massachusetts sends Ted Kennedy back to the U.S. Senate with more than 60 percent of the popular vote, despite the tarnish left on his image by the Chappaquiddick incident.

1971: The administration of British prime minister Brian Faulkner enacts the Special Powers Act, which permits incarceration for individuals suspected of terrorism in Northern Ireland.

January 1971: Several instances of rioting among minority Catholics occur this month in neighborhoods throughout Belfast.

"The idea of raising money on Second Avenue to buy guns so that an 18-year-old in Derry can kill an 18-year-old British soldier, a soldier from Manchester who knows nothing of the reasons for the fight he is in, this notion to me is sickening."

—NEW YORK CITY JOURNALIST AND IRISH AMERICAN JIMMY BRESLIN, SPEAKING TO A 1972 CONGRESSIONAL SUBCOMMITTEE ON NORTHERN IRELAND

British troops turn on Catholics After the Battle of the Bogside, the British government dispatched troops to Northern Ireland because officials had decided that the overwhelmingly Protestant police force was incapable of handling the rising violence. Many weary Catholics greeted the troops as protectors who would shield them from Protestant mobs—including the police. But after the Bloody Sunday massacre in Derry, the troops no longer were considered impartial peacekeepers. They were seen as an occupying army, even by moderates who opposed the IRA.

Bloody Sunday in Derry Northern Ireland exploded in violence in the late 1960s when the province's Catholics, inspired by the civil rights movement in the United States, demanded an end to discrimination in employment and housing. On January 30, 1972, some 15,000 people marched in Derry—despite an official ban on the demonstration—to protest the mass arrests of Catholics. British paratroopers opened fire on the crowd, killing 13 people outright and wounding 18 in what was dubbed "Bloody Sunday." The victims' coffins were put on display on February 2. Meanwhile, public opinion around the world turned against British policy in the North.

**The Chieftains'
Irish music** More
than any other
group, the Chief-
tains popularized
Irish traditional
music in the United
States. Formed in
1963, the group, led
by Paddy Moloney,
delivered Irish music
in constantly new
and varied ways to
audiences around

the world. In a sense, the Chieftains did for the traditional
Irish sound what "Riverdance" later accomplished for dance.
Winners of many awards, including a clutch of Grammys and
an Oscar, the Chieftains expanded their appeal beyond the
strictly traditional by collaborating with rock and pop artists,
including Van Morrison.

Americans support NI's Catholics Irish America has
always been part of the struggle to win Ireland's freedom
from British rule. But after the founding of the Irish Free
State in 1921, many Irish Americans considered the national
question closed. The unrest of the 1960s, however, led to
greater American involvement concerning Northern Ireland. Marchers, such as these pictured in a South Boston
St. Patrick's Day parade, rallied to the cause of the North's
oppressed Catholics. They demanded an end to Britain's
presence on the island of their ancestors.

Young radical Bernadette Devlin, seen here on a bus in
London in 1972, was elected to the British House of Commons in 1969, when she was 21 years old. A native of
County Tyrone, she was active in Northern Ireland's civil
rights movement and brought the cause of the province's
oppressed Catholics to the House floor. Outspoken and
unconventional, she became a transatlantic celebrity because
of her youth, her radical politics, and her willingness to con-
front powerful politicians. She punched a House member,
Reginald Maudling, after Maudling had defended the Bloody
Sunday killings. In 1969 Devlin caused a sensation in New
York when she received the ceremonial keys to the city and
then gave them to members of the Black Panther Party.

McGovern's run in '72
The descendant of both
Irish Catholic and Scots-
Irish Protestant fore-
bears, South Dakota
senator George McGov-
ern was the Democratic
Party's presidential nominee in 1972. McGovern,
a decorated World War
II bomber pilot, won
the nomination on the
strength of his opposi-
tion to the Vietnam War.
But his campaign against
President Richard Nixon—
also an Irish American

Protestant—was an uphill struggle from day one. McGovern
carried just one state—Massachusetts, with its heavily Irish
Catholic enclaves—giving Nixon one of the biggest landslides
in U.S. history.

January 3, 1971: Father Robert F. Drinan takes his seat in the U.S. House, representing Massachusetts. He will serve five terms and become the first Catholic priest to cast a congressional vote.

January 12, 1971: The groundbreaking series *All in the Family* premieres on CBS. Carroll O'Connor will win four Emmy Awards for his portrayal of Archie Bunker.

April 23, 1971: The day after becoming the first veteran of the Vietnam War to testify about the war before Congress, future presidential candidate John Kerry throws his medals over a fence onto the Capitol steps in protest.

June 27, 1971: Colonel David Hackworth, a decorated war veteran and career Army man, gives an interview on ABC's *Issues and Answers* in which he calls for U.S. withdrawal from Vietnam. The retribution from his Pentagon superiors will virtually put an end to his military career.

September 30, 1971: Ulster politician Ian Paisley assumes leadership of the Democratic Unionist Party.

December 4, 1971: Fifteen Catholic civilians die when the UVF bombs McGurk's Bar in north Belfast.

1972: In west Belfast, John McKeague forms the Red Hand Commandos, a paramilitary group that is essentially an offshoot of the UVF. It will be outlawed the following year.

January 30, 1972: In a tragedy that will come to be known as Bloody Sunday, British soldiers gun down 26 unarmed Catholic civil rights demonstrators. The dead include six youths.

March 28, 1972: The British Parliament's Northern Ireland Act takes effect. The act suspends the Parliament of Northern Ireland and establishes direct rule over the region.

An Irish-Jewish TV couple In the fall of 1972, CBS offered a new comedy series called *Bridget Loves Bernie,* starring Meredith Baxter as Bridget Theresa Mary Colleen Fitzgerald, the daughter of a wealthy Irish Catholic family. She is in love with a Jewish cabdriver and struggling writer named Bernie Steinberg, played by Irish American actor David Birney. Although the show garnered critical acclaim and strong ratings, it was canceled after one season when religious organizations representing both faiths protested this picture of a happy interfaith marriage. Ironically, Baxter and Birney later married each other.

New Jersey's beloved governor A graduate of Princeton University and Harvard Law, Brendan Byrne served as a prosecutor and a judge. While on the bench, he developed a reputation for integrity in a state plagued by corruption. In 1973 he was elected governor of New Jersey. During his tenure, Byrne signed a controversial bill that mandated a state income tax to fund New Jersey's public schools. He was reelected in 1977 and subsequently became one of the state's most beloved political figures. Under Byrne's watch, the Meadowlands Sports Complex opened and casino gambling was legalized in Atlantic City.

Boston's underworld

George V. Higgins was well suited to write a novel about Boston's Irish underworld. Born and raised just outside Boston by Irish Catholic parents, he knew the Massachusetts Irish well. As a federal prosecutor in the late 1960s and early '70s, he came into daily contact with the hoodlums and thugs who made up its outlaw society. When *The Friends of Eddie Coyle* appeared in 1972, it was an instant literary success. It depicts in fine detail and superb dialogue the life of small-time hood Eddie Coyle, who gets squeezed when he tries to play both ends against the middle. In 1973 the story was made into a movie starring Robert Mitchum and Peter Boyle.

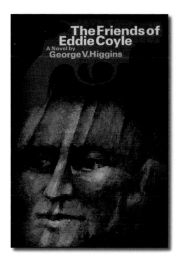

The first priest in Congress The Vietnam War years saw a marked increase in the level of political activity on the part of American Catholic priests. But only one, Father Robert Drinan, took his politics directly and successfully to voters. In 1970 Drinan became the first priest in Congress when he was elected as a Democrat in a Massachusetts House district. Drinan would serve five consecutive terms before an impending Church law brought an end to "our father who art in Congress." He remained active, however, as a lawyer and as a writer for the *National Catholic Reporter*.

Flamethrower Nolan Ryan, who credited his parents with instilling in him tenacious work habits from an early age, was blessed with an arm that could throw a 100-mph fastball. For the California Angels in 1973, Ryan broke the major-league record for strikeouts with 383. He went on to become the most prolific strikeout pitcher of all time, fanning 5,714 batters over an epic 27-year career. He also tossed seven no-hitters—three more than anyone else.

Rooney's Steelers Talk about luck of the Irish! Art Rooney, Sr., the son of immigrants from Newry, Northern Ireland, won more than $300,000 at New York racetracks in two days in 1936. He used it to keep his football team, then called the Pittsburgh Pirates, afloat. Rooney renamed the club in 1940, and his vision eventually turned the Steelers into one of the NFL's most successful franchises. Under the watch of their popular owner, the Steelers were the 1970s' dominant franchise, winning four Super Bowls during the decade.

November 7, 1972: Democratic presidential candidate George McGovern suffers one of the worst presidential defeats in history, garnering only 17 electoral votes to 520 for Republican Richard Nixon.

January 1, 1973: Both the Republic of Ireland and the United Kingdom are accepted into the European Common Market.

June 7, 1973: President Richard Nixon nominates Clarence Kelley to succeed J. Edgar Hoover as director of the FBI.

June 24, 1973: Eamon de Valera retires as president of Ireland. In his 90th year, he is the world's oldest head of state.

December 9, 1973: The Sunningdale Agreement, an attempt to bring peace to Northern Ireland by dividing power between Protestant loyalists and Catholic nationalists, is signed.

December 31, 1973: Notre Dame defeats Alabama 24–23 in the Sugar Bowl to secure an undefeated season and the national championship.

April 2, 1974: Two Irish American actors earn Academy Awards this year. Jack Lemmon is named best actor for his work in *Save the Tiger,* while Tatum O'Neal is recognized as best supporting actress for her role in *Paper Moon.*

May 1974: The Sunningdale Agreement is abandoned in the face of utter lack of cooperation between its signatories.

May 17, 1974: In Ireland, four car bombs explode in the morning—three in Dublin and one in Monaghan. With 33 dead, it is the single bloodiest day of The Troubles.

June 17, 1974: An IRA bomb detonates in Westminster Hall, causing considerable damage to the British Houses of Parliament.

Day Hicks says no to busing Anti-busing advocate Louise Day Hicks, shown here in dark glasses while leading a protest march in 1975, held seemingly contradictory political views. While serving in the U.S. House of Representatives in the early 1970s, this Irish Catholic had strongly supported passage of the Equal Rights Amendment. But back home in Boston, she resisted moving children out of neighborhood schools, which was intended to give black students equal educational rights. Day Hicks argued that in the public schools in Boston's Italian North End, students were all Italian; in Irish "Southie," they were mainly Irish; and in African American Roxbury, they were all black. To her, forced busing was an attack on community.

Boston's four-term mayor When populist Kevin White (*foreground*) ran for mayor of Boston in 1967, one of his slogans proclaimed: "When landlords raise rents, Kevin White raises hell." Bostonians liked the sound of that, and they kept him in office for 16

years—a record for a Boston mayor. White was the son, grandson, and son-in-law of city council presidents, and his Irish roots served him well in his run of victories. He became mired, as did his entire city, in the 1974 busing imbroglio. But although White opposed busing, his role was mostly that of mediator.

"Eighty percent of the people in Boston are against busing. If Boston were a sovereign state, busing would be cause for a revolution."

—BOSTON MAYOR KEVIN WHITE

Busing in Boston

Ted Kennedy was a member of the Irish American royal family—brother of the beloved John and Bobby Kennedy. In 1974, however, Ted was nearly mauled by a mob in an Irish neighborhood. The busing crisis had turned Boston upside-down. When the crisis broke out in 1974, much of the country came to view Boston as filled with Irish bigots who were violently resistant to change.

In reality, Boston's Irish Americans experienced a range of complex emotions. In J. Anthony Lukas's book *Common Ground*, an Irish American mother of seven, who lived in a housing project, wondered: "If she asked herself whom she really detested in all this, it wasn't the blacks, who in many ways were as much victims as she was; it wasn't the Yankees from the suburbs, who were just as out of touch with urban reality as she'd always known they were. It was the Irish Catholic traitors, the people who should have known better but who had allowed wealth, comfort, power, or patronage to lure them from their basic allegiance to turf and tribe." The deep class and racial tension that gripped Boston in the mid-1970s was yet another episode in the history of Irish Americans in which they felt trapped between the rich and poor.

The saga began in June 1974 when federal district court judge W. Arthur Garrity ruled that Boston had maintained a segregated school system, which was unconstitutional. The solution? Black and white students would have to be bused from their own neighborhoods to achieve a better racial balance. There were numerous layers of Irish opposition to this initiative. There were racists who did not want to associate with blacks. But other parents—black and white—wondered why their children had to be removed from a nearby school to attend a distant school, just because some judge said so.

Other working-class Irish Bostonians felt they had enough problems to worry about. Now, the one thing in which they took a fierce pride—their turf—was being tampered with by outsiders. And why, they wondered, weren't more-affluent neighborhoods affected by this?

An attack on pro-busing marchers, May 3, 1975

The controversy reached a fever pitch when school opened in September 1974. Rocks were thrown, slurs were screamed, prayers were chanted. Many Irish and other white parents launched a boycott, aiming their rage at leaders of all political stripes. The street struggle eventually became a political one. Matronly Irish American politician Louise Day Hicks became a symbol of the anti-busing movement. She "tapped a much broader sense of grievance," according to Lukas, that the Irish "had been abandoned by the very institution—City Hall, the Democratic Party, the Catholic Church, the popular press—that until recently had been their patrons and allies."

Mayor Kevin White struggled to balance his support among his fellow Irish with a desire to uphold the law. Despite the uproar, courts later ordered Boston to expand its busing program.

Perhaps the most tragic outcome of the busing controversy is that it did little to improve the academic performances of the city's African Americans. When the busing program officially ended in 1999, even supporters wondered if this had been a well-intended but ill-advised venture that had altered Boston's history for the worse.

Shooting star Irish American Rick Barry was one of the best pure shooters in basketball history. His underhanded free throw style netted a 90.0-percent career success rate, which stood for years as an NBA record. From the floor, his picture-perfect jump shot and incredible range gave defenders fits. The eight-time NBA All-Star is the only player in history to have captured NCAA, ABA, and NBA scoring titles. Barry scored an NBA-high 35.6 points per game in 1966–67, and he led Golden State (*pictured*) to the 1975 NBA championship.

The new Governor Brown Jerry Brown was elected governor of California in 1974. He succeeded Ronald Reagan, the man who had defeated Brown's father, Governor Pat Brown, in 1966. He served two successful terms and ran for the Democratic presidential nomination three times—in 1976, 1980, and 1984. In his last two presidential races, Brown emerged as one of the nation's most-liberal mainstream politicians, advocating universal health care and greater federal support for solar power. Brown served as mayor of Oakland from 1999 to 2007 before becoming attorney general of California.

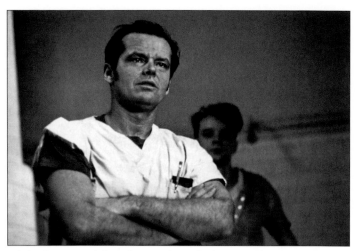

Nicholson's Irish roles Jack Nicholson, Irish American on his mother's side, ranks among Hollywood's most prolific actors. Nicholson began his career with bit roles in the late 1950s and went on to win three Academy Awards and garner 12 nominations. Nicholson won his first award in 1976 for his starring role in *One Flew Over the Cuckoo's Nest,* in which he played Irish American criminal Randle P. McMurphy (*pictured*), who pretends he's insane. Nicholson's film credits include *Ironweed,* based on William Kennedy's Pulitzer Prize-winning novel, and *The Departed,* in which he played an Irish American mob boss.

"Irish" as a selling point Print and TV ads for Irish Spring soap were so ubiquitous in the 1970s and beyond that they became part of American pop culture. Such ads demonstrated that images of "Irishness" had come full circle in America. Once widely seen in a negative light, Ireland and the Irish were now viewed favorably: The Irish were jocular, friendly, and down to earth, and their land was of unparalleled beauty. Thus, ad campaigns for faux Irish goods, such as Lucky Charms cereal and Irish Spring soap, and for genuine Irish products, such as Guinness Stout and Bushmills Irish Whiskey, all turned on a positive image of Ireland.

Trendsetting skater With a bright smile and youthful enthusiasm, Dorothy Hamill captured America's hearts when she won the gold medal in women's figure skating at the 1976 Winter Olympics in Innsbruck, Austria. Her short, bobbed haircut influenced a generation of young American women who came of age in the late 1970s. Her signature move on the ice, a camel spin followed by a sit spin, became known as the "Hamill camel." The Irish American skater, who was born in an "Irish ghetto" in Chicago, spent most of her childhood in Greenwich, Connecticut.

The IRA reemerges When unrest began in Northern Ireland in the mid-1960s, the Irish Republican Army was virtually moribund. A campaign in the mid-1950s had achieved nothing, and the outlawed paramilitary group faded into obscurity. But when British soldiers and Northern Ireland's security forces tried to crush the civil rights movement, the main faction of the IRA, known as the IRA's Provisional wing, found a new pool of recruits among the province's young people living in the slums of Derry (*pictured*) and West Belfast. By the mid-1970s, Northern Ireland was a war zone, and several generations of young people reached maturity having never known peace.

Playmate of the Year Irish beauty had come a long way from the caricatures of the mid-19th century. Patti McGuire was a student at Southern Illinois University, majoring in political science, when she was featured in the November 1976 issue of *Playboy* magazine. Her sultry good looks earned her Playmate of the Year honors in 1977, launching a career as a model and producer. In 1980 she married Jimmy Connors, an Irish American tennis star who won eight Grand Slam titles in the 1970s and '80s.

Leader of the longshoremen Thomas "Teddy" Gleason, a dockworker and union leader for 73 of his 92 years, was the dominant figure on the New York waterfront for half a century. Through his leadership of the International Longshoremen's Association from 1963 to '87, he changed the way in which America's ports worked. Tough and outspoken, Gleason—the eldest of 13 children—turned an undisciplined union into a force to be reckoned with in American labor. He was the grand marshal of the New York St. Patrick's Day parade in 1984.

June 21, 1974: Judge Arthur Garrity orders the integration of Boston public schools via a mandatory busing program. The tension between the Irish community of South Boston and the largely black community of Roxbury will persist for several years.

July 17, 1974: One person is dead and 41 are injured when an IRA bomb explodes in the White Tower at the Tower of London.

July 29, 1974: Irish American Jimmy Connors is the top-ranked tennis player for the week, a spot he will hold for 160 consecutive weeks.

August 9, 1974: Facing impeachment over the fallout from the Watergate scandal, President Richard M. Nixon resigns from office.

November 21, 1974: Twenty-one die when IRA bombs explode in two Birmingham pubs—Tavern in the Town and the Mulberry Bush.

December 24, 1974: John Glenn, the Mercury 7 astronaut who became the first American to orbit Earth, takes office as U.S. senator (D-OH).

January 6, 1975: Following in the footsteps of his father, Pat, Edmund Gerald "Jerry" Brown, Jr., takes office as governor of California.

July 31, 1975: A UVF detail accidentally detonates a bomb while attempting to smuggle it onto the Miami Showband's tour bus at a false checkpoint in Newry, Northern Ireland. Two of the terrorists are killed, while those remaining murder three of the band members.

1976: Pittsburgh Steelers owner Dan Rooney and former Heinz CEO Anthony O'Reilly establish The Ireland Fund to raise money for their stated goals of peace, culture, and charity.
• Leon Uris releases *Trinity,* a novel about Ireland from the Great Famine to the Easter Rising.

The writings of Dunne and Didion Irish American John Gregory Dunne (*pictured*) brought a critical East Coast eye to his writings about the Irish of California, including Hollywood. The Connecticut-born Dunne penned the best-selling *True Confessions* in 1977, a murder tale featuring Irish American brothers—a priest and a cop. Dunne was married to novelist Joan Didion (*right*), who was part Irish, and father of Quintana (*left*). In her 2005 bestseller, *The Year of Magical Thinking,* Didion wrote about coping with the loss of her husband, who had died of a heart attack at the dinner table in 2003. Quintana died two years later.

A new kind of television
Phil Donahue is considered the father of substantive daytime talk shows. For three decades, he hosted shows for housewives that emphasized serious issues—as opposed to the mindless game shows and soap operas that had filled the morning and afternoon time slots. Born in Cleveland, Donahue became a TV news anchor in the late 1950s, and he landed his
first TV talk show in Chicago in 1967. Donahue once said: "We found that women were interested in a lot more than covered dishes and needlepoint." Donahue dominated daytime TV until he retired in 1996.

Hamill chronicles New York If the title "Irish America's Bard" existed, it would settle easily on the shoulders of Pete Hamill. The son of immigrants from Belfast, Brooklyn-born Hamill was a combative liberal. Beginning in the early 1960s, he marched steadily through the worlds of newspapers, magazines, and books. As a newspaper editor, essay-

ist, and author, he emerged as one of the great chroniclers of his native city. His best-selling works include *Forever, Downtown: My Manhattan,* and the autobiographical *A Drinking Life.*

Chicago's funny man For more than three decades, Bill Murray has been one of Hollywood's top comic actors. Raised in the Chicago suburbs, Murray was one of nine children (several of them actors, including Brian Doyle Murray) and often got into trouble at school. His big break came when he joined Chicago's influential Second City comedy troupe, which led to a starring role on TV's *Saturday Night Live.* His movie breakthrough was the 1979 comedy *Meatballs.* A string of hits followed, including *Caddyshack* (pictured), *Ghostbusters,* and *Groundhog Day.* Murray's serious role in 2004's *Lost in Translation* earned him an Oscar nomination.

George Carlin's perspective Did you ever notice, comedian George Carlin would ask, that mice have no shoulders? No, we didn't, because only the skewed mind of Carlin could conceive of such things. Carlin's observational humor and bug-eyed delivery earned him regular gigs on *The Tonight Show* in the 1960s. He rose to greater heights in the '70s and beyond with his hilarious rants against America's Establishment and hypocrisies—as well as the Catholic faith (in which he had been raised). In 1972 Carlin was arrested for verbalizing the "seven words you can never say on television"—a routine that led to a 1978 U.S. Supreme Court decision regarding free speech.

Flanagan's Irish novels
Thomas Flanagan taught English for many years at Cal-Berkeley and the State University of New York at Stony Brook. In 1979 he achieved literary acclaim with the publication of his first novel, *The Year of the French.* The story centers on the Rebellion of 1798, when a small French army landed in County Mayo to support Irish rebels. Flanagan followed up this success with two other

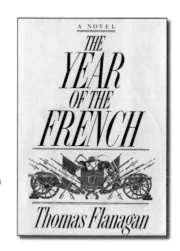

novels that completed the story of Ireland's quest for independence: *The Tenants of Time* and *The End of the Hunt.*

February 13, 1976: U.S. figure skater Dorothy Hamill wins a gold medal at the Olympic Winter Games in Innsbruck, Austria.

March 29, 1976: Jack Nicholson earns best actor honors for his portrayal of Randall Patrick McMurphy in the film adaptation of Ken Kesey's *One Flew Over the Cuckoo's Nest.*

April 5, 1976: Irish American industrialist, aviator, and film producer Howard Hughes, who is perhaps best known for being a spectacularly wealthy recluse, dies while being transported in his airplane at age 70.

November 1976: Chicago mayor Richard J. Daley wins election to his fourth term of office.

January 3, 1977: Montana senator Mike Mansfield leaves office after 24 years in the U.S. Senate. He spent 16 of those years as the Senate majority leader, longer than anyone else in Senate history. • Daniel Patrick Moynihan, a New York Democrat, takes the U.S. Senate seat that he will hold for the next 24 years.

December 10, 1977: Betty Williams and Mairead Corrigan are awarded the Nobel Peace Prize for founding the Peace Movement of Northern Ireland.

September 1978: Andy Rooney launches his humorous essay segment "A Few Minutes with Andy Rooney" on the CBS news program *60 Minutes.*

1979: The Progressive Unionist Party is formed in Belfast as the political arm of the Ulster Volunteer Force. • *The Year of the French,* Thomas Flanagan's book about the Irish Rebellion of 1798, is released to critical acclaim. It will win the National Book Critics Circle Award.

December 9, 1979: Archbishop Fulton Sheen dies, two months after receiving high praise from Pope John Paul II for his service to the church.

Byrne blazes a trail Jane Byrne, the first female mayor of a large American city, entered Chicago politics in the 1960s and was taken under the wing of Mayor Richard J. Daley. After Daley died, Byrne became disenchanted with his successor (Michael Bilandic) and ran for mayor in 1979. She won a surprising victory. She then garnered national headlines when, as mayor, she moved into a housing project to highlight the need for better low-income housing. Byrne, however, was never able to build a coalition among reformers and machine Democrats, and she lost the following election.

The Irish Celtic It was only fitting that Kevin McHale, the son of an Irish American father, wound up a Boston *Celtic.* But it was his remarkable ability to score in the post more than his heritage that endeared him to fans in Boston. Joining Larry Bird and Robert Parish on one of the best frontcourts in NBA history, McHale helped power the Celtics to three NBA titles in the 1980s. The seven-time All-Star and 1999 Hall of Fame inductee averaged 17.9 points per game over his career.

"Four Horsemen" Push for Peace

The Troubles in Northern Ireland forced a great divide in Irish America. Some sympathetic Americans asserted that violence was the only way to secure Irish unity, while others believed that peaceful political change was the only justifiable way forward. As violence escalated in the 1970s, the former method was in the apparent ascent.

Northern Ireland's moderate politicians, most especially John Hume, were concerned about the potential destabilizing effects that American-based support for the IRA might have on constitutional politics on both sides of the border in Ireland. Working with the Irish government's diplomats in Washington, they moved to rally support for a peaceful solution in Northern Ireland. One notable result of this effort was the emergence in the late 1970s of a group of Irish American leaders dubbed the "Four Horsemen."

Senators Ted Kennedy and Daniel Patrick Moynihan, Speaker of the House Tip O'Neill, and New York governor Hugh Carey first rode into public view with a 1977 St. Patrick's Day statement that condemned Irish American support for the IRA. The Four Horsemen appealed to Americans to embrace the goal of peace "and to renounce any action that promoted the current violence or provided support or encouragement to organizations engaged in violence." The statement would be the first of many from the group and its individual members, who would play a growing role in the efforts during the 1980s to secure a constitutional settlement in Northern Ireland.

The Horsemen would spur the formation of a congressional caucus known as the Friends of Ireland, formed in 1981. The Friends would be a political counterpoint to the House of Representatives-based Ad Hoc Committee for Irish Affairs. That committee also condemned violence, but it was more sharply critical of British policy and more inclined to listen to the arguments of militant Irish Americans. The personalities in both groups changed over the years, as the peace process brought about an inevitable melding of views between them.

One of the "Four Horsemen" Hugh Carey, New York governor from 1975 to '82, was one of the most influential Irish American politicians of his day. As a governor, Carey seemed the odd man out in the Irish American power quartet known as the "Four Horsemen," the others being senators Daniel Patrick Moynihan, Ted Kennedy, and Tip O'Neill. But Carey, who as governor helped rescue New York City from bankruptcy, had himself served seven terms as a congressman. The Horsemen condemned Irish American support for the IRA (because of the group's use of violence) while simultaneously calling for a more interventionist U.S. role in Northern Ireland.

Kennedy dogged by Chappaquiddick After the deaths of his brothers, U.S. Senator Ted Kennedy (D-MA) carried the torch for Irish America's most famous family. Though a run at the presidency was inevitable, winning it proved beyond the powers of even this consummate politician. Kennedy's 1969 misadventure at Chappaquiddick, in which passenger Mary Jo Kopechne had died after he drove a car into a pond, dogged Kennedy's political ambitions. In 1980 it doomed his attempt to wrest the Democratic nomination from President Jimmy Carter. His Senate career, by contrast, flourished. On Irish American issues, Kennedy, an uncompromising opponent of violence in Northern Ireland, became a dominant figure. It was said that any visiting Irish politician had three ports of call in Washington: the White House, Capitol Hill, and Ted Kennedy's office.

> **"I am the great-grandson of a Tipperary man. I'm the president of a country with the closest possible ties to Ireland."**
> —PRESIDENT RONALD REAGAN, ADDRESSING A JOINT SESSION OF THE IRISH PARLIAMENT IN DUBLIN, JUNE 4, 1984

Ronald Reagan

In June 1984, Ronald Reagan visited Tipperary and said: "My great-grandfather left here in a time of stress, seeking to better himself and his family. From what I'm told, we were a poor family. But my ancestors took with them a treasure: an indomitable spirit that was cultivated in the rich soil of this county." Millions of Americans could have made these comments. This one happened to be the president, whose Irish roots were as strong as his support among Irish American voters.

Reagan's great-grandfather, Michael, was born in Ballyporeen, Tipperary, and moved to London during the Great Famine. The Reagans eventually settled in California, and Ronald was born in Tampico, Illinois, in 1911. His father, John, was a practicing Catholic who converted after marrying a Protestant.

Reagan famously made a name for himself as an actor in Hollywood. He was politically active in the Screen Actor's Guild before becoming a rising Republican star as governor of California. One of his great skills was winning over voters who had traditionally voted Democrat.

In fact, in 1980, Irish Catholics were considered an integral part of the so-called "Reagan Democrat" coalition, which put "The Gipper" in the White House. For many Irish, Reagan was the first Republican they had ever voted for. The appeal went beyond Reagan's vaunted communication style, which some attribute to his Irish background. Following the excesses of the 1960s and '70s, many Irish Catholics were attracted to Reagan's cultural conservatism.

Reagan was a controversial president. Though credited for ending the Cold War, he was accused by opponents of creating huge budget deficits, favoring the rich, siding with big business over labor, and supporting questionable regimes. During his visit to Ireland, a folk singer greeted him with a song critical of U.S. policy in Central America. Reagan's famous humility and optimism would not be dimmed. "My roots in Ballyporeen, County Tipperary, are little different than millions of other Americans who find their roots in towns and counties all over the Isle of Erin," he said. "I just feel exceptionally lucky to have this chance to visit you."

An inch from death President Ronald Reagan is shot as he departs the Washington Hilton on March 30, 1981. Wounded under his left arm, Reagan was rushed to George Washington University Hospital, and it was only then that the true gravity of his injuries was discovered. The would-be assassin's bullet had missed Reagan's heart by less than an inch, and the president nearly bled to death during surgery. Reagan reportedly told his wife, Nancy, after he regained consciousness, "Honey, I forgot to duck." The 70-year-old president was back at his desk in less than a month.

Brady calls for gun control Events on March 30, 1981, forever changed the life of Irish American James Brady, President Reagan's White House press secretary. On that day, a shot fired in an assassination attempt on the president struck Brady in the head, partially paralyzing him. Confined to a wheelchair, Brady and his activist wife, Sarah, became staunch supporters of strict gun-control laws. Through their efforts, Congress in 1993 passed the Brady Handgun Violence Prevention Act (the "Brady Bill"), which required background checks on prospective purchasers of handguns. In 1996 President Clinton awarded Brady the Presidential Medal of Freedom.

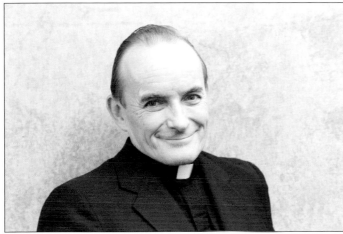

Father Greeley's words of wisdom A prolific writer and sociologist, as well as a parish priest, Father Andrew Greeley published some 150 books on a wide range of topics. Born in Illinois in 1928, Greeley began publishing sociological studies of the priesthood in the 1970s. Then in 1981 came the influential *Irish Americans: The Rise to Money and Power*. Since then, Greeley has churned out mystery novels as well as books and articles on politics and history. He also has written about sex and child abuse in the priesthood. He is one of America's foremost Catholic intellectuals.

Dying for their cause Hunger strikes have a long, tragic, and revered place in Irish history. In 1981 imprisoned members of the IRA and another paramilitary group, the Irish National Liberation Army, began turning away their meals in an effort to gain status as prisoners of war. Led by Bobby Sands, the strike began on March 1. As the world's media converged on Northern Ireland, Sands won election to the House of Commons while on strike—a startling show of support for the protest. Sands lingered for 66 days before he died on May 5. Nine more prisoners starved themselves to death. Irish Americans were galvanized by the dramatic sacrifice, and renewed protests against British rule in the North took place in several U.S. cities.

August 1980: Senator Ted Kennedy withdraws from the presidential race.

September 9, 1980: Brothers Philip and Daniel Berrigan, both Roman Catholic priests, launch the "Plowshares Movement." The antiwar group will stage dozens of nonviolent protests over the course of the next decade.

November 2, 1980: Inveterate Irish American bank robber Willie Sutton dies after spending nearly half his life in prison. In his final years, he consulted with banks about improving security measures.

January 20, 1981: Former actor and California governor Ronald Reagan is sworn in as the 40th president of the United States.

February 28, 1981: Imprisoned Provisional IRA member Bobby Sands enjoys his last meal. He will launch a hunger strike the next day in an effort to have himself and his comrades regarded as political prisoners, not criminals.

April 9, 1981: Well into his hunger strike, Bobby Sands is elected to Parliament.

May 5, 1981: Bobby Sands dies at the age of 27, 66 days into his hunger strike, while imprisoned near Belfast.

July 4, 1981: John McEnroe of New York captures the title at Wimbledon, defeating Bjorn Borg in the final round. Despite his impressive play, the event is distinguished by McEnroe's frequent outbursts, including heckling the judges with calls of "You cannot be serious!"

March 29, 1982: Warren Beatty's film *Reds* earns him a best director statuette as well as best supporting actress accolades for Maureen Stapleton. The film receives nominations in all four acting categories.

McEnroe whines and wins Called a "petulant loudmouth" by the British tabloids, John "Superbrat" McEnroe was also among the most successful tennis players of all time. His words and antics on the court did not always hold up to Wimbledon standards for gentlemanly conduct. Still, he counted three Wimbledon and four U.S. Open singles titles among his 17 Grand Slam crowns (including doubles). Before a 1983 Davis Cup match in Dublin, McEnroe said his ancestry gave him a purer pedigree than Ireland's No. 1 player.

O'Connor breaks the barrier On July 7, 1981, President Reagan nominated Arizona Appeals Court judge Sandra Day O'Connor as an associate justice of the U.S. Supreme Court. Confirmed by the Senate by a 99–0 vote, O'Connor became the first woman ever to serve on the highest court in the land. Here she descends the court's steps with Chief Justice Warren Burger. Though she was a moderate on the bench, controversy enveloped O'Connor in 2000 when it was reported that she did not want to retire while a Democrat could appoint her replacement. She was one of five justices who voted in favor of George Bush in the contested 2000 election. She finally retired in 2006.

The "Great White Hope" Promoter Don King was among those who called Gerry Cooney the "Great White Hope" prior to his much-hyped heavyweight championship fight against Larry Holmes in 1982. Before losing that bout by TKO in Round 13, the product of a large, Irish Catholic family in Huntington, New York, had never been

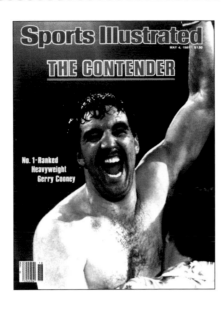

forced to fight past the eighth round during his unbeaten pro career. A winner of two New York Golden Gloves titles, Cooney went 28–3 with 25 knockouts as a pro.

Burning topics A chronicler of the rich and powerful, Dominick Dunne was one of six children born to an Irish American family in Hartford, Connecticut. After serving in Word War II, he worked at a number of show business jobs, including movie producer. Dunne was thrust into the public eye in 1982 when his daughter, actress Dominique Dunne, was murdered by her former boyfriend. After publishing several novels, Dunne used his own experiences with criminal justice to cover the high-profile murder cases of Claus von Bulow and O. J. Simpson for *Vanity Fair* magazine.

Notre Dame's revered president Father Theodore Hesburgh was born to an Irish American mother and German American father. However, his long tenure as president of the University of Notre Dame made this high-impact religious figure, civil rights activist, and political leader as "Fighting Irish" as they came. Father Hesburgh served for 35 years (1952–87) as Notre Dame's revered president—the longest tenure in the school's history. While leading the university to national prominence as an academic institution, he also made lasting contributions to the Catholic Church and stood side by side with the likes of Dr. Martin Luther King in the struggle for human freedoms.

A few funny minutes Would there be anything ridiculous left in the world if Andy Rooney was in charge? Certainly, the resident curmudgeon on CBS's *60 Minutes* has a keen eye for the absurd and a double-barreled tongue to match. Beginning in 1978, and lasting for three decades, "A Few Minutes with Andy Rooney" has

served as the humorous conclusion to the Sunday evening news show. Before entering broadcasting, the Albany-born Rooney nailed down his journalistic reputation during World War II while writing for *Stars and Stripes*.

The MacBride Principles

Northern Ireland experienced profound changes in the final decades of the 20th century. But while violence grabbed the biggest headlines, significant change was also pushed through on paper by a set of nine fair-employment guidelines known as the MacBride Principles. The principles served as a code of conduct for companies doing business in Northern Ireland.

The MacBride Principles were named after Irish statesman and Nobel laureate Dr. Sean MacBride. But the MacBride campaign's engine was U.S.-based and primarily driven by a Washington, D.C.-based lobbying group, the Irish National Caucus. The INC, headed by Irish-born priest Father Sean McManus, forged alliances with sympathetic members of Congress and the office of the New York City comptroller.

The MacBride campaign demanded job equality for all in Northern Ireland. During the 1980s, more than a dozen U.S. states and 30 cities adopted the MacBride Principles and urged U.S. companies doing business in Northern Ireland to follow the principles.

Opposition from the British government, and even some nationalist politicians in Northern Ireland, was vociferous and included extensive lobbying by British officials and diplomats in the U.S. Crucially, however, MacBride backers were able to argue that their nonviolent, civil rights-based campaign was not only consistent with American ideals, but a good way of energizing Irish Americans who might otherwise have been tempted to support the IRA.

The MacBride effort spurred the British government to pass legislation aimed at tackling discrimination in Northern Ireland, where unemployment among Catholics had been two and a half times higher than among Protestants. The MacBride campaign in America reached a symbolic mountaintop in 1998 when President Bill Clinton signed a federal MacBride Principles bill into law.

The Provos' deadly campaign The IRA's Provisional wing—or the Provos, as its members were called—carried out a relentless campaign against British targets throughout the 1980s. Hundreds of innocent civilians were killed, as were security forces and members of the IRA and of Protestant paramilitary organizations. The IRA brought its campaign to the British mainland in 1982. On July 20, a nail bomb exploded during a parade of the Queen's Household Cavalry in London's Hyde Park. Media images of dead and wounded horses (*pictured*) horrified the world. Two soldiers also died, and 17 civilians and soldiers were wounded.

Ford rockets to stardom Of mixed Irish and Jewish parentage, screen star Harrison Ford once said that he felt "Irish as a person but Jewish as an actor." For Ford, the road to stardom was rocky. Through much of the 1960s and early '70s, he worked as a carpenter in Los Angeles while picking up bit parts in movies and TV. A chance meeting with director George Lucas won him the part of Han Solo in *Star Wars* and launched his mammoth cinematic career. Ford rose to superstardom with his portrayal of an adventurous archaeologist in the Indiana Jones series. He is pictured here in *Indiana Jones and the Temple of Doom*.

Sullivan walks in space It was one giant leap for womankind. New Jersey-born Dr. Kathryn Dwyer Sullivan joined NASA's astronaut team in 1979 and quickly made her mark in the Space Shuttle program. On October 11, 1984, she became the first American woman to walk in space after being launched into orbit aboard the *Challenger*. Sullivan undertook two subsequent Space Shuttle missions, including one in 1990 as part of the crew that deployed the Hubble Space Telescope. In all, Sullivan logged 532 space hours before retiring from orbital flight.

$1 billion worth of pizza Raised by nuns in an orphanage after his father's death in 1941, Tom Monaghan served in the Marines before buying a pizza parlor in Ypsilanti, Michigan, in 1960. He built Domino's into America's second largest pizza chain (and also bought the Detroit Tigers). After selling the pizza company in 1998 for an estimated $1 billion, he used his wealth to advance conservative Catholic causes. He has given millions to support pro-life organizations and Catholic schools. His most ambitious and controversial projects have been the establishment of a Catholic law school in Michigan and the creation of a Catholic city and university, both called Ave Maria, in Florida.

Walsh leads 49ers to glory "If [Bill] Walsh were a general," ESPN analyst Beano Cook once said, "he would be able to overrun Europe with the army from Sweden." The son of a day laborer who once got him a job in a garage near the Los Angeles Coliseum, Walsh knew that hard work and a keen intellect formed a winning combination. He spent countless hours perfecting what became known as the West Coast Offense, which he used to mold the San Francisco 49ers into a 1980s juggernaut. He won three Super Bowls in 10 seasons with the Niners.

November 16, 1982: Lenny Murphy, UVF member and leader of the gang of sociopaths known as the Shankill Butchers, is assassinated by the IRA.

1983: Belfast Catholic Gerry Adams is named president of the nationalist political party Sinn Féin.

May 30, 1983: Irish prime minister Garret FitzGerald convenes the New Ireland Forum, a meeting of political interests on both sides of the ongoing conflict, in an effort to achieve a framework for peace.

1984: Father Sean McManus, president of the Irish National Caucus, promotes the MacBride Principles, a code governing the conduct of American interests doing business in Northern Ireland.

April 9, 1984: Irish American actors Shirley MacLaine and Jack Nicholson earn best actress and best supporting actor Oscars for their roles in *Terms of Endearment*.

January 1985: Prominent antiwar veteran John Kerry is sworn in as the junior senator from Massachusetts.

November 15, 1985: The Anglo-Irish Agreement, which attempts to gain peace by offering the Republic of Ireland a nominal role in Northern Ireland's government, is signed at Hillsborough Castle by British prime minister Margaret Thatcher and Irish prime minister Garret FitzGerald.

1986: An amendment to the Immigration Reform and Control Act provides for several thousand "Donnelly visas," named for the Massachusetts congressman (James Donnelly) who sponsored the amendment, to be distributed via lottery. Due to targeted advertising, nearly half the visas are won by Irish nationals. • Irish American investigative journalist, columnist, and author Jimmy Breslin is awarded the Pulitzer Prize for Commentary.

Geldof creates LiveAid Dublin-born rocker Bob Geldof (*pictured*) was the architect of the LiveAid famine relief concerts of July 13, 1985. Geldof conceived of "a global juke box"—overlapping concerts at London's Wembley Stadium and Philadelphia's JFK Stadium that would be broadcast worldwide to raise funds for Ethiopian famine victims. Among the dozens of American acts at JFK Stadium were Bob Dylan, Neil Young, Tom Petty, Joan Baez, and B. B. King. Ireland donated more per capita than any other nation, and the total LiveAid contributions reportedly topped $200 million.

Fire on ice Joe Mullen grew up a gritty competitor in Manhattan's rugged Hell's Kitchen area, dominating street hockey games in which a roll of electrical tape sometimes served as the puck. He stayed close to his Irish American roots by playing for Boston College on a partial scholarship. There and in the NHL, his tenacity served him well. In 18 NHL seasons for the Blues, Flames, Bruins, and Penguins, Mullen won three Stanley Cups and became the first American-born player to amass 500 career goals.

McAuliffe and *Challenger* People around the world mourned the loss of the seven-member *Challenger* crew after the Space Shuttle exploded seconds after takeoff on January 28, 1986. Many were particularly touched by the death of Christa Corrigan McAuliffe, who a short while earlier had stepped aboard *Challenger* as the first civilian bound for space. A schoolteacher in New Hampshire, McAuliffe had been chosen for the flight from thousands of applicants eager to be the first member of NASA's Teacher in Space Program. A fellowship for outstanding teachers now bears her name.

Speaker of the House Thomas Phillip "Tip" O'Neill was the last of the truly commanding urban politicians to emerge from Irish America. O'Neill was born in Cambridge, Massachusetts, and served in the state House of Representatives before being elected to Congress in 1953. A New Deal liberal who never wavered from his belief that "all politics is local," O'Neill served 17 terms in the House and was the speaker of the

House from 1977 to '87. As speaker, O'Neill opposed the rising conservative tide embodied by the election of President Ronald Reagan in 1980.

An economics whiz James Tobin's ability to analyze the intricacies of an economy reached its academic height in 1947, when he earned a doctorate in economics from Harvard. Tobin took his qualifications to Yale, where he lectured during the fast-changing early years of the baby boom. At the request of President Kennedy, Tobin sat on the Council of Economic Advisers in 1961 and '62. He won the Nobel Prize for economics in 1986 for his work on the relationship between financial markets, expenditure decisions, employment, production, and prices.

New generation of Kennedys Joseph P. Kennedy III, son of Robert and Ethel Kennedy, was elected to the House of Representatives in 1986, taking the seat previously held by Speaker of the House Tip O'Neill and by Kennedy's famous uncle, John F. Kennedy. Joseph was part of a third wave of Kennedys who played prominent roles in public life. His sister Kathleen Kennedy Townsend served as lieutenant governor of Maryland from 1995 to 2003; his brother Robert F. Kennedy, Jr., became a prominent environmentalist; and his cousin Patrick Kennedy (Ted Kennedy's son) became a congressman from Rhode Island. While in Congress, Joseph Kennedy was active in housing and energy issues.

January 28, 1986: The Space Shuttle *Challenger* disintegrates moments after takeoff, claiming the lives of seven astronauts. Christa Corrigan McAuliffe, who was meant to be the first teacher in space, is among those who perish.

March 24, 1986: Anjelica Huston, daughter of director John Huston, earns a best actress Oscar for her work in *Prizzi's Honor*.

November 6, 1986: President Ronald Reagan signs the Immigration Reform and Control Act, which grants amnesty to illegal aliens who have been continually in residence since 1981.

January 3, 1987: Speaker of the House Thomas P. "Tip" O'Neill retires after representing Massachusetts for nearly 35 years in the U.S. House of Representatives.

January 29, 1987: William Casey, director of the CIA, resigns his post after six years in office.

March 17, 1987: President Reagan hosts a White House event at which the merger of The Irish Fund and the American Irish Foundation is announced. The new organization is called the American Ireland Fund.

November 1987: Joseph Kennedy, the oldest son of Robert F. Kennedy, wins election to Tip O'Neill's former seat in the U.S. House of Representatives.

December 17, 1987: *The Dead,* director John Huston's ambitious adaptation of the James Joyce book of the same name, is released.

1988: President Reagan appoints Irish American jurist Anthony Kennedy to the U.S. Supreme Court.

April 29, 1989: Jodie Foster is named the year's best actress for her work in *The Accused,* while Kevin Klein is awarded best supporting actor for his comedic performance in *A Fish Called Wanda*.

A wave of immigration Irish citizens wait in line at the U.S. Embassy in 1987 to apply for visas to emigrate. That generation's youth had been reared with expectations that were higher than those of their parents. But the Irish economy floundered in the 1980s, and tens of thousands of Irish left for America in the second half of the decade. However, many of them faced a major problem: They found that they had missed the amnesty offered in the 1986 immigration reform bill. These illegal aliens joined the Irish Immigration Reform Movement and campaigned for visas. More than 70,000 would ultimately secure green cards.

HELPING OUT THE NEW ARRIVALS

Angie McCarthy, a friend from the neighborhood...[told me that] newly arrived Irish immigrants were having trouble getting bank accounts and were getting mugged a lot, because they carried their cash around, up in the Bronx.... So I said, 'Gee, that's not right, why don't we send them in....' We had to have ID, and a lot of them did not have ID, so I said [we could accept an] Irish passport, or something like that. So, I was doing a lot of informal things. Cutting corners, to the point of legality, we'd get a lot of accounts for them. And...we took care of a lot of Irish kids coming over, and helped them with accounts. Once you get an account established, have a checking account, you're getting interest and you have a domicile, and your money is safe, most importantly. I mean, working hard for six or seven hundred a week and getting hit on the head and getting it stolen from you—not much worse than that. So, I think we stopped some of that.

—DONALD A. KELLY, A RETIRED SENIOR VICE PRESIDENT OF EMIGRANT SAVINGS BANK AND AN EMERALD ISLE IMMIGRATION CENTER EXECUTIVE COMMITTEE MEMBER, ABOUT HELPING UNDOCUMENTED IRISH IMMIGRANTS IN NEW YORK DURING THE 1980s

Illegal Immigrants

The arrival of thousands of Irish immigrants during the 1980s stood out from previous migrations. In this new wave, many of the newcomers overstayed visitors' visas and became undocumented. Irish fled their homeland due to a sharp economic downturn in both the Republic and Northern Ireland, where The Troubles were a constant fiscal dampener. They headed for America, whose economy was booming.

Fiona McConnell, a one-time illegal immigrant

As was the case with previous waves, the new Irish immigrants hooked up with family members and acquaintances. Due to so many recent immigrants, cultural groups flourished and Irish American newspapers flew off the newsstands. But something was amiss. As Irish America became more familiar with the newcomers, it was being told—quietly at first, and then loudly—that few of them had been offered America's official welcome mat. This was because most had arrived after an amnesty for illegal immigrants (contained in the 1986 Immigration Reform and Control Act) had been granted.

The problems faced by these new but clearly different Irish led to the birth of the Irish Immigration Reform Movement (IIRM), a vocal, energetic lobbying group that quickly demonstrated a knack for attracting national media and political attention. The IIRM began in 1987, primarily as the creation of two undocumented arrivals from County Cork: Sean Minihane and Pat Hurley. In the years that followed, the IIRM startled Irish America into the realization that what had been accepted for generations—the near automatic processing of Irish immigrants into American society—was no longer a reality.

The IIRM's campaign prompted congressional action, which led to the Donnelly and Morrison visa programs. The result of these programs was more than 70,000 green cards for the Irish by the early 1990s. But even this bonanza failed to bring relief to all the undocumented Irish of the '80s. On their behalf, another organization—the Irish Lobby for Immigration Reform (ILIR)—has launched another visa campaign.

Americans behind the IRA This mural in South Boston, which includes the Irish language rendering of the words *Irish Republican Army* below the Celtic cross, mimicked the pro-IRA graffiti on many walls and buildings in Northern Ireland. But Irish American support for the IRA sometimes went beyond pictures. For example, militant leaders Michael Flannery and George Harrison were accused of supplying the IRA with weapons and money in the 1970s and '80s. They were indicted in 1980 but found not guilty, even though they admitted their role as conduits for the IRA. Their lawyers persuaded a jury that they believed they had the support of the Central Intelligence Agency.

Reagan's CIA director William Casey was director of the Central Intelligence Agency during the Reagan administration. Fiercely hostile to the Soviet Union, Casey had a strong influence on Reagan's hostility toward Moscow. As director, Casey was a pivotal figure in the Iran-Contra Affair, although he fell terminally ill before being called to testify on his role in the scandal. Despite his New York Irish Catholic background, Casey was exceptionally pro-British. Bob Woodward, in his 1987 book, *Veil, The Secret Wars of the CIA 1981–1987,* described Casey as a "certified Anglophile."

Downey's trash talk Before Jerry Springer and Maury Povich, there was Morton Downey, Jr. Born in 1932, Downey was the son of two popular singers. He found his own niche in radio, then television, where his abrasive style paved the way for a new kind of programming, the "trash" talk show, in the 1980s. Often smoking and screaming, Downey became hugely popular before the novelty wore off. He developed lung cancer in the 1990s, and he became an anti-smoking activist before dying in 2001.

Voice of the Dodgers A New York native, Vin Scully inherited his Irish mother's red hair and the tireless work ethic of both parents. Blessed with a soothing voice, poetic eloquence, and a passion for radio and baseball, Scully joined the Brooklyn Dodgers broadcast team at age 22 in 1950. The Dodgers moved to Los Angeles in 1958, and Scully went with them. Incredibly, in 2008, he celebrated his 59th consecutive season as the "Voice of the Dodgers." He has also worked for NBC and CBS, broadcasting major baseball, football, and golf events. In 2000 the American Sportscasters Association named him Broadcaster of the Century.

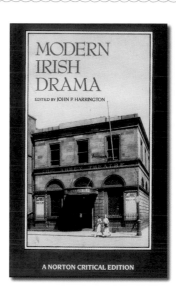

Kennedy rises to Supreme Court Along with Sandra Day O'Connor, Supreme Court Justice Anthony Kennedy often provided a pivotal swing vote on key rulings regarding abortion and the death penalty. Born in California to a family of practicing Catholics, Kennedy attended Stanford and Harvard before taking over his father's law practice. In 1975 he was appointed to the U.S. Court of Appeals for the Ninth Circuit. Ronald Reagan appointed him to the Supreme Court in 1987 after the previous nominee, Robert Bork, was deemed too conservative. Kennedy's centrist rulings have, at times, angered conservatives.

Studying the Irish Beginning in the 1960s, interest in Irish studies soared in the United States. Part of this came about because an ever-growing number of college-educated Irish Americans sought to better understand the Irish experience. Out of this interest grew the establishment in the early 1960s of two scholarly organizations, the American Committee for Irish Studies and the Irish American Cultural Institute, both of which were dedicated to advancing knowledge of Irish culture in the U.S. By the late 1980s, about 25 percent of all American colleges and universities offered courses or programs in Irish studies.

Black Mountain poet In 1962 Robert Creeley gained critical acclaim with a collection of poems entitled *For Love.* He already had been writing and teaching for a decade, during which he became friendly with famous Beat writers Allen Ginsberg and Jack Kerouac. Creeley, who lost his left eye in an accident at the age of four, wrote dozens of books—both poetry and prose. He was among the originators of the avant-garde Black Mountain school of poetry. Advanced by the experimental Black Mountain College, this poetic style was characterized by shorter lines that could be spoken in one utterance, forming a distinctive style of poetic diction. Creeley served as poet laureate of New York from 1989 to '91.

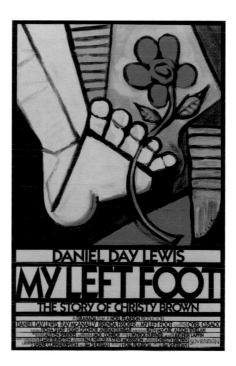

A poignant tale *My Left Foot* (1989) is the film biography of Irish painter and poet Christy Brown. In 1932 Brown was born with cerebral palsy into a huge working-class family in Dublin. He was able to control only one of his limbs—his left foot—but he learned to write and paint with it. The movie, based on Brown's autobiography, *Down All the Days,* was a hit in both Europe and America. Daniel Day-Lewis, son of Irish-born British poet laureate Cecil Day-Lewis, won an Academy Award for his portrayal of the moody and often cantankerous Brown.

Going Strong
1990–TODAY

> **"You never forget your homeland. You never forget your birth land. But I'm loyal to America. I would never think of going back [to Ireland]. My children are here. Their roots are here."**
>
> —IRISH IMMIGRANT
> MARY JO LENNEY, 1996

On an April evening in 1994, two young Irish American step dancers performed an original seven-minute piece during the televised talent show *Eurovision*. The program, which originated in Dublin, was watched by millions of viewers throughout Europe. The dancers were not part of the competition. They were merely providing entertainment between acts, but they stole the show. Jean Butler, a Long Island native, and Michael Flatley, of Chicago, became international superstars that night in Dublin. The piece they performed was called "Riverdance," and it became the centerpiece of a show that has toured the world several times over in the years since.

Few would have guessed it at the time, but "Riverdance" was just the beginning of an extraordinary and utterly unexpected flowering of Irish and Irish American culture in the 1990s—a Gaelic revival that carried into the new millennium. Several years after Butler and Flatley's debut, Irish American Thomas Cahill published a book entitled *How the Irish Saved Civilization* that became wildly popular. Frank McCourt followed with the enormous bestseller *Angela's Ashes,* an evocative story of his childhood in Brooklyn and Limerick and final immigration to the states. Alice McDermott won a National Book Award for *Charming Billy,* a story of suburban Irish America. Film directors Jim Sheridan and Terry George, both immigrants, hit the big time in Hollywood with several Irish-themed hits, including *Some Mother's Son.* Journalist Maureen Dowd of *The New York Times* won a Pulitzer Prize and became the best-read and most-imitated political columnist in the country.

Girls from the Woods School of Irish Dance perform in front of the Boston Convention & Exhibition Center in March 2005. Due largely to the success of "Riverdance," Irish cultural activities, particularly Irish dancing, flourished in the 1990s and 2000s.

Remarkable though these achievements were, they represented just a portion of the Irish story in the last decade of the 20th century. In 1994 the IRA announced a cease-fire in its violent campaign to end British rule in Northern Ireland. President Bill Clinton seized the moment, reaching out to all sides but especially to Gerry Adams, leader of Sinn Féin, the political party aligned with the IRA. In late 1995, as a fledgling peace process took hold in the North, Clinton and his wife, Hillary Rodham Clinton, visited Belfast to show their support for the province's peacemakers. Clinton was welcomed with the kind of enthusiasm and affection that the Irish had showed John F. Kennedy during his visit in 1963.

U.S. president Bill Clinton (*right*) meets with Sinn Féin president Gerry Adams on November 30, 1995. Hoping to broker a permanent peace in Northern Ireland, Clinton appointed former Senate majority leader George Mitchell to head the negotiations. The talks culminated in the historic Good Friday Agreement of 1998, an accord reached by the governments of Ireland and the United Kingdom and the political parties of Northern Ireland.

President Clinton, with Irish roots on his mother's side, sent a personal envoy—former U.S. senator George Mitchell of Maine—to the North to serve as a mediator among the contending parties. Irish American political figures, such as Congressman Peter King of Long Island and U.S. ambassador to Ireland Jean Kennedy Smith (sister of the slain president)—as well as such business leaders as Charles Feeney and Bill Flynn—kept all parties engaged and talking. Finally, with Washington's help, London, Dublin, and Northern Ireland's Catholic and Protestant political parties agreed on a framework for peace and power sharing in 1997. Years of continued negotiations followed, but at last an unlikely scenario unfolded in Belfast: Catholic and Protestant enemies joined together to jointly administer Northern Ireland.

To the south and west of Belfast, equally astonishing events were unfolding in the Irish Republic. Long an economic backwater, the Republic's investments in education and technology began to pay off in the mid-1990s. Young people no longer looked across the Atlantic for opportunities. Instead, opportunity kept them home—and made many of them rich. Thousands of young Irish immigrants who had revived old urban neighborhoods in America in the 1980s now did something utterly new and unexpected: They returned home. And they were not the only people who saw a chance to better themselves in Ireland, home of an economy dubbed the "Celtic Tiger." In yet another astonishing development, poor and unemployed people from Poland, Nigeria, Romania, and other countries moved to Ireland to find a better life. Ireland was no longer a source of immigration. It was a compelling destination.

And just as Irish America experienced a reawakening of culture and accomplishment, so too did the Irish in Ireland. The Irish rock band U2 became a global phenomenon. Irish poet Seamus Heaney, a native of Derry in Northern Ireland, won the Nobel Prize for literature in 1995. Politicians John Hume and David Trimble, who brought warring parties to the negotiating table in Northern Ireland, won the Nobel Peace Prize in 1998. And two Irish women, Mary Robinson and Mary McAleese, were successively elected president of Ireland.

Cultural and economic dynamism on both sides of the Atlantic have reinforced the ties that bind the Irish in America with the Irish in Ireland. Writers, rock bands, business leaders, politicians, shoppers, and the just plain curious have traveled between the New World and the new Ireland with ease and comfort, enriching the cultures of both nations. Time has not diminished the relationship between the United States and Ireland. Incredibly, and unexpectedly, the connections have never been stronger.

Perhaps that explains another phenomenon of the 1990s: the dedication of memorials to the Great Famine and its victims in the old cities of America in conjunction with the famine's 150th anniversary. The story of Irish America in the late 20th and early 21st centuries surely is one of achievement and influence. But Irish America's commemoration of the famine during the late 1990s reminded the world, and itself, of the tragedies that preceded prosperity.

Rescue workers remove the body of Father Mychal Judge, a chaplain with the Fire Department of New York, from the North Tower of the World Trade Center on September 11, 2001. The son of poor Catholic immigrants from Ireland, Judge rushed to the site to help victims. He was killed by falling debris.

One other event also reminded Irish America that sacrifice was not relegated to the struggles of the past. On September 11, 2001, nearly 3,000 people were killed when terrorists slammed two airliners into the World Trade Center skyscrapers in Lower Manhattan. Those who died were brokers, government workers, and dishwashers; they were Americans of European, Asian, and Hispanic descent. But it was the sacrifice of the Fire Department of New York, which lost 343 members, that symbolized the tragedy and the heroism of that day. It was hard not to notice the number of Irish American names among the FDNY's dead. Nearly half the firefighters were members of the department's Emerald Society, its Irish American fraternal group.

Heartbreak and hardship were no strangers to the Irish before 9/11, and no doubt there will be further unwelcome visits in the future. But the Irish in America also have learned the importance of resilience, determination, hard work, and faith.

They will not back down, because, after all, they never have.

1990–TODAY

1990: The Ulster Volunteer Force and the Ulster Defense Association join forces with the Combined Loyalist Paramilitary Command. • American computer giant Dell opens a manufacturing facility in Limerick, Ireland.

November 29, 1990: The Immigration Act of 1990 is enacted. It raises the maximum number of annual legal immigrants from 500,000 to 700,000 and restructures the visa lottery to more fairly distribute visas to traditionally less-favored nations.

1991: New York's St. Patrick's Day parade is consumed by controversy when the parade's organizer rejects the application of the Irish Lesbian and Gay Organization to participate in the parade.

August 28, 1991: United Artists releases *The Commitments,* an Alan Parker film about a group of Dublin drifters who form a soul band.

March 30, 1992: Jodie Foster wins best actress honors for her portrayal of Clarice Starling in the chilling Jonathan Demme film *The Silence of the Lambs.*

November 3, 1992: William Jefferson Clinton, of Irish ancestry, wins the presidential election, defeating incumbent George H. W. Bush.

1993: Van Morrison of Belfast is inducted into the Rock and Roll Hall of Fame.

September 22, 1993: Nolan Ryan, a flamethrowing Irish American pitcher with the Texas Rangers, takes the mound for the last time. He will retire with a major-league record 5,714 strikeouts.

December 15, 1993: The *Downing Street Declaration* is issued. It reestablishes the right of the people of Northern Ireland to determine if their province will be affiliated with the United Kingdom or the Republic of Ireland.

A pioneer in organ transplants What is today the almost routine medical procedure of human organ transplant owes much to the pioneering efforts of Dr. Joseph Murray. In the early 1950s, Murray sidelined his work in plastic surgery and turned his attention to the plight of patients suffering from kidney failure. In a procedure involving identical twins, Murray performed the first kidney transplant in 1954 at what is now Boston's Brigham and Women's Hospital. Murray's work progressed to transplants involving unrelated donors and recipients. In 1990 he won a Nobel Prize for his continued efforts in human organ transplants.

A comedy with soul In 1991 *The Commitments* hit U.S. theaters with an improbable and joyous mix of American rhythm and blues, Irish soul, and comic genius. The film relates the quest of a would-be North Dublin music impresario, Jimmy Rabbitte, to form a new band. Forsaking rock 'n' roll, Jimmy sets about recruiting musicians and singers for a soul ensemble. Why? As Jimmy explains it: "The Irish are the blacks of Europe. And Dubliners are the blacks of Ireland. And the Northside Dubliners are the blacks of Dublin." Featuring astonishing musical performances with a bittersweet plot, *The Commitments* remains a cult favorite.

Beautiful voice, strong convictions Dublin-born singer Sinead O'Connor exploded onto the American music scene in 1990 with her passionate version of the Prince song "Nothing Compares 2 U." But behind the beautiful voice was a woman of strong convictions, which often got her into trouble. Most famously, in 1992, O'Connor shocked America on *Saturday Night Live*. After performing, she held up a photo of Pope John Paul II and said, "Fight the real enemy," before tearing up the photo. O'Connor claimed to be protesting child sexual abuse within the Catholic Church.

Clancy under fire Tom Clancy penned some of the top-selling books of the 1990s and 2000s. Like the Baltimore native, Clancy's fictional hero, Jack Ryan, is Irish American. But many Irish were upset with the tenor of one of his best-sellers-turned-movie, *Patriot Games*. Unlike Clancy novels that are set against the Cold War, *Patriot Games* deals with the Irish Troubles. Critics claimed that all the British characters in the story were morally upstanding while all the Irish ones, except for Jack Ryan, were portrayed as psychotic killers.

The upper middle class Beginning in the 1960s, the children of Irish America began entering college and the professions in unprecedented numbers. By the time Ronald Reagan was elected president in 1980, Irish Americans were living in upper-middle-class suburbs, such as Birmingham, Michigan, with its tennis courts, golf courses, and tidy downtown. Birmingham's Brother Rice High School held an annual "Irish Night" auction that raised large sums for the school. Here, well-off locals play blackjack at a Birmingham Junior League fundraiser event.

GE's guiding light Jack Welch, one of the most successful and famous corporate leaders of his generation, is credited with transforming General Electric. Born in Salem, Massachusetts, he began working for GE in 1960 as an engineer. Over the years, he gained an intimate knowledge of what he saw as the company's rigid bureaucracy. Throughout the 1970s, he swiftly rose up the corporate ladder until becoming CEO in 1981, when the company's market value was $12 billion. By 2001, GE's value was $280 billion. That year, Welch penned a best-selling memoir entitled *Jack: Straight from the Gut.*

1994: The Peter Quinn novel *Banished Children of Eve* is released to strong reviews. Set in 1863 New York City, the story evokes the urban Irish Catholic immigrant experience during the Civil War. • Patrick Joseph Kennedy, Senator Ted Kennedy's second son, is elected to represent Rhode Island in the U.S. House of Representatives.

January 6, 1994: Irish American figure skater Nancy Kerrigan is clubbed on the knee by a goon hired by the husband of Tonya Harding, Kerrigan's rival. Kerrigan will recover in time to win Olympic silver the following month.

February 25, 1994: *In the Name of the Father,* a powerful film based on the true story of Gerry Conlon, a young Belfast man falsely accused of an IRA bombing, is released. The film's lead, Daniel Day-Lewis, will earn a best actor statuette for his portrayal of Conlon.

February 28, 1994: The Brady Handgun Violence Prevention Act takes effect. The "Brady Bill" is named for James Brady, President Reagan's Irish American press secretary who was critically injured during the 1981 assassination attempt on Reagan.

April 30, 1994: Michael Flatley and Jean Butler introduce their Irish step dancing routine, "Riverdance," on European television.

August 31, 1994: The IRA announces a cease-fire of indefinite duration.

1995: Robert McNamara, defense secretary under presidents Kennedy and Johnson who was chiefly responsible for the execution of the Vietnam War, publishes *In Retrospect,* his memoirs. It is widely regarded as an effort to apologize for Vietnam. • *The Brothers McMullen,* an Ed Burns film about three New York Irish Catholic brothers struggling with their personal lives, wins the Grand Jury Prize at the Sundance Film Festival.

The place to go

The Irish pub served generations of immigrants as a place to escape from the harder world—and conduct business to better advance in it. Bars were the third leg of the social stool in urban Irish immigrant communities, the others being parish and family. In

the bar you met friends, reached deals, overindulged, and sorted out your problems and those of the world. This is no less the case today than when Irish America was born. Bars with Irish names dot the American landscape, from Mr. Dennehy's in New York to the Irish Oak in Chicago to Kennedy's in San Francisco.

Ambassador to Ireland Jean Kennedy Smith, John F. Kennedy's youngest sister, served as ambassador to Ireland during the crucial years of the 1990s, when the violence in Northern Ireland finally drew to a close. Born in 1928, Kennedy married Stephen E. Smith in 1956 and had four children. President Clinton nominated her to serve as Irish ambassador on St. Patrick's Day in 1993. She helped persuade the Clinton administration to grant Sinn Féin leader Gerry Adams a visa, a step seen as crucial to opening up the Irish peace process. Kennedy was awarded honorary Irish citizenship in 1998.

Quinn's historical novels The novels of Bronx-born Peter Quinn have proved enormously popular with an Irish America that has undergone a renewal over how it sees itself in the context of America's history. Quinn's novel *Banished Children of Eve* (1994) was a tale set against the Civil War and draft riots in 1863. Quinn's second novel, *Hour of the Cat* (2005), uses New York and Berlin in the years just before World War II as its stage. His books, though fiction, incorporate real-life historical figures. In his earlier years, Quinn served as a speechwriter, most notably for famed orator Mario Cuomo, the governor of New York.

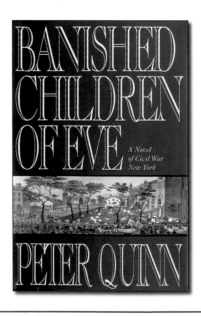

Money for Ireland

The American Ireland Fund (AIF) is the linchpin of a global fundraising network for Ireland. Part of the worldwide Ireland Funds, the AIF taps the resources of people of Irish ancestry (and friends of the Irish) to support programs of peace and reconciliation, arts and culture, and education and community development throughout the island.

The Fund is rooted in the 1963 meeting in Ireland of U.S. president John F. Kennedy and Irish president Éamon de Valera. The two formed the American Irish Foundation, the mission of which was to foster connections between Irish Americans and the land of their forebears.

In 1976 Dr. Anthony O'Reilly, former CEO of H. J. Heinz Co., formed The Ireland Fund with fellow Pittsburgh businessman Dan Rooney, owner of the Pittsburgh Steelers football team. With the goals of peace, culture, and charity in their sights, the duo appealed for support from all Americans, particularly those of Irish descent.

On St. Patrick's Day, 1987, The Ireland Fund and the American Irish Foundation merged to form The American Ireland Fund, thus becoming the world's largest private organization funding positive change in Ireland. In subsequent years, a network was developed in more than a dozen U.S. cities. Fund events in those cities have raised hundreds of millions of dollars.

Many see the AIF as an Irish counterpart to the considerable financial aid that Jewish Americans have long given to Israel. Actually, for a number of years the fund was guided by Loretta Brennan Glucksman, a Pennsylvania-born Catholic, and her Jewish and Hungarian American husband, the late Lew Glucksman, who was once described by a leading Irish newspaper as "one of Ireland's greatest benefactors."

Leary's serious side The son of Irish immigrants and a native of Worcester, Massachusetts, actor and comedian Denis Leary is known for his angry persona and politically incorrect habits, such as being photographed while smoking a cigarette. But he also has a serious side. After a friend and a cousin were among six Worcester firefighters killed in a roof collapse in 1999, Leary started a foundation to assist families of fallen firefighters. After 9/11, Leary created a drama called *Rescue Me,* in which he plays a New York firefighter named Tommy Gavin. He was nominated for an Emmy in 2005.

Preserving Irish heritage This townhouse on New York's fashionable 5th Avenue has housed the American Irish Historical Society (AIHS) since 1940. In 1897, a group of 50 Irish Americans in Boston founded the AIHS. Their mission was to counter nativist prejudices against the Irish by extolling the achievement of the exiled sons and daughters of Erin. The society's motto is "That the World May Know." One of the founders was Teddy Roosevelt, who had Irish roots on his mother's side. Today, part of the AIHS's mission is to educate Irish Americans about their heritage.

The life and death of JFK, Jr. As son of a slain president and scion of the greatest Irish American political dynasty, John F. Kennedy, Jr., occupied a unique place in national life. Born in 1960, two weeks after his father was elected president, "John-John" Kennedy brought Americans to tears with his salute during his father's funeral. Thereafter, he was never far from the public eye. Trained as a lawyer, he turned to magazine publishing in his mid-30s. A perennial "most eligible" bachelor, he finally married in 1996. Kennedy, along with his wife, Carolyn Bessette, and her sister, Lauren Bessette, died on July 16, 1999, when he crashed his plane near Martha's Vineyard, Massachusetts.

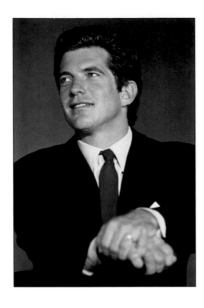

Foster's fame One of the most popular and respected screen actresses of her generation, Jodie Foster began her career as a young girl. She later earned raves when she played an underage prostitute in *Taxi Driver* in 1976. However, she garnered unwanted attention in 1981, when the would-be assassin of President Reagan claimed to have pulled the trigger in order to impress Foster (whom he had never met). Foster, who won Oscars for her roles in *The Accused* (1988) and *The Silence of the Lambs* (1991), is also a director and producer. Here she is pictured in the 1994 film *Maverick*.

Columnist and novelist Born in Philadelphia, journalist Anna Quindlen went on to become an op-ed columnist for *The New York Times* in the 1980s. Insightful and strongly opinionated, with an eloquent writing style, Quindlen won the Pulitzer Prize for commentary in 1994. She also authored several best-selling novels, including *Object Lessons* and *One True Thing*. Quindlen left the *Times* in 1995 and currently writes a column for *Newsweek* magazine.

An extreme conservative Pat Buchanan came to prominence in the 1980s and '90s as a different kind of Irish American politician: an extreme conservative who confronted the major U.S. political parties on issues ranging from abortion and gay rights to gun rights and immigration. Buchanan served as a speechwriter for President Richard Nixon and as communications director for President Ronald Reagan. He ran unsuccessfully for the Republican presidential nomination in 1992 and '96. Buchanan was a pioneering conservative commentator on cable TV, and he continues to produce a syndicated column.

President Mary Robinson

Change was in the Irish air in 1990, but many were taken aback by the election to the country's presidency of a woman. Mary Robinson, an independent, won the presidency when the campaign of her chief rival imploded. Once elected, Robinson was determined to push the bounds of the office beyond the limits adhered to by her six male predecessors.

A lawyer, academic, and former member of the Irish Senate, Robinson seemed to be a perfect fit for a constitutionally limited job. But from the start, she used the presidency as a pulpit to speak out on issues in a way that would radically alter the world's image of Ireland and its people. "The Ireland I will be representing is a new Ireland—open, tolerant, inclusive," Robinson said in her inauguration speech.

Robinson also looked beyond Ireland, addressing such international issues as poverty and AIDS. Photos of her visits to Africa and other parts of the developing world sparked reactions that British royalty would have envied. Robinson turned her nation's attention to those Irish liv-

ing illegally in America and those living in poverty in Britain—as well as to the millions of people around the globe who claimed familial ties to the island. She burned a candle in the window of her official residence for this diaspora, all the while dispensing political heartburn to Irish politicians.

During her seven-year term, Robinson used the world as her stage. When she shook hands with Northern Ireland loyalist paramilitary leaders, it was not in Belfast or Dublin, but New York. "Irishness, she will tell you, is global," *U.S. News & World Report* stated in 1996.

Robinson left office in 1997 to become United Nations high commissioner for human rights. She was followed into office by another woman, Mary McAleese, marking the first time in world history that a woman succeeded another as an elected head of state. McAleese, a Belfast Catholic, announced the theme of her presidency to be "building bridges," continuing Robinson's issues of tolerance and inclusivity. She was reelected in 2004.

An irresistible story

Thomas Cahill, a brilliant editor and writer, arrived on the bestseller list in 1995 with an unexpected hit entitled *How the Irish Saved Civilization*. Cahill told the story of St. Patrick and the Irish monks he inspired—men who preserved and then taught the great works of classical Europe after the fall of the Roman Empire. Cahill's book not only brought new light on an old story, but it showed that Irish Americans were interested in reading about their heritage. Besides, how could anybody resist that title?

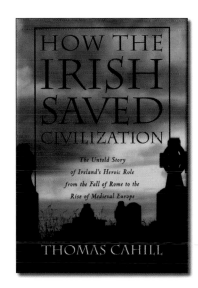

A rose for Mrs. Kennedy

The matriarch of the Kennedy dynasty, Rose Kennedy was born in Boston's North End in 1890. Her father was a congressman and Boston mayor. As a teenager, she met Joseph P. Kennedy, whom she married in 1914. Rose gave birth to nine children over the next 18 years while coping with her husband's overt infidelity. She endured tragedy when her son Joseph died in World War II. Her daughter Kathleen also died, in a 1948 plane crash, and sons Bobby and John were later assassinated. Rose persevered through all of the family's triumphs and tragedies until January 22, 1995, when she died at age 104.

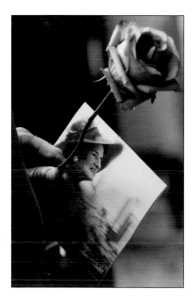

January 18, 1995: Kathleen Kennedy Townsend, the eldest of the 11 children of Robert Kennedy and his wife, Ethel, is sworn in as the lieutenant governor of Maryland.

January 22, 1995: Rose Kennedy, the widow of Joseph Sr. and the Kennedy family matriarch, dies at age 104.

February 3, 1995: The space shuttle *Discovery* lifts off with Irish American astronaut Eileen Collins—the first woman to pilot a space shuttle—at the helm.

February 22, 1995: The governments of Britain and the Irish Republic issue a joint declaration called the Framework Documents, which present a framework for agreement between the two nations.

March 1995: The U.S. State Department grants a visa to Sinn Féin leader Gerry Adams, despite his group's status as a designated terrorist organization.

March 17, 1995: President Clinton hosts Sinn Féin leader Gerry Adams at the White House.

November 1995: President Clinton arrives in Belfast, becoming the first sitting U.S. president to visit Northern Ireland.

1996: Irish American insurance executive Thomas J. Moran is awarded the Ellis Island Medal of Honor, which pays tribute to the immigrant experience and individual achievement. • Notre Dame football coach Lou Holtz leaves the storied football squad. One given reason is that he does not wish to surpass the legendary Knute Rockne in career victories with the team.

January 22, 1996: The International Body on Arms Decommissioning releases the Mitchell Report. The report details the Mitchell Principles, six agreed-upon rules to be adhered to during peace talks between Britain and Ireland.

Burns's cinematic gem Jack Mulcahy, Edward Burns, Maxine Bahns, and Mike McGlone (*left to right*) perform in 1995's *The Brothers McMullen*. Burns wrote and directed the film, which revolves around the late coming-to-maturity of three Irish American brothers from Long Island. Though the film cost just $25,000 to produce, the results were spectacular. The movie took top honors at the 1995 Sundance Film Festival, grossed more than $10 million at the box office, and launched Burns on a successful acting, writing, and directing career.

Murphy builds media empire One of the most admired media executives of the last four decades, Thomas S. Murphy helped build Capital Cities/ABC into an international powerhouse. Born in Brooklyn, Murphy served in the Navy and attended Harvard. He began working in TV in the mid-1950s for a small upstate New York company, which eventually became Capital Cities. Murphy was named company president in 1964, and he became chairman and chief executive officer two years later. Murphy oversaw Capital Cities' merger with ABC in 1985, and he retired when that company merged with Disney in 1996.

**Ignatiev ignites contro-
versy** Descended from Russian Jews, Noel Ignatiev was
trained in the highest circles
of U.S. academia and in the
gritty realities of American
working life. As a Marxist
scholar of race, he produced
a challenging new view of
Irish America's history in
1995's *How the Irish Became
White*. Ignatiev argued that
Irish immigrants who arrived
in the United States before
the Civil War managed to
gain acceptance in U.S. society only by joining in the oppression of blacks. Ignatiev's work posed penetrating questions
about race and the Irish American experience. However, it
was widely criticized among mainstream historians as incon-
clusive and doctrinaire.

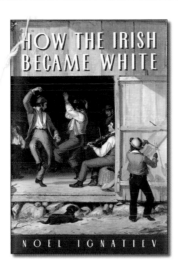

**Remembering the
famine** The com-
memoration of the
Great Hunger's
150th anniversary in
1997 brought a flurry
of interest in famine
memorials across
the country and the
world. From Bos-
ton and Cambridge
(*pictured*) to Rhode
Island and Philadel-
phia, the memorials
depict stark, often
gaunt figures that
capture the suffer-
ing endured by Irish
immigrants. But the
memorials came in many forms. The much-acclaimed memorial in downtown Manhattan is a recreation of a famine-era
cottage that has been abandoned by its starving residents.

Reclusive philanthropist
Chuck Feeney doesn't respond
to those who ask for a
donation from the fortune
he has accrued in the duty-
free shopping business. He
chooses his deserving causes.
One of those causes has been
peace in Northern Ireland. In
the 1990s, the reclusive New
Jersey-born Feeney briefly
stepped into the public eye
as part of an Irish American
delegation that blazed a trail
in the early days of the peace process. Feeney's Atlantic Phi-
lanthropies is pledged to give away all of his estimated
$4 billion by 2020.

Chicago's green river New York has its long, green line up
Fifth Avenue on St. Patrick's Day, but Chicago claims that it
makes an even bigger splash by dyeing the Chicago River green.
The tradition began in the early 1960s when it was discovered
that the dye used to detect unwelcome leakages into the river
turned a bright shade of green when added to the water. In
1966 the composition of the dye was changed to protect the
river's fish. Since then, the Chicago Journeymen Plumbers
have maintained a ritual that is now famous the world over.

February 9, 1996: An IRA bomb explodes in London's Canary Wharf, claiming two lives and injuring more than 100 civilians.

March 1996: Renowned Irish American peace broker William Flynn is named grand marshal of New York City's St. Patrick's Day parade.

March 25, 1996: Susan Sarandon is named best actress by Oscar voters for her role as Sister Helen Prejean in *Dead Man Walking,* the true story of a nun who finds herself comforting a death row inmate.

June 10, 1996: The United Kingdom and the Republic of Ireland convene another round of All-Party Talks in an effort to curb the ongoing sectarian violence in Northern Ireland.

July 2, 1996: *Lord of the Dance,* a musical production created and fronted by Michael Flatley—the American-born Irish step dancing champion—premieres in Dublin.

September 5, 1996: Frank McCourt's Pulitzer Prize-winning memoir, *Angela's Ashes,* is published. In 1999 Paramount Pictures will release a film based on the book.

November 1996: Kathleen Kennedy Townsend fails in her bid to win a seat in the U.S. House of Representatives, marking the first time a Kennedy has lost a general election.

1997: The National Committee on American Foreign Policy awards its first Initiative for Peace Award to its chairman, William Flynn, for his efforts to promote peace in Northern Ireland.

March 24, 1997: Frances McDormand wins a best actress Oscar for her work in *Fargo.*

May 2, 1997: Thanks to a landslide victory for Britain's Labour Party, Tony Blair takes over the prime minister's office from defeated Conservative leader John Major.

"[I]f I were in America, I could say, 'I love you, Dad,' the way they do in the films. But you can't say that in Limerick for fear you might be laughed at. You're allowed to say you love God and babies and horses that win. But anything else is a softness in the head."

—AUTHOR FRANK McCOURT

McCourt's memoir Frank McCourt was an obscure retired teacher from New York when his memoir, *Angela's Ashes,* hit bookstores in 1996. His unblinking look at his poverty-stricken childhood in Brooklyn and Limerick, told with elegance and wit, won the hearts of readers—as did McCourt himself, with his low-key manner and storytelling abilities. The book won a Pulitzer Prize, sold millions of copies throughout the world, and was turned into a movie. McCourt became the face of Irish America, regularly featured on television programs about the Irish at home and abroad. His subsequent memoirs, *'Tis* and *Teacher Man,* also won critical acclaim.

Ireland fights for women's rights

Patricia Ireland, with a name that seems appropriate for the fray, has been one of America's leading voices for women's rights and political advancement. Her involvement dates back to the 1960s and her early work for the National Organization for Women (NOW). Ireland's discovery that women were often treated as second-class citizens came when, as a flight attendant, she found that her insurance coverage was largely determined by her gender. The Illinois-born Ireland was NOW's president from 1991 to 2001. Her autobiography, *What Women Want,* was published in 1996.

The "Peculiar" Novelist

William Kennedy once told *Irish America* magazine: "My father's father came from Tipperary. Dad was on the edge of senility at this point and he's telling this story. And he just starts speaking in a brogue. It was a terrific brogue."

Kennedy's greatest novels, such as *Legs, Ironweed,* and *Roscoe,* are filled with such moments, when the past collides with the present in an otherworldly manner. In his acclaimed "Albany cycle," Kennedy spans the decades and treats his native city much as Joyce treated Dublin and Faulkner portrayed the South.

William Kennedy

Born in Albany in 1928, Kennedy was an only child. His father was a town deputy sheriff, so William knew a thing or two about the city's political machine. Much of Kennedy's fiction revolves around the Irish Democratic organization, its flexible moral code, and the colorful scoundrels who supported it for decades. As the titular character in *Roscoe* (2002) says: "Honesty is the best policy for people striving to be poor."

As a young journalist, Kennedy was asked to write a 26-part series about Albany neighborhoods. He himself was struck by the mythical quality of this material. "It explained my own history to me," he said. *Ironweed,* which won the 1984 Pulitzer Prize, is probably Kennedy's best work. It follows a ghostly hobo named Francis Phelan who once played baseball and now spends his days drinking and talking to the dead. Francis, in the end, seems like a figure out of both vaudeville comedy and Greek tragedy. (*Ironweed* was later turned into a Meryl Streep/Jack Nicholson movie.)

Among the great mysteries surrounding Kennedy's brilliant novels is how a gentleman of such humble beginnings produced them. "There were no writers in my family," he said. "I don't know where I came out of. I was hatched in a peculiar way."

This seems a fitting answer. As Kennedy wrote in *Legs:* "The Irish always wrote the best letters. When they could write at all."

PBS, Disney laud the Irish As the Irish in America became a hot cultural topic in the late 1990s—thanks to successful journalists, artists, and writers—the Public Broadcasting Service and the Disney empire collaborated for a four-part televi-

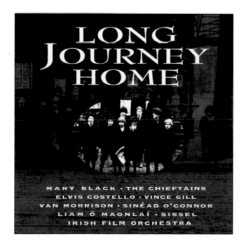

sion series in 1998 entitled *The Irish in America: Long Journey Home,* directed by Thomas Lennon. To go along with the series, Disney produced a CD of the show's soundtrack (*pictured*), featuring such artists as Van Morrison and the Chieftains. The project also included a coffee table book, written by Terry Golway and edited by Michael Coffey.

The films of John Sayles John Sayles built a career as a respected Hollywood scriptwriter and an award-winning independent moviemaker. Born in Schenectady, New York, the son of two half-Irish parents, Sayles got his start writing low-budget sci-fi/horror flicks. He went on to write and direct his own films, including *Return of the Secaucus Seven, Brother from Another Planet, Matewan, Eight Men Out,* and *Lone Star.* His interest in his

Irish heritage played a part in the moving and lyrical *The Secret of Roan Inish,* the story of a young girl's coming of age, set on the coast of County Donegal.

U.S. Brokers Peace in Northern Ireland

In his 1894 poem "Lake Isle of Innisfree," William Butler Yeats wrote about peace "dropping slow," and few Irish would dispute his observation. The Normans invaded Ireland in 1169, and peace seemed even more elusive 800 years later when The Troubles entered their modern phase.

During The Troubles in Northern Ireland (late 1960s to 1990s), more than 3,000 people (mostly civilians) lost their lives. Yet the effort to secure a lasting peace somehow managed to make progress when none seemed evident or even possible. By the mid-1980s, the Irish and British governments had reached a previously unattained level of adherence to the Anglo-Irish Agreement. But the peace process, as it would later be dubbed, was like a recipe missing a key ingredient.

That ingredient was the United States. Irish Americans had agitated for change in Ireland from the first days of the American Republic, and this activity reached new heights during the peak years of The Troubles. Efforts such as the MacBride Principles' fair employment campaign were a foot in Northern Ireland's door that successive British governments sought to keep closed. Irish America alone, however, could never force profound historical change. But America, the world's only superpower, could.

As if on cue, or by Irish luck, a group of Irish American activists led by Paul O'Dwyer drew answers about Northern Ireland from two presidential candidates in 1992,

George Mitchell and N.I. secretary of state Patrick Mayhew

Jerry Brown and Bill Clinton. That November Clinton was elected president, and so began America's engagement, at the highest level, on behalf of peace and functional politics in a land that had not known either since the Middle Ages.

Clinton's special envoy, Senator George Mitchell, guided and cajoled the warring sides to embrace the 1998 Good Friday Agreement. The accord was the start of a new phase in a process that would lead to the end of the IRA's violent campaign and, by 2007, to an unprecedented power-sharing government in Belfast. Peace had "dropped slow," but it had finally landed.

Trimble aids the peace process

As leader of the Ulster Unionist Party, David Trimble was an implacable foe of Irish republicanism and nationalism. Nevertheless, and with the support and encouragement of the United States, Trimble led his party into negotiations with those forces that he believed were attempting to wrest Northern Ireland from the United Kingdom. By so doing, he played a vital role in securing passage of the 1998 Good Friday Agreement. Trimble was joint winner of the 1998 Nobel Peace Prize (with Irish nationalist politician John Hume), and he was later awarded a British peerage.

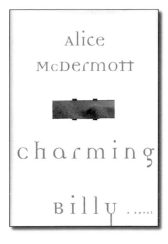

McDermott's suburban perspective In her novels, Alice McDermott picks up the story of Irish America as it moves from the old city neighborhoods to the postwar suburbs. McDermott herself was born in Brooklyn, but she grew up amid the tract houses, lawns, and shopping centers of Long Island. In her novels, she narrates a new chapter in Irish American history, a time of widespread prosperity, home ownership, and hope for the future. Still, her books are not without familiar heartaches and tragedies. Her novel *Charming Billy* won a National Book Award in 1998.

Irish music fests Irish rocker Elvis Costello plays an acoustic set at the 1999 Guinness Fleadh in San Francisco. The San Francisco Fleadh (the Irish word for "festival"; pronounced *flah*) was part of the Irish cultural revival that swept the United States in the 1990s. The Guinness Fleadh, also held in New York, Chicago, and other cities, featured both Irish-born stars and non-Irish performers. Those who graced the Guinness Fleadh stages included Sinead O'Connor, Van Morrison, The Chieftains, John Lee Hooker, and Taj Mahal.

Big Mac attack St. Louis Cardinals slugger Mark McGwire belts his 70th and last home run of the 1998 season, off Montreal's pitcher Carl Pavano. "Big Mac" and the Chicago Cubs' Sammy Sosa electrified the nation that season in the "Great Home Run Chase." Each eclipsed Roger Maris's major-league record of 61 home runs (McGwire was the first to do it), and Mac outhomered "Slammin' Sammy" 70–66 thanks to five big flys on the final weekend. The immensely muscular McGwire belted 583 career home runs, but accusations of steroid use—and his unwillingness to address those accusations—tarnished his legacy.

Master of suspense A self-described "nice redheaded Catholic girl from the Bronx" and the daughter of an Irish bar owner, Mary Higgins Clark built a fabulously successful writing career on pure perseverance. A mother of five who wrote short stories, she was widowed in her mid-30s. To pay the bills, she turned to writing radio scripts—then tried her hand at novels. After one disappointment (a romance about George and Martha Washington), Clark found success with a suspense novel, *Where Are the Children?* (1975). Since then, her best-selling thrillers have enthralled Americans, who have bought 85 million of her books.

1990–TODAY

June 13, 1997: Robert "Basher" Bates, a member of the Shankill Butchers—a gang that randomly kidnapped, tortured, and murdered Catholics in the 1970s—is shot dead on the streets of Belfast, likely by a relative of one of his many victims.

July 19, 1997: The IRA reestablishes a cease-fire and sits down at the negotiating table with Ulster and Irish Free State officials.

October 13, 1997: Ulster Protestants are enraged when British prime minister Tony Blair shakes hands with Sinn Féin's Martin McGuinness and Gerry Adams.

January 26, 1998: The miniseries *The Irish in America: Long Journey Home* premieres on PBS.

March 23, 1998: Jack Nicholson nets another best actor award, this time for his portrayal of Melvin Udall in *As Good as It Gets*.

April 10, 1998: The Good Friday Agreement, also known as the Belfast Agreement and the Stormont Agreement, is signed. Containing various provisions, the agreement is a major stepping-stone on the path to peace.

June 28, 1998: The city of Boston unveils its Irish Famine Memorial, a $1 million city park situated along the popular Freedom Trail.

July 1, 1998: David Trimble takes office as the initial first minister of Northern Ireland.

August 15, 1998: A bomb rocks Omagh, Northern Ireland, claiming 29 lives and wounding more than 200. An IRA faction calling itself the "Real IRA" claims responsibility.

September 8, 1998: Slugger Mark McGwire of the St. Louis Cardinals belts his 62nd home run to break Roger Maris's single-season major-league record. "Big Mac" will finish the season with 70 four-baggers.

Ties to America When a replica of the famous Vietnam War memorial toured Ireland in 1999, thousands of Irish citizens paid their respects. Many of them looked for the names of distant relatives or friends who had died during that long, bitter conflict. Here, Olive Hartney of Dublin finds the name of a cousin, Michael David Jalbert of Rhode Island, who was killed in action. The moment was a small but poignant reminder of how close are the ties between Ireland and America.

Billionaire Flatley gives back A quintessential immigrant success story, Thomas J. Flatley (*left*) was born in County Mayo and went on to become a billionaire businessman. Flatley immigrated to the U.S. in 1950 and, after settling in Boston, built his fortune in real estate. He also became a prominent philanthropist, contributing to many Catholic charities. Flatley also served as chairman of the committee responsible for constructing a memorial in Boston commemorating the 150th anniversary of the Irish famine. Here, on March 16, 1999, Flatley participates in a candlelight vigil to honor those who perished in the Great Hunger.

Exploring our roots Where did we come from? Many Irish Americans can answer instantly, down to the precise village or town in a particular county. Others frequently mount searches for their family roots, such as amateur genealogist Joseph Silinonte (pictured at the grave of his great-great-great grandfather). Such quests have been aided enormously in recent years by technological advances and the inclusion of family migration records on various Web sites. These sites have been created by the likes of the emigration museum in Cobh, just outside Cork City, and Ellis Island in New York Harbor.

FBI wants Bulger In 1999 notorious Irish American mobster James "Whitey" Bulger was placed on the FBI's Most Wanted List. Bulger, whose brother William served as president of the Massachusetts State Senate, was wanted for the deaths of 19 people, who had been killed from 1973 to 1985. One case involved the murder of John McIntyre, an admitted IRA gunrunner who disappeared

in November 1984. Bulger had been an FBI informant even as he headed Boston's bloodthirsty Winter Hill Gang. Since he vanished in 1995, there have been "Whitey" sightings on almost every continent. In 2008, he was No. 2 on the FBI's Most Wanted List, behind Osama Bin Laden.

A fireman remembers A product of New York's East Side, Dennis Smith—like many other sons of poor Irish families—grew up to become a fireman. In 1974 he published the electrifying book *Report from Engine Co. 82,* about life in his South Bronx firehouse. It sold more than two million copies. Smith authored other bestselling books and founded the successful *Firehouse Magazine.* His book *A Song for Mary,* a tribute

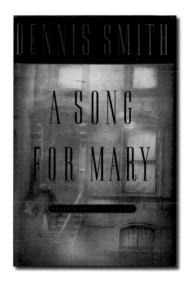

to his mother's devotion to her family during the long years of his father's mental illness, was chosen by the Book of the Month Club as the best memoir of 1999. His 2002 book, *Report from Ground Zero,* is the definitive account of the 2001 terrorist attack on the World Trade Center.

AIF honors Clinton President Bill Clinton, who has Irish roots on his mother's side, received the Millennium Peace Award from the American Ireland Fund (AIF) in March 2000. The Clinton administration is widely credited for assisting the peace process in Northern Ireland. AIF president Loretta Brennan Glucksman (*left*) presented the award to Clinton, who was the first sitting president to visit Northern Ireland. AIF is part of a charitable network that has raised more than $300 million. Glucksman and her husband, Lew, are active in many charitable causes, and they helped found the Glucksman Ireland House at New York University.

October 1998: The MacBride Principles, a code governing the conduct of U.S. business interests operating in Northern Ireland, becomes federal law.

December 10, 1998: John Hume, leader of the Social Democratic and Labour Party, and David Trimble, head of the Ulster Unionist Party, are jointly awarded the Nobel Peace Prize.

January 1, 1999: The euro becomes the official currency of the European Union, and Ireland is one of the 11 member nations to adopt it on this day.

July 16, 1999: John F. Kennedy, Jr., along with his wife, Carolyn, and her sister, Lauren Bessette, die when the plane he is piloting to his cousin Rory's Massachusetts wedding goes down in Rhode Island Sound.

August 19, 1999: Irish American mobster James J. "Whitey" Bulger, leader of the Winter Hill Gang and brother of Massachusetts state senator emeritus William Bulger, is added to the FBI's Ten Most Wanted list.

August 3, 2000: Having bested Arizona senator John McCain in all but a handful of states, George W. Bush (of Irish ancestry) is officially nominated as the Republican candidate for the presidency.

January 3, 2001: Daniel Patrick Moynihan retires after representing New York for 24 years in the U.S. Senate.

September 11, 2001: Islamic terrorists attack the World Trade Center in New York, murdering hundreds of members of the largely Irish New York police and fire departments along with more than 2,000 civilians.

2002: Dublin native Patrick Burke signs with the Orlando Magic and becomes the first Irish native to play in the NBA. • *In America,* a film about an Irish immigrant family trying to make a new life in the United States, is released.

> **"[Ireland] through a combination of good luck, good timing and good policies, has caught the crest of a geographical and technological wave, and has ridden it to a prosperity nobody expected."**
>
> —ECONOMIST AND WRITER PAUL KRUGMAN, 1997

The "Celtic Tiger" Lab technicians work at Intel Ireland in Leixlip, County Kildare. Reversing years of economic backwardness, the Republic of Ireland's growth accelerated in the mid-1990s at a phenomenal rate. More than once, the annual Gross National Product rose by more than 10 percent, turning the Republic from one of the poorest countries in Europe to eventually the richest in terms of individual disposable income. Low corporate taxes, a well-educated young workforce, European Union membership, and U.S. corporate investment all contributed to the peak "Celtic Tiger" years, roughly from 1994 to 2001.

Regis loves the Irish Regis Philbin is a New Yorker of mixed ethnic heritage. But the veteran talk and game show host leaves little doubt which familial strand is the one that leads the others. Philbin, who has notched up more hours on television than just about any of his contemporaries, is best known as host of *Live* (he is pictured with former co-host Kathie Lee Gifford) and *Who Wants to Be a Millionaire.* With his upbeat persona and invariable good cheer, Philbin frequently reminds viewers of his Irish identity by proclaiming his allegiance to Notre Dame's Fighting Irish football team.

Lord of the Dance Dancer Michael Flatley performs in his show "Feet of Flames" in 2000. From an Irish family in Chicago, Flatley was trained as a youth in step dancing. He combined eye-popping physical skill, creativity, and showmanship to transform an essentially conservative traditional art into a spectacle of color and movement. Flatley, who was a champion flautist and a Golden Gloves boxer, became the first non-European to win the All-Ireland World Championship for Irish dance. In 1994 he and Jean Butler introduced "Riverdance," the groundbreaking Irish dance show. Flatley later created the acclaimed "Lord of the Dance," "Feet of Flames," and "Celtic Tiger" productions.

Irish America's newspaper First published in 1928, *The Irish Echo* grew over the next few decades into Irish America's dominant weekly newspaper. The New York-based *Echo* itself faced challenges from newer arrivals following the 1980s surge in Irish immigration. But the paper, with a 50-state Irish American readership, has continued to change with the times. It sometimes raises the eyebrows of even veteran readers with its imaginative composite covers, such as the one that adorned this 2001 St. Patrick's Day issue.

HOW'VE YOU BEEN, ANNIE?

Pouring rain. My wife is sitting in the passenger seat, and my mother behind me. And we had to stop because of cows coming down this lane.... And as the cows were walking by...a man, driving the cows, came behind them in the rain, using a burlap bag to cover his head.... I opened the window and said hello. He stuck his head in the window with the burlap bag, and he completely soaked me. Completely. And he looked at my mother in the back seat and said, "Oh, Annie, how've you been?" Forty years. Stunned, she had no idea who he was, not at all. White hair, blue eyes. She was about 70 at the time, and he was about the same. Childhood friends, you know. But in his life, nothing had changed. Nothing.... It was stunning. And everything was like that in the homecoming, you know.

—PROFESSOR ROBERT SCALLY, RETIRED DIRECTOR OF
IRELAND HOUSE AND THE IRISH STUDIES PROGRAM AT
NEW YORK UNIVERSITY, ABOUT TAKING HIS MOTHER, ANNE,
BACK TO HER HOMETOWN IN WESTERN ROSCOMMON

Visiting and moving to Ireland The age of jet flight sent the American Irish back to the "old sod" in annually increasing numbers. The Irish were never slow to throw out the welcome mat for their visiting cousins, though the plaid brigade of the 1970s drew occasional derisory comments. Today, Americans continue to visit the island in large numbers. In recent years,

an increasing number of Americans, not just of Irish descent, have moved to the economically vibrant Ireland as a result of marriage or relocation within a company, thus giving the island a new and indigenous American flavor.

44 Million Irish Americans

How many Irish Americans are there? It's a question that is impossible to answer, but millions of Americans claim family ties to Ireland, with 44 million (as of 2008) being the most oft-quoted total.

So how was this sum reached? Both the 1980 and 1990 U.S. censuses asked Americans to reveal what they considered to be their primary ethnic ancestry. Based on the 1990 census, the Census Bureau in 1998 logged in a figure for Irish Americans of 22,721,252, of which 22,451,511 were listed as born in the United States. This total included only people who considered themselves wholly Irish American in their ethnicity.

The bureau also posted a graph showing a figure of 39 million citizens who considered themselves primarily and/or partially Irish American. This total came under the heading "Top 15 Ancestry Groups: 1990." The 39 million Irish Americans comprised 16 percent of the U.S. population. German Americans were the only larger ethnic group.

Parade in Washington, D.C., 2003

The Census Bureau lists Irish as an ethnic category, but it also lists Scots-Irish as an entirely separate category. There were, according to the bureau's assessment of the population in 1990, 4,334,197 Scots-Irish Americans. Adding that figure to the 39 million brings the total close to the 44 million mark.

Clearly, there is an element of choice with regard to every American's ethnic makeup. Family trees in America are complex, but "Irish" as a No. 1 selection seems to have stood the test of time. Come St. Patrick's Day in the U.S., it may seem like everyone is wearing green.

In the fall of 2007, while accepting the credentials of the new Irish ambassador to the United States, President George W. Bush alluded to the nation's growing Irish American community. "The ties between Ireland and the United States are deep and broad," Bush said, "as deep as the Irish family roots that 45 million Americans proudly claim."

St. Patrick's Day parades The first St. Patrick's Day parade was held in New York—not Ireland—in 1762. As Irish immigration to the United States increased, so did the number of parades, with the celebrations in New York (*pictured*) and Boston proving to be the largest throughout the 19th century. Eventually, the tradition spread across the U.S., with Savannah, Georgia, showcasing one of the nation's largest parades and Chicago famously dyeing the city's entire river green every March 17. America's Irish parade tradition proved so popular that many other nations—including Ireland—began staging their own St. Patrick's Day parades.

Bono and U2 Bono (*left*) and U2 guitarist The Edge perform in a 2001 concert in Switzerland. U2 rose from schoolboy beginnings in the 1970s to become the world's most successful band. The Dublin group was known early on for a hard-edged sound and politically tinged lyrics in songs such as "Sunday Bloody Sunday." U2 proved immensely popular in the United States, winning 22 Grammy Awards, more than any other band in history. Bono, born Paul David Hewson, parlayed his star status into a second career as a social activist. His organization DATA (Debt AIDS Trade Africa) is dedicated to finding long-term solutions for crises besetting that continent.

Black Irish This striking woman exhibits traits said to typify the "black Irish." The term is believed to be of American origin and refers to Irish with black or very dark brown hair, very pale or olive skin coloring, and blue or dark brown eyes. The origin of this type—and even whether it is a type—is a subject of debate and speculation. Experts reject one widely held belief: that the black Irish descended from Spanish Armada survivors. Scientists studying the origins of those who settled Ireland may one day answer the "black Irish" conundrum.

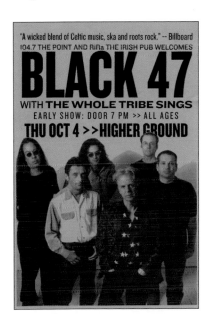

"A wicked blend of Celtic music, ska and roots rock." -- *Billboard*
104.7 THE POINT AND RíRá THE IRISH PUB WELCOMES
BLACK 47
WITH **THE WHOLE TRIBE SINGS**
EARLY SHOW: DOOR 7 PM >> ALL AGES
THU OCT 4 >> HIGHER GROUND

Black 47 New York City's Black 47 is a politically inclined Irish American rock band whose name refers to the darkest year of Ireland's Great Famine (1847). Wexford-born Larry Kirwan says Black 47's mission is "to create music that would reflect the complexity of immigrant and contemporary Irish American life and to banish 'When Irish Eyes Are Smiling.'" The band's Celtic-tinged rock includes uilleann pipes, penny whistles, saxophone, and trombone in addition to guitar, bass, and drums. Their albums include rollicking party songs and left-wing anthems drawn from Irish history.

Hollywood heartthrob Kentucky-born George Clooney has propelled himself through the ranks of screen stars to the very highest tier. Both an actor and director, Clooney has demonstrated dramatic diversity even while carrying the often burdensome tag of Hollywood sex symbol. A nephew of singer Rosemary Clooney, the actor has mixed lighter works, such as *Ocean's Eleven* (*pictured*), with more dramatic films, such as *Syriana* (for which he won an Oscar). Clooney, a political activist, also has won acclaim for his work behind the camera. He earned a best director Oscar nomination for *Good Night, and Good Luck*.

Irish victims of 9/11 Due to the terrorist attack on the World Trade Center on September 11, 2001, 343 members of the Fire Department of New York lost their lives. About half of them were members of the FDNY's Emerald Society, an organization of Irish Americans. Here, the Society's Pipe and Drum Corps pays tribute to the fallen during a ceremony at Ground Zero on October 7, 2001, the day on which the United States and Great Britain launched their invasion of Afghanistan.

Magazine targets affluent Irish *Irish America* magazine, published in New York, was a clear and glossy signal that the new generation of Irish Americans would see themselves differently than all others before them. Emerging in the middle of the 1980s, the magazine targeted an affluent Irish America. It has featured the work of new and established writers to present a contemporary image of the American Irish—even while frequently reaching back into history for its story content. The magazine annually stages a highly popular Irish America Top 100 awards ceremony.

The Bushes' Irish blood The Irish roots of President George H. W. Bush and his son, President George W. Bush, have been traced to counties Down and Cork. Some have even asserted that the presidents are descendants of Strongbow, who led the 12th century Norman invasion of Ireland. Though their Irish ancestry might be in the distant past, it was brought home to the two Bushes every St. Patrick's Day of their combined three terms. The American presidents were presented annually with a bowl of shamrocks by the Irish prime minister, in this case Bertie Ahern in 2002.

Scandal rocks the Church One of the worst scandals in the history of the American Catholic Church broke in early 2002, when news reports revealed that the high-ranking clergy had not taken action against priests accused of molesting minors. Defrocked priest John Geoghan (*pictured*) was accused of abusing more than 100 youngsters in New England before being sent to jail, where he was murdered in 2003. The heavily Irish Catholic hierarchy came under intense criticism for its handling of the pedophile scandal. Similar scandals rocked the Church in Ireland at around the same time.

Coming to America

The Irish will always come to America. The question is simply in what numbers and under what legal circumstances. Irish immigration during the 20th century occurred in roughly 30-year cycles, with the last big arrival decade being the 1980s. On that basis, the flow westward across the Atlantic should start to pick up momentum in the years after 2010.

However, events have occurred that will likely interrupt the cyclical pattern. First and foremost has been the extraordinary economic development of Ireland over the last two decades. Secondly, U.S. immigration laws have continued to become more stringent, particularly after 9/11. Additionally, Irish immigrants tend to be single, whereas current law favors reuniting family groups. The presence in the United States of a significant number of undocumented Irish has kept the immigration issue on Irish America's front burner.

Immigrant Stephen Masterson

No matter how advanced an economy, there will be people living within its boundaries who feel the urge to move. And if there is one thing that matches, indeed exceeds, the push effect in Ireland, it is the pull exerted by America—the glow that promises so much over the western horizon. A possible way to accommodate this push and pull phenomenon in the future is a flexible, bilateral migration treaty, one that will make it easier for the Irish to live legally in America and Americans to live and work in Ireland.

Film captures immigrants' struggles In the 2002 film *In America,* writer and director Jim Sheridan drew on personal experience to present the story of an illegally immigrated Irish family. After they smuggle themselves across the border from Canada, the mother (played by Samantha Morton), father (Paddy Considine), and two daughters (Emma Bolger, *left,* and Sarah Bolger) embark on an undocumented life in New York City—one filled with struggles and hardships. While the story ends with the promise of better times, *In America* is a reminder that immigrant life is challenging and positively perilous when in the shadow of illegality.

Left-wing documentarian Filmmaker Michael Moore's path to fame and controversy began near Flint, Michigan, where he was born in 1954 to parents he describes as "Irish Catholic Democrats, basic liberal good people." Moore's father was a longtime General Motors employee, but Moore embarked on a career as a journalist and documentarian. His first film focused on the same GM plant that employed his father. Moore's documentaries, including *Roger and Me, Bowling for Columbine, Fahrenheit 9/11,* and *Sicko,* are provocative because of their left-wing critique of U.S. life. The aforementioned films explore, respectively, corporate behavior, America's gun culture, George W. Bush and the 2001 terrorist attacks, and America's health care system.

September 14, 2002: The effort to have Archbishop Fulton Sheen canonized begins in earnest, as the Congregation for the Causes of Saints opens his cause and officially names him a "Servant of God."

November 2002: Kathleen Kennedy Townsend loses her bid to become governor of Maryland.

December 20, 2002: Martin Scorsese's *Gangs of New York* is released. Set in 1860s New York, the film recreates the violent Irish gang culture of the historic Five Points neighborhood.

February 25, 2003: Richard M. Daley, son of longtime Chicago mayor Richard J. Daley, is elected to his fifth term of office. He will be reelected again in 2007, setting him on course to succeed his father as the longest-serving mayor in Chicago history.

June 2, 2003: Irish American Harrison Ford, one of the highest-earning actors in entertainment history, receives his star on the Hollywood Walk of Fame.

November 3, 2004: Democratic senator John Kerry, who is incorrectly perceived by many as Irish, concedes defeat in the presidential race to incumbent president George W. Bush.

2005: U2, one of the world's most successful rock bands since its premiere in Dublin in 1976, is inducted into the Rock and Roll Hall of Fame.

July 28, 2005: The Provisional IRA announces that it will lay down weapons and work to achieve its goals through diplomacy and nonviolent means.

November 2006: In California, former governor Jerry Brown is elected as the state's attorney general.

2007: NBC launches *The Black Donnellys*, a series about the Irish Donnelly brothers and their forays into New York's criminal underbelly.

Insights into the mind Massachusetts-born Dr. Paul McHugh (*left,* with attorney Robert S. Bennett) is considered one of the brightest minds in the field of clinical psychiatry. A graduate of Harvard Medical School, McHugh worked at a number of medical institutions, where he pioneered new techniques in neuroscience. In 1975 he joined the faculty at Johns Hopkins University. McHugh was not averse to taking issue with others on analysis of disorders and treatment methods. His coauthorship (with Philip Slavney) of the groundbreaking 1983 book *The Perspectives of Psychiatry* won McHugh widespread acclaim.

Cheer for old Notre Dame The storied University of Notre Dame football program has been a source of pride among Irish Americans for more than a century. No school has captured more Associated Press national titles (eight) or Heisman Trophies (seven) than the Fighting Irish, whose legacy includes many of the greatest names in the history of college football—such as coaches Knute Rockne and Frank Leahy and players George Gipp, Joe Montana, and the Four Horsemen. Notre Dame football games have sold out for decades, and the school's national popularity resulted in a multi-million dollar national television contract that no school can rival.

O'Connor's Irish themes Dublin-born novelist Joseph O'Connor, brother of singer Sinead O'Connor, won critical acclaim with his first book, the novel *Cowboys and Indians*, in 1991. Five years later, O'Connor published a work of nonfiction based on his journeys through the United States. *Sweet Liberty: Travels in Irish America* won O'Connor attention and a large audience on this side of the Atlantic due to his witty and touching word pictures of Irish American icons. O'Connor's novel *Star of the Sea*, published in 2002, is a fictional account of a transatlantic voyage in 1847, during the famine.

Sheehan's personal war Cindy Sheehan became a leading voice against the U.S. war in Iraq after her oldest child, Army Specialist Casey Sheehan, 24, was killed in Baghdad in April 2004. Sheehan is best known for her long vigil outside President George W. Bush's Crawford, Texas, ranch in the summer of 2005. The following year, she visited Ireland to urge the government to not allow CIA planes to use Shannon Airport. In 2007, Sheehan decided to run for Congress in California's 8th District (represented by House Speaker Nancy Pelosi). In summer 2008, she successfully secured enough signatures to get on the ballot.

Reporter dies in Iraq War Born on St. Patrick's Day in 1957, Michael Kelly emerged from the Persian Gulf War in 1991 as one of his generation's finest reporters. After filing memorable pieces for *The New Republic* and *The Boston Globe,* he went on to write for *The New Yorker* and serve as an editor with *The New Republic* and *Atlantic Monthly.* Fiercely opinionated in print but gentle in private, Kelly supported the American invasion of Iraq in 2003. He left his desk to report on the war first-hand, and was killed while under enemy fire on April 3, 2003. He left behind a wife and two young children.

Boston's Irish college

Boston College is one of a group of leading American universities established by Catholic religious orders in the 19th century that have strong associations with the Irish. By virtue of its original location in the city's South End, Boston College lays particular claim to an Irish American heritage and ethos. Now located in Chestnut Hill, just west of the city, BC is home to the Burns Library, a renowned center for Irish American studies. The Jesuit-run college is one of the most academically rigorous universities in the United States.

Comic king of late night After a successful few years as a writer for television (including *The Simpsons*), Conan O'Brien was plucked from relative obscurity in 1993 to host a late-night talk show on NBC: *Late Night with Conan O'Brien*. Born in Brookline, Massachusetts, to Irish American parents, O'Brien graduated *magna cum laude* from Harvard University. Though he stumbled through his early *Late Night* shows, he gradually won over audiences with his remarkably quick wit, funny facial expressions and body movements, and hilarious sketches. He was scheduled to replace Jay Leno on *The Tonight Show* in 2009.

Ferrell's funny films Comedian and actor Will Ferrell joined the cast of *Saturday Night Live* in 1995. His imitations of political figures and celebrities, from Harry Caray to Janet Reno, won him a large following. Ferrell made the transition to feature-length films and became a huge box office attraction, displaying his physical-comedy gifts in such movies as *Elf, Talladega Nights,* and *Blades of Glory*. His role as dimwitted newscaster Ron Burgundy in the 2004 film *Anchorman: The Legend of Ron Burgundy* (pictured) was right up his alley. In 2008, Ferrell won the James Joyce Award from the Literary and Historical Society of University College Dublin.

The opinionated O'Reilly After stints at CBS and ABC, broadcast journalist Bill O'Reilly joined the fledgling Fox News Channel in the late 1990s. His show, *The O'Reilly Factor,* quickly became one of the highest rated programs on cable television due to its host's acerbic, conservative commentaries and his eclectic mix of guests. O'Reilly's in-your-face style has earned him criticism from colleagues and media watchdogs, but his influence is undeniable. He also hosts a highly rated radio show, writes a newspaper column, and has written several bestsellers about contemporary politics.

The leprechaun, transformed Beginning in 1963, "Lucky the Leprechaun" graced the cover of Lucky Charms and pitched the cereal on TV commercials. The leprechaun has undergone a major makeover in his voyage to America. An ancient trickster in Irish folklore, often taking the form of a ragged cobbler, the leprechaun is a character known for his slyness, magical abilities, and miserliness. After crossing the Atlantic, the leprechaun became a jolly shadow of his former clever self. Although he is still beloved by Irish Americans, marketers have transformed him into a clownish and, to some, mildly offensive caricature of the Irish.

Staging Plays at the Irish Rep

Irish theater travels the world well, but it sometimes needs a home base—even one far from the island of its inspiration. Founded in 1988 by Ciaran O'Reilly and Charlotte Moore, the Irish Repertory Theatre (IRT) has been an Irish cultural cornerstone in New York City. Broadway had staged the plays of Shaw, Synge, and Friel, but the IRT has introduced theatergoers to many other Irish playwrights, old and new, who continue to tell the story that makes the worldwide Irish experience a truly dramatic one.

The Irish Rep, as it is popularly known, is first and foremost a company, though now one with a permanent home in the Chelsea district of Manhattan. In its early years, it borrowed space from the Irish Arts Center, New York's

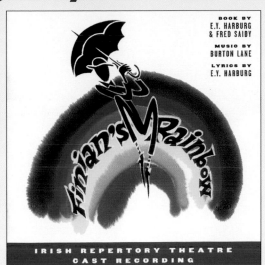

BOOK BY
E.Y. HARBURG
& FRED SAIDY

MUSIC BY
BURTON LANE

LYRICS BY
E.Y. HARBURG

IRISH REPERTORY THEATRE
CAST RECORDING

A 2004 revival of the classic musical

other Irish theatrical wellspring. The Irish Repertory Theatre is so respected that the Irish government has contributed funds to the company.

The Irish Repertory's mission is, in its own words, "to bring works by Irish and Irish American masters and contemporary playwrights to American audiences; provide a context for understanding the contemporary Irish American experience; and encourage the development of new works focusing on the Irish and Irish American experience, as well as a range of other cultures."

Its entertainment values go without saying. The Irish Rep's first play of 2008 was *Take Me Along*, a romantic musical based on Eugene O'Neill's *Ah, Wilderness!*

Adams vital to peace process Gerry Adams (*right*) carries the coffin of veteran Irish republican Joe Cahill, who died of natural causes in 2004. History will acknowledge Adams as the man who pledged to take the gun out of Irish politics—and mostly succeeded. Though the Sinn Féin leader denied ever leading the IRA, Adams was regarded by the Irish and British governments as the man who could steer the entire republican movement toward peace. Marathon negotiations eventually led, in 2007, to power-sharing governance in Belfast.

Dowd's acerbic wit
The daughter of an Irish American police officer, Maureen Dowd gained fame and a Pulitzer Prize in 1999 with her witty political commentary in *The New York Times*. Her ability to find absurd humor on the campaign trail and her unflinching descriptions of the nation's top political leaders have made her columns must-read material throughout the country. Dowd is famous for her use of harsh nicknames, such as "Darth" and "Shooter" for Vice President Dick Cheney.

Premier playwright Writer John Patrick Shanley took an unusual path to Broadway. The son of Irish immigrants, Shanley was expelled from school in the Bronx and had to take a break from college to cool himself down—in the United States Marine Corps. What followed was a stellar career as a play-

wright. From the late 1980s onward, Shanley's star rose over Broadway to the point where he was being compared to Eugene O'Neill. His 2004 play *Doubt* won a Pulitzer Prize for drama as well as four Tony Awards, including best play. He also won an original screenplay Oscar for *Moonstruck* (1987).

Labor boss AFL-CIO president John J. Sweeney (*right*) is pictured during a New York City labor protest in 2005. Born in the Bronx in 1934 to Irish immigrants, Sweeney grew up close to the realities of working families: His father was a city bus driver, and his mother was a cleaning woman. A longtime organizer, Sweeney became chief of the labor federation in 1995 by promising an aggressive campaign to reverse the long slide in U.S. union membership. But the decline continued through 2007. The AFL-CIO saw some of its biggest unions leave because of dissatisfaction with Sweeney's leadership.

ILGO demands the right to march Into the 1980s, the New York St. Patrick's Day parade was known solely as a boisterous celebration of all things Irish. But then each parade came with protests launched by gay activists, such as the Irish Lesbian and Gay Organization (ILGO). (Pictured are protesters in New York in 2005.) They wanted the right to march, but parade organizers, including the Ancient Order of Hibernians, argued that homosexuality was against the teachings of the Catholic Church. The ongoing debate illustrates the diversity—and, at times, rancor—of the Irish experience in America.

The genius behind Southwest A charismatic and visionary executive, Herbert Kelleher turned Southwest Airlines into one of the most profitable airlines in the country. Born in 1931 in Camden, New Jersey, Kelleher co-founded Southwest in 1967 with the then-revolutionary concept of streamlining services and slashing fares. In 1982 he became president and CEO of Southwest, earning a reputation as a vibrant leader and one of the best CEOs in the country. Kelleher, at age 77, stepped down as Southwest chairman in May 2008.

A pioneer in space The first woman to pilot the Space Shuttle, Eileen Marie Collins was born in Elmira, New York, in 1956. Initially a member of the Air Force, Collins became an astronaut in 1991. Four years later, she piloted a shuttle mission, and in 1999 she served as shuttle commander. It is estimated that she has flown more than 6,700 hours in 30 different kinds of aircraft. Collins, pictured here in 2005, retired from NASA a year later.

 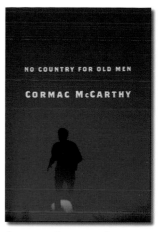

McCarthy grapples with heavy themes At an early age, Charles McCarthy changed his name to Cormac in honor of a king of ancient Ireland. A Roman Catholic education probably informed McCarthy's preoccupation with the human struggle to reconcile sinfulness and the inevitability of suffering with a belief in God. His novels regard evil as a force that sets its practitioners apart from the rest of society—spiritually and often physically. But McCarthy makes clear that any of us are apt to fall prey to temptation, and that if we do, the road to redemption will be tortuously difficult. His best-selling 2005 novel, *No Country for Old Men,* swings on greed, and the remorseless, strangely honorable perseverance of murderer Anton Chigurh, one of the most frightening figures in all of modern literature.

Magees help children smile In 1982 Dr. William P. Magee and his wife, Kathleen, a nurse, went to the Philippines as part of a volunteer effort to repair cleft palates and other ailments rampant in the region. The need for more assistance was so great that the Magees founded Operation Smile, whose sole mission is to repair children's facial deformities. The group, whose slogan is "Changing Lives One Smile at a Time," has treated more than 115,000 children worldwide. Irish actress Roma Downey (*pictured between the couple*), the star of TV's *Touched by an Angel,* is one of the group's spokespersons.

The younger Daley Chicago mayor Richard M. Daley marches during the city's St. Patrick's Day parade in 2006. The son of longtime Chicago mayor Richard J. Daley, the younger Daley has established his own legacy during two decades in office. He has won plaudits for his environmental policies, and he has presided over a massive wave of upscale development in Chicago's downtown and many neighborhoods. He has left no doubt he is a Daley. Though he doesn't wield the nearly absolute power that his father enjoyed, he is tough—and some say autocratic—in carrying out his agenda.

1990—TODAY

March 26, 2007: Sinn Féin head Gerry Adams meets Democratic Unionist Party leader Ian Paisley. The once-bitter enemies will agree to terms for the Northern Ireland power-sharing executive.

May 8, 2007: Democratic Unionist Party head Ian Paisley is named the first minister of Northern Ireland.

August 1, 2007: Irish folk singer Tommy Makem succumbs to lung cancer at age 74 in Dover, New Hampshire.

October 2007: Irish American mobster James "Whitey" Bulger is named the second most wanted man in America, after only Osama Bin Laden. • Henry Hill, the Irish mafia associate whose life story inspired the film *Goodfellas,* opens a restaurant, Wiseguys, in West Haven, Connecticut.

January 2008: Senator Ted Kennedy, along with his son Patrick and niece Caroline Kennedy Schlossberg, officially endorses U.S. senator Barack Obama (D-IL), partly of Irish ancestry, for the Democratic presidential nomination. In June, Obama will defeat Senator Hillary Rodham Clinton in the race for the Democratic nomination.

January 18, 2008: Irish American actor George Clooney, one of Hollywood's biggest stars, is named a United Nations peace envoy.

March 4, 2008: Irish American senator and war hero John McCain becomes the presumptive Republican nominee for president by clinching the majority of delegates.

May 20, 2008: Doctors announce that longtime U.S. senator Ted Kennedy has a malignant brain tumor.

June 22, 2008: Irish American George Carlin, a legendary counter-culture comedian, dies of heart failure at age 71.

Cusack shines in Hollywood At times quirky, at other times dramatic, John Cusack has built an impressive Hollywood career. He has starred in teen flicks, such as *Say Anything,* as well as dramas, including *The Grifters* and 2007's *Grace Is Gone* (which Cusack produced). Born in Evanston, Illinois, to an Irish Catholic family with strong artistic and political impulses, John—as well as his actress sister, Joan—appeared in the 1984 hit *Sixteen Candles.* Since then, he has starred in more than 40 films. Off camera, Cusack is known for his down-to-earth personality and outspoken liberal views.

Determined to preserve St. Brigid's Demographic changes have led to the closing of many parishes in Catholic urban enclaves. Some closures have been resisted, and this has been very publicly the case with St. Brigid's in Manhattan, a church dating to the time of the Irish famine. Its preservation has been supported by

those who see St. Brigid's in both historical and religious terms. Despite warnings by the Archdiocese of New York that St. Brigid's was in danger of literal collapse, the venerable church survived partial demolition of its rear gable wall. Its future was assured in May 2008 when an anonymous donor gave $20 million, half of which would go to restore the church.

Prosecutor of the powerful Born in Brooklyn to parents hailing from County Clare, Patrick Fitzgerald was named U.S. attorney for the Northern District of Illinois in 2001. Beginning in 2003, he gained renown for a series of high-profile court cases, securing convictions against former Illinois governor George Ryan on corruption charges as well as several close associates of Chicago mayor Richard Daley. Later, Fitzgerald successfully prosecuted vice presidential aide Scooter Libby (in the Valerie Plame CIA leak case) on obstruction of justice charges.

McCain's support for immigrants Two of John McCain's great-great-great-great grandparents, John and Mary Young, lived in County Antrim. While McCain's immigrant roots may be not be of recent vintage, he emerged as a strong advocate of immigrant rights in the years leading to his nomination as the Republican Party's presidential candidate in 2008. The Arizona senator was vocal in his support for illegal immigrants, a group that includes thousands of Irish who came to the United States before Ireland's economic boom in the mid-1990s. Here, McCain addresses supporters at an Irish American awards reception in 2007.

A passion for politics Each week on *Meet the Press* and other NBC News outlets, Tim Russert shared his passion and deep knowledge of Washington politics with millions of American viewers. Presidential elections

especially excited him. He predicted that "Florida, Florida, Florida" would be the pivotal state in the 2000 election, and he introduced "red states" and "blue states" to the American vernacular. Due largely to Russert's tough questioning of political heavyweights on *Meet the Press, Time* named him one of the 100 most influential people in the world in 2008. Russert, an Irish Catholic from Buffalo, wrote two No. 1 bestsellers, *Big Russ & Me* and *Wisdom of Our Fathers.* He died at age 58 in 2008.

Obama's Irish blood Barack Obama's historic presidential campaign in 2008 recalled another precedent-shattering campaign in 1960, when John F. Kennedy became the first Catholic to win the White House. Not coincidentally, Obama won the support of President Kennedy's brother, Massachusetts senator Ted Kennedy, and daughter, Caroline Kennedy. Obama himself is part Irish on his mother's side, with family roots in County Offaly. Chicago alderman Ed Burke was not surprised to learn that Obama was of Irish heritage. "I could tell from the very first time I saw him," Burke said. "He's got such a way with words."

Preserving her father's legacy Caroline Kennedy Schlossberg was just five years old when her father, President John F. Kennedy, was assassinated. She grew up in the public eye, yet she avoided the tabloid-ready scandals that plagued other Kennedys. She became a respected legal scholar and author whose books include a biography of her father (for young readers) and a collection of her mother's favorite poems. As president of the John F. Kennedy Library Foundation, she has been a close guardian of her father's legacy. Kennedy married Edwin Schlossberg in 1986. They have three children.

Index

Index

Picture Credits

Picture Credits

(bottom), 174, 180 (top), 183 (top left), 217 (bottom left), 235 (center), 236 (top left), 237 (left center & right center), 239 (bottom left), 248 (top), 249 (top left & top right), 250 (top right), 252 (top), 254 (bottom right), 261 (top left), 270 (bottom left), 271 (bottom), 277, 288 (bottom), 290 (top right), 292, 293 (bottom), 294 (bottom right), 299 (bottom left), 300 (top), 303 (bottom right), 323 (bottom right), 325 (bottom left), 334 (top & bottom right), 339 (bottom left), 344 (top left), 361 (top), 371 (top right), 375 (left), 379 (bottom right), 382 (top left & bottom), 386 (top right), 393 (top left), 397 (top), 400 (bottom), 408 (top), 411 (top), 413 (center), 414 (bottom right), 417 (bottom right); **AFP,** 383 (top right), 398 (bottom), 402 (top), 405 (bottom right), 410 (top & bottom); Focus on Sport, 367 (bottom left); David E. Klutho/*Sports Illustrated,* 403 (bottom left); Neil Leifer/*Sports Illustrated,* 370 (top left); Meet the Press, 419 (top right); Michael Ochs Archives, 321 (top left), 322 (bottom left), 332 (bottom right), 363 (top left & top right); Peter Read Miller/*Sports Illustrated,* 381 (bottom left); NBAE, 374 (bottom); Popperfoto, 279 (top right), 364 (top); Retrofile, 319 (top left); Time Life Pictures, 101 (bottom), 243 (top left & bottom right), 278, 279 (bottom right), 287 (left), 288 (bottom), 289 (bottom right), 295 (top left & top right), 297 (right), 299 (top right & bottom right), 302 (bottom), 303 (top right & bottom left), 304 (top), 307 (bottom right), 313 (top left & bottom left), 314 (top), 316, 317 (top right & bottom right), 320 (top), 321 (bottom right), 323 (top right), 327, 328 (top right), 330 (bottom), 331 (top), 332 (left center), 333 (bottom center), 335 (top right), 338 (top left & top right), 339 (top left), 340 (top), 342 (bottom right), 348-349, 350, 353 (top right), 358 (bottom), 363 (bottom right), 365 (bottom right), 372 (top), 374 (top), 381 (bottom left), 384, 385 (top), 392 (bottom), 405 (top left); Tony Triolo/ *Sports Illustrated,* 379 (top left); Roger Viollet, 32; **The Glens of Antrim Historical Society:** 261 (bottom right); **The Granger Collection, New York:** 20, 25 (bottom), 34, 40-41, 45 (top & right center), 46 (top), 49 (bottom left), 50 (top), 55 (top), 56-57, 60 (top), 63 (bottom right), 66 (bottom), 67 (top left), 69, 94 (bottom), 96 (bottom), 103 (bottom), 111, 112 (left center), 116 (top), 117 (top left), 119 (bottom right), 121 (top left), 122, 123 (top right), 124 (left center), 139 (top left & top right), 141 (bottom), 144 (bottom), 147 (bottom right), 148 (bottom left), 149, 150 (top), 151 (bottom left & bottom right), 158 (bottom), 163 (bottom right), 164 (bottom), 166 (left), 167 (top left), 168 (top left & bottom), 171 (bottom right), 179 (bottom left & bottom right), 181 (bottom left), 182 (top left & bottom left), 189 (top left), 190 (top), 193 (top), 194 (top), 195 (top right, bottom left & bottom right), 196 (bottom), 197 (top left & top right), 198 (bottom right), 214 (top), 216 (bottom), 217 (top), 219 (top), 221 (top), 243 (bottom left), 251 (top right), 252 (bottom), 254 (bottom left), 255 (bottom right), 258 (top right), 260 (bottom), 291 (top right), 294 (bottom left); Reu des Archives, 258 (bottom right); **Harry S. Truman Library & Museum:** 306 (bottom left); **The Herb Block Foundation:** 291 (bottom right); **Heritage Resources, Saint John:** 108 (bottom); **Historical Art Prints:** Don Troiani, artist, 130 (top), 135 (top); **David J. Hogan Collection:** 220 (top), 266 (top left & bottom right), 283 (top left), 318 (bottom left), 333 (top left & top right & bottom right), 338 (bottom right), 342 (top left), 345 (top center & top right), 365 (top left), 367 (top left), 394 (bottom), 399 (top left), 400 (top right), 403 (top left), 417 (top right); **Image Source:** 407 (bottom); **The Image Works:** AAAC/Topham, 15; Ann Ronan Picture Library/Heritage Images, 98 (top left); Ann Ronan Picture Library/HIP, 107 (right); Mark Godfrey, 121 (top right); HIP-Archive/Topham, 140 (bottom), 151 (top right); Lebrecht Music and Arts, 313 (bottom right); Mary Evans Picture Library, 19, 21, 23, 25 (top), 29, 35, 38 (bottom), 43, 54 (bottom right), 55 (bottom), 76 (bottom), 78 (bottom), 79 (top right), 90, 93, 103 (top), 104 (bottom), 114 (bottom), 115 (bottom left), 119 (top), 121 (right center), 133 (bottom), 215 (bottom right), 233 (top left), 237 (top), 250 (top left), 271 (right center), 334 (bottom left); Mary Evans Picture Library/Arthur Rackham, 104 (top); Mary Evans Picture Library/Edwin Wallace, 26; National Media Museum/SSPL, 272 (top); Roger Viollet, 85 (top left); Topham, 165 (top), 189 (bottom), 294 (bottom center); Werner Forman Archive/Topham, 14, 16; **International Potato Center:** Rebecca Nelson, 97 (top left); *The Irish Echo,* 407 (top left); **Irish National Archives:** 227 (center); **Courtesy Richard J. Jensen:** 76 (top); **joyceimages. com:** 58, 61 (top), 85 (top right), 179 (top left); **Mort Kunstler, Inc./mkunstler. com:** "Hancock the Superb" by Mort Kunstler ©2002, 126-127; "Rebel Sons of Erin" by Mort Kunstler ©1996, 131 (top); **Lehigh University Digital Library:** 142 (bottom); **Library and Archives Canada:** 161 (left); James Francs Kenney Fonds, 147 (top left); William Notman, 150 (bottom); **Library of Congress:** 18, 49 (top & bottom right), 52, 53 (bottom left), 59, 61 (bottom left), 62, 63 (top left & bottom left), 67 (bottom left), 75, 77 (top), 79 (bottom left), 84 (right center), 85 (bottom), 87 (right center), 92, 94 (center), 95 (top), 99

(top right), 105 (bottom left), 112 (right center & top right), 114 (top), 116 (left center), 117 (bottom), 120, 121 (left center), 124 (top), 129; 131 (bottom), 132 (top), 135 (bottom left), 138 (bottom), 139 (bottom left), 143 (top), 145 (top right & bottom left), 146, 147 (top right), 148 (top right & bottom right), 151 (top left), 155, 157 (top), 159 (bottom right), 162 (bottom), 170 (top left & top right), 171 (top left), 172 (top), 176, 181 (top), 182 (top right), 184, 186 (bottom left & bottom right), 187 (top), 189 (top right), 192 (top left), 195 (top left), 197 (bottom right), 198 (bottom left), 200 (bottom right), 201 (top left & top right), 202 (top), 203 (left), 207 (bottom right), 208 (bottom left), 209 (bottom left), 218 (top), 220 (bottom), 221 (bottom), 222, 223 (bottom), 226 (bottom), 227 (right), 228 (left, top right & bottom center), 229 (top), 230, 231 (top), 233 (top right), 236 (top right & bottom left), 238 (top), 239 (top left, top right & bottom right), 240 (top left & bottom), 243 (top right), 253 (bottom), 256 (top left), 257 (top), 263 (top right), 265 (top), 273 (top), 282 (bottom), 300 (bottom), 301 (top), 326 (top), 345 (top left); **Maryland Historical Society:** 74 (bottom); **The McClatchy Company:** 99 (bottom left & bottom right); **Minnesota Historical Society:** Thomas M. Swem, 201 (bottom right); **Missouri Historical Society:** 148 (top left); **National Archives, and Records Administration:** 302 (top); **National Baseball Hall of Fame, Cooperstown, N.Y.:** 214; **National Library of Ireland:** 180 (bottom); **National Museum of American History:** 160 (bottom); **National Museum of the United States Air Force:** 274-275; **New Bedford Whaling Museum:** 166 (right); **New York Public Library, Astor, Lenox and Tiden Foundations:** 158 (top), Art & Architecture Collection, 201 (bottom left); Billy Rose Theatre Division, 165 (bottom right), 171 (top right), 183 (top right), 208 (bottom right), 231 (bottom); Emmet Collection, 67 (right center), 73, 87 (left center); Humanities and Social Sciences Library, 260 (top), 263 (top left); The Lionel Pincus and Princess Firyal Map Division, 84 (top left); Mid-Manhattan Library Picture Collection, 248 (bottom); Miriam and Ira D. Wallach Division of Art, 84 (bottom left), 169 (top), 183 (bottom left), 224 (top); Music Division for the Performing Arts, 202 (bottom), 204 (bottom), 209 (bottom right), 235 (top right); New York Public Library Archives, 223 (top right); Picture Collection, The Branch Libraries, 54 (top), 80 (bottom), 82 (bottom), 115 (bottom right), 137 (top), 144 (top), 145 (top left), 159 (bottom left), 165 (bottom left), 178 (bottom), 196 (top), 199 (right), 215 (top), 225 (left); Science, Industry & Business Library, 173 (top); **The Newberry Library:** 142 (top left), 178 (top), 192 (top right), 220 (center); **NewspapersARCHIVE. com:** 267 (bottom left); **North Wind Picture Archives:** 36, 38 (top), 39 (top), 48 (top), 62 (top), 100 (bottom), 113 (left), 163 (bottom left), 168 (top right); **Notre Dame Archives:** 293 (top); **Courtesy Maureen O'Hara:** 8; **Philadelphia Museum of Art:** 194 (bottom); **Photofest:** 322 (top); **PIL Collection:** 101 (top), 143 (bottom left), 177, 191 (top), 200 (top), 204 (top), 228 (right center), 238 (bottom right), 251 (bottom left), 271 (top right), 279 (top left & bottom left), 283 (bottom left), 284 (left center), 286 (top left & bottom left), 295 (bottom), 296 (top), 301 (bottom), 314 (bottom), 315 (bottom left) (bottom right), 318 (top left), 321 (top right), 325 (bottom right), 332 (top left), 342 (top right), 344 (top right), 345 (bottom center), 362 (bottom left), 366 (top), 370 (bottom right), 373 (bottom left) (bottom right), 387 (top right & bottom left), 392 (bottom), 397 (bottom left), 401 (bottom left), 405 (top right), 409 (bottom left & bottom right), 410 (left center), 411 (left center), 413 (top left), 414 (bottom right), 415 (top); **Playboy ©1976:** Pompeo Posar, 371 (bottom left); **Public Domain:** 145 (bottom right), 147 (bottom left); **Purdue University Libraries, Archives and Special Collections:** 270 (top right); **Courtesy Peter Quinn:** 9; **Radioarchives.org:** 284 (right); **Rutgers University:** Courtesy Jack Lynch, 53 (top right); **Schuylkill County Historical Society:** 161 (right); **SuperStock:** Christie's Images, 94 (top); **Transcendental Graphics:** Mark Rucker Collection, 235 (top left); **United States Army:** 319 (bottom right center); **United States Army Center of Military History:** H. Charles McBarron Jr., artist, 47; **United States Marine Corps:** 319 (bottom left center); **U.S. Naval Historical Center:** 46 (bottom), 182 (bottom right), 305 (bottom); **University at Buffalo Libraries and Illuminations:** 110 (top); **University College Cork:** 125 (right); **University of California at Berkeley, Bancroft Library:** 123 (bottom right), 188 (top), 199 (bottom), 223 (top left); **University of Michigan Library:** 143 (bottom right); **University of Notre Dame Archives:** 412 (bottom); **University of Southern California, on behalf of the USC Specialized Libraries and Archival Collections:** 229 (bottom right); **Utah State Historical Society:** All rights reserved. Used with permission, 236 (bottom right); **Ed Vebell Collection:** 78 (top right); **Villanova University, Falvey Memorial Library:** 251 (top left); **Washington University, Warshaw Collection of Business Americana, Archives Center:** 53 (top left); **John Weedy/www.Iln.org.uk:** 97 (top right); **Lynn Wright:** 117 (top right).